HOSTILITY
and
AGGRESSION

DOLF ZILLMANN

Indiana University

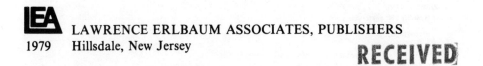

LAWRENCE ERLBAUM ASSOCIATES, PUBLISHERS
1979   Hillsdale, New Jersey

DISTRIBUTED BY THE HALSTED PRESS DIVISION OF
JOHN WILEY & SONS
New York   Toronto   London   Sydney

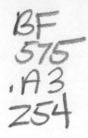
Lawrence Erlbaum Associates, Inc., Publishers
365 Broadway
Hillsdale, New Jersey 07642

Distributed solely by Halsted Press Division
John Wiley & Sons, Inc., New York

Library of Congress Cataloging in Publication Data

Zillmann, Dolf.
  Hostility and aggression.

  Bibliography: p.
  Includes indexes.
  1. Aggressiveness (Psychology) 2. Hostility
(Psychology) 3. Violence. 4. Psychology,
Comparative. I. Title.
BF575.A3Z54   152.4   79-18641
ISBN 0-470-26832-8

Printed in the United States of America

Contents

Preface

A cursory inspection of theory and research on aggression may well leave the impression that aggression is a well understood phenomenon. Treatises on the subject abound, and several seemingly all-encompassing theoretical models have been presented in recently published monographs. In addition, the sheer amount of research information that has been generated by many investigators in a variety of disciplines is truly overwhelming. In the face of these circumstances, it might be surmised that the topic of aggression has been exhausted in terms of theoretical accounting and empirical testing, and that little, if anything, is left to be investigated. Or to put it somewhat more conservatively: It may appear that at least all significant aspects of aggression have been dealt with in considerable detail and that any attempt to discover a hitherto neglected major domain of aggression—one that is in dire need of theoretical and empirical exploration—is doomed to failure. And accordingly, it may seem that writing a book on aggression could only be an exercise in redundancy.

Obviously, I have taken exception to this assessment. I felt that upon closer examination anybody would be convinced that, despite of the immensity of available research information, there remain many facets of aggression about which we know very little. Regardless of the presumed convictions of others, however, and granted that great progress has been made in recent theorizing and research, I felt that our understanding of aggression in animal life and especially in human affairs is quite rudimentary, and that there is ample fundamental and challenging work left, not only for myself, but for entire generations of investigators.

After a critical examination of theory and research on aggression, I was particularly dissatisfied with the following aspects: the vagueness of prevalent conceptualizations of aggression in animals and man, the unwarranted extensions of theoretical models of severely restricted scope, the questionable validity of much research information together with the selective use of the evidence, the absence of specific models in which common violent outbursts are considered and treated as emotions, and the far-reaching recommendations for the control of aggression that are based on scanty data. I felt that, if I could correct at least some of the misconceptions I thought I had detected, my efforts in writing a book on aggression would constitute a worthwhile investment.

The book was written mainly in three consecutive "long" summers. Early in 1975, I took on the tedious assignment of reconceptualizing aggression, my objective being to avoid the inconsistencies that have plagued many definitional approaches and to generate a useful terminology that would permit finer and more reliable distinctions than the definitions that were available.

In the summer of that year, I reviewed the literature on aggression in subhuman species. I concentrated on the evidence that pertains most directly to the identification of characteristic features of aggression in animals, thus preventing the mere aggregation of empirical data. My main objective was to extract the principles that govern aggressive behaviors in animals and to show how well, at this time, we comprehend aggression in nonhumans. But I was equally intent on showing how little our knowledge of animal aggression teaches us about human aggression. In fact, my greatest discontent with "general" theories of aggression is with regard to the obvious overextension of models that may well be valid in a restricted context. This overextension is most obtrusively manifest in the inferential leaps, from animals to humans, that are at the core of some of the most popular theories of aggression. A considerable portion of my writing efforts was consequently aimed at showing why such generalizations are invalid and at explaining exactly which aspects of human aggression can and cannot be validly inferred from the knowledge of aggression in other species.

I spent the summer of 1976 analyzing the major theories of human aggression and surveying the research evidence pertinent to their evaluation. My objective was to reconstruct the theories in the most formal terms possible under the circumstances, to inspect the claims made regarding the generality of the theories, to evaluate the theories in the light of the available evidence, and to specify the conditions under which they are valid—and, if necessary, the conditions under which they are not.

With few notable exceptions, I found these theories wanting in their account of the phenomenon of aggression at large. It seemed to be widely assumed that a sound theory of aggression must be constructed on the basis of just one fundamental mechanism. Accordingly, in one theory, all aggression is projected as resulting, ultimately, from frustration; in another, from operant learning; in yet another, from classical conditioning; and so forth. And although qualifying comments are made at times, the proponents of particular theories tend to suggest, or at least imply, that invoking additional mechanisms does not appreciably further our understanding of aggression. Only recently, it seems, has it been fully recognized that any theory that seeks to explain the enormous complexity of aggression must involve numerous independent and interrelated mechanisms.

"One-mechanism theories" of aggression have usually been supported by empirical evidence that derives from a rather limited set of manifestations of aggression. These models thus appear to be capable of explaining a particular form of aggression. If they had not been extended beyond their scope, there would be little cause for concern. Characteristically, however, these simple theories of aggression have entailed universal claims: Practically all conceivable manifestations of aggression were considered to be explained; and, what turned out to be particularly distressing, far-reaching solutions for the control of aggression in society were explicitly offered or implied. Also, the appraisal of a theory's merits has all too often confounded the theory's explanatory capacity with its implications for curbing violence. Ample precedent, then, cautioned me not to follow such a practice. I consequently have given much attention to the separation of a theory's explanatory power from its implications for the control of destructive behavior, and I have made every effort to evaluate the theory proper in the light of the available research evidence only. Following this evaluation of a theory in purely epistemological terms, I have, however, detailed the theory's implications for aggression control—whether or not these implications were recognized by those who proposed or promoted the theory in question.

Presumably because of procedural restrictions that make the collection of decisive empirical data very difficult, theories of human aggression have often been considered supported by findings that are of doubtful validity and that only loosely relate to the propositions tested. Frequently, and in my judgment regrettably, investigators have cited as evidence anything that passed the criteria of peer review—which is practically everything that has been published. The result seems to be that more findings than should be are considered valid, and more theoretical rationales than should be are considered supported. It also seems that, if we had been a little more critical in our appraisal of the validity of research information, we would be confronted with fewer "theoretical dilemmas": sets of incompatible theoretical propositions, all of which, as it now stands, enjoy some empirical support. I thought that much could be gained from a critical, detailed analysis of the empirical work and from an in-depth analysis of key studies. I therefore decided to scrutinize research designs and procedures. Often I could confirm what had been claimed, but in numerous cases I found myself in disagreement with earlier conclusions. In fact, my analysis of the research evidence led me at times to strongly disagree with the appraisals and claims of fellow investigators. I can only hope that my criticism will be received in the constructive spirit in which it is offered, and I sincerely hope that I will not alienate any of my friends and colleagues in aggression research with my interpretations and reinterpretations of the significance of research findings.

In the summer of 1977, I formalized my own views of human aggression. I started with the delineation of distinct, principal forms of aggression and then proceeded with the construction of a theoretical account of each of the basic forms I had distinguished. As a point of departure from other approaches, I did not attempt to propose a single-mechanism theory for all conceivable manifestations of aggression. Instead, I developed a set of complementary and interrelated theoretical propositions, each designed to explain a specific domain of destructive behaviors. I would think, however, that since the interdependencies of the various rationales have been specified, the combined set of theoretical propositions could appropriately be characterized as "a theory."

I have dealt in considerable detail with the interactions between cognitive and excitatory processes. I feel that we have made good progress in understanding the role of arousal in aggression. We know under what conditions arousal will intensify aggressive behavior and under what conditions it will not; and we know at least some of the conditions that control the magnitude of excitatory reactions. In contrast, however, we know very little about the way in which changes in arousal alter cognitive capabilities and very little about the implications of altered cognitive capabilities for aggressive behavior. I was painfully aware of this state of affairs when I was dealing with the topic of destructive emotional outbursts in developing a model of impulsive aggression. Given the great social significance of "emotional aggression" in human society, I very much hope that my theoretical speculations will encourage others to further pursue the exploration of the intricate interdependencies between cognition and excitation involved in impulsive behaviors.

I finished writing this book in the summer of 1977 with a note on the control of aggression. I had been bewildered by the many careless projections of remedies for the problem, and I was motivated to show how little cause there was to trust certain "solutions" for the curtailment of violence. In the following summer, I found myself expanding this note, not merely to show which remedies to be wary of, but to specify, in a positive manner, what recent theorizing and research have to offer in terms of guidance in the control of aggression. The remainder of my time during the summer of 1978 went into updating and revising the manuscript into its present form.

In addressing as complex a phenomenon as aggression, I have considered myself both fortunate and privileged because of the diverse training I have received. Although in recent years I have worked exclusively with human subjects, and have used mainly the methodology of social psychology, I have benefitted greatly from my earlier involvement in ethological work and from a great deal of exposure to biological, anthropological, and—maybe most importantly—psychophysiological research. I feel that this background has enabled me to analyze the critical research on both animal and human aggression with what I hope is adequate and equal sensitivity, and to integrate mechanisms that derive from different disciplines into one unified theoretical approach. I hope, in fact, that it is this integration of the contributions from various independent theoretical and empirical traditions that will recommend this book to the attention of students of aggressive behavior—and to those interested in the complexity of behavior in general.

I am greatly indebted to many friends and colleagues who have assisted me in writing this book. Professor Joanne Cantor has scrutinized the initial draft in its entirety. She has given much of her time, suggesting numerous changes to improve clarity and removing uncounted stylistic ideosyncracies stemming from my native language. The resulting manuscript has been read in full by Professors Brendan Rule and Robert Baron. Both provided many insightful comments, and I gratefully feel them responsible for many improvements in the presentation of theories and research data. Professor John Paul Scott read the portions of the manuscript that concern animal aggression. I am greatly indebted to him for the much needed feedback he provided with his meticulous, superbly informed, insightful commentary. Professors José Delgado and Albert Bandura read the sections of the manuscript that deal with their own theoretical positions and experimental work. I am grateful to both for their helpful comments. Finally, I am greatly indebted to my editor, Professor Robert Krauss, for his extremely careful analysis of the manuscript. He has been most perceptive, and his insightful comments and suggestions—none of which I had any disagreement with—have helped me and this book immensely. Needless to say, however, I solely am to be held responsible for any errors that may have escaped our concerted efforts to eliminate them, and for any shortcomings the reader may detect in the interpretations and proposals that I have presented.

I also would like to acknowledge a different kind of assistance I have received: The financial support of our work on aggression that came mainly from the National Science Foundation and the National Institute of Mental Health. Although the various grants we have received were primarily intended to support our experimental investigations, this book could not have been written without the sustained support these grants provided.

Last, but by no means least, I must express my great gratitude toward my family. My wife, Valtra, proved to be a most valuable collaborator. She has carried the major burden of the necessary, extensive library work, and she has helped in numerous secretarial functions—from typing to proofreading and indexing. But most importantly, she motivated me to persevere, giving me comfort and encouragement at times when the task I had taken on appeared to be overwhelming and the goals I had set myself seemed unattainable. My two sons, Martin and Tomas, were equally supportive, never—not even for a moment—giving me cause to regret my decision to write this book. They have been extremely patient with me, and they have earned my respect—if for nothing else, for sacrificing without much ado their trip to Hawaii for three years in a row, and settling for a few days in Kentucky instead.

DOLF ZILLMANN

1
The Issue at Hand

Aggression seems a pervasive and ubiquitous phenomenon in animal and human life. In the so-called fight for survival, animals kill their prey and are in turn killed by their predators. All the essential functions of their lives, particularly feeding and mating, appear to entail continual battle with rivals of their own kind. Plant life seems to be destroyed indiscriminately by animals of a vast variety of species. Man, unquestionably the most effective predator of all species, has brought immense destruction upon his environment, fauna and flora alike. Most notably, however, man has wrought devastation upon himself. This destructiveness is evident throughout history in the countless wars that have decimated populations, accompanied by atrocities that only man seems capable of performing. More telling evidence comes from the records of violent crime in every known culture. It appears that man—in furthering his self-interest—has shown little reluctance to inflict pain, injury, mutilation, and death upon his fellow man.

Aggression, possibly because of its obtrusiveness in nature but more probably because of its profound role in human affairs, has always been a central theme of human discourse and reflection. As literary records show, the poets and philosophers of every era have addressed the issue. With little systematic observation, they have attempted to comprehend the apparent propensity for destructive behavior of animals and man. Characteristically, their efforts have resulted in proclamations of the existence of aggressive instincts and instinctlike drives and in moral pronouncements about them. The assumption of some unspecified and unmeasurable inner force that compels the organism to perform the aggressive behavior that has been observed is without explanatory value, of course; and whatever value there

1

may have been in the descriptive accounts of destructive behavior is greatly diminished by the encroachment of value-laden anthropomorphic interpretations. Much of the early reasoning on aggression seems to have been guided by philosophical and theological convictions, and these convictions frequently led to the aggregation of observations that was highly partial to particular doctrines and the "views of nature" contained in them.

The emergence of scientific technology in the biological and behavioral sciences, especially the refinement of observational methods and experimental procedures, has produced major changes in the study of aggression. Manifestations of aggression in animal and man came to be recorded with greater precision and reliability, and the significance of the antecedents of aggression as well as its consequences was explored in experimental investigations. An enormous amount of relevant information has been accumulated in recent decades, and it would appear that contemporary students of aggression—unlike their poorly informed colleagues of earlier times—could draw upon this wealth of knowledge to refute unwarranted speculations and ill-advised recommendations concerning aggression. This impression would be highly misleading, however. It is true that great progress has been made in the study of aggression. But it is also true that particularly in the study of human aggression, the most crucial, decisive investigations have not been and probably will never be conducted. The reason for this is as obvious as it is inevitable. The experimental investigation of situations that may cause a person to attack, injure, and eventually kill another person, as well as the experimental exploration of circumstances that may lead to riots and wars, is intolerable in any society in which personal safety is considered the individual's inalienable right. The creation of sets of natural conditions that would permit the unambiguous determination of what, in the short or long run, causes what kind and what amount of destructive behavior is simply beyond the range of employable methods. Investigators of human aggression—like their colleagues studying natural disasters or the spread of dangerous, infectious diseases in man—are severely restricted in their ability to manipulate the conditions required for the crucial testing of relevant propositions. These investigators have to ensure that none of their subjects is made to suffer unmanageable stress or risk permanent physical or psychological injury. Thus confined, the investigators must resort to methods that produce less decisive results.

Since the investigators are relatively free to collect data on events and circumstances after destructive behavior has occurred under natural conditions, many have attempted to implicate functional relationships by the use of correlational methods. Other investigators have employed simulations of the phenomenon studied, using analogous but artificial social situations or computer techniques in efforts to generate expected outcomes from sets of antecedent conditions. The results have been suggestive, but they typically have not been capable of establishing definitive causal relationships. Most experimental investigations of human aggression have also employed simulations of destructive behavior rather than destructive behavior itself. In children, aggression has been operationalized, among other things, as the desire to see a balloon pop, as the manipulation of fighting dolls, and as the frequency of punches directed at the stomach of a toy clown. The operationalization of aggression in adults has involved procedures such as the writing of complaints about mistreatment by others and the ostensible delivery, under some guise, of electric shock to another person. The construct validity of these operationalizations has been convincing to some investigators, but it has left many others skeptical. The experimental analogues of aggression have been challenged, and the generalizability of experimental findings has often been called into question. All this is not to say that the investigation of human aggression has not progressed. Our understanding of the antecedent, concurrent, and subsequent conditions of aggression and of the aggressive process itself has greatly advanced in recent years. It is apparent, however, that the methodology employed in the study of human aggression has produced considerable controversy among investigators and that many findings are open to criticism, to reformulation, or to alternative interpretations.

Given these constraints, it may appear promising to study human aggression through the analysis of aggression in animals. This approach, which has been used with great success in the investigation of many other aspects of behavior, enables investigators to circumvent most of the restrictions placed upon research with human subjects. Comparatively unconcerned with the potential damage done to their subjects, animal researchers can explore aggressive behavior directly and thus avoid the "artificiality" of experimental work with humans. However, when one considers the basis for drawing conclusions about human aggression from findings on aggression in animals, the advantage of greater realism vanishes. Clearly, generalizations from animal to human behavior are valid only under the assumption that all factors contributing to the occurrence and the particular manifestation of aggression are present and equally salient in the animal species involved and in man. But no one has seriously endorsed this assumption. Instead, it commonly has been assumed that among vertebrates, there is sufficient similarity among the factors causing aggression to warrant inferences about aggression from animals to man. Those who feel comfortable with this assumption have claimed animal and human aggression to be homologous, and those who find the assumption unacceptable have charged that findings on aggression in animals at best constitute interesting analogies for aggression in man. Apparently, one man's homology is another man's analogy, and depending on one's point of view on the matter, such inferences will be accepted or rejected. Since no sound criteria have been developed for determining the degree of similarity of factors contributing to aggression in animals and man, conclusions cannot be considered definitive. The controversy over the contribution of animal studies in the understanding of human aggression thus promises to continue. And as long as it continues, generalizations from animal studies—and particularly the sweeping implications for human aggression that tend to come with them—must be viewed with considerable skepticism.

The gist of the argument here is that although great progress has been achieved in the study of aggression in animals and man, our understanding of the process of human aggression is still quite fragmentary and incomplete. Because of this, the area is open to conjecture and speculation. Such a state of affairs certainly prevails in many other domains of inquiry. But in the study of aggression, unlike the other domains, speculation seems to have gotten in the way of progress. Speculation is most productive if it promotes hypotheses that can be subjected to empirical testing. The verification or falsification of these hypotheses then permits the successive delineation of viable, accurate explanations and the elimination of unfounded, erroneous views. Such a process, which signifies the true advancement of knowledge in a field of inquiry, is characteristic of disciplines in which the phenomenon under investigation is directly manipulable and measurable. As pointed out earlier, however, the study of human aggression has relied heavily on indirect assessments of the object of investigation. The resulting ambiguities in the interpretation of findings seem to have greatly impeded the successive reduction of the number of proposals and theories that are being entertained.

Another characteristic of the investigation of human aggression that occasionally seems to obstruct the advance of knowledge is the concern of some investigators with the objectionable aspects of aggression in human affairs. More specifically, it is the ambition of some to contribute solutions to pressing problems, such as the control of violence. This is certainly understandable, particularly at a time when most, if not all, highly developed cultures are undergoing rapid increases in violent crime and when the decision of a few men and women—subject to all "human" weaknesses—can activate weapons with potentially enormous destructive consequences. Many investigators have sought to affect public policy on such matters as educational practices, mass communication, and penal reform, and their research has become preoccupied with demonstrating the undesirable consequences of prevailing practices and the desirable outcomes of recommended changes. It is true that there is a great need for rigorously conducted applied research on human aggression. Decisions that need to be made now, in the face of ambiguities and uncertainty, can be assisted and guided toward the more probable achievement of desirable ends. In fact, applied research has recently made valuable contributions to the formation of aggression-related policies. There is thus ample pragmatic justification for it.

The objectionable element of the concern about violence in society lies in the fact that it has become customary for investigators to propose remedies that relate to their findings in only the loosest manner and the effects of which have not been determined in any acceptable way. A disproportionate amount of academic discussion has been devoted to the criticism and the defense of recommended solutions. Investigators have advocated and defended their value positions, their hopes, and their recommendations more than the particular factual evidence they have obtained. And similarly, investigators have been criticized not so much because of the findings they have reported but because of their views of the nature of aggression and its implications for the curtailment of violence. In sum, much of the controversy about aggression in man has been value-laden, and the development of theories addressing the principal processes of aggression has, at times, become a secondary objective. This is not to say that the social implications of knowledge gained about aggression should be neglected by the social scientist. (On the contrary: Social scientists should recognize their obligation to articulate the implications of their work—in social, political, even philosophical terms. Many investigators, in fact, may be criticized for having been negligent on that count.) Rather, it is argued that the securement of definitive causal relationships must be the foremost objective in the study of aggression. The projection of social implications is productive only when it is founded on sound knowledge. If based on tentative data or even on sheer speculation, any recommendations amount to risky propositions indeed; they could be misleading and if adopted, cause more harm than good.

If some writers have been preoccupied with social concerns, others seem to have enjoyed themselves and thrilled their audiences by depicting incidents of violence in animal and man and particularly by projecting the hopelessness of man's lot and the ultimate inevitability of disaster. Aggression, undoubtedly, has always had dramatic qualities. Aggressive action and drama seem inseparable. It is thus not surprising to find that the vivid exposition of the drama of aggression in animal and man, especially when coupled with "revelations about human nature," has emerged as a best-seller formula. Numerous books on aggression that have employed this formula have become popular and highly influential. Although their main impact has been on the interested layman, they have not been without effect in scholarly circles. As the hostile reactions from aggression researchers of different persuasions would seem to attest, they have further aggravated the value-laden debate, adding to the confusion concerning aggression in animal and man.

Finally, in the discussion of aggression, there has been considerable heterogeneity in the use of basic concepts. The term *aggression* itself has been defined in very different ways. In fact, it has been defined in so many ways that a journalist who was covering a recent convention on aggression felt compelled to report that the various researchers "can't agree on what aggression is" and to conclude that "they don't know what they are talking about." Matters are not that bad, however. There is consensus on the phenomenon, on what constitutes overt manifestations of aggression as such. The diversity of definitions is a consequence of the diversity of approaches to the study of aggression. Some biologists have given primary attention to the purpose of aggression and its adaptive or nonadaptive function for various species. Others have opposed such preoccupation and have pursued a deterministic motivational analysis of aggression in the investigation of contributing exogenous and endogenous factors, independent of teleological considerations. Some psychologists have approached aggression in a strictly behavioral fashion, conceiving of it only in terms of variables that can be directly observed. Others have found it necessary to invoke hypothetical constructs, such as specific intent or expectations of outcomes. Both the antecedents and consequences of aggression have thus been conceptualized differently by different investigators, and the differences in conceptualization have been expressed in seemingly incompatible definitions. At close inspection it becomes apparent, however, that there is considerable overlap among the behaviors that the various definitions accept as manifestations of aggression, and this overlap makes for a reasonable degree of consensus on the phenomenon. Nonetheless, the heterogeneity of definitions has—at times at least—hampered the reconciliation of conflicting positions, and in this sense, it has not aided in the understanding of aggression.

In the face of these difficulties, it seems advisable first to establish some conceptual clarity regarding the phenomenon under investigation. In Chapter 2, this tedious task is undertaken in a critical analysis of commonly employed conceptualizations of aggression and the development of definitional criteria to be considered in the conceptualization of animal and human aggression. These criteria are then employed in defining various forms of hostility and aggression. The defined concepts, in turn, are employed in the subsequent treatment of theories and analysis of research findings. It is hoped that the consistent use of the concepts developed (i.e., specific forms of hostility and aggression) will help to avoid much confusion and aid in reconciling disagreements based on differing conceptualizations.

Chapter 3 serves a dual function. First, it provides an account of what is known about hostility and aggression in animals other than man. Phylogenetic speculations and "grand theories" that span aggression in all species are subjected to a critical analysis. The specific theories of hostility and aggression available (together with those theories that bear on these behaviors) are presented and appraised in light of the evidence regarding the mechanisms that govern the behaviors. Second, the distinguishing characteristics of hostility and aggression in humans—especially the unique features of hostility- and aggression-mediating mechanisms in humans—are delineated and contrasted with the mechanics of hostile and aggressive behaviors in subhuman species. The contrast drawn between the mechanics of human and subhuman hostile and aggressive behavior is then used to specify where generalizations from animal to man are unwarranted and why.

The reader should be prepared for a rather drastic change in Chapter 3 regarding the relationship between theory and evidence. The amount of relevant data on animal aggression from both laboratory and field investigations is nearly overwhelming. In sharp contrast, research findings concerning the specific differences between animals and man in the mechanics of aggression are virtually nonexistent. Comparative data on the antecedents and consequences of hostility and aggression are not available, and as will become clear later, they would be quite useless anyway. Data on the unique human characteristics that probably influence hostility and aggression abound, but they generally have been obtained in connection with other behaviors. All this is to say that the initial discussion of human aggression in Chapter 3 is not nearly as well substantiated by data as is the discussion of aggression in animals that precedes it. For example, evolutionary considerations obviously can only be supported by the scantiest of anthropological findings. The discussion of the likely role of aggression in the ascent of man thus is necessarily highly speculative. Furthermore, the discussion of man's unique characteristics (i.e., mainly his advanced conceptual and communication skills) may appear largely speculative in Chapter 3, but it can actually be substantiated to a considerable degree. A large portion of Chapters 4 and 5, in fact, amounts to a substantiation of the general contentions expressed in the discussion of the animal–man differences regarding the mechanics of aggression presented toward the end of Chapter 3. The reader should keep this in mind while being introduced to this differentiation.

In Chapter 4, the major theories of human aggression are presented and subjected to a critical appraisal. Similarly, theoretical approaches that directly relate to aggression without having been identified as theories of human aggression specifically are discussed. The change from a preoccupation with aggression instincts to an emphasis on aggressive drives is traced, and the gradual replacement of the concept of specific aggressive drive by that of generalized drive as a response energizer is detailed. The acquisition, maintenance, and extinction of hostile and aggressive modes of behavior are discussed, and the various specific learning mechanisms that have been implicated in these functions are analyzed and evaluated in the light of pertinent research evidence. The notion of punishment is subjected to a detailed theoretical examination, and the consequences of punishment—especially of its controversial use for the purpose of controlling aggression—are projected on the basis of available research findings.

Throughout Chapter 4 and the following chapters dealing with human hostility and aggression, much attention is given to research procedures and their adequacy. This is done to guard against the possible misinterpretation of findings. As indicated earlier, in research on human aggression, the measures of aggression often have only a weak connection with what they are supposed to measure. This substantial discrepancy between the concept and its operationalization is reason enough to be particularly cautious in making generalizations. Much attention is also given to the involvement of values. In the discussion of theories and research findings regarding human hostility and aggression, the explanatory adequacy of theoretical propositions and the social implications of theories or findings are separated conceptually and considered independently.

In Chapter 5, cognitive response guidance in human hostility and aggression is analyzed. The involvement of attributional processes and moral judgments is detailed and integrated in a system of response guidance through the anticipation of consequences. The likely dependency of this system of cognitive guidance on favorable excitatory conditions is then shown. A model is developed according to which the effective cognitive guidance of hostility and aggression is restricted to conditions of intermediate, "normal" sympathetic activity. The model projects the impairment of cognitive guidance for extreme levels of excitation, especially for extremely high levels, and a return of response guidance to the more elementary mechanics of learning—mainly to stimulus control.

Thereafter, two relatively independent motivational systems governing human hostile and aggressive behavior are recognized. On the basis of a distinction between incentive motivation and annoyance motivation, two different but complementary theories are proposed to account for the various forms of hostile and aggressive behavior in man. Both the theory of incentive-motivated hostility and aggression and the theory of annoyance-motivated hostility and aggression are discussed in terms of the available research evidence. In connection with the latter theory, the phenomenon of "impulsive" hostility and aggression is investigated.

In Chapter 6, the theory of annoyance-motivated hostility and aggression proposed in the preceding chapter is further developed and refined. Annoyance and the hostile and aggressive actions it promotes are treated as emotions. The specific interplay of cognitive and excitatory processes in these emotional states and emotional behaviors is scrutinized. Special attention is given to the behavioral implications of excitatory activity prior to, during, and following acute annoyance. Much attention is also given to the formation of hostile and aggressive habits that serve the alleviation of annoyance. A theory that details the cognitive and excitatory mechanics of emotional hostility and emotional aggression is proposed and appraised in the light of pertinent research findings.

Finally, in Chapter 7 some of the implications of the preceding explorations in theory and research regarding hostility and aggression are outlined. The need for the correction of various popular misconceptions is pointed out, and some strategies for the control of human hostility and aggression are suggested.

2 Aggression and Hostility Conceptualized

In this chapter, we review commonly employed conceptualizations of aggression and discuss their utility. We delineate the conceptual ambiguities in the various available definitions and then develop definitions that seek to avoid these ambiguities. In the conceptual approach taken, the basic similarities in animal and human aggressive behavior are acknowledged, but fundamental differences are also recognized. In this conceptualization, fighting in animals and aggression in man are, in fact, viewed as sufficiently distinct to warrant independent definitional treatments. The point of departure between animals and man is mainly the intent construct, which is dismissed for the definition of aggression in animals but employed for that of human aggression. Another principal distinction between this and common conceptualizations is the definitional separation of aggression (i.e., behavior seeking to inflict physical damage upon an organism) and hostility (i.e., behavior seeking to inflict harm in a more general sense, that is, harm that does not entail the infliction of physical damage specifically).

I. CONCEPTUALIZATIONS OF FIGHTING IN ANIMALS

The common use of the term *aggression* with regard to fighting in animals confounds various definitional criteria. Characteristically, aggression is conceived of as behavior that inflicts *destruction* upon some entity. This entity is usually an animal other than the agent inflicting the destruction. However, on occasion, the term *aggression* is used when the recipient of the destruction is the destructive agent itself, a living organism other than an animal, or even an inanimate object. The degree to which destructive behavior is perceived as aggressive is dependent on the extent of destruction observed. Other things being equal, degrees of aggressiveness thus appear to be a simple function of the magnitude of destruction.

At times, however, behavior is perceived as aggressive not so much because of its destructive consequences as because of its extraordinary *vigor*. Of similarly destructive or nondestructive animals, those which perform more forcefully in social encounters are likely to be considered more aggressive. To the extent that so-called threat displays involve vigorous motor behavior, animals that employ such displays with the effect of preventing destructive behavior will consequently appear to behave in a highly aggressive manner.

The perception of aggressiveness in animals seems also to depend on the particular circumstances under which behaviors with potentially destructive consequences occur. An assault in the absence of apparent *provocation* usually is considered more aggressive than the performance of the same behavior in response to provocation. Similarly, the attribution of an acceptable *purpose* for the destruction exerts an influence on the assessment of aggressiveness. Destructive behavior that apparently fails to serve the maintenance of the species directly, such as wasteful predatory killing or the mutilation of conspecifics, tends to be perceived as more aggressive than the same behavior whose consequences are somehow "put to good use." In addition, the assessment of aggressiveness tends to be colored by a sense of *fairness* and an esteem for *courage*. Both assaults upon weak, defenseless victims and attacks by overpowering, strong antagonists have been interpreted as more aggressive than assaults upon opponents of equivalent strength.

None of these considerations that affect the perception of aggression in animals is without its problems. Destructiveness usually can be readily assessed. However, as a criterion, it can be applied only after aggression has occurred, and it is therefore insensitive to potential aggression. The vigor of motor behavior is similarly obtrusive and measurable. However, vigorous activity in and of itself, which is not associated with destruction, is generally not considered aggression. The information required for the other criteria that affect the perception of aggression is less accessible. The sufficiency of a provocation, the legitimacy of a purpose, the unfairness of an attack, and the courage needed for an assault—all are considerations that go far beyond the descriptive assessment of destructive behavior. These considerations imply an understanding of the ecological function of the destructive behavior and require complex evaluations of the circumstances under which the behavior occurs. Clearly, when such criteria are applied, human values are being projected into animal behavior, resulting in a truly anthropomorphic assessment of aggression.

The use of these criteria in combination—leaving unclear the extent to which particular considerations are being invoked—has created considerable conceptual ambiguity. This ambiguity has motivated the development of more or less formal conceptual definitions and, along with them, of particular operationalizations of the phenomenon under investigation and their implications for the generalizability of research findings. As we will see, efforts to conceptualize aggression in animals in more formal terms have led to the removal of most anthropomorphic considerations but generally have failed to produce a nomenclature that could be agreed upon by investigators of different methodological persuasions in the biological and behavioral sciences.

A. Predation and Interspecific Fighting

Disagreement is evident in the treatment of predation and nonpredatory interspecific fighting as contrasted with conspecific fighting. Aggression in animals would seem to be most apparent in the behavior of the predator killing his prey. In terms of the destructiveness criterion, a cheetah running down and subduing an impala or, for that matter, a cat catching a mouse certainly would be examples of aggression. Many biologists, however, have excluded predation, by definition, from the category of aggressive behaviors and have reserved the term *aggression* for fighting among members of the same species. Carthy and Ebling (1964) noted considerable agreement among biologists on this distinction. According to such a view, the realm of aggression consists solely of conspecific fighting. Predatory behavior—although generally far more destructive in its consequences—and inter-specific nonpredatory fighting—no matter how destructive—are considered to fall outside this realm.

The distinction between predation and other forms of potentially destructive behavior is certainly a basic one. Predation, by definition, is behavior that serves the procurement of food. Nonpredatory fighting serves other ends. There are extreme differences in the manifestations of these behaviors and probably also in the underlying mechanisms. For example, several investigators (Hutchinson & Renfrew, 1966; Roberts & Kiess, 1964; Wasman & Flynn, 1962) have noted substantial differences between predatory behavior and "affective aggression" in the cat. Predation involves few, if any, emotional displays such as hissing and growling. The cat slinks to the floor, remains relatively motionless and silent, and suddenly makes a deadly assault upon its prey. In the case of nonpredatory, affective fighting, in contrast, the cat displays pronounced sympathetic arousal. It hisses and growls, moves about, arches its back, and attacks with a barrage of scratches and bites. Similarly, predatory behavior differs from nonpredatory behavior in group attacks. Wolf packs, for example, subdue their prey by getting behind their victim and hamstringing it. In social fighting, in contrast, the approach is always head to head, and the wolves seek to seize each other by the back or the neck (Murie, 1944). Defensive movements against predators also exhibit differences from those used against conspecifics. Tinbergen (1953a), for example, has reported that deer use their antlers only in social combat with rivals and use their front hooves to ward off predators.

There is reason, then, to believe that predatory behavior and nonpredatory aggression differ not just in degree but in character. It follows that a thorough understanding of nonpredatory aggression cannot be developed through extrapolation from predatory behavior, and in this sense, it seems justified to investigate the two types of behavior independently. The apparent need for independent exploration does not suggest or require, however, that predation not be considered aggression.

The tendency to separate predation and, more importantly, nonpredatory interspecific fighting from the study of aggression per se derives from a preoccupation with hostile conspecific encounters. This preoccupation, in turn, results from the dominant interest in human aggression and also from characteristics of particular research procedures. To those who seek to reveal the nature of aggression among humans through the exploration of fighting in animals, aggression within a species provides the closest analogue. For these researchers, the exploration of predation and conflict between members of different species holds little promise. In terms of research procedure, aggression between conspecifics has been extensively studied for reasons of parsimony and convenience. In laboratory investigations of social behavior, allelomimetic as well as aggressive, conspecifics have received the most attention. Natural predator–prey relationships have been of some interest, too. In contrast, the study of nonpredatory interspecific fighting and predation that does not naturally occur has had little appeal, mainly because it requires the potentially endless probing of species combinations without sound theoretical guidance or assurance of meaningful findings. In field studies, the investigation of predation and interspecific fighting seems to have been hampered by the presence of the researcher. His presence, concealed as it may have been from the group being studied, may have kept predators and rivaling species away. This possibility led Washburn and Hamburg (1968) to suggest that "predation and interspecies conflict may have been under-estimated in the field studies so far available [p. 469]."

B. Conspecific Fighting

The preoccupation with conspecific fighting and consequent neglect of predation and nonpredatory interspecific fighting, for whatever reason, seems to have guided the conceptualization of aggression rather than vice versa. The practice of equating aggression with conspecific fighting has led to the development of formal definitions of the former concept in terms of the latter. In turn, such definitions have guided further conceptualizations and influenced our thinking about aggression in general. Technically speaking, definitions are no more than arbitrary labeling conventions. Once in use, however, they have a tendency to shape approaches and channel research activities. The recognition of this effect of definitions has led to objections to equating aggression with conspecific fighting. Washburn and Hamburg (1968) have suggested that predation and other forms of fighting may not be as independent as commonly assumed and that the various forms of fighting may well be related. These researchers insist that in the study of aggression, predation "should be kept open for investigation and not ruled out by definition [p. 463]." The same argument can be made against ruling out nonpredatory interspecific fighting. Such fighting does occur in invertebrates (e.g., Cloudsley–Thompson, 1965), in vertebrates (e.g., Wynne–Edwards, 1962), and in primates (e.g., Teleki, 1973). At present, the possibility of a relationship between interspecific and conspecific fighting, particularly in primates, cannot be ruled out on the basis of available data, and the definitional elimination of interspecific fighting from the study of aggression in animals can only perpetuate the prevailing ignorance about this relationship.

It may appear that the study of destructive behavior in animals would best be served by a conceptualization of aggression that gives primary consideration to the destructiveness criterion. Predation and nonpredatory fighting between different species and within particular species could be comparatively assessed on this criterion, and any empirically determined similarities and interdependencies between these destructive behaviors could be incorporated in pertinent definitions. In order to avoid any misconceptions, types of aggression could be denoted as predatory, interspecific, or conspecific. However, as stated earlier, since the destructiveness criterion can be applied only after the overt manifestation of fighting, such a definition would be insensitive to the potentiality of aggression. If aggression among animals were to be defined as *behavior by which an animal inflicts destruction upon another animal,* conspecific fighting that manifests itself in the effective display of threats could not be considered aggression. The chief domain of past and contemporary research on aggression in animals would thus be reduced to the consideration of conspecific fighting that has notable destructive consequences. Such fighting is generally thought to be very rare (cf. DeVore, 1965; Eibl–Eibesfeldt, 1970; Hinde, 1970).

It seems to have been well recognized that the straightforward application of the destructiveness criterion would exclude from consideration many behaviors that are typically thought of as aggressive. In order to include these behaviors, the definitional criterion has been modified to accommodate the *potentiality* of aggression. This accommodation has taken quasi-descriptive form. Hinde (1970), for example, defined aggressive behavior in animals as follows: "behavior directed towards another individual which could lead to physical injury to the latter [p. 335]."

This definition is another way of saying that in order to be considered aggressive, behavior need not result in actual destruction but must have the potential for so doing. More characteristically, however, definitions have involved notions of intent or purpose more or less directly. The involvement of such notions is apparent in a much-cited definition of aggression proposed by Carthy and Ebling (1964): "An animal acts aggressively when it inflicts, attempts to inflict, or threatens to inflict damage on another animal [p. 2]."

According to this definition, the actual infliction of destruction, unsuccessful efforts toward that end, and the emission of signals conveying a threat of possible destruction all qualify as aggressive behavior.

Definitions such as Hinde's, which avoid assumptions about behavioral intent and purpose, create problems at the operational and conceptual level. Who is to judge which kind of skirmish between animals *could* lead to injury and which kind *could not?* Nonhostile encounters—those involving vigorous group play, in particular—result in injury now and then. Should they therefore be classified as aggression? On the other hand, should ferocious, apparently hostile skirmishes that nonetheless seldom produce detectable injury be excluded? Clearly, the observer's judgment concerning the possibility of injury from an encounter is highly subjective. It may depend largely on potentially irrelevant considerations such as the vigor of the behavior displayed. Definitions that involve ambiguity to this extent tend to produce unreliable classifications, and they certainly do not help to resolve existing classificatory confusions.

Definitions that explicitly or implicitly involve notions of intent or purpose create more serious problems not only at the operational level but also at the conceptual level. In the formulation offered by Carthy and Ebling, who is to judge if damage was attempted, that is, was intended? Who is to judge if a particular display was meant as a threat and specifically, as a threat to inflict damage? Such judgments cannot be made on the basis of observational data. They require knowledge of the animal's destructive intentions, which—lacking information for valid inference—can only be conjectured upon. Thus, at the operational level, the definition is not workable.

At the conceptual level, the problems associated with definitions involving the intent construct become apparent when efforts are made to make such definitions workable. If intent is approached through a contingency analysis of purely observational data, destructive attempts can be defined as those behaviors that, when not disrupted, lead with great regularity to destructive behavior. Similarly, threats can be defined as behaviors that, when ignored by the animal toward which they are expressed, are regularly followed by destructive behavior directed against the animal threatened. A high transition probability for destruction does not ensure, however, that destruction was initially intended or that it was the ultimate goal response. A skirmish may start harmlessly but escalate toward destruction. Given this possibility, it would seem to be misleading to read, as a rule, attempts to inflict damage into the initial phases of encounters.

Concerning threats to inflict damage, the possibility of misconceptions is even more disturbing. Threats of destruction, when they function in the way they are commonly assumed to function, will *prevent* destruction by making it unnecessary. When a state of discomfort is discontinued or a particular goal is achieved by the use of threat, there is no reason for the threatening animal to engage in actual fighting with its threatened-away opponent. If it did fight, the animal would only risk injury and losing what its threat had accomplished. Effective threat should thus be associated with low transition probabilities for destruction. Only in situations in which threat fails should there be cause for an escalation of conflict and should destructive behavior become more likely.

In cases in which threat fails, the conceptual problem is comparable to that associated with attempts at destruction. If an escalation from threat to injurious fighting occurs, it does not necessarily follow that the infliction of damage was initially threatened. The true conceptual dilemma, however, is created in the case of effective threat. Should the display of any behavior or the emission of any signal that either prevents the approach of a potential opponent or induces his withdrawal be considered an effective threat of destruction? Clearly, approach may fail to occur, and withdrawal may occur for many reasons other than threat; and if it does, the attribution of retreat to particular displays and signals preceding it would be erroneous. There exists an entire class of behaviors, the so-called submission and appeasement gestures, which—as far as withdrawal is concerned—may be expected to produce consequences quite similar to those achieved by effective threats. Considering displays or signals and nonapproach or withdrawal alone, there is no way in which a threat function can be validly distinguished from an appeasement function. The fact that most investigators seem at great ease in deciding between threat and submission displays shows only that in such classifications, for better or worse, additional criteria that have not been stipulated in the definition are being used.

Finally, the conceptual equation of threat of destruction with threat per se may be called into question. It is possible that at least some threat displays are not preludes to the execution of destructive behavior at all but instead serve an expressive function only. They may be protective expressions or expressions of claims aimed at warding off opponents and rivals. If they fail, the animal may be as much inclined to yield and flee as to fight. There seems to be no need whatsoever to assume that the animal who emits such expressions seeks to convey a readiness to engage in actual fighting for the declared purpose of inflicting damage.

It appears that the interpretation of threat displays in animals has been guided to a great extent by a uniquely human appraisal of the function of threat. In general, it has been presumed that animals are incapable of using "empty" threats. It may be closer to the truth to assume that what in animals appears as threat is almost always empty in the sense that this behavior is not linked to any destructive goal response. Threat of destruction implies an appreciation of the threat's lack of power if not followed up with the threatened consequences. Since such appreciation cannot be taken for granted in animals, it seems appropriate to treat threat displays according to how they function in their immediate context, namely as a form of defensive or offensive move in themselves. Considering threat displays as aggression can only cause confusion, and to avoid this likely confusion, it appears desirable to supplement the concept of aggression with that of hostility.

In conclusion, the involvement of the intent concept in the conceptualization of aggression in animals is not only unworkable but potentially misleading. It seems preferable to discard this concept entirely (for the consideration of aggression in animals only!) and to construct definitions on the basis of purely descriptive data. Furthermore, in building definitions upon descriptive data, the empirical estimation of typical, most probable outcomes promises to be superior to an impressionistic treatment of possible outcomes. These considerations have guided the construction of the definitions now proposed.

C. Definition of Aggressive and Hostile Behavior in Animals

1. Any and every activity of an animal that is directed toward another animal and that inflicts partial or complete destruction upon that animal or that is associated with a high probability of so doing constitutes *aggression*.
2. Any and every activity of an animal that involves behavioral elements characteristic of aggression without, however, involving the infliction of destruction upon another animal and that is enacted in situations of social conflict constitutes *hostility*.

These definitions do not rely on an appraisal of intent or purpose but instead depend on empirically derived knowledge concerning the probable consequences of fighting and the social conditions that lead to skirmishes. Without taking into account such knowledge, which every experienced investigator has and in fact uses anyway, behavioral assessments of aggression and hostility are likely to be confusing and unreliable.

The definition of aggression stipulates that destruction actually be inflicted or—based on prior observation—at least be highly likely under the circumstances. A cat, for example, that performed all predatory motions toward a mouse would be considered to have behaved aggressively even if the mouse managed to escape injury. However, kittens that inflict minor injuries upon each other at play are not considered to aggress because of the extremely low likelihood of injury associated with their behavior. The definition also stipulates that destruction need not be fatal or even serious. It can be minimal in the sense that some tissue of the organism is at least temporarily damaged. Pain, in the absence of notable damage, is not considered a sufficient condition of destruction. Although pain may be considered a construct of great behavioral relevance, it has not been invoked, because its assessment in animals is problematic, and this would only make the definition less workable.

Secondly, the definition stipulates that for a behavior to be considered aggressive, the destruction need be directed against another animal—not just living matter or inanimate objects. This restriction, which seems to put the major burden of aggressiveness upon the carnivores, is applied mainly to achieve a relatively close correspondence between the defined concept and the general use of the term *aggression*. Commonly, the destruction of plant life by herbivores is not considered aggression. The term as generally used seems to presuppose a struggle between assailant and victim. This struggle is apparently absent when destruction is directed against unresisting plants. The idea of struggle has, in fact, so strongly influenced common conceptions of aggression that the struggle-free destruction of animals by animals is often not considered aggression. A bird's catching and gulping of a fly is hardly considered an attack. In contrast, a spider's catching and eating of the very same fly tends to be conceived of as merciless aggression. In the definition proposed here, the interpretation of aggression differs sharply from such common views. The defined concept is independent of considerations of the efficiency of destruction, the victim's limitations in defending itself, and its ability to express distress in a way that will make man take notice.

Thirdly, the definition stipulates that the destructive activity *be directed toward* potential victims. This stipulation was involved to prevent the accidental destruction of animals from being classified as aggression. The elephant, for example, who lumbers across the plains, no doubt behaves destructively, crushing and injuring ants, grasshoppers, small lizards, and the like. Such destruction, which is accidental in the sense that it is performed against animals that are not perceived by the destroying agent, is generally not considered aggression. The stipulation that aggressive behavior need be directed toward another animal eliminates accidental destruction from consideration by requiring that at the very least, the aggressive animal perceive the potential victim. At the most, it requires that particular responses be aimed at the victim. The stipulation, it should be noted, does not allude to any intent to harm in the aggressor. Independent of any consideration of intent, the elephant's seemingly unmotivated trampling of a snake that it has detected in its path is to be considered aggression.

Finally, the definition makes no provision for the possibility of self-injurious behavior. Such behavior was not included because among animals, it constitutes a negligible phenomenon.

The concept of hostility was introduced in order to accommodate the fact that nonpredatory interspecific and conspecific fighting is rarely injurious. Treating such noninjurious behavior as aggression implies that it is closely related to destructive behavioral tendencies, which may prove incorrect. As suggested earlier, nondestructive fighting may as readily result in withdrawal and flight as in an escalation toward destruction. Hinde (1970) noted that "a tendency to attack is often associated with a simultaneous tendency to flee, and many threat postures are associated with both these tendencies. Furthermore, threat postures likely to be followed by an attack on the rival intergrade with submissive ones [p. 336]." In the concept of hostility, these circumstances are recognized. It is not implied in any way that in the final analysis, the opponent's destruction is being pursued. On the contrary, the concept of hostility leaves open to empirical determination the conditions under which hostility leads to aggression and those under which it does not.

The definition of hostility stipulates that hostile behavior have some affinity with aggressive behavior. Characteristically, the hostile animal approaches an opponent or behaves in a way that signals that an approach is forthcoming. This approach or pseudoapproach resembles an attack in that it involves expressive elements of destructive fighting. These expressive elements may also accompany retreat. There is thus no contradiction in the notion of hostile retreat. It should be clear, however, that communicationlike behaviors that could be construed as conveying threats—such as, for example, territorial "claims" by bird song (cf. Howard, 1920) or by odor markings in mammals (cf. Uexküll, 1956)—are not considered hostile.

According to the definition, hostile behavior in animals is nondestructive fighting in direct encounters. Such fighting is usually conducted in pursuit of vital needs, and the recognition of these needs helps to delineate conditions of social conflict. The presence of social conflict, in turn, seems a useful additional criterion in determining the hostile character of behavioral exchanges.

D. Definition of Types of Aggressive and Hostile Behavior in Animals

Once aggression is conceived of as fighting in which destructive consequences are certain or highly probable, the question of conceptual refinements through subdivisions of the basic concept arises. Any such refinements may also be deemed desirable for the concept of hostility.

Moyer (1971) has proposed a detailed subclassification of aggressive and hostile behaviors on the basis of physiological distinctions. By tracing the involvement of neural and humoral structures in various behavioral manifestations of aggression and hostility, he arrived at seven or eight kinds of destruction-related behaviors: (1) predatory aggression, (2) intermale aggression, (3) fear-induced aggression, (4) irritable aggression, (5) territorial defense, (6) maternal aggression, (7) instrumental aggression, and (8) sex-related aggression, which is listed as a likely class. Moyer hastened to point out that these classes of aggression are not mutually exclusive and that there may be considerable overlap between the various classes of aggression in any given situation. But he maintained that "there are different neural and endocrine bases for each of the above aggression classes [p. 30]."

The evidence for such a one-to-one correspondence between types of aggression and distinct neural and humoral structures is by no means conclusive, however. But even if it were and distinctly different structures were involved in distinctly different ways in the various proposed kinds of aggression, the classification would seem to have limited value in a behavioral analysis of aggressive and hostile behavior. Conceptually, any distinct behavioral manifestation of aggression or hostility should, in the final analysis, be associated with distinct neural and humoral processes. The particular manifestations of aggression or hostility, together with the particular circumstances under which they occur, should thus be redundant with specific physiological ones—if those should exist—and should provide equivalent criteria for classification. The categorization of forms of aggression on the basis of the involvement of neural and endocrine structures, as proposed by Moyer, is certainly justified and offers a potential means for controlling aggression by intervening in physiological processes. If there should be distinct physiological states associated with distinct types of aggressive and hostile behavior in animals, these types of aggression and hostility would have to be controlled in different ways. This in fact is Moyer's primary interest and concern. In the behavioral analysis of aggressive and hostile behavior, however, classifications based on overt manifestations of the behavior must be considered superior to those based on physiological criteria, because the information needed for classification is more readily accessible and, more importantly, because the overt behavior is the actual phenomenon under investigation.

The conceptualization of specific types of aggression and hostility in behavioral terms must be based on at least three principal questions—all of which ask for information about directly observable behavior only.

1. Which animal aggresses against or expresses hostility toward which other animal?
2. Under what prevailing conditions does aggressive or hostile behavior occur?
3. What are the consequences of the aggressive or hostile behavior?

Concerning the involvement of animals in aggressive or hostile encounters, the categories of conspecific and interspecific fighting are obvious:

1. Aggression or hostility is *conspecific* when such behavior occurs between members of the same species.
2. Aggression or hostility is *interspecific* when such behavior occurs between members of different species.

Fighting in particular social aggregates (*individual-individual, individual-group,* and *group-group aggression,* etc.) can be similarly specified by qualifying the primary concepts.

Concerning prevailing conditions, the initiation of aggressive or hostile activities serves as the criterion for determining attack and defense.

3. Aggression or hostility in an animal is *offensive* when such behavior is initiated by the animal, that is, when it is not performed in response to prior aggression or hostility directed against that animal.
4. Aggression or hostility in an animal is *defensive* when such behavior is performed in response to prior aggression or hostility directed against that animal.

According to the latter definition, a potentially injurious assault by an animal that has been the target of offensive hostility is to be considered defensive aggression. It is not stipulated that in order to be considered defensive, aggression need be provoked by aggressive activities only. This is to ensure that the animal that initiates a hostile exchange is identified as the offensive party even if its opponent is the first to actually inflict destruction.

It should be noted that these definitions concerning the initiation of fighting are not consistent with the widely adopted definitions proposed by Scott (1958). Scott reserved the term *aggression* for the act of initiating an attack. Fighting is thus either aggressive or defensive. In view of the fact that the offensive attacker is not always successful in the infliction of injury to the attacked animal, it seems unwarranted to exclude defensive fighting, which may be as destructive as offensive fighting, from the domain of aggressive behavior. As far as the infliction of destruction is concerned, only predation seems to favor the attacker. In much of interspecific fighting, and certainly in conspecific fighting, destructive outcomes appear to be independent of the initiation of aggression. The definitional approach taken here, that is, the qualification of the primary concepts as offensive vs. defensive, was chosen to involve secondary considerations, which may be of significance for particular research interests, without dismissing any aspect of aggression from consideration.

The analysis of conditions prevailing when aggressive or hostile behavior occurs can further be used to determine the degree of sympathetic activation preceding the performance of such behavior. The animal's general activity is commonly used to judge activation levels. *Low-activation* could thus be distinguished from *high-activation* types of *aggression* or *hostility,* and intermediate levels could be specified in between. Such a distinction would accommodate the concept of "affective aggression" without, however, involving anthropomorphic elements associated with the notion of affect.

Concerning the consequences of aggressive or hostile behavior, other major distinctions are apparent.

5. Aggression is *predatory* when the aggressing animal regularly ingests, partially or completely, the destroyed animal.

Cannibalism could be defined as predatory aggression that victimizes conspecifics. Cannibalism is frequently cited, although incidents of conspecific killing and ingesting occur only rarely. Incidents in which animals eat conspecifics without having killed them are often referred to as cannibalism. In light of the fact that such behavior usually does not involve conspecific aggression, it should be considered *scavengerism* rather than cannibalism.

6. Aggression or hostility is *antagonistic* when such behavior is terminated with the resolution of social conflict.

Characteristically, resolution is accomplished by the withdrawal of one party. However, antagonistic aggression may continue until one or more of the animals involved is disabled or killed.

These qualifications of the principal concepts of aggression and hostility could, of course, be expanded to accommodate more specific research interests without involving such considerations as purpose, instrumental value, exogenous or endogenous causal factors, or behavior control by incentives or punishments. For our present purposes, it suffices, however, to distinguish first between potentially destructive aggressive behavior and nondestructive, aggressionlike, hostile behavior, and then between conspecific and interspecific, offensive and defensive, low-activation and high-activation, and predatory and antagonistic behaviors.

II. CONCEPTUALIZATIONS OF AGGRESSION AND HOSTILITY IN MAN

In discussions of human aggression, as in analyses of fighting in animals, behavioral and social scientists have tended to restrict the notion of aggression to conspecific destructive behavior—that is, to destructive behavior among humans. There has rarely been any mention of the fact that man, unlike any other species, has considerably broadened and expanded his predatory behavior. The truism that animals kill because they have to—meaning that such behavior directly serves their survival—certainly does not apply to man.

A. Man Against Animal

A great portion of interspecific destruction committed by man no doubt serves the purpose of securing food. Although such destruction is usually not discussed as aggression, the killing involved, in a general sense, may legitimately be considered *predatory aggression*. However, man's interspecific aggression differs from that of other animals in his destruction of much animal life for purposes other than food getting. There are at least four types of assaults by man upon animals other than man that seem uniquely human.

First, unlike animals, who typically either escape or defend themselves only when acutely endangered by others, man has frequently taken the offensive by destroying other species that only occasionally pose a direct threat to his life or health. This kind of destruction, which we refer to as *aggression serving man's safety,* has been systematically directed against dangerous animals such as lions, bears, poisonous snakes, and scorpions. Unquestioned in its value for man, it has been practiced for centuries and has resulted in the decimation of the species in question in all areas densely populated by man.

A second type of assault, which serves a similarly vital interest of man, is called *aggression serving man's well-being*. This label subsumes systematic attacks directed against any species that interferes with the procurement of food or other essential commodities or that itself provides products with survival value. Examples of the former are insects and rodents, which may spoil crops, and termites, which may damage homes; duck embryos, which are used in the production of a rabies vaccine, are an example of the latter.

Third, there exists a type of destruction that is less universally condoned. This type is called *aggression serving man's convenience*. This category includes any destruction that fails to serve vital needs but that provides "peace of mind" or some valued commodity. In this category, the species assaulted range from pesky flies and moles in the backyard to animals whose fur is in fashion. The near extinction of the snowy egret for its haute-couture feathers comes to mind as an example of this type of destruction. In recent years, killing for luxury, particularly when it threatens to wipe out an entire species, has been severely criticized in the media and by groups and individuals concerned with the environment. The fact remains, however, that man continues to practice this type of destruction.

Fourth and finally, unlike any other species, man kills other species for the declared purpose of obtaining enjoyment. We thus may talk about *aggression as a leisure activity*. People engage in the popular "sports" of hunting and fishing primarily for the fun of it. The fact that successful hunting and fishing also produce food is usually secondary, since comparable or equivalent food typically can be obtained with far less effort and expense. As long as there has been assurance that any victimized species would survive in sufficient numbers, such killing for enjoyment has been socially sanctioned and generally conceived of as having recreational value.

The various forms of interspecific aggression committed by man may or may not be related to his conspecific aggressive behavior. As in the case of animal–animal aggression, this question should be kept open for empirical exploration rather than being dismissed by definition. Conceivably, there are interdependencies between the two types of behavior. A number of theoretical notions have, in fact, assumed that interdependencies exist. Hunting, for example, has been said by some to have cathartic value and by others to constitute disinhibition training, and accordingly, it has been expected either to lower or to heighten human aggressiveness generally. The initial evidence has failed to disclose any particular relationship, however (Buss, Booker, & Buss, 1972).

B. Man Against Man

The issue that has generated the most discussion and controversy is, of course, the conceptualization of conspecific human aggression. What, precisely, do we mean when we talk about aggression in man? What behaviors does this concept involve?

There seems to be general agreement regarding the principal characteristic of aggressive behavior: the infliction of partial or complete destruction upon the entity aggressed against. Such destruction is alternatively referred to as damage, injury, harm, or noxious stimulation. But whatever the particular choice of words, some form of destruction is considered the defining property of aggression (cf. Bandura, 1973a; Berkowitz, 1965a; Buss, 1971; Feshbach, 1970; Kaufmann, 1970; Rule, 1974). The principal issue, namely that *aggression constitutes injurious behavior,* thus seems settled. Disagreements arise, however, in the interpretation of what, precisely, constitutes injury or damage, who or what constitutes the target of aggression, and last but not least, what motivational circumstances underlie any such effects.

1. Aggressive Intent. Beginning with the latter factor, the questions of whether or not destructive behavior need be *intended* in order to be considered aggression and whether or not the eventual involvement of the concept of intent is methodologically sound and useful have produced considerable debate. Buss (1961) suggested that the assessment of intent could only be unreliable and argued that the use of the intent concept, because of its teleological character, would be entirely inconsistent with behavioral research methodology. Consequently, he dismissed intent and proposed a definition of aggression in pure stimulus–response terms: Aggression is "a response that delivers noxious stimuli to another organism [p. 1]."

The adequacy of this definition has been severely challenged (e.g., Bandura & Walters, 1963b; Feshbach, 1964; Kaufmann, 1970). Obviously, according to this definition, any accidental (meaning unintended) response of an individual that noxiously stimulates someone else is to be considered aggression. So is any noxious stimulation administered for beneficial reasons. This makes a baseball fan's being hit by a foul ball and a patient's being surgically treated genuine instances of aggression. The latter example makes it especially clear that the sole consideration of the effect of a particular behavior upon a target is an insufficient criterion for aggression. Apparently, if only damage to tissue (or the noxious stimulus quality thereof) is critical, the acts of a sadistic torturer and a surgeon are equivalent conceptually. By giving consideration only to the immediate consequences of behavior, definitions that disregard intent create considerable conceptual confusion, as has been amply demonstrated elsewhere (e.g., Kaufmann, 1970). This confusion in the conceptualization of human aggression, it appears, can only to be resolved by giving full consideration to antecedent conditions, of which intent may be regarded a crucial element.

Modifying his earlier position, Buss (1971) has more recently accepted intent as a concept necessary to deal effectively with human aggression. He has, in fact, incorporated it in a new definition: Aggression is "the attempt to deliver noxious stimuli, regardless of whether it is successful [p. 10]."

In contrast to definitions that avoid the intent concept, this formulation does not entirely rely on the actual performance of injurious behavior. All it requires is that efforts, futile though they may be, be made toward that end. The definition thus addresses behavior that potentially has certain consequences, not solely the consequences themselves. Most importantly, however, by stipulating that efforts be made toward an end, it involves the concept of goal-directedness, which is generally considered an equivalent of intent.

With such a change of position, Buss has in effect returned to the influential conceptualization of Dollard, Doob, Miller, Mowrer, and Sears (1939), which stresses the goal-directedness of aggressive behavior: Aggression is "an act whose goal-response is injury to an organism [p. 11]."

In one form or another, this goal-response formulation of injurious intent has been adopted or adapted in most definitions of human aggression formulated by more recent investigators (cf. Bandura, 1973a; Berkowitz, 1962; Feshbach, 1970; Sears, Maccoby, & Levin, 1957). The intent concept seems thus to have become generally accepted. However, the resolution of the intent controversy concerns the general notion only. With regard to specifics of goal-directedness or intent, there remain many ambiguities.

First, it is usually unclear what precisely is meant by saying that injury was intended or, for that matter, that it constituted the goal response. One interpretation is that the response causing injury was nonaccidental in the sense that the aggressor failed to make an effort to avoid the damage. The response was thus not deliberate but not against the aggressor's will, either. A more common view is that any injurious act committed voluntarily, whether unplanned or deliberate, is intended. Implicitly, the person is credited with *free will* (to aggress or not to aggress) and is consequently held responsible for all aggressive responses under his or her control. Another interpretation is that injurious intent is characterized by a disposition to commit a variety of damage-inflicting behaviors that are enacted as the individual is confronted with the target toward which he or she is so disposed. In this view, aggressive intent reveals itself only as opportunities for aggression arise. This is in contrast to yet another interpretation, which maintains that injurious intent involves the active seeking out of opportunities for aggression. Consequently, intent is conceived of as a predisposition to approach and attack certain general or specific targets—a predisposition that the individual may or may not be aware of. With the possible exception of the view presented first, all these interpretations have been used, typically implicitly and rather inconsistently, by investigators of human aggression.

A second source of ambiguity concerns the theoretical status of the intent concept. Many investigators have hesitated to employ intent as a purely hypothetical construct that could be tested in derived implications. Instead, they have sought to establish intent empirically. Buss (1971), among others, has categorically asserted that "intent is inferred by examining the stimulus antecedent to the response and its consequences [p. 10]." He has given the example of a boy who, after being taunted by another boy, becomes angry, fights, and hurts his tormentor. He feels that in such a case the inference of intent to do harm is simple and straightforward. This seems to appeal to common sense, and for all practical purposes it probably is adequate most of the time. The inference is not compelling, however. In line with commonly made assumptions concerning animal behavior, it could be argued that the boy was responding at all times to stimuli in his immediate environment— that he was reacting, so to speak, on impulse. He may not have had any specific anticipation of future states or notion of purpose, as some interpretations of intent would require. The fallacy of the intent inference is more apparent, however, in cases such as when a student who has been publicly demeaned by his instructor later jostles him in a crowded hallway. The collision might have been purely accidental, but knowledge of the antecedent conditions would suggest aggressive intent. Given sufficiently complex situations, knowledge of some form of prior provocation would, in fact, lead to the conclusion that retaliatory intentions were behind any behavior potentially producing adverse consequences.

It should be noted in passing that if the analysis of the antecedents of aggression were to permit decisive and valid inferences about intentions (and this would resolve a good portion of the problems in the administration of criminal justice), the intent concept would become expendable, since it would be entirely redundant with the information contained in the analysis of antecedents. Aggression could thus be explained by direct reference to these antecedents.

Inferences about aggressive intent seem deceptively plausible, because they are habitually practiced by every mature person. As is discussed later in more detail, aggressive acts are perceived, evaluated, and in fact, overtly responded to as a function of the attributions of intent or purpose a person makes, in part by projecting his or her own reactions to similar circumstances onto others. Such attributions are subject to considerable distortion and error. There is little cause to believe that if made by scientists, they would constitute a more "objective" (or less subjective) basis for implicating intent than would self-critical introspective reports furnished by aggressors. In view of the ill repute of introspection in the early stages of psychology, the behavioral scientists' reluctance to use insight-type data is understandable. So also is the haphazard manner in which they have come to accept the intent concept for the study of human aggression. However, the notion of intent probably has survived, not because of its inferential rigor and the compelling quality of conclusions based upon it, but because of its intuitive appeal based on introspection. At times people know that they feel like hitting their tormenter or that they are waiting for a chance to get back at him or her when a safer opportunity arises. Generally speaking, this state of affairs can be articulated by the individual, and potentially valuable information can be obtained from self-reports. The real problem is to devise procedures that guard against the acceptance of distorted reports—not to dismiss such data in perpetuation of historically based prejudices. Error-reducing procedures, no doubt, also must be applied to attributions of intent to the behavior of others. The introspective report of intent is of course nothing other than the self-attribution of intent. In all likelihood, both these types of attribution involve highly related, interdependent cognitive processes. The empirical investigation of these processes seems imperative to a full understanding of human aggression. Eschewing the use of introspective data certainly does not facilitate matters. Moreover, the intuitive inference or attribution of the intent or purpose of aggression from its antecedents and consequences cannot be considered to be independent of introspection, and thus it does not constitute an alternative approach.

This is not to say that a thorough analysis of reliable introspective reports of aggressive intentions is likely to reveal all the critical factors contributing to human aggression. Man's beliefs about his intentions may have little relevance for his behavior. But then again, they may be truly significant. This certainly is an open empirical issue that should not be decided prematurely, one way or the other, by any one-sided conceptualization of aggression. Conceivably, man's ability to use a coding system to represent to himself what he wants and means to do is a principal factor that separates man and animal—at least as far as the study of aggression and hostility is concerned. The animal responds to its immediate environment, that is, to characteristic stimuli that elicit attack or defense motions through innate or learned connections. There is no evidence that nonhumans engage in searches for retaliatory opportunities, delay reprisals, or obtain gratification from witnessing misfortunes befall their antagonists. The idea of retaliation, which certainly holds a central position in the discussion of human aggression, appears to be uniquely human. It seems intricately related to his ability to analyze and evaluate his own behavior as well as that of others and most importantly, to conceive of a plan or program of his future behavior and to execute it at will as the required conditions arise (cf. Miller, Galanter, & Pribram, 1960). If aggressive intent functions, in fact, as a plan of action that is likely to be executed, it would still remain to be shown to what extent such a plan is accessible through introspection and to what extent it may be influenced by it. It is conceivable that introspection is not a determining factor at all and that its sensitivity is limited. Some plans may be recognized, others may be misread, and others may go unnoticed. In short, introspective data may or may not provide valuable information about behavioral dispositions. In order to resolve this conceptual dilemma, it would seem indicated to treat intent as a hypothetical construct (rather than an empirical entity) and to establish the merits of introspection and attributions in deduced consequences.

A final comment concerning intent is in order. The inclusion of this concept in definitions of human aggression effectively eliminates the misclassification of the accidental infliction of injury, but it does not help to distinguish between aggression based on malevolent and benevolent motives. According to all definitions of human aggression thus far presented, the surgeon who performs an operation and the mother who resorts to spanking to train a child not to put his hands on the stove, for example, perform aggressive acts. Any more discriminative definition will have to involve the consideration of *specific* intentions, goals, or purposes. Efforts toward this end are apparent in recent publications (e.g., Bandura, 1973a; Buss, 1971; Feshbach, 1970; Rule, 1974; Rule & Nesdale, 1974). As a result, various subclasses of human aggression have been proposed. This issue is addressed following a discussion of the more basic question: What, in the definitions offered, constitutes injury, damage, or noxious stimulation?

2. Infliction of Injury. In conceptions of aggression in animals, the stipulation that injury be inflicted upon another animal means that damage, defined as the destruction of tissue, must occur. Aggression in man is generally conceived of very differently. In definitions of human aggression, the infliction of injury may but need not be directed toward another person or even another organism, and it may but need not involve actual physical injury. This definitional stipulation, in short, means different things to different people, investigators included.

Dollard et al. (1939) seem to have set the general direction for the conceptualization of the universe of manifestations of aggression in man. They qualified their major definition of aggression by specifying that the injurious goal response may be directed against an organism or an *organism surrogate*. Obviously following psychoanalytic ideas, they considered the target of aggression to be substitutable. If, for whatever reason, a frustrator cannot be attacked directly, his affiliates and belongings are seen to stand next in line. Any inanimate object can thus become a target for an aggressive outburst. A doll, for example, can be ripped to pieces. According to Dollard et al., such behavior constitutes genuine aggression, "provided that the acts would be expected to produce injury were the object animate [p. 10]." Aggression, then, need not inflict injury upon any living being but may cause the *destruction of inanimate objects.*

A related issue is the extent to which an attack upon another person need be injurious in order to be considered aggression. Dollard et al. felt that in aggressive assaults on frustrators, it is of little moment "whether the weapon is a business deal, a gun, a malicious rumor, or a verbal castigation [p. 10]." Consequently, *nonphysical assaults,* such as disadvantaging, embarrassing, humiliating, or scorning someone, qualify as aggression, although they are not destructive to the tissue of the target. Dollard et al. have gone even further by suggesting that, for example, fantasizing and dreaming about "getting even" with a frustrator and swearing after striking one's own thumb with a hammer constitute aggressive behavior. Clearly then, the meaning of "injury" in stretched to accommodate the *autistic commission of destruction* and the *expression of annoyance,* both of which do not inflict actual damage upon anybody or anything.

In more recent definitional efforts, the meaning of injurious behavior has similarly been expanded to accommodate attacks against nonorganisms, nondestructive attacks, or both.

Feshbach (1970) conceived of aggression as any behavior that results in injury or damage to *inanimate objects* as well as organisms. Boelkins and Heiser (1970), who sought to tighten up other definitions of aggression by modifying Carthy and Ebling's formulation, stipulated that threatened, attempted, or actually inflicted damage to an individual or to *property* be considered aggression. Bandura (1973a), who also considers the destruction of property aggression, proposed that in humans injury can be of a mental sort: Aggression is "behavior that results in personal injury and in destruction of property. The injury may be psychological (in the form of devaluation or degradation) as well as physical [p. 5]."

Similarly, Buss (1971) feels that, for example, "the 'bite' of verbal aggression may be as sharp (psychologically) as the serpent's sting [p. 7]" and suggests that aggression need not be physical. In fact, Buss has proposed that on occasion, *passive behavior* can constitute aggression. He has proposed three independent dichotomies of aggressive behavior: (a) physical-verbal, (b) active-passive, and (c) direct-indirect. Eight types of aggression are derived from the interaction of these dichotomies. Out of this entire scheme, only two classes deal with the infliction of injury (in Buss' terms, with the infliction of noxious stimulation, which involves the experience of physical pain, publicly expressed or privately suffered). The combination physical-active-direct subsumes shooting, stabbing, punching, and the like; the combination physical-active-indirect involves such things as practical jokes and booby traps. Sit-ins and similar obstructions of passage are said to constitute direct, passive, physical aggression; and refusals to perform necessary tasks indirect, passive, physical aggression. Verbal assaults, all considered aggression, range from direct insult (verbal-active-direct), through malicious gossip (verbal-active-indirect), to refusals to speak (verbal-passive-direct), and refusals to consent (verbal-passive-indirect). In this view, for example, aggression is committed by the girl who says "no" and by the mother who denies her child a foolish request.

Other writers (e.g., Lorenz, 1963; Storr, 1968) who have equated aggressiveness to a high degree with the striving for self-assertion have given prime consideration to *competitive activities*. Such activities are of course predominant in games and sports, and consequently, participation in such activities, whether the competitor ends up on the winning or the losing side, is considered to constitute aggression. In fact, even the enthusiastic spectatorship of such activities is considered aggressive.

All this should make it very clear that the concept of human aggression has not been restricted to the infliction of physical injury or physically painful stimulation. Investigators have tended to stretch the concept so as best to accommodate the particular notions about aggression they have entertained or to bring the definition into line with the methodologies they have employed. As a result, the meaning of aggression has become blurred. What, precisely, are manifestations of aggression in man? There is no doubt about the intentional killing and wounding of others. But what about pushing and jostling among youngsters, which does not cause any damage to tissue? More importantly, what about committing a murder in fantasy, smashing a vase in anger, or saying to someone: "You idiot!" "I'll kill you!" "I hate you!" or simply "No!" in noncompliance with a request? Should such events be considered aggression?

Definitions being arbitrary labeling conventions, there is certainly nothing wrong with stretching the aggression concept to any point one desires. The practicality of such extensions may be seriously questioned, however. Much disagreement among investigators (and among interested laymen, for that matter) seems to result from discrepant conceptualizations. If *A* restricts him- or herself to the consideration of injurious behavior but *B* considers playing tennis and resisting the draft acts of aggression, it is easy to see that they will not be able to agree on any general statement concerning aggression. There is thus much to be gained, pragmatically speaking, from some scrutiny of the concept of human aggression.

The primary concern with aggression as a phenomenon in human affairs has always been man's propensity to inflict bodily damage upon his fellow man. In speaking of aggression, one speaks mainly of killing, wounding, and hurting others—physically, not in a metaphorical sense. This type of destructive behavior could, of course, be specified as "physical aggression." But it would seem more parsimonious and potentially less misleading to consider it aggression per se and to label seemingly related types of behavior either by qualifying them ("nonphysical," "verbal," "indirect," etc.) or by using other concepts. The use of distinct concepts has the advantage of not implying great affinity when in fact only analogy may exist. As the excursion on the thorny road of definition should have revealed, investigators have proposed or implied that many forms of noninjurious but harm-inflicting behaviors are very closely related to destructive aggression. Being mean, obnoxious, or oppressive in nonphysical ways has often been treated as if such behaviors had the same motivational origins and behavioral objectives as overt physical aggression. In conceiving of particular relationships, investigators have gone far beyond what has been empirically established. What, precisely, is the relationship between competition and aggression or between passive resistance and destructiveness? There are, no doubt, some common aspects. But there are substantial and fundamental differences, too. And these differences tend to be obscured once behaviors are subsumed under the same general heading. Also, after some time, relationships that have been assumed come to be taken as proved. They are no longer open to empirical determination. But they must be if we are to progress in our understanding of aggression.

C. Definition of Aggression and Hostility in Man

The principal distinctions of interest, which were not made in the conceptualizations already discussed, concern (a) the infliction of bodily injury versus the infliction of harm in more general terms, (b) the intention to inflict injury or harm versus the expression of anger or annoyance, and (c) the communication of threat versus the infliction of harm and the expression of anger or annoyance.

In discussing the infliction of injury, many investigators have freely assumed that as far as man is concerned, the infliction of bodily damage is just one manifestation of aggression among many potentially *equivalent forms.* They have implied that noninjurious acts that thwart another person's attainment of desired goals, deprive him or her of cherished objects, or cause his or her disparagement or humiliation can "hurt" as much as, for example, a punch in the nose. With the ultimate "ends" thus conceived of as highly similar or equal, noninjurious means have been seen as alternatives potentially equivalent to those means that involve the infliction of bodily damage. The ends are, of course, not equal but only similar in certain ways. Obviously, the state produced by receiving a severe beating differs from that produced by being deceived in a business deal. Yet according to certain criteria, these actions may produce similar or equal effects. The two actions may, for example, yield comparable emotional reactions of anger or depression or the same loss of time, energy, or money. The two experiences may even be reported as equally "painful." There are, then, experientially relevant dimensions on which the impact of injurious and noninjurious behaviors can be assessed and compared, and such comparisons may reveal considerable similarities. The most frequently implied dimension of comparability is, no doubt, the degree to which an inflicted experience, no matter what kind, *is suffered by the victim.* In accord with this criterion, it can indeed be considered more "aggressive" for the legendary rich uncle to disinherit his spoiled nephew than to slap his face. If the ultimate object of all aggressive behavior were to inflict suffering, it would stand to reason to conceive of actions, whether they are injurious or not, as equivalent and *interchangeable* as long as they inflict the same degree of suffering. It cannot be reasonably assumed, however, that human aggression is generally motivated by a desire to bring suffering to the victim. There are strong alternative motives for committing aggressive acts (cf. Buss, 1961, 1971). Additionally, it has been proposed (e.g., Berkowitz, 1965a, 1974) that even in cases where the desire to make the victim suffer predominates, persons who have set their minds on inflicting injury will strive toward the completion of the contemplated acts. They will, so to speak, not rest until they see the target of their efforts injured, and they will not settle for noninjurious substitutes regardless of how much suffering they cause. On the basis of research evidence, the possibility that certain aggressively instigated persons are intent upon seeing bodily damage done cannot be ruled out. Research has failed to address the substitutability issue directly. Given the lack of relevant evidence, it would seem premature to jump to conclusions about equivalent means in the conceptualization of aggression. The intent to inflict bodily damage should not be treated as necessarily functionally related to the intent to inflict suffering in more general terms. We accordingly distinguish between the infliction of physical injury and the infliction of *harm*, where harm denotes any experience associated with suffering not resulting from physical injury. We then conceputalize human aggression as the infliction of injury and conceptualize human hostility as the infliction of harm; we leave open to empirical determination whether and to what extent aggressive and hostile activities in humans are functionally equivalent and interchangeable.

Investigators have generally failed to separate definitionally the expression of anger and annoyance from aggression and hostility. The tendency to lump the concepts together seems to derive from the widely held belief that anger consistently produces aggression (cf. Dollard et al., 1939). This belief is erroneous, however. As Buss (1971) pointed out, anger need not lead to aggression, and aggression may occur in the absence of anger. Anger is thus neither a necessary nor a sufficient condition for aggression. If anger is conceived of as an emotional state associated with elevated sympathetic excitation and certain cognitive processes, there is no need to assume that these cognitive processes necessarily serve the preparation of aggressive or hostile acts. A person may be enraged without contemplating such acts. He or she may instead be upset with the circumstances at large or with him- or herself in particular. He or she may covertly curse and swear, feel "disillusioned," and make preparations to avoid getting into the same mess again. The dominant cognitive process in a state of anger may consist of verbalizations such as "I'm stupid, stupid, stupid, . . ." rather than a search for someone to "let it out on." However, even when retaliatory activities are contemplated in a state of anger, such "fantasy behavior" need not result in overt hostility or aggression. The "will I get him for that!" for example, may remain a presumably pleasant private experience and never affect overt behavioral exchanges. But whatever the effect of cognitive processes in states of anger or annoyance may be, as long as these states are not expressed in some form, they obviously cannot convey hostile or aggressive inclinations and thus cannot confuse the classification of hostile or aggressive behavior. Only verbally and/or nonverbally *expressed* emotional states can affect such classifications.

At this point it becomes important to distinguish between: (a) the expression of anger or annoyance as such, (b) threats of hostility or aggression, and (c) actual hostility. The comments "I'm mad at you" or "You are obnoxious" together with particular intonation and gestures may be nothing but a way of expressing to another person that his or her behavior has produced anger or annoyance. They may be used in seeking the discontinuation of the stimulation in question, without any consequences whatsoever for hostility or aggression. Similarly, the refusal to speak—which Buss (1971) has classified as verbal-passive-direct aggression—may be just another way of expressing persisting annoyance about an earlier conflict. Furthermore, attacklike motions such as kicking objects around or banging one's fist on the table may merely serve the expression of anger. This reasoning relates to Feshbach's (1964) distinction between expressive and hostile aggression, which he derived from presumed desires *to hit* versus *to hurt*. Since only the latter type of motive is defined as aggression in the present conceptualization, the expressive behavior in question should be referred to as expressive anger rather than expressive aggression.

The expression of anger and annoyance can, of course, involve *threats of hostility and aggression*. The statement, "I'll get you for this!" for example, expresses the potential attacker's readiness to await retaliatory opportunities and to engage in hostile or aggressive acts at a later time. Such an expression of threat may or may not convey anger. Threats can no doubt be made "in cold blood." In fact, they may take conditional form (if you do this, I'll do that), in which case they are made to avoid future states of anger and annoyance rather than to remedy present ones (cf. Tedeschi, 1970). The conditional form of threat plays an extremely significant role in bargaining at the personal and organizational level. It constitutes the basis of international agreements such as truces and peace treaties. Characteristically, agreements of this kind are made for the declared purpose of preventing destruction. If they are followed, they do prevent destruction not just in spite of the conditional threats of aggression and hostility involved but presumably because of them. Threats of aggression, particularly conditional ones, should thus not be plainly equated with aggression. If they do not inflict injury or harm, they cannot be considered aggression or hostility.

Finally, expressions other than threats may inflict considerable suffering. Insults, malicious gossip, dishonesty that inflicts loss, and the like are to be considered forms of hostility—not aggression. Needless to say, behavioral dispositions to commit aggressive, hostile, or threatening acts are not to be considered aggression, hostility, or threats as long as these acts are not performed.

These considerations, together with others discussed later, suggest the following definitions of human aggression, hostility, and related forms of behavior:

1. Any and every activity by which a person seeks to inflict bodily damage or physical pain upon a person who is motivated to avoid such infliction constitutes *aggressive behavior*.

2. Any and every activity by which a person seeks to inflict harm other than bodily damage and physical pain upon a person who is motivated to avoid such infliction constitutes *hostile behavior*.

3. Any and every communicative activity conveying a person's intention to behave in an aggressive or hostile manner toward a person, either dependent

on certain conditions or unconditionally, constitutes a *threat of aggression* or a *threat of hostility,* respectively.

4. Any and every activity resembling aggressive or hostile behavior but by which a person does not seek to inflict injury or harm upon a person constitutes *expressive behavior* that may or may not be associated with a state of anger or annoyance.

5. Any and every state of readiness or willingness to aggress against, be hostile toward, or threaten a person constitutes an aggressive, hostile, or threatening disposition, respectively.

In order to make these definitions apply to human aggression against animals, the word *animal* should replace *person* whenever the latter word refers to the object or the target of the behavior in question.

In the present conceptualizations of aggression, hostility, threat, and the purely expressive components of these behaviors, the definitions involve the specification of both the aggressor's and the victim's motivational states. In other definitional efforts, usually only the aggressor's motivational state has been taken into account. However, the motivational states of both parties seem critical in generating satisfactory conceptualizations.

The conceptual stumbling blocks for definitions of aggression seem to be the classifications of *accidental, prosocial,* and *masochistic* behaviors. With the stipulation of injurious intent, the accidental infliction of bodily damage or physical pain has generally been eliminated from consideration as aggressive. Prosocial injurious behavior, in contrast, has remained a source of disagreement. Most definitions are simply not sensitive to this type of behavior. Consequently, the surgeon's prosocial services, for example, must be considered incidents of aggression. Although it has been recognized (e.g., Feshbach, 1971; Rule, 1974) that the perception of prosocial motives, in contrast to personal ones, tends to make aggressive activities appear more acceptable, prosocially motivated injurious behavior, even when extremely beneficial to the victim, has remained within the definition of aggression. Finally, definitions have generally ignored the case in which bodily damage or physical pain is desired or sought by the recipient and either provided by others or inflicted by the self. The related case in which pain and possibly minor injuries are tolerated rather than sought is undoubtedly more typical. It should not be considered aggression, for example, when in connection with sexual activities, one party—knowing that the other party enjoys it or at least does not object to it—inflicts sensations on the other that under different circumstances would be considered painful.

The proposed definitions resolve the issue of the prosocial, benevolent infliction of injury or harm and the issue of the consent of the recipient by stipulating that the victim be motivated to avoid the injury or harm. The definitions thus address the element of coercion in aggression, hostility, and threat. Aggressive or hostile behavior is *imposed* upon someone. Injury or harm is *forced upon the victim*. If it is consented to, the phenomenon vanishes. In one of those "possible worlds" in which people would agree to hurt, torture, or kill each other, there would be considerable destruction; but without coercion, the notions of aggression, hostility, and threat would be alien.

The inclusion of the element of coercion in the conceptualization of aggression, hostility, and threat relates to a recent attempt to reinterpret aggression in terms of coercive action. Tedeschi, Smith, and Brown (1974) charged that the concept of aggression is inadequate and useless; they suggested that it be abandoned and replaced by the more inclusive and, in their view, less value-distorted concept of coercion. As a superior way of delineating aggression, they proposed the specification of the forceful and potentially harmful and destructive use of power (i.e., the specification of a particular form of coercion).

Although the criticism of the aggression concept by Tedeschi et al. disclosed many definitional problems, it is difficult to see how the concept of coercion eludes these problems. For example, the concept of coercion seems just as vulnerable to the potential encroachment of human values as that of aggression. With regard to the difficulties that follow the necessary involvement of intent or purpose, coercion seems to fare worse than aggression rather than better. Because of its close association with intent and purpose in the use of power, the notion of coercion appears to be especially prone to the involvement of intangibles. It thus has little utility for the analysis of aggressive behavior in animals, and in the conceptualization of human aggression, it at best offers an alternative definitional approach. In defining human hostility and aggression, it seems to matter little whether one starts with the element of destruction and harm and then considers coercion, or whether one begins with the element of coercion and then involves destruction and harm. What is important is that both elements of hostility and aggression—namely, the infliction of harm and injury on one hand, and the coercive nature and function of this infliction on the other—be recognized. The value of the reconceptualization of aggression by Tedeschi et al. (1974) lies in its focusing of attention on an important, hitherto neglected component of hostility and aggression rather than in its rendering superfluous the notion of aggression as such.

Returning to the stipulations in the definitions already presented, the implications should be obvious. Suicide, for example, is to be considered a destructive but not an aggressive act. Similarly, sadomasochistic behavior, no matter what destructive consequences it has, is not to be considered aggression. The infliction of pain in interpersonal competition does not constitute aggression, either, as long as the agreed-upon rules are not violated. The stipulation also prescribes that benevolent injurious acts not be classified as aggression. The surgeon, for example, does not commit an act of aggression, because he generally has the consent of his patient to produce injuries necessary to achieve beneficial ends. The determination of consent seems preferable to stipulations based on personal utility (e.g., that in aggression, the negative utility outweighs the positive), because the assessment of utility—which necessarily involves highly subjective judgments on the part of the potential victim—would create immense practical problems. Apparent consent for the reception of injury or harm, which may be conceived of as the final outgrowth of personal utility considerations, seems more readily accessible.

At the pragmatic level, the assessment of goal-seeking behavior and potential avoidance motivation presents many difficulties. As discussed earlier, intent cannot be rigorously inferred from an inspection of the antecedents and consequences, in purely behavioral terms, of any particular injury- or harm-inflicting act. Observed persistence either in seeking to perform such an act or in efforts to avoid its impact would be highly suggestive. However, in most instances, there will be little or no evidence of persistence, and the investigator will have to accept introspective reports, even retrospective ones, to learn about intentions (to inflict) in the potential aggressor and intentions (to avoid) in the potential victim. At times, he or she will have to use intentions as hypothetical constructs to be validated by determining whether observed events correspond with deduced implications. Generalizations from these assessments will then provide a basis from which inferences about intentions can be drawn in a probabilistic fashion.

The basis for drawing inferences about intent is a point of distinction between conceptions of animal and human aggression and hostility. As will be recalled, the notion of intent was not involved in definitions regarding animal behavior. This course was chosen mainly because intent cannot be adequately inferred from behavioral observation alone. In the conceptualization of human aggression and hostility, intent was involved because observational records can be complemented by introspective reports and introspection-based constructs and because this concept resolves part of a conceptual dilemma. More importantly, it was involved because the human capacity to rehearse cognitions related to intentions conceivably affects dispositions and behavioral manifestations in ways that are unique to organisms capable of arbitrarily representing events to themselves via a coding system. This aspect of human behavior is discussed in some detail in later sections of the book.

The definitional approach taken here is in accord with the methodological tradition in which a definition is viewed as the specification of a set of principal characteristics that potentially distinguish the defined entity from all others (e.g., Reichenbach, 1947). Following this approach, the imposed infliction of injury or harm emerges as the principal characteristic of aggression or hostility, and this characteristic serves as the criterion for classification. The definitions thus constitute *classification rules* that—when strictly adhered to by investigators of potentially different moral convictions and idiosyncrasies—should yield an identical (or at least highly similar) classification of events as aggressive vs. nonaggressive, hostile vs. nonhostile, etc. According to agreed-upon criteria, particular behaviors are to be considered aggressive, hostile, or neither. Personal views are considered independently, but they can of course be related to the defined concepts. These personal views may greatly overlap with the defined concepts, but they also may have little in common with them.

This approach differs considerably from the one taken by Bandura (1973a). This investigator, who carefully analyzed the various factors that influence a person's perception of injurious acts, arrived at the formula that "aggression is characterized as *injurious and destructive behavior that is socially defined as aggressive* [p. 8]." This amounts to saying that aggression is what people say is aggression. There are thus no definitional rules to follow but people to consult instead. In order to decide whether or not an injurious act is aggressive, the investigator has to sample people's views of the act in question.

Rather than eliminating the ambiguities and inconsistencies in common views of aggression, as other investigators have attempted to do in their definitional efforts, Bandura in fact uses these common views as the very basis of his conceptualization. Such a procedure may have great practical merit. It assures that by definition, the scientist's view is no longer deviant from that of the layman, and since aggression concerns the lives of most laymen directly, the exchange of ideas and facts concerning aggression would seem to be greatly facilitated. From the standpoint of theory and research, however, the approach has severe drawbacks. Clearly, common views of aggression do not emerge as the result of people's search for reliable classifications of phenomena. They are instead subject to numerous potentially distorting influences. In line with Bandura's (e.g., 1973a) view, they are acquired rather uncritically, and the acquisition is controlled by such processes as social learning (where the reinforcement contingencies involved generally apply to factors other than the adequacy of particular discriminations). In general terms, common views of aggression, vague as they may be, are adopted and modified in many ways and for a variety of reasons. To the extent that these views change, any reliance on them amounts to the endorsement of a floating reference point. Many behaviors that were considered aggression a couple of years ago may now be designated differently, and vice versa. The changes in designation, then, would cause changes in aggression to be ascribed to unchanged situations, and they would generally distort any record of the development of human aggression. Comparisons of this type are more meaningful when a more stable reference point is used, such as that provided by definitions that specify criteria for behavioral characteristics of aggression.

The same assessment applies to comparisons between groups or individuals. Views of aggression are clearly different in different social groups within any complex society and between societies (cf. Wolfgang & Ferracuti, 1967). Finally, the aggressor's view of an injurious act need not be identical or even similar to the victim's. A bystander may see the act in yet another way. A husband, for example, who makes a cynical comment about married life to his wife may feel that he is being hostile to her. The wife, on the other hand, may miss the intent and interpret the comment as a general statement. Conversely, the husband may make just such a general statement, and the wife may read hostile intent into it. The interpretation of a witness may fail to correspond to the view of either of the parties involved. If people's views are to be consulted, an act's designation as aggressive or hostile will thus greatly depend on who is being asked.

All this, of course, is not to say that the views people have of the injurious acts they inflict, suffer, or witness are not of interest in the study of aggression. Obviously, these views constitute a person's belief that he or she has aggressed or not, has been aggressed against or not, or has witnessed an aggressive or a nonaggressive act. These beliefs generally have definite behavioral implications, and they thus must be of great interest to anyone who attempts to explain behavior. However, a person's beliefs about a particular incident should not be mistaken for an unbiased, highly specific, and accurate assessment of it. Beliefs are not valid merely by virtue of their existence. If, instead, a less personal assessment is pursued (one that meets the standards of behavioral research), beliefs concerning aggressive acts can be analyzed more meaningfully in that they can be related to potentially valid external criteria. In summary, conceptualizations of aggression that are based on social judgment necessarily involve distorting factors (e.g., ethical considerations) and constitute unstable reference points; conceptualizations that are based on specified characteristics to be judged following methodologically sound observational procedures define a comparatively stable reference point to which personal assessments can be compared. Only the latter type of conceptualization permits the investigator to trace changing views of aggression and changes in manifestations of aggression itself. Similarly, only this type permits the meaningful assessment of any existing differences between views and manifestations of aggression.

It should be recognized that the foregoing discussion of the social-judgment approach to the conceptualization of aggression applies mainly to the definition of the primary concept. Any deliberate, coercive, injurious assault upon another person—regardless of particular distributions of personal views of it—should be classified as aggressive. This classification should be sustained even if all such views disagree with it, as they well might in a case where the assault duly punishes a wrongdoer. As long as classifiers can readily concur on the relationship between a behavior to be classified and the criteria advanced in a definition, there seems to be no reason to abandon formal definitional approaches in favor of assessments in which criteria are being employed in an entirely uncontrolled fashion. Formal definitional approaches, as the consensus stipulation shows, are not devoid of elements of social judgment, but incorporate them in a structured manner so as to improve on the reliability of classification. Formal definitional and social-judgment aproaches are thus by no means independent. Indeed, it should be clear that in the definition of many subclasses of hostility and aggression, especially those involving value and moral considerations, the two approaches converge and lead to very similar classification procedures.

D. Definition of Types of Aggression and Hostility in Man

Given these primary definitions of aggression and hostility, we can now delineate more specific categories by qualifying the primary concepts. We define only the most basic subclasses here. It should be clear, however, that other subclasses, which may be required in the pursuit of specific research objectives, can be formed in an analogous manner.

1. Aggression is *offensive* when a person seeks to inflict injury upon a person who is not attempting or has not been attempting to inflict injury upon him or her; hostility is *offensive* when a person seeks to inflict harm on a person who is not attempting or has not been attempting to inflict harm upon him or her.

2. Aggression is *defensive* when a person seeks to inflict injury upon a person who is attempting or has been attempting to inflict injury upon him or her; hostility is *defensive* when a person seeks to inflict harm upon a person who is attempting or has been attempting to inflict harm upon him or her.

According to these definitions, aggression enacted in response to another person's hostility is to be considered offensive. In order to be defensive, aggression must be provoked by aggression and hostility by hostility. This stipulation ensures that the person who crosses the line from hostile exchanges to injurious behavior is identified as the offensive aggressor. It should be noted that no such stipulation was made for animal behavior. Such a stipulation would be unworkable, because for animals—unlike for humans—hostility and aggression were conceived of as having similar overt manifestations.

In general, defensive activities are aimed at warding off an attack; that is, their goal is to prevent the infliction of injury or harm. In pursuit of this objective, they can, however, develop into full-fledged counterattacks. The possibility that the offensive aggressor may suffer more injury than the defensive aggressor is not in conflict with these definitions.

Both offensive and defensive activities are thus conceptualized at the descriptive level. However, to deal with uniquely human aspects of aggressive and hostile behavior, it becomes necessary to go beyond this level and to involve constructs. The notions of retaliatory, provoked, and unprovoked aggression and hostility seem to be meaningless in the absence of social judgment by an evaluator of the activities that produce injury or harm.

3. Aggression or hostility is *retaliatory* when the action is undertaken to compensate for injury or harm suffered in an earlier attack.

Clearly, this notion implies that an attack that has inflicted a certain degree of suffering has taken place and that whoever assesses the status of retaliation perceives the counterattack to be aimed at the reciprocation of this degree of suffering. The concept is thus based on a primitive form of justice (cf. Heider, 1958). Retaliatory actions seem "justified" or "called for" by an earlier attack. The principle of justice involved is that of "an eye for an eye," and the fact that many moral systems condemn justice of this type does not contradict the fact that this principle constitutes a form of justice. Needless to say, the principle is an ideal projection. Retaliation aims at "getting even," but efforts toward this end can of course fall short of or overshoot the objective.

4. Aggression or hostility is *provoked* when in the judgment of the attacker, the victim, or a witness, the attacker has been the victim of acts that deserve to be compensated for by aggressive or hostile means.
5. Aggression or hostility is *unprovoked* when in the judgment of the attacker, the victim, or a witness, a person aggresses against or treats in a hostile manner someone who has not done anything that deserves to be compensated for by such action.

As formulated, then, the notion of provocation is intricately related to considerations of justice. Unprovoked acts are seen to create an inequity in suffering. Retaliation potentially removes this inequity, thereby recreating the initial equitable state. Provoked acts are, of course, those that serve the restoration of an equitable state. The notion of equitable compensation for injury or harm implies that the magnitude of suffering caused must be judgmentally assessed in some manner. Similarly, the magnitude of the compensatory suffering inflicted by retaliatory acts must be judged. For retaliation to be perceived as equitable, these judgments must assign comparable valence to similar or dissimilar acts. A student, for example, must feel that his letting the air out of his teacher's car tires is roughly equivalent to the teacher's flunking him in a course (undeservedly, no doubt). Such judgments seem to be highly dependent on particular social norms and standards. The concept of retaliation is thus inseparably linked to moral judgment, and differences or changes in moral convictions should be reflected in views of the legitimacy or justifiability of retaliation.

The concepts of retaliatory, provoked, and unprovoked aggression and hostility, by involving aspects of social judgment, manifest a desirable sensitivity to aggression and hostility as they "objectively" may exist while taking into account the manner in which they are perceived by the various parties involved. However, in contrast to some other definitional approaches (e.g., Bandura, 1973a), it does so without rendering the primary concepts spurious by making them entirely dependent on social judgment.

Further classes of aggression and hostility concern objectives or goals other than retaliation. A principal dichotomy of aggression types has been proposed by both Buss (1961, 1971) and Feshbach (1964, 1970). These investigators distinguish between *angry* (or "hostile") aggression on one hand and *instrumental* aggression on the other. The former type subsumes acts whose goal it is to make the victim suffer or to hurt him or her. The latter subsumes activities that are engaged in to ensure or to facilitate the achievement of nonaggressive goals. As Buss (1971) described the concept, in instrumental aggression the aggressor commits an aggressive act in order to acquire some "reinforcer."

This distinction acknowledges the fact that whereas some aggressive acts are committed in a state of rage without regard for the acquisition of extrinsic incentives, other aggressive acts are committed "in cold blood" for the declared purpose of obtaining valued objects or services. Angry aggression seems to be motivated by the experience of a noxious state, and aggressive behavior aims at terminating this state. Termination of the noxious state, in turn, removes the motivation to aggress. Instrumental aggression, in contrast, is motivated by the desire to secure extrinsic incentives, and aggression provides access to these incentives. The attainment of the incentives, in turn, terminates the motivation to aggress. In these terms, angry aggression is *annoyance motivated* and instrumental aggression *incentive motivated.*

The distinction between angry and instrumental aggression, although widely used and rarely challenged, has recently come under criticism. Bandura (1973a) noted that the dichotomy is forced and that in this connection, the term *instrumental* is vague and misleading. He pointed out that in general, aggressive acts not only make the victim suffer but also produce a variety of incentives for the aggressor. Further, he discussed the semantic ambiguities of the term *instrumental.* The anger-motivated disablement of an attacker can, after all, be considered highly instrumental in removing an annoyance. It can also be argued that the termination of annoyance constitutes the instrumentality of angry aggression. In Bandura's view, the distinction between angry and instrumental aggression thus "reflects differences in desired outcomes, not in instrumentality [p. 3]." He suggests that it would be more accurate to distinguish aggressive acts in terms of their objectives rather than in terms of whether or not they are instrumental.

Bandura's criticism seems well justified. However, instead of discarding the distinction in question altogether, it would appear to be more desirable to accommodate the criticism by revising the potentially useful conceptual distinction. In fact, the proposed labels of annoyance-motivated and incentive-motivated aggression and hostility seem to accommodate this criticism reasonably well. These labels acknowledge behavioral objectives. In addition, rather than specifying whether or not instrumentality exists, they specify the particular utility of a behavior, and these specifications can be further refined as needed. Concerning the instrumental–noninstrumental dichotomy, it must be acknowledged that for most practical purposes, the two classes are not mutually exclusive. The motivation to reduce annoyance and the motivation to acquire incentives may coexist in many aggressive or hostile activities. The degree to which these motivational forces combine or interact is of course an empirical issue of great significance.

We thus redefine the conceptual distinction between angry and instrumental aggression.

6. Aggression or hostility is *annoyance motivated* when its primary function is to reduce or terminate a noxious state.

7. Aggression or hostility is *incentive motivated* when its primary function is to acquire extrinsic incentives.

The distinction drawn might also be conceived of as punishment-escaping versus reward-seeking behavior.

Since the escape from annoyance presupposes annoyance, and since the suffering of annoyance involves emotional responses associated with elevated physiological excitation, we alternatively refer to annoyance-motivated behavior as *emotional aggression* or *emotional hostility*. This is not to say that incentive-motivated behavior is necessarily nonemotional. Affect is seen to be involved to a substantially smaller degree in the latter type of behavior, however.

Finally, another distinction between types of aggression and hostility has been promoted by Feshbach (1971) and Rule (1974). These investigators have distinguished between *personally motivated* and *socially motivated* aggression. This distinction relates to moral considerations and their influence on the perception of aggressive acts. Generally, aggression committed in pursuit of personal gain or in connection with private vendettas is viewed as more objectionable than aggression enacted for the social good. The latter type of aggression is at times referred to as *prosocial*, although it should be clear that it is usually antisocial as far as the victims are concerned. The idealistic but hostile advocate of revolution and the well-meaning but aggression-inciting leader of a social movement, for example, may thus enjoy the benefit of mitigating circumstances in the evaluation of their behavior. The need for qualifications in the assessment of hostility or aggression is more apparent in the case of a judge who sentences a convicted criminal or a guard who subdues a prisoner who is trying to escape. In these latter examples, the acts committed are—according to our definitions—truly hostile or aggressive because the victim fails to consent. The lack of consent is, however, compensated for by a public mandate to perform these acts for the public good. The principal reason for reevaluating prosocial hostile or aggressive acts, then, is to determine the extent to which such behavior is *socially sanctioned.*

It appears that the consideration of whether and to what degree a particular hostile or aggressive act is sanctioned provides a more meaningful, reliable criterion for the classification of such acts than does the analysis of personal or social motivation. Prosocial motives that are not intertwined with selfish interest are difficult to envision and to determine empirically (cf. Krebs, 1970). The seemingly unselfish revolutionary, for example, may do whatever he does because he gains political recognition, prestige, and power; because he impresses the opposite sex; or simply because he enjoys the "ego trip" of entertaining a crowd. His behavior may thus be totally incentive motivated in a highly personal sense. Similarly, the behavior of prosecutors, policemen, and soldiers seems to be motivated, for the most part, by obvious personal incentives rather than the pure desire to behave in the public interest. In fact, the prosocial nature of the behavior of public servants, if their actions remain within the bounds of their mandate, can be quite independent of their personal motivation. The policeman, for example, who risks his life in subduing a murderer in order to get a medal or to impress his grandmother nevertheless commits a prosocial act. It appears, then, that the distinction between personal and social motivation, whatever the latter may be, is not a useful criterion for definitions. We thus avoid this distinction and instead define related classes in terms of existing or perceived legitimacy.

8. Aggression or hostility is *sanctioned* when it serves socially agreed-upon objectives and is performed within socially agreed-upon confines.

Social agreement characteristically takes the form of explicit regulations arrived at by legal processes. Thus, to the extent that they pursue socially agreed-upon objectives, judges who inflict harm and policemen who inflict injury perform sanctioned hostile and aggressive acts. Social agreement can, however, be conceived of as rather informal, serving as "unspoken law" in any social aggregate. A juvenile gang may agree on the value of aggression against competing gangs, thereby sanctioning such behavior within their group.

There is, of course, a crucial difference. In the first case, aggressors execute a public mandate; whereas in the latter case, a group—in a partisan manner—speaks for itself only and disregards the interests of others. Nonetheless, it should be noted that such disregard for the interests of others can also manifest itself in due legal process—the legitimacy of killing in a war against another nation being a case in point. In view of the special role of legal sanctions in the curtailment of hostility and aggression in society, it seems warranted to distinguish between sanction by public mandate and the partisan, self-produced sanction of hostility or aggression in groups of any kind. This is readily done by refining the foregoing definition.

9. Sanctioned aggression or hostility is *legal* when its objectives and the enforcement of those objectives are agreed upon by due legal process within a society or between societies.

Thus far, aspects of legitimacy have been considered in social terms. Legitimacy was conceived of as granted via a social process. However, considerations of legitimacy also apply to the individual's assessment of hostile or aggressive activities. Whether or not acts are socially sanctioned, they can be perceived as justified, unjustified, or justified to a certain degree. A soldier's shooting of an enemy, for example, although sanctioned and legal, may be considered unjustified by the aggressor, the victim, a bystander, or someone who is merely told about the act. In another vein, the riots in Watts or Milwaukee may be considered justified by some and unjustified by others. The personal judgment of justification is, no doubt, dominated by personal moral considerations. No matter how primitive such considerations may be, they relate to antecedent conditions and perceived objectives, and they result in a verdict of "good" or "bad." If hostile or aggressive behavior is witnessed, good or bad motives are attributed to it. In short, if the ends seem warranted under given circumstances, hostile and aggressive means may be endorsed. Such a process is formalized in the following definition:

10. Aggression or hostility is *justified* to the degree that its objective is perceived as acceptable or desirable by the attacker, the victim, or a witness.

In the presumed judgmental process that guides the evaluation of harm- or injury-inflicting acts, the perception of provocation and the attribution of motives should be important. Generally, the perception of provocation will tend to make hostile and aggressive acts appear more justfied. Also, given the broad agreement concerning the positive value of prosocial acts, the attribution of prosocial motives, erroneous though it may be, should make hostile or aggressive acts generally appear more justified.

3

Aggression and Hostility in Animals and Man

As indicated earlier, views of animal aggression have often been highly anthropomorphic. An intuitive appreciation of the workings of aggression in man has been projected onto animals, causing them to be viewed as ferocious, vicious, malicious, merciless, vengeful, and so on. However, as also noted earlier, there appears to be firm agreement among behavioral scientists that such thinking is futile. In general, investigators keep an alert watch for anthropomorphisms and avoid them whenever they suggest themselves in insights or findings. Thus, there is great reluctance to account for animal aggression by drawing inferences from knowledge of human aggression. In contrast, there is no such reluctance concerning the drawing of inferences in the opposite direction: from knowledge of animal aggression to human aggression. In fact, efforts to account for the phenomena of human aggression through the study of analogous behaviors in animals have received broadest attention in publications on aggression. These publications have featured existing and presumed similarities between animals and man. Important differences, which also exist, have been largely neglected. The prevalent views of human aggression have suffered from this selectivity, and it seems that a more critical analysis of similarities and differences between animal and human aggression is in order. In this chapter, we first take a look at unwarranted claims of parallelism and then elaborate on crucial discrepancies that must be recognized in any sensitive and potent theory of human aggression.

I. ON PHYLOGENETIC SPECULATION

Since Darwin's (1859/1887) revolutionary proposal concerning the origins of species, it has become quite customary among biologists, especially among zoologists and ethologists, to place every behavior under consideration into an evolutionary perspective. According to morphological or functional criteria, species are mapped onto an evolutionary scale, and aspects of the behavior of a species are evaluated in terms of that species' relative position on that scale. It should not be surprising, then, to find the aggressive behavior of a species treated in the same manner. Many biologists were apparently discontent with purely descriptive accounts of aggression within species and with purely descriptive comparisons between species. They felt compelled to "explain" manifestations of aggression by tracing them to presumed primal roots. They were also eager to claim a survival value for aggression in order to document its adaptive function. In this conceptual framework, human aggression has commonly been conceived of as a direct extension of emerging trends in phylogenetic classifications from lower to higher vertebrates.

The evolutionary approach to human aggression is most evident in the popular work of a group of European ethologists, chiefly Lorenz (1963, 1965c), Tinbergen (1951, 1953b, 1968), Morris (1968), and Eibl-Eibesfeldt (1970, 1971), together with an extraethological following (e.g., Ardrey, 1966; Storr, 1968). Of this group, Lorenz has been particularly insistent that a true understanding of human aggression, as well as of any other form of behavior, can be achieved only through phylogenetic analysis (e.g., 1950, 1954/1965, 1961, 1965a). Although the validity of this approach has remained highly controversial, it has been freely employed by these investigators in efforts to illuminate the nature of human aggression.

Phylogenetic speculation has led Lorenz (1963, 1964, 1965c) to propose that aggression in man is both *instinctive* and *spontaneous* (1964): "There cannot be any doubt, in the opinion of any biologically-minded scientist, that intraspecific aggression is, in Man, just as much of a spontaneous instinctive drive as in most other higher vertebrates [p. 49]."

Lorenz arrived at this sweeping proposal mainly by reviewing findings on conspecific aggression in birds and fish. There is some evidence that in these animals, particularly in fish (cf. Tinbergen, 1968), this type of aggression is not learned and in this sense is instinctive. Cullen (1961) showed that male sticklebacks that were reared from the egg in isolation from other animals displayed the complete and appropriate fighting behavior of males reared under normal conditions. Similarly, Eibl-Eibesfeldt (1963a, 1963b) reported that grey Norway rats that were reared in isolation displayed normal threat and fighting behavior. With instinctive conspecific aggression in lower vertebrates thus in evidence, Lorenz proceeded to proclaim aggression to be instinctive for all higher vertebrates as well. Although he acknowledged, at times (e.g., 1965a), the more highly developed organism's capacity to learn to respond to environmental settings related to aggression, he totally disregarded the potential biological significance of this capacity, particularly in the context of conspecific aggression. Lorenz made it very clear that in his view, aggression in higher vertebrates, in the primates, and finally, in man is not acquired in response to particular environmental conditions but is built into the organism. He posited that (1965c): "Man has inherited instincts, too; and the instinct to aggress is not a reactive one, but is a *spontaneous* activity within ourselves [p. 297; author's translation]."

With the propensity for aggression thus built into the organism, the role of the environment, in Lorenz's view, is to provide key stimuli that elicit fighting and to furnish other highly specific displays that stop it. As might be expected, the organism's sensitivity to such releasers and counterreleasers is conceived of as innate. Releasers are said to fit the innate releasing mechanisms as keys fit locks (Koehler, 1968). As a consequence, the function of such stimuli in triggering or stopping intraspecific fighting is considered rigid and practically unmodifiable by learning.

The existence of releaser mechanisms in lower vertebrates is not in doubt. One of the major contributions of ethology has been the delineation of such mechanisms. Ethologists have specified stimulus configurations that elicit so-called fixed action patterns—that is, relatively invariant characteristic behavior sequences (cf. Eibl-Eibesfeldt, 1970; Marler & Hamilton, 1968; Tinbergen, 1951). In the context of conspecific fighting, the function of releasing stimuli has been abundantly documented for a great variety of species. For example, it has been shown that in fence lizards, the male attacks models of its kind only if they display the male's blue throat (Noble & Bradley, 1933) and that male sticklebacks attack only models that show the red belly of the male in breeding condition (ter Pelkwijk & Tinbergen, 1937). Similarly, it was observed that when the female of a pair of American flickers was provided with an artificial mustache (the unobtrusive distinguishing characteristic of the male), she was attacked by her own mate until the mustache was removed (Noble, 1936). Similarly, changing the color of the chest of the female chaffinch from grey-brown to the male's orange-brown resulted in attacks from males in close proximity (Marler, 1956). Such findings have been employed to demonstrate the overriding importance of innate response mechanisms in the elicitation of aggressive behavior in general. The proposed innateness of these mechanisms has remained a controversial issue, however, because in the judgment of many biologists (cf. Lehrman, 1953, 1970; Schneirla, 1959), the involvement of learning in the ontogenesis of seemingly instinct-controlled behaviors has not been ruled out decisively. The rigidity or stability of the releasing mechanisms has also been challenged, since the perceptual systems involved have been found to change considerably in the process of ontogenesis (Hailman, 1970).

Evidence demonstrating characteristic displays that serve the inhibition or the cessation of fighting is less abundant. In fact, there is no systematically produced evidence of the function of such displays. Instead, Lorenz has contributed some informal observations. He reported (1963) that in young rails, the back of the head is equipped with a naked spot that shows a skin area of high blood concentration. Presentation of this spot to adult rails, he suggested, inhibits attack. The presentation of "blood spots" is not claimed to function as a universal inhibitor, however. It is pointed out that in cranes, for example, the display of such spots serves as an aggression releaser. Lorenz believes that he has detected inhibiting stimuli not so much in relatively stable, long-lasting stimulus configurations but in transient characteristics of behavior—more specifically, in behavioral changes during fighting. Encounters between fish, for example, may result in fighting when the animals involved display their colors, move in a conspicuous, abrupt manner, or present themselves as large as possible. The fight, he suggested, can be discontinued at any time by the removal of these releasers—that is, by a participant's turning pale, remaining relatively motionless, or positioning himself so as to appear small. A further illustration of the cessation of fighting through the removal of releasers is given in the case of a defeated fighting rooster that seemed to attempt to hide its comb, the presumed releaser, in order to discontinue the elicitation of its opponent's attack.

Lorenz's most spectacular and most frequently cited illustration of a counterreleaser, the exposure of the jugular vein in a defeated wolf or dog to stop the attack of the victorious opponent, has been faulted. What Lorenz considered an aggression-ceasing submission display that renders the animal extremely vulnerable to potentially fatal injury was found to be a challenging posture that characteristically leads to further attack and fighting (Schenkel, 1967). Considering acceptable evidence, the claim of counterreleasers—that is, of bodily features or innate behavioral displays that cause the discontinuation of fighting through innate releasing mechanisms—is in no way supported (cf. Barnett, 1967). Generally speaking, conspecific fighting seems to be discontinued not so much because of the display of highly specific behaviors that signal surrender and defeat but simply because one of the antagonists withdraws or displays relatively nonspecific signs of submission, thereby removing any aggression-promoting releasers.

Despite the troublesome status of the evidence concerning counterreleasers as a particular type of releaser, many biologists (cf. Hinde, 1970; Marler & Hamilton, 1968) have employed the concept of aggression releasers for the study of the behavior of invertebrates and lower vertebrates. Since both the characteristic stimuli that elicit aggressive reactions and the aggressive reactions themselves show little if any variability due to learning, such stimulus–response connections can be treated as unlearned or innate without loss of predictive accuracy. However, Lorenz and his followers stand alone in suggesting that similar connections govern aggressive behavior in higher vertebrates, primates, and man in particular. Lorenz's insistence that such releasers (or counterreleasers) are "innately known" (e.g., 1942, 1965b) has stirred up considerable controversy.

Besides Lorenz, both Eibl-Eibesfeldt (1971) and Morris (1968) have supplied many illustrations of what they consider universal releasers and counterreleasers in man. Threat displays shown to be used in many cultures, such as a man sticking out his chest or wearing attire designed to make him look taller, broader, or more muscular, are said to be directly related to the fighting behavior of fish and birds. Appeasement gestures such as bowing or retreat are similarly interpreted. So confident are these investigators of the "innate knowledge" of the meaning of particular human gestures and postures that they render specific advice regarding what to do or not to do to incite an attack or to pacify an attacker. Morris recommends, for example, that to calm a policeman whom we have aroused by violating a traffic regulation, we should display abject submission in words, body posture, and face and get out of and away from our car to prevent feelings of territorial rivalry from developing. The implied causal relations are of course pure conjecture. There is no assurance of successful appeasement. The policeman might well interpret any overly obvious submission as deliberate ingratiation and react with increased rather than decreased hostility. Also, the notion of territoriality as applied to these circumstances may prove to be nothing but a theoretician's idiosyncrasy. Given the obviously extreme variability of circumstances that can trigger or prevent aggressive outbursts in humans, it appears highly unreasonable to expect that because of *innate* releaser mechanisms, everybody always quits fighting when the opponent bows "in humiliation" or that everybody always picks a fight when the opponent flexes his muscles or "invades his territory."

The search for aggression releasers and counterreleasers in man has made for entertaining reading but has altogether failed to reveal acceptable evidence for their existence. A wealth of broad analogies between animal behavior on one hand and anthropological case studies, informal observations, and occasional anecdotes on the other cannot possibly be considered to document reliably that for man, configurations of external stimuli exist that universally elicit and stop aggressive behavior. The search for releasers and counterreleasers in man seems, if anything, to have accomplished the opposite of what it was meant to achieve: It has shown that there are apparently no universal stimuli that set off or break up hostility or aggression with great regularity under all circumstances. If such stimuli did exist, they should have been detected readily, because they would have been associated with highly obtrusive behavior. Even if these hypothetical stimulus situations were highly complex, one would expect them to have been delineated by now because of the necessary consistency of the stimulus–response relationship.

Indeed, the fact that there are no known universal aggression releasers in man indicates that in order to arrive at a satisfactory theory of human aggression, it will be imperative to consider the learning of aggressive reactions to particular external (and internal) stimuli as well as the learning of the inhibition of aggressive reactions to such stimuli.

The lack of evidence for universal releasers in man and other higher vertebrates, damaging as it may seem to the analogy between the function of innate releasers in lower and higher animals, has done little to deter Lorenz from proclaiming aggression as instinctive in man. This is because of the concept of *ritualized aggression,* which plays a crucial role in the instinct claim. Lorenz (e.g., 1942, 1963, 1964) proposed that in order to curb aggressive behavior that produces dysfunctional, nonadaptive consequences for a species, nondestructive, pseudoaggressive forms of behavior evolved and came to serve the purpose of the more archaic destructive behavior. The concept of ritualization was introduced mainly to accommodate the conspicuous fact that in much conspecific fighting the antagonists rarely injure each other. In Lorenz's view, nondestructive conspecific fighting is genuine aggression, because the animals involved draw upon a repertoire of aggressive action patterns that greatly overlaps with that of the action patterns of destructive aggression—at least at the outset of the ritualization process. However, in conspecific fighting over territory, social rank, mates, and the like, the antagonistic animals are seen to operate under "innately known" constraints so as not to inflict damage upon one another. The fight for first rights is thus seen as ritualistic rather than real. Bruising as it may be, such fighting is viewed as constituting tournaments rather than battles with potentially fatal consequences.

The documentation of ritualistic or tournamental fighting is extensive (e.g., Eibl-Eibesfeldt, 1963a, 1970; Lorenz, 1963, 1964). It ranges from the ceremonial combat of lizards—who take turns grasping each other's necks until one party seems exhausted (Kitzler, 1942)—to gazelles' snout-pushing maneuvers—which are said to have evolved from biting (Walther, 1958). The more spectacular illustrations come from species equipped to kill or mutilate with ease. Rattlesnakes, for example, do not bite each other but determine conspecific dominance in elaborate wrestling matches (Shaw, 1948). Oryx antelopes, who use their spearlike horns to stab predators, do not use these weapons in their conspecific head-to-head pushing contests (Walther, 1958).

The impression these examples create—that ritualized surrogates for destructive conspecific fighting have evolved in all species—is erroneous, however. In many species, if conditions prevent the separation of the antagonistic parties—that is, if the endangered animal fails to escape—fighting continues until mutilation or death. For example, lions have been observed to kill lions of other prides (Schaller, 1969; Schenkel, 1966) and African wildebeests have been witnessed using their horns against their rivals, putting their eyes out and otherwise injuring them severely (Estes, 1969). Among numerous other species—such as cichlid fish, hamsters, langurs, baboons, and gorillas—if the flight of the subordinate animal is unsuccessful, the victorious animal is likely to fight to the point of the opponent's physical incapacitation or death (Dart, 1961; Eibl-Eibesfeldt, 1970; Hall, 1968a; Lawick-Goodall, 1968; Sugiyama, 1967; Yoshiba, 1968). The apparent harmlessness of conspecific fighting is often not so much the result of the seemingly marvelous evolution of nondestructive substitute behaviors as it is the consequence of speedy flight on the part of the defeated animal and the limited capacity of the victorious one to inflict injury upon a conspecific. The latter is partly dependent on an injury-resistant anatomy—on sturdy skulls and thick hides (cf. Johnson, 1972).

Notwithstanding such "primitive" resolutions of the injury problem in conspecific fighting, it is generally accepted that conspecific skirmishes typically are settled without serious physical injury to the participants (cf. Hinde, 1970). The evolution of obviously adaptive, nondestructive con-specific fighting for various purposes is thus not in question. Rather, the issue in controversy is the way in which such fighting is said to have evolved and into what behavioral forms it is considered to have evolved. Lorenz and his followers (e.g., Eibl-Eibesfeldt, 1970; Lorenz, 1963) apparently have assumed that the destructive forces of instinctive aggression were initially directed indiscriminately both at members of other species and at conspecifics. The contention, then, is that to assure survival of a species, destructive aggression against conspecifics has been redirected and channeled into less destructive forms—such as ritualized fighting—for determining conflict-resolving dominance. In terms of specific behaviors, for example, biting has evolved into snout pushing in gazelles, and striking and biting into wrestling in rattlesnakes. However, in liberal extensions of the notion of ritualized aggression, the evolution of redirected behavior is not confined to the removal of destructive elements from fighting. Behaviors that do not involve physical contact or that do not bring harm or even disadvantage to opponents—such as territory-marking bird songs (cf. Marler & Hamilton, 1968)—are also conceived of as ritualized aggression. The full scope of forms of redirected aggression becomes most apparent in the discussion of human aggression (e.g., Eibl-Eibesfeldt, 1971; Lorenz, 1963; Storr, 1968). The desire to perform a task better than others, to achieve success professionally or in private life, or simply to come out a winner in competition involving skill or chance is seen to derive directly from instinctive aggression. Similarly, a person's willingness to defend his personal values or those endorsed by the culture into which he finds himself born is also considered to have evolved and to be inherited (Lorenz, 1963, 1965c). And last but not least, even bonding behavior in man—that is, love—is said to have evolved by way of ritualization on the basis of aggressive instinct (Lorenz, 1964). Thus, it should be clear that at the very least, all competitive, self-assertive behaviors in man are pronounced aggressive activities, and all are presumed to have evolved from a primal force of instinctive aggression. Put somewhat more dramatically, aggression is seen as the force of life itself.

Lorenz's grand theory proves wanting on several counts. There are serious conceptual ambiguities in the principal propositions, and the far-reaching projections from invertebrates and lower vertebrates onto higher vertebrates seem entirely unwarranted and unjustifiable.

First, the implicit assumption of initially indiscriminate aggression is highly questionable. It is difficult to imagine how any species could have survived such an archaic state of conspecific fighting. More importantly, however, the concept of evolution has been applied quite arbitrarily and selectively. Whereas aggressive behaviors were apparently free to evolve into any ritual form, seemingly without constraints, the motivational forces behind them were treated as immutable. Whereas in any given species, nonadaptive conspecific aggression is considered to have fallen by the wayside in the process of evolutionary advancement, conspecific destructive urges are still presumed to be alive and active. Bigelow (1972) has considered such reasoning an inversion of the concept of evolution: "Because we have evolved from lower animals, our 'animal' responses have not evolved [p. 18]."

The attempt to relate potentially all of an organism's behavior to a single, unitary force is certainly not novel. Freud (1930/1948) is presumably best known for such an attempt. He sought, initially at least, to account for all human behavior on the basis of so-called libido energy, the force of a presumed primal sex drive. Clearly, what the sex drive was to Freud, the aggression instinct is to Lorenz: a hypothetical construct, treated as though it were empirically established, that serves as a universal energizer of all behavior. Such unitary forces have held great appeal for the theoretician and the interested layman alike. To theoretical minds, a unitary force seems to assure parsimony in an approach—not to mention that it also appeals to a widespread aesthetic conviction that upon sufficient reflection, nature reveals a marvelous simplicity. The layman's preference for accounts based on unitary forces seems to derive from convenience: the avoidance of the difficulties of complex, elaborate explanations. Be this as it may, the proposal that most if not all behavior of potentially all species, man included, is driven by instinctive aggression has proven persuasive to many, in spite of a lack of critical evidence.

Considering the needed empirical evidence, a *universal* instinctive aggressive force has of course never been shown to exist in any organism (cf., e.g., Bandura, 1973a; Hinde, 1970; Scott, 1969a). The fact that specific aggressive behaviors have been shown to be independent of social learning, as reported earlier, is irrelevant here. These behaviors merely demonstrate that animals, such as fish and birds, are equipped with the neural and humoral apparatuses for particular fixed action patterns and that these action patterns can be elicited by appropriate stimuli. They do not support the claim that animals are generally endowed with instinctive forces that motivate aggression (e.g., Eibl-Eibesfeldt, 1970). (In this connection, the acknowledgment that proof of such an inborn aggressive drive in man has not yet been presented [also Eibl-Eibesfeldt, 1970] is reassuring.) To establish a universal force, the needed, crucial evidence concerns the hypothesized conversion or transformation of motivational energy from aggressive to pseudoaggressive and finally nonaggressive energy. Has it ever been demonstrated that a person who seeks high accomplishment or simply tries to show himself in a favorable light is spurred by inherited, initially destructive forces? Or in considering the smallest conceivable redirection, has it ever been shown that snout pushing to determine social rank in animals derives from injurious biting used in pursuit of the same objective? Very plainly, there is no acceptable supportive evidence. The claim of the evolutionary redirection of presumed instinctive aggression rests solely on intuitive judgment. The illustrations employed to make such judgments convincing—specifically, the unsystematic eclectic comparison of similar, related species, which shows incidents of nondestructive conspecific fighting in the seemingly more advanced species—are at best suggestive of evolutionary changes toward ritualization. In these illustrations, species are compared that characteristically differ according to a variety of behavioral criteria, and the presumed initial identity regarding aggression mechanisms is, for obvious reasons, merely assumed and never documented. Under such circumstances, compelling demonstrations of behavioral homology are inconceivable (cf. Atz, 1970). But no matter how suggestive the type of illustration discussed may be, there are no grounds for believing that as nondestructive forms of fighting evolved, the associated motivational forces remained unchanged. In fact, there is little reason to believe that prior to the presumed evolutionary separation of overt forms of aggressive behavior, these behaviors were governed by identical or highly similar mechanisms (cf. Lehrman, 1970).

The notion of redirected instinctive energy not only is empirically unfounded; it leads to a conceptual dilemma as well. If Lorenz's (1963, 1964) contention that socially constructive behaviors—bonding behavior and caretaking in particular—have likewise evolved on the basis of an aggression instinct is taken seriously (and it apparently is not by most of his critics), the totalistic, all-encompassing scheme of instinctive aggression becomes obvious. It is unclear how any phylogenetic classification could possibly prevent anybody from arbitrarily pronouncing aggression to be the force behind any and every behavior. If supportive evidence for the proposals made were not required, all nonaggressive behaviors—by virtue of their existence— could be declared to have evolved from instinctive aggression by virtue of the presumption of such a universal basis. The notion of ritualization is thus a patent formula that, although in actuality explaining nothing, seems to make matters plausible to those who are the least critical.

A final comment concerning Lorenz's propositions is in order. Lorenz (e.g., 1942, 1961) suggested that the force energizing any instinctive behavior—aggressive behavior being a case in point—is cumulative. Specifically, he posited that if the energy assumed to be associated with specific aggressive behaviors is not regularly discharged in appropriate actions, it accumulates to increasingly higher levels. He further proposed that the energy dammed up in this manner induces appetitive behavior in the animal, causing it to engage in an active search for an appropriate target for the behavior in question or if such a target is not encountered, triggering the behavior without apparent external stimulation. Consequently, in the absence of appropriate aggression releasers in the environment, the aggression-deprived animal is expected to seek out aggression opportunities, to be ready to attack in response to increasingly less appropriate releasers, and finally to erupt in a stimulus vacuum (e.g., Lorenz, 1963, 1965c). This assertion of *spontaneity* in instinctive aggression, which was readily adopted by others (e.g., Eibl-Eibesfeldt, 1970, 1971; Storr, 1968), has drawn strong negative reactions from a great many highly competent biologists and psychologists (e.g., Bandura, 1973a; Berkowitz, 1969b; Hinde, 1967; Lehrman, 1953; Scott, 1967). The critics of Lorenz's proposal point out that there is no neurophysiological evidence of any organismic structure that—in the absence of regular discharge—accumulates behavior-specific motivating energy to a point at which the specific behavior is forced upon the organism independent of external stimulation; nor is there evidence of a mechanism by which any accumulated behavior-specific motivating energy could enter other structures and—again in a stimulus vacuum—force out alternative related or unrelated specific activities (cf. Hinde, 1960; Scott, 1969a, 1971, 1973).

The documentation provided to back the notion of spontaneous drive is extremely questionable. Lorenz initially reported the informal observation that a presumably aggression-deprived, tame jackdaw "attacked" a pair of black swim trunks (1935/1965) and that a similarly deprived starling in the absence of insects in the environment behaved so as to "catch flies" (1963). Somewhat more systematically inclined, Eibl-Eibesfeldt (1971) cites studies by Kruijt (1964), von Holst and von Saint Paul (1959), and Rasa (1969) to demonstrate both appetitive aggressive behavior and vacuum aggression. Kruijt, who worked with fighting cocks reared in isolation, observed that these animals displayed the normal conspecific fighting patterns when permitted to combat rivals. More importantly, when deprived of opportunities to fight, they attacked their own tails or struck at their own shadows with their spurs. Von Holst and von Saint Paul found that electrical stimulation of specific brain areas induces motor restlessness in chickens and that the presence of any target, either appropriate or inappropriate, results in attacks. In these studies, increased habitual mobility is taken to document appetitive behavior, and the attack upon seemingly any target is taken to show that increasingly less appropriate targets take on the stimulus quality of a releaser. However, Rasa's study on cichlid fish is considered to provide the most direct demonstration thus far of the spontaneity of aggression. Rasa placed pairs of cichlids during the reproductive phase into one of three conditions: (a) together with other conspecifics so that fighting could occur naturally, (b) separated from other conspecifics by a glass partition so that fighting was restricted to visual engagements, and (c) isolated from conspecifics. It was found that when males were prevented by the glass from directly attacking male rivals, the average frequency of attack upon their mates increased slightly. More importantly, however, it was found that when males are deprived altogether of the opportunity to attack rivals, the average frequency of attack upon their mates increased by more than a factor of 3. Indeed, under the latter circumstances, the males' attacks upon their mates, unlike ritualized fighting, tended to be continued to the mate's destruction. These findings are certainly in accord with Lorenz's notion of spontaneous aggression. However, aside from some methodological problems with the study (e.g., reproductive events were not entirely parallel, and time of observation differed notably—discrepancies that could have biased the conditions in terms of critical aggression-laden periods), the findings are open to alternative explanations. For example, since under natural conditions the mate is by no means free from attack (in Rasa's study, nearly one-fourth of all attacks were directed against the mate), the fact alone that she—in contrast to male rivals—uninhibitedly continued to approach the hostile male while potentially aggression-diverting males were absent accounts for the reported increased attack frequencies. But whatever the ultimate explanation of the findings may be, it appears to be a tremendous leap indeed to generalize from the tentative findings on cichlid fish to all higher vertebrates. Lorenz's assertion that *all species, man included*, are equipped with instinctive aggressive forces that—when not discharged by appropriate external stimuli—will result in a discharge toward potentially inappropriate targets or *in vacuo* can only be considered unfounded and unwarranted.

Given this state of affairs, it appears rash, if not naive and irresponsible (cf. Schneirla, 1973), for anyone to project instinctive (and spontaneous) aggression upon all species irrespective of their placement on the evolutionary scale. In principle, such a projection assumes: (a) that ontogenetic development is confined within the narrow bounds of an aggression-specific phylogenetic dictum, and (b) that behavioral organization is essentially the same at all levels of evolutionary advancement. It would appear that only Lorenz's preoccupation with lower vertebrates could have led him to make these assumptions. If the aggressive behavior of higher vertebrates—especially primates and man—is given adequate scrutiny, both assumptions appear quite indefensible.

Although Lorenz (e.g., 1965a) has more recently come to acknowledge the significance of ontogenetic factors in the development of aggressive behavior, his major contention remains that aggression is nearly entirely phylogenetically controlled and that ontogenesis involves only a minor potential to modify innate behavioral dispositions. Considering fish and birds, this may well prove to be a workable assumption. But the extension to such species as mice, rats, cats, and dogs is already troublesome and reveals the inadequacy of the assumption. For example, it has been demonstrated convincingly that when the attacks of mice are made to be consistently successful, the mice develop into extremely aggressive, ferocious fighters and that—more importantly here—when mice are made to be consistently unsuccessful in fights, they develop into nonaggressive, timid animals who will not attack others (Kahn, 1951; Scott, 1958, 1966). Contrary to expectations that follow from the assumption of spontaneity in aggression, in the absence of external stimulation to fight (e.g., the infliction of pain by another animal), mice trained to live nonaggressively display no ill effects whatsoever (Scott, 1971; Scott & Marston, 1953). Dogs have also been trained to be arbitrarily either peaceful or vicious in competing with members of their own species (Kuo, 1967). It thus has been shown that experiential factors can have an enormous influence on the development of conspecific aggressive behavior. With regard to interspecific aggression, predation in particular, the significance of ontogenetic processes has been demonstrated even more dramatically. For example, Kuo (1930) studied behavior that is quite universally regarded as innate: rat killing in the cat. He investigated the degree to which such behavior depends on experiential factors by raising kittens from birth to maturity under the following controlled environments: (a) the kittens occasionally witnessed their mother chase and kill rats; (b) the kittens were brought up in isolation from rats; and (c) the kittens grew up in company with rats without ever witnessing rat killing. Under the quasi-natural conditions in which rat killing was witnessed, 86 percent of the kittens became rat killing adults. Of those growing up in isolation from rats, only 45 percent spontaneously killed rats as adults. And of those who grew up along with rats but never witnessed killing, only 17 percent killed rats as adults. Similarly, neutral contact—particularly friction-free social interaction between animals that are usually in a predator-prey relationship—was found to reduce the predator's aggressive assaults upon its potential prey almost totally (Kuo, 1938). By creating the appropriate environmental conditions during the course of ontogenetic development, Kuo (1938, 1967) was furthermore able to rear kittens so that as adults, they would either fear such customary prey as rats and birds, affiliate with them, affiliate with one kind of rat and kill others (shaved ones), or kill mice and be "friendly" to rats. Similar studies have been conducted more recently to explore nonpredatory interspecific aggression. It has been shown, for example, that although rats ordinarily attack mice, few if any will attack and kill mice if the two species have been raised together (Denenberg, 1966; Denenberg, Hudgens, & Zarrow, 1964; Denenberg, Paschke, & Zarrow, 1968; Myer, 1969). Finally, cross-species attachments caused by atypical ontogenetic development in animals that are commonly hostile toward one another have been reported for many species, including monkeys with rats (Mason & Green 1962) and dogs with lambs (Cairns, 1966).

Taken together, these findings are clearly at variance with the view that ontogenesis merely serves to develop specific aggressive behaviors that are phylogenetically fixed in the various species. It is obvious that ontogenesis can greatly modify the development of aggressive behavior. Its power to modify is in fact so extreme that it becomes difficult to see what, precisely, should be considered phylogenetically determined. In the study by Kuo (1930), which half of the cats reared in isolation from rats behave in the "phylogenetically proper" manner—those that kill rats or those that do not? Or as Kuo (1967) put it: "Which of these two types of behavior pattern is the result of nature and which of nurture [p. 116]?" In looking at Scott's (1958) work on fighting in mice, it is equally unclear whether the mice trained to be vicious fighters or those trained to live peacefully approximate more closely any assumed phylogenetic mold. The findings have made it evident that the inference of specific genetic molds, based on the observation of behavior under the particular environmental conditions that commonly prevail, is premature and potentially misleading. As has been demonstrated, such species as mice, rats, cats, and dogs have the capacity to adapt to different environments in different ways. The animals seem equally capable of coping with specific environments by developing aggressive modes of behavior as by developing nonaggressive modes. They clearly are not caught in a "phylogenetic trap" that requires them to aggress against members of other species and conspecifics alike—irrespective of experiential factors and the appropriateness of the behavior for adaptation.

This point is eloquently made in Kuo's theory of behavioral potentials (1967). Kuo's theory stresses the enormous possibilities or potentialities for behavior development with which every species, but particularly the vertebrates, is provided genetically. It treats these potentialities as physical capabilities without implying any inborn behavioral dispositions. Genetic factors thus merely determine the boundaries of the range of behavioral potentials. During the course of behavior development, some of these potentials manifest themselves as a function of environmental conditions, and the remainder—a vast number of potentials—maintain latent status. A newborn kitten is thus seen as having no genetic endowment that would make it a rat killer but as possessing the potentialities for becoming both a rat killer and a rat lover. Similarly, the kitten is not genetically predisposed to affiliate with conspecifics but has the potentiality for so doing, along with the potentiality to reject its own kind and to become attached to members of a great many other species.

In Kuo's theory, the flexibility of adaptation at the ontogenetic level is a function of the phylogenetically determined reservoir of behavioral potentials. To the extent that this reservoir increases with organismic complexity, it should be expected, generally speaking, that the more highly developed organism will be characterized by greater adaptive flexibility. As Kuo has argued, this potential adaptability is generally unknown, because behavioral development—as it has been recorded—has been confined to just a few sets of environmental conditions. Regarding aggressive behavior, it is not known whether or not a particular species could adapt to specific environments in such a way that predatory, interspecific, or conspecific aggression would be substantially reduced or altogether prevented from developing. The relevant behavioral potentials simply have not been staked out. However, it seems that the model and the evidence at hand would justify the greatest caution when it comes to projecting instinctive aggression onto the primates and man.

Conceivably, ontogenetic adaptability in invertebrates and lower vertebrates is extremely limited and can be neglected without loss. For example, a praying mantis might be unable to adapt to an environment by feeding on seeds instead of killing and ingesting the insects it commonly preys on. Similarly, cichlid fish might display their conspecific fighting behavior in all imaginable environments. In contrast, ontogenetic adaptability in mice, rats, cats, and dogs has been shown to be pronounced enough that claims of instinctive aggression are not reasonable. It seems fair to say, consistent with available evidence, that for these species, aggressive behavior is primarily *ontogenetically controlled.* Both aggressive and nonaggressive modes of adaptation can be seen as phylogenetically determined, but the crucial adaptive selection of one or the other mode is an ontogenetic process. Considering that ontogenesis thus dominates behavior development in subprimate species, and in view of the immensely greater adaptive flexibility of the primates and man, it appears conservative and safe indeed to infer even stronger ontogenetic dominance in the behavior development of primates and man. If mice, rats, cats, and dogs can become nonattackers, primates and man must be expected to be capable of accomplishing the same. Genetically speaking, monkeys and apes are as much affectionate, attachment-seeking creatures as they are vicious killers, and every human being is as much endowed with the capability of being a pacifist as with the capability of being a mass murderer. The choice out of this vast range of potentialities is a matter of individual development.

The outlined projection of maximal ontogenetic adaptability in man sharply contrasts with Lorenz's proposal. It denies man's inheritance of instinctive aggressive forces that must find outlet. Unlike Lorenz's speculations, it is in accord with the major findings concerning the ontogenetic control of aggressive behaviors, and as mentioned earlier it is a highly conservative projection onto primates and man. There is thus heuristic justification in preferring one projection over the other, and it is unwarranted to contend that the instinct proposal is usually rejected on moral grounds alone—in consideration of implications—and in the absence of contradictory evidence (Eibl-Eibesfeldt, 1970). It is true, however, that most critical evaluations of Lorenz's propositions—this lengthy discussion included— were prompted by the consideration of the profound implications of these propositions not only for the investigation of human aggression specifically but more importantly, for human aggression per se and civilization itself.

The claim of aggressive instinct in man—by promoting the belief that in the final analysis, *aggression is inevitable* at the individual or societal level— constitutes a ready-made rationalization for anyone's violent acts, and it potentially provides a convenient excuse for anyone who contemplates such acts. Lorenz (1963) considered the popularity of his views on aggression to be due to the fact that so many people had recognized the instinctive nature of aggression on their own, and he saw himself simply as the spokesman for common knowledge. It is equally plausible, however, to believe that this popularity results from the instinct notion's promise of aggression amnesty. People who are troubled by their own violent impulses and occasional outbursts must be comforted indeed when they learn that they really can't help themselves because they are built to behave that way. Be this as it may, to the extent that the belief in the innateness of aggression can promote aggressive behavior in individuals and ultimately in society, the proposal of an aggression instinct in man—particularly since it is unsupported by empirical evidence—is a cause for great concern. Considered in heuristic and pragmatic terms, the value of the grossly oversimplified phylogenetic speculations on aggression in man, as promoted by Lorenz and his followers, is extremely questionable.

II. ANTECEDENTS AND CONSEQUENCES OF FIGHTING IN ANIMALS

As mentioned earlier, discussions of aggression in animals have usually dealt with conspecific fighting. Predation, for the most part, either has been definitionally excluded or has been treated as an independent, special kind of destructive behavior whose relationship to other forms of aggression was left unclear. However, although the need for a distinction between predatory and nonpredatory aggression is generally recognized, the two types of aggression are occasionally lumped together. On such occasions, it has been implied that both types of behavior derive from a common mechanism, and this implication has led to some confusion in the interpretation of research findings. To avoid similar confusion, we briefly discuss the principal differences between predation and nonpredatory interspecific and conspecific aggression.

A. Predatory Aggression

The most obtrusive behavioral criterion that distinguishes predation from other forms of aggression is its characteristic consequence: the ingestion of the victim of a predatory attack. An intuitive appraisal of such behavior would suggest that predatory behavior is precipitated by food deprivation, which motivates the carnivorous animal to seek out and subdue appropriate prey, and that the ingestion of this prey removes the motivation for further foodgetting until the state of acute deprivation reappears. If the carnivorous animal were not to engage in the behavior in question, it would no doubt soon be weakened and die of starvation. There is thus an obvious, direct connection between food deprivation or hunger on one hand and predatory aggression on the other. Clearly, among the various conceivable forms of aggressive behavior, predation is unique in that it is strongly associated with a state of bodily need as a motivational force (cf., e.g., Bindra, 1959; Brown, 1961; Morgan, 1959).

In an extensive review of the literature on brain mechanisms and aggressive behavior, Kaada (1967) presented considerable evidence showing that predatory attack and defensive fighting are distinct processes and are quite independent anatomically. Whereas structures associated with fear and anger (e.g., Ursin, 1965; Ursin & Kaada, 1960) seem generally more closely related to defensive aggression, there is evidence that predatory killing is connected with feeding mechanisms. This research generally corroborates the behavioral differentiation between predation and "affective" aggression detailed by Wasman and Flynn (1962) and by Egger and Flynn (1963). The most direct demonstration of the kill-and-eat connection comes, however, from a study by Hutchinson and Renfrew (1966), who found that in the cat, both predatory attack and eating can be elicited by stimulation of identical sites in the hypothalamus. The connection is also in evidence in studies on the effects of food deprivation and competition for food (e.g., Heimstra, 1965; Heimstra & Newton, 1961; Paul, 1972; Paul, Miley, & Baenninger, 1971; Whalen & Fehr, 1964). Both situations were found to promote predatory attacks on mice by rats, largely independent of whether these rats were mouse killers or nonkillers. Also, predatory killing has been observed to decrease with satiation (e.g., Kulkarni, 1968). There are, however, several studies that have produced apparently conflicting findings. For example, the observation that lesions in the hypothalamus that abolish eating behavior inhibit predatory attack only temporarily, not permanently (Karli & Vergnes, 1964), has been interpreted as showing that predatory behavior is not entirely based on hunger (Moyer, 1971). In line with this interpretation are reports of starving nonkiller rats (Karli, 1956) and nonkilling "predatory" mice (Clark, 1962) who fail to respond to predatory opportunities. Clearly, food deprivation does not lead to predatory behavior by necessity. The animal must be exposed to stimuli that either trigger a specific unlearned reaction or, more likely, elicit behavior that has been acquired through social learning. Independent of the particular mode of the stimulus–response connection, food deprivation should be expected to mobilize predatory behavior in animals in which such connections are established—not in those in which they are not established.

The relative independence of predation from other forms of aggression is also evident in the analysis of endocrine processes that precede, accompany, and follow aggressive behaviors (cf. Brown & Hunsperger, 1963). Conner (1972), who provided a thorough review of the pertinent literature, concluded that the aggression-modifying effect of various hormones and biogenic amines is not at all uniform but is substantially different for predatory and nonpredatory aggression. Whereas hormones of the pituitary-gonadal system, especially the androgens, have generally been found to potentiate conspecific aggression, particularly intermale aggression (e.g., Beeman, 1947; Fredericson, 1950; Hutchinson, Ulrich, & Azrin, 1965; Levy & King, 1953; Powell, Francis, & Schneiderman, 1971), these hormones seem to have only negligible consequences for predatory attack (e.g., Beeman, 1947; Karli, 1956, 1958; Kuo, 1960; Leaf, Lerner, & Horovitz, 1969). Moyer (1971) has arrived at essentially the same generalization. Regarding the effects of changes in the pituitary-adrenal system and the effects of biogenic amines, the findings generally corroborate the principal distinction between predatory and nonpredatory aggression, but they are less clear-cut mainly because of inconsistencies among findings of investigations of predatory aggression (e.g., Goldberg & Salama, 1969; Leaf, Lerner, & Horovitz, 1969; Sofia, 1969).

It is generally held that the state of bodily need brought about by food deprivation, whatever its particular neural and humoral manifestations may be, motivates the animal to move about as though engaging in an active search for objects capable of satisfying the need. This deprivation-motivated behavior, which is known as "precurrent" (Sherrington, 1906) or "appetitive" (Craig, 1918), is characterized by an increase in general motor activity (e.g., Bolles, 1965; Teghtsoonian & Campbell, 1960) and more importantly, by a heightened sensitivity to stimuli associated with food (e.g., Amsel & Work, 1961; Bolles, 1963; Mendelson, 1966; Sheffield & Campbell, 1954). The animal thus comes to respond selectively to specific need-related stimuli in its environment. Concerning predatory attacks, findings obtained in brain-stimulation research suggest that such attacks are generally dependent on highly specific stimuli. With only a few reported incidents of stimulation resulting in attacklike behavior directed toward empty space (Brown & Hunsperger, 1963; Yasukochi, 1960), the bulk of evidence shows that stimulation of specific areas triggers attacks on appropriate targets only (cf. Moyer, 1971). For example, Wasman and Flynn (1962) have demonstrated that during stimulation of the lateral hypothalamus, cats that normally do not attack rats will ignore alternative stimuli and display predatory reactions toward a rat: They will quietly stalk the rat, jump it, and kill it, characteristically by biting it in the neck. Such stimulation contrasts sharply with stimulation of the medial hypothalamus, which produces nonpredatory attacks associated with pronounced sympathetic excitation. These attacks involve tearing at the stimulus object with unsheathed claws and a high-pitched screaming. Moreover, in the presence of a predatory target such as a rat, attacks can be directed at highly dissimilar targets in the environment—such as a human (Egger & Flynn, 1963). The critical specificity of the target in predatory attack has further been shown in a study by Levison and Flynn (1965). The likelihood of attack was found to decrease with the target object's dissimilarity to the appropriate target, namely a rat: Cats stimulated in the lateral hypothalamus assaulted stuffed rats less frequently than anesthetized ones, and in turn, they assaulted hairy toy dogs and rat-sized styrofoam and foam-rubber blocks less frequently than stuffed rats. Whereas hairy toy dogs drew some attacks, the cats showed very little inclination to attack the blocks. In the absence of suitable targets for attacks, the animals merely displayed general motor restlessness.

The appetitive phase of predatory behavior is quite variable. In probing for food in its environment, the animal may initially behave in a quasi-random manner. However, in most species this archaic pattern of locomotion is rapidly modified by learning. Through selective reinforcement, the animal develops characteristic ways in which to probe for food in its environment—an obviously adaptive change toward greater efficiency in food gathering. Nonetheless, it should be clear that this ability to adjust to specific distributions of food in the environment brings considerable behavioral variability with it. In contrast, as many ethologists have noted (cf. Eibl-Eibesfeldt, 1970; Hinde, 1970), the variability of the final, search-terminating behavior—known as the "consummatory" response (Craig, 1918; Sherring-ton, 1906)—is far less pronounced. The predatory attack is usually triggered by a relatively small number of stimuli, and it consists of a characteristic, relatively invariant sequence of reactions, which form what has been termed a "fixed action pattern" (cf. Hinde, 1970; Lorenz, 1965a). Generally speaking, the fixed action patterns of predatory attacks show comparatively little variation. They seem to have developed into efficient forms of incapacitating the prey. A rat, for example, does not make several approaches in its efforts to subdue a mouse; it simply kills with a bite through the spinal cord.

A final comment concerns the obvious consequence of predation. Successful attack is followed with extreme regularity by the ingestion of the incapacitated prey. The theoretical significance of this consequence of destructive attack is that predatory aggression is associated with highly potent reinforcement. A primary reinforcer, food, is coupled with deadly assault (cf. Skinner, 1938, 1969), and by removing a state of acute deprivation, the kill-and-eat sequence proves drive reducing (cf. Hull, 1943, 1952).

In summary, then, the relevant characteristics of predatory aggression are: (a) the deprivation-motivated appetitive phase during which the animal is hypernormally active and selectively sensitive to highly specific, deprivation-related stimuli; (b) the relatively invariant consummatory attack upon prey; and (c) the ingestion of the prey, which removes the acute deprivation and reinforces the predatory behavior.

B. Conspecific Fighting

Scott (1973) considers withdrawal to avoid injury—along with ingestive, sexual, exploratory, and shelter-seeking behavior—a fundamental, near-universal form of behavior, and he views the more complex forms of social fighting as having evolved from this basic withdrawal reaction. Conspecific fighting, as such, is seen to be limited in its distribution across species by two major factors. First, there must be sufficient individual variation or polymorphism within a species and adequate sensory faculties to permit individual recognition (cf. Caspari, 1967). These conditions are required since indiscriminate conspecific attack should have proved highly maladaptive and should have effected selection against the species. Second, the species must be equipped with motor organs enabling its members to inflict pain and injury upon fellow members.

Given these limitations, conspecific fighting—although common in some arthropods (e.g., decapods such as crayfish and orthopterans such as grasshoppers)—is most highly developed in the vertebrates. Social fighting is in evidence in all major classes of vertebrates, including fish, reptiles, birds, and mammals, and it seems most characteristic and pronounced in those species that have achieved complex social organizations.

As discussed earlier, conspecific fighting rarely results in severe injury or death (cf. Eibl-Eibesfeldt, 1970; Hinde, 1970). The fighting is typically not continued to the point of the opponent's incapacitation. However, the suggestion that this is so because nondestructive, "ritualized" forms of conspecific aggression have *evolved from* the destructive forms of interspecific fighting—predation included (e.g., Eibl-Eibesfeldt, 1970, 1971; Lorenz, 1963, 1964)—is insufficiently documented. The illustrations provided to support it fail to implicate the proposed evolutionary redirection of destructive aggression in any decisive way. It seems that unique forms of noninjurious conspecific fighting can be explained more parsimoniously by a straightforward application of evolutionary reasoning (cf. Bigelow, 1972; Scott, 1971, 1973). Effective, interspecifically directed predatory behavior and nondestructive conspecific fighting are equally adaptive, and the *combination* of both features should have selectively advantaged subpopulations within a species and ultimately the species itself. This is to say that in all likelihood, nondestructive forms of conspecific fighting have evolved *along with* destructive interspecific aggression.

However, independent of evolutionary possibilities, there are highly parsimonious, plausible explanations for the fact that conspecific fighting generally does not lead to incapacitation. Unlike predatory behavior, in which the predator characteristically has a marked physical advantage over the prey, the combatants in conspecific skirmishes have similar capabilities of performing injurious attacks and of avoiding their impact. In many species, the avoidance capability is far superior to that of inflicting injury, and to the extent that this holds true, noninjurious outcomes of fights among conspecifics are to be expected. Furthermore, in species with sufficient learning capacity, actual fighting in which injury could be inflicted seems generally restricted to an initial encounter between any two individual animals (cf. Etkin, 1964). In such initial encounters, the inferior fighter will escape, presumably when it experiences pain resulting from minor tissue damage inflicted by its opponent. In future encounters, the inferior fighter will acknowledge the superiority of its opponent by withdrawing before the antagonistic parties reach the proximity necessary for fighting. Moreover, the inferior fighter's yielding behavior seems to generalize readily to initial encounters with potentially superior fighters: The animal will display subordination to other animals who are, for example, larger or more vigorous (cf. Collias, 1944; Guhl, 1962). Much of conspecific fighting, then, consists less of aggression (as we have defined it) than of noninjurious, *hostile* behavior. Barnett (1967) has expressed this point of view as follows: "The word 'aggression,' in its colloquial sense, does not adequately describe conflict among animals of the same species. Encounters are usually restricted to displays, and superiority is acknowledged by withdrawal before either party is injured [p. 45]."

Largely on the basis of an analysis of findings concerning fighting in lower vertebrates, which had led others to suggest instinctive aggression as a patent explanation, the pioneering ethologist Craig (1921) proposed that all conspecific fighting is *motivated by aversions*. Specifically, he posited: (a) that there is no appetence for fighting; (b) that animals fight only when attacked or threatened or when their vital interests are interfered with; (c) that during fighting, they give indication that the behavior itself is aversive; and (d) that as the animal succeeds in warding off attack, threat, or interference with its interests, it discontinues fighting. Craig thus denies any "biological" urge for conspecific fighting and declares such fighting secondary to various fundamental needs of the animal. He suggests that if these general needs could be satisfied without "conflict of interest" with other animals, fighting would not occur. Since such conflict is unavoidable, however, fighting—a "necessary evil"—is engaged in as a last resort. Many other investigators have arrived at essentially the same assessment and have provided further data consistent with it (e.g., Andrew, 1957; Marler, 1957; Sabine, 1959; Scott & Fredericson, 1951).

The analysis of fundamental needs and the ends ultimately served by conspecific aggression has led to various specific classifications (e.g., Cloudsley-Thompson, 1965; Collias, 1944; Etkin, 1964; Johnson, 1972; Lorenz, 1964; Scott, 1958; Wynne-Edwards, 1962). However, notwithstanding differences in emphasis and nomenclature, there is general agreement on its basic functions: (a) the procurement of food, and (b) the safeguarding of reproduction.

These basic functions are not necessarily independent. In fact, they are usually interrelated. The interrelationship becomes apparent as the more specific functions of fighting are considered. Many investigators (e.g., Lorenz, 1964; Marler & Hamilton, 1968; McBride, 1964) have stressed the role of fighting in spacing out the members of a species over the available habitat. At the species level, spacing assures that all of the suitable environment is utilized (cf. Cloudsley-Thompson, 1965), and it thereby minimizes maladaptive crowding that would place the satisfaction of fundamental needs in jeopardy. At the level of the individual animal, spacing amounts to the allotment of a particular territory in which the animal can pursue vital objectives with minimal interference from conspecifics. With regard to fundamental needs, the territory potentially provides food and shelter. For many species, territory indeed coincides (at least for the period of time associated with reproductive activities) with both food and shelter. Song birds, for example, establish feeding-and-breeding territories (Marler & Hamilton, 1968). In such cases, fighting for territory is largely redundant with fighting for food and reproductive success. In many other species, however, territory relates to shelter only. Marine birds, for example, share the ocean as a feeding ground but establish and vigorously defend a small territory around the nest site (cf. Etkin, 1964). In this case, fighting for territory merely serves to safeguard reproduction.

Fighting for mates may or may not be closely related to territorial fighting. In many birds, for example, the male establishes at the beginning of the breeding season a territory to which a female is then attracted (cf. Hinde, 1970). In such cases, the male "fights for mates" by keeping other males out of his territory. Territorial fighting thus makes the male's actual fighting for a mate unnecessary. In this connection, Cloudsley-Thompson (1965) indicated that contrary to common belief, males generally fight not over mates but over territories (instead, females fight over mates).

Fighting over mates can, however, be independent of territorial considerations. In the red deer of Europe (Darling, 1937), for example, herds of males and herds of females separately establish group territories. During rut, the adult males abandon their territories and wander considerable distances through the territories of female herds. They round up a group of females by constantly patrolling the group and forcing those who attempt to return to their own territories back with the others. The male leaders of the herd ward off other adult males, fighting them if necessary. This fighting is clearly not linked to any geographically fixed territory but simply accommodates the particular position held by the herd at a given time.

In social vertebrates, a considerable amount of fighting revolves around the determination of social ranks (cf. Allee, 1951; Collias, 1944; Etkin, 1964). In any social aggregate, an animal establishes dominance over others by defeating them—usually in initial encounters that involve competition over food. Defeat is operationalized simply as withdrawal in response either to the display of threat or to actual fighting. On these hostile or aggressive terms, the most effective fighter becomes the most dominant animal, commonly referred to as the first-ranked or alpha animal. Analogously, the second most effective fighter obtains second rank and is referred to as the beta animal. All animals in the aggregate are so classified, down to the most subordinate one, the so-called omega animal. The resulting dominance hierarchies, which are in evidence in a great variety of species, seem to assure privileges of food and shelter to those of higher rank, clearly disadvantaging those of lower rank (cf. Johnson, 1972). As we will see, there is some ambiguity concerning reproductive privileges, however.

Rank-associated food and shelter privileges are characteristic in many species. The "peck order" of hens (Guhl, 1956) has become proverbial: The alpha animal feeds first or gets the first choice of perches and is followed by those of successively lower rank. However, in many related species—such as doves and pigeons—ranking may exist in rudimentary form only. Whereas the alpha animal emerges, further reliable differentiations in rank may not become manifest (Etkin, 1964).

Presumably, perfect hierarchies can be formed only when fighting behavior is well differentiated in the animals involved. Fighters of similar physical constitution and fighting skills are bound to engage repeatedly in skirmishes to determine rank. Their respective rank positions may change with the outcome of such fighting, which in turn should introduce some unreliability into the hierarchical organization of the group.

Granted that dominance hierarchies are subject to change, they nonetheless prove, generally speaking, to be relatively stable over considerable periods of time (cf. Candland & Bloomquist, 1965). In rats, for example, when dominance relationships are established early, they remain stable throughout life (Baenninger, 1966). In species as diverse as electric fish (Westby & Box, 1970), chaffinches (Marler, 1955, 1971), sheep (Scott, 1945), goats (Hafez & Scott, 1962), dogs and wolves (Scott, 1950), and dairy cattle (Schein & Fohrman, 1956), dominance relationships of substantial duration have been documented. In monkeys and apes, social hierarchies are generally well established. Their development and maintenance becomes increasingly complex, however. In rhesus monkeys, for example, rank seems to be a simple function of the number of fights brought to successful conclusion (Sade, 1967). In some macaques, however, rank is partly determined by social affiliation: A low-ranking animal is able to improve its relative rank position by its association with a high-ranking one that might come to its defense (Varley & Symmes, 1966). Similarly, in langurs (Jay, 1965), females who associate themselves with dominant males advance their own ranking. Furthermore, a female's rank improves as she progresses in the reproductive cycle. In the last week of pregnancy, she enjoys a high dominance position. However, a female with a newborn infant, by avoiding dominance interactions, virtually removes herself from the dominance hierarchy. In baboons (Hall & DeVore, 1965; Washburn & DeVore, 1961), dominance over a troop need not be exerted by a single male; quite commonly, several high-ranking males join forces in dominating a troop. Finally, the formation of coalitions between males has been observed in this species. Animals cooperate in order to maintain their rank position relative to subordinate third parties. Such coalitions have also been observed in macaques (Altmann, 1962; Imanishi, 1960).

With such modifications in dominance systems, the fact remains that dominance—no matter how it is established or maintained—brings food and shelter privileges to the animal. It appears that reproductive privileges are similarly rank bound. This, however, does not hold true universally. In baboons (Hall & DeVore, 1965), for example, it has been observed that the alpha male was the only one to copulate with adult females as they came into estrus and turgidity was at a peak. Though possessive with regard to high-ranking females, he showed little interest in low-ranking young females, even when they were in full estrus and presented to him. Also, the alpha male allowed the next-ranking males to share in the mating of high-ranking females before and after they reached full turgescence. In macaques (Simonds, 1965) and gorillas (Schaller, 1965), by contrast, sexual behavior seems to be entirely unrelated to rank, with high-ranking males being extremely tolerant of the copulatory activities of low-ranking ones.

Such findings on the sexual behavior of primates suggest that fighting for dominance may serve the reproductive function less directly than is commonly believed. It is not necessarily the best fighter who "passes on his genes," and consequently, selection does not necessarily favor the fighter. In socially organized animals, the primary function of fighting for dominance may be the determination of the one animal who is best qualified to protect and lead the group—a function Lorenz (e.g., 1964) has stressed. The dominant male's role as a protector of the group has, in fact, been abundantly documented. In baboons (Hall & DeVore, 1965), for example, the alpha male frequently breaks up skirmishes between troop members regardless of their rank and sex. He is the one who threatens and if necessary combats potential dangers to the troop, such as approaching alien baboons or predators. Females with recently born infants cluster near him, and any attack on them prompts his immediate counterattack. Similar behavior patterns are evident in many other primates (e.g., Hall, 1964; Schaller, 1965; Simonds, 1965). Dominance does not necessarily confer leadership, however. In sheep, goats, and many other ruminants, it is the oldest female that leads the herd, although males may be more dominant (Scott, 1976).

Finally, it has been suggested that both territorial and dominance fighting are means to *control* aggressive behavior within a species (Etkin, 1964). Such a suggestion may seem odd and self-contradictory at first, since it entails the claim that aggression functions to curtail aggression, but it proves very meaningful upon closer inspection.

Regarding territorial fighting, the spacing of antagonistic males, which is accomplished with the delineation of territories, should greatly limit the frequency of encounters in which fighting can ensue. Aggression is thus limited to an initial period, and once its very objective—the distribution of territories—is achieved, fighting is effectively curtailed.

Similarly, fighting for dominance curtails aggression, once its objective—the formation of reliable and stable dominance and subordination relationships within a group—is accomplished, by making repeated skirmishes over food, shelter, and mates unnecessary. The mechanisms of curtailment are different in principle, however. Whereas spacing reduces aggression by minimizing the occurrence of conflict, dominance reduces it by placing inhibitions upon the subordinate animal as it pursues motivated activities in situations of conflict. The previously noted peace-keeping function of dominant males in primate groups further illustrates this mechanism: some aggression is used to force upon others the inhibition of potentially many more incidents of aggression.

Thus, regarding territorial and dominance fighting, there is no contradiction in the proposal that aggressive behavior may function to control aggression of greater magnitude. Aggressive behavior that serves in such a function should be considered adaptive.

As indicated earlier, biochemical analyses show the pituitary-gonadal system to be profoundly involved in conspecific fighting. The pituitary-adrenal system also affects (and is affected by) fighting in unique ways. Generally speaking, the two systems are interdependent in exerting their influences.

The emergence of fighting among males, which is generally far more pronounced than among females or between sexes (cf. Bronson & Desjardins, 1971; Collias, 1944), largely coincides with puberty, at which time the amount of circulating androgen sharply increases (e.g., Fredericson, 1950; Hutchinson, Ulrich, & Azrin, 1965; Levy & King, 1953). Levy and King demonstrated that in mice, when the androgen level is prematurely raised by administration of testosterone propionate, fighting occurs equally prematurely.

The relationship between androgen and fighting has been investigated in numerous castration studies. Beeman (1947), for example, reported that in mice, castration virtually abolishes fighting but that with the administration of testosterone propionate, fighting reappears. As Bevan, Bevan, and Williams (1958) noted, castration does not completely abolish fighting in all mice, however. There is, in fact, conflicting evidence concerning the unqualified effect of gonadal hormones on aggressive behavior. For example, whereas Hutchinson, Ulrich, and Azrin (1965) found that in rats, castration is followed by a steady, gradual decline in the frequency of fighting, Powell, Francis, and Schneiderman (1971) failed to observe any increment in fighting when testosterone propionate was administered over a 2-week period. Furthermore, Powell et al. reported that the castration of young rats led to a decrement in fighting during adulthood if the castrates had previous fighting experience. The effect diminished over time, and fighting returned to more normal levels. In castrates without prior fighting experience, in contrast, a decrement in fighting emerged only very slowly during adulthood. Studies by Uhrich (1938) and Yen, Day, and Sigg (1962), which have shown that prepubertal castration decreases adult fighting to a far greater extent than postpubertal castration, are similarly suggestive of an involvement of experiential factors. Given the inconsistent findings concerning the consequences of postweaning castration and androgen administration, it appears that the aggression-potentiating, long-lasting influence of gonadal hormones manifests itself most reliably and most strongly when these hormones are present in sufficient quantity at the time the organism acquires aggressive habits in response to aversive stimuli. Recent findings accord with this interpretation. Conner and Levine (1969), for example, found that male rats that had been castrated neonatally displayed in adulthood the fighting behavior characteristic of females. Even when later treated with testosterone propionate, these animals failed to develop the typical male fighting pattern. In males castrated at weanling age, by contrast, the administration of testosterone propionate entirely restored the male fighting behavior. Similarly, Powell et al. (1971) showed that neonatally administered testosterone propionate resulted in elevated levels of fighting during adulthood, and Bronson and Desjardins (1968) observed increased intersex fighting in neonatally androgenized females.

The apparent fact that in most mammalian species, the aggressive behavior of males surpasses that of females seems to have fostered the belief that estrogens may serve the inhibition of aggression. Studies on mice tend to confirm this speculation. Terdiman and Levy (1954) and Suchowsky, Pegrassi, and Bonsignori (1969) found that although the administration of estrogen to male mice at weanling age had no appreciable effect on later fighting, its administration to adult males did in fact reduce aggressive behavior. Additionally, Mugford and Nowell (1970a, 1970b) demonstrated that the incidence of males' attacks upon females increased substantially when the females were treated with testosterone. These investigators have suggested that male attacks upon females are normally inhibited by a pheromone that is released in the females' urine and that is suppressed by androgen. If this account should hold true, the effects of estrogen would be inhibitory, indeed, and it would only manifest itself peripherally.

Considering other species, the evidence regarding the effect of estrogen is quite mixed. Whereas there was indication of an inhibitory effect in lizards (Evans, 1936) and in domestic fowl (Davis & Domm, 1943), aggression was found to be enhanced in hamsters (Kislak & Beach, 1955) and chimpanzees (Birch & Clark, 1946). Mirsky (1955) found that implants of estrogen in rhesus monkeys did not lead to changes of rank within groups. Michael (1969), also working with rhesus monkeys, reported that following ovariectomy, the female of a male–female pair became somewhat more hostile, but this hostility was not notably altered by the administration of estrogen. However, when the female was made sexually receptive by the combined treatment of estrogen and progesterone, her aggressive behavior increased twofold. In fact, it eventually increased to such an extent that the pair had to be separated to avoid mutual injury. In view of such data, the role of estrogen in the mediation of aggression remains unclear.

The pituitary-gonadal system both effects changes in the pituitary-adrenal system and is affected by changes in that system. The former is evident in the fact that pituitary-adrenal activity is greatly altered by the removal of the gonads (e.g., Sigg, 1969; Wurtman, 1971). This, in fact, shows that the effect of gonadal hormones on aggression may be mediated to some extent by the pituitary-adrenal system. The latter has become increasingly apparent in studies on the effects of crowding (cf. Christian, 1950, 1963; Christian, Lloyd, & Davis, 1965; Davis, 1958). The emerging chain of events is as follows:

1. Increases in population density effect increases in the incidence of conflict and fighting.

2. Increased fighting is associated with increased adrenal activity, which causes the adrenal cortex to enlarge until—under conditions of extreme activity—exhaustion occurs.
3. Aside from various endocrine consequences of negative survival value, such as increased susceptibility to infection and reduced production of antibodies, adrenal hyperactivity causes the suppression of reproductive functions.

According to Christian et al. (1965), the reduction of reproductive activity is partly caused by the adrenocorticotrophic hormone and the adrenal cortical steroids that act back to interfere with gonadotrophin production. The corresponding variation of population density and size of adrenal cortex has been shown in species such as mice, rats, voles, woodchucks, and monkeys (cf. Davis, 1964), and the impact of high densities on reproduction has been documented in lower mammals, mainly in rodents (cf. Christian et al., 1965). There is no evidence that similar endocrine, self-regulatory mechanisms of population control exist in higher mammals, however. In fact, it has been suggested that these mechanisms are lacking in higher mammals such as the primates and that any regulatory function would be of a social kind (Rothballer, 1967).

Activity in the pituitary-adrenal system is also related to social rank. Adrenal weight has been found to vary inversely with rank. This relationship has been demonstrated in mice (Davis, 1964; Davis & Christian, 1957) and in sexually mature White Leghorn chickens (Flickinger, 1961). The latter study failed to reveal such a relationship in grouped hens and in sexually immature cocks but showed a tendency for dominant males to have the largest testes and for spermatogenic function to be retarded in subordinate animals.

Louch and Higginbotham (1967) conducted an experiment in which they placed mice in groups for a prolonged period of time and after determining the dominant and subordinate animals, sacrificed them in order to ascertain plasma corticosterone levels. It was found that compared to control animals, corticosterone levels in dominant animals were only slightly and unreliably elevated. In subordinate animals, by contrast, they were more than two times those of the controls. Adrenal response thus seems to be associated with defeat, and the larger adrenals of repeatedly defeated subordinate animals appear to synthesize and release greater amounts of adrenocorticoids (cf. Bronson & Desjardins, 1971; Nagra, Baum, & Meyer, 1960). Focusing on the "winner" rather than the "loser," Davis (1964) arrived at the following generalization: "An important consequence of aggressive behavior is the physiological advantage gained from winning, since the adrenals of winners are normal in size rather than hypertrophied and thus have normal function [p. 67]."

The relationship between rank and adrenal responsiveness in rhesus monkeys has been studied longitudinally by Sassenrath (1970). Over a period of 2 years, groups of three males and two females were caged together, and various changes in the social environment were introduced. Adrenocortico-trophic hormones were exogenously administered, and adrenal response was measured in urinary 17-hydroxycorticosteroid levels. It was found that when the dominance structure was stable, the alpha male showed lower adrenal responsiveness than the subordinate animals. Within groups, social rank and adrenal response were inversely related. Removal of the alpha male resulted in marked decreases in adrenal responsiveness in the female cagemates; it did not appreciably affect responsiveness in the subordinate males, however. Removal of the most subordinate female led to marked decreases in her adrenal response. Furthermore, when consort pair formation occurred between an alpha male and a number 3 female, the female's rank rose to number 2, and there was a concomitant decrease in her adrenal response. At the same time, the other female cagemate became the omega animal of the group, a change that promptly effected increased adrenal responsiveness.

There is considerable evidence, then, that in various species, including primates, the dominant animals, which are typically the most aggressive ones (cf. Collias, 1944; Etkin, 1964; Hall & DeVore, 1965), exhibit normal adrenal functioning, whereas the subordinate ones suffer from adrenal hypertrophy. It is quite unclear, however, to what extent the observed hypertrophic adrenal activity results directly from fighting or, more specifically, from defeat in hostile and aggressive encounters. The findings thus far discussed leave it similarly unclear whether or not—and if so, to what degree—normal adrenal functioning potentiates aggression.

Regarding hypertrophic action, a low ranking, which presumably results from repeated defeats in competitive situations, entails numerous, at least temporary deprivations. Under conditions of severe shortages of food, the low-ranking animal's life is placed in jeopardy. Shortages of life-preserving shelter may also jeopardize the animal's existence, and mate shortages may eliminate its involvement in the reproductive process. More common conditions—in which access to available food, shelter, and mates is competitive—characteristically require the low-ranking animal to engage in continued efforts to obtain vital commodities and conditions. Whereas the dominant animal invests comparatively little effort in need satisfaction and generally suffers only short periods of deprivation, the low-ranking animal exerts far more energy in such efforts, potentially exhausting itself, and it suffers deprivations for much longer periods of time. The continuous burden of prolonged deprivations and excessive energy expenditure may be conceived of as *stressful* to the low-ranking animal, and in accord with Selye's (1950, 1956) concept of a general adaptation syndrome, increased activity in the pituitary-adrenal system should be expected. The adaptation concept stipulates that in order to provide the organism with the energy needed to meet long-term stresses, various essential metabolic and other changes are induced by the action of adrenocortical hormones, particularly the glucocorticoids. Through the increased production of these corticoids over extended periods of time—accomplished via a feedback system that keeps the level of adrenocorticotrophic-hormone synthesis in the anterior pituitary elevated—the organism maintains effective operation under the particular stress conditions. Adaptation is thus dependent on continued increased activity of the adrenal cortex. As a consequence, it is possible that adrenal hypertrophy in animals of lower social rank results entirely from the stress factors associated with the discussed prolonged deprivations and excessive energy expenditure. Conceivably, then, hypertrophy could develop in the absence of competition and aggression in socially isolated animals who are made to experience the deprivations and expend amounts of energy comparable with low-ranking, grouped animals. On the other hand, the low-ranking animal's continuous acquiescence to the dominant others and particularly, its frequent yielding to them in situations where the animal is disposed to perform a need-satisfying goal response (e.g., readiness to eat in the presence of food) may well prove to be a potent stressor in itself.

Regarding the effect of adrenal activity on aggression, the observation that normal function in dominant animals tends to correspond with increased aggressiveness (and hypertrophy presumably corresponds with a lower incidence of attack) has to be dealt with cautiously. Changes in rank and changes in adrenal function were most often confounded in the investigations discussed. It could thus be argued that instead of adrenal activity having changed as a function of rank, there may have been a propensity for adrenal hypertrophy in those animals that subsequently dropped in rank. Conversely, however, the coincidence of normal adrenal function, high social rank, and high aggressiveness may result entirely from superior fighting abilities that lead to the dominance position, which in turn leads to minimal stresses and thus normal function. The correlational nature of the data simply does not permit the implication of a definite causal linkage between the various factors involved, particularly not between normal adrenal activity and increases in aggression.

There are, nonetheless, some findings that could be interpreted as indicating a greater incidence of aggression at normal or, more accurately, subnormal *general* levels of adrenal activity. It has been well established that in male mice (cf. Garattini & Sigg, 1969) and to a far lesser extent in female mice (Ginsburg & Allee, 1942; Weltman, Sackler, Schwartz, & Owens, 1968), social isolation promotes fighting. Isolation, presumably because it removes all social stresses from the animal, has been observed to produce adrenal atrophy (cf. Conner, 1972). More specifically, Welch and Welch (1969b) have shown that isolation produces changes in levels and utilization rates of catecholamines: In the brain, norepinephrine levels are lowered, and utilization rates for norepinephrine and dopamine are reduced; peripherally, both levels and utilization rates of adrenal medullary norepinephrine and epinephrine are reduced. These investigators (Welch, 1964; Welch & Welch, 1969a) have suggested that generally reduced adrenal function may accentuate the magnitude of the adrenocorticoid response to stress, making the animal more easily aroused and hyperresponsive to stimulation (cf. Sigg, 1969). Increased aggressiveness following isolation could thus be accounted for as the result of possible hyperresponsiveness in the stressful confrontation with a conspecific.

Such an account raises the question of whether or not the proposed hyperresponsiveness would be specifically related to aggression. Does low-level adrenal activity—by accentuating (adrenal) responsiveness to stress—exclusively promote fighting, or does it enhance *any* behavior called for by immediate stimuli? For example, in a mouse's confrontation with a cat, would it facilitate fear and flight behavior? There is no evidence that adrenal atrophy and hyperresponsiveness in mice produce effects specific to fighting, and it would thus be premature to consider these effects aggression-specific.

The phenomenon of isolation-induced fighting in mice, as such, calls for considerable caution concerning cross-species generalizations. Apparently, the phenomenon is restricted to mice. It is not in evidence in rats (cf. Conner, 1972) or dogs (cf. Scott & Fuller, 1965), and in higher mammals, particularly the primates, isolation generally induces withdrawal-type reactions rather than attack (cf. Harlow & Harlow, 1965; Rowland, 1964).

Independent of adrenal functioning as a relatively steady antecedent condition of aggression, adrenal activity concurrent with aggression has also been investigated. High adrenal activity levels have been found to facilitate fighting. Kostowski (1967) demonstrated that corticosterone increases pain-elicited aggression in mice. Similarly, Jacobs and Farel (1971) showed elevated adrenal activity to potentiate pain-elicited aggression in rats. Such demonstrations of aggression-facilitating effects of heightened adrenal action in animals are, however, relatively rare. Investigators seem to have concentrated instead on changes in the pituitary-adrenal system as a consequence of fighting.

If aggressive behavior is considered a stressful condition, increased adrenal activity during fighting is to be expected. Various investigators have reported findings corroborating this expectation. Following hostile and aggressive encounters, high levels of plasma adrenocorticoids have frequently been observed in mice (e.g., Bronson & Eleftheriou, 1965a, 1965b; Yen, Day, & Sigg, 1962). Similarly, fighting causes elevated levels in various biogenic amines. For example, Welch and Welch (1969b) reported sharp increases in serotonin levels. However, increased adrenal activity again cannot be considered to be specific to fighting. All marked changes in stimulation tend to increase adrenal activity (e.g., as observed by Welch and Welch [1968a, 1968b], serotonin levels also rise as the result of an animal's exposure to cold and similar stressors). Regarding adrenal changes concurrent with fighting (or immediately subsequent to fighting), aggressive behavior is to be considered comparable to innumerable conditions that—exogenously or endogenously—induce stress in the organism. It should be clear, nonetheless, that the findings on adrenal activity associated with fighting accord with the generalization that aggressive behavior as such is stressful.

The biochemical analysis of the not-so-immediate consequences of fighting leads to a somewhat different assessment. One would expect that after fighting—a strenuous activity that necessitates elevated adrenal function— indices of this function would reveal a slowing down of operation. Consistent with this expectation, Welch and Welch (1969b), for example, showed that in mice, adrenal medullary levels of epinephrine decline following fighting, with levels of norepinephrine remaining relatively stable. In the brain stem, but not in various other areas such as the diencephalon–midbrain region, levels of norepinephrine also decline. This pattern of adrenal slowdown after fighting proved to be distinct from the biochemical consequences of another stressor— namely, restraint. The question remains, however, whether adrenal slow-down after a nonaggressive activity producing a degree of exertion comparable to that of fighting would have critically differed. This question also relates to the finding that in male mice, short daily episodes of fighting— not of winning or losing—lead to long-term elevations of adrenal function and ultimately produce cardiac hypertrophy (Welch & Welch, 1971).

Conner, Vernikos-Danellis, and Levine (1971) have documented that during fighting, adrenocorticotrophic-hormone levels increase markedly and apparently continuously—in rats, for at least a period of 5 minutes. Following fighting, these elevated levels decline steadily and return to prior levels.

In their investigation, Conner et al. employed the paradigm of shock-induced fighting (cf. Ulrich, 1966). In this procedure, fighting is initiated by placing the animals into a relatively small, restrictive enclosure and then administering electric shock through the grid of the floor. The procedure thus requires the delivery of shock to the animal—a treatment that must be considered highly stressful. To control for the adrenal reaction to shock, Conner et al. (1971) involved a control condition in which individual animals received a shock treatment identical to that which the fighting animals received. Except for no-shock, no-fight controls, all animals were treated according to the following scheme: They received either 50 shocks in the initial 2.5 minutes, or they received this treatment plus 40 further shocks in the next 2.5 minutes. All animals were sacrificed to obtain measures of levels of adrenocorticotrophic hormones and adrenocorticosteroids from plasma concentrations. The animals were killed at the following critical times: (a) after 2.5 minutes of shock treatment, (b) after 5 minutes of shock treatment, (c) 2.5 minutes after termination of the 5-minute shock treatment, and (d) 10 minutes after the 5-minute shock treatment. It was found that both the fight treatment and the shock-only treatment—as compared to the no-shock, no-fight controls—resulted in elevated levels of adrenocorticotrophic hormones after 2.5 minutes, in further elevated levels after 5 minutes, and in a steady decline thereafter, with recovery not complete 10 minutes after the shock or shock-and-fight treatment, however. (Changes in adrenocorticosteroid levels were partly similar but generally inconsistent and unreliable.) In line with expectations, these parallel changes simply show both shock and fight treatments to be stressful. Comparisons of the effect of these treatments at the various time points proved much more revealing. Since fighting in itself is stressful and shock is equated in both treatments, it is to be expected that adrenal activity should be highest in the fighting condition. The findings show, however, that this is the case only after 2.5 minutes of fighting. At this time, adrenocorticotrophic hormone levels in the fight condition were reliably above those in the shock-only condition. Unexpectedly, after prolonged fighting—that is, after 5 minutes—this difference was reversed, and the higher levels now associated with shocking only were in evidence throughout the recovery period. It has thus been shown that fighting, although initially causing a greater elevation in adrenal activity than nonfighting, results in a more effective recovery from this elevation than nonfighting. Since both the fighting and the shock-only treatments induced similar vigorous motor and vocal reactions in the rats, it is difficult to dismiss the findings as resulting from a confounding of the treatments with skeletal-motor responses.

Stolk, Conner, Levine, and Barchas (cited in Conner, 1972), who studied the metabolism of brain catecholamines under the experimental conditions already described (Conner et al., 1971), reported findings that are partly consistent with those discussed. During and immediately following fighting, there were only insignificant changes in catecholamine levels in various areas tested. By contrast, the shock treatment alone resulted in an increased rate of norepinephrine utilization in the brain stem. The shock-plus-fight treatment thus appears to be less stressful than the shock-only treatment. Further data are somewhat confusing, however. In the hour following the treatment manipulations, animals who had fought showed increased norepinephrine metabolism in various areas, whereas animals who had received shock only showed decreased utilization rates of norepinephrine in the brain stem but no changes in other areas. Still later, this relationship partly reversed. The treatments thus led to structural differences in catecholamine metabolism, but it is unclear which recovery pattern should be considered more effective.

Conner et al. have suggested that the superior adrenal recovery after fighting (and the possibly less intense adrenal reaction) is due to a *coping value of aggression*. Fighting is considered stress reducing (and in this sense, it is considered adaptive), because it constitutes—in contrast to the disorganized escape attempts in the condition of nonfighting—an organized behavior pattern. Conner (1972) related this notion of aggression as a coping response to Miller's (1969b) work, which shows an attenuation of the behavioral and/or physiological reactions to aversive stimulation when the animal is provided with a coping response such as escape. It seems, however, that in categorizing aggressive behavior along with other coping responses, some caution is indicated. In the procedures employed by Conner et al. and Stolk et al., the shocked animal was confined in a way that prevented any organized reaction. If an organized, yet unsuccessful, escape response had been permitted, nonfighting might have resulted in more effective recovery from elevated adrenal activity than fighting. In other words, the findings merely show that organized aggressive behavior is potentially more adaptive than disorganized nonaggressive behavior. They certainly do not demonstrate that organized aggressive behavior is more adaptive than organized nonaggressive behavior. Thus, the respective adaptation values of various forms of aggressive and nonaggressive coping reactions in particular species remain to be shown.

By way of overview, it can be said that the biochemical analysis of conspecific fighting reveals the following:

1. The pattern of endocrine processes associated with conspecific fighting differs substantially from that associated with predatory behavior.

2. Elevated activity in the pituitary-gonadal system potentiates aggressiveness mainly when it prevails during the developmental stage in which the organism is acquiring aggressive modes of behavior. Counter to common beliefs, later changes in androgen levels do not consistently facilitate aggression.

3. Prolonged elevated activity in the pituitary-adrenal system—that is, adrenal hypertrophy—is generally associated with defeat and subordination. Adrenal atrophy, resulting from social isolation, may cause hyperresponsiveness to stimulation and thereby promote fighting in some lower mammals; in higher mammals, it is likely to promote withdrawal reactions.

4. Adrenal activity concurrent with fighting enhances aggressiveness.

5. Aggressive behavior elevates adrenal activity. It thus is to be considered stressful.

6. Aggressive reactions usually constitute well-organized behavior. The performance of organized aggressive reactions seems less stressful than the performance of disorganized nonaggressive reactions but not less stressful than the performance of similarly organized nonaggressive behaviors such as escape.

7. Neither the effect of adrenal activity on fighting nor the effect of fighting on adrenal activity appears to be specific to aggression. Both probably apply to a variety of vigorous nonaggressive behaviors as well.

The biochemically supported view that fighting—unless it entails the relatively effortless, consistent domination of conspecifics—constitutes a stressful, potentially aversive state seems to conflict with occasional pronouncements that conspecific aggression has reinforcing qualities. Skinner (1969), for example, has argued that an "innate capacity to be reinforced by damage to others [p. 211]" could be derived from certain phylogenetic contingencies. The evidence for such an innate capacity is quite equivocal, however.

First of all, the reinforcement value of aggression is evident mainly in predatory behavior—not in conspecific fighting. For example, Roberts and Kiess (1964) showed that hypothalamic stimulation of cats, which caused predatory attacks on rats, also facilitated the learning of a Y-maze when a rat was provided for attack and thus served as a reinforcer. Similarly, Myer and White (1965) and Van Hemel (1972) reported that in rats, the opportunity to kill a mouse can serve as a reinforcer in maintaining learned responses. Other experiments (Huston, DeSisto, & Meyer, 1965; Tellegen, Horn, & Legrand, 1969; Van Hemel & Myer, 1970) have made essentially the same point. It is unclear, however, whether predatory attack functions as a primary reinforcer or simply serves as a secondary reinforcer based on food as the primary reinforcer. Roberts and Kiess (1964) suggested that food was not the source of the reinforcement and backed this view with the observation that hypothalamic stimulation during eating caused cats to relinquish their food and attack an available mouse. This reasoning is not compelling, however, since the specific areas stimulated in the study referred to were associated with attack—not with eating. More importantly, Van Hemel's (1972) findings are supportive of an explanation that favors food rather than aggression per se as the primary reinforcer. This investigator placed killer rats in an operant paradigm in which mice were presented whenever the rats pressed a key. All animals learned the response and killed consistently throughout the training period. Moreover, they maintained the response when continuous reinforcement was changed to a variable schedule of reinforcement. Interestingly, however, these animals pressed the key as readily for anesthetized mice, and even for dead mice, as they did for live mice—in contrast to rat pups for which they exhibited significantly lower response rates. Obviously, if the reinforcement values of live, anesthetized, and dead prey are equal, predatory attack in itself cannot be considered the critical reinforcer.

In light of such findings, it appears somewhat premature to accept the notion that predatory attack serves as a primary reinforcer—independent of food intake. Moyer (1971), for example, has suggested that "just as food is reinforcing to the animal whose 'feeding system' is activated, the opportunity to attack is reinforcing to an animal whose 'predatory system' is activated [pp. 15–16]." Such a suggestion is tautological in that reinforcement is equated with elicitability (by brain stimulation): If a behavior can be elicited, it must be reinforcing. By the same reasoning, if escape or similar withdrawal-type reactions can be elicited, they must be reinforcing. The term *reinforcement* apparently is being used in ways alien to learning theory, and this leads to eventual misunderstandings. Notwithstanding the different interpretations of "reinforcement," it remains to be shown that predatory attack has the qualities of a primary reinforcer in the sense of facilitating the acquisition of any neutral behavior by contingent placement without having itself first been facilitated by a primary reinforcer.

Regarding conspecific fighting, there are a number of studies that have been interpreted as demonstrating that aggression is reinforcing. However, it appears that in all these investigations, certain conditions have prevailed that restrict generalization and, in fact, render unwarranted and spurious the claim that aggressive behavior is *universally* reinforcing.

Working with mice, Lagerspetz (1969) reported two experiments in which fighting promoted further fighting. In the first study, fighting was interrupted at the point at which the animal of interest had been defeated or was at a standoff with its opponent. The animals were then provided with an opportunity to continue fighting. Under these conditions and when the initial fighting was intense, it was found that undefeated mice were more inclined to continue fighting than defeated ones or, more importantly, than mice who had not fought before. In the second study, animals fought briefly or did not fight and were then provided with the "opponent" in such a way that they had to cross an electrified grid to attack the opponent. It was observed that those animals whose fighting had been disrupted crossed the grid more rapidly and more often than those who had not fought initially. Dreyer and Church (1970) reported that when rats received inescapable electric shock, they turned to the arm of a T-maze that contained a rat they could fight. Azrin, Hutchinson, and McLaughlin (1965) found that after being shocked, squirrel monkeys emitted an operant response such as chain pulling to obtain an inanimate object they could attack. Finally, Thompson (1963, 1964) showed that fighting fish and fighting cocks would perform operant responses in order to achieve merely visual contact with a conspecific.

The latter findings are rendered somewhat equivocal because they involve animals known for hyperaggressive conspecific behavior. Additionally, concerning the fighting cocks, there is the question of whether the observed behavior was prompted by a history of victorious fights rather than defeats or just struggles. Most importantly, however, the studies on fighting fish and fighting cocks are more directly supportive of the notion that the presence of a conspecific is reinforcing than they are of the proposal that aggression is reinforcing. After all, the behavioral contingency employed did not involve fighting.

The behavior observed by Azrin et al. (1965) is also uncomfortably remote from actual fighting. Strictly speaking, the findings show that when an animal is in pain, the opportunity to bite into something—if this is the only choice of directed action—is reinforcing. The studies by Dreyer and Church and by Lagerspetz are less artificial in that, as is characteristic in fighting situations, the animals involved placed themselves at risk when choosing to attack.

Be it merely the provision of an object to bite or of a target for full-fledged attack that is being considered a reinforcer, the studies just discussed show that the reinforcement function depends on the infliction of pain or the prior initiation of attack. Apparently, attack is only "rewarding" when the animal has been or is being *aversively stimulated*. The animal seems to draw upon unlearned or learned stimulus–response connections to terminate or alleviate this state of aversion—by continuing to fight in order to exert dominance or by attacking the only object the environment provides. In the latter case, the animal behaves *as if* a causal connection were made between the aversive state and any animal or substitute in the immediate vicinity. Ulrich (1961) noted that aggression in response to shock was extremely likely if—and only if— another animal was close by, and he suggested that the organism might be endowed by heredity with the tendency to attack when in pain (Ulrich & Symannek, 1969). Such a tendency would certainly appear adaptive, since under nonlaboratory circumstances, the aversively stimulated animal who assaults the closest thing in its vicinity will probably be attacking the agent responsible for the infliction of the pain. Under laboratory conditions, by contrast, confusions are likely, and it should not be surprising that an animal in pain will eventually attack a canvas ball—as in the study by Azrin et al. (1965)—if this is the only object accessible.

Returning to the reinforcement issue, it should be clear that broad and unqualified generalizations such as "fighting is enjoyable" or "aggression is rewarding" are not supported by animal research. As Azrin et al. (1965) carefully pointed out, any reinforcement value of fighting is dependent on aversive stimulation. The proposal that aggression may reinforce certain behaviors that are instrumental in providing attack opportunities is thus not inconsistent with the view that aggression is principally based on aversions. However, Azrin et al., by suggesting that aggression is a distinctive motivational state that is produced by aversive stimulation and "which can be used to condition and maintain new behavior [p. 171]," have created the impression that attack is just another reinforcer, similar to food and water. It is this potentially misleading impression that calls for clarification.

As an aversion-induced "motivational" state, aggression differs in principle from deprivation-based motivations. The most crucial difference is with regard to the time period of any "appetitive" phase. Whereas deprivation-based motivations successively and rather slowly build up to maximum force, intense aversive stimulation constitutes an emergency that immediately motivates with maximum and then with quickly diminishing force. As a consequence, deprivation-based motivation spans comparatively large time periods in which the organism can pursue behaviors that ultimately result in the reduction of the motivating deprivation. There is thus a relatively long appetitive phase in which the animal's behavior can be shaped and modified by the provision of adequate reinforcers. In an aversion-based motivation, by contrast, the behavioral emergency demands immediate action. The action may be reflexive in character, as Ulrich (1961) suggested. At any rate, there is no appetitive phase to speak of between the infliction of pain and the attack upon a nearby animal or object. As the animal is aversively stimulated, it tends to perform what could be considered the consummatory response. This fact shows how restrictive the provision of an opponent (or an inanimate object) for attack would be in the conditioning of neutral behaviors. Also, the suffering animal is placed in a state of increased sympathetic excitation (cf. Cannon, 1929; Sternbach, 1968), which narrows the repertoire of spontaneously occurring behaviors that can be reinforced, thus further restricting the use of attack for the purpose of reinforcement. Reinforceable behaviors may well be confined to immediate actions such as pulling, pushing and kicking. Hutchinson (1972) has referred to the reinforcement in question as "target contact." This designation seems appropriate, because it points out the lack of time or space separation between the onset of aggression-motivating pain and the resultant aggressive act as such.

Quite independent of these implications for conditioning, the findings discussed—together with others discussed later—reveal a clear tendency for pain to induce attack and attacklike behavior in various species. Consistent with Glickman and Schiff's (1967) model, it appears that if attack upon an apparent annoyer is viewed as an immediate consummatory response evoked by intense aversive stimulation, such defensive fighting may be reinforcing in its own right—perhaps because the consummatory reaction neutralizes the neural activity incited by pain. Conceivably, however, in the case of pain, this neutralization of neural activity is not specific to fighting. The neural activity may be as readily neutralized by flight and possibly even more effectively. Since experimental investigations of fighting generally do not compare the fight and flight options, this issue cannot be decided at present.

Concerning the relationship between pain and aggression, Scott (1971) noted that pain instigates defensive fighting with extreme regularity in a great variety of species, and he suggested that with the exception of amphibia, which are limited to escape reactions, the pain–aggression connection is nearly universal in vertebrates. In Scott's (1971) view, "defensive fighting in reaction to painful stimulation is the most basic type of social fighting [p. 12]." Less intense aversions may prompt nonaggressive withdrawal or hostile displays as adaptive reactions, but pain is seen to demand fighting as an adaptive reaction. The justification for such an interpretation is apparent: In animals, the mutual infliction of pain by shoving, clawing, or biting entails physical contact; consequently, if pain is inflicted, the agent who has inflicted it is immediately present and in a position to inflict further damage. Given this condition, attack—even if only to provide a better opportunity for later escape—is superior to immediate escape, because it provides perceptual control of the opponent's behavior and thereby permits effective counter-measures. By confronting the antagonist in a fight, the animal minimizes the opponent's infliction of further pain and, more importantly, bodily damage. This is not to say that prolonged combat serves this adaptive function but that brief fighting that provides the physically inferior animal ample opportunity to withdraw without risk of injury does so.

As indicated earlier, there is considerable evidence that pain does, in fact, induce aggressive reactions in a great variety of species. Pain-elicited aggression has been observed in such diverse species as wasps, crayfish, mice, rats, snakes, turtles, gamecocks, alligators, opossums, ferrets, foxes, raccoons, and squirrel monkeys (cf. Azrin, 1964; Hutchinson, 1972). As suggested by the finding of pain-elicited aggression in wasps and crayfish, this phenomenon may apply to many species of invertebrates as well. However, it seems not to be entirely universal in vertebrates: The phenomenon could not be demonstrated in guinea pigs, for example (cf. Ulrich, 1966).

Pain may be the most basic and reliable inducer of defensive fighting, but it certainly is not the only one. In fact, if it were considered the only inducer of fighting, the initiation of fighting could only be explained as accidental. If all animals were to avoid inflicting pain upon others, pain obviously would have to be accidentally inflicted upon the one beginning the fight. It can, nonetheless, be argued that such "accidental" initiations of fighting are easily brought about in characteristic conflict situations. In the struggle over food, for example, actual fighting might be triggered as soon as one of the animals involved experiences pain. However, observations in laboratory and field studies do not confirm this. In order to obtain or maintain control of vital commodities (i.e., food) or conditions (i.e., shelter), animals generally resort to fighting *before* pain is inflicted by competitive action.

The study of competitive and spontaneous fighting in mice (Fredericson, 1950), for example, shows that fighting over food starts with the introduction of food and is independent of the specific physical proximity of the animals at that time. When the animals were placed in conditions of severe food depriva-tion, such fighting started immediately with the presentation of food—whether or not the competing animals were in physical contact. Satiated animals fought to a lesser extent, again independent of initial physical proximity. Similarly, it has been demonstrated (Azrin, Hutchinson, & Hake, 1966) that pigeons who peck for and ingest food will attack a nearby pigeon once food is withheld. Obviously, the attack is not elicited by pain. The animal responds *as if* it were warding off a competitor for food. The observation that prior satiation reduced attack is consistent with this interpretation. Field studies on rhesus monkeys (Southwick, 1966, 1969) further corroborate this view. Food-elicited fighting increased when the amount of food was adequate but its distribution restricted. Again, fighting began when food was placed in sight rather than with the accidental infliction of pain.

Ulrich, Hutchinson, Azrin, and their associates have generated a research program in which potentially all critical antecedent and subsequent conditions of aggression are being systematically investigated. Since comprehensive and detailed reviews of their work have been published (e.g., Azrin, 1964; Hutchinson, 1972; Ulrich, 1966), we discuss the essential findings in summary fashion only.

In categorizing the environmental causes of aggression, Hutchinson (1972) distinguished between (I) *antecedent conditions* (i.e., a class of causal events that precede instances of aggressive behavior) and (II) *subsequent conditions* (i.e., a class of causal events that follow aggressive behavior and that may influence the occurrence of future aggression). He further distinguished between the two principal types of stimulation: (1) *aversive stimulation* (i.e., exposure to painful and noxious events or to other previously neutral stimuli that—as a result of being paired with aversive events—have come to be conditional aversive stimuli), and (2) *beneficial stimulation* (i.e., exposure to pleasant and need-satisfying events or to other stimuli that have come to be conditional beneficial stimuli); and between (a) the *onset or increase* and (b) the *offset or decrease* of stimulation. Obviously, not all combinations of these dichotomous conditions are of interest when the elicitation and potentiation of aggression are being considered. Only categories IIa, I2b, II2a, and III1b concern us here. This conceptual scheme appears to be helpful in structuring environmental influences on aggression and the wealth of relevant findings.

I1a. As attested by numerous studies, aversive stimulation is a potent antecedent condition for aggression. Aggressive reactions have been found to be elicited by the delivery of aversive stimuli such as a physical blow (Azrin, Hake, & Hutchinson, 1965), intense heat (Ulrich & Azrin, 1962), air blasts (Ulrich, Hutchinson, & Azrin, 1965), loud noise (Hutchinson & Emley, 1972), electric shock (O'Kelly & Steckle, 1939; Renfrew, 1969; Ulrich & Azrin, 1962), and conditioned aversive stimuli (Hutchinson, Renfrew, & Young, 1971; Vernon & Ulrich, 1966). Pain-elicited attack will be directed against conspecifics if they are present (Ulrich & Azrin, 1962). In their absence, a substitute such as a toy animal (Azrin, Hutchinson, & Sallery, 1964) or simply a rubber hose (Hutchinson, Azrin, & Hake, 1966) may draw the attack. However, as Ulrich (1966) noted, some species (e.g., pigeons and monkeys) will readily accept inanimate substitute targets for attack, whereas others (e.g., rats) will not.

I2b. The removal of beneficial stimulation proved to be a potent antecendent of aggression in several investigations. Aggressive reactions were elicited by the removal of beneficial stimuli such as food (Azrin, Hutchinson, & Hake, 1966), morphine (Boshka, Weisman, & Thor, 1966; Emley, Hutchinson, & Brannan, 1970), and conditioned beneficial stimuli (Hutchinson, Azrin, & Hunt, 1968; Hutchinson & Pierce, 1971). Attacks were directed toward such targets as conspecifics (Azrin, Hutchinson, & Hake, 1966), a model of a conspecific (Azrin, Hutchinson, & Hake, 1966), and a rubber hose (Hutchinson, Azrin, & Hunt, 1968).

II2a. Aggressive behavior, like any other behavior, can readily be strengthened by the subsequent administration of appropriate reinforcers—future manifestations of the behavior thus becoming more likely. The subsequent delivery of beneficial stimulation such as food (Azrin & Hutchinson, 1967; Reynolds, Catania, & Skinner, 1963), water (Ulrich, Johnston, Richardson, & Wolff, 1963), and target contact (Azrin, Hutchinson, & McLaughlin, 1965) has been found to potentiate aggressive responses.

II2b. The subsequent removal of aversive stimulation has also been observed to potentiate aggression. Aggression can be viewed as instrumental (cf. Hokanson, 1969) in that it seems to be effective in terminating the aversion. This is apparent in the aggression-facilitating effect of the termination of an attack by a conspecific—which amounts to a pseudovictory (Scott & Fredericson, 1951)—and in the termination of electric shock (Azrin, Hutchinson, & Hake, 1967; Miller, 1948).

There are profound differences between the overt manifestations of aggressive behavior that is elicited by antecedent conditions and those of aggression that is effectuated by subsequent events. Hutchinson (1972) noted that antecedent-elicited attack, whether it is produced by the onset of aversive stimulation or by the offset of beneficial stimulation, "is accompanied by autonomic vocal and facial responses characteristic of the reaction pattern commonly referred to as anger [p. 177]." By contrast, consequence-fostered attack, whether facilitated by the onset of beneficial or the offset of noxious stimulation, is generally not accompanied by signs of emotional arousal. This difference in sympathetic excitation associated with potentially equally destructive behaviors relates to the distinction, developed earlier, between annoyance-motivated and incentive-motivated behavior. Antecedent states that elicit spontaneous attack in animals—whether such attack is learned or unlearned—are intensely experienced annoyances or emergencies. The utility of the attack is the alleviation of the annoyance. As alleviation is achieved, the utility of fighting terminates. Quite to the contrary, incentive-motivated attack is not performed in emergency situations, and it is not linked to high arousal states. Its utility is, not to alleviate *now,* but to provide vital commodities and conditions *later,* and without apparent termination. (The teleological note derives from the fact that [as in all learning] the animal behaves *as if* consistencies in past events will extend into the future: Since fighting has brought incentives, it will do so again.)

It is worthy of note that aggressive reactions also can become classically conditioned to initially neutral stimuli. This phenomenon has been demonstrated in investigations by Ulrich, Hutchinson, and Azrin (1965); Creer, Hitzing, and Schaeffer (1966); Vernon and Ulrich (1966); and Farris, Gideon, and Ulrich (1970).

Numerous brain-stimulation studies have generally corroborated the discussed findings. Aggressive reactions have been elicited by the antecedent onset of noxious stimulation and the antecedent termination of pleasant stimulation, and they have been potentiated by the subsequent onset of pleasant stimulation (cf. Hutchinson, 1972).

Considered as a whole, the evidence presented by Azrin, Hutchinson, and Ulrich, their co-workers, and others has greatly furthered our understanding of the influence of environmental conditions and contingencies on aggressive behavior in various species. However, some caution is indicated in generalizing about the likelihood of attack among conspecifics in their natural habitats. Research findings, primarily those of Delgado and his associates, have made certain qualifications necessary.

As mentioned earlier, the experimental investigation of aggressive behavior is largely associated with procedures that severely confine the animal and restrict its environment, usually eliminating important behavioral options such as escape. In the extreme, the animal is physically confined to a particular position and confronted with just one object into which it can bite. Behavioral freedom is thus reduced to biting vs. nonbiting. Such procedures, of course, permit the determination of environmental influences upon *differential* biting attacks, but by limiting or preventing alternative reactions, they foster artificially high attack rates. In this connection, Ulrich (1966) acknowledged a tendency for animals under intense aversive stimulation to make futile attempts to escape. Apparently, the animals fight as frequently as they do only when "cornered."

Delgado was able to bypass the seemingly unavoidable confinement of animals for the purpose of experimentation by exploiting modern communication technology: the radio transmission of signals in combination with the miniaturization of receivers. Delgado (e.g., 1967a) implanted electrode assemblies in the brains of experimental animals, mainly rhesus monkeys, and equipped the animals with small, lightweight receivers and stimulators or skin shockers. The assemblies were fixed to the skull, and the receiver-stimulator or receiver-shocker unit was held by a collar. Radio-controlled electrical stimulation could thus be applied to any electrode point of interest, and most importantly, it could be done via remote control, with the animal free in its customary social environment.

There is some indication from brain-lesion studies (e.g., Plotnik, 1968; Rosvold, Mirsky, & Pribram, 1954) that aggressive behavior varies as a function of the particular social conditions under which it occurs. Such findings suggested that the identical stimulation might result in highly different reactions under different environmental circumstances. That this is indeed so has been convincingly demonstrated in Delgado's work.

The restricted generalizability of studies in which conspecific attack is assessed in restrained individual animals became apparent with the demonstration (Delgado, 1967a, 1967b) that the identical stimulation (of points in the nucleus ventralis posterior lateralis of the thalamus or points in the central grey) has quite different consequences in rhesus monkeys depending on whether the animal is: (a) restrained in a chair, (b) free but alone in its colony cage, or (c) free to interact with other colony members. In the restrained animals, the stimulation simply resulted in staring, minor head movements, the opening of the mouth, and low-pitched vocalizations. In the free but isolated animals, it led mainly to increased walking and circling and also to low-pitched vocalizations. In striking contrast, the stimulation profoundly affected attack and defense in the animals who were free in their colony. The specific effect was entirely dependent on the social rank of the animal stimulated—a significant discovery in itself. Stimulation of the alpha animal of the group produced well-organized attacks upon subordinate animals, including chasing, striking, and biting. These attacks were launched primarily against an animal that had previously clashed with the stimulated animal. Another animal, with whom the stimulated animal was "on friendly terms," was never attacked. Disposition toward particular individuals thus proved to be a key factor in the observed aggressive behavior. Stimulation did *not indiscriminately* cause aggressive action. Its effect was *guided by earlier experience with the potential targets.* It is also of interest that whereas "aggressive intent and aim were constant" (Delgado, 1967b, p. 388), the overt manifestations of aggressive responses were highly variable—an observation that shows that social fighting in monkeys does not conform to so-called fixed action patterns. Stimulation of the beta animal also produced well-organized attack. The assaults of this animal were directed against all other animals in the group, including the alpha animal. After several stimulations, the social status of the beta animal had improved to the point where it became dominant over the former alpha animal. Interestingly, the identical stimulation in low-ranking animals did not produce aggressive responses at all. It merely induced restlessness, causing the animals to run around in the cage following each stimulation. Strangely enough, as they did, they were attacked more often than usual by more dominant animals, thereby becoming even more submissive. It is evident, again, that *prior experience guides* the effect of stimulation. If aggressive reactions are not habitually performed under specific social conditions, presumably because they have been associated with intense aversions in the past (i.e., they have led to painful defeats), they are apparently readily suppressed. The impulse may be there, but it is of no consequence.

These findings have been confirmed with rhesus monkeys in other investigations (Delgado, 1967a, 1967b, 1969), which have taken a somewhat different approach. It has been shown, for example, that aggressiveness elicited by the identical stimulation will vary with the individual animal's place in a social hierarchy. In one study, a particular animal was either: (a) alone and restrained in a chair, (b) free in a large cage with a subordinate animal, or (c) free in this cage with a dominant animal. Stimulation (of the right pedunculus cerebellaris medius, close to the lateral lemniscus) produced marked restlessness but neither threatlike nor attacklike behavior in the socially isolated and restrained animal. When the animal was in company with the subordinate, the stimulation produced, with considerable regularity, both effective threat displays and actual attack. In contrast, when the animal was in the company of the dominant animal, stimulation did not produce a single threat display or attack. In another study, different groups of four were composed to effect variations in an animal's rank: The animal to be stimulated was placed: (a) in the omega position, (b) in the number 3 position, and (c) in the number 2 position. It was found that the same stimulation produced negligible reactions when the animal was lowest in rank, that it produced increasing aggressiveness with improved ranking, and that the aggressiveness was consistently directed toward animals of lower rank. Additionally, it was observed that as the animal became more aggressive as a consequence of its improvement in rank, it was aggressed against less frequently by the other animals of the group.

These findings have made it very clear (a) that "results obtained in isolated or restrained animals often do not apply to more normal, social situations" (Delgado, 1969, p. 118), and (b) that aggressive behavior in socially organized animals, particularly in the primates, crucially depends on prior experience. In this connection, Delgado's (1967a) demonstration that in rhesus monkeys, stimulation of specific areas failed to produce hostile and aggressive behavior between previously friendly animals, whereas it readily incited aggressive reactions in previously friendly cats is of interest. The aggression-modifying and aggression-controlling effect of social affiliations appears to be restricted to species in which social structures of greater complexity than the male–female unit are formed and exert a regulatory influence on behavioral interactions. Consequently, a great deal of caution is indicated in the generalization of observations on socially organized animals to relatively unorganized ones, and vice versa. In recognition of this problem, Delgado (1969) advised that "results obtained in lower species such as rats or cats should not be unduly generalized [p. 118]."

Research aimed at the determination of specific, central brain structures that elicit or inhibit aggressive reactions when excited has been pursued in brain-lesion studies and in electrical and chemical brain-stimulation studies. Moyer (1971) has provided a comprehensive review of this research, which is not detailed here. This work is excluded from the present discussion for two reasons. First, the research has concentrated on predatory attacks and thus is largely uninformative as far as conspecific aggression is concerned. Second and more importantly, the findings are not very instructive from the point of view of a general behavior analysis. For example, demonstrations that bilateral lesions in the amygdala eliminate intense aggressiveness in wildcats

(Schreiner & Kling, 1953), that in cats, highly aggressive behavior can be produced by lesioning the ventromedial hypothalamus (Wheatley, 1944), that stimulation of the posteroventral nucleus of the thalamus in alpha rhesus monkeys enhances aggressiveness, and that aggressiveness in these animals is inhibited by stimulation of the caudate nucleus (Delgado, 1967a) are certainly important in their own right. They are valuable contributions to the mapping of connections between the excitement of specific sites in the brain and modes of behavior in the various species. As indicated earlier, they also have major implications for the control of aggression by surgical intervention. However, they are not what some investigators suggest they are—namely, proof that aggression is innate and internally propelled. The fact that eating, drinking, mating, and fighting can equally be induced by the excitation of certain intact areas in the brain (provided a supportive environment) does not ensure that "the basic mechanisms are essentially the same" (Moyer, 1971, p. 12); nor does it warrant the conclusion that "there must also be internal impulses to aggression [p. 12]." The demonstration of specific, innate excitation-response connections merely shows that the organism is endowed with such connections. Considering aggressive behavior, it is conceivable that many species are equipped to react violently when a great many specific areas of the brain are excited. The real issue is whether or not these areas ever become excited under ordinary circumstances. Can environmental stimuli, as they interact with endogenous conditions, sufficiently excite the critical areas and thereby produce the aggressive response? This is the principal question from the point of view of a general behavior analysis, and it is usually not answered in brain-lesion and brain-stimulation research. As long as this issue is avoided (as it seems generally to be), the artificial isolation or excitation of particular brain structures only demonstrates behavioral potentialities for aggression (cf. Kuo, 1967) and says very little or nothing about the elicitation of aggression in typically prevailing environments.

Plotnik, Mir, and Delgado (1971) have recently taken a new approach in using brain-stimulation research to study conspecific aggression. This approach, which addresses the relationship between external and central or noncentral internal stimulation, holds great promise in elucidating the uncertain linkage between the internal and the external elicitation of aggressive behavior.

Plotnik et al. distinguish between *primary* and *secondary* aggression. The former involves aggressive reactions that can be elicited by brain stimulation through cerebral mechanisms that are independent of aversive sensations. The latter involves aggressive reactions elicited either by brain stimulation or by peripheral stimulation that *first produces noxious sensations,* which in turn produce the overt manifestations of the behavior in question. Secondary aggression is thus mediated through aversion, with primary elicitation centers presumably becoming excited in the second phase of a hypothetical two-step process. (It should be noted that the qualifier *secondary* relates to brain mechanisms only. It does not imply that secondary aggression, which we call aversion-induced aggression to avoid confusion, is of lesser import than some primary form.)

There is evidence that nonaversive brain stimulation can induce aggression (Robinson, 1968). In most investigations on conspecific fighting, however (e.g., Adams, 1968; Delgado, 1968; von Holst & von Saint Paul, 1960; Phillips, 1964), primary and secondary elements of aggression have been confounded. It is thus unclear whether or not aversion was a critical or contributing factor. The research by Plotnik et al. constitutes a first effort to partial out secondary or aversion-induced aggression and to explore it independently.

Plotnik et al. (1971) implanted a multitude of intracerebral electrodes in rhesus monkeys and then determined the reinforcement value for each stimulation point. The rewarding or punishing properties of the stimulation were assessed by observing the animal's operant behavior in obtaining or avoiding each stimulus. The animal's behavior in response to brain stimulation was compared to that performed in response to a known reward (food) and a known punishment (foot shock). The animal's general behavior served as a basis for evaluating the neutrality of stimulation. Aversion thus refers to the characteristic of a stimulus that the animals work to avoid. Since avoidance can be motivated by fear as well as by pain, this operationalization is one of *noxiousness* rather than one of pain specifically. Nonetheless, it was observed that the stimulation points showing aversive properties were located mainly in brain structures that are known to be involved in the central mediation of pain.

The main findings on aggression once more bear out the significance of prior experience within a social organization. Both aversive brain stimulation and skin shock induced aggressive behavior as a function of the social situation: They prompted attacks upon subordinate monkeys but failed to result in any kind of aggressive activity toward dominant partners. In the latter condition, the animal not only failed to attack but gave no indication of redirected aggressive activities or of submission; overt behavior showed no discernible effect of stimulation.

Further data concerning the effects of aversive, neutral, and positive (i.e., reinforcing) brain stimulation reveal that aversive stimulation generally disrupts prosocial activities such as grooming and that neutral and positive stimulation generally suppresses aggressive behavior elicited earlier. The finding that neutral stimulation leads to the discontinuation of fighting appears to implicate mere distraction as a force capable of intervening in ongoing aggressive activities.

Taken together, the findings reported by Plotnik, Mir, and Delgado (1971) leave no doubt about the power of *aversive* stimulation, as such, to promote and potentiate aggressiveness within the confines of established social structures. Although it seems possible to bypass aversion in eliciting social fighting through brain stimulation (cf. Robinson, 1968), the findings generally corroborate Scott's (1971) view of intense aversion as the principal source of conspecific fighting.

Generally speaking, conspecific fighting almost always takes place between two individual animals (cf. Scott, 1969a). Within groups of conspecifics, ganging up against a particular animal—in the sense of an organized attack— is extremely rare. Fighting between groups of conspecifics is not common but occurs occasionally.

Intergroup fighting might be expected in those species whose members live in socially organized groups that are not bound to specific territories. The primates are a case in point. It is quite common that the ranges of different bands of animals of the same species overlap, making the occasional confrontation of bands unavoidable. Strangely enough, these confrontations are usually resolved by threat displays alone (cf. Hall, 1968a). As Hall (1964) noted, the inferior group yields to a superior one (i.e., the larger group, or in the case of similar-sized groups, the one with the greater number of mature fighters) much as a subordinate animal yields to a dominant one. The animals behave *as if* they can compare the strength of their own group to that of the rivaling one and elect to withdraw if the outcome is not in their favor.

There is only one peculiar exception to the no-intergroup-aggression rule: Rivaling groups of rhesus monkeys have been observed to engage in injury-producing battles. Southwick, Beg, and Siddiqi (1965) studied the behavior of bands of this species in Northern India. They found that in temple areas in an urban environment, bands that usually avoided one another could find themselves—because of prevailing distractions or general inattentiveness— suddenly in confrontation. When this happened, fighting erupted. Characteristically, the adult males initiated the fighting, but females and juveniles became involved as well. The fights were ferocious and produced injuries— mainly in the male adults—on the face, shoulders, and rump. Fighting of this severity is possibly limited to the conditions of crowding (in urban environments) under which it has been observed. This limitation has, in fact, been suggested by Southwick et al., who noted that wounds due to group fighting were far less evident in rhesus monkeys living in rural habitats and forest areas.

Granting this exception, the evidence regarding conspecific group fighting makes it nonetheless very clear that: (a) it is not sought out (cf. Scott, 1969a); (b) it is actively avoided; and (c) threats generally suffice as a means of conflict resolution (i.e., to make one party yield).

Finally, with regard to the use of tools to assist conspecific fighting, the status of the evidence is clear: Instances of weapons use have not been reported (cf. Hall, 1968b). This applies to both individual and group fighting.

In the following, the most relevant characteristics of conspecific aggression that have emerged during this discussion are briefly summarized:

1. Social encounters that produce states of intense aversion constitute the primary source of social fighting. The infliction of pain is a particularly effective elicitor.

2. Intense aversion induces fighting. Responses are generally aimed at warding off the aversion suffered.

3. The removal of aversive stimulation terminates fighting. The infliction of pain or injury upon the opponent is not the ultimate goal response of social fighting.

4. Fighting is not sought out. There is no apparent appetitive phase in conspecific fighting.

5. Fighting as consummatory behavior is highly variable. Though clearly species specific in its motor manifestations, it generally does not conform to fixed action patterns, such as those observed in predatory attack.

6. Most confrontations and skirmishes are resolved with threat displays alone. Actual fighting is relatively rare. When it does materalize, it usually is terminated by the withdrawal of the inferior party before serious injury occurs. Injury resulting from conspecific fighting is comparatively rare.

7. The reinforcement value of social fighting is not uniform. It depends entirely on the outcome of the fighting. Victorious fighting, which apparently is rewarding, increases the readiness for fighting on future occasions. Fighting resulting in defeat, which apparently is punishing, reduces this readiness.

8. Fighting generally is stressful. With the possible exception of consistently victorious fighting, it constitutes an aversion. Repeated defeats have profound adverse effects upon the organism.

9. In socially organized species, social fighting results in the formation of hierarchies within groups. Social rank, once determined, is relatively stable and prevents fighting in future conflict situations.

10. In such species, rivaling groups generally resolve conflicts by displays of threats. Actual fighting is quite rare.

11. In conspecific fighting, aggression-assisting tools are not used by any nonhuman species, including all subhuman primates.

C. Nonpredatory Interspecific Fighting

The analysis of nonpredatory interspecific fighting reveals two distinct instigatory conditions: (a) social conflict ensuing in the interspecific competition for vital commodities and conditions, and (b) defense against predatory attack. However, it appears that although these aggressive behaviors vastly differ in terms of their specific antecedents, their overt manifestations, and their particular consequences, they largely derive from the same motivational source: aversive stimulation.

1. Interspecific Rivalry. Interspecific fighting for the procurement of food and shelter closely parallels conspecific fighting that serves these objectives. Quite commonly, an animal or a group of animals competes with an animal or a group of animals of another species, with the interspecific rivalry being just as intense as that of conspecifics. A redbellied woodpecker, for example, may have to defend a nest site against intruding redheaded woodpeckers as intensely as against intruding conspecifics. At a different level, a hyena may have to protect its food supply from many other scavengers.

When fighting occurs, it follows the pattern of conspecific skirmishes. Threat displays and defensive attacks are employed to ward off the intruder. When this is accomplished, the state of aversion is terminated, and fighting ceases; again, the ultimate goal response is not the infliction of pain or injury upon the rival. When efforts to ward off the intruder fail and this intruder obtains control of the object or condition in contention, the defender yields to the superior animal and withdraws. Presumably because of effective escape early in the skirmish, interspecific fighting of this sort, like conspecific fighting, very rarely leads to injury.

The rarity of injury in interspecific skirmishes has still another cause, however. Unlike conspecific encounters, the confrontation between members of different species is likely to bring together animals with vastly different fighting capabilities. Differences in sheer size and in the vigor of motor reactions generally induce the inferior animal to yield without fighting or even without being confronted with a threat display. Whereas downy woodpeckers, for example, engage in intense skirmishes over food among themselves, they timidly surrender the food to somewhat larger birds of different species. The phenomenon of interspecific fighting for food and shelter thus seems to be limited to confrontations between equipotent species. In fact, differences in the overall fighting capability of species have been observed to produce stable dominance–subordination relationships between species occupying the same habitat (cf. Cloudsley–Thompson, 1965). Leopards maintain dominance over cheetahs, for example, walruses over seals, and chimpanzees over baboons. The consideration of fighting strength as the principal criterion for dominance may prove somewhat misleading, however. Many skirmishes over food involve animals of vastly different strengths. For example, a lion usually has to defend its kill against a number of scavengers, all of which are of considerably lesser strength. These animals may engage in a continued struggle and not submit, even though the lion is clearly superior in strength. The failure of subordination seems to result from a balance in attack–escape efficiency. That is to say, a dominance–

subordination relationship may not materialize when the superior attack abilities of one party are matched by the superior escape abilities of the other.

With these differences between interspecific and conspecific fighting in mind, it is nonetheless clear that both kinds of fighting are equally motivated by aversive stimulation. There is no need, then, to propose a different underlying mechanism.

2. Defense Against Predators.   Predatory attack ultimately involves the infliction of pain, and pain has been discussed as a highly potent elicitor of fighting. There is no doubt about the aversive nature of the stimulation that the attacked animal seeks to terminate by escape or—if escape is prevented— by counterattack. Thus, defense against predators is also aversion motivated, and there is no reason to propose a distinct underlying mechanism.

There are, however, some forms of defensive fighting that seem unique to predatory defense. Disregarding species-specific motor reactions of animals in pain, these characteristic forms involve: (a) socially organized defense and attack, and (b) the use of tools. Both forms of fighting are restricted to socially organized species. The latter form is limited to primates.

It has been observed that many mammals living in social aggregates form defensive bands when confronted with predators (cf. Cloudsley-Thompson, 1965). Particularly when faced with an organized attack, the animals group in shoulder-to-shoulder position, taking full view of the attackers. This behavior partly depends on the size of the aggregate. For example, when attacked by wolves, American pronghorn antelopes stampede if there are only a few of them, but if they number a dozen or more, they assume the described organized defensive position. In this formation, they effectively resist attack and even manage to drive off the predators. The similar, well-known defensive behavior of the bison turned out to be highly maladaptive against hunters' rifles.

In the primates, the organized defensive fighting of baboons is noteworthy (cf. DeVore & Hall, 1965). Baboons range in the open, away from the protective cover of trees, and are thus highly vulnerable to attack by a variety of predators. They have developed a protective formation that proves very effective: The immature animals, the primary targets of predatory attack, cluster together with the females of the band and are surrounded by the adult males. The males fight off potential threats to the group. It has been observed (DeVore, 1972) that when threat displays fail, the males launch a joint, organized assault at top speed upon such predators as cheetahs. These attacks, which are usually effective in warding off the threat to the group, constitute the socially most organized aggressive behavior known in nonhuman primates.

Regarding the use of tools to assist fighting, there is some evidence that occasionally has been interpreted as indicating that primates make intelligent use of weapons—in the sense that tools are used in anticipation of increased fighting effectiveness (cf. Kortlandt & Kooij, 1963). However, the findings neither call for nor warrant such an interpretation.

In both monkeys and apes, numerous incidents of the following sort have been described: As an intruder—a potential predator—approaches a group of animals, the animals become increasingly agitated, engage in threat displays, break off branches or turn rocks over, and drop branches on the intruder or roll rocks downhill toward it. The dropping of branches has been observed in orangutans (Schaller, 1961; Wallace, 1902), howlers (Carpenter, 1934), red spider monkeys (Carpenter, 1935), patas (Boulenger, 1937), gibbons (Carpenter, 1940), cebus (Kaufmann, 1962), and gorillas (Merfield & Miller, 1956; Schaller, 1963). Orangutans and cebus also drop fruit from above, and howlers defecate and urinate upon intruders below. The seemingly deliberate rolling of stones down a slope toward intruders has been reported for baboons (Brehm, 1916; Hornaday, 1922) and macaques (Hingston, 1920; Joléaud, 1931). The common element in these observations is that *objects are put into motion in the general direction of an intruder.* The objects are not thrown, an act that requires far greater coordination of limb motion and release than has been observed in these species. Some reports indicate, however, that direction is imparted on the objects by a swinging motion of a limb prior to the release of the object. This possible guiding motion and also the possible delay of a barrage until an opportune time seem to indicate an anticipation of effects and, in this sense, the comprehension of the purpose of the action. However, it is this practice of aiming and timing that is very much in doubt.

In a careful analysis of tool use in antagonistic encounters, Hall (1968b) provided a parsimonious explanation for the discussed behavioral phenomenon. His account does not involve assumptions about a comprehension of means–ends relations. Hall posited: (a) that behaviors such as the breaking of branches are carry-overs from threat displays (e.g., tree shaking) and general agitation; and (b) that "the delay in dropping and the imparting of direction to the branches is 'purposive' or 'instrumental' in the elementary sense that the consequence of this variation is anticipated as being more rewarding than the consequence of no aiming [p. 135]." The latter amounts to the application of the operant-conditioning paradigm to aiming (and timing): The intruder's withdrawal—the presumed reinforcer—is occasioned by hits and near misses, which result from aimed drops rather than arbitrary ones, and this contingency should favor aiming over nonaiming. Aiming (and timing) are thus accounted for very simply.

Given this account, one wonders why "aiming" at intruders did not develop into full-fledged throwing at them—throwing, after all, being just a gradual extension of the aimed guiding and releasing of objects. According to the theory, the animals should readily have advanced to throwing as a highly reinforced type of fighting. The fact that throwing did not materialize in any nonhuman primate seems to indicate that the form of tool use discussed, mainly the dropping of branches, was an entirely ineffective means of fighting. Near misses and not-so-near misses seem to have been equally inadequate inducers of the intruder's withdrawal. Painful or injurious hits, if they ever occurred, must have been far too infrequent to effect learning. "Aiming" was thus *not* consistently reinforced. Hall's analysis, which attempts to account for the assumed aiming in releasing objects downward upon intruders, can thus be used to call into question the very assumption it seeks to explain.

Be this as it may, the use of tools in the defensive fighting of primates is very poorly developed. The dropping of branches and fruits and the rolling of rocks constitute restrictive, comparatively ineffective fighting maneuvers. They can hardly be considered to enhance the animal's natural potentiality for aggression. Hall (1968b) is quite correct in pointing out that "because the use of objects as missiles has tended to be confused with the use, and even fashioning, of objects as offensive weapons, the complexity of the behavior involved seems to have been greatly exaggerated [p. 138]."

III. HOSTILITY AND AGGRESSION IN MAN

In evolutionary speculations about the transition from ape to man, the use of tools—especially weapons for fighting—has always been assigned a crucial role (cf. Clark, 1955). To some extent, this emphasis may be the result of the fact that in contrast to transient events that were lost forever, weapons left their traces behind for the paleozoologist to discover. The discovery of crushed skulls and bones and the recovery of the weapons themselves left little doubt about the ability of prehominids and early hominids to use weapons effectively. Since, as we have seen, present-day monkeys and apes are extremely inefficient users of "weapons," the question of what might have made for the obvious change in the behavior of the prehominids has immensely intrigued anthropologists and interested laymen alike.

It seems that all conspicuous anatomical and ecological differences between apes and man have been explored in advancing hypotheses about the evident evolutionary transition. The numerous explanatory efforts have included brain expansion, bipedal locomotion, hand versatility, reduction of the temporal muscle, lack of natural weapons such as adequately sized canine teeth and claws, defense against predators, lack of safe shelter, competition for food, and a number of other factors, alone or in combination. Since we cannot consider them all here, we concentrate on those that are most consistent with the available data.

The popular notion that ill-equipped, early man was forced into social life, cooperation, and tool use by the urgent need to protect himself and especially his young from powerful predators such as lions, leopards, and cheetahs appears to be unfounded. Although the evidence is still somewhat tentative (cf. Leakey, 1967), it seems likely now that the prehominids and early hominids were never endangered by the large carnivores. With the exception of some baboons, which are customarily preyed upon by leopards, the primates are protected from attack by being unpalatable to the carnivores. Generally speaking, humans do not constitute "good food" for them. Man-eating animals are rare deviants. According to Leakey, only one out of 100,000 carnivores is a man-eater. Hall's (1964) suggestion that the social organization of baboons (as discussed earlier) most closely approximates the protective communities that must have been formed by early man thus appears questionable in light of the discrepancy between the prey status of baboons and man. Man seems not even to be palatable to scavengers such as hyenas. In the past, many African tribes put out the bodies of their dead to be eaten by these carrion feeders—seemingly proving that human flesh was acceptable to them. Leakey observed, however, that feeding on the dead bodies is delayed by 36 to 40 hours, a period sufficient for putridity to take effect and to change both odor and taste.

If it is true that the prehominids were protected against predation by their odor, there was indeed little need for them to form protective social groupings and to develop weapons. In evolutionary terms, this condition failed to give a selective advantage to the behaviors in question. It must thus be considered unlikely that coordinated fighting in which weapons were employed evolved in connection with defensive aggression.

Most comprehensive accounts agree in implicating the prehominids' competition for food and ultimately their development of carnivorous feeding habits with the emergence of tool use and weapon use specifically (cf. Dart, 1926, 1949b; Leakey, 1951, 1959). It is presumed that the scarcity of edible vegetation forced the prehominids into carnivorous habits. Grubs and beetles are likely to have formed the initial carnivorous diet. The prehominids then became scavengers. In the African savanna, they competed with hyenas, dogs, and vultures for carrion residues left behind by the large carnivores. Being relatively ill equipped to separate flesh from bones, they may have resorted to the use of sharp-edged stones or ready-made scrapers in the form of available jawbones. According to Leakey (e.g., 1967), it was the competition for carrions that inspired the first hurling and throwing of objects: The prehominids had to hold off the competing scavengers. Also, since single manlike animals could readily be driven away from these carrions by groups of hyenas or jackals, there was an apparent advantage to feeding in groups. The initial impetus for the use of tools and weapons may thus have come from the interspecific defense of food rather than from its procurement.

Dart (1925a, 1925b, 1948, 1949a, 1953) has stressed the anatomical differences between monkeys and apes on one hand and the prehominids on the other and has proposed an account of the achievement of hurling and throwing on the basis of certain unique physical characteristics of protoman. The study of *Australopithecus africanus* led Dart to conclude that protoman was essentially too clumsy for efficient defensive behavior. In particular, he suggested that the ability to leap sideways, thereby avoiding assaults without losing a position advantageous for counterattack, was limited in the prehominids. Prehominids were instead provided with *bipedal fixity*. In Dart's view, accuracy in hitting and hurling, which monkeys and apes lack but which man universally possesses, is due to the ability to stand firm and still on two legs and to use the added height resulting from erect posture to apply blows with fists clenching objects and to hurl projectiles. This ability in turn derives from the following anatomical features (Dart, 1953): "a short and enlarged pelvis, such as the *Australopithecinae* possessed, capable of rotating on two columnar limbs about powerful ankles, above feet that have planted heels and big toes capable of adhesion to the ground [p. 210]." Whereas the greater agility of monkeys and apes permits them to hurl themselves around trees and branches, protoman and early man came to hurl these objects around themselves. Thus, according to Dart, it was mainly an anatomical characteristic that eventuated in the use of weapons in the prehominids. Dart (1953) pointed out that the mental capacity required for hitting and hurling is minimal: human microcephalic idiots with mental capacities assumed to be below that of *Australopithecinae* can readily handle such tasks. He consequently suggested that brain development was a secondary factor—not the primary one. Brain expansion may have followed rather than preceded the use of weapons.

If there is indeed an anatomical difference between apes and man that favors aiming in the latter and tends to preclude it in the former, the earlier discussed application of the operant-learning paradigm (cf. Hall, 1968b) becomes revealing. Apparently for anatomical reasons, monkeys and apes never achieved aiming at a sufficient level of accuracy to place reinforcement upon superior performance. By contrast, the anatomically advantaged prehominids reached such a level. Superior hurling performances were consistently reinforced, so that the aiming and throwing of projectiles could evolve rapidly. The increasingly efficient use of natural weapons—such as the long limb-bones of antelopes as clubs, their horns as daggers, and stones as projectiles—can thus be explained by operant conditioning. This account, it should be noted, does not necessitate the assumption that the development of weapons was in any way dependent on or assisted by the explicit anticipation of ends. However, it does appear that the later invention of novel, artificial weapons such as bolas (i.e., stones connected by string) required a comprehension of purpose (cf. Leakey, 1951, 1959).

The study of *Homo habilis,* who used bolas among an arsenal of less sophisticated weapons, led Leakey (e.g., 1967) to conclude that early man was indeed a scavenger but that his weapon-based success in defensive aggression was soon followed by the offensive use of weapons. Apparently, the early hominids were highly effective, organized hunters. Their prey was no longer limited to small and relatively defenseless animals but now included species that were large in size and far superior in physical strength. Leakey (e.g., 1967) has provided evidence (i.e., skulls fractured by blows from blunt objects, marrow bones cracked by tools, etc.) that supports his suggestion that *Homo habilis* regularly attacked and killed now-extinct giant baboons. Since man had carried his aggression against other primates, armed aggression against his fellow man, in Leakey's view, was too similar not to emerge.

According to this proposal, then, armed interpersonal aggression with potentially severe destructive consequences is an outgrowth of predatory behavior. Paleontological investigations leave it entirely unclear, however, whether predation was a factor in interpersonal aggression. Unlike the situation concerning the large carnivores, human flesh is quite palatable to humans, and cannibalism was an extremely widespread phenomenon. It prevailed until recently in West and Central Africa, South America, China, Tibet, Australia, New Guinea, Melanesia (particularly Fiji), New Zealand, the Polynesian Islands, Sumatra and other East Indian Islands (cf. Dart, 1953). Intergroup aggression may thus have been facilitated by cannibalistic inclinations, but it appears reasonable to assume that it was not the only or even the primary cause of such aggression. Conceivably, as in other species, intergroup conflict had many sources related mainly to food and shelter— both largely coinciding with territory or range. Paleontological analyses leave it also unclear, for obvious reasons, whether social conflict within groups prompted the use of available weapons, thereby furthering the destructiveness of interpersonal aggression well beyond that found in other primates.

The evidence for interpersonal killing during the Pleistocene has been surveyed by Roper (1969). The remains of 169 individuals, all pre-*Homo sapiens,* were subjected to detailed analysis by specialists who evaluated apparent injuries. In 56 cases—that is, in 33% of the sample cases—apparent injuries (e.g., skull fractures likely to have been inflicted by a blow with a blunt object) were attributed to interpersonal aggression. This is a remarkably high ratio, indeed. For the *Australopithecinae* included in the sample, this ratio was even higher: 20 out of 36; that is, 56%. These data, like most paleontological findings, are not entirely unequivocal, however. Injuries may have been the result of accidents, such as falling off a tree. On the other hand, the ratios may be conservative in that the bones fail to reveal many injuries that might have happened nonaccidentally. A spear through the heart would have gone undetected as would a drowning or a hanging. Be this as it may, the findings indicate at least that protoman and early man frequently died violent deaths and that many of these violent deaths probably did not come about accidentally.

The way in which the use of weapons may have influenced human evolution—that is, the selection of some hominids over others—no doubt makes for fascinating speculation. *Neanderthaloids,* for example, emerged and vanished. Did they fail to control armed intragroup fighting? Or did they weaken themselves in intergroup battles? Did they fail to achieve adequate social organization when fighting with contemporaneous *Homo sapiens?* Did their rivals develop superior fighting methods? Or were all these factors involved? We will probably never know for certain. But given the records of weapon-inflicted injuries in prehominids and early hominids, the view of early man as the basically peaceful "noble savage" who used his weapons only in a rational manner seems untenable. More likely than not, some varieties of humans became extinct by the actions of other varieties and to some extent by their own doing. As Bigelow (1969, 1972) has stressed, inefficient interspecific aggression *and* inadequate control of intragroup and intergroup aggression are negatively selective. Conceivably, those early hominids who vanished did so not only because they failed to organize themselves for combat as well as their opponents but also because they could not control intragroup and intergroup aggression, which had become devastating through the use of arms. *Homo sapiens,* who—in a not-so-noble manner—may have greatly expedited the extinction of other hominids, may have been distinguished not so much by superior skills of aggression but, as Bigelow has suggested, by the intelligent control of intragroup and intergroup fighting.

The intelligent control of nonadaptive aggression and the intelligent cooperation in adaptive aggression—the latter involving both offensive fighting in predation and defensive fighting against dangers—have probably evolved along with increasingly efficient *coding systems.* Paleontological analysis of course fails us here, since the emergence of signaling behavior of greater complexity than that of the primates left no lasting traces. We can only guess that this development coincided with the enormous expansion of the brain during the Pleistocene. But independent of when it happened, it is clear that it happened and that it profoundly affected both aggression and the control of aggression.

The ascendance of both imperative and descriptive modes of communication must have enormously enhanced the coordination of group attack and group defense, and the efficiency of such fighting must have improved immensely as a direct consequence. Superior communication skills in armed combat, then, must have been the mark of troops best suited for survival under competitive circumstances. Alexander (1971) and Bigelow (1972) have applied evolutionary reasoning to intergroup conflict among early hominids and have suggested that superior communication skills—which resulted in superior coordination and, in turn, superior ability for intergroup combat (and also for control of intragroup aggression)—effected a selection toward larger and larger brains. Thus, brutal as it may appear, the extinction of human groups of inferior cognitive capacity by human groups of superior cognitive capacity may have greatly accelerated the evolution of today's man.

The advent of language must also have greatly facilitated the comprehension of means-ends relationships. The use of naturally provided weapons such as stones, sticks, and bones for throwing, clubbing, and stabbing can be adequately explained as accidental in origin, with operant conditioning shaping the final behavioral form. The manufacture of weapons, from bolas to bows and arrows, can hardly be similarly explained, however. The invention of tools to improve the efficiency of killing—tools that are artificial in the sense that the environment does not provide a model that can be copied—seems to require some form of comprehension of purpose. This comprehension of purpose, in turn, seems to have been possible only because of the availability of a coding system that permitted the arbitrary representation of events. Unlike his predecessors, man with linguistic competence was not tied to the events as they were physically manifest "then and there" but could "manipulate" events freely, probing for novel configurations of entities and circumstances. Most importantly, however, man could take note of *if-then relationships* with greater accuracy and reliability, and he could *anticipate outcomes* on the basis of his superior assessments.

The invention of weapons is, of course, just a case in point. Given the linguistically enhanced capacity for innovation, curious probing resulted in the development of tools in all domains of human activity. Equally, if not more importantly, it led to the great agricultural innovations: the planned production of crops and the domestication of animals for food and services. Finally, the newly gained communication competence was no doubt crucially involved in the ascent of communal living. Baboons have been observed to form colonies of up to 200 members (cf. Hall, 1964), and the prehominids may have lived in far smaller groups or similarly sized hordes. But with linguistic competence, man could and did form more and more complex societies.

In terms of conspecific aggression, innovative man brought upon himself an entire set of new conditions fostering the use of force. Whereas man's predecessors lived "from hand to mouth" with nothing worth retaining, the planned and organized manufacture of food and other vital commodities produced possessions of potential value to others. The ancient communities on the outskirts of the African savanna, presumably the first to enjoy the yield of cooperative agricultural efforts, proved vulnerable to organized attack. Intercommunal conflicts erupted, and armies of fighting men were mobilized to commit "agricultural theft"—the principal motive behind the early wars of mankind (cf. Bronowski, 1973). The fight over possessions is of course not restricted to the communal level. Within his own community, the individual presumably was in similar danger of assault because of his possessions. The ancient theft motif in aggression may have undergone changes regarding the target objects, but it obviously has not changed in principle. Theft—and defense against it—at the individual, family, communal, and societal level is the impetus for a good portion of interpersonal aggression.

Man's immediate predecessors have been characterized by Dart (1953) in colorful language as "confirmed killers: carnivorous creatures, that seized living quarries by violence, battered them to death, tore apart their broken bodies, dismembered them limb by limb, slaking their ravenous thirst with the hot blood of victims and greedily devouring livid writhing flesh [p. 209]." Such gruesome ancestry has, as one might expect, invited much speculation about residual savagery in modern man and the role of intelligence in controlling violence. One line of argumentation points to obtrusive incidents of recent violence—devastating war practices, bizarre atrocities, rioting and looting, and staggering crime rates—and leads to the conclusion that things have not changed very much. More specifically, it suggests that the ascendance of language-mediated intelligent behavior in man seems irrelevant to the development of violent behavior. The opposite line of reasoning takes a more statistical approach. It is suggested that in spite of the availability of enormously destructive weapons, recent wars have claimed fewer lives—relative to the size of the populations involved—than ever before, that humanitarian care for the wounded and otherwise victimized has greatly improved, that atrocities still occur but have become comparatively rare, that revolutions are less bloody, and that the crime figures appear moderate if one takes a closer look at earlier times. From this line of reasoning, it appears that intelligent behavior has led to a general decline of violence.

The look back into prehistoric times may be revealing in many ways, but it may be quite misleading when applied to the understanding of contemporary human aggression. Those who have derived human destiny, as far as aggression is concerned, from the carnivorous habits of the prehominids have committed a conceptual error in treating predatory aggression as aggression per se. Granted that our predecessors were savage hunters, it does not necessarily follow that they were similarly vicious in their interactions with conspecifics. But then again, they may have been savage with alien troops of conspecifics, yielding to predatory impulses in cannibalistic habits. The fact is that we know very little about their aggressive interactions with conspecifics. There is simply no data basis to remove the conceptual ambiguities, and this renders all related speculations idle.

The roundabout connection between predatory behavior in prehominids and aggression in modern man is similar to the projection of conspecific aggression in nonhuman primates, mammals, vertebrates, or animals in general onto human aggression, in that both fail to recognize the principal differences between animal and human aggressiveness. This is not to say that man differs from other animals in some unspecified, mystical fashion. Statements about the uniqueness of man have come to be suspect in the community of scholars. Too often in the past, man has been treated as unique without adequate justification. However, regarding aggression, man *is* unique, for reasons that have been indicated in this discussion and that are further developed here. To satisfy those who feel that unique characteristics should not be attributed to man per se, it is pointed out that the uniqueness to be discussed applies to all species that exhibit the characteristics in question: linguistic competence with its cognitive correlates and the presumably dependent innovativeness in producing vital commodities and conditions. Since only man is on record as having exhibited these characteristics, this concession obviously makes a moot point.

At the anthropological level, man's condition is unique in that he is confronted with seemingly ever-increasing temptations to take control of valued objects. Nonhuman primates have and the prehominids had, so to speak, comparatively little to fight about: limited supplies of food; access to water, shelter, and mates. The tendency for hoarding started to change this. The quasi-domesticated herds of the nomads amounted to food supplies of considerable magnitude. As one would suspect, such aggregations of vital resources prompted others to attempt theft by violent means and forced those controlling these resources to develop defensive measures. This situation is far more apparent in stationary agricultural communities. The systematic, largely cooperative manufacture of food tended to produce surpluses, at least temporarily, that spurred others to combat and the communities to fortify their dwellings. Maybe more significantly, man produced not only perishables but objects of considerable permanence—that is, objects that were of value for a relatively long period of time. To the extent that such objects involved laborious production or rare materials, they had to be retained. Man thus started to surround himself with objects of value—first weapons and essential tools, then drays, carts, carriages, boats, ships, furniture, clothes, embellishments, and finally, rare minerals and metals, which seemed to last forever. Nonperishable food, livestock, land, and artifacts—man accumulated it all. He took possession of these objects—by violent means, if necessary or opportune—and controlled whatever he obtained, again by violent means. Presumably in a direct expansion of the control of livestock, man came to possess, by violent means, even members of his own species. Through objectlike possession, he controlled the services of animals and his fellow man alike. The point here is that man, by aggregating "objects of value," created *a new dimension for violent conflict*. Unlike his predecessors, man competes not just for vital commodities and conditions but for less immediately essential and even trivial objects and services—potentially by violent means.

In conceptual terms, the impulse to control may be not so much a simple response to objects and services that avail themselves in the environment as a result of *unique cognitive capabilities in man*. It has been suggested earlier that man's linguistic competence may be mainly responsible for his apparent ability to *anticipate* outcomes. The declarative use of linguistic elements forced the formation of concepts. The explicit formation of concepts, in turn, facilitated discrimination skills and, more importantly, the comprehension of relationships between concepts. If–then and causal relations are cases in point. Linguistic man could *recognize* consistencies—not just respond to them mechanically as his predecessors did. The recognition of relationships enabled him to anticipate the consequences of events. He could anticipate how he would react to particular stimuli, how others would react, and how his behavior might affect others. Imperfect as his anticipations may have been, *he could consider alternatives concerning his own behavior and choose the one best suited to satisfy his needs without entailing undesirable repercussions.*

Linguistic man became an efficient optimizer. In contemplating action, he could maximize desirable ends while minimizing undesirable consequences. This cognitive skill has two significant implications for aggression.

First, the capability of anticipating one's own reaction to stimuli, potentially novel stimuli, results in the motivation to control these stimuli whenever there is the promise of gratification. Man not only suffers deprivation from circumstances that have proved rewarding in the past, but he may acutely suffer de facto deprivation from a multitude of objects and services he deems desirable but has never experienced directly. The control of these objects or services by others comprises a powerful source of social conflict. This potential for conflict is increased by the fact that gratifications accessible through the services of others may be thwarted by the failure of these others to cooperate. In short, unlike other species, man—seemingly unrestricted by his immediate environment—can "imagine" or "envision" a wealth of gratifications. In more technical terms, he is distinct in his ability to arbitrarily generate expectations concerning potential rewards. It is this ability to *anticipate gratifications* that traps him in uncounted temptations to get his way by whatever means avail themselves—violent means included.

Man is equally able, however, to *anticipate the aversive consequences* for himself of his own actions. He is thus not doomed to pursue the promise of gratification regardless of the circumstances. He is not caught up in *what could be* but can compromise with *what would be*. By relating expected gratification to likely aversions, man can estimate the net yield and act accordingly. In other words, man will come to pursue only those anticipated gratifications that outweigh the anticipated aversions to be encountered in their pursuit. Regarding the use of violent means, he can take into account the risk of injury to himself, the strenuous activity required, the likelihood of reprisals, and other aversive consequences and then employ such means only when the net yield is in his favor.

There is no assumption of built-in inhibitions against conspecific aggression in this construct. As a look at the violent past of mankind (cf. Freeman, 1964) readily attests, there is scant evidence for such inhibitions. In pursuit of incentives, man is at apparent ease in killing, mutilating, and torturing his fellow man—even today (cf. Washburn & Hamburg, 1968). If he restrains his violent behavior, it is presumably because violence fails to produce the net yield of anticipated gratifications or because there are more efficient ways of reaching the same ends. The phrase "man *resorts* to violence" is probably very misleading. More likely, man is violently inclined in getting things his way, and he resorts to nonviolent tactics whenever environmental conditions are such that violence is an inferior means.

In this context it has to be stressed that *incentive-motivated aggression is intelligent behavior*—generally speaking. In fact, it can be argued that *man's unique propensity for violence is the consequence of superior intelligence.* If the prolonged, monotonous, strenuous expenditure of energy—the standard condition of labor—is considered aversive, it is a highly *economical,* intelligent act, for example, when a horde of "savages" invests a day's work and robs an agricultural community of its crops and livestock. Irrespective of moral considerations, it is also intelligent to club a person to death and take his life's earnings, to force a person at gunpoint to render sexual services that cannot otherwise be obtained, or to cut the throat of a witness whose testimony could result in aversive treatment. As Buss (1971) puts it, "aggression pays"—as long as the aggressor gets away with it. In the psychological investigation of conditions that lead to aggression, much attention has been given to *what is done to the potential aggressor* (e.g., Dollard, Doob, Miller, Mowrer, & Sears, 1939), but the question of *what aggression does for him* has been largely neglected.

The fact that incentive-motivated aggression (like other incentive-motivated behaviors) is basically intelligent, rational behavior does not mean, of course, that all aggressive attempts of this kind must appear intelligent to the outside observer. The rationality involved is subjective. The aggressor's assessment of the gratifications and repercussions that will result from his or her contemplated action may well be imprecise or erroneous, and as a consequence, his or her aggressive efforts may fail to serve their objective. Surely, aggression does not always pay! It should be clear, however, that incentive-motivated aggression is generally undertaken because the aggressor expects to succeed. Cases in which the transgressor hopes to get caught and suicide missions are certainly exceptions to the rule.

It appears that incentive-motivated aggression is generally contemplated in the absence of acute annoyance and that these circumstances favor the rational construction of behavioral plans for execution at a later time (cf. Miller, Galanter, & Pribram, 1960). In contrast, annoyance-motivated aggression is quite commonly considered irrational. The noxious state suffered seems to interfere with rational, intelligent behavior, and a person is liable to commit him- or herself to action that he or she may regret as soon as he or she is relieved of the aversive stimulation. In the sense that the annoyed person is compelled to take action that may prove disadvantageous in the long run (i.e., it may induce the withdrawal of incentives, the thwarting of access to gratifications, and further increases in annoyance), annoyance-motivated aggression or hostility seems to be unintelligent behavior. If intelligence is taken to mean the conception of plans whose execution produces advantageous consequences, this assessment is correct. Characteristically, annoyance-motivated aggression is not thoroughly premeditated; nor is it aimed at improved later conditions. It is instead an *emergency reaction* that has the immediate objective of *terminating an aversion by fight* (Cannon, 1929). Such behavior may be unintelligent but has obvious utility. It may not pay, but it relieves the suffering at least temporarily. For example, in view of the probable long-range consequences (a likely prison term), it may not be intelligent for a wife to shoot her husband when he tortures her with accusations of her sexual inadequacy, but the aggressive action at least puts an end to her acute misery.

The difference in contemplating acts of aggression to obtain incentives vs. to remove annoyances becomes less clear, however, when the *anticipation of annoyance* is considered. The individual who has been annoyed by particular circumstances in the past can prepare for future encounters with these circumstances. He or she can conceive of a plan of action in the absence of acute annoyance and then execute it when reexposed to the noxious treatment. As in the contemplation of incentive-motivated assaults, the individual can give consideration to probable consequences and in so doing, minimize undesirable repercussions. Under these circumstances, annoyance-motivated aggression and hostility would both have to be considered intelligent behaviors. This seems to hold true even in the extreme case of suicide. Persons take their lives because it seems "the only way out" of acute aversion; but more characteristically, suicide is contemplated and planned because intense aversions seem not to end and are anticipated to extend indefinitely into the future. Self-assertion comes to an end because it cannot be anticipated to be successful.

Man's conceptual skills are most apparent in his *capacity to delay* the execution of the aggressive and hostile activities he is disposed to perform. Unlike aggression in other species, human aggression is distinguished by the fact that the aggressor need not display his or her attack in response to stimuli in the immediate environment but is capable of *inhibiting the attack until more favorable conditions for the assault arise*. The same applies to human hostility. Once an aggressive or hostile disposition is formed, man can await the opportune moment at which his opponent displays a weakness and attack is relatively safe. Animals fight their own kind almost exclusively on an individual-vs.-individual, face-to-face basis (cf. Scott, 1969a). Man, on the other hand, has shown a preference for mobbing and ambush. Killing those who are outnumbered over a distance from a secure position, ideally with the proverbial "shot in the back," is uniquely human. Disregarding the moral properties of the action, it has one important characteristic: It is intelligent behavior.

The ability to maintain plans for attack independent of contemporaneous external stimulation is presumably due to a process of rehearsal in which the individual represents to him- or herself key stimuli associated with past events and, specifically, with his or her disposition to perform particular acts or to achieve certain ends. Whatever the specifics of such a rehearsal mechanism may be, the ability to rehearse past events has further important implications for aggression. Whereas animals react to aversive stimulation here and now (cf. Boelkins & Heiser, 1970), man can *acutely suffer an annoyance far beyond the time at which the aversive external stimulation is removed.* The individual can rehearse any mistreatment and by brooding over it, prolong and possibly intensify the noxious experience. However, man's conceptual skills may also help him to cope with annoyance. In animals, the accidental infliction of noxious stimuli is not distinguished from its intended infliction. Man can readily make allowances for accidents and thereby *reduce or eliminate reactions of annoyance.* The individual can consider the specific circumstances that accompany aggressive or hostile treatment by another person or group and infer mitigating circumstances or attribute the treatment to obvious or nonobvious ultimately benevolent motives. Whether correct or not, such considerations potentially provide a means of reducing the impact of mistreatments.

Another distinct characteristic of man is that he not only can anticipate what *could* be and what in all likelihood *will* be but he also can develop definite expectations as to *what should be.* He entertains notions of justice, primitive as they may be, and applies them to the social circumstances he encounters (cf. Heider, 1958). In aggression-theoretical terms, intuitive justice has a simple and revealing basis: In his competition for valued commodities and services, *man is generally unwilling to grant privileges that he is denied.* If others (i.e., the person's peer group, community, society at large) deny a person access to potential gratifications by setting up aversive contingencies, this person wants to see those contingencies applied to the behavior of these others as well. The person watches alertly to be sure that what others would do to him or her under certain circumstances is done to others under the same circumstances. If he or she suffers aversive treatments after some transgression of social percepts, others should suffer them too. The arbitrary, selective application of punishment—that is, of socially sanctioned aggression or hostility—disturbs the "intuitive sense of justice." It violates expectations of *what should happen* under the circumstances, and it proves irritating and disturbing to a point where it can readily promote hostility and aggression aimed at rectifying the situation.

At first glance, the moral principle involved, "he or she shall not enjoy what is denied to me," seems primitive in comparison to more idealistic formulations of ethical standards. At closer inspection, however, the principle is largely in accord with more positive-sounding proposals. Clearly, the principle promotes a uniform distribution of privileges—a condition that is in line with, for example, Bentham's (1789/1948) formula of "the greatest happiness of the greatest number" or Kant's (1785/1922) maxim that stipulates that one's own behavior be such that it can serve as a societal standard. There is one important difference, however. The formal construction of ethical principles characteristically seeks to establish a reasoning paradigm for "inner guidance": Because a certain state of affairs is good (by declaration) for some specified social aggregate, the individual should behave in a manner that serves this state or at least that does not interfere with it. The individual "derives" a behavioral imperative from the contemplation of desirable social functioning. Altruism—that is, the unselfish and self-negating benefaction of others—is readily implicated as the ultimate ethical reaction. By contrast, the justice principle of aggression and hostility appears not to require any explicit reasoning process. It can be viewed as the *de facto projection of the individual's experience with prevailing reinforcement contingencies onto his or her social environment.* This projection is effectuated by external events in which the individual is involved or that he or she witnesses rather than by conceptual processes. Existing social control is thus promoted, with the individual making him- or herself an agent of enforcement. In this enforcement, the individual is biased in a selfish way: He or she is annoyed and possibly impelled to action when the transgressions of others are not promptly punished but seems relatively undisturbed when their "good deeds" are not promptly rewarded. Generally speaking, it appears that man has little concern for the deserved benefaction of others. The individual seems very eager, however, to see deserved punishment applied. This bias points to the source of man's basic moral considerations: the social denial of arbitrary gratification. It is assumed that there is no desire to construct a better world or the best of all possible worlds but rather an urge to see to it that in the competition for limited valued commodities and services, no one is advantaged. The intuitive notion of justice is thus one of competition and rivalry. It is concerned with self-enhancement (more accurately, with the prevention of the undue enhancement of others), and unless altruism can serve this objective, altruistic behavior is alien to it.

Considerations of justice, it seems, not only can produce annoyance in case of failure to punish transgressions, but they may invoke a similar reaction in the case of benefaction that is perceived as unwarranted. Because of his conceptual skills, man is again unique in his ability to suffer the agony of discriminatory rewarding treatments. Hostility and aggression may be sparked when two parties receive incentives and one considers the benefaction too small in comparison to that of the other—whatever the absolute value of the benefits may be. For example, a boy may be abundantly rewarded with Christmas gifts but have a violent temper tantrum because he feels his brother got more; or a professor may exhibit considerable hostility because a colleague has—undeservedly in his view—received a somewhat greater salary increase. These situations are theoretically revealing, because they show that under certain social conditions, the receipt of gratifications may prove an aversive treatment.

The concept of retaliation directly derives from the discussed notion of justice. A misdeed is to be punished. A transgressor has to get his or her "just deserts." Any advantage that may have been obtained by the transgression has to be nullified. Any setback the transgressor has inflicted on others is to be compensated for by his or her being set back in turn. Only man can hold grudges and plan to get even. And only man is capable of rejoicing after having retaliated effectively for an earlier provocation, and only man is capable of applauding witnessed reprisals. By the same token, only man can suffer the persistent, nagging irritation of unavenged transgressions. Retaliation is contemplated, purposive behavior, and as such, it is uniquely human.

Finally, man's conceptual skills permit him to assess the relative magnitude of suffering and damage inflicted by hostile and aggressive actions. People have notions as to the severity of the consequences of such actions. To be beaten and stabbed to death, for example, is generally considered worse than to die of a "clean" shot in the chest. To suffer a broken arm or a gaping flesh wound is worse than to get a black eye. Internal bleeding is worse than the transitory pains resulting from a slap in the face. Having one's car stolen and wrecked is worse than just having the tires flattened. Being verbally demeaned is worse in front of friends than in front of strangers, and being insulted by one's children is worse in public than in the privacy of the home. Assessments regarding aggression effects seem relatively uncomplicated. The degree of behavioral impairment, the duration of this impairment, and the pain and discomfort associated with it appear to be the primary criteria. Assessments concerning the effects of hostility are more elaborate. The degree and duration of behavioral impairment are factors. For example, the discomfort caused by having to have punctured tires unmounted, fixed, and remounted exceeds that of having to clean soaped windows. However, consequences resulting from mental torment cannot be evaluated in this manner. Behavioral impairment may exist, but it cannot readily be assessed. It appears that the *amount of suffering* is inferred mainly on the basis of projection; that is, the individual judges the aversive reactions of others to particular stimuli in terms of his or her own past reactions to these or similar stimuli. If the individual has suffered from demeaning treatment by colleagues more than by family members, he or she will tend to believe that everybody does. The assessment of suffering may thus be highly subjective—a circumstance that does not detract from the fact that it is generally practiced.

It is noteworthy that the assessment of the amount of suffering caused, subjective and interpersonally variable though it may be, crosses the boundaries betwen aggression and hostility. A punch in the nose, for example, may be compared to socially debasing comments, and dependent on the specific circumstances, it may be considered to inflict suffering of smaller, similar, or greater magnitude. Conceptually, *the consequences of aggressive and hostile actions can be mapped onto a unitary dimension: degree of aversive stimulation.* Man seems to be able to conceive of the impact of actions in such terms. He entertains notions of the amount of aversive treatment a particular transgression calls for. He has ideas of the magnitude of punishment a transgressor "deserves." This *conception of magnitude* is potentially disturbing when punishment for transgression or retaliation for provocation falls short or is excessive. However, man's conceptual skills allow that punishment or retaliation need not take the behavioral form of the transgression or the provocation. The rule of "an eye for an eye" is not as "human" as it has been suggested. Because *aggressive and hostile means can be equivalent aversive treatments,* they are *interchangeable.* A murderer, for example, need not be killed but may be punished by being deprived of privileges and condemned to unpleasant labor. A child who has hit a peer need not be hit in return but may be punished by being excluded from activities he or she enjoys. Conversely, an insult may be avenged by a punch in the nose, and a child's purposeful destruction of objects may be "corrected" by a spanking. Hostile action can thus punish aggression, and aggressive action can punish hostility.

The principal antecedent and subsequent conditions that govern inter-individual aggression and hostility also control this behavior between groups. Groups fight to obtain incentives and to end and avert annoyance. Future fighting is—as in individuals—a function of past success. With increasing size and the concomitant increase in organizational complexity, this control functions less directly, however. Early hominids may have formed socially homogeneous parties comprised of members who were equally motivated to loot, rape, and kill or to defend against intruders who were so motivated. It is equally likely, however, that they formed social hierarchies like other primates, with alpha members forcing those of lower rank into line. At some point, the fight-or-flight decision came to be executed by dominant individuals or leaders, and the other members came to be coerced, if necessary, to cooperate in fighting ventures. The aggressiveness of a group thus became a function of the aggressiveness of its leadership rather than that of its membership.

Much intercommunal and intersocietal conflict in the past was the rather personal affair of sovereign leaders. Armies of fighting men were responsive to their leader's command, and war itself became a tool (cf. Scott, 1969a) of the leaders. Under these conditions, aggression was indeed not indicative of any aggressiveness prevailing in the social aggregates controlled by the sovereigns.

In modern times, the relationship between leaders and fighters has become blurred by the increasingly complex organization of decision-making institutions. Absolute sovereigns have become rare, and where they have remained in power, they seem to have become increasingly sensitive to the inclinations of their subjects. More importantly, however, in the complex societies of today, it has become unclear—at times at least—whose war it is that is being fought. It has been suggested that war between modern nations has nothing to do with the aggressiveness of individuals but rather reflects the aggressiveness of institutions (cf. Rapoport, 1966). This observation is certainly correct in that the decisions concerning war and its procedural aspects are not under the immediate control of the population involved. Wars are generally not decided on by referenda. Characteristically, the people involved delegate decisional powers to leaders who are organized in institutions. It is thus not incorrect to say that in modern society *the people fight wars through institutions.* However, the relative autonomy of decision making by the leaders who run these institutions may produce situations in which substantial numbers of the people dissent from official decisions. In such cases it may appear that *the institutions fight wars through the people.* Which of these extreme positions provides the more accurate description of a particular situation will depend on the extent to which the people control their institutions. If these institutions are responsive to the people's inclinations, war will reflect the aggressiveness of the people. By the same token, since war would be based on public consent, it would be difficult for the institutions to promote and pursue wars in the face of pronounced public dissent. On the other hand, if these institutions—once created by whatever means—are highly autonomous decision-making bodies, the people might well find themselves fighting the wars of institutions.

Consideration of aggression-related decisional processes in the relevant institutions of a complex society tends to give the impression of enormous diffusion. This impression may prove somewhat misleading, however. Institutions are generally hierarchically organized, with all essential decisions made by the person (or just a few persons, at most) at the top. The downward diffusion of directives, which may affect the entire system, does not change the fact that the actual decision making is concentrated. Societal advancement beyond the rule of sovereignty may thus be more ostensible than real.

Quite often, even in complex societies, one person may decide on war and peace. That individual's being advised in various ways does not detract from this fact; the sovereigns of earlier days also consulted with others. With the de facto concentration of decision-making powers in just a few hands, a nation's readiness to engage in war with another nation may still to a considerable degree be determined by the aggressiveness of its supreme leadership, and the complexity of governmental institutions may be less consequential than commonly thought. But be this as it may, it is clear that the phenomenon of planned, organized intersocietal warfare is unique to man (cf. Hall, 1964; Scott, 1969a).

By way of overview, this conceptual analysis of human aggression and hostility—based on general, well-established relationships and several eventualities yet to be addressed in terms of available data—shows man's position to be a unique one in the following principal ways:

1. By producing valued artifacts, man has created a new, highly salient sphere of social conflict.

2. Man has superior conceptual skills that enable him to anticipate the consequences of particular actions; he can anticipate both gratifications—immediate or delayed—and aversive consequences—again immediate or delayed.

3. Man's anticipatory skills enable him to choose between alternative means to attain goals; as a consequence, he will tend to take aggressive or hostile actions toward these goals only when they appear to him to constitute the superior means in terms of behavior economy.

4. Because of the latter condition, aggression and hostility—for the most part—are to be considered intelligent behaviors.

5. Because of rehearsal skills, man can suffer from acute annoyance after the removal of the treatment that initially induced this reaction; annoyance not only can be perpetuated and possibly intensified, but it can also be reinstated at later times in the absence of the initial external inducers.

6. Man can consider the particular circumstances of an aversive treatment and make allowances for intent and purpose, thereby controlling, to some extent at least, his annoyance reaction and its hostile and aggressive consequences.

7. Man entertains intuitive notions of justice that demand punishment (i.e., counteraggression or counterhostility) for the transgression of social precepts.

8. Man can conceive of aversions in terms of degrees.

9. Because of the latter, aggressive and hostile acts that produce equal amounts of aversion, although of different kinds, are potentially interchangeable.

10. With aggressive and hostile means being thus interchangeable, intuitive justice seems to demand that transgressions be punished by aversive stimulation that at least equals in magnitude that which was inflicted by the transgression.

All these principal characteristics of human aggression and hostility are intimately linked to man's communication efficiency. The superior conceptual capabilities of man—which with regard to aggression, give him a unique position among the earth's species—are founded on his language competence. This fact has been recognized and stressed by numerous investigators (e.g., Bandura, 1973a; Barnett, 1967; Washburn & Hamburg, 1968). In comparison with monkeys and apes (and presumably the prehominids), the human brain's association areas concerned with recall, anticipation, planning, and the inhibition of inappropriate reactions have tripled in size; whereas other structures, mainly those related to tooth fighting and bodily displays (not involving manual skills) of inferior communication efficiency, have diminished in volume (cf. Lancaster, 1968). These dramatic anatomical changes prompted Washburn and Hamburg (1968) to suggest that the human body can to some extent be considered "the product of language and of the complex social life that language made possible [p. 476]." But whatever effect the emergence of language may have had on physical structures, it evidently led to profound changes in the psychophysiological mechanisms of aggressive and hostile behaviors.

This brings us back to the question of the extent to which human aggression and hostility can be inferred from animal studies. Is there sufficient similarity in the psychophysiological constitution of organisms and consequently in the antecedents and consequences of aggression to warrant such inferences? Clearly not! Aggression in animals and humans is not homologous by anybody's standards. Cognitive processes in man, with their implications for aggression and hostility, have no parallel in other species. On the basis of the obvious discrepancies at this level, one might question the value of analogies as well (cf. Barnett, 1967). Since most, if not all, species inflict some degree of destruction upon their environment, favor their own kind over others, and behave in a self-asserting manner at the individual level, there *must* be some behavioral similarities. A multitude of analogies thus emerge by necessity. They can be freely and selectively sampled, it seems, to make any point one cares to make (cf. Hinde, 1967). However, as Scott (1969a) argued, similarities in overt behavioral manifestations do not imply in any compelling way that these manifestations derive from the same or similar underlying mechanisms; there need not be a common mechanism, and the mechanisms of overtly similar behaviors may differ vastly. Broad analogies may intrigue analysts and their audiences, but they prove nothing.

Analogies are no substitute for the comparative analysis of aggressive and hostile behavior in the various species. Only careful comparative analysis can determine what elements of behavior and its associated mechanisms are universal or widespread. Equally important, only this type of analysis can reveal principal differences in the behavior and its underlying mechanisms. All indications are that human aggression and hostility are unique. There is thus no shortcut to their *direct* investigation. Man may have "inherited the biological basis" for violence and hold it in common with many other species. But he also is endowed with the unique capability for intelligent behavior, and this capability applies to aggression and hostility as it does to various other forms of behavior. The analysis of aggression in animals fails to account for the potential effect of man's intelligent behavior on aggression and is consequently bound to mislead us whenever the superior human conceptual skills exert their influence—which is nearly always. The analogue of aggression in animals provides, at best, interesting working hypotheses (cf. Scott, 1969b). Regarding aggression and hostility, man is on his own course, and to understand his behavior, it will have to be man who is studied. After the extensive, detailed comparison of aggression in a great many species, Scott (1969a) similarly concluded: "If we are to understand human behavior from the biological viewpoint, we must study human beings as human beings and not try to derive all our information from distantly related animals [p. 129]."

4 Principal Theories of Aggression and Hostility

This chapter seeks to provide an overview of the theoretical approaches to aggression that have proved to be the most influential. Although the theories discussed may address aggression in both animals and humans, we concern ourselves primarily with *interpersonal* human aggression and hostility. In fact, we pursue this selectivity in interest throughout the remainder of the book.

The grouping of theoretical approaches into various categories (i.e., instinct, drive, learning, and social learning) uses the major emphasis of each theoretical notion as a sorting criterion. It is hoped that this categorization facilitates the overview. It should be kept in mind, however, that the various theories are not necessarily confined entirely to the features suggested by their category heading; nor are they fully independent of one another. Drive theories of aggression, for example, involve learning considerations, and the learning of aggression to some extent involves considerations of drive.

I. AGGRESSION AS INSTINCTIVE BEHAVIOR

Not long ago, it was quite common to see psychologists proclaim instincts as the basis of any and every characteristic behavior pattern. James (1844/1890), for example, talked about 32 different instinctive behavior tendencies. McDougall (1908), who spoke of about a dozen instincts, is probably best remembered for his proposal that more or less all social behavior is under instinctive control. In a review of the psychology literature of the first quarter of this century, Bernard (1924, 1926) detected 5,684 behavior patterns that were designated as instinctive. Not surprisingly, then, hostile and aggressive behaviors were subsumed under this heading. It soon became apparent, however, that labeling has nothing to do with explaining. The assumption of an instinct underlying particular behavioral phenomena does not help to predict whether or not the phenomena will manifest themselves under given circumstances, and in this sense, it fails to explain anything. With increasing demands on the predictive and explanatory power of theories, instinct psychology fell into disrepute as a psychology of imaginary forces (cf. Lashley, 1938).

There have been numerous suggestions, nonetheless, that assign a central role in life to a presumed aggressive instinct. Adler (1927a, 1927b), for example, proposed that all human behavior, in the final analysis, derives from one single instinct—the "will to power," which he later referred to as the "striving for superiority." Similarly, Ardrey (1966) posited that human behavior is spurred by one major force—in this case, a possession or property instinct—the so-called territorial imperative. Schultz–Hencke (1940, 1951) acknowledged these two instincts and added sexuality as a third, thus arriving at a three-instinct proposal of sex, power, and possession to accommodate all human behavior. These and similar suggestions seem to have had little influence on contemporary views of aggression in comparison with the instinct proposals made in connection with more orthodox psychoanalytic and ethological theory. Freudian thinking and the writings of Lorenz have proved immensely influential, particularly in view of their practical implications for psychotherapy and everyday life. We therefore focus on these two positions.

A. Aggression Instinct in Psychoanalysis

In developing psychoanalytic theory, Freud (e.g., 1905/1942, 1915a/1946, 1917/1940) initially sought to derive all manifestations of human behavior from one basic life instinct, designated as *Eros*. This life instinct was conceived of as a force referred to as *libido* that promoted the *integration of the organic*—its declared function being the enhancement, prolongation, and reproduction of life. In the context of this one-instinct approach, aggression was viewed as a reaction to the thwarting of the successful pursuit of libidinal inclinations. It was not considered an innate force, nor a vital force of great significance. As noted by several investigators (e.g., Jakobi, Selg, & Belschner, 1971), Freud exhibited very little interest in aggression as such in his earlier writings. It has been speculated that Freud's reluctance to acknowledge the importance of aggression until quite late resulted from the fact that it had been stressed by Adler, who had defected from the orthodox position of psychoanalysis (Storr, 1968). It has also been conjectured that Freud's later interest in aggression was stimulated by the events of World War

I (Buss, 1961) or by the need to accommodate theoretically such behaviors as sadism and, especially, masochistic and self-destructive tendencies (Marx & Hillix, 1963). Whatever the motive, Freud (e.g., 1915b/1946, 1920/1940, 1933/1950) revised his earlier position regarding instincts. He proposed a dual-instinct theory in which the life instinct was matched by a death instinct, designated as *Thanatos*. In direct opposition to the life instinct, this death instinct was conceived of as a force urging the *disintegration*, that is, the *destruction of the organic*. The function of the death instinct, Freud proclaimed, was to return the organic to its original inanimate form. The relationship between the life and the death instinct is thus one of polarity, and any destructive or nondestructive activity can be construed as the specific interaction of the antagonistic forces. Freud apparently hoped to explain human behavior more completely as the result of the interplay of these two presumed instinctive forces than as the product of the life instinct alone (cf. Jones, 1955).

The most remarkable aspect of Freud's death instinct is the fact that he considered it to be *directed against the self.* In contrast to the quite common view that man readily engages in destructive behaviors against rivals, Freud posited in no uncertain terms that the ultimate objective of the death instinct was the death of the self. However, since in comparison with outward-directed hostile and aggressive activities, explicit self-destructive behaviors are relatively rare occurrences, he drew upon such psychoanalytic mechanisms as displacement—which had been conceived of earlier, independent of aggression—to convert the potential attack on the self into an attack upon others. In Freud's view, then, the death instinct forces the individual to direct aggressive acts against the social and physical environment in order to save him- or herself from self-destruction. Outward-directed aggression, interpersonal aggression in particular, is thus a derivative of self-directed aggression and not a primary force.

As noted by Marx and Hillix (1963), Freud's self-centered death instinct constitutes the most controversial element of psychoanalytic theory. The concept has been accepted in full by only a few followers (e.g., Klein, 1950, 1957; Nunberg, 1955). Some followers have applied minor modifications (e.g., Waelder, 1956). Other psychoanalytically inclined investigators have accepted the notion of instinctive aggressiveness but have transformed Freud's concept of primary self-aggression into an aggressive instinct that is primarily directed outward (e.g., Beres, 1952; Hartmann, Kris, & Loewenstein, 1949; Loewenstein, 1940; Mitscherlich, 1963). Still others in the psychoanalytic movement have rejected the notion of instinctive aggression altogether, replacing it with the conception of aggression as primarily reactive behavior (e.g., Fenichel, 1945; Horney, 1939; Stone, 1971). For a more detailed discussion of the various psychoanalytic views, the reader is referred to Buss (1961).

The death instinct has been criticized mainly on intuitive grounds. Stone (1971), for example, noted that the concept entirely neglects the behavioral significance of flight, which is always an alternative in conspecific and interspecific aggression, and he considered this fact in itself an a priori difficulty in the concept of a destructive instinct. Similarly, one might detect conceptual problems with the displacement or sublimation of self-destructive tendencies. According to psychoanalytic theory (cf. Toman, 1954), these mechanisms are forced into operation by the blockage of basal inclinations; they are not spontaneously activated. With the death instinct, however, the basal urges of self-destruction are never blocked. The avenue to self-inflicted death is always open. Thus, the proposal that displacement and sublimation are constantly involved in warding off self-annihilation by redirecting the immanent destructive forces toward the outside world is less than compelling intuitively.

Such objections may raise doubts, but they are not crucial. Freud's concept of the death instinct evades decisive criticism because it is sufficiently vague (cf. Nagel, 1961). It involves nothing concrete that can be operationalized. This vagueness applies equally to the transformed death instinct—the aggressive instinct accompanying libidinal urges rather than opposing them (cf. Hartmann, Kris, & Loewenstein, 1949). In psychoanalytic theory, both the death instinct and the aggressive instinct have remained imaginary forces. As such, they are generally employed to "shed light" on behavior that has already manifested itself. Since the forces are hypothetical and *unmeasurable*, behavior cannot be predicted on the basis of specific variations in the instincts in question. Post facto accounts of behavior may sound plausible, but they should not be confused with explanation that is established mainly by the accuracy of the prediction of outcomes. In psychoanalytic terms, any aggressive act can be readily "accounted for" by mapping it onto the continuum of antagonistic libidinal and destructive energy (i.e., Freud's model) or that of jointly operating libidinal and destructive forces (i.e., the model of Hartmann et al.). Also, the distinction between primary inward-directed and primary outward-directed aggression is heuristically less relevant than it might appear. Since redirecting mechanisms are invoked in both cases, plausibility can be equally achieved by both reasoning procedures. Sadism, for example, "results" in Freud's model from redirected self-destructive energy that dominates libidinal impulses, and in the model of Hartmann et al., from dominant destructive urges. In the case of masochism, the former model posits self-destructive urges that dominate the libido, and the latter model, the redirection of originally outward-directed, dominant destructive energy. Additionally, the notion of simultaneous cathexis—that is, the simultaneous concentration of libidinal and destructive energy on a particular object—which has been entertained by Hartmann et al., seems to be reduced to an exercise in semantics. In terms of the death-instinct paradigm, any combination of sexual and aggressive behavior tendencies can readily be "explained" as a compound of life and death instinct in which either the life or the death component is dominant. Given these conceptual ambiguities, the two models are equally adequate or, more correctly, inadequate. With regard to the death instinct specifically, it becomes a matter of taste whether to endorse or to condemn it. Epistemically, the assumption of such an instinct is simply pointless. It fails to further our understanding of aggression.

The element of Freudian theory that has proved most influential concerns the *relief* from libidinal or destructive pressures by appropriate consummatory action. It deals with the purgation of violent urges, an effect that may be transitory or may endure over longer periods. This phenomenon is best known as *catharsis*.

Although in Freud's dual-instinct theory, the forces of life and death are antagonistic, both instincts are conceived of as mechanisms that serve the conservation of energy. Both instincts actuate behavior that, at the very least, *averts prolonged states of elevated energy mobilization.* More characteristically, however, they actuate behavior that *effects a reduction of such states.* In Freud's view, the reduction of tension associated with a state of need (Reduzierung der Bedürfnisspannung) is a primary function of an instinct. The behavior is actuated to reestablish the state (generally associated with minimal tension) that prevailed before the instinctive forces were potentiated and to remove the stimuli that impinged upon the instinctive propensity. It is thus consistent with the model to say that libidinal energy is absorbed, neutralized, or reduced by the performance of direct sexual behavior or sex-related activities in a broader sense. More importantly here, it is equally consistent with the model to speak of the absorption or *reduction of destructive energy by aggressive action.*

The concept of catharsis is not simply identical to that of tension reduction, however. Freud discussed catharsis in connection with the expression of emotion. This relates, in fact, back to the original meaning of the concept, which grew out of Greek dramatic theory. In relation to drama, particularly tragedy, catharsis referred to a feeling state caused by witnessing tragic events. "It meant the stillness at the center of one's being which comes after pity and fear have been burned out. The soul is purified and calmed, freed from the violent passions" (Schaar, 1961, p. 320). In the Freudian application of this notion, catharsis became the purging of hostile and aggressive inclinations brought about by the mere affective display—not the actual execution—of such inclinations (cf. Feshbach, 1970). Unlike in Greek dramatic theory—where the purgation of "violent passions" is viewed as resulting from *witnessing* emotional expression—in Freudian reasoning, purgation is expected to come from the *expression* of aggression-related emotions, primarily hostile feelings and anger. By means of the presumed purgation, that is, by a reduction of destructive energy, the mere expression of hostile and aggressive feelings is seen to prevent truly harmful and injurious behaviors—or at least to lower their strength and the likelihood of their occurrence. This points out what must be considered the principal element of the cathartic process: *Destructive behavior can be weakened or eliminated by some form of less destructive or nondestructive substitute action.*

Many investigators (e.g., Berkowitz, 1962; Buss, 1961) have taken Freud's treatment of instinctive and cathartic processes to mean that Freud conceived of destructive energy as a finite, well-defined quantity, which fluctuates markedly with particular expenditures of energy. They attributed the so-called hydraulic energy model, in which forces are treated as analogous to liquids in a container, to psychoanalytic reasoning. In the hydraulic model, any increment in energy is associated with an increase in the amount of liquid held in the container, and any decrement is associated with a decrease. Liquid can be released through regular outlets. If it is not released, the reservoir may grow and build pressure to intolerable levels. By the same token, if liquid is drained through nonhabitual outlets, only the remaining reservoir can be discharged through the regular channels.

With regard to the cathartic process, this analogue suggests that if a nondestructive behavior absorbs destructive energy, less energy remains to motivate destructive behaviors. There is thus a purgation of hostile and aggressive forces. Obviously, the analogue also suggests that the motivation for hostile and aggressive activities is lowered by the performance of independent or related truly destructive behaviors.

Jakobi, Selg, and Belschner (1971) have taken issue with this interpretation of Freudian theory. They criticized Berkowitz (1962), in particular, for arguing that the notion of a reservoir of aggressive energy that can be drained and *abreacted* through aggressive action is an integral, essential part of the psychoanalytic theory of aggression. Jakobi et al. insist that in Freudian reasoning, there is "no direct connection between catharsis and aggression which would lead to the expectation that certain aggressive acts (e.g., socially sanctioned ones) could effect a reduction in others (e.g., socially disapproved ones) [p. 44; author's translation]." Indeed, Freud was rather inexplicit and roundabout in discussing the relationship between behaviors that could induce catharsis and behaviors that could be curbed by catharsis. Furthermore, the extent of cathartic tension reduction, in terms of both magnitude and duration, was left entirely unclear. Freud not only did not specify which particular emotional expressions satisfy the conditions of tension relief for which behaviors, but he also was highly ambiguous with regard to the degree and time course of the potential effects. According to Freud's writings, the expression of hostile feelings toward one's spouse, for example, should prove cathartic in lowering the likelihood of the actual infliction of harm. If the potential assaulter manages to "displace" his or her hostility onto another target—that is, subconsciously to confuse the real target with an alternative one—the expression of hostile feelings by, say, the proverbial smashing of china should also induce catharsis. In such cathartic behavior, the involvement of the skeletal musculature was considered to facilitate greatly the discharge of energy (e.g., Freud, 1915a/1946). However, there is apparently a limit to cathartic relief. Characteristically, emotion-laden hostile and aggressive exchanges are preceded by extensive engagements in expressive activities. The expression of hostile feelings, if it reduces the likelihood of actual hostility at all, obviously does not neutralize larger portions of destructive energy. How much and what kind of actual hostility can be curbed by hostile expressions remains unclear in Freudian writings. In some current psychoanalytically inspired therapeutic techniques (e.g., Bach & Goldberg, 1974; Lowen, 1967, 1970, 1971; Perls, 1969a, 1969b), however, the cathartic powers of hostile expression are treated as unquestionable and seemingly unlimited—in spite of decisively negative research evidence on this point (cf. Berkowitz, 1973a).

Returning to Freudian reasoning on catharsis, it is especially unclear over what period of time any eventual cathartic effect would extend. Is the reduction of tension a matter of seconds, minutes, hours, days, or months? How quickly is destructive energy regenerated? Does it happen in the next breath, or is the recovery as slow as that of a healing wound? The illustrations provided by Freud seem to warrant the inference that the effect of cathartic processes is extremely short-lived. The expression of hostile inclinations may prevent the further pursuit of these inclinations for now, but tomorrow they may become revived. This inference of the short-lived nature of the cathartic reduction of destructive energy would explain why Freud did not propose that the performance of particular hostile or aggressive acts now would reduce the motivation for related or unrelated hostile or aggressive activities to be performed at a later time—a fact noted by Jakobi et al. (1971). It also would explain Freud's general pessimism regarding the role of violence in human society (1920/1940, 1930/1948, 1933/1950). According to Freud, the never-ceasing self-destructive impulses of the death instinct have to be transformed continuously into outward-directed hostility and aggression to ward off the ever-impending discontinuation of life. Aggression is thus inevitable, and attempts to control and eliminate it can only be futile (cf. Bandura, 1973a). Man cannot escape his violent nature. If interpersonal aggression were, in fact, successfully curbed, the unchecked self-destructive inpulses would cause man's self-annihilation. In theory, then, the choice is between the destruction of man by homicide or by suicide. The supposal of a death instinct thus leads to a dim view, indeed, of man's prospects.

In summary:

1. Freud proclaimed a death instinct whose goal is to return the organic to its original inanimate form.
2. He proposed that the energy of this instinct has to be continually converted into outward-directed aggression to prevent the destruction of the self.
3. He entertained the notion of tension reduction in connection with destructive energy.
4. He conceived of catharsis as a process in which the affective, nondestructive display of hostile and aggressive inclinations can discharge destructive energy and thereby reduce the strength of these inclinations.
5. Finally, he presented the view that aggression is, in the final analysis, inevitable.

He did not, however, suggest that the individual is provided with a certain limited amount of destructive energy. Nor did he suggest that aggressive action, which he nonetheless considered to effect a discharge of destructive energy, appreciably reduces the presumed instinct reservoir of destructive energy for any length of time.

With regard to the catharsis notion, Freud seems to have been erroneously credited, for better or worse, with a paradigm of greater specificity than that which he proposed. His treatment of tension reduction has been "forced" into a model in which: (a) the amount of available destructive energy is finite, (b) the discharge of energy by aggressive action drains the reservoir to a point where other destructive behaviors are deprived of their motivational force, and (c) the reservoir is not immediately replenished after energy discharge. According to this model, aggression against a particular target should indeed result in reduced subsequent aggressiveness against *any other target*. This is not what Freud suggested. If he had entertained this view, he should have had great hopes for the control of violence by the harmless *abreaction* of destructive impulses toward specially selected targets. There would, in fact, have been little cause for painting the bleak picture of inevitable violence. As Jakobi et al. (1971) suggested, the more specific model of the cathartic process just outlined is not due to Freud but derives instead from the work of Dollard, Doob, Miller, Mowrer, and Sears (1939) on frustration and aggression. However, erroneous as the accreditation may be, the notion of catharsis as a mechanism by which aggression or pseudoaggression generally lowers subsequent aggressiveness has become integrally associated with psychoanalytic theory. The basic concept has been promoted with enormous success by Dollard et al., who were very much under the influence of Freudian thought. The instinct component was eventually replaced by *drive* forces. In this form, the catharsis concept is very much alive in contemporary psychology (cf. Feshbach, 1970). As we proceed, we will continue to encounter the more recent form of catharsis theory.

B. Aggression Instinct in Ethology

If Freud was vague and ambiguous regarding the specifics of instinctive energy, Lorenz was not. As discussed earlier in connection with phylogenetic speculation, Lorenz (e.g., 1942, 1963, 1964, 1965c) posited very explicitly that instinctive aggressive energy, if it is not regularly discharged through aggressive action, accumulates to a point where it will force out aggressive behavior in the absence of appropriate environmental stimuli. Aggression in a stimulus vacuum—which seems to be at the center of the controversy concerning Lorenz's proposals—is commonly related to the hydraulic energy model and interpreted as an overflow of the energy reservoir or the rupture and bursting of the container. In actuality, Lorenz (1950) detailed a hydraulic analogue of instinctive energy that is somewhat more elaborate.

In his energy model of instinctive actions, Lorenz conceived of energy as a liquid stored in a container. Energy is continuously provided through an input pipe. There is a constant flow of energy into the reservoir. The reservoir is drained through an output pipe. The outflow of energy is regulated by a valve that is controlled by a spring. This spring responds (a) to the pressure inside the reservoir and (b) to the pull of external stimulation. The latter is represented by an outside weight that exerts a pull on the valve. Energy exits through a horizontal spout. Dependent on the pressure inside the container, it may drop close to the container (at low pressure) or shoot farther away from it (at higher pressures). The energy passes through a scale grid and finally reaches a trough with a leaning, perforated bottom. The holes in the bottom correspond to instinctive actions. Holes in the lower area of the trough are associated with more basic instinctive actions than those in higher areas. The more characteristic forms of behavior are thus advantaged by the downward flow of energy in the trough. The more specific forms are elicited only at high energy levels.

Specific and complete as the analogue may appear, it leaves some questions unanswered. A principal ambiguity that cannot be resolved concerns the closing of the valve. When is the exit flow of energy shut off? After the entire reservoir is drained? Is a constant or pressure-dependent amount released? Or is there a point of standard pressure at which the valve closes? It seems that another basic ambiguity can be resolved, however. Lorenz failed to specify the way in which the valve operates. It could control the outflow of energy either in a gradual manner or in an all-or-nothing fashion. Since Lorenz considered the pressure of exiting energy to represent the pressure inside the container, gradual release is ruled out. The valve apparently is conceived of as operating in an open-or-closed manner, with a certain force being necessary to effect the change from closed to open. Since Lorenz stipulated that energy release is possible in a stimulus vacuum, the pressure inside the container can apparently reach the level of this needed force.

Applied to instinctive aggression, this model leads to the following propositions:

1. Aggressive energy is produced spontaneously and continually at a constant rate within the organism.

2. The evocation of aggressive behavior is a joint function of the amount of accumulated aggressive energy available and the strength of aggression-releasing stimuli impinging upon the organism.

Although it seems inconceivable that powerful aggression releasers could elicit aggression at zero levels of energy, it is conceivable that aggressive energy could accumulate to a point where it would trigger instinctive aggressive actions at zero levels of stimulation. Characteristically, however, the pressures of aggressive energy and the pull potential of releasers combine in the evocation of aggressive behaviors.

3. The specific manifestations of aggression and the intensity of evoked behaviors are largely a function of the amount of prevailing aggressive energy.

Small amounts of energy will elicit characteristic aggressive reactions. Large amounts will elicit both characteristic and more specific reactions.

In Lorenz's model, the evocation of aggression is apparently not entirely in accord with the standard releaser-reaction paradigm, which links specific stimuli with specific responses. The changing amount of available energy is seen to effect a corresponding change in the elicitation threshold for aggressive action: As the reservoir of instinctive aggressive energy increases, this threshold is lowered, and as it decreases, the threshold is raised. As a consequence, reactions are not stimulus specific. Independent of the specificity and potency of releasers, at low levels of available energy, only basal fixed-action patterns of aggression can be elicited. At high levels, in contrast, weak and usually inappropriate releasers will trigger, in addition to the more basal forms, highly specific and intense destructive behaviors. Lorenz (1950) described this relationship between stimulus and response as follows: "The longer the normal stimulation is withheld, the less necessary it becomes, in order to set off the reaction, to supply *all* of the stimuli pertaining to it [p. 247]." At extreme levels of accumulated energy, the elicitation threshold is said to reach a "theoretical zero point." The removal of the threshold then produces what is known as vacuum behavior or an explosion reaction, that is, aggression in the total absence of releasing stimuli.

As discussed earlier, Lorenz has been severely criticized for proposing that aggression is *spontaneous* in the sense that it may occur in a stimulus vacuum. This criticism, although valid, seems somewhat misdirected. The stimulus vacuum can be considered a contrived situation. Under prevalent environmental conditions, the organism is in all likelihood exposed to potential releasers frequently, and this prevents the presumed aggressive energy from ever damming up to "explosion levels." The more relevant condition thus is that in which energy accumulates to relatively high levels and then finds outlet through minimal stimulation. As the organism is deprived of opportunities to behave aggressively, minimal provocation, so to speak, becomes increasingly likely to trigger outbursts of considerable intensity. The *time of aggression deprivation*, a word combination that is very meaningful in Lorenz's model, can convert a weak releasing stimulus into a highly potent one. This is the crux of Lorenz's conception of aggressive instinct. Trivial releasers, too weak to incite aggressive action, grow into powerful ones that force violent eruptions. The reason for this change in releaser potency is obvious: It is the constant influx of energy into the reservoir. The spontaneity of aggression is a direct outgrowth of the more basic assumption that within the organism, aggressive energy is (a) *spontaneously produced at a constant rate* and (b) *capable of accumulating.* The nonviability of this assumption has been detailed earlier.

Lorenz's energy model of instinctive aggression is unambiguous in projecting that aggression is inevitable, yet modifiable. With regard to the inevitability of aggression, Lorenz's view parallels that of Freud. With regard to its modifiability, the views differ. A principal implication of Lorenz's model is that if energy is continuously prevented from accumulating to higher levels, dangerous violent outbursts cannot occur, since they require larger amounts of energy. Gross destruction, it appears, can thus be curbed by frequent participation in minor hostile and aggressive activities (which, taken together, are nonetheless as energy absorbing as the grossly destructive behavior). In man, a violent outburst, dramatically speaking, can be averted by a thousand naughty actions. Seemingly in accord with this interpretation, Lorenz (1963) has expressed great hopes for the curtailment of violence in society by such activities as the active or passive participation in competitive sports events. These hopes may appear to be a straightforward implication of the energy model; in fact, they are not. As was the case in Freudian reasoning concerning the death instinct, the rate of replenishment of drained energy is left entirely unclear in Lorenz's model. It can only be speculated that similarly to the operation of a toilet tank, the reservoir was thought to be rapidly drained and not so rapidly refilled. Only if it is assumed that the replenishment of energy is a time-consuming process does it become meaningful to expect benefits from the drainage of energy by minor aggressive actions. In Lorenz's model, the treatment of the period of time that follows energy discharge and during which aggressiveness, as a consequence, is potentially reduced is far too vague to permit anything more than superficial analogizing.

Finally, Lorenz's conception of instinctive aggression involves a principal behavioral characteristic that is not an element of the energy model and that, presumably because of this, is usually overlooked. Lorenz (e.g., 1950) was most insistent that aggressive behavior, conspecific and nonpredatory interspecific fighting included, has an appetitive component. In the context of the energy model, this proposal implies that the organism is provided with feedback of accumulating pressure. As the energy reaches a certain threshold, this feedback triggers search activities. It is said that the organism *seeks out* opportunities to engage in aggressive behavior and that it may invest considerable efforts in so doing.

The implications of this reasoning are twofold. First, it could be suggested that the posited search behavior has adaptive value because—within Lorenz's instinct theory—it shortcuts the energy accumulation. Locomotion generally increases the likelihood of encountering a releaser, and energy discharge thus occurs before the buildup of extreme levels. However, since vacuum behavior, like a safety valve, is there to prevent abnormal and intolerable levels, searching for aggression opportunities would seem to result in trivial gains only. The opposing argument, namely that the search, by increasing the frequency of encounters, places the individual at greater risk of injury and thereby ultimately endangers the species, appears more compelling. Second, the search proposal can be seen to supplement the notion of spontaneously accumulating, instinctive aggressive energy in that it once more stresses the inevitability of aggression. As in Freudian thought, there is absolutely no escaping violence. According to Lorenz, if aggression does not find us, we will find it—because of the way we are built.

Suffice it to say, at this point, that Lorenz's proposal of spontaneous and accumulating instinctive aggressive energy is without empirical foundation. (The reader is referred to the more detailed discussion under "Phylogenetic Speculation" in Chapter 3.) The biology of aggression instinct, as promoted by Lorenz and his immediate followers, has remained a dynamic of imaginary forces. This assessment applies equally to the psychology of instinctive aggression as presented in psychoanalytic theory—whether the presumed instinct is directed against the self or others.

II. DRIVE AND AGGRESSIVE BEHAVIOR

With the rather harsh attack upon instinct notions in American psychology (e.g., Lashley, 1938), it became increasingly difficult to carry such concepts into contemporary theories of aggression. Generally speaking, the concept of instinctive aggression in man has been abandoned in American psychology. Specifically, the notion of spontaneity in aggression, that is, the endogenous buildup of aggressive energy, has been dismissed. The energy concept, however, has been maintained. In fact, energy has remained an imaginary force in some theoretical notions. In others, the energy concept, which was eventually relabeled the drive concept, has undergone important theoretical transformations. These theoretical adjustments were accompanied and followed by increasing efforts to achieve workable operationalizations of the drive concept.

In this section, we briefly trace this transformation of aggressive drive from a purely hypothetical construct to a potentially measurable entity.

A. Frustration and Aggression

In 1939, Dollard, Doob, Miller, Mowrer, and Sears published a monograph on aggression in which they presented what has come to be known as the frustration–aggression hypothesis. This hypothesis proved to have an immense impact. It appears to have influenced current Western thinking on aggression more profoundly than any other single publication. For more than three decades, the frustration–aggression hypothesis has guided, in one way or another, the better part of the experimental research on human aggression (cf. Geen, 1972). Perhaps more importantly, however, the views of aggression that it involves seem to have become widely adopted and accepted; they have become commonplaces. This popular success may have various sources. First, the principal hypothesis is uncomplicated and easy to grasp. The theory is generally well structured and clearly articulated, a fact that again facilitates comprehension. Second, the theory does not involve overly abstract concepts or elaborate procedures. It is very close to common sense—seeming to be built on it. Finally, as Selg (1971) observed, the theory tends to provide a justification for behaving aggressively: "Being frustrated made me do it!" Like the aggression amnesty provided by instinct notions ("It can't be helped because we're built that way!"), although not as strong, this kind of justification can be drawn upon as a ready-made excuse for uncontrolled (or premeditated) hostile or aggressive actions.

As to the principal hypothesis, Dollard et al. (1939) posited "that the occurrence of aggressive behavior always presupposes the existence of frustration and, contrariwise, that the existence of frustration always leads to some form of aggression [p. 1]." Frustration, in this context, was specified as the thwarting of a goal response, and a goal response, in turn, was taken to mean the reinforcing final operation in an ongoing behavior sequence. At times, however, the term *frustration* is used to refer not only to the process of blocking a person's attainment of a reinforcer but also to the reaction to such blocking. Consequently, "being frustrated" means both that one's access to reinforcers is being thwarted by another party (or possibly by particular circumstances) and that one's reaction to this thwarting is one of annoyance.

It was soon recognized that the initial claims—(a) that aggression is *always* based on frustration and (b) that frustration *always* leads to aggression—were far too general. These claims made frustration both a necessary and a sufficient condition for aggression. Miller (1941) was quick to retract the latter part of the proposal. Quite obviously, frustrations do not cause hostile or aggressive outbursts by necessity. Potential outbursts may be effectively inhibited or may result in alternative actions, such as the pursuit of other, more readily available reinforcers. Miller therefore rephrased the second part of the hypothesis to read: "Frustration produces instigations to a number of different types of response, one of which is an instigation to some form of aggression [p. 338]."

According to this reformulation, frustration actuates motivational forces that are *diffuse* rather than specific to aggression. It is assigned the properties of a *general* drive. Such apparent moderation has not been applied to the first part of the original frustration–aggression hypothesis, however. Miller (1941) found the generality of this claim both defensible and useful.

The revised frustration–aggression hypothesis thus maintains the following: (a) *Frustration instigates behavior that may or may not be hostile or aggressive.* (b) *Any hostile or aggressive behavior that occurs is caused by frustration.* In other words, frustration is not a sufficient, but a necessary, condition for hostility and aggression.

It should be noted that the revised hypothesis retains a good deal of the original, sweeping claim. Because of its sweeping nature, the hypothesis proved most controversial (cf. Bandura & Walters, 1963a, 1963b; Buss, 1961). After considering the more specific elements of frustration–aggression theory, we briefly review the main arguments in this controversy.

In developing a comprehensive theory of aggression, Dollard et al. (1939) specified that the motivational strength toward aggression is a function of: (a) the reinforcement value of the frustrated goal response, (b) the degree of frustration of this goal response, and (c) the number of frustrated response sequences. The first two of these propositions are straightforward. Aggression-potentiating annoyance is seen to increase with the incentive that could be obtained or the aversion that could be terminated by the blocked goal reaction. Furthermore, frustration can be incomplete, and thus a goal reaction can be partially completed. The third proposition is less direct, however. It is meaningful only if it is assumed that frustration-induced annoyance is cumulative. It is apparently held that "aggressive drive" resulting from frustrations is somehow maintained within the organism and adds up to a level at which an otherwise tolerable frustration evokes aggression. Dollard et al. were, in fact, very explicit about the assumed additivity of aggressive forces. They posited that the strength of a hostile or aggressive reaction depends in part on the "amount of *residual instigation from previous or simultaneous frustrations* [p. 31; italics added]." "Minor frustrations," they suggested, "add together to produce an aggressive response of greater strength than would normally be expected from the frustrating situation that appears to be the immediate antecedent of the aggression [p. 31]." Dollard et al. acknowledged the significance of the temporal aspect of this summation of "aggressive drive" but quickly dismissed the issue by pointing out the lack of relevant data.

The theoretical treatment of the inhibition of aggression is related to the time issue, in that the lack of immediate, overt manifestations of aggression is assumed to lead to prolonged covert consequences that eventually "break out" in different form. Dollard et al. recognized that *not all* frustrations produce *overt* aggression, and to account for this fact, they posited inhibitory forces whose strength was said to vary positively with the severity of the punishment anticipated to result from the particular contemplated goal reaction. It was proposed that if punishment (a notion that was broadened to include such things as injury to a loved object and failure to achieve desired objectives) was anticipated to outweigh any incentives that could be gained, overt aggression would be inhibited. However, consistent with the original conviction that all frustrations produce some form of aggression, Dollard et al. insisted that it would be "clearly false [p. 32]" to view inhibited overt aggression as nonaggression. Being "furious inside," for example, is interpreted as nonovert aggression, which apparently can linger on and erupt in overt manifestations at a later time.

Put concisely, then, anticipated punishment, which is a primary source of frustration, effects the inhibition of overt aggression when it exceeds anticipated gratifications. The *inhibition is incomplete,* however, in the sense that: (a) it fails to control covert elements of aggression, and (b) it fails to terminate the instigation to aggression.

A significant element of frustration–aggression theory concerns the redirection or *displacement* of aggression. Dollard et al. were very explicit in their treatment of this phenomenon. They proposed that a particular frustration instigates aggression primarily against the source of the frustration but also instigates aggression against targets that are to some degree related to that source. The strength of the instigation was seen to vary as a function of associative ties between the actual source of frustration and the alternative target. The Freudian displacement mechanism was thus interpreted in terms of stimulus affinities. With the source of frustration constituting the primary target for aggression, closely associated targets evoke similar aggressive reactions; generally, the strength of the instigation to aggression diminishes as the similarity between the original and alternative target decreases. Dollard et al. further proposed that the more punishment is anticipated to follow contemplated acts of aggression against a particular target—that is, the more severe the inhibition placed upon such behavior—the more likely it becomes that the "inhibited" aggressive actions will be: (a) replaced by alternative, less punishment-burdened acts, and/or (b) displaced upon other targets. These propositions make it clear once again that in the framework of frustration–aggression theory, the inhibition of aggression is always incomplete. The frustrated individual who is forced to inhibit contemplated acts against particular targets (this inhibition in itself being considered frustrating and thus increasing the frustration suffered) is viewed as motivated to find other outlets for his or her aggressive inclinations. Only hostile or aggressive activities, transformed or displaced as they may be, are capable of reducing this instigation to aggression. Since the theory fails to stipulate other mechanisms for the reduction of such instigation, frustration must be viewed as a force that *"drives" the organism for an indefinite period of time,* ultimately until hostile and aggressive acts are performed.

This state of affairs is not entirely consistent with Miller's (1941) revision of the frustration–aggression hypothesis. The suggestion that frustration instigates nonaggressive as well as aggressive reactions seems to imply the possibility of instigation reduction by nonaggressive goal reactions. Miller actually addressed this issue, but he did so in conditional form. He cautiously argued that if a nonaggressive reaction *were* instigation reducing, then the instigation to aggression would also be reduced. Theoretically, this argument is of interest in that it implies that the instigating force resulting from frustration is not specific to aggression but has more general motivational properties. It is entirely noncommittal, however, and fails to rid frustration–aggression theory unambiguously of the stipulation that only hostile or aggressive acts can reduce the instigation to aggression.

Concerning the reduction of the instigation to aggression as such, Dollard et al. (1939) categorically declared that it is achieved, at least in part, with any and every act of aggression. These investigators further proposed an "equivalence of forms" of instigation-reducing means, positing "an inverse relationship between the occurrence of different forms of aggression [p. 51]." They qualified this postulated reciprocal relationship by suggesting that it applies especially to the dichotomies of overt vs. covert and self-directed vs. outward-directed aggression. In this context, the notion of *catharsis* is equated with the reduction of the instigation to aggression in general, irrespective of specific targets.

A violent assault upon a frustrator is thus seen as cathartic. More significantly, however, the expression of minor, less direct, and possibly covert acts of "aggression" are viewed as alternative, powerful means to bring about catharsis. The mere expression of annoyance, which does not harm anybody, is also considered an aggressive act capable of producing catharsis. Furthermore (and very significantly), since according to the theory, aggression can be displaced, attacks upon alternative targets are seen to reduce the instigation to aggression against the actual frustrator. Finally, aggression against the self, in overt or covert form, may prove cathartic as well. (In contrast to Freudian thought regarding the death instinct, Dollard et al. consider self-aggression a last resort, however. "Other conditions being constant, self-aggression should be a relatively nonpreferred type of expression which will not occur unless other forms of expression are even more strongly inhibited [p. 48]." This proposition leaves no doubt that aggression as a reaction to frustration is viewed as primarily self-assertive.)

In frustration–aggression theory, the treatment of catharsis principally parallels that of the instigation to aggression: Whereas instigation is conceived of as cumulative, with various independent frustrations heightening its level successively, catharsis is cumulative in the sense that independent cathartic incidents successively lower the level of instigation. "Drive" is built up by frustrations and "worn down" by catharsis. According to Dollard et al., this *frustration-induced drive is aggression specific without being specific to particular aggressive forms, and it is not specific to particular targets.* Miller's revision of frustration–aggression theory affects only the first part of this assessment: Frustration-induced drive is conceived of as a nonspecific motivating force. The two remaining, outstanding features of the theory have been retained. We refer to these two features as: (a) the *interchangeability of aggressive forms* and (b) the *interchangeability of targets.*

As noted by various investigators (e.g., Buss, 1961; Selg, 1971), the treatment of the temporal component of both instigation and catharsis in frustration–aggression theory is vague and ambiguous. How long can the instigational effect of frustrations ensue? How long does catharsis exert its instigation-reducing impact? The answers can only be inferred from illustrations provided by Dollard et al. (1939). According to these illustrations, both instigational and cathartic effects can be either transitory or long-term. Typical short-term effects are, for example, when a boy is denied the ice cream he has expected to get (frustration) and in his annoyance, he rips his sister's doll to pieces (catharsis); when a business executive misses his plane and angrily stamps his foot on the floor; or when a young scientist discovers that her funding has been discontinued and she throws a notebook across the laboratory. All these examples involve an emotional reaction from which a person seems to recover by employing expressive, hostile, or aggressive means. We later analyze such emotional processes in great detail. At this point, suffice it to say that the instigation to aggression—via frustration—and the diminution of the instigational experience—seemingly due to cathartic action—may coincide with the induction and dissipation of acute emotional states. This correspondence seems incidental, however, because according to frustration–aggression theory, the instigation to aggression often outlasts acute emotional states. For example, the student who fails to obtain admission to the college of his choice may not be just briefly annoyed. He may hold a grudge against "the system" for years to come. Consistent with Dollard et al., the many denials of gratifications suffered during childhood can accumulate to intense juvenile frustration, and the struggle of the working class can build up to levels at which it incites revolution. In disadvantaged minorities, the instigation to aggression grows with every frustration until it ultimately leads to violence. These are typically cited long-term effects.

The proposed additivity of instigational forces is meaningful only if it is assumed that individual frustrations have extremely long-lasting consequences. In terms of aggressive drive, this means that the drive state, once activated, remains active within the organism for an indefinite length of time. Under these circumstances, drive is a purely hypothetical construct without physical embodiment in the organism. The construct of instigation to aggression, which Dollard et al. preferred, is similarly without embodiment but can, as a motivational force, be approached empirically through self-reports. However, whether the concept of aggressive drive or aggressive instigation is employed, the long-term effects of frustration are without identifiable organismic changes; they are—if at all measurable—difficult to trace, and they have opened the door for considerable speculation. For example, Plack (1969) derives virtually all the evils of society, especially violence, from the abundance of denials in childhood and early adolescence. Since a good portion of these denials are likely to be employed even in societies far more permissive than ours (the point being that some will have to be employed), such interpretations, which are principally founded on the presumed accumulation of frustrations with long-term instigational effects, come very close to the projection of instinctive aggression. If aggressive drive is assumed to accumulate steadily with the unavoidable frustrations of everyday life, its consequences become indistinguishable from those of a spontaneous instinctive type of aggression. In this connection, it is of little moment that aggression is *reactive* in frustration–aggression theory.

All this is not to say that extended periods of deprivation from valued objects and experiences cannot promote hostility and aggression. Bandura and Walters (1959), for example, presented evidence showing that aggressive juveniles tended to have suffered a greater incidence of frustration during childhood than nonaggressive ones. At a more extreme level of aggression, Palmer (1960) has suggested that murder can result from frustrations inflicted by illness and accidents. Generally speaking, the belief that nagging frustrations, resulting mainly from the ever-present societally imposed pressures to inhibit relatively minor activities, can eventuate in violent crime in "overcontrolled" persons has grown popular among psychiatrists and lawyers (cf. Lunde, 1975; Megargee, 1966, 1971). The issue at hand, however, is whether or not observed violent transgressions occur *because of the accumulation of residual instigatory effects of frustrations.* The aggressive behavior of frustrated people is not by necessity the result of their frustrations, and the account of their actions on the basis of frustrations is usually open to alternative explanations. Violent youths, for example, may behave aggressively, not because of remote childhood frustrations, but because they have developed aggressive dispositions through the modeling of their typically more aggressive parents and because they have come to experience less intense guilt feelings regarding aggresssion (Bandura & Walters, 1959). Similarly, crippling illnesses or accidents may cause violent eruptions not so much because instigational forces are steadily built up but because the person so affected, as a result of the handicap, is denied gratifications he or she once obtained readily. The person may be largely deprived of his or her earlier means of nonaggressive appeal and resort to violence as the only effective means left to change the behavior of others as desired. Even in "overcontrollers," aggressive outbursts may come after the realization that nonaggressive ways have failed to achieve vital objectives. The roundabout hint at frustrations as the ultimate source of all violence, epitomized in Berkowitz's contention (1962) that "the person who kills generally does so because he has been frustrated [p. 318]," is far too simplistic to be acceptable as an explanatory account. Such a formula merely rephrases the necessity postulate of frustration–aggression theory (i.e., frustration is a necessary—though not a sufficient—condition for aggression), which not only fails to be enlightening but is also erroneous (cf. Buss, 1961, 1971).

The ambiguities concerning the time course of the instigation to aggression following a frustration have plagued frustration–aggression theory in that they have fostered far-reaching and farfetched interpretations and applications. Although the theory is equally vague about the time course of cathartic effects, this has not resulted in similarly broad or farfetched interpretations. Dollard et al. (1939) suggested that catharsis is generally of short duration, with likely frustrations soon again building up the instigation to aggression. This suggestion, it seems, has been universally accepted. According to common interpretations, catharsis at best brings aggressive drive to a zero level. It cannot accumulate a negative "counterforce" that could hold instigational forces below zero. However, consistent with the theory, repeated instances of catharsis should lead to successive decrements in the prevailing instigation to aggression. Catharsis should thus be as additive and cumulative in lowering instigational forces as frustration is in elevating them. Also, the mechanism assumed to govern the posited sustenance of instigational forces following frustration should equally affect their sustenance after catharsis. This is to say that if frustration effects are long-lasting, cathartic effects should be long-lasting as well. Interestingly, these implications of the theory have been largely neglected. In contrast to the specific recommendations that have been derived from Lorenz's instinct theory of aggression, in frustration–aggression theory proper, it has not been suggested that violence in society can be curbed effectively by a battery of minor catharses; and it has not been claimed that extreme acts of violence—for example, the murder of an annoyer—could induce supercatharses that would cause extended periods of nonhostile, nonaggressive behavior in individuals. Only the somewhat careless interpretation of frustration–aggression theory, it seems, has led to the occasional projection of such and similar cathartic effects.

1. Restrictions. Although the frustration–aggression hypothesis initially was widely accepted without much modification (e.g., Berkowitz, 1958; McNeil, 1959), there were early critics of the universal claims expressed in it. Both Maslow (1941) and Rosenzweig (1944), for example, suggested that frustrations instigate aggression only when they are associated with threat. More recently, Buss (1961) similarly insisted that the thwarting of a goal reaction in and of itself does not instigate aggression and that in order to evoke aggressive behavior, frustration must involve the element of attack. Buss also stressed the instrumental value of aggression in the overcoming of frustrations. The initial use of the concept of frustration was thus considered to confound thwarting and attack. Berkowitz (1958), for example, initially subsumed insult and attack under the general heading of frustration, arguing that the various interlocking components could not be separated operationally. Subsequent research showed, however, that the factors in question could be isolated both conceptually and operationally. This research has been competently reviewed by several investigators (e.g., Bandura, 1973a; Buss, 1961). We do not present a further exhaustive review but instead concentrate on a few selected studies that characterize the trend of relevant findings and exemplify the limitations of frustration–aggression theory.

Buss (1963) conducted an investigation in which three types of frustration were created: (a) task failure with no apparent repercussions, (b) task failure associated with the failure to obtain a monetary reward, and (c) task failure associated with both the denial of an incentive (i.e., improvement of course grade) and the infliction of punishment (i.e., reduction of grade). The subjects were to teach another person a concept through the appropriate use of punishment. When errors were made by the learner, who was actually an experimental accomplice, the subjects were to deliver electric shock to him. Frustration was produced by setting a standard of performance for the teacher and then having the learner perform so poorly that the standard would not be attainable. In a control condition, no such goal for performance was set.

The three types of frustration employed were considered to produce different levels of frustration, with (a) constituting the lowest level, (b) the intermediate level, and (c) the highest level. Frustration–aggression theory leads to the expectation that the levels of aggression should correspond to the levels of frustration. Such a correspondence was not found, however. In females, level of frustration had no reliable effect on aggressiveness. In males, frustration associated with the denial of an incentive led to significantly more aggression than did simple frustration, but frustration associated both with the denial of an incentive and with punishment failed to do so. The findings thus do not unequivocally support the notion that aggressiveness increases with level of frustration.

Further, it was found that compared to the no-frustration control condition, aggressiveness increased in all frustration conditions. The increase was observed in both males and females. This finding needs to be qualified, however. Given the experimental procedure described, aggression clearly had instrumental value: It was a means that ostensibly helped to attain the desired goal. The results therefore support the conclusion that frustrations promote aggression that has instrumental value. They leave unclear the effect frustrations would have if the possible aggressive reactions were without this instrumentality.

In a later study (Buss, 1966b), this effect of frustration on instrumental aggression was not replicated. The procedures employed were essentially the same as those used in the earlier investigation. In the frustration variation, the condition of monetary incentive was omitted, but other variations, which concern us later, were added.

Compared to the no-frustration control, frustration failed altogether to enhance aggressiveness. Whether frustration was produced by task failure without apparent repercussions or by task failure linked with the denial of an incentive and with punishment, and whether or not the instrumentality of aggression was stressed, aggressive behavior in the frustration conditions did not reliably differ from that in the control condition. Clearly, these findings lend no support whatsoever to frustration–aggression theory. Considering the results of the two discussed studies together, Buss (1966b) concluded that "frustration is at best a weak determiner of aggression [p. 161]."

More recently, Rule and Percival (1971) conducted a further study of the effect of frustration. These investigators, using a slightly modified version of the procedure devised by Buss (1963, 1966b), obtained findings that (as in Buss' first study) supported the notion that frustration promotes aggressive behavior—provided that the aggression is instrumental in overcoming the frustration.

An experiment by Haner and Brown (1955) is frequently cited as the first demonstration that frustration potentiates aggressive responses that are not instrumental in overcoming the frustration. Working with children, these investigators thwarted their subjects by preventing them from successfully completing a task. Specifically, the subjects' task was to place marbles into holes on a board until all the holes were filled. If they completed the task in an allotted period of time, they were to receive a reward. The experimenter signaled the end of the time period at different levels of closeness to completion (as defined by the number of holes still not filled) by sounding a loud buzzer. The subject was to terminate this buzzer by pushing a plunger. The pressure exerted on the plunger was taken to reflect the child's aggressiveness.

Haner and Brown observed that the closer the subject was to completion when the buzzer sounded, the more pressure was exerted on the plunger. This finding has been considered supportive of the claim of proportionality between degrees of frustration and levels of aggression, as advanced in frustration–aggression theory.

Such an interpretation is based on the assumption that plunger pressure is, indeed, indicative of aggressive behavior. In view of the fact that the procedure employed to measure aggressiveness neither involves the intent to harm or injure someone nor the intent to destroy something, however, this assumption appears highly questionable. The lack of an acceptable construct for the validity of this measure has been pointed out repeatedly (e.g., Buss, 1961; Geen, 1972). Conceivably, the children were more annoyed and in turn more sympathetically excited, the closer they were to completion when the buzzer sounded. The greater degree of excitation may have intensified the required motor reaction—without any destructive inclination being involved. It is even possible that the subjects were not aversively aroused but became increasingly excited with the anticipation of success on the trial.

The findings of a recent investigation by Kelly and Hake (1970) seem consistent with the view that frustration elevates sympathetic arousal and that this arousal in turn intensifies subsequent motor behavior, possibly effecting a selection of more vigorous responses. In this investigation, subjects concurrently performed several tasks: They pulled a knob, awaited visual signals, and inserted coins into a slot in order to obtain a monetary reward; additionally, they manipulated one of two devices in order to avoid or escape a tone. Avoidance of or escape from the tone was achieved either by pressing a button, an operation that required only minimal effort, or by punching a cushion, an operation that required considerable effort. Kelly and Hake observed that when subjects were provided with the rewards, they tended to press the button in order to avoid or escape the tone. However, when the rewards were discontinued, the rate of cushion punching increased in most subjects.

As in the experiment by Haner and Brown, the dependent response cannot be accepted as a measure of interpersonal aggression. At best, it can be considered an index of expressed annoyance. The investigation shows, however, that frustration brings about a preference for vigorous over less intense motor reactions, presumably because of elevated sympathetic excitation. To the extent that a subject experienced annoyance, these reactions may well have served to express his emotional state.

The point that frustration does not necessarily lead to aggression has been made in numerous investigations. In an early experiment, Davitz (1952) observed that the response to frustration varies greatly with the prior training and personality characteristics of the respondent. In an environment similar to that in which frustration was to occur later, children were either encouraged to interact aggressively in a competitive situation and were rewarded for doing so or they were treated in this manner for behaving constructively and cooperatively. After the training and an initial assessment of aggressiveness, all children were frustrated and then placed under observation to determine the effect of the training on aggressive behavior. It is important to note that in this procedure, aggressive reactions were without instrumental value in the overcoming of frustration. Specifically, after the children had seen one enjoyable film and were given candy bars, the viewing of a second film (five had been promised) was disrupted at a climactic point by the experimenter, who—without apparent reason—took away the children's candy and ushered them into a playroom. The experimenter told them that they could not have any more candy or see any more films but that they could play with anything in the room. A screen door between the playroom and the projection room was closed in such a way that the children could still see the projector running but were unable to see the movie screen. The frustration thus not only was without any justification, but it also was maintained in an acute form by reminding the children continuously of what they were missing. Under these circumstances of rather severe frustration, it was found that most of the aggressively trained subjects displayed increased aggressiveness (14 of 20), but some showed a substantial decline (5 of 20). More importantly, however, only a small fraction (6 of 20) of the constructively trained children showed increased aggressiveness; the larger fraction (11 of 20) exhibited pronounced decreases. The latter finding, in particular, is highly inconsistent with the original frustration–aggression hypothesis. It suggests that aggression is only one of potentially many coping reactions to frustration.

A recent, more complex study by Christy, Gelfand, and Hartmann (1971) makes essentially the same point. Boys either: (a) were exposed to an aggressive model, (b) were exposed to a nonaggressive but highly active model, or (c) engaged in social interaction. They then: (a) experienced failure in a competitive game, (b) experienced success in such a game, or (c) played noncompetitively. Free-play behavior was observed thereafter to obtain measures of both aggressiveness and nonaggressive vigorousness. Similar to the effect of the aggressiveness training in Davitz's investigation, exposure to an aggressive model resulted in a greater incidence of subsequent aggressive behavior than did either exposure to a nonaggressive but highly vigorous model or to social interaction. Counter to what would be predicted by the frustration–aggression hypothesis—that is, maximal aggressiveness following failure in the competitive game—aggressiveness was found to be most pronounced in the condition combining aggressive modeling and successful competition. Aggressiveness after both success and failure in competition was significantly higher than in the no-competition control condition, and the two competition conditions did not reliably differ from each other. However the strong effect in the condition combining aggressive modeling with successful competition may be explained, it is clear that frustration–aggression theory is at a loss to account for it. The fact that under conditions of nonaggressive modeling and no modeling, the frustration treatment failed to produce reliable effects further documents the weakness of frustration per se as an inducer of aggression.

The analysis of vigorousness in the study by Christy et al. is also revealing. The nonaggressive but highly active model proved to affect the vigor of the boys' behavior: Vigorousness in these active-model conditions exceeded that in the aggressive-model and social-interaction conditions. Furthermore, under conditions of active modeling, both success and failure in competition produced a significantly greater incidence of vigorous behavior than that which occurred in the remaining conditions, without any appreciable difference between success and failure. By contrast, under conditions of aggression modeling and prior social interaction, there were no reliable differences in vigorousness between the competition conditions and the no-competition condition or between the conditions of successful and unsuccessful competition.

This pattern of effects on vigorous behavior is of interest in that it mirrors the pattern of aggressive behavior. In both measures, the interactive consequences of modeling and successful or unsuccessful competitive activities are clearly in evidence. Presumably, the invigorating effect of competition facilitated modeled activities—those that were nonaggressive as well as those that were aggressive. The pattern of results clearly cannot be accounted for by frustration–aggression theory. Again, the findings urge the rejection of the view that frustration generally leads to aggression. In the Christy et al. (1971) experiment, aggressive reactions had no instrumental value in overcoming the frustration, and under these circumstances, frustration had no discernible effect on aggression. The study further shows that invigorating activities do not necessarily lead to a greater incidence of vigorous actions that could be construed as the expression of some emotional state.

These and many other experiments (cf. Bandura, 1969, 1973a, 1973b) suggest that aggression is just one of potentially many coping reactions to frustration. After an exhaustive review of the pertinent research literature, Bandura concluded (1969) that "when thwarted, some people become dependent and seek help and support, some display withdrawal and resignation, some experience psychosomatic dysfunctions, some seek refuge in drug-induced experiences and anaesthetic doses of alcohol, some respond aggressively, and most simply intensify constructive efforts to overcome the obstacles they face [p. 384]." The fact that some studies reported findings supportive of the frustration–aggression connection—that is, increased aggressiveness after frustration (e.g., Buss, 1963; Geen, 1968; Rule & Percival, 1971)—is probably due to the involvement of supplementary factors such as personal attack or the instrumental value of aggressive reactions. Perhaps equally important, the procedural restriction to aggressive reactions in these studies—that is, the elimination of potentially preferred alternative responses—may have led to the observed increments in aggressive reactivity.

There is considerable evidence supporting the view that frustration becomes a potent inducer of aggression when it is associated with personal attack. In a number of investigations, which are discussed in greater detail at a later point, it has been shown that frustration produces hostility or aggression more readily when it is perceived as arbitrary, unjustified, intentional, or unmitigated rather than accidental or warranted (e.g., Burnstein & Worchel, 1962; Cohen, 1955; Kregarman & Worchel, 1961; Mallick & McCandless, 1966; Pastore, 1952; Rothaus & Worchel, 1960; Zillmann, Bryant, Cantor, & Day, 1975; Zillmann & Cantor, 1976b). These investigations generally corroborate Buss' (1961, 1971) contention that personal attack rather than the blocking of a goal response per se is the principal aggression-potentiating element in frustration—when the popular, broad meaning of this concept is used. The investigations also point up the importance of cognitive considerations in the control of hostility and aggression. For example, Mallick and McCandless (1966) showed that retaliatory behavior is reduced when a reasonable explanation for the provoker's misbehavior is supplied subsequent to provocation, and Zillmann and Cantor (1976b) demonstrated that prior knowledge of mitigating circumstances associated with a provocation can prevent the development of anger, thereby holding down the level of retaliatory hostilities.

In summary, research on the frustration–aggression hypothesis leaves no doubt about the indefensibility of the original proposal that presented frustration as both a necessary and a sufficient condition for aggression. Miller's revision may have made the hypothesis defensible, but it also made it quite unworkable as a predictive notion. If, as Miller posited, frustration produces instigations to various different types of behavior—aggression being just one of many alternative routes of action—it becomes unclear when, if ever, frustration will lead to aggression. Since frustration–aggression theory has failed to detail the conditions under which frustration will evoke aggression and those under which it will not, Miller's revision deprives the theory of much of the predictive power it originally held. Also, the part of the hypothesis not altered by Miller, namely that the occurrence of aggression always presupposes prior frustration, appears to obscure the phenomenon of aggression rather than clarify it. This roundabout claim can only be considered to create semantic ambiguities that potentially hamper the development of refined conceptualizations and thus obstruct the empirical determination of specific factors that contribute to the evocation of hostility and aggression.

In light of the relevant research findings, the following restrictive propositions concerning the relationship between frustration and aggression seem to be in order:

1. The blockage of a goal reaction, in and of itself, may prompt the expression of an affective reaction such as disappointment, annoyance, or anger, but it generally will not induce interpersonal hostility or aggression.

2. The blockage of a goal reaction is likely to evoke behaviors through which the blockage can be terminated and the initial goal reaction executed. If aggressive responses hold promise for such an overcoming of the frustration, their execution becomes likely, particularly in the absence of undesirable repercussions. If aggressive responses have proved in the past to have instrumental value in the overcoming of frustrations, aggressive acts (like nonaggressive, instrumental actions) will acquire habit strength, and the probability of their execution in the face of frustration will increase. Thus, hostile and aggressive reactions in response to the blockage of a goal response are likely only if the specified instrumental value of such reactions exceeds that of nonhostile and nonaggressive alternatives or if this condition has prevailed in the past with some consistency.

3. When coupled with personal attack, goal thwarting is likely to evoke feelings of annoyance and anger, which in turn increase the likelihood of hostile and aggressive reactions. In this context, goal thwarting that the frustrated person perceives as intentional, arbitrary, and unjustified is conceived of as personal attack.

2. Extensions. The application of Miller's conflict model (1944) to aggressive behavior, specifically to the displacement of aggression onto substitute targets, proved to be a highly influential extension of frustration-aggression theory. Miller (1948, 1959) proposed that both the substitute target and the intensity of the attack directed against it could be predicted on the basis of three antecedent conditions: (a) the strength of the drive that motivates aggression against the original target, (b) the strength of inhibitory response tendencies, and (c) the degree of stimulus similarity between the original and substitute targets. More specifically, he posited the following relationships:

1. Aggressive responses to the original stimulus generalize to similar stimuli, with the amount of generalization becoming smaller for increasingly dissimilar stimuli.

2. Responses that conflict with aggressive reactions to the original stimulus also generalize to similar stimuli, becoming weaker for increasingly dissimilar stimuli.
3. The gradient of generalization of inhibitory, conflicting responses falls off more steeply with stimulus dissimilarity than does that of aggressive responses.
4. An increase in the drive associated with either gradient will raise the overall height of that gradient.
5. Given alternative response avenues, the responses that will be executed are those associated with the greatest net strength—net strength being defined as the response strength of aggression minus the response strength of incompatible inhibitory reactions.

The predictions deriving from this model become immediately apparent when one envisions various critical gradient constellations in graphs. In fact, Miller (1948) provided such graphs. In these graphs, potential targets are placed along the abscissa, and the strength of aggressive and competing responses is mapped on the ordinate. The original target is placed to the left, and on some hypothetical scale of stimulus similarity, substitute targets are placed to the right, with their degree of similarity to the original target declining successively. The gradient expressing the strength of aggressive responses, then, declines with increasing target dissimilarity. So does the gradient expressing the strength of conflicting responses, its decline being more pronounced, as stipulated in the model.

In this model, it is of course possible that the two gradients of interest do not intersect. The gradient of aggressive drive may lie entirely above that associated with the strength of competing responses, or alternatively, it may lie entirely below it. In the first case, competing response tendencies fail to effect the inhibition of aggression against any target, including the original one. The instigated attack should consequently be directed against the original target. In the second case, competing response tendencies totally dominate aggressive inclinations toward all possible targets. Inhibition is thus all-encompassing, and direct or displaced aggression should not occur at all. Clearly, these predictions are secondary as far as the model is concerned, since they do not involve displacement. The model's characteristic features emerge when intersecting gradients are considered. In this case, aggression is expected to be inhibited as long as the gradient associated with the strength of competing response tendencies lies above the drive gradient, and displacement becomes possible as soon as this situation reverses. Most importantly, in the region of displacement, the point of greatest vertical discrepancy between the two lines is the "point of strongest displacement." The target associated with this point (on the abscissa) constitutes the one against which displaced aggression will be directed, with the magnitude of aggression being determined by the discrepancy between the gradients.

In its simplest form, Miller's displacement model is expressed in intersecting linear gradients. For linear generalization gradients, the strongest displacement is defined as the point at which the gradient associated with the strength of competing responses touches the abscissa. At this point, aggressive drive is unimpaired by inhibitory forces, and the response strength of aggression is above that for all other target points associated with negligible inhibitory forces. Additionally, the net response strength of aggression—that is, the residual strength left after subtraction of the strength of competing responses—is above that of all target points associated with higher, yet impaired, aggressive drive. Miller stipulated, however, that the gradients could be nonlinear. More specifically, he suggested that they probably are negatively accelerated. Since the gradient associated with the strength of competing responses is expected to drop to negligible strength very rapidly and then to approach the zero level at an increasingly slow rate, the predictions are essentially the same. The point of strongest displacement remains associated with negligible inhibitory forces.

The unique prediction, then, of Miller's displacement model is that *when aggression against the instigator is inhibited, aggression will be directed against the target (out of potentially many available targets) for which*: (a) *the strength of competing nonaggressive responses is negligible and* (b) *the stimulus similarity with the instigating target is the greatest.* In this context, the inhibition of aggression is assumed to result from conflict, that is, from the dominant strength of aggression-opposing response tendencies. Miller distinguished this type of precondition for displacement from the prevention of aggression by the unavailability of the instigator as a target. He proposed that when the strength of aggressive responses against the original target dominates the strength of competing reactions and the original target is removed, aggression will generalize to the most similar target in line. This prediction follows directly from the stipulated relationship between the gradients involved: From the appropriate target to increasingly dissimilar substitute targets, the strength of aggressive drive can never be reached or even approached by that of the inhibitory forces.

With regard to interpersonal human aggression, the following principal propositions inherent in Miller's displacement model are significant:

1. The prevention or the inhibition of aggression against a particular instigator occasions aggression against other persons.

2. The unavailability of the aggression instigator as a target for attack leads to aggression against highly similar persons. Relative to the strength of the attack that was prevented, the strength of the attack upon the highly similar substitute person is only trivially reduced.

3. Given that aggression against the instigator is inhibited by conflicting response tendencies, aggression is displaced against persons of greater similarity to the instigator, the higher the aggressive drive and/or the lower the inhibitory forces. Conversely, aggression is displaced against persons of greater dissimilarity to the instigator, the lower the aggressive drive and/or the higher the inhibitory forces. Although the strength of the displaced attack is not a simple function of similarity between the instigator and the substitute, attacks upon persons who are highly dissimilar to the instigator tend to be of substantially lower intensity than the potential strength of the inhibited attack on the instigator.

These propositions have far-reaching implications. The first proposition restates the familiar notion that once aggressive drive has been aroused, the prevention or the inhibition of aggression will ultimately fail. Apparently, drive is viewed as sustaining itself until an opportunity for appropriate behavior arises with the occurrence of stimuli that exhibit some degree of similarity to the original target. Displaced aggression, then, is potentially evoked by "innocent bystanders" who happen to display certain physical characteristics of the aggression instigator and/or who happen to be in an environment that is similar to that in which the instigation occurred. Whereas the initial induction of drive can be considered reactive, the drive energizing the displaced attack cannot. This drive is maintained as an aggressive force that awaits release by appropriate stimuli.

The second proposition, which has been largely neglected, actually stipulates that the person who has meant to attack but who has somehow let the instigator get away will have to assault the next best target that comes along—granted that there is some degree of similarity. A person who is physically very similar to the instigator, coincidental as this similarity may be, should trigger intense aggression. A less similar person should still trigger an assault, but thanks to the decline of the drive gradient, this assault should be less intense.

The third proposition, which has been extensively discussed (cf. Bandura, 1973a), favors the similar over the dissimilar target with increasing drive— other things being equal. However, for high levels of inhibition, it entails a corollary of great significance: The stronger the inhibitory forces placed on aggression against the proper target, the farther out on the similarity continuum will be the target for displaced aggression. Strong inhibitions are thus expected to promote aggression against persons who exhibit little similarity with the aggression instigator.

The displacement model thus projects a rather gloomy view of efforts to control interpersonal aggression. It would appear that the control of aggression would best be served by letting the aggressively instigated person attack his or her tormentor. (Such an attack might at least be morally warranted.) Clearly, if this retaliatory attack does not occur, for whatever reason, aggression will victimize someone who is innocent. And since it seems inconceivable to control the instigated person's environment (to prevent him or her from being provided with substitute targets), it can only be hoped that target similarity will be minimal, so that drive generalization will be weak.

All these implications of Miller's model hinge on one crucial assumption: that inhibitory responses generalize less than aggressive ones. Miller derived this assumption from findings on conflict. Specifically, he drew upon the demonstration (Miller, 1944) that if a hungry animal is first trained to find food at the end of an alley and then given electric shock there, the tendency to avoid this location is weakened by distance more than the approach to food that it inhibits. The spatial gradient of avoidance is thus steeper than that of approach, and Miller felt that stimulus dissimilarity should function in a manner analogous to spatial separation. As far as interpersonal aggression is concerned, this suggestion is still entirely without empirical foundation, however. The lack of critical testing of this particular proposal is mainly due to what proved to be the major inadequacy of the displacement model: its vagueness with regard to the operationalization of stimulus similarity. In the transformation of the conflict model, the precision of the variable of spatial separation—that is, of physical distance—was lost, and the measurement of "stimulus similarity" posed seemingly insurmountable problems. The stimulus–response nomenclature leads one to expect a degree of precision in the similarity variation far beyond that which has been accomplished. Miller himself (e.g., 1948) invited unrestrained use of the similarity construct by espousing a form of semantic generalization (cf. Maltzman, 1968). He proposed (1948) that "if the individual learns to respond to two quite different situations with the same verbal response, the stimuli produced by this response will be a common element mediating an increased amount of generalization from one situation to the other [p. 174]." The process was referred to as the *acquired equivalence of cues* (Miller & Dollard, 1941), and it was considered to produce *secondary generalization* (cf. Hull, 1943). In other words, the generalization of aggressive responses, or of competing reactions for that matter, no longer was restricted to perceptual similarities based on the physical manifestations of original and substitute targets, but it could bridge vast perceptual discrepancies as long as there were some common verbal or nonverbal denoting or connoting qualifiers. To use one of Miller's (1948) illustrations, the mechanism of secondary generalization permits Mr. Johnson, when forced to inhibit aggression against Mr. Bartlett, to displace his attack on Mr. Bartlett's dog.

It should not be surprising, then, to find stimulus similarity experimentally manipulated along "semantic" dimensions rather than perceptual ones. In early investigations of the displacement mechanism, for example, Murray (1954) and Murray and Berkun (1955)—in assigning degrees of similarity between a client's mother and others—perceived greater similarity between the mother and an aunt than between the mother and people in general. Similarly, Ferson (1958) manipulated stimulus similarity along lines of academic rank: The inhibited hostility of students toward a professor was expected to generalize in decreasing degrees to a teaching assistant, an exam grader, and finally, fellow students. Such similarity assessments show that perceptual similarities between targets were, by and large, not considered crucial. Apparently, nobody felt it worthwhile to test whether or not inhibited aggression against a red-haired, freckle-faced person would be more readily displaced toward red-haired, freckle-faced people than toward other people. Although perceptually obtrusive racial characteristics were considered important in the so-called scapegoat theory of prejudice (cf. Berkowitz, 1962), similarity has generally been derived from conceptual criteria. Assessments have been made on intuitive grounds, leaving room for considerable interpretative variation. This interpretative tolerance has permitted very liberal applications of the displacement model as an explanatory mechanism. In fact, it has made for a model that was nearly infallible in making past events appear plausible. Given that everybody has to inhibit aggression once in a while, observed aggression can all too easily be accounted for with the post hoc placement of substitute targets on the similarity continuum. However, as Buss (1961) emphasized, such accounts are not to be confused with explanation. Explanation requires, of course, that the targets be placed on the abscissa of the displacement model and that predictions of yet unobserved aggressive reactions be based on their placement. Under these conditions, the model suffers greatly from the discussed ambiguities concerning the assessment of "stimulus similarity" (cf. Feshbach, 1970).

Since the earlier work relating to the displacement model has been extensively discussed by many investigators (e.g., Bandura & Walters, 1963b; Buss, 1961) and also since the evidence is generally considered equivocal at best (cf. Bandura, 1973a), we refrain from covering it here once more. Instead, we pursue some more recent work on displacement, and we do so in connection with modified versions of Miller's model. More specifically, since Miller's reasoning has been incorporated into much of Berkowitz's (e.g., 1962, 1965a) theorizing, we continue to discuss considerations of target similarity, together with pertinent research, in the context of revisions of frustration–aggression theory.

3. Revisions. There have been several attempts to modify frustration–aggression theory in order to accommodate some of the emerging findings. For example, Barker, Dembo, and Lewin (1941) proposed a frustration–*regression* hypothesis. These investigators had observed a tendency for frustrated children to display "primitive" behavior patterns. The children's behavior gave the impression of a regression back to an earlier developmental stage. The reformulation simply emphasized this apparent regression without, however, changing the frustration–aggression relationship specified in the original hypothesis. Similarly, the basic relation between frustration and aggression was not changed by Maier (1949), who proposed a frustration-*fixation* hypothesis. This hypothesis was developed to deal with the finding that frustrated rats develop a tendency to perform a noninstrumental response very persistently—such as turning to a particular side. Clearly, these are minor, negligible modifications.

An attempt to revise frustration–aggression theory in a more sweeping manner was made by Berkowitz (1962, 1965a, 1969a). Berkowitz (1965a) proposed: (a) that frustration induces an emotional reaction—anger—that "creates only a *readiness* for aggressive acts"; and (b) that "aggressive responses will not occur, even given this readiness, unless there are suitable cues, stimuli associated with the present or previous anger instigators. Objects having some connection with aggression generally may also have this cue property [p. 308]." Furthermore, Berkowitz sought to restrict the universal claim that all aggression presupposes frustration by suggesting that in the absence of frustration, exposure to suitable cues can lead to the formation and evocation of aggressive habits.

Except for the latter qualification, Berkowitz's revision to a large extent rephrases frustration–aggression theory as amended by Miller (1941, 1948). The earlier concepts of aggressive drive and response strength for aggression have been replaced by those of emotional anger and aggression readiness, and the stimulus dependence, which was stressed by Miller, is similarly emphasized. It is the involvement of the concept of *suitable cues* then, that constitutes a point of departure from the earlier model.

In Berkowitz's revision, this concept of "suitable cues" is central, yet highly ambiguous. The definition of these cues (i.e., stimuli associated with present or previous anger instigators or with aggression generally) says nothing about the minimal strength of "association" necessary to make a cue a suitable one. If matters are taken literally, all stimuli connected with the frustrating experience as such and with aggression in general become potent aggressive cues that are sufficient to evoke aggression in the frustrated individual. In every immediate social encounter that involves the frustration of one person by another, suitable cues are thus undoubtedly abundant. Such encounters, then, should *always* lead to aggressive exchanges—an implication that runs counter to the objective of the revision. Furthermore, if any aggression-linked stimulus, as proposed, indeed suffices as a cue in evoking aggressive reactions, one would assume that the frustrated person will be induced to aggress against some available person or object unless he or she is placed in a highly artificial, restrictive environment. This is to say that the standard human environment is so laden with cues that somehow relate to hostility and aggression that it becomes difficult to see how any frustrated person can avoid cues suitable for the evocation of aggression. Incidentally, this line of reasoning shows that Berkowitz's notion of suitable cues can readily accommodate the displacement of aggression. Where Miller's model required target similarity or cue equivalence, Berkowitz's notion calls for suitable cues—a seeming, rather than actual, difference from Miller's model because similarity or equivalence assures a degree of association between targets and, consequently, the suitability of cues.

Berkowitz's insistence on the involvement of suitable cues in the evocation of aggression is not to be confused with the notion of the availability of appropriate targets or the possible suggestive power of the availability of aggressive means. The revision does not so much suggest that a person who is motivated to aggress against his or her instigator will attack as soon as encountering both the target and the necessary means as it stresses that aggression can be "pulled out" of the generally motivated and possibly even unmotivated aggressor. The individual is thus partly driven (by a state of anger) and partly pulled (by the environment) into violent action. Berkowitz (1965a) stipulated that the strength of an attack made in response to suitable cues is a joint function of: (a) "the aggressive cue value of this stimulus—the strength of the association between the eliciting stimulus and the past or present determinants of aggression," and (b) "the degree of aggression readiness—anger intensity or strength of the aggressiveness habits [p. 308]."

Although Berkowitz (1969b) has been a vehement critic of Lorenz's instinct theory of aggression, the model just outlined obviously shares some principal features with it. Both approaches assign an elicitation power to certain stimuli. In Lorenz's model, the connection between releaser and aggressive response is characteristically assumed to be innate. In Berkowitz's model, this connection between suitable cues and aggressive response is generally assumed to be learned. The latter model thus seems to accommodate the human capacity for learning, which is largely ignored in the former. In spite of this difference, however, both models lead to the expectation that the organism is "forced into" aggression when certain key stimuli are encountered. This evocation of aggression by key stimuli is seen as relatively independent of the level of aggression instigation; in fact, according to Berkowitz (e.g., 1970, 1973b, 1974), it can occur in the absence of annoyance. The person is, so to speak, surprised by a salient suitable cue and, as in Lorenz's model, cannot help but launch an attack. In Berkowitz's terms, the attack is "pulled out of" the organism.

The pulling analogy would acceptably describe the process of the evocation of aggression if the aggressive reaction triggered were strictly interpreted as a conditioned response. Nearly any initially neutral stimulus can, no doubt, be made to trigger an aggressive response by the proper application of conditioning procedures. The analogy is not restricted to conditioning, however. Berkowitz suggested that the mere *association* of stimuli with aggression may provide suitable cues—that is, cues that pull aggression out of the organism. A knife or club, for example, can hardly be considered a stimulus to which specific aggressive reactions have been conditioned. Such potential weapons are nonetheless considered suitable cues for the evocation of aggression, especially in frustrated persons. The exact process assumed to mediate this proposed effect has not been made entirely clear. Presumably it works through the general associative linkage between the suitable cues and a person's actually established stimulus–response connections in the domain of aggression. It should be clear at this point that Berkowitz's reasoning on associative linkages is far broader than the related reasoning in frustration-aggression theory. It is, for example, not restricted—as it was in Miller's displacement model—to connections between the instigator and substitute targets.

According to Berkowitz's reasoning, weapons generally are highly suitable cues in the elicitation of aggression. In somewhat dramatic language, he suggested (1968): "Guns not only permit violence, they can stimulate it as well. The finger pulls the trigger, but the trigger may also be pulling the finger [p. 22]."

The frustrated person's exposure to such cues as weapons should thus constitute conditions for a direct test of the effect of aggressive cues. Berkowitz and LePage (1967) have, in fact, used this paradigm. In their investigation, subjects performed a task that was evaluated by another subject who actually was a confederate of the experimenter. The evaluation was carried out by the administration of electric shock to the subject: either only 1 shock—to indicate the confederate's satisfaction; or 7—to indicate his dissatisfaction with the performance. The number of shocks was of course independent of the subject's actual performance. The shock variation was employed to create a variation in anger levels. As required, the subjects who had received the larger number of shocks reported a greater degree of anger than those who had received just 1 shock. The angry or nonangry subjects then had to evaluate the confederate's performance on the task. The subjects were seated at the apparatus where they would deliver shock. At this point, the crucial variation in cues was introduced. In one condition, a shotgun and a revolver were placed near the apparatus. The subjects were told that these weapons belonged to the confederate and that they should disregard them. In another condition, the weapons were also present, but the subjects were told that they belonged to someone other than the confederate. In the control condition, the weapons were not present. Another control condition was added with angry subjects only: Badminton rackets were placed near the apparatus, and subjects were told that this equipment belonged to someone else. It was found that in nonangry subjects, the presence of weapons and their association with the aggression target had no discernible effect on aggressive behavior as measured in the number of electric shocks given to the confederate. In angry subjects, by contrast, the variation in cues resulted in differences in aggressiveness. Angry subjects behaved significantly more aggressively in the presence of weapons associated with the target than in the presence of the badminton rackets or in the absence of either set of gear. There was no appreciable difference in aggressiveness between the conditions of associated and unassociated weapons. Subjects in the condition in which the weapons were present but not associated with the target behaved significantly more aggressively than those in the condition in which the sports gear was present. However, subjects in the unassociated-weapons condition did not behave reliably more aggressively than those in the condition in which no gear was present.

It should be noted that these findings were not obtained as the result of mere incidental exposure to weapons. The weapons were singled out, and their belonging to a particular owner was mentioned. They were thus placed at the center of attention—at least for some time. This element of procedure has sparked considerable controversy and in fact has led to the faulting of the original findings.

In an attempt to extend the research concerning what has come to be known as the "weapons effect," Ellis, Weinir, and Miller (1971) failed to replicate the findings reported by Berkowitz and LePage. Ellis et al. experienced extreme difficulties in making subjects believe that the weapons belonged to the other subject, that is, the confederate. Subjects generally recognized the purpose of the weapons, even when somewhat more credible cover stories were used (e.g., they replaced the original cover story—that the other subject needed the weapons for an experiment he was conducting—with one that stated that the confederate was about to go hunting). Because of these difficulties, the condition of target-associated weapons was omitted from the experiment. The replication varied only the presence vs. the absence of target-unassociated weapons. The weapons—three pistols, a blackjack, and a knife—were placed conspicuously without any particular explanation being given. Ellis et al. employed three levels of anger instigation: no shock, 2 shocks, and 8 shocks. Consistent with the findings reported by Berkowitz and LePage, the presence of weapons had no discernible effect under conditions of mild irritation (2-shock treatment). However, in contrast to the original weapons study, there was also no discernible effect under conditions of more severe irritation (8-shock treatment). In the absence of irritation (no-shock treatment), the presence of weapons had a significant inhibitory rather than facilitatory effect on aggression. This latter finding, though not decisively opposing the cue model, is certainly not consistent with it.

In an effort to create a more credible cover story for the obtrusive presence of guns, Ellis et al. (1971) employed conditions in which the other subject was presented as a policeman who either had just taken off his weapons in order to be comfortable or who had come in uniform but without arms. Again unlike the original findings, the presence of weapons had no discernible effect.

Buss, Booker, and Buss (1972) also reported unsuccessful attempts to replicate the weapons effect. In order to improve on the credibility of the cover story concerning the presence of weapons, these investigators told the subjects that the weapons belonged to the other subject, who was going to lend them to a friend who was in another experiment. Regarding the cue variation, the replication involved only the presence of target-associated weapons vs. the absence of weapons. In all other respects, the design and procedures employed by Berkowitz and LePage were strictly followed. Under these conditions, Buss et al. obtained a significant main effect for the weapons variable and a negligible interaction between the presence vs. absence of weapons and the degree of anger instigation: The presence of weapons *reduced* rather than increased aggressive behavior, and it did so equally for instigated and noninstigated subjects.

Buss et al. speculated that in the face of destructive weapons, subjects might have considered the administration of shock of relatively high intensity as too painful and therefore inhibited their shocking. Since such concern was most likely to develop in the anger-instigation condition (7-shock treatment), these investigators decided on yet another replication: Subjects were again tested under the discussed conditions, this time with shock levels being reduced to "barely painful." Once more, the findings failed to confirm Berkowitz's weapons effect. The indices of aggressiveness, frequency of shock ostensibly delivered to the other subject, were virtually identical in the presence and absence of target-associated weapons.

Buss, Booker, and Buss also conducted several investigations in which guns not only were present but were actually used by the subject. The subject either did or did not participate in a target-shooting session before being provided with the opportunity to behave aggressively. The use of weapons must be considered to be laden with aggressive cues, and the aggression-evoking potential of these cues should be expected to carry over into immediately subsequent aggressive behaviors. The highly inconsistent and equivocal findings do not support such a view, however. In only one of four studies did the use of weapons facilitate subsequent aggressiveness. In the three others, it had no discernible effect.

Page and Scheidt (1971) approached the elusive weapons effect in terms of experimental artifact. These investigators argued that the subjects who were aggressively instigated, exposed to weapons, and then given an opportunity to aggress against their annoyer might have readily recognized the purpose of the placement of the weapons. Knowing what the experimenter hoped to prove, they might have played along and delivered more shock. This yielding by the cooperative subject is an experimental bias introduced by the so-called demand characteristics (cf. Orne, 1962; Rosenthal, 1966) of the procedure.

As Buss et al. (1972) had done, Page and Scheidt selected the conditions of target-associated weapons for replication. An initial study revealed no discernible effect of weapons at either low or high levels of instigation. In this study, the subjects were undergraduates who were taking their first course in general psychology. These subjects were comparatively naive with regard to the deceptions about the actual purpose of a study—deceptions that are characteristic of social psychological experiments. To obtain experienced, more "sophisticated" subjects, Page and Scheidt decided to sample subjects from a more advanced social psychology course for another replication attempt. This attempt involved the variation of the presence vs. absence of weapons at the higher level of aggressive instigation only. A significant inhibitory effect of the presence of weapons was observed under these conditions. Half the subjects in the weapons condition recognized the purpose of the weapons' presence. According to Page and Scheidt, many subjects were suspicious of deceptions and showed hostility toward the experimenter rather than the confederate. This, they feel, may account for the findings, in that the more sophisticated subjects were noncooperative, seeming eager to thwart the experimenter's efforts and to "louse up" the experiment. Since so many recognized the purpose of the presence of the weapons, another possibility is that some subjects decided to administer fewer shocks in order to be considered "a nice, nonaggressive person" by the experimenter. This behavioral tendency of individuals—that is, their striving toward the best possible impression they can make under the circumstances— is referred to as yielding to evaluation apprehension (cf. Rosenberg, 1965, 1969). Finally, Page and Scheidt separated experienced, sophisticated subjects from experimentally naive subjects and replicated once more what they considered to be the critical part of the weapons study: the presence vs. absence of target-associated weapons at the higher level of aggression instigation. In this replication, they observed a significant increase in aggressiveness due to exposure to weapons in the sophisticated subjects. In naive subjects, by contrast, exposure to weapons failed to have this effect, and in fact, a tendency toward the opposite effect was noted. This tendency proved not to be statistically reliable, however. The findings of this last replication are complicated by the fact that whereas in the presence of weapons, naive and sophisticated subjects exhibited aggressiveness at nearly identical levels, in the absence of weapons, sophisticated subjects displayed far less aggressiveness than naive ones. The latter seems to indicate that sophisticated subjects reduced the administration of shock because they experienced evaluation apprehension when they inferred the experimenter's interest in measuring retaliatory behavior. In the presence of weapons, this same apprehension presumably fostered cooperation with the largely recognized purpose of the weapons' presence. This interpretation is in apparent contrast to the hostile "screw you" attitude (Masling, 1966) that was invoked by Page and Scheidt to explain the opposite finding in an earlier replication attempt.

Given such inconsistencies, Page and Scheidt (1971) proposed "a complex interplay between sophistication, demand awareness, and evaluation apprehension [p. 304]" in the experimental investigation of aggressive behavior. Subjects may be cooperative, not because they are altruistically inclined, but because they yield to evaluation apprehension. The altruistically cooperative subject may indeed be a myth, as has been suggested (e.g., Berkowitz, 1971; Sigall, Aronson, & VanHoose, 1970). On the other hand, the subjects may be noncooperative and malicious. The weapons studies leave it rather unclear, however, why at times subjects are cooperative and why at other times they seek to thwart the experimenter's efforts.

Since the possibility of artifact in the discussed research on the weapons effect is symptomatic of research on interpersonal aggression in general, a comment on demands and apprehensions in aggression research seems to be in order. Critics of experimental work have come to use such concepts as demand characteristics and evaluation apprehension in a very roundabout fashion. The detection of any demand or apprehension is frequently taken as sufficient justification for branding the results of an investigation as artifactual. Such condemnation is not necessarily warranted, however. Generally speaking, it is certainly good advice to employ experimentally naive subjects in aggression research and to avoid sophisticated subjects whenever possible (e.g., Turner & Simons, 1974). On the other hand, it would be quite unrealistic to believe in the existence of truly naive subjects. Normally acculturated human subjects (who would be the most appropriate for most experimental purposes) will respond to demands and display bias because of apprehensions. They will do this outside the laboratory as well. The laboratory is thus "just another place" in which social interactions with all their psychological ramifications occur. Laboratory subjects respond to instructions as a set of demands; they may like or hate the task they are made to perform; and they may have a positive or negative "gut" reaction to the experimenter. College students, no matter how naive they are, will entertain hunches about the purpose of the experiment in which they are participating, and even elementary school children will venture to guess what the study is about. All this is quite acceptable. As long as the demands and apprehensions exert only an overall, nondifferentiated influence, they generally do not impair the validity of experimental investigations. This is so, because such investigations characteristically do not seek to establish absolute or normative levels of performance but instead are designed to determine the relative effects of various circumstances or treatments. The crucial precondition for the validity of comparisons of this kind is that the demands and apprehensions not produce *differential* effects in the various conditions being compared. In other words, it is imperative that demands and apprehensions not favor some conditions or treatments over others. Only if the differentiation of observed effects of particular experimental conditions coincides with the effects that are to be expected on grounds of demand characteristics or evaluation apprehension (or other potentially biasing factors) should the findings be considered faulted on such grounds. This reasoning may appear self-evident to the experimentally minded investigator, but apparently it is not an obvious matter to the many interpreters of research on human aggression who continue to perceive intolerable artifact and artificiality in most laboratory investigations.

In the experimental analysis of human aggressive behavior, it is imperative, then, to guard against the potential confounding of procedural influences with the effects of the experimental variations under investigation. It might appear that this is readily taken care of in a postexperimental interview in which the subject reports any suspicions. Such a view is overly optimistic, however. If the subject yields to demands and apprehensions in the experiment, he or she should do so in the subsequent interview as well. There is no reason to believe that the biased subject will suddenly become unbiased in the interview, as some investigators—among them Page and Scheidt— seem to have assumed. The principal problem is that demands and apprehensions encroach upon the study of these very demands and apprehensions. For example, when Page and Scheidt probed for the subject's awareness of the purpose of the weapons in their experiment, the subject was asked by the experimenter, among other things, whether the subject's hypothesis was that the gun on the table was to increase his aggressiveness toward his partner. In terms of demands and apprehensions, this question seems suggestive in that it makes the student who admits that he did not recognize the experimental hypothesis appear stupid, particularly in the condition of the more severe aggressive instigation, where he perhaps should have recognized it more readily. Awareness of the guns' purpose is thus *created,* to some extent at least, by asking the question, and reported awareness is spuriously high as a consequence.

Recently, Tannenbaum (cf. Tannenbaum & Zillmann, 1975) has suggested a procedure that promises to reduce greatly the bias in the determination of bias. His procedure has various stages:

1. After the subject has completed all experimental tasks, he or she meets a confederate who has ostensibly just been a subject in the same experiment. The confederate notes any spontaneous comments made by the subject concerning the experimental procedure.
2. If none are forthcoming, the confederate voices his or her own bewilderment about the study, expressing curiosity about the actual purpose of the study.
3. If the subject still fails to express any suspicions or hunches, the confederate expresses his or her own doubts, suggesting that the stated purpose could not have been the real purpose.
4. Finally, if the subject still has not volunteered his or her own views on what might be the actual purpose, the confederate states the actual purpose as his or her suspicion and notes the subject's reaction.

Another appropriate procedure to guard against procedural bias is to solicit guesses about the research objective from pilot subjects who have participated in the various conditions of an experiment. The most frequently occurring "hypotheses" are then presented, in randomized sequence, to the actual subjects, who rate the extent to which they believe the various notions to be true.

Procedures such as these should be used in the study of interpersonal aggression. They will reveal bias and thereby guide the development of ultimately unbiased procedures. Once bias is eliminated, these procedures will provide information with which possible accusations of bias can be refuted. Generally speaking, the actual purpose of a study—that is, the variation whose effect is being studied—has to be well disguised in order to avoid the confounding of effects with demands and apprehensions. On this count, the weapons studies are particularly troublesome. As is apparent in the investigations by Ellis et al., Buss et al., and Page and Scheidt, the presence of guns in the laboratory did strike most subjects as peculiar; and in the immediate context of the annoyance-retaliation paradigm, it made many of them "put two and two together." This transparency of purpose is the crux of the problem. If the transparency had not been there, the discussed biasing effects of demands and apprehensions could not have come into play in the way they evidently did.

In a recent field experiment on the effect of weapons on aggression, Turner, Layton, and Simons (1975) bypassed the awareness problems of laboratory research. These investigators frustrated car drivers by having a confederate block traffic. Specifically, the confederate drove a truck up to a stoplight and failed to move it for some time after the light had turned green. A gun either was or was not displayed on a rack in the rear window of the truck. Additionally, a bumper sticker reading either "vengeance" or "friend" was employed. These stickers were used to assure that the guns would have either aggressive or nonaggressive connotations (cf. Berkowitz & Alioto, 1973). Furthermore, the driver was either clearly visible or concealed by a curtain. The extent of horn honking of the driver in the car immediately behind the confederate was taken to reflect aggressive behavior.

Before we consider the findings, a look at the measure of aggression employed seems indicated. Is horn honking an acceptable index of aggression? Turner et al. (1975) presented data that show that drivers consider themselves to be readily annoyed by the behavior of nonalert and discourteous fellow drivers. These drivers also reported little reluctance to express their annoyance. The question, however, is whether horn honking is more than such an *expression of annoyance*. There are no correlational data that show that a person who honks is out to inflict real harm or injury. The validity of the measure thus rests on a construct, and this construct appears questionable. Honking is commonly practiced by drivers, whether they are annoyed or not, when they realize that the person ahead has missed the signal change—presumably because of distraction rather than malice. Honking may well be a *prosocial* communicative act that merely tells the other driver that he or she can move on. At times, however, it may be employed to express anger, and we thus treat horn honking as a measure of the expression of annoyance. Since there is no apparent infliction of harm or injury involved, we cannot consider it a measure of hostile or aggressive behavior.

Turner et al. observed that when the driver was not visible, the presence of a gun together with the "vengeance" sticker resulted in more frequent honking than the presence of the gun with the "friend" sticker and the absence of the gun and sticker. When the driver was clearly visible, no such effect was obtained, however. Also, whether or not the driver was concealed, the presence of the gun together with the "friend" sticker failed to elevate the frequency of honking. In a second study, Turner et al. (1975) reported that the gun alone had a consistent tendency to reduce honking frequency. (This comparison was not evaluated statistically, however, presumably because it was not of central importance to these investigators.) In male drivers of new vehicles, the rifle together with the "vengeance" sticker resulted in more frequent honking than the average of the remaining conditions (i.e., no gun and no sticker, sticker but no gun, and gun but no sticker). However, the frequency of honking in the gun-plus-sticker condition was comparable to that in the condition in which both were absent. (The investigators again failed to supply a statistical evaluation.) In male drivers of old vehicles, the presence of the rifle and the "vengeance" sticker had the opposite effect: It produced significantly less honking than the remaining conditions combined. These variations produced only negligible effects in females, whether they were driving new or old vehicles.

Taken together, the findings reported by Turner et al. fail to lend support to the notion that guns, as potent aggressive cues, evoke expressions of annoyance. In the absence of suggestive stickers, the presence of a gun consistently tended to lower the frequency of such expressions. In the presence of the "vengeance" sticker, the effect of a gun was highly inconsistent. It varied with the sex of the respondent and reversed with the age of the respondent's car. It also varied with the degree of visibility of the person toward whom the expression of annoyance was directed. The dominant effects of these secondary variations attest to the fragility and nongenerality of the weapons effect. In this regard, the field-experimental findings of Turner et al. are similar to the laboratory investigations reported earlier. As it stands, the available research evidence concerning "aggressive cues" such as weapons is largely negative, inconsistent, and contradictory. Berkowitz's proposal that such cues universally possess aggression-evoking powers cannot be considered to have been decisively supported under these circumstances.

Regarding the degree to which cues are associated with the instigation of aggression and are correspondingly capable of evoking aggressive reactions, the evidence is similarly equivocal.

Berkowitz and his co-workers conducted a series of studies in which aggressive cues were connected with a target, thereby increasing this target's potential to evoke aggressive reactions from a frustrated subject. It has been shown (Berkowitz, 1965b), for example, that annoyed subjects, after seeing a film of a prizefight, rated their annoyer as more hostile when he was identified as a former college boxer than when he was introduced as a speech major. "By associating this person with the aggressive scene, the 'boxer' label had presumably heightened his cue value for aggressive responses [p. 359]." Rated hostility was not affected by the differential identification of the target when subjects had seen a neutral film or when they had not been annoyed earlier. In another study, subjects' aggressiveness was measured by the ostensible delivery of electric shock to the target person. The findings obtained on the number of shocks administered corroborated those of the earlier study. On shock duration, the label-mediated enhancement of aggressiveness after exposure to the prizefight was also observed in nonannoyed subjects. In a third study, the aggressive action in the prizefight was initially described either as justified or as relatively unjustified. Independent of the degree of justification of the violent acts witnessed, the identification of the annoyer-target as a boxer produced consistently higher frequencies than did his identification as speech major.

Since there was an overall tendency for the delivery of a greater number of shocks and shocks of longer duration to the target person when he was labeled a "boxer" than when he was labeled a "speech major," alternative explanations became apparent (cf. Berkowitz, 1965a). For example, the identification of the person as a boxer might have made him appear tough, and this perceived toughness, made especially salient by the prizefight, in turn may have counteracted inhibitions against shocking. Such interpretations were ruled out in a subsequent study by Berkowitz and Geen (1966), in which the researchers took advantage of the fact that there was a well-known actor, Kirk Douglas, in the prizefight film employed. They sought to "mediate" aggressive cues from the film to the target person by giving the target part of this actor's name—*Kirk* Anderson. In the control condition, this name was changed to *Bob* Anderson. A factorial design was employed, varying high-vs. low-aggression instigation, exposure to an aggressive vs. a nonaggressive film, and the identification of the confederate as Kirk vs. Bob. It was found that name mediation facilitated aggressiveness, as measured in the frequency of shocks delivered, when subjects had been aggressively instigated and had then seen the aggressive film. This effect was also observed when the fictitious name of the aggressive protagonist was used for mediation (Geen &

Berkowitz, 1966). As Midge *Kelly,* Kirk Douglas was shown to be brutally beaten by a fighter named Johnny *Dunne,* played by an unknown actor. The confederate's name thus was either Bob Kelly, Bob Dunne, or—in a control condition—Bob Riley. The Kelly mediation was found to increase the number of shocks delivered, but the Dunne mediation did not. This study was interpreted as showing that mediation is particularly potent when it relates to the depicted victim of aggression. In contrast to these supportive findings, the mediating effect of cues (i.e., *Kirk* over *Bob*) was not obtained in a later study by Geen and Berkowitz (1967). Also, when the revelation of the name association was delayed until after the viewing of the film (Berkowitz & Geen, 1967), it failed to produce the mediation effect. (In the latter study, there was no discernible effect when all subjects were considered. A significant differentiation was reported only after the dismissal of an arbitrary number of subjects from each condition. We have to consider such a procedure unacceptable.)

These name-mediation studies are thus not entirely consistent in supporting the notion that a particular target's potential to draw out aggressive reactions increases with the extent to which it has been associatively linked to independent aggressive cues. More importantly, however, the findings are as much open to criticism on grounds of demands and apprehensions as the original weapons study. The effects of name mediation reported were not obtained as the result of the merely incidental name sharing between an aggressive protagonist and the confederate. Rather, the experimenter "casually but pointedly remarked that the accomplice happened to have the same name as one of the people . . . in the film" (Geen & Berkowitz, 1966, p. 459). As in the weapons study, the crucial experimental variation was made the focus of attention. The experiment's purpose may have been similarly transparent, allowing for the encroachment of artifact into the findings. In other words, the purported aggression-enhancing effect of name mediation has not yet been demonstrated as the consequence of the mere commonality of the names of aggressive persons and annoyers, and it is quite conceivable that the effect would not materialize under these circumstances.

As might be expected, the mediation paradigm has also been employed in the investigation of the displacement of hostility. Berkowitz and Knurek (1969) conducted an experiment in which negative attitudes were conditioned to certain first names. Subjects were subsequently either annoyed or not annoyed by a trainer and then placed in a discussion group with two experimental accomplices. One of the accomplices had a first name toward which a negative attitude had been conditioned, and the other did not. Subjects later evaluated these accomplices, and negative evaluations were taken to reflect hostility. It was found that annoyed subjects evaluated the accomplices more negatively when they had the negative name than when they had a neutral one. In nonannoyed subjects, the negative name failed to exert a notable influence. These findings are compromised, however, by the fact that for some unexplained reason, annoyed subjects were altogether far less negative in their evaluations than nonannoyed subjects. Given this finding, the validity of the ratings as a measure of hostility appears questionable.

Fenigstein and Buss (1974) have recently provided a direct test of the involvement of associative bonds in the displacement of aggression. In their investigation, subjects were either angered or not angered by a confederate and then given an opportunity to aggress against two other persons. These other persons entered the scene after the subjects had been subjected to the provocation treatment. One of them interacted with the confederate in a manner that made it apparent that the two were longtime friends. The other gave no indication of knowing the confederate. After the confederate left, the subject had to teach something to the two newcomers, who had to cooperate with each other on a task. The subject was to deliver shock to one of the two learners for every error made by the team.

Clearly, Berkowitz's mediation model leads to the expectation that aggressive behavior should be readily displaced toward the annoyer's friend. This is because this person's associative linkage to the annoyer makes him a potent aggression-evoking cue. In other words, it makes him a highly suitable target who pulls aggressive behavior from the frustrated subject. Fenigstein and Buss failed to obtain data that would support this reasoning. Their findings show no discernible effect of a person's association with an annoyer on the displacement of aggression. In their study, the friends of an annoyer simply did not constitute more suitable targets for aggression than other people. Needless to say, these findings also fail to support Miller's displacement theory.

In summary, then, the overall evidence concerning Berkowitz's mediation or association model is not unequivocal. The findings that are the least suspect of being confounded with demands and apprehensions are not supportive. Under these circumstances, the mediation model should be used with considerable caution, especially so in view of its far-reaching social implications. These implications are discussed in a later section as we encounter more recent formulations of the eliciting-cue notion.

B. Aggressive vs. Generalized Drive

Miller's (1941) retraction of the claim in frustration–aggression theory (Dollard et al., 1939) that frustration necessarily induces aggressive drive, which in turn necessarily results in some form of hostility or aggression, seems to have led the way in the dismissal of the concept of specific aggressive drive. In contemporary psychology, this concept—as originally employed in the frustration–aggression hypothesis—generally has been abandoned. This, however, does not mean that all characteristic features of a hypothetical aggressive drive have been discarded nor that the alternative of a nonspecific diffuse drive has been universally accepted. As the drive concept in frustration–aggression theory (and more generally, in behavior theory) was challenged, investigators became understandably reluctant to commit themselves to a nomenclature that could make their theoretical positions vulnerable. The drive concept was henceforth treated with caution. The concept was neither abandoned nor necessarily altered. The word *drive*, however, was largely shunned. If used, it was frequently placed in quotation marks, and when avoided, substitute terms were freely drawn upon. These practices unfortunately have not helped to clarify the reasoning on aggression, since the changes were more apparent than real. Many investigators maintained elements of aggressive drive in their theories, but they did so without clearly identifying them as such. Elements of aggressive drive are thus obscured, and our task here is to reconstruct them explicitly in those approaches in which they have survived. More importantly, however, our task is to determine the transformations that the drive concept has actually undergone in aggression theories. Of particular interest is the relationship between anger and drive, the notion of drive as a universal energizer, and the theoretical status of drive itself. The discussion of research pertaining to the issue of specific vs. nonspecific drive is delayed, however. The theoretical model developed later in the text relates directly to the issue in question, and pertinent investigations that bear on it are considered in connection with this model.

1. Appetitive Drive. Aggressive drive has been conceived of, essentially, as an internal state of energy that: (a) is produced by aversive stimulation, (b) compels the organism to aggressive action, and (c) is diminished or terminated after the execution of such action. The drive state is thus *reactive* rather than spontaneous, and it has *appetitive* properties that define particular appropriate *consummatory* acts. Thus conceived, the notion of aggressive drive has continued to be used mainly in the writings of Berkowitz (e.g., 1965a) and Feshbach (e.g., 1970).

In his reinterpretation of the frustration–aggression relationship, Berkowitz (1969a) expressed the conviction that frustration induces a motivational state that favors aggression over alternative response routes. "Basically," he said, "I believe a frustrating event increases the probability that the thwarted organism will act aggressively soon afterward, and that this relationship exists in many different animal species, including man [p. 2]." This statement, in fact, largely reverses Miller's (1941) retraction of the claim that frustration always fosters aggression. Apparently, frustration is viewed as making aggression the likely reaction most of the time. However, more importantly here, the statement attributes appetitive properties to the frustration-induced state—*drive, force, anger,* or whatever label is used to denote it. In Berkowitz's (1965a, 1969a, 1970) conceptualization, then, aggressive drive predisposes the organism to aggression. It constitutes a state of aggression readiness, sensitizing the organism to releasing cues that are said to be necessary for aggression actually to occur.

With regard to consummatory aggressive reactions, Berkowitz has taken an extreme stand. He has posited a "completion tendency" (1965a) for aggressive behavior. Specifically, he proposed that for the individual in an acute state of aggression readiness, the infliction of injury upon the tormentor is the ultimate goal reaction and that only this goal reaction can terminate the state of aggression readiness. He furthermore suggested that such a completion tendency exists even though the response readiness may be purely autistic. Once the organism is "primed to aggress" and "aggressive responses are set into motion, even if only implicitly in the person's thoughts, " he wrote (1965a), "then an individual will not attain completion until the goal object has been aggressively injured [p. 324]." Bandura (1973a) has taken issue with this proposal as far as the autistic function is concerned, and the interested reader is referred to his discussion of it. Here, we continue to concentrate on the completion tendency as such.

In contrast to frustration–aggression theory, which permits the substitution of targets, Berkowitz's argument implies that in order to terminate an acute state of aggressive drive, aggression need be directed against the appropriate target. Berkowitz hastened to point out that because of man's conceptual abilities, the injury need not be inflicted personally by the instigated individual and that it need not be inflicted in exactly the way in which it was contemplated. In other words, aggressive agents and means may be substituted, but targets and intended injuries may not.

This argument is of critical theoretical consequence. Most importantly, it categorically *denies catharsis through displaced aggression.* Berkowitz's reasoning, generally speaking, adheres very closely to frustration–aggression theory, but with regard to catharsis, it obviously does not. Only aggression against the tormentor is assumed to function as drive-reducing consummatory behavior. As a consequence, aggression cannot be displaced in the sense of taking the place of another, originally motivated attack. An alternative target that draws an attack because—according to Berkowitz's cue model—it is associated with aggression-triggering stimuli thus cannot substitute for the original tormentor. Attacks upon alternative targets, then, simply constitute excess violence motivated by the readiness to aggress against a specific tormentor.

In this connection, Berkowitz (1965a, 1973b) has developed an interesting rationale that predicts that if anything, attacks upon alternative targets will heighten the probability of an assault upon the actual tormentor. He proposed that since the infliction of injury on the tormentor constitutes the ultimate goal reaction for the aggressively instigated individual, failure to hurt the intended victim is frustrating in itself. This frustration adds to the torment suffered initially, thus increasing the individual's aggression readiness.

Although Berkowitz does not suggest this, his argument can be applied recursively: Every increment in aggression readiness makes the failure to inflict injury all the more frustrating, adding further to aggression readiness, and so forth indefinitely. Since the proposal fails to indicate a mechanism by which this drive escalation can be disrupted, aggression against the tormentor seems largely to be inevitable and only a matter of time. What starts as an "aggressive thought" must ultimately become overt violence—a challenging, controversial idea indeed (cf. Bandura, 1973a).

Attacks upon alternative targets relate to this escalation model in two ways. First, the emphasis on goal achievement rather than goal response—that is, on hurting rather than hitting—led Berkowitz (e.g., 1973b) to propose that especially for the acutely instigated person, the infliction of injury generally reinforces aggression. Attacks upon alternative targets thus make further attacks, including those directed toward the original target, more likely. Second, attacks upon alternative targets are viewed as lowering "aggression anxiety," and this anxiety reduction leads to the same expectations.

Finally, Berkowitz (1970, 1973b) suggested that the desire to hurt motivates the aggressively instigated person to enjoy witnessing others inflict injury upon others and that mere exposure to violent activities reinforces aggression. The angry person is said to develop an appetite for injurious activities, and the observation of such activities is considered aggression enhancing because it elicits "aggression-related anticipatory goal responses" (Berkowitz, 1973b, p. 134). In other words, witnessing aggression reminds the angry person of his or her desire to hurt the tormentor, and this reminder further instigates the desire to hurt that tormentor.

In summary, Berkowitz projects a highly specific aggressive drive that, once set in motion, is strengthened by additional frustrations, by attacks made upon irrelevant targets, and by exposure to violent actions. Further, the drive dissipates only after the object toward which it is directed has been harmed or injured.

Feshbach (1955, 1961, 1964, 1970), an outspoken proponent of the notion of aggressive drive, has arrived at a substantially different proposal. In agreement with Berkowitz, he views frustration as the major source of aggressive instigation. His view of the drive-motivated goal activities is also very similar to that of Berkowitz. The infliction of pain and injury upon the tormentor is seen to terminate the drive state. Additionally, the mere observation of the infliction of this pain and injury is seen to be reinforcing for the individual in whom aggressive drive is activated (Feshbach, 1970;

Feshbach, Stiles, & Bitter, 1967). In sharp disagreement with Berkowitz's position, however, Feshbach (e.g., 1970) proposed that any activity, overt or covert, that "functionally relates" to the goal behavior constitutes a substitute act and that the performance of substitute acts diminishes aggressive drive. The consequence of this diminution of aggressive drive is, of course, a reduced likelihood of aggression against the original tormentor and against all other targets. The important aspect of this cathartic process is that it is best attained by aggressive activities. Engaging in hostile fantasies, deliberately anticipating aggressive acts, witnessing violence, assaulting an inanimate object, and hurting a defenseless victim—all these activities are expected to reduce aggressive drive because they relate to the thwarted goal reaction more closely than do nonaggressive activities. In the Lewinian nomenclature (e.g., Lewin, 1951) preferred by Feshbach (e.g., 1970), only aggressive activities have *substitute valence* for goal responses the aggressively instigated person is motivated to perform, and consequently, only such activities can absorb and reduce specific aggressive drive.

Essentially, then, Feshbach has adhered to the concepts of aggressive drive and catharsis as they were developed in frustration–aggression theory. To accommodate recent findings, he has modified and redefined his views, however. We discuss these changes in the following sections.

2. Diffuse Drive. The principal weakness of drive theories of aggression is their inability to account for the fact that (a) aggressive drive can facilitate nonaggressive activities (cf. Bandura, 1973a), and (b) nonaggressive drive can facilitate aggressive behavior (cf. Zillmann, 1978). Aggressive drive, it seems, can readily be discharged through nonaggressive actions. Moreover, aggressive actions apparently feed not only on aggressive drive but on other sources of drive as well. Under these circumstances, as Bandura (1973a) pointed out, the involvement of an aggressive drive in theories of aggression has created more conceptual problems than it has resolved. To deal with recent findings, it apparently has become necessary to abandon the assumed one-to-one correspondence between aggressive instigation, aggressive drive, and aggressive behavior.

In an effort to accommodate findings that show that frustrations potentially facilitate a multitude of behaviors—nonaggressive as well as aggressive activities—Feshbach (1970) conceptually separated anger from aggressive drive. Anger is considered to have drive properties "in the sense of an energizer of ongoing behavior [p. 162]," and it is made clear that this response-energizing function is not specific to aggression. Feshbach thus views anger as a diffuse drive, whereas aggressive drive is seen as specific. Such a dual system helps to cope with findings that cannot be accounted for in terms of aggressive drive, but it does so only in a postmortem analysis. For explanatory purposes, the differentiation between anger and aggressive drive is too ambiguous to permit the formulation of clear-cut predictions. Specifically, it remains unclear when the presence of diffusely energizing anger predominates over specific aggressive drive. When does frustration produce just anger, and when does it produce anger plus aggressive drive? It seems to be assumed that acute anger can be aroused in the absence of aggressive instigation and that this condition prevails when nonaggressive activities are intensified by anger. Such an assumption is not only conceptually troublesome, but it also largely fails to meet the specific experimental conditions under which the findings to be accommodated by the revision were obtained.

Most contemporary investigators of aggression have shown more willingness than Feshbach to abandon the notion of specific aggressive drive altogether. The major impetus for their readiness to accept the alternative concept of drive as a diffuse, universal energizer seems to have come from behavior theory. Hull (1943, 1952) had proposed a *generalized drive,* that is, a nonspecific, undifferentiated drive state that integrates components of drive from various sources. In his view, the strengths of simultaneously active drives combine into an effective drive state. The entire accumulated force of this state then energizes the behavior that is prepotent in the habit structure. Thus, there is no one-to-one linkage between a particular drive and associated behaviors. Dependent on prevailing stimulus conditions that control habit, elements of drive *a* can facilitate behavior associated with drive *b,* and vice versa. In principle, any behavior can be facilitated by *irrelevant drive*—that is, by energy that in the past has not been connected with the behavior it is energizing.

The application of these propositions to aggression is not as straightforward as it may appear. Hull dealt primarily with deprivation-based drive states such as hunger and thirst. These states are associated with well-defined consummatory reactions. The situation is obviously very different for aggression. Aggression is not based on deprivation; nor are there unquestionable, highly specific, and ultimately drive-reducing associated activities. These differences, which are all too easily overlooked, have been acknowledged by Brown and Farber (1951), who undertook the task of applying Hullian theory to aggression. Specifically, Brown and Farber conceived of emotions as intervening variables, and they dealt with frustrations in this context. They posited that "frustration-produced drive has *the functional status of an irrelevant drive* [p. 488]." This amounts to saying that frustration induces a drive state that, in the absence of preestablished drive-specific habits, potentially energizes aggressive and nonaggressive behaviors alike. In short, conceiving of frustration as an irrelevant drive removes all elements of aggression specificity from frustration, making it a source of purely diffuse drive.

For some reason, Brown and Farber's efforts have attracted little attention. Investigators have drawn directly on Hull's model, ignoring the problems deriving from differences in the status of drive. Hull's notion of generalized drive was simply transformed into the proposal that drive (or arousal) will facilitate the behavior that holds a prime position in the response hierarchy (e.g., Geen & O'Neal, 1969) or the proposal that arousal (or drive) enhances any and every behavior a person comes to perform (e.g., Tannenbaum, 1972).

Such formulations remove the burden for the causation of aggression from drive and place it on habit. Under given circumstances, established aggressive habits are activated, and the strength of drive present at that time comes to energize the activated habit. Consequently, drive is not viewed as pushing toward a specific behavior, but once a specific behavior is determined— mainly by environmental stimuli that trigger a learned reaction—this behavior is seen as being powered by prevailing drive. This position on drive has been concisely expressed by Hebb (1955), who treated generalized drive and arousal as synonymous: Drive "is an energizer, but not a guide; an engine but not a steering gear [p. 249]." This view contrasts sharply with Miller's (1959) conception, which, as will be remembered, assigned strong stimulus properties to a drive state.

The view that prevalent drive diffusely energizes any and every behavior performed has a significant corollary that is often overlooked: *The degree to which behavior will be energized is a monotonic function of the strength of diffuse drive.* In the proposed additive integration of various sources of drive, the specificity of these sources is entirely lost. The notion of partial energization, due to incompatible elements of drive, would be contradictory to the very notion of a generalized drive. The full force of drive must thus come to play. With regard to aggression, the theoretical expectation is not ambiguous, then: Diffuse drive operates as a unitary force, *intensifying—in proportion to the magnitude of drive or arousal prevailing at that time—any aggressive reaction performed.*

3. Drive Reduction. The principal features of drive theory are, of course: (a) that increases in drive level increase the motivation to seek out conditions under which consummatory activities can be performed and enhance the motivation to perform such activities; and (b) that the performance of these consummatory activities effects a reduction in drive level and consequently decreases the associated motivation. In the hungry animal, for example, the motivation to seek and consume food is assumed to increase with drive, which in turn is assumed to increase with time of food deprivation. Food consumption, that is, the performance of the consummatory response, is considered to lower drive and consequently to relax the animal's food-gathering activity until drive levels rise again, and so forth. Whatever the merits of employing the drive concept in this context, the analogy with aggression must appear forced. As has been pointed out earlier, and notwithstanding Lorenz's convictions to the contrary, aggression is not based on deprivation. Because it is not, consummatory actions that would eliminate a deficiency, and that would thereby necessarily reduce the motivation to aggress, cannot be specified. To consider the infliction of pain or injury upon an antagonist a consummatory, drive-absorbing act thus means overextending a model designed to explain behavior that differs fundamentally from aggression. Nonetheless, presumably because the drive model proved to be so very plausible for behaviors that are motivated by bodily changes resulting from deprivation, the analogy of specific drive in aggression seems to have been broadly accepted. People tend to consider it a truism (a) that the aggressively instigated person is out to hurt his or her tormentor, and (b) that ultimately, only a successful attack will make that person feel better. As discussed earlier, Berkowitz (e.g., 1965a, 1969a) has formally expressed this popular view.

In terms of drive reduction, this view is extreme in suggesting that once aggressive drive is activated, it will remain active until the specific goal to be achieved by the goal reaction has been accomplished, that is, until injury has been inflicted. In fact, drive must be assumed to be maintained at its original level until injury has been inflicted.

Frustration–aggression theory, as will be remembered, has promoted a different view. Dollard et al. (1939) held that the expression of any act of aggression is drive reducing in that it lowers the instigation to all other acts of aggression. This makes any hostile or aggressive act, no matter what target it is directed against, a partial or possibly total substitute for the initially motivated aggressive goal response. The aggressive goal response is partially deprived of its associated drive and hence is less likely to occur. This drive reduction through substitute hostility or aggression is of course the thrust of the catharsis proposal.

Feshbach (1970) has more narrowly defined the conditions under which a reduction of specific aggressive drive can occur. He stipulated that there "needs to be a functional relationship between the goal behavior and the substitute act [p. 238]," but he failed to specify what exactly is meant by this functional relationship. Feshbach suggested that a high degree of similarity between the substitute act and the goal response for which it serves as a substitute would ensure drive reduction, but the basis for similarity was left unclear. Presumably, a high degree of similarity in the patterns of motor activity associated with the goal response and its substitute would meet the stipulation. But would incidental stimulus similarities between the original and the substitute target also qualify?

In the light of such conceptual and ultimately operational difficulties with the variables upon which the very prediction of catharsis is based, one might expect that the explanatory power of this notion would be considered limited. This is not the case, however. In Feshbach's reasoning, the discharge of aggressive drive through substitute activities is treated largely as an undeniable truism. This becomes quite clear in Feshbach's recent discussion of the research evidence pertaining to catharsis theory.

Feshbach (1970) proposed that substitute aggression may have several independent effects that together determine the level of subsequent aggressiveness. First, such aggression should reduce the level of aggressive drive and, in turn, aggressiveness. At the same time, however: (a) it may lower the strength of inhibitions upon later aggression; (b) it may be reinforcing through the attainment of feedback relating to the motivated goal response (e.g., the substitute attack may produce the victim's expression of pain, which is considered reinforcing because it is part of the originally intended goal reaction); and (c) it may be reinforcing because of its instrumental value (e.g., it may prove to yield incentives). A finding in which the performance of aggression is followed by reduced aggressiveness can thus be viewed as a case in which a reduction in aggressive drive dominated the aggression-enhancing factors. A finding in which the performance of aggressive acts fails to alter subsequent aggressiveness can be seen as a case in which the effect of drive discharge was counteracted and neutralized by the opposing effects indicated. Last but not least, a finding in which aggression is followed by increased aggressiveness can be interpreted as a case in which the aggression-enhancing forces dominated the impact of drive drainage. Clearly, no matter what effect is observed, it can be accounted for post facto by such a model. Even in the face of what would appear to be counterevidence, a claim can be made that catharsis occurred. Within Feshbach's model, catharsis theory eludes the possibility of falsification. As long as the effect on aggression of the various presumed subprocesses cannot be isolated and assessed independently, the catharsis hypothesis cannot be subjected to decisive empirical testing (cf. Bandura, 1973a).

We now turn to the consideration of the energization of aggressive behavior by diffuse drive and its implications for drive reduction. It will be remembered that the concept of generalized drive is based on the assumption that elements of relevant and irrelevant drive inseparably combine into an effective drive that diffusely energizes behavior associated with a prime location in a hypothetical hierarchy of responses. In this theoretical framework, a reduction in drive level is considered to come about with the performance of energy-absorbing activities. It is secondary here that in behavior theory, such a reduction in drive is said to reinforce the behavior that precipitated the drive discharge. What is important is the view that a reduction in drive level can be brought about by *any* energy-absorbing activity. It is of little moment whether or not the energy-absorbing behavior is aggressive. Aggressive and nonaggressive activities alike effect a reduction in drive as a function of energy discharge. As a consequence, aggressive behavior that consumes little energy should have little if any impact on subsequent aggressiveness, and nonaggressive acts that absorb considerable energy should reduce subsequent aggressiveness.

A major factor in the discharge of energy through behavior is the involvement of skeletal-motor activity. Generally speaking, the amount of energy discharged increases with the number of skeletal-motor structures involved in a response sequence, with the vigor of the responses in the sequence, and with the length of time the response sequence is performed. The reduction of diffuse drive should thus be more pronounced, the more strenuous the behavior performed.

This reasoning has interesting implications for aggression. As already indicated, it leads to expectations that sharply contrast with those deriving from the notion of a specific aggressive drive. First, the infliction of injury does not necessarily reduce drive level. Pulling a trigger, for example, consumes so little energy that it can hardly be considered to effect a notable discharge of diffuse drive. Consequently, shooting someone should fail to lower drive level by very much, and if aggressive responses remain in a prime location in the response hierarchy, diffuse drive should be carried along to energize such responses. Also, no matter how much harm is inflicted by hostile activities, these activities should generally not reduce drive notably. Dropping a devastating remark, for example, is simply not very strenuous. A vigorous aggressive struggle, in contrast, should constitute an optimal condition for drive discharge, whether or not it leads to the infliction of injury. Second, and of equal importance, the performance of vigorous *non*aggressive activities must be expected to reduce the level of diffuse drive, thus depriving subsequent behavior of much of the irrelevant drive that could have energized it. This expectation relates to the suggestion by Freud (1915a/1946) and Hartmann, Kris, and Loewenstein (1949) that intense skeletal-motor activities can purge the organism of aggressive urges. It seems also to relate, although more loosely, to Lorenz's (1963) conjecture that participation in sports can help curb violence by draining off a hypothetical reservoir of spontaneously increasing aggressive energy.

In summary, then, models of aggression that explicitly or implicitly endorse the notion of a specific aggressive drive tend to emphasize the importance of goal attainment (the infliction of injury) in the reduction of drive. Drive reduction has been expected, in principle: (a) with the actual goal attainment, (b) with the performance of the goal reaction against a substitute target, and (c) with the performance of a modified, yet inherently similar, goal reaction against a substitute target. The performance of responses that fail to inflict harm or injury of some sort is considered to leave the level of aggressive drive unaltered. Aggressive drive is thus assumed to persist at given levels for indefinitely long periods of time. Models that embrace the notion of a diffuse, generalized drive, by contrast, stress the energetic aspects of behavior. Drive reduction is expected to follow both aggressive and nonaggressive activities that are energy consuming. Since diffuse drive is unrelated to specific goal reactions, the infliction of harm or injury in and of itself is not considered to effect drive discharge. Aggressive goal reactions reduce drive level only to the extent that they are precipitated by and directly involve strenuous activities. Finally, since diffuse drive is viewed as varying freely with energy expenditures, drive levels are generally not considered stable for any length of time.

4. From Drive to Arousal.   In behavior theory (e.g., Hull, 1943, 1952; Spence, 1956, 1960), drive has, strictly speaking, the status of a hypothetical construct. Hull (1943) conceived of drive as an *intervening variable* that is "never directly observable [p. 57]." On many occasions, however, Hull suggested a physical embodiment of drive, although he was relatively imprecise on the matter. He suggested, for example, the following (1943):

Most, if not all, primary needs appear to generate and throw into the blood stream more or less characteristic chemical substances, or else to withdraw a characteristic substance. These substances (or their absence) have a selective physiological effect on more or less restricted and characteristic portions of the body... which serves to activate resident receptors. This receptor activation constitutes the drive stimulus [p. 240].

Suggestions of this kind tended to equate drive with activity in the autonomic nervous system. The assessment of drive in terms of such activity has remained an unresolved issue, however (cf. Cofer & Appley, 1964).

With the advent of activation theory (e.g., Duffy, 1957, 1962; Lindsley, 1951, 1957; Malmo, 1959), the emphasis changed to activities in the brain-stem reticular formation. The ascending reticular activating system had been shown to project diffusely to thalamic, hypothalamic, and cortical regions (e.g., Magoun, 1954; Moruzzi, 1964; Moruzzi & Magoun, 1949). The fact of essentially diffuse projection, which has survived later modifications and refinements in the delineation of the specific structures involved (cf. Thompson, 1967), was interpreted as inconsistent with the assumption of specific, motivating drives. Activation was conceived of as a nonspecific, behavior-energizing force that could be measured through the electroen-cephalogram. Most importantly, activation was treated as a measurable unitary variable, ranging from death through coma, deep sleep, light sleep, drowsiness, relaxed wakefulness, and alert attentiveness to strong, excited emotions (e.g., Lindsley, 1957). All these levels of activation were shown to be associated with characteristic wave patterns and rhythms in the encephalogram.

The concept of activation was readily incorporated in theories of motivation. Brown (1961) accepted the possibility of assessing drive through arousal in the reticular formation, and many others did likewise (e.g., Berlyne, 1960; Bindra, 1959). It should be clear, however, that drive was not simply equated with such arousal. Rather, arousal in the reticular system was treated as a reliable, convenient index of activation at large. It was considered to reflect the degree of excitation of all organismic structures: "the extent to which the organism as a whole is activated or aroused" (Duffy, 1934, p. 194). Arousal in the reticular formation, although it was considered a superior index of the level of motivation (e.g., Malmo, 1965), was thus assumed to correlate highly with arousal in other structures (cf. Duffy, 1957).

The changing status of drive, from a construct to a measurable entity, is similarly evident in aggression theory. The explicit use of the drive concept has become comparatively rare. The concept of arousal, on the other hand, seems to have become successively more popular. In one way or another, all contemporary theories of aggression try to explain the phenomenon in terms of an interaction of cognition and arousal. The student of this topic may thus readily come to the conclusion that the theories are very similar, at least as far as arousal is concerned. Such an impression is quite erroneous, however. Confusion arises from the fact that the concept of arousal is used very broadly and assumes different meanings in different theories—occasionally even in the same theory.

In Berkowitz's reasoning, for example, arousal designates both a state of acute physiological excitation (e.g., 1970) and an energizing force that apparently only loosely corresponds with excitation (e.g., 1965a). The latter use of the arousal concept plays a part in the proposal of a completion tendency in aggression. As will be remembered from the earlier discussion of this proposal, thwarting the attainment of an aggressive objective is considered to add aggression-enhancing frustration, presumably until the goal is achieved. Berkowitz stated (1965a) that this additional frustration "leads to a heightened arousal state. In turn, the increased arousal (a) is felt as an unpleasant tension, and (b) strengthens the ongoing but blocked aggressive response sequence [p. 323]." Presumably, some form of physiological activity was the intended meaning of arousal. But since no time restrictions were stipulated for this process of arousal escalation and since the heightened arousal state is viewed as being capable of motivating aggression for extended periods of time (i.e., potentially until response completion is achieved), arousal cannot have been conceived of as something that closely corresponds with acute physiological excitation in the organism. Independent of the effect of disruptive intervening stimulation, homeostatic control alone makes it impossible for response-energizing activation to be maintained at high levels for extended periods of time (e.g., Cannon, 1932;

Freeman, 1948; Richter, 1942). At times, then, Berkowitz has used the concept of arousal as a substitute for the instigation to aggression or aggressive drive. On the other hand, more recently he has employed this concept as synonymous with diffusely energizing, acute physiological excitation (e.g., 1970). Regardless of the particular interpretation of arousal, Berkowitz (e.g., 1965a, 1969a) has considered the relationship between the instigation to aggression and aggression—and for that matter, between arousal and aggression—as partly based on innate connections and partly learned. Feshbach (e.g., 1970) has expressed a very similar view.

In his social learning theory of aggression, Bandura proposed (1973a) that aversive treatments produce "a general state of emotional arousal that can facilitate a variety of behaviors, depending on the types of responses the person has learned for coping with their stress and their relative effectiveness [p. 53]." This proposal is entirely consistent with Hullian behavior theory, as Rule and Nesdale (1976a) have pointed out. Emotional arousal is conceived of as a universal, diffuse energizer of behavior controlled by established stimulus–response connections. Concerning this concept of emotional arousal, Bandura has not been very specific, however. He has acknowledged the response-potentiating properties of acute arousal without specifying exactly what comprises such arousal or how it exerts its behavior-modifying influence. Regarding the latter, he has not developed a mechanism by which arousal can facilitate, as proposed, nearly every kind of behavior. The specific operation of arousal, then, remains unclear. In particular, it is difficult to see how a high-activation state can facilitate a low-activation response to provocation. How can, for example, acute arousal "energize" withdrawal, resignation, or apathy—all these reactions to frustration being used as illustrations by Bandura? Regarding the theoretical status of the arousal concept, Bandura has employed arousal as a construct. He has equated level of arousal with level of activation or level of physiological excitation without committing himself to particular operationalizations. Arousal generally was not measured in his research.

Bandura's analysis of arousal as a facilitating force in aggression has several distinguishing characteristics. First, in sharp contrast to other positions in which the treatment of arousal largely parallels that of drive, Bandura stressed the short-lived nature of acute arousal. He directed attention to the noncathartic dissipation of arousal and to factors that influence and control this dissipation. Second, Bandura felt it necessary to qualify to some extent the notion of arousal as a *universal* energizer. Whereas arousal from adverse experiences is expected to energize socially constructive behaviors as well as hostile or aggressive activities, arousal deriving from joyful or rewarding experiences is expected to inhibit rather than facilitate hostility and aggression. This expectation, which severely restricts the generality of arousal as an energizer, is based on the contention (1973a) that euphoric arousal is *"incompatible* with hostile actions [p. 56; italics added]." In Bandura's view, then, only arousal deriving from adverse experiences can function as the universal energizer referred to in behavior theory. Arousal from pleasant experiences may facilitate similar experiences, but it is seen as incapable of combining with noxious arousal in the facilitation of aggression. In short, the impact of noxious arousal crosses hedonic lines; the impact of pleasant arousal does not. Finally and maybe most importantly, Bandura views the role of arousal in aggression as entirely secondary. He feels that aggression is almost totally controlled by reinforcement contingencies, independent of the arousal prevailing at the time of instigation or at the time of performance of aggression. "By arranging social learning determinants such that arousal-linked aggression is negatively sanctioned but aggression without arousal is well received, one could undoubtedly reverse the relationship between physiological state and action" (Bandura, 1973a, p. 56). Arousal is thus merely a cue that may coincide with aggressive inclinations. If, as presumably is the case in most if not all human cultures, arousal facilitates aggression, it does so only because at high levels of arousal, aggression has tended to have greater reward value. If we were consistently rewarded for aggressing when calm and punished for aggressing when aroused, we should come to be greatly inhibited by the arousal that prevails when we are aggressively provoked. It should be clear at this point that Bandura considers the relationship between arousal and aggression to be *entirely learned.*

Notwithstanding Bandura's approach to arousal, in recent years investigations of the function of arousal in aggression have shown a strong tendency to assess arousal rather than assume it to exist at particular levels. Arousal has been measured in motor activity (e.g., Gallup & Altomari, 1969; O'Neal, McDonald, Hori, & McClinton, 1978), in task performance (e.g., Burgess & Hokanson, 1964; Doob & Kirshenbaum, 1973), and in various physiological reactions—mainly cardiovascular changes (e.g., Doob & Kirshenbaum, 1973; Hokanson & Burgess, 1962b). It appears that this tendency will persist and ultimately lead to a compelling separation of the concept of arousal from the concept of drive as a force that remains elevated after activation has dissipated.

In recent research on aggression, then, the concept of drive, especially aggressive drive, has been replaced by the concept of arousal. At times, arousal is used as a synonym for aggressive drive; at others, for generalized drive. More frequently, however, it is employed in the sense of an acute state of physiological excitation with diffuse, energizing properties. The arousal-aggression relationship has been considered by some to be partly inherent and partly learned and by others to be entirely learned. Arousal has been operationalized in a variety of ways, and with increasing frequency it has been subjected to measurement.

III. AGGRESSION AS LEARNED BEHAVIOR

In animal studies, the modification of aggressive behavior by learning processes has been amply documented (cf., e.g., Cairns, 1972; Hutchinson, 1972; Kuo, 1960; Scott, 1958, 1973). Both the acquisition and the extinction of aggressive responses evidently are greatly influenced by reinforcement contingencies. More specifically, the learning of aggression has been shown to follow the classical and the instrumental conditioning paradigms, and it has been suggested that respondent and operant processes in aggression can operate concurrently (e.g., Ulrich, Dulaney, Arnett, & Mueller, 1973). Concerning human aggression, no one seems to deny that learning is critically involved in the acquisition and maintenance of hostile and aggressive modes of behavior. There is considerable disagreement and controversy, however, with regard to the adequacy of explanatory attempts that rest solely or primarily on the basic learning paradigms. There are investigators who seem to feel that human aggression is indeed controlled by the very mechanisms that control aggression in any other animal species and who consequently advocate the straightforward application of these mechanisms to human aggression (e.g., Ulrich et al., 1973). But there are many others who stress the mediating function of complex cognitive structures in humans and who assign limited explanatory value to the use of the basic learning paradigms alone (e.g., Bandura, 1973a; Feshbach, 1970; Pepitone, 1964; Zimbardo, 1969). Zimbardo has stressed the element of volition in aggression, viewing man as unique among animals because his capacity to determine his own behavior may largely defy reinforcement control. Bandura, on the other hand, has advanced the development of more specific learning mechanisms to accommodate those facets of human hostile and aggressive behavior that seem to elude strict reinforcement control.

This section seeks to provide a brief overview of principal stands and recent developments concerning learning paradigms in aggression theory. The section is structured by paradigms, and the various theoretical positions are dealt with under paradigm headings. The grouping is accomplished in accordance with a theory's emphasis upon a particular paradigm, and it should not be taken to imply that the theory necessarily relies solely on this paradigm. Additionally, since the distinction between the basic paradigms has become somewhat blurred in recent theoretical reasoning (e.g., Herrnstein, 1969; Rescorla & Solomon, 1967; Schoenfeld, 1966), the grouping should not be taken as a commitment to an irreconcilable conceptual differentiation.

A. Instrumental Learning of Aggression

Based on his experimental work on aggression in animals, which we discussed earlier, Scott concluded (1958) that the "motivation for fighting is strongly increased by success, and that the longer success continues, the stronger the motivation becomes [p. 126]." In terms of learning theory, this proposal translates to the statement that *the likelihood for aggression to occur increases as aggression is reinforced.* Given the enormous amount of research support for the reinforcement formulation in general (e.g., Honig, 1966), one might consider its application to aggression noncontroversial. At closer inspection, however, this turns out not to be the case.

Without the basic notion being challenged in any way, there is considerable controversy over *what, exactly, constitutes reinforcement in successful aggression.* Scott's experiments have convincingly demonstrated that success in fighting is reinforcing, but they have left it unclear which specific aspect of success constitutes the critical reinforcer. For all practical purposes, it may well suffice, in animal aggression, to use the overall outcome of a fight as the operationalization of success. Under natural conditions, successful fighting tends to confound several more specific outcomes, and some of these outcomes may not even be free to vary independently. The fact is, however, that different theoretical proposals have singled out different aspects of successful fighting as the crucial reinforcers of aggression, and these differential emphases have proved to have far-reaching implications. Because of these circumstances, successful fighting must be discussed in greater detail.

1. Alleviation of Aversion vs. Attainment of Rewards. If successful fighting in animals is conceived of as an exchange of potentially injurious behavior that, for the successful animal, terminates with the submission, the escape, or the incapacitation of the defeated animal, success may be considered to be composed of at least the following elements: (a) the diminution or cessation of the acute aversive state associated with the hostile and aggressive confrontation; (b) the diminution or cessation of any pain that may have been inflicted upon the successful fighter in the course of fighting; (c) access to the valued but scarce resources, such as food, a mate, or shelter, that were in dispute and thus led to the fighting; and (d) the submissive displays of the defeated animal, escape as a form of this display, or the infliction of injury upon the defeated animal.

How much, if anything, do these various elements contribute to the reinforcement value of success; and which element, if any, plays the dominant, crucial role? Since totally unambiguous data do not exist on this point, answers to this question seem to be very much a matter of theoretical orientation. Investigators who espouse the notion of aggressive drive in one form or another, and who consequently conceive of the infliction of injury as a consummatory response, tend to claim that the infliction of injury is the drive-reducing act and hence, that it is the critical reinforcer of aggression. We have seen earlier that both Berkowitz (e.g., 1969a) and Feshbach (e.g., 1970) advocate such a view. Interestingly, entirely unrelated to drive considerations, Skinner (e.g., 1969) has made himself a rather radical proponent of this idea that injury is the ultimate reinforcer of aggression. His views, which are seldom acknowledged in the aggression literature, are discussed in some detail later (see Section IIIA2 of this chapter).

The proposal that the infliction of injury constitutes the primary reinforcer of aggression is in apparent conflict with the fact that intraspecific fighting rarely leads to injury. From the most prevalent consequences of such fighting, one would tend to conclude that submission or flight is its principal reinforcer. This, oddly enough, has not been claimed.

In contrast to those who have emphasized the reinforcing role of injury, many investigators (e.g., Patterson & Reid, 1970; Scott, 1958) have suggested that *aggression is primarily reinforced by the termination of the noxious state associated with fighting.* This termination usually coincides with the physical separation of the antagonistic parties and is thus confounded with it.

It is important to recognize that the beneficial effect of the disengagement of the aggressive parties is brought about by submission and escape as well as by success. The termination of the noxious state associated with fighting, then, can be seen to reinforce withdrawal in the loser as much as it reinforces attack in the winner. An analysis of the pain associated with fighting leads to a similar conclusion. Following disengagement, this pain—which can be considered a salient element of the noxiousness of fighting—should diminish in both successful and unsuccessful fighters, and consequently, it should reinforce disengagement in both parties. Obviously, the associative linkage between fighting and pain should generally reinforce the avoidance of aggressive engagements, the only exception being the extremely skillful fighter who manages to defeat his or her opponent without ever suffering pain.

Such an interpretation is entirely consistent with Scott's (cf. 1958) experimental findings. The animals in his study could not avoid aggressive engagements, and for the animals in which aggression was reinforced, aversion-reducing disengagements were made contingent upon attack. Generally speaking, animals tend to avoid potentially painful behavioral exchanges. Only when aggression "holds promise" to terminate aversive conditions effectively will it become a dominant mode of behavior. This is exactly what Scott has demonstrated. Conditions were set up in which aggression proved repeatedly effective in quickly terminating a noxious situation. The removal of noxiousness, not the incapacitating infliction of injury, constituted the reinforcement in the aggression training. Once aggressive responses had become likely under aversive conditions, however, they could generalize to nonaversive situations. Scott (1958) expressed this view as follows: "Defensive fighting can be stimulated by the pain of an attack, but aggression, in the strict sense of an unprovoked attack, can only be produced by training [p. 20]."

At this point, it should be clear that training is a selective application of reinforcement. If reinforcement contingencies are created in such a way that aggression consistently or predominantly terminates aversion, aggression will become an increasingly likely reaction. If, on the other hand, fighting prompts withdrawal and this withdrawal consistently or predominantly terminates aversion, this nonaggressive reaction should become more likely. The thrust of the argument here is that the diminution of pain and the cessation of aversion have the potential to reinforce nonaggressive as well as aggressive behavior.

In terms of theory, then, the issue of whether aggressive or nonaggressive behavior will be reinforced by the termination of an acute annoyance is decided mainly by situational factors associated with aggressive encounters—particularly those encounters that occur early in the organism's development, when responses to aversions are being developed. An animal may develop into a vicious fighter, for example, because it is anatomically advantaged or has superior motor skills. As a consequence of its physical superiority, it may fight defensively with success. This success should lead to increased utilization of the aggressive response mode, which may ultimately become so prepotent that annoyance no longer is a necessary condition for the evocation of an attack. Theoretically speaking, this chain of events may be set into motion by an accidental strike in initial aggressive encounters. At the same time, it is conceivable that even a well-equipped animal—that is, a potentially successful fighter—could get off to a poor start, suffering the infliction of pain by an inferior opponent. To the extent that this pain induces submission or escape, the potentially superior fighter may be on its way to becoming a generally submissive, timid animal. The theoretical analysis of reinforcement by the alleviation of aversion thus yields a dual projection: (a) *If aggression accomplishes alleviation, aggression is reinforced;* and (b) *if submission accomplishes alleviation, submission is reinforced.* Under natural conditions, the physically advantaged animal seems to be destined to become aggressive, whereas the weak individual appears doomed for a submissive role. The contingencies of reinforcement can of course be arbitrarily altered by an intervening, physically superior agent. Parental guidance, as has been documented in many species, particularly in the primates, is one such source of intervention in the reinforcement process.

There seems little reason to doubt that the development of annoyance-motivated aggression in humans progresses along similar lines, at least in its initial phases. Patterson, Littman, and Bricker (1967) have presented data on aggressiveness in children that seem highly consistent with the discussed theoretical suggestions. These investigators observed that initially timid children who were occasionally the target of attack by peers and whose defensive aggression often proved effective in terminating aversions increased their defensive fighting considerably. In addition, they started to attack peers without first being attacked. At the same time, timid children who succeeded in avoiding being attacked through withdrawal and those whose efforts in warding off an attack failed remained submissive.

These findings are very suggestive of the reinforcement function of the alleviation of annoyance, but they do not decisively implicate this function because of conceptual ambiguities. Unlike in much animal research (cf. Hutchinson, 1972), aversive treatments in studies with humans are typically not operationalized in noxious stimulation of a measurable response intensity. Nor are aversions characteristically conceived of as experiential states with specific motivational properties. Instead, in the operant-learning tradition, aversions usually are defined in situational terms—as environmental (rather than internal) conditions that produce strong avoidance tendencies in the organism. Technically speaking, the termination of such a condition is expected to reinforce the behavior (or operant) that preceded the termination. Under these conditions, the noxiousness of a particular stimulus has often been assumed rather than empirically ascertained, and as a consequence, the offset of noxious stimulation has frequently been implicated as a reinforcer when other factors may have served in this function. In addition, the interpretation of aversion as pain has been liberally extended for humans. In the extension, environmental changes that impair the control of a valued and rewarding commodity or condition are also considered aversions. More specifically, aversions have been viewed as situations that constitute a threat to the acquisition or maintenance of some form of extrinsic reward. The finding that children's aggressiveness increases with the repeated successful defense of valued conditions—say, of toys or of a corner of a room where play proved rewarding—can thus be taken to support two different views equally well: (a) that the reduction of annoyance is reinforcing, and (b) that regaining a reward that was in jeopardy or temporarily lost constitutes the reinforcement. The case in which annoyance is operationalized as an impairment of efforts to obtain an extrinsic reward further illustrates the conceptual ambiguity: Children who, for example, fight over a toy or a candy bar may be considered to fight to terminate annoyance or to gain access to the reward. The demonstration that successful fighting increases subsequent aggressiveness again can be taken to mean either that the reduction of annoyance or that the attainment of a reward is reinforcing.

The described interpretational dilemma concerns, of course, the differentiation between *negative* and *positive reinforcement*. Many events in human affairs that prove to have reinforcement value apparently can be viewed either in terms of aversions (and thus as negative reinforcement) or in terms of rewards (and thus as positive reinforcement). The choice can be quite arbitrary. And although it does not affect the empirical assessment of the fact of reinforcement per se, it permits the display of idiosyncratic "philosophical" bents in the theory of human aggression. It seems that as long as aversions are not dealt with as experiential states, measurable in terms of their psychological and physiological manifestations, it is difficult if not impossible to determine the exact nature of reinforcement in human aggression. To dramatize this point in an illustration: Is the juvenile who robs a bank positively reinforced by the wealth he obtains, or is he negatively reinforced by the poverty he terminates? Apparently, the onset of elation coincides with the offset of misery, and the attribution of reinforcing properties to one or the other component in the change of experiential state becomes a matter of intuitive appeal. And the intuitive appeal of one or the other interpretation seems to vary as a function of one's personal convictions.

For all practical purposes, it may suffice to determine the fact that reinforcement value accrues to the *transition from aversive to less aversive or positive stimulation* as manifested in specific consecutive environmental conditions. In fact, the entire issue of whether reinforcement is negative or positive may be viewed as moot by those who are solely concerned with the prediction of outcomes on the basis of empirically assessed circumstances. The shift in emphasis—from aversions to rewards—has immense interpretative implications, however. Those who consider aggression to be primarily the result of conflict generated in the pursuit of extrinsic rewards, and who also employ instrumental learning as an explanatory mechanism (e.g., Buss, 1961, 1971), should be inclined to reassess much of the aggression others have declared to be reinforced by the alleviation of aversion and consider it to be *reinforced by the attainment of rewards or satisfiers.*

When the view that aggression is primarily reinforced by extrinsic rewards is taken, offensive aggression can be readily explained. It will be recalled that if the reduction of aversion is the designated reinforcer of aggression, the initial attack upon an opponent cannot be directly accounted for. It can be explained as stimulus–response generalization based on successful defensive fighting or, alternatively, as due to the fact that in the competition for valued commodities and conditions, at least among animals, the possibly incidental mutual infliction of aversive treatments is largely unavoidable. Placing the emphasis on rewards very much reverses this assessment. Competition over valued commodities and conditions leads to threats and attacks to ward off rivals. If these behaviors prove effective, the fighting individual gains control over the rewards and consumes them. Consumption of the obtained commodities ultimately reinforces fighting, because it serves vital needs that are entirely extrinsic to aggression itself. In terms of drive-reduction theory, aggression is not considered to be motivated by a deprivation-based drive that is reduced by fighting, but it effects drive reduction in other domains in which deprivations have induced drive states. Aggression in the hungry animal, for example, will be reinforced by securing the food being fought for. Once offensive fighting has become a habit, it may be expected to generalize to defensive aggression. This process completes the discussed reversal in the assessment of what constitutes the primary reinforcement in aggression. The reversal is not a total one, however. Although the view that aggression is aversion based can be seen as all-encompassing, with aversions inevitable in the individual's pursuit of vital objectives under naturally prevailing conditions, the alternative view that aggression is reward motivated cannot be applied successfully to situations in which rewards are not immediately apparent. As a consequence, the reward argument is usually supplemented by the notion that the termination of aversive stimulation also reinforces aggression. This supplementation is of course not contradictory at all.

The most significant aspect of the reward rationale is the assertion that *aggression is reinforced by conditions not inherent in aggression itself.* Aggressive behavior is not viewed as generating built-in satisfiers; nor is it seen as containing its own rewards. Instead, it is considered to be reinforced by any condition that satisfies a vital need. In animals, such needs concern mainly food, shelter, and mating. The satisfaction of such basic needs functions as unlearned *primary reinforcement.* However, in animals, particularly in the higher vertebrates, conditions that are contiguous with primary reinforcers may acquire reinforcement value and then serve as *secondary reinforcers* in the reinforcement of aggression (cf. Nevin, 1973). In human aggression, secondary reinforcement is considered the rule rather than the exception (e.g., Buss, 1961; Skinner, 1969). Although in some human societies, conditions that attach primary reinforcers such as food, clothing, or shelter to aggressive behavior may still exist, however, the standard of living in nearly all contemporary societies has been elevated to a point at which the basic needs (i.e., food, clothing, and shelter) are almost always satisfied without resorting to violent means. Aggression in humans, then, is hardly ever strengthened through primary reinforcers.

This state of affairs is actually rather troublesome in that it conflicts with the argument that the secondary reinforcement of aggression can readily be traced to contiguities with primary reinforcement. In general, neither the developing child nor the mature adult in our society ever fights to satisfy the most basic needs. Aggression in children (and later in adults) centers around rewards that, biologically speaking, can only be considered nonessential. The fact that early aggression in children concerns things such as toys and "territories" (cf. Patterson, Littman, & Bricker, 1967; Patterson & Reid, 1970) suggests either that the control of objects or places is intrinsically reinforcing or more likely, that their control already has acquired reinforcement value through learning mechanisms that do not necessitate contiguity with primary reinforcers (see Section C of this chapter). Given the rarity of aggression that is reinforced by basic, primary reinforcers in human ontogenesis, the proposal that the reinforcement of human aggression is generally of a secondary kind constitutes an act of faith in the theory of instrumental conditioning rather than a documented fact.

Whether particular rewards are considered primary or secondary (positive) reinforcers, there seems little doubt that in their attainment, successful aggression is favored over yielding and submission. Unlike the case of negative reinforcement through the termination of an aversion—which was viewed as potentially reinforcing submission and escape as well as successful fighting—in the competition for scarce resources, yielding is obviously not reinforced by the attainment of rewards. *Incentive-motivated successful fighting is selectively reinforced by the attainment of rewards.* This selectivity gives the advantage to the individual who is superior to his or her competitor in terms of anatomy and motor skills. In theory, it turns the strong animal or person into a vicious fighter—even in cases in which rewards were initially incidental to fighting.

The purpose of this section has been to point out the main conceptual problems regarding the application of the reinforcement concept to aggression. The discussion can be summarized as follows:

1. The modification of aggressive behavior through the contingent placement of reinforcement is not in doubt. The instrumental-learning paradigm applies to all behaviors, and aggression must be seen as just one of potentially many behavioral manifestations of interest.

2. Concerning human aggression, the alleviation of aversions and the attainment of rewards are largely appraised on intuitive grounds. As a consequence, it is often unclear whether reinforcement is negative or positive, and statements about the nature of reinforcement can be misleading.

3. The alleviation of aversion potentially reinforces both successful aggression and submission.

4. The attainment of rewards tends to selectively reinforce successful aggression.

5. Concerning the ontogenesis of human aggression, it is unclear how secondary reinforcement can be established on the basis of contiguity with primary reinforcers.

For the following sections, some pertinent research has been selected for discussion, mainly to document the type and strength of the evidence that has been aggregated in support of or in opposition to specific proposals. More comprehensive reviews of the literature on instrumental learning in aggression have been presented by Buss (1961) and Bandura (1973a).

2. Is the Infliction of Injury Reinforcing?   As indicated earlier, Skinner (1969) is a proponent of the view that aggression is mainly reinforced by the infliction of injury. He suggested (1969) that the "stimuli which reinforce aggressive action are to be found in the behavior of the recipient as he weeps, cries out, cringes, flees, or gives other signs that he has been hurt [p. 210]." Most importantly, however, he proposed that this reinforcement function of the described stimuli is innate as well as acquired.

Skinner has drawn a distinction between *phylogenic* and *ontogenic* aggression. He conceives of phylogenic aggression as aggressive behavior that is accompanied by autonomic responses. Autonomic reactions, in turn, are seen to enhance the survival value of aggression in the naturally selective "tooth-and-claw competition" by providing the energy for vigorous activity. The infliction of injury in phylogenic aggression is considered a primary reinforcer. In an illustration, Skinner in fact suggests that hurting is as natural to the angry individual as eating is to the hungry one. Ontogenic aggression, in contrast, is conceived of as aggressive behavior that is individually acquired. It is considered autonomically flat or "cold," comparable to such behaviors as food getting. Damage to others (1969) "may function as a conditioned reinforcer because signs of damage have preceded or coincided with reinforcers which do not otherwise have anything to do with aggression [p. 210]." However, autonomic reactivity is seen to enter ontogenic aggression rather freely, providing the basis for feelings associated with this type of aggression. The excitatory component of ontogenic aggression, then, is considered phylogenic. In ontogenic aggression, as Skinner (1969) put it, "an *innate capacity to be reinforced by damage to others* traceable to phylogenic contingencies may give rise to the autonomic pattern associated with phylogenic aggression [p. 211; italics added]."

In Skinner's view, the topography of fighting is more effectively shaped and maintained by immediate feedback of damage than by eventual success. Aggression is thus seen to be reinforced most directly by the infliction of injury. Later reinforcement, through the attainment of rewards not related to aggression as such or through the alleviation of an aversion, seems to serve mainly to strengthen the more immediate reinforcers—signs of damage, that is.

Signs of damage are also considered to reinforce behavior that does not itself inflict damage. And though it is unclear how the presumed re- inforcement value of witnessing the infliction of injury by others upon others can be systematically and constructively utilized in human affairs, Skinner feels that the popularity of aggressive sports such as boxing, wrestling, and football is best explained by the fact that patronage of the spectacle is reinforced by the signs of damage.

Finally, Skinner proposed that hostility is entirely ontogenic. In his view, hostile actions that inflict harm upon an opponent through, for example, personal insult, cursing, or the bringing of bad news may be reinforced by contingencies arranged by a so-called verbal community. These contingen- cies, however, are seen as not having prevailed long enough, phylogenetically speaking, to warrant the assumption that the infliction of harm functions analogously to the infliction of injury. The autonomic component of phylogenic aggression is apparently considered lacking in hostility. Hostility, it seems, is by necessity "cool." This view is also taken with regard to the use of recently developed weapons. The infliction of injury with such weapons is considered acquired and not inherited. In Skinner's view, then, the elements of phylogenic aggression that enter ontogenic aggression clearly favor the tooth-and-claw variety of fighting. Apparently, along with other aggressive species, man is seen as deeply entrenched in this kind of archetypal aggression.

The assertion that the infliction of injury may serve as a primary reinforcer of aggression is rarely put forth in contemporary psychology, but the notion that signs of damage can acquire reinforcement value is more widely held. Concerning human aggression, Sears, Maccoby, and Levin (1957) suggested that signs of pain and injury may become rewarding: (a) because of their repeated association with relief of the tensions deriving from the conflict between aggressive inclinations and fear of adverse consequences, or (b) because of their consistent association with the overcoming of frustrations (cf. Sears, 1958). In either case, signs of damage are seen as coinciding with the termination of an aversion, and consequently, the nature of the reinforcement acquired by these signs is viewed as negative.

Bandura (1973a) has also suggested that if signs of damage should prove reinforcing, this reinforcement is likely to derive from the relief of discomfort. "The alleviation of aversive treatment from an injured oppressor rather than his suffering may be the primary source of satisfaction [p. 198]." The possibility that signs of damage become positive reinforcers of aggression through their repeated connection with extrinsic rewards is left open, however. Bandura has furthermore stressed a contingency that has been largely overlooked by those who consider the role of the cues of pain and injury to be critical: He proposed that when aggressors suffer reprisals or self-contempt for hurting others, signs of suffering should come to function as a deterrent to aggression rather than a reinforcer.

Feshbach (1970) has recently taken a very different approach to the presumed reinforcement value of signs of pain and injury. He posited that through observational learning and precept, the individual acquires norms of retaliation. Once adopted, these norms exert a certain degree of control over behaviors related to self-esteem. In Feshbach's view, being successfully aggressed against tends to lower self-esteem, and retaliatory actions provide the means to regain the lost esteem—and possibly to enhance the self. The norms of retaliation demand the reciprocation of aversive stimulation: An eye for an eye! If an aggressor has inflicted injury, he or she must be injured in return. It is the feedback from successful retaliatory efforts that, according to Feshbach, restores self-esteem and hence is gratifying and reinforcing.

In contrast to suggestions that signs of damage reinforce aggressive behavior (positively or negatively, as the case may be), it has also been proposed that such signs generally inhibit aggression. The argument has its roots in ethology and in common observation.

In ethology, Lorenz (e.g., 1963) has taken the view that in intraspecific aggression, signs of damage frequently function as unlearned signals that prevent further assault. Such signals simply are considered to have evolved as, for example, in the case of the "blood spots" in young rails discussed earlier. At times, the inhibitory effect of signs of damage is viewed as partly acquired through learning, however. Morris (1968) regards the expression of pain and the display of injury as specific manifestations of a more general category of signs: submission gestures. Submissive behavior functions, of course, to prevent or terminate rather than to further instigate aggression.

Common observation leads to similar expectations. Since signs of damage usually occur near the end and immediately after a fight, the interpretation that these signs were causally involved in the termination of aggression is understandable. Cultural norms concerning aggression tend to make this "intuitive appraisal" even more compelling: Strictly enforced social norms prohibit further aggression against opponents who apparently have been defeated. In other words, the inhibition of aggression is trained as a response to submission, especially when the submission is associated with pain and injury; and this training may prompt the belief that signs of damage are, in fact, inhibitory. The individual may "detect" feelings of pity—feelings that, in self-assessment, prevent him or her from further attacking the victim.

Finally, the inhibition of aggression can also be predicted from an empathy point of view. Investigators of empathy, from McDougall (1908) to Stotland (1969), have suggested that witnessing distress in another person induces a comparable affective reaction in the observer. If so, the aggressor continuing an attack upon a person in pain would place him- or herself in a greater state of discomfort (e.g., Baron, 1971b, 1971d). The aggressor can avoid this noxious experience by stopping the fight.

Interestingly, all these suggestions of an aggression-inhibiting effect of signs of damage are not, as it might appear, contradictory to the proposal that such signs reinforce aggression. Reinforcement affects the *recurrence* of aggression, and the possibility that signs of damage cause the inhibition of aggression does not exclude the possibility that the likelihood of subsequent aggression will increase. In fact, from the point of view of instrumental learning, it could be argued that if these signs serve the inhibition of aggression, the inhibitory function is an important prerequisite for the signs' acquisition of reinforcement value: The inhibitory function assures a close association between signs of damage and the termination of fighting. The acquisition of reinforcement value of the signs fully depends on the contingencies of reinforcement that prevail after the termination of fighting, and these contingencies are clearly not altered by the immediate impact of the signs. In short, there is no contradiction in the view that signs of damage can serve a dual function: They effect the immediate inhibition of aggression and promote later aggression. However, many investigators who believe that signs of pain and injury serve the inhibition of aggression have implied that at least as far as human aggression is concerned, the inhibiting exposure to such cues will come to effect the inhibition of aggression generally. Exposure to signs of damage, together with the anticipation of social disapproval, seems to be considered a highly aversive condition. If this aversive condition is treated as a form of punishment contingent upon the successful yet injurious execution of aggressive activities, one should indeed expect that aggression would be generally discouraged by the display of the damage.

The foregoing discussion shows that many notions about the possible effects of the knowledge that one has hurt someone are being entertained. In contrast, there are only a few empirical investigations that could help decide which notions are to be favored and which are to be discarded. The grand speculations concerning the evolution of the function of signs of damage, to be sure, have eluded decisive empirical evaluation altogether. Skinner (1969) based his proposal that man is equipped with an innate capacity to be reinforced by such signs on a single study done on squirrel monkeys (Azrin, Hutchinson, & McLaughlin, 1965). This study is ambiguous as far as evolutionary considerations are concerned (for a detailed discussion, see Chapter 3, Section B), as are other animal studies that could be drawn upon (e.g., Cole & Parker, 1971; Dreyer & Church, 1970; Legrand, 1970). Lorenz (1963) based his suggestion that signs of damage may inhibit aggression on some informal observations of lower vertebrates. The phylogenetic proposals of the discussed function of the cues are thus entirely without an acceptable empirical foundation in animal research. Phylogenetic speculation aside, we now turn to investigations of human aggression to determine which view is favored by the available evidence.

Patterson and his associates (Patterson, Littman, & Bricker, 1967; Patterson & Reid, 1970) have investigated aggressive exchanges in children through participant observation. Observers, who were placed in groups of interactants, recorded the occurrence of various behaviors of interest as unobtrusively as possible. Their records were used to determine the frequency of specific activities that precipitated and followed aggression. Under these conditions, it was observed that the infliction of pain by a "skilled" aggressor characteristically prompted the victim: (a) to yield his or her territory, (b) to give up his or her toy, or (c) to cry. "When any of these *positive* consequences occurred, the attack terminated" (Patterson & Cobb, 1973, p. 155; italics added). Patterson et al. (1967) explicitly treat the witnessed expression of pain, that is, *crying,* along with the attainment of extrinsic rewards as a *positive reinforcer of aggression.*

Such an interpretation is highly questionable, however, for several reasons. Most importantly, the observational data presented fail to document that crying is, as suggested, a reinforcer of aggression. The research method employed simply does not permit a conclusive evaluation of the effect that crying, in and of itself, may have had on the successful fighter's subsequent aggression. Furthermore, since there is no stipulation that witnessed crying be considered a secondary reinforcer nor any indication of a process through which it may acquire reinforcement value, crying is apparently treated as a primary positive reinforcer. This assessment seems quite arbitrary. The finding that the victim's crying tended to coincide with the termination of fighting, particularly in view of the uncertain reinforcement value of such crying, can alternatively be seen to confirm the proposal that the expression of pain inhibits continued attack and possibly acquires reinforcement value for the successful attacker through its connection with the attainment of rewards. Independent of alternative considerations, the findings reported by Patterson et al. (1967) clearly do not demand that the victim's crying be viewed as a reinforcing positive consequence of an aggressive assault. All the data show is that crying, at least for the victim of aggression, is a characteristic subsequent condition of fighting. Reinforcement value aside, the data even leave unanswered the question of whether crying is a critical cue in the cessation of attack. It is conceivable that in humans, as in many other animal species, further attack is averted mainly because the opponent stops resisting and yields embattled objects or conditions. It is doubtful that crying, if not associated with yielding, would terminate an aggressive struggle over sought-after rewards or, for that matter, that it would promote later aggression by the attacker. Unfortunately, unequivocal data on this point are not available, and thus the "biological" signal function of crying in children, be it the inhibition or the reinforcement of aggression or both, remains to be demonstrated.

Concerning the more general proposal that signs of damage function as reinforcers of aggression, whether the sign function is presumed inherent or acquired, some experimental data have been collected on human adults, and the findings do permit an evaluation of this proposal.

In a first investigation pertinent to this issue, Buss (1966a) explored the consequences of inflicting bodily damage upon a victim on subsequent aggression against another victim. Subjects were called upon to serve as "experimenters" conducting a learning study. They were to provide feedback to the learners: light signals for correct responses and shock for erroneous ones, with the intensity of shock to be determined by them as experimenters. Both learners, that is, both victims, were experimental confederates who presented all subjects with the same schedule of "errors." The critical experimental manipulation was applied at the end of the first learning session. In the harm condition, the first victim—who ostensibly had received the shocks via a finger electrode that the subject had attached to him or her—

looked perplexed and somewhat upset when the subject removed the electrode. He or she complained of having no sensation in the finger and of not being able to move it. The victim insisted that the actual experimenter be called and that his or her finger be treated immediately. The first victim was ushered away, and the second victim was introduced. The subject then conducted the learning session with the second victim. In the control condition, the first victim reported no damage and voiced no complaints. During the second session, subjects thus either believed or did not believe they had inflicted injury upon the learner in the first session. Sex of subject and sex of victim were factorially varied with the experimental treatment, with both victims of any one subject being of the same sex.

The findings show that when no harm was inflicted upon the first victim, the magnitude of punitive measures directed against the second victim differed only negligibly from that directed toward the first victim. If anything, there was a tendency for aggressiveness, as measured in the intensity of shock delivered, to increase slightly from the first to the second victim. In sharp contrast, when the first victim had apparently suffered some bodily damage, the magnitude of punitive measures directed against the second victim decreased substantially. This effect was not uniform across sex conditions, however. The infliction of damage proved to reduce aggressiveness more in female than in male subjects. It also proved to reduce aggressiveness more for female than for male victims. These effects were additive. The largest reduction of aggressiveness was thus observed in the condition in which both the subject and the victim were female. Both mixed-sex arrangements yielded intermediate levels of reduction. Finally, in the condition in which both the subject and the victim were male, the reduction proved negligible and nonsignificant. Buss suggested (1966a) that the lack of an effect in the latter condition derives from differences in the acculturation of the sexes with regard to aggression. "Evidently, men are expected to be able to take considerable pain and perhaps even harm and the aggressor's awareness that he has hurt or harmed a male victim apparently has no effect on subsequent aggression [p. 254]." Granted that in male-male aggression, the infliction of injury may be of little moment, Buss' findings provide strong evidence that signs of damage do not reinforce aggression. In fact, with the exception of intermale aggressiveness, signs of damage clearly inhibit subsequent aggression.

In another investigation, Buss (1966b) examined the consequences of the victim's expression of pain on subsequent aggression against the same victim. The basic experimental procedure was as described earlier, but there was only one victim. The feedback from the subject's punitive responses was manipulated as follows: In the condition in which the victim expressed suffering, he or she gasped, groaned, or cried out in pain whenever the subject used high shock levels (8, 9, or 10). He or she also gave similar feedback half the time when the subject used intermediate shock levels (6 or 7). At lower shock levels, the victim gave no feedback. In the control condition, the victim remained silent throughout the learning session. The experiment also involved variations in sex of subject, sex of victim, and degree of frustration.

The victim's expression of pain was found to reduce aggression against him or her substantially. Unlike in the case of bodily damage, the expression of pain had a highly uniform effect. Neither the sex of the subject nor the sex of the victim modified the impact, and degree of frustration exerted only a minor influence. This assessment is corroborated by the analysis of shock blocks. Of particular interest is the finding that the expression of pain *successively* lowered aggressiveness. That is, during the learning session, the gradient associated with aggressiveness following the expression of pain fell more and more below that associated with aggressiveness in the control condition. Under conditions that must be considered ideal for the demonstration of the reinforcing effect of pain, the evidence is counter to the reinforcement notion. Buss' findings, taken together, not only deny the reinforcement claim but show pain to be a potent inhibitor of subsequent aggression.

Geen (1970) reported data that confirm Buss' findings. Male subjects were aggressively instigated by receiving a seemingly unfair number of shocks from a confederate, the later victim, in evaluation of their opinions. Control subjects were treated by the confederate in a neutral manner, receiving no shocks at all. In the experimental procedure devised by Buss (e.g., 1966b), subjects then delivered shock to the victim. In the feedback condition, the victim registered discomfort by making short exclamations whenever shock was delivered. In the control, he remained silent. Under these conditions, Geen observed that the victim's expression of pain significantly reduced aggressiveness as measured in the intensity of shock delivered. Whether subjects had been aggressively instigated or were treated in a neutral manner, signs of pain lowered aggression to equal degrees.

The aggression-inhibiting effect of pain cues was further documented in a series of studies conducted by Baron. Baron (1971d) investigated the effect of the magnitude of the victim's pain on subsequent aggression. Male subjects were led to believe that the victim was hooked up to a "psychoautonomic pain meter," a fictitious apparatus said to integrate physiological responses. The procedure devised by Buss was employed, and in this context, the subject had to deliver shock for "errors" made by the victim. The subject was exposed to the pain meter, and it was his job to record the readings. He was thus made aware of the pain suffered by the victim. The bogus apparatus was controlled by the experimenter as follows: In a low-pain condition, the needle was made to point to "none," "mild," and "moderate" whenever the subject used shock intensities 1–3, 4–6, and 7–10, respectively; in a moderate-pain condition, the needle deflected to "mild," "moderate," and "strong" whenever the subject used the aforementioned intensities; in a high-pain condition, the needle jumped to "moderate," "strong," and "very strong" whenever these intensities were used. In a procedure analogous to the one employed by Geen (1970), the subjects were aggressively instigated or treated in a neutral manner beforehand.

Baron observed that aggressiveness, as measured in the intensity and duration of shock delivered, was inversely proportional to the magnitude of pain ostensibly experienced by the victim. Aggressiveness decreased as the intensity of pain increased, and it did so equally for provoked and unprovoked subjects. The findings are thus in total agreement with those reported by Geen (1970).

In a very similar investigation with male subjects, Baron (1971b) included a variation in the social relationship of aggressor and victim: student against student compared with student against a blue-collar worker. Information about the victim's intense pain again proved to reduce aggression substantially, whether or not the subjects were aggressively instigated and whether or not they had the same socioeconomic and educational status.

A study by Rule and Leger (1976) gives further evidence that pain cues inhibit rather than reinforce aggressive behavior. These investigators employed the pain-meter procedure devised by Baron (e.g., 1971d), providing both provoked and unprovoked male subjects with feedback of the victim's minor or severe pain reaction. The indication that the victim suffered pain acutely was found to reduce aggressive behavior in provoked and unprovoked subjects alike. This uniform inhibitory effect was assessed in both the intensity and duration of electric shock delivered to the victim.

In yet another related study with males, Baron (1974a) stepped up the subject's aggressive instigation in order to learn if at least at higher levels of anger, the provision of information about the victim's suffering would reinforce aggression. In the provocation condition, the subject's performance on a task was reprimanded and additionally "evaluated" with a seemingly unfair number of electric shocks. In the control condition, the subject received a favorable evaluation and no shocks at all. Feedback of the victim's pain was again provided through the bogus pain meter. The study also included conditions in which the subject first witnessed another person deliver shock to a victim, with either no feedback from the victim or with pain feedback that was totally ignored by the aggressor.

Witnessing the aggressor, whether he did not receive feedback from the victim or ignored the feedback of pain, increased aggressiveness. However, this effect was independent of the effect of receiving feedback of pain from the subject's own victim. More important here, regardless of whether or not an aggressive model had been witnessed, feedback of the victim's suffering failed to exert an overall effect. Its effect was found to vary as a function of the level of instigation to aggression. Aggressiveness, measured by both the intensity and duration of shock delivered, tended to be reduced by information about the victim's pain only in nonangry subjects (according to a significant differentiation of these conditions on shock duration). In angry subjects, such information failed to exert any reliable effect.

As far as unprovoked persons are concerned, these findings further corroborate the earlier ones: Signs of damage and pain inhibit rather than reinforce subsequent aggression. With regard to aggressively instigated persons, however, the findings show that acutely angry people—in this study, males—may well continue to punish their tormentor even though he displays signs of discomfort and pain. Granted that under these circumstances, signs of damage do not inhibit aggression, it should be clear that the data on hand in no way support the contention that such signs reinforce aggression.

An investigation on human subjects by Feshbach, Stiles, and Bitter (1967) seems to have generated some tentative support for the contention that in the aggressively instigated individual, information about a tormentor's suffering can reinforce other behaviors, although not necessarily aggression. Feshbach et al. adapted a research paradigm employed in studies of verbal conditioning (cf. Greenspoon, 1955, 1962; Kanfer, 1968; Krasner, 1958). They suggested that witnessing the infliction of pain upon an annoyer should function as a positive reinforcer for verbal responses in a manner similar to the placement of verbal and nonverbal signs of approval (e.g., "good," "mm-hmm," and head nodding) that proved effective in verbal conditioning. It was thus expected that the frequency of an utterance would increase if it was followed by exposure to the annoyer's expression of pain.

In the study by Feshbach et al. (1967), female subjects were initially either treated rudely and evaluated in a highly derogatory fashion by a male accomplice or treated politely by him. This accomplice then was to perform a task in the adjacent room, and the subject's assignment was to observe him through a one-way mirror and rate the degree to which he appeared relaxed or tense at various times. The subject was told that the other person would be performing the task under conditions of stress. The stressor was to be electric shock applied at random intervals. In a control condition, a light signal replaced the shock treatment. Purportedly as a distraction to avoid a set effect in the stress ratings, the subject was instructed to form sentences between ratings. These sentences were to involve stimulus words provided by the experimenter. The stipulation was to use the verb and one of six pronouns—*I, we, they, he, she,* or *you*—that were presented on a card. Whenever the subjects used "we" or "they" in a sentence, the shock vs. light treatment was applied. After using one of these words, the subjects either witnessed the confederate jerk up his arm in apparent pain or saw a light flash behind the confederate without any notable impact on his behavior.

The findings are suggestive and puzzling at the same time. Feshbach et al. (1967) observed that compared to preconditioning frequencies, the combined frequency of the use of "we" and "they" increased for subjects who had been provoked and were exposed to the annoyer's shock treatment and that this frequency declined for subjects who had not been provoked yet witnessed the other person's suffering. With the margin of increase in the former condition being roughly the same as that of the decline in the latter one, the frequencies in these two conditions were reliably different. The combined frequency of the use of "we" and "they" dropped considerably for subjects who had been provoked but witnessed only their annoyer's exposure to nonaversive light flashes. Frequency levels in this condition were similar to those in the condition combining the subject's neutral treatment with witnessing the other person suffer. In comparing the effect on provoked subjects of witnessing the annoyer suffer from shock and his merely being exposed to light signals, the frequency of the utterances followed by these contingencies was significantly higher when pain cues were provided than when the events were entirely innocuous.

At this point, the data appear reasonably clear-cut. Exposure to an annoyer's expression of pain seems to function as a positive reinforcer of precipitating behavior—exactly as proposed. One may consider it problematic, however, that the reinforcement effect derives partly (about half of it) from the frequency-depressing effect in the control conditions. Roughly speaking, witnessing the other person suffer functioned as much as a deterrent for unprovoked subjects as it did as a reinforcer for provoked ones. Only the combined deterrent–reinforcement effect proved reliable. A convincing demonstration of the reinforcement value of the annoyer's suffering requires that it unilaterally produce a significant increase in the occurrence of the reinforced behavior over preconditioning levels. Such an effect was not obtained, however.

The findings are further compromised. First, witnessing the light flash behind the other person proved nearly as reinforcing for unprovoked subjects as witnessing him suffer pain was for provoked subjects. The reinforcement value of these contingencies was statistically equivalent; that is, the reinforcement value of pain cues for angry subjects never reliably exceeded that of light signals for nonangry ones. Assuming that irrelevant light flashes cannot contain much reward value, the rewarding power of pain cues must appear quite limited. Second, the findings seem quite fragile in that they are based entirely on the frequency of just one word used—the word *they*. For some unidentifiable reason, the word *we* eluded conditioning altogether. Feshbach et al. reported two earlier tests in which the word *we* also yielded only unreliable findings. Given such inconsistencies, the findings should be treated with caution.

Although the findings reported by Feshbach et al. (1967) fail to demonstrate convincingly that seeing one's annoyer suffer is reinforcing, they do show that the reinforcement value of witnessing an annoyer in pain exceeds that of witnessing a neutral person in pain. However, with equal justification it can be said that the data show the deterrent value of seeing a neutral person suffer exceeds that of seeing an annoyer suffer. The former experience, according to the findings, tends to be as much avoided as the latter exposure tends to be sought out. If we give credence to the positive and negative changes in the frequency of the operant brought about by the conditioning procedure, the provoked subject's exposure to the tormentor's pain can be viewed as pleasing, satisfying, and rewarding to some extent. At the same time, the unprovoked subject's exposure to the neutral person's pain must be considered unpleasant, disturbing, and noxious.

Such an interpretation is consistent with recent findings on affective reactions to the display of pain by others (Zillmann & Cantor, 1977). In an investigation with children, it was observed that witnessing a nasty person suffer is enjoyable, whereas witnessing a nice person suffer is not only not enjoyable but annoying. Interestingly, the suffering of a neutral, but not particularly nice, person proved disturbing rather than enjoyable.

Together with the findings reported by Feshbach et al., these and other observations (e.g., Bramel, Taub, & Blum, 1968) suggest that the annoyed person may well enjoy seeing his or her annoyer suffer. This enjoyment should constitute reward value, which in turn should function as a reinforcer. However, when the reinforcement of aggression through exposure to pain cues is being considered, conceptual problems arise. Information about an annoyer's suffering seems to be particularly appreciated, and hence reinforcing, when the angry person him- or herself fails to act aggressively upon the annoyer. Retaliatory aggressive action, if taken, may also provide feedback of suffering, but as discussed earlier, the possible reinforcement value of this feedback is almost necessarily confounded with a variety of potentially more powerful positive and negative reinforcers. The case of the infliction of damage upon the tormentor by others, particularly the case of his or her accidental victimization, is of interest because it provides conditions under which the presumed reinforcement effect of pain cues can manifest itself without the indicated confoundings. In terms of theory, these cases have revealing implications: If, for the provoked individual, signs of his or her annoyer's suffering should prove to have reinforcement value, the infliction of suffering through events not controlled by the angry person would reinforce his or her *non*aggressive behavior. To the extent, then, that annoyers get the treatment they deserve through the action of others or by accident, signs of damage should reinforce the provoked person's patience, self-control, and belief that things will turn out all right without his or her resorting to violent means. The point to be made here is that whereas the presumed reinforcement value of signs of damage could promote aggression in certain situations, in others, it could increase the likelihood of nonaggressive activities.

In summing up, it can be said that the search for the reinforcement value of signs of damage has produced mainly negative results.

1. Signs of damage failed to reinforce aggression. With the possible exception of intermale aggression, signs of damage proved to exert a strong inhibitory effect on later aggression.

2. The victim's experience and expression of pain failed to reinforce aggression. In unprovoked and in slightly provoked individuals, information about the victim's suffering inhibited subsequent aggression. In more severely provoked individuals, the victim's suffering did not inhibit subsequent aggression, but neither did it reinforce it.

3. Witnessing an annoyer suffer seems pleasing, whereas witnessing a neutral person suffer seems disturbing. The former condition may function as a reinforcer, the latter as a deterrent. The control of aggression by such reinforcers or deterrents has not been demonstrated, however.

4. There is no evidence whatever that could be construed as support for the notion that signs of damage and expressions of pain are inherently reinforcing.

3. Incentive Theory.   We will refer to the notion that aggression is primarily committed in order to control positive reinforcers as "incentive theory." Buss (1961, 1971), who is the main proponent of this view, has suggested that in our society and in most others, aggression is so ubiquitous a phenomenon because it generally yields a significant payoff. In short, *aggression pays.* It produces benefits for the aggressor, and the experience of being benefited reinforces aggression. Or alternatively, the experience of having been benefited by aggression creates the anticipation of additional benefits, thereby motivating further aggression. Buss acknowledges the realm of "angry," emotional aggression, that is, of annoyance-motivated aggressive behavior directed at terminating the annoyance (or at negative reinforcers, if a Skinnerian terminology is preferred). He feels, however, that "instrumental" aggression, committed "in cold blood" to obtain incentives, is the more important phenomenon. In what appears to be a reaction against the pervasiveness of the frustration–aggression hypothesis in aggression theory, Buss suggested (1971) that "angry aggression has probably been over-emphasized in theoretical accounts of aggression," and that "most aggression appears to be instrumental [pp. 10, 11]." It is his contention that instrumental aggression is predominant: (a) because of an ever-present competition for rewards; and (b) because in this competition, an aggressive maneuver "tends to guarantee acquiring the reinforcer [p. 11]," whereas possible nonaggressive actions hold only a low probability for success. Observational data on children largely confirm the conclusion that aggression indeed pays more often than not (e.g., Patterson & Cobb, 1971; Patterson, Littman, & Bricker, 1967), but the data on violent actions among children, among adults, and between adults and children generally do not support the claim that incentive-motivated aggression is more characteristic than annoyance-motivated aggression. This issue is taken up in Chapter 5.

Regardless of whether incentive-motivated or annoyance-motivated aggression predominates, the view that aggression is often controlled by incentives is widely held in aggression theory (cf. Bandura & Walters, 1963b; Patterson & Cobb, 1973). In fact, irrespective of theoretical considerations, the notion is so broadly accepted that it may appear to be common sense. Obviously, killers kill, robbers rob, and muggers mug for money, and children fight over candy and toys.

It would be an oversimplification of incentive theory, however, to say that only such apparent, tangible rewards are being viewed as incentives. Incentives are equated, in theory at least, with all types of positive reinforcers. Any condition that proves to exert the influence of a positive reinforcer is thus to be considered an incentive. Nevertheless, in practice, the incentive status of particular conditions is determined mainly on intuitive grounds rather than on the basis of the documentation of reinforcement value. If an object or condition appears desirable and a high degree of consensus among people can be assumed, it is declared an incentive. The magnitude of an incentive is similarly assessed: Incentive value increases with the degree to which objects or circumstances are deemed desirable.

Buss (1971) has proposed three major classes of incentives: gain of money, prestige, and status. Bandura (1973a) distinguished tangible rewards and social or status rewards. Incentives are thus not restricted to corporeal entities but involve such intangibles as increased self-confidence and self-enhancement through the approval of others. The inclusion of intangibles has broadened the scope of incentive theory far beyond skirmishes over food, mate, and shelter. It has made it possible to apply the theory to uniquely human situations: to conflicts over commodities with no survival value whatsoever, to social benefits of similar distinction, and to desirable traits with little "cash value."

At the same time, however, this extension has created many ambiguities both at the conceptual and the operational levels. Conceptually, it seems again to be a mere act of faith in the theory of operant learning to believe that all nontangible rewards can be considered secondary reinforcers readily traceable to linkages with primary reinforcement. More importantly, at the operational level it is frequently difficult to reach agreement on whether or not something is an incentive for a particular person and if it is, on how much incentive value it holds. The ambiguity concerning the magnitude of incentive also applies to the seemingly best defined tangibles: monetary incentives. The reward value of money apparently varies inversely with a person's wealth: A given amount is a greater incentive for the poor than for the rich. The ambiguity here appears trivial, however, when compared to such intangibles as prestige and "making a good impression on the opposite sex." Returning to conceptual matters, the issue of positive vs. negative reinforcement discussed earlier also seems to plague intangible incentives. It is difficult to decide, at least at times, whether aggressive actions are being reinforced by the attainment of what appear to be incentives or whether the seemingly positive reinforcers are simply prominent signals that terminate an aversion, thus reversing the nature of reinforcement to negative. For example, is a gain in prestige rewarding because it makes life more enjoyable or because it ends the humiliations associated with inferior status? Such questions tend to be decided in favor of whatever is more noticeable—the aversive experience or the euphoria following self-enhancement.

In spite of these conceptual and operational difficulties concerning incentives, incentive theory has proven valuable. Historically, it has helped to correct the preoccupation with "aggression because of aggravation" and has drawn attention to "aggression for self-enhancement." Common observation certainly confirms that aggression in pursuit of furthering the individual's "quality of life" is widespread. In accounts of aggression, incentive-motivated aggression must therefore be recognized as a unique domain of aggressive behavior. It should be kept in mind, however, that the overly liberal interpretation of incentives—that is, the detection of reward value for almost every aggressive act—would be as futile as the overly liberal use of the frustration concept. After all, the overcoming of frustration via aggression can almost always be interpreted as self-enhancing, and aggressive self-enhancement through incentives can almost always be interpreted as overcoming frustration.

Incentive theory is unequivocally supported by a bulk of empirical data. Evidence that would challenge the notion is conspicuously absent. The relevant literature has been competently reviewed elsewhere (e.g., Bandura, 1973a; Bandura & Walters, 1963b; Buss, 1961). Suffice it here to indicate some of the pertinent findings.

In research with animals, food is, as one would expect, a potent incentive for the hungry animal. Essentially, aggressive responses, like nonaggressive responses, can be controlled by the frequency and the specific placement of positive reinforcement. It has been shown, for example, that animals readily fight when reinforced by food and moreover, that their specific fighting action can be quite arbitrarily shaped by the appropriate placement of incentives (Reynolds, Catania, & Skinner, 1963). The placement of food after fighting not only converts nonaggressive animals into aggressive ones, but the animal's aggressiveness also increases with the frequency of reinforcement. These effects can be reversed, however. When the provision of food is made noncontingent upon specific responses, aggressive reactions are soon extinguished, and the once aggressive animal returns to its initial nonaggressive behavior (Azrin & Hutchinson, 1967). On the other hand, aggressive modes of behavior, once established, can be maintained by the occasional administration of incentives (Stachnik, Ulrich, & Mabry, 1966a, 1966b).

In studying the effects of incentives on the aggressive behavior of children, Walters and his associates employed marbles as tangible rewards. Cowan and Walters (1963) explored the consequences of different reinforcement schedules. Boys were rewarded for attacking an automated clown: (a) after every punch they threw at it, (b) after every 3rd punch, or (c) after every 6th punch. All schedules elevated attacking behavior. After the administration of incentives was discontinued, boys who had been continuously rewarded for punching attacked the least, whereas existinction manifested itself comparatively slowly in boys who had been intermittently rewarded. Boys who had been rewarded only for 1 punch out of 6 persisted the longest in their attacks on the clown. Walters and Brown (1963), in an important investigation, further demonstrated that the intermittent reinforcement of specific attack responses may generalize to other attack reactions. Boys received "aggression" training; that is, they attacked a clown and (a) were rewarded for every punch they landed, (b) were rewarded for every 6th punch, or (c) were not rewarded at all for punching. An additional group did not get an opportunity to punch the clown. The children then either were severely frustrated (the movie they were watching was interrupted, and their candy was confiscated) or were permitted to engage in pleasant activities. Thereafter, their behavior was observed in competitive games and in unrestricted play situations, with every act of interpersonal hostility and aggression being recorded. Under these conditions of interaction, it was found that the boys who had been intermittently rewarded for punching behaved far more aggressively than those in all other conditions. Continuous reward failed to generalize from clown punching to other situations. The aggressiveness of boys in this condition was at a level comparable to that of boys who either had never been rewarded for punching or who had not had the opportunity to punch the clown. Frustration failed altogether to exert a reliable effect on aggressiveness—a finding that further corroborates our earlier assessment of the likely consequences of this variable.

Buss has conducted several investigations on the instrumental value of aggression (1963, 1966b, 1971) that bear on the function of incentives in adult aggression. He (1963) observed that in males and females alike, the prospect of gaining a favorable self-evaluation, a monetary incentive, or a better course grade elevated the level of aggressiveness above that of conditions in which such prospects were absent. Unlike females, males proved particularly susceptible to monetary incentives. Later studies (1966b, 1971) confirmed that aggression indeed increases when it holds promise for a more favorable self-evaluation. In the latter of the two investigations, after committing highly aggressive responses, the subjects actually received information about the successful approach of their goal. They were made to see aggression work.

And as aggression worked toward an incentive condition, its intensity increased.

Gaebelein (1973b) provided monetary incentives for intense aggressive responses and observed that this treatment markedly elevated the level of aggressiveness in males. Additionally, she (1973a) confirmed the sex differences encountered by Buss regarding the incentive value of money. Men were again found to be far more susceptible to monetary incentives than women. Money proved to have only a negligible effect on the aggressive behavior of females, a finding that seems in accord with the demonstration that money is altogether less salient for females than it is for males (cf. Garland & Brown, 1972; Wernimont & Fitzpatrick, 1972).

Observational data on juvenile gangs seem to suggest that prestige and superior social status, as incentives, motivate much aggression (e.g., Miller, 1958; Short & Strodtbeck, 1964), with intergang rivalry following similar lines (e.g., Wolfgang & Ferracuti, 1967; Yablonsky, 1962). At the same time, such data show that status-determining skirmishes, which make up far more than half of all "aggressive" encounters in gangs, are for the most part verbal battles (e.g., Miller, Geertz, & Cutter, 1961). The incentive of status thus seems mainly to promote hostility—even in outspokenly violent gangs.

Social approval and encouragement, frequently referred to as "social reinforcement," have also been shown to promote aggression. Aggressiveness in children was found to increase substantially as the children were praised for aggressive assaults (Patterson, Ludwig, & Sonoda, 1961). Females were observed to deliver increasingly intense shocks when "rewarded" by the experimenter's saying "good" (Staples & Walters, 1964). Similarly, males were found to become increasingly aggressive as a result of the experimenter's expression of approval in the comments, "that's good" and "you're doing fine" (Geen & Pigg, 1970). This observation was confirmed and extended by the finding that male subjects having received this reinforcement tended to persist in an aggressive mode of behavior for some time after verbal support was discontinued (Geen & Stonner, 1971). Persisting aggressiveness seems to be restricted, however, to situations that are laden with aggressive connotations (Geen & Stonner, 1973).

In the light of this supportive evidence, the effect of social approval and encouragement on aggression is not in doubt. There is some controversy, however, as to whether enforcing a response by saying "good" or nodding one's head should be considered operant conditioning (cf. Buss, 1971; Dulany, 1961). The possibility that subjects become aware of the reinforcement contingency placed upon them (cf. Spielberger, 1965) and become apprehensive in ways that bias the results has not been eliminated conclusively and thus raises questions of validity. More importantly, however, the findings are open to alternative interpretations. Geen and his colleagues (e.g., Geen & Stonner, 1973), for instance, have accepted the reinforcement formulation and suggested that social reinforcement *increases the strength of aggressive habits.* Such an interpretation would explain their finding that reinforced aggression to some extent generalizes to novel situations. Bandura (1973a), on the other hand, has taken issue with this account and favors the view that the findings reflect differential *restraint reduction.* According to this notion, the subjects became more aggressive as they were exposed to approving and encouraging comments and interjections, because their inhibitions against aggression were removed—without necessarily altering habit strength. In support of this view, Bandura cites the finding, reported by Staples and Walters (1964), that females who showed particularly strong inhibitory tendencies became only slightly more aggressive in response to praise for highly aggressive reactions, whereas females not so strongly inhibited showed substantial increments in aggression when praised. Assuming that comments such as "good," if rewarding at all, are equally rewarding for strongly aggression-inhibited and not so strongly inhibited females, this finding is indeed at variance with the proposal that the observed effects of social approval on aggression result from increments in habit strength.

A recent investigation by Borden (1975) provides more compelling evidence against the habit-strength interpretation of the aggression-facilitating effect of social approval. Borden employed a task (cf. Taylor, 1967) in which the subject sets the level of shock his or her opponent will receive if the opponent is defeated on the next trial of a reaction-time competition. The opponent, actually an accomplice administering a prepared schedule of responses and outcomes from an adjacent room, ostensibly also sets a level of shock. After each reaction-time trial, the subject is informed of having been faster or slower than his or her opponent. In either case, he or she learns about the intensity of shock the opponent has chosen, and if the subject has lost the competition, he or she actually receives shock.

In a first study, male subjects performed the task in the presence of either a male or a female observer. It was found that aggressiveness, as measured in the intensity of shock set for delivery to the opponent, was higher in the presence of a male than a female observer. Interestingly, the removal of the male observer effected a significant reduction of aggressiveness, bringing the subject's aggressiveness to a level comparable to that displayed by his opponent. In contrast, the removal of the female observer proved of little consequence. These data would seem to suggest that at times, social approval and encouragement may be assumed rather than explicitly articulated. The male subjects appear to have felt that onlooking male peers would approve or possibly even expect their aggressive reactions against the opponent. Males, in other words, seem to display a good deal of apprehension in their efforts to make a favorable impression on other males by being tough and aggressive. Females seem not to produce such apprehensions.

A second study shows this effect of evaluation apprehension more directly. Again, both male and female observers were used. In addition, however, these observers were identified either as proaggressive or as antiaggressive. A shoulder patch on the observer's jacket was pointed out to introduce the proaggressive observer as a karate instructor who was fascinated with this aggressive sport. Analogously, the antiaggressive observer was introduced as an activist in a worldwide peace organization. The findings show that males' aggressiveness in the presence of a proaggressive observer, whether male or female, is far more pronounced than in the presence of an antiaggressive observer, again whether male or female. Paralleling the findings of the first study, there was a tendency for male observers, independent of their apparent views on aggression, to foster higher aggressiveness than female observers. This main effect of sex was trivial, however, in comparison with that of the observer's ostensible attitudes toward aggression. Most importantly, it was further observed that after the removal of the male or female proaggressive observer, aggressiveness declined significantly, to a level comparable with that displayed by the opponent. The removal of the male or female antiaggressive observer, by contrast, had no discernible effect: Level of aggressiveness remained close to that exhibited by the opponent.

The demonstration that aggressive behavior is to some extent under the control of apprehensions set up by observers, besides having immediate practical implications, seems to reconcile earlier conflicting findings. Borden and Taylor (1973) had observed that the presence of a small audience of male and female peers facilitated aggressiveness, whereas Baron (1971a) reported that the presence of a visiting professor and his research assistant who wanted to learn about the experiment reduced the intensity of aggressive responses. If it is assumed that the involvement of male peers in the audience of the former investigation created expectations of evaluative gains through increased aggression, whereas the presence of "critical minds" in the latter investigation produced expectations of evaluative losses, the discrepant effects can be accounted for.

Of special interest here is Borden's demonstration that evaluation apprehension can produce aggression-modifying effects usually attributed to "social reinforcement" and furthermore, that the removal of this apprehension terminates the effect of the reinforcement. Most earlier investigations of the effect of social reinforcement, it seems, can alternatively be explained in terms of evaluation apprehension. Prompting aggressive responses by saying "good" or "you are doing fine," for example, is just another way of telling the subject that the experimenter approves of such action and that he or she takes a favorable view of the person who performs it. As long as the experimenter remains present, reports of the "generalization" of aggressiveness to novel situations should thus not be surprising. In Borden's study, the apprehension contingency was discontinued more convincingly than in earlier investigations, and the immediate decline of aggressiveness following the removal of the aggression-facilitating presence of apparently approving others was repeatedly observed. This immediate decline constitutes evidence against the view that social reinforcement builds aggressive habits that, once established, tend to persist.

The proposal that the aggression-facilitating effect of social approval and encouragement results from a reduction in the subject's hesitation to aggress against another person is quite consistent with the findings. It is fully in accord with the observation that the presence of a proaggressive peer promotes aggressiveness, and it does not conflict with the observation that the presence of an antiaggressive peer does not further the inhibition of aggression. The findings show, however, that the aggression-enhancing effect of restraint reduction depends on the presence of the agent through whom this reduction in restraint is achieved. In other words, the evidence at this point does not favor the view that restraint reduction carries with it sufficient reinforcement value to affect persisting aggressiveness habits.

Our discussion of incentive theory in aggression thus leads us to the following conclusions:

1. Aggression is strongly reinforced by the attainment of tangible rewards.

2. Aggression is reinforced by the attainment of various nontangible incentives. The nature of this reinforcement cannot always be determined, however. It appears that conceptually at least, positive reinforcement is characteristically confounded with elements of negative reinforcement.

3. Marked sex differences seem to exist with regard to the reinforcement value of both tangible and nontangible rewards.

4. The social approval and encouragement of aggression promotes aggressiveness. It is not necessarily reinforcing, however, and the effect is open to alternative explanations. The treatment of social approval and encouragement as factors that reduce aggression constraints adequately explains the pertinent findings. So does the treatment of these factors in terms of evaluation apprehension.

4. Punishment as a Deterrent.   Punishment, in one form or another, has been used in all known human societies to shape and correct the behavior of adults, children, and domesticated animals. Throughout the ages, punishment and the threat of punishment seem to have functioned as the principal deterrents to transgressions—especially those of a hostile or aggressive nature. In light of the apparent effectiveness of such measures, one might expect their behavior-modifying power to be well established in theory and research. This is not the case, however. On the contrary, the effectiveness of punishment and the threat of punishment have been severely challenged. In psychological theory, punishment has been a highly controversial issue, and this controversy seems to have been considerably clouded by humanitarian considerations. What is equally important, however, is that pertinent data have been scarce, and misleading generalizations have resulted. Only recently, as more relevant data have become available, has it been possible to correct erroneous earlier views (cf. Azrin & Holz, 1966; Fantino, 1973; Solomon, 1964). Concerning the function of punishment in human affairs, the scarcity of critical evidence still persists to a large degree. Experimental research, when not ruled out entirely, is greatly restricted for obvious moral reasons, and most observational studies do not allow unequivocal determinations of causal relations. The available evidence on punishment and aggression is largely based on the behavior of deviants, that is, on clinical and criminal cases; what is known about normally adjusted individuals is generally limited to rather mild forms of punishment. Under these conditions, it is indeed difficult to arrive at definitive evaluations of theoretical proposals.

In the consideration of human behavior, the punishment issue is further complicated by conceptual ambiguities. The punishment concept is used in common discourse to refer to measures taken to bring justice to a situation. A transgressor is punished for a violation of precepts. Only transgressions are punished. The punishing, aversive stimulation inflicted on the transgressor would be considered a simple hostile or aggressive assault if it were not precipitated by a transgression. Punishment thus seems to be inseparably connected with moral judgment.

At other times, however, punishment is conceived of as aversive stimulation—independent of moral considerations. This is the predominant usage of the concept in psychology. Punishment is the counterpart of reward. In operational terms, *punishment* is the arrangement of a response consequence that reduces the likelihood of this response. The stimulus that is arranged as a consequence is referred to as a *punisher*. Punishment is thus the exact opposite of reinforcement. This parallel extends to the distinction between positive and negative punishment. *Positive punishment* denotes the delivery of noxious stimuli, whereas *negative punishment* denotes the partial or total removal of a reinforcer. The symmetry in the reinforcement–punishment terminology would seem to project a symmetry of function. It is at this point, however, that theoretical views diverge. We now briefly discuss the major views on the effect of .punishment.

Historically speaking, it was Thorndike (1911, 1913) who in the so-called *law of effect* proposed a symmetrical model of reinforcement and punishment. Thorndike operationalized *satisfaction* as a state of affairs that the organism does not actively avoid but makes efforts to extend and renew. Analogously, he operationalized *annoyance* as a state of affairs that the organism does not actively preserve but engages in efforts to end. Employing these concepts, he then posited that of several responses made in the same situation: (a) those that are accompanied or closely followed by satisfaction will be strengthened, so that when the situation recurs, these responses will be more likely to recur; and (b) those responses that are accompanied or closely followed by annoyance will be weakened, so that when the situation recurs, they will be less likely to occur. Whereas reward increases the likelihood of a response, punishment decreases it. This is the Thorndikean maxim that "pleasure stamps in, pain stamps out." Reinforcement and aversive control of behavior are thus viewed as producing directionally opposite effects, but otherwise they are treated as functionally equivalent.

The apparent symmetry of the function of punishment and reinforcement was not claimed for very long, however. Thorndike (1932) himself amended the law of effect so as to de-emphasize the significance of punishment in the control of behavior. He modified the model after conducting a series of studies that seemed to demand the correction. In verbal-learning experiments, Thorndike employed the response "right" as a reinforcer and the response "wrong" as a punisher. In support of the reinforcement portion of the law of effect, he observed that the contiguous placement of "right" increased the frequency of the rewarded response. Surprisingly, however, the placement of "wrong" also increased the frequency of the associated response—compared to the frequency of the response when not "punished." Punishment apparently did not weaken responding. On the basis of this negative evidence, Thorndike dismissed the punishment portion of the law of effect. Aversive control seemed uncertain and in no way the inverse of reinforcement.

Later experimentation corroborated Thorndike's initial findings. It was again observed (Stone, 1953; Stone & Walters, 1951) that a subject's response is indeed more likely to recur when followed by the comment "wrong" than when followed by no comment. More surprisingly, even mild electric shock was found to strengthen rather than weaken the subject's responding. "Wrong" and mild shock apparently functioned as positive reinforcers.

Dinsmoor (1954, 1955) has taken issue with these verbal-learning studies on punishment, suggesting that all they really show is that comments such as "wrong" do not function as punishers. He argued that according to the empirical law of effect, a punisher is an event that lowers the likelihood of the recurrence of a response, and if "wrong" fails to do so, it simply is not a punisher. Although this suggestion may seem plausible with regard to the comment "wrong," it raises some questions when shock is considered. If it can be ascertained that shock is an aversive stimulus (via the demonstration of efforts to avoid and escape it), it must be expected, in accordance with the law of effect, that it would function as a punisher, "stamping out" the punished response. If, as Dinsmoor suggests, a purely empirical determination of "punisher" is accepted, the law of effect becomes true by definition. The punishment portion of the law can be maintained, because the postulated response-weakening effect of a punisher is necessarily "confirmed" with every observation of some discernible event following a reduction in response rate. The law of effect would be infallible, since the stamping out of a response by a punisher is expected only after the stamping out of the response by the punisher has been observed. The possible falsehood of the punishment portion of the law could only be suggested by the possible scarcity of events that qualify as punishers.

Accepting a definition of "punisher" in strictly functional terms (i.e., any stimulus condition that has been shown to lower the frequency of a preceding response) would mean abandoning the classification of stimulus events as reinforcers and punishers based on experiential criteria. Food would not necessarily constitute a positive reinforcer, and painful shock would not necessarily be a positive punisher. Generalizations about reinforcers and punishers, deriving from the analysis of stimulus characteristics (satisfier vs. annoyer), would appear to be unwarranted, and the determination of the status of a stimulus event would have to await the seemingly endless probing of its impact on the rate of particular responses. In conceiving of punishment, it seems to be more parsimonious, both in theory and practice, to preserve the linkage between aversive stimulation and the punishment function. It may be assumed that by and large, the degree of aversiveness of a stimulus is proportional to the degree to which it will function as a punisher. In making this assumption, situational differences can readily be granted. In fact, it has been demonstrated that the reinforcement and punishment value of stimulus events can vary greatly from one situation to another (e.g., McKearney, 1969; Premack, 1962) and that it depends on the subject's experiential history (Ayllon & Azrin, 1968; Holz & Azrin, 1961). It would seem farfetched, however, to assume that in Stone and Walters' investigation, mild shock was perceived as pleasant and thus functioned as a reinforcer. The findings that prompted the dismissal of the punishment portion of the law of effect, together with those that corroborated this dismissal, appear to be more readily explained as experimental artifact: The punishment, in spite of its potentially noxious properties, may have cued the subject to respond to certain stimuli, fostering discrimination (cf. Azrin & Holz, 1966).

The notion of asymmetry between reinforcement and punishment, at which Thorndike had arrived, found an impassioned proponent in Skinner. Skinner (1953, 1971) flatly denied that punishment is an effective means of controlling behavior, and he has probably been the most influential advocate of this view. Specifically, Skinner asserted: (a) that punishment is relatively ineffective compared to reinforcement, (b) that its effect is highly transient, and (c) that it has potentially maladaptive side effects. These conclusions were based mainly on two experiments with animals.

Skinner (1938) conducted an experiment with rats relating to this issue. In the first phase of his investigation, the animals received intermittent positive reinforcement for pressing a lever. After the animals had acquired the lever-pressing response, they were run in extinction sessions during which lever pressing was no longer reinforced (two 2-hour sessions on 2 successive days). In this second phase, the animals were either punished or not punished for lever pressing in the initial period of the first extinction session (10 minutes). The punishment consisted of a hard slap to the foot, administered via a spring on the lever, for every lever press response. Under these conditions, it was found that punishment depressed the rate of lever pressing during the period in which it was consistently administered. The surprising finding, however, was that when the punishment was discontinued, the rate of lever pressing rose temporarily above that of the animals who had not been punished. Additionally, there was no appreciable difference in the total number of lever-pressing responses during the entire extinction period (the two sessions combined) between animals who had been punished and those who had not. The temporary depression in response rate during punishment seemed to be compensated for by the temporary elevation following the removal of the punisher.

A similar experiment with rats was conducted by Estes (1944). The first phase was the same as in Skinner's study. In the second phase, punishment was administered via electric shock, and further extinction sessions were added. Estes entirely replicated Skinner's findings when using mild shock. The pattern of findings changed considerably, however, when more intense electric shock was employed as the punisher: The lever-pressing response virtually vanished within the first few minutes of the punishment period. More importantly, the rate of this response remained extremely low after punishment was discontinued. The response rate was depressed throughout three extinction sessions, and only afterwards, in four further sessions, did it gradually increase to levels comparable to those of unpunished animals. Severe punishment thus had a more lasting effect, and the "reversal"—that is, the temporary increase in responding observed after the discontinuation of mild punishment—did not materialize. Estes further noted that severe punishment reduced the rate of lever pressing and held down the rate of the response for several extinction sessions whether or not the punisher was made contingent upon lever pressing. The intense shock evidently produced a state of immobilization that seemed to impair the lever-pressing response only incidentally.

Together with Thorndike's data, these findings led to Skinner's sweeping generalizations concerning the ineffectiveness of punishment. In building a case against punishment, Skinner (e.g., 1938, 1953, 1971) has provided a theoretical proposal that goes far beyond the data, however. Since the more recent theories of punishment appear largely to be different modifications of Skinner's initial propositions, we discuss his proposal in greater detail.

According to Skinner, the *primary effect of punishment* is the disruption of ongoing behavior through the elicitation of incompatible responses. This effect of punishment is said (1953) to be "confined to the immediate situation [p. 186]." The notion that punishment produces maladaptive by-products is based mainly on the fact that punishment is indiscriminate with regard to incompatible responses. It blindly drives the organism into response modes that may be maladaptive as well as adaptive. Skinner emphasizes, of course, the maladaptive response choices and draws freely upon Freud's defense mechanisms and the notion of psychosomatic illness to illustrate the inadvisability of punishment. A *second effect of punishment* is said (1953) to be that "behavior which has consistently been punished becomes the source of conditioned stimuli which evoke incompatible behavior [p. 187]." The response to a punisher is thus seen to become classically conditioned to the stimuli that precede the impact of punishment. Among the stimuli that can acquire the power to elicit responses directly connected with punishment, Skinner listed proprioceptive cues deriving from activities in glands and smooth muscles. At times, however, the emotional reaction that should trigger the behavior directly connected with punishment is considered the incompatible reaction itself. Be this as it may, Skinner hastened to point out that any such secondary effect of punishment also merely suppresses the punished behavior temporarily. Finally, Skinner (1953) posited a *third effect of punishment,* suggesting: (a) that the aversive properties of the punisher become conditioned to concurrent stimuli, and (b) that " *any behavior which reduces this conditioned aversive stimulation will be reinforced* [p. 188]." Conditioned negative emotional reactions, most importantly fear, are thus seen to motivate the avoidance of the punisher and to serve as negative reinforcers for any mode of behavior that accomplishes this avoidance. According to Skinner (1953), "to establish aversive conditions which are avoided by any behavior of 'doing something else'" is "the most important effect of punishment [p. 189]." This acknowledgment of importance is quickly put back in line with the asserted overall ineffectiveness of punishment. Skinner notes that this third effect of punishment tends to eliminate itself: As punishment is repeatedly avoided because of conditioned aversion, the conditioned negative reinforcer undergoes extinction; unpunished behavior is thus reinforced less and less, and the punished behavior should soon recur. In concluding his theoretical analysis of punishment, Skinner insisted (1953) that "punishment does not actually eliminate behavior from a repertoire [p. 190]"—a resolution he considers to be in agreement with Freud's discovery of the survival of repressed wishes. (The intrusion of moral considerations in Skinner's assessment [1953] is evident in ideas such as that the temporary achievement of punishment "is obtained at a tremendous cost in reducing the over-all efficiency and happiness of the group [p. 190].")

Skinner's contention that punishment is an ineffective means of behavior control has more recently been faulted. As Fantino put it (1973): "Although Skinner has made an impressive case against the effectiveness of aversive control, his position has not been borne out by empirical data [p. 243]." In animal studies, with punishment being operationalized in the delivery of electric shock, it has been convincingly demonstrated that the suppression of a response rate: (a) can be complete, and (b) can last over considerable periods of time (e.g., Appel, 1961; Appel & Peterson, 1965; Azrin, 1960; Azrin, Holz, & Hake, 1963; Storms, Boroczi, & Broen, 1962). The degree and duration of response suppression have been found to be a simple function of the intensity of punishment (e.g., Appel & Peterson, 1965; Azrin, 1960), and the frequency of punishment has been found to function analogously (e.g., Azrin, 1956; Azrin, Holz, & Hake, 1963). Generally speaking, the more intense or the more frequent the punishment, the greater and the longer the suppression of the punished response. Additionally, if the punishment is sufficiently severe, punished responses can be entirely eliminated. These generalizations are in apparent conflict with Skinner's claim of the ineffectiveness and impermanence of punishment effects.

Animal studies have further revealed that punishment, in producing the opposite effect of reinforcement, functions analogously to reinforcement. The effect of noncontingent punishment is the inverse of noncontingent reinforcement (e.g., Azrin, 1956; Filby & Appel, 1966). As is the case with reinforcement (e.g., Neuringer, 1969; Skinner, 1938), strong and enduring effects of punishment depend on the immediate placement of the punisher following the punished response; delays in punishment were found to impair the punisher's effectiveness greatly (e.g., Azrin, 1956; Cohen, 1968). The effect of reintroducing punishment after its discontinuance mirrors the effect of reintroducing reinforcement (e.g., Holz, Azrin, & Ulrich, 1963). With regard to stimulus control, stimuli associated with punishment have been found to generalize to other stimuli just as stimuli associated with reinforcement do (e.g., Honig & Slivka, 1964). Conditioned punishment functionally parallels conditioned reinforcement. It has been shown that a neutral stimulus, through the contingent placement of a positive punisher, readily acquires the properties of a conditioned suppressor (e.g., Hake & Azrin, 1965). It has also been demonstrated that conditioned suppression can be accomplished by the withdrawal of the opportunity to respond for positive reinforcement, that is, by negative punishment (e.g., Ferster, 1957). As is the case with conditioned reinforcers, the effect of conditioned punishers is transient but can be maintained indefinitely by the occasional reinstatement of the stimulus-punisher contingency (e.g., Hake & Azrin, 1965). Finally, Estes' (1944) finding that was mainly responsible for the belief that punishment depresses responding in a blind, indiscriminate manner—the finding that punishment suppressed response rate whether or not it was contingent upon the response—has been qualified. It has been shown that in general, contingent punishment suppresses responding to a far greater degree than noncontingent, "free" punishment (e.g., Azrin, 1956; Schuster & Rachlin, 1968). More importantly, it has been shown that when animals are provided with response choices, they display reactions that secure the least punishment, whether or not this punishment is contingent upon these reactions (Schuster & Rachlin, 1968). In other words, the animals behave so as to minimize aversive stimulation. Independent of immediate contingencies, punishment exerted the strongest effect, in the long run, on whichever response tended to reduce it the most. These findings again parallel those on reinforcement (e.g., Ferster & Skinner, 1957).

In the light of such evidence, the contention that punishment is ineffective simply does not hold up. It is apparently true that the effects of punishment are largely transient, but this is equally true for the effects of reinforcement. The contention that punishment obeys laws that are fundamentally different from those governing reinforcement is at variance with the findings. After a careful review of the pertinent recent research, Fantino (1973) concluded that the principles that apply to reinforcement apply to punishment as well. "Aversive stimuli function in the same manner as do positive reinforcers. Rewards and punishments are events that are identical but opposite in sign in their effect on behavior. No separate laws need to be constructed to understand the effects of aversive stimuli [p. 275]."

The functional parallels between reinforcement and punishment, as initially proposed in the first version of Thorndike's model, are similarly stressed by Schuster and Rachlin (1968) when they say that the "empirical symmetry dictates a corresponding conceptual symmetry in terms of a positive law of effect accounting for response increments and a negative law accounting for response decrements [p. 777]."

Given that punishment is an effective means of behavior control, a fact that has only recently gained acceptance, it remains to be seen how, exactly, punishment achieves its effect. It has become customary (cf. Bolles, 1967; Dunham, 1971; Solomon, 1964) to classify the theories that address this issue into one-process and two-process theories. In trying to provide a brief overview of the major theories of punishment, we also follow this scheme. We do so with some reservations, however. The scheme, based on what is being emphasized in the various notions, often oversimplifies matters by neglecting secondary propositions.

In the so-called one-process theories of punishment, only one learning mechanism is held responsible for the response-depressing effect of punishment. Since either classical or instrumental learning could be implicated in this function, one expects and finds two types of one-process theories. Estes and Skinner (1941) are credited with the proposal that emotional responses elicited by the punishing event become classically conditioned to stimuli that precede this punishing event; the conditioned emotional responses compete with the punished response and cause its suppression. Miller and Dollard (1941) are credited with the proposal that any response linked with the termination of the punishing stimulation becomes instrumentally conditioned as an alternative to the punished response.

In the far more popular, so-called two-process theories of punishment, the two learning mechanisms are both involved to account for the avoidance of the punishing event. Mowrer (1947; Mowrer & Lamoreaux, 1946) proposed that fear is classically conditioned to stimuli preceding the occurrence of the punisher. Any response that alleviates this aversive state of fear is then instrumentally conditioned through negative reinforcement. Dinsmoor (1954, 1955) translated this view into more behavioral terminology. He posited that the aversive properties of the punisher are classically conditioned mainly to the proprioceptive stimulus feedback from the punished response and that any alternative response that diminishes or removes this conditioned aversive stimulation becomes instrumentally conditioned. Similar two-process theories have been proposed by Anger (1963) and Rescorla and Solomon (1967).

The common feature of all these two-process theories is apparent: First, the stimuli preceding the punisher become conditioned punishers. The different notions stress different stimuli in this function, however. Some investigators emphasize spatial and temporal cues, others proprioceptive cues such as the incipient movements of the punished response. These stimuli are presumed to produce aversive autonomic reactions. Second, the performance of non-punished responses, by removing the conditioned punisher, is then reinforced, thus fostering effective avoidance of the punisher. Clearly, two-process theories assign a crucial role to the conditioned aversive autonomic reactions. It is this aversive arousal that motivates the organism either to terminate a chain of responses that would lead to punishment or not to display any particular overt reaction.

This placement of emphasis—which, as will be remembered, has also been promoted by Skinner (1953)—has stirred up considerable controversy. What is the crucial element effecting avoidance? What reinforces nonpunished, alternative reactions? How important is the classical-conditioning component of two-process theory? How important is its component of instrumental conditioning? And finally, could it be that neither component is particularly significant? Could the avoidance of the unconditioned punisher itself be the crucial reinforcer?

At this point, the evidence accumulated in investigations with animals: (a) is not supportive of the view that avoidance reactions become classically conditioned to stimuli preceding punishment, (b) assigns only a minor role to conditioned aversion in the reinforcement of avoidance reactions, and (c) favors the proposal that the omission of the unconditioned punisher itself is the most potent reinforcer of avoidance reactions. The classical conditioning of avoidance has been employed as a post hoc explanation of findings (e.g.,

Hendry & Hendry, 1963). In a careful, direct test of this proposal (Wahlsten, Cole, Sharp, & Fantino, 1968), it was shown, however, that environmental cues associated with punishment are not a determining factor in avoidance. Numerous studies show that the removal of the conditioned punisher has only a weak effect on avoidance. The studies suggest that this effect results mainly from the fact that the removal of the conditioned punisher signals the omission of the unconditioned punisher (e.g., Bolles & Grossen, 1969; Bolles, Stokes, & Younger, 1966; D'Amato, Fazzaro, & Etkin, 1967). The power of the sheer omission of the unconditioned punisher in controlling avoidance reactions has been documented in several studies (e.g., Herrnstein & Hineline, 1966; Kamin, 1956, 1957). The accumulating evidence favoring the view that the nonoccurrence of punishment is the crucial reinforcer in avoidance has been discussed by Herrnstein (1969).

Taken together, these findings have been interpreted as strong evidence against two-process theories of punishment (cf. Fantino, 1973). Emotional processes, fear, anxiety, apathy, guilt, or whatever else (cf. Mowrer, 1947; Skinner, 1953, 1971) seem not to play the important part in mediating the effect of punishment that some theoreticians have ascribed to them. The evidence obtained on animals does not support the view that aversive control is a highly emotional affair. Animals simply behave so as to maximize the time free of aversion (e.g., Herrnstein & Hineline, 1966), and in so doing they seem to be as "cold-blooded" as in their efforts to minimize periods of nonreinforcement (e.g., Herrnstein, 1964; Squires & Fantino, 1971). One can, of course, take the position that in the study of punishment and avoidance in animals, the experiential component of aversion has not been directly assessed and that statements about emotional disturbances and ill effects are thus not disconfirmed. In fact, two-process theories of punishment have been considered incapable of being disproved and hence untestable, because "all the critical events are assumed to occur within the organism being punished" (Schuster & Rachlin, 1968, p. 784), with the covert reactions involved being considered unobservable. But whatever view is taken, it should be clear that the evidence from animal studies does not support the proposal that punishment, provided it can be avoided through unpunished, alternative responses, causes disturbing emotional and motivational problems. In the light of this evidence, the generalization that the aversive control of behavior, for more or less all species, is ultimately maladaptive and causes neurotic behavior (Skinner, 1971) appears to be a myth.

This assessment certainly does not apply to situations where the organism is exposed to aversive stimulation for extended periods of time without being able to avoid it. Continued stress undoubtedly can have maladaptive consequences in both animals and man (cf. Brady, 1970; Oken, 1967). Also, the assessment may have to be qualified for the aversive control of aggressive behavior. As discussed earlier, the infliction of pain in animals is a nearly universal elicitor of aggressive reactions. Scott (1958) has questioned the effectiveness of punishment in the curtailment of aggression for this reason. The suppression of aggression through aggression, that is, through the infliction of at least physical pain, seems contradictory indeed. From a theoretical point of view, it can hold promise only if the aggression-instigating impact of the infliction of pain is overpowered by its avoidance-motivating effect. We further discuss this problem in connection with punishment and human behavior.

Turning now to the aversive control of human behavior, it appears that a careful analysis of the behavior characteristics unique to man provides the best protection against making hasty, misleading generalizations from the findings in other species. A most critical difference between man and other species concerns his superior communication skills. These skills have to be acknowledged, and their potential consequences for the effectiveness of punishment have to be taken into account in order to achieve an adequate understanding of aversive control in human affairs.

Generally speaking, punishment and moral judgment, as reflected in the common usage of the punishment concept, seem inseparably linked in human behavior. The deliberate application of aversive stimulation for the purpose of behavior control is perceived as differentially appropriate or inappropriate, justified or unjustified, as soon as the individual has developed the competence to make such judgments (cf. Kohlberg, 1964; Piaget, 1932). Conceivably, the effect of aversive stimulation or "punishment" on the individual depends on whether he or she can accept this treatment as deserved or has to reject it as undeserved. On this point, a large number of investigations (e.g., Burnstein & Worchel, 1962; Cohen, 1955; Kregarman & Worchel, 1961; Mallick & McCandless, 1966; Pastore, 1952; Zillmann, Bryant, Cantor, & Day, 1975; Zillmann & Cantor, 1976b) have shown with great consistency that an aversive treatment, whether aggressive or hostile in character, that is perceived as arbitrary and unjustified tends to instigate hostility and aggression to a far higher degree than the same treatment when it is perceived as unintended or justified to some extent. We discuss the amassed evidence concerning such moral considerations in greater detail later. Let it suffice at present to consider it established that the degree to which an aversive treatment is perceived as justified is a critical factor in the determination of its impact on behavior. Dependent on the perception of the treatment—or more precisely, dependent on the perceived moral justifiability of the "punishing" agent's application of aversive stimuli—the response can be hostile or aggressive, or it can be quietly accepted and can possibly suppress the punished response. The indicated evidence strongly suggests that for mature individuals who habitually apply moral considerations, aversive treatments that cannot be considered "deserved"—that is, that cannot be seen as called for by transgressions committed—will tend to elicit hostile and aggressive behavior. In accord with Scott's concern about the aggression-instigating effect of aversive stimulation, it seems extremely unlikely that hostile and aggressive measures perceived in this way can effectively curtail human hostility and aggression. It seems that aversive treatments *must* be perceived as not arbitrarily inflicted or as justified in the context of prevailing precepts and social norms in order for them to have in humans the response-suppressing effect that has been documented in other species.

All this is not to say that by and large, man's behavior deviates from the maxim that stipulates that aversion be minimized. Presumably, along with the other species, man behaves so as to minimize exposure to unconditioned and conditioned punishers. Aversive stimulation that the environment imposes upon the individual is generally avoided. At the very least, efforts are made to reduce this type of stimulation as far as possible. The child, for example, should quickly learn not to touch a hot stove a second time and after being bitten, to avoid the neighbor's ferocious dog. Similarly, the adult who becomes nauseated on the roller coaster should be inclined to seek pleasure elsewhere. This type of aversive control undoubtedly exerts an enormous influence on human behavior, and there is every reason to believe that the mechanism governing this influence closely parallels that in other species. However, because this type of aversion cannot be considered *manipulative* in the sense that *someone deliberately sets up punishment contingencies to influence someone else's behavior,* it is generally not considered central to the punishment issue. We can readily accept that *nonmanipulative aversive control* in humans functions analogously to that in other species, but we have to reject any implication that the difference between humans and other species is similarly trivial for *manipulative aversive control.*

The issue at hand is that of *coercion:* An individual, a group, or a society sets up contingencies of punishment; that is, arranges aversive stimulation through hostile or aggressive actions to follow (a) the performance of acts that have been declared prohibited, or (b) the failure to perform acts that have been prescribed. Conceiving of punishment in these conceptual terms elucidates the unique characteristics of aversive control in humans.

First, it shows that there is an entirely novel use of punishment—namely, to *force compliance with directives.* This usage is obviously based on a capability that is not developed in other species: the ability to *communicate specific behavioral expectations.* The fact of this capability alone makes general statements about the effect of punishment in all species, man included, untenable. Bolles (1967), for example, concluded his discussion of the effect of punishment on behavior by stressing that punishment cannot produce alternative reactions "other than the particular response it elicits. Therefore punishment is not effective in altering behavior unless the reaction to punishment itself competes with the response we wish to punish [p. 433]." This assessment, which is very similar to that of Skinner (e.g., 1953), may well apply to most species. The aversively stimulated animal, particularly in the restricted laboratory box, can hardly be expected to select specific adaptive routes (without being reinforced for such responses) when preoccupied with escape from an acute aversion. The situation in the coercive use of punishment in humans is very different: Alternative response routes are explicitly designated; characteristically, the recipient of punishment knows exactly what he or she has failed to do and can readily direct and redirect his or her behavior in compliance with directions in order to avoid the punishment. Unless punishment is used indiscriminately and without any direction (as, for example, in the "educational" efforts of maladjusted, sadistic parents), conditions are simply not parallel to the animal case, and generalizations are thus unacceptable and potentially misleading. Regardless of what holds for other species, the use of punishment in the coercion of behavior may prove highly effective in human affairs.

Second, because of superior communication skills, man can arbitrarily establish specific punishment (and reinforcement) contingencies simply by pronouncing them "in effect" without requiring any prior learning trials. In coercion, the *threat of punishment* amounts to an informal contractual arrangement. Such a contractual arrangement is nothing more than a *communicated punishment contingency:* If you do what you were instructed not to do, or if you don't do what you were told to, we will produce these aversive consequences for you. It has been pointed out earlier that contractual arrangements of this kind are involved in nearly all of human affairs, especially in the curtailment of violence. They permeate all aspects of family life, interaction with peers, and education. When formalized, they apply as legal sanctions to all members of society, functioning as a deterrent to violent assaults on other members of the society (but also as a deterrent to the refusal to perform such assaults on members of other societies in times of war). In the curtailment of violence, particularly criminal violence, the threat of punishment is generally considered effective. It is widely believed that if the punishment contingencies set forth in criminal law were discarded and abandoned, violence would reach catastrophic levels very quickly (cf. Bandura, 1973a). This view is shared even by extreme opponents of punitive measures in the control of aggression. The important point here is that it seems to be possible to suppress violent behaviors on a grand scale by the sheer threat of aversive treatments, that is, *without the actual instrumental learning of avoidance.* Even under conditions of very severe provocation, most people, without ever having been punished for such behavior, refrain from inflicting injury or death upon their tormentors. In fact, it is the effect of the actual application of punishment for transgressions of this sort that is in dispute. The effectiveness of rehabilitation programs in particular is in question (cf. Zimring, 1971). Thus, although it appears that human beings, like other species, behave so as to minimize aversive stimulation for themselves, they do so mainly through the seemingly deliberate *anticipation of consequences* rather than on the basis of learning trials. Even granting that this anticipation is subject to considerable judgmental error (i.e., the likelihood and the magnitude of anticipated aversions may be misjudged), such behavior cannot be considered parallel to that of other species. Again, the hasty generalization of findings deriving from animal behavior must appear unwarranted and potentially misleading.

Third, there is the discussed ability in humans to pass moral judgment. As soon as social and societal precepts are recognized, the child can readily detect violations of them; and if punishment contingencies are known to exist for such violations, the child can project the amount of punishment appropriate for the transgression. Knowing the rules that govern the aversive consequences of one's actions is, of course, critical in the individual's arrangement of an aversion-free environment. Accepting the rules is another issue, however. Here it is important to distinguish between at least two levels of development: one at which punishment is treated as an unquestionable "natural" mandate and one at which punishment contingencies are recognized as totally arbitrary (cf. Kohlberg, 1964; Piaget, 1932). The child at the former stage accepts punishment as an atonement or a reparation for offenses and thus should accept being punished for transgressions. The magnitude of the punishment called for is determined mainly on the basis of the obtrusive aspects of the misdeed, with little regard for motivational circumstances. As the child advances to the superior stage, usually between the ages of 5 and 7 (dependent on the individual's mental maturity), the motivational circumstances become increasingly salient. Considerations of intent become crucial; corrections are applied in the punishment of accidental transgressions. The assessment of the magnitude of punishment for transgressions is also refined. The expiation rule "the sterner, the juster" (Piaget, 1932) is abandoned in favor of equity considerations that, roughly speaking, stipulate that the aversive treatment to be applied as punishment compensate for that inflicted upon others through the transgression. The assumed effectiveness of the punishment in correcting the undesirable behavior may also enter into the assessment of the punishment's appropriateness.

This analysis of the development of moral reasoning leads to the following expectations:

1. In children who have achieved neither the comprehension of precepts nor the recognition of prevailing punishment contingencies, aversive control, whether manipulative or nonmanipulative, should function as it does in other species.

2. In children at the developmental level of expiatory retribution, punishment should be readily accepted for apparent transgressions. The

application of punishment should produce reactions appropriate to the aversive stimulation involved but otherwise leave the individual undisturbed. In other words, punishment should not constitute an instigation to aggression beyond its immediate stimulus impact. Such is not the case, however, for manipulative aversive control that cannot be perceived as punishment for a transgression. Attempts at coercion, especially when they do not come from an authority apparently commissioned with the enforcement of precepts, are likely to be perceived as transgressions themselves, which deserve to be punished.

3. In the more mature child and in the adult, punishment is, generally speaking, accepted only when it is applied by an agent who is more or less formally commissioned with the enforcement of precepts and when the kind and amount of punishment applied is strictly within socially sanctioned limits. If punishment is perceived as unduly harsh, the recognition of its inappropriateness is likely to instigate the recipient to hostile or aggressive actions against the agent applying the punishment. This is to say that punishment may readily be perceived as undeserved, at least to some extent, and that in this case, it is likely to function as an instigation to hostility and aggression in and of itself, in addition to the impact of the aversive stimulation as such. This situation is further complicated by the fact that there may be little consensus on the justifiability of some punishment contingencies; the punished individual may not approve of the contingencies used to control his or her behavior. Under this condition, it seems that punishment can only function to provoke the individual severely. Finally, manipulative aversive control—that is, the administration of aversive stimulation in the absence of any behavior that could be construed as a transgression—will be perceived as an infringement of behavioral freedom. Unless it is enforced by punishment contingencies that the individual cannot escape, it is likely to elicit hostile or aggressive efforts toward the restoration of the threatened behavioral freedom and possibly toward retaliation.

On the basis of the foregoing discussion, it is suggested that unqualified statements of the effect of punishment on humans, especially the broad generalizations of findings in animals, are unjustified. In humans, the impact of punishment is apparently a function of its acceptance in judgmental terms, and this acceptance in turn seems to depend largely on moral considerations. This is not to say that the individual necessarily engages in explicit moral reasoning as he or she responds to punishment. Rather, it is assumed that he or she habitually matches coercive attempts and punitive measures against the precepts and social norms known to apply to the particular circumstances. Aversive treatments employed in accord with these precepts and norms may well achieve the effect observed in other species. But the application of such treatments in violation of precepts and norms can only foster hostile and aggressive reactions in the person toward whom punishment is directed and who perceives the violation. This should also hold true when the precepts and norms are rejected by the individual. The use of punishment in the curtailment of hostility and aggression, then, may be expected to be effective in children and in potentially maladjusted adults who fully accept any punishment contingencies imposed on them. In more mature children, in adolescents, and in adults, the effect of punishment probably depends largely on its *perceived legitimacy*. Presumably, this subjective assessment of legitimacy varies considerably from situation to situation and from individual to individual. To the extent that it does, punishment will prove effective in suppressing the punished responses on some occasions but will instigate hostile and aggressive reactions on others.

Although the proposal that the effect of punishment is mediated by the subjective assessment of its legitimacy has not undergone decisive testing, it can aid in reconciling much conflicting evidence concerning the effectiveness or ineffectiveness of punishment (e.g., Bandura & Walters, 1959; Becker, Peterson, Luria, Shoemaker, & Hellmer, 1962; Eron, Banta, Walder, & Laulicht, 1961; Sears, Maccoby, & Levin, 1957; Sears, Rau, & Alpert, 1965). Perhaps more importantly, together with the conceptual distinction between nonmanipulative aversive control, manipulative aversive control, punishment, and the threat of punishment, the proposal may be able to alleviate confusion and prevent unwarranted and misleading generalizations. We now apply this conceptual scheme to some pertinent experimental investigations on the effect of aversive control and punishment in the curtailment of human hostility and aggression.

In an important, representative study of the effect of "punishment" on children conducted by Deur and Parke (1970), first-, second-, and third-grade boys first were: (a) continuously rewarded, (b) intermittently rewarded, (c) not rewarded, or (d) intermittently rewarded and punished for hitting a Bobo doll; thereafter, the hitting response was (a) placed in extinction or (b) continuously punished. Marbles, obtained through a dispenser, constituted the reward: a noxious buzzer noise constituted punishment. Both the frequency and the force of punches against the Bobo doll were measured. Deur and Parke found that punishment slowed the rate of hitting and decreased the intensity of the responses in the acquisition period and that the response intensity remained comparatively low after acquisition. The rate of hitting in the second phase was substantially lower under continuous punishment than under extinction. Finally, subjects who were intermittently punished (and rewarded) in the acquisition period exhibited greater resistance to extinction and greater persistence under continuous punishment than those who had been continuously rewarded during acquisition.

The study demonstrates that nonmanipulative aversive control in children functions as should be expected on the basis of the evidence from animal studies. Apparently, in behaving "aggressively," children quickly recognize an aversive contingency and then act so as to minimize aversion. Aversive stimulation thus effectively impairs the acquisition and maintenance of aggressive responses. When it becomes apparent that aggression no longer has any payoff, the behavior is discontinued; and when it holds some promise, as in the condition of intermittent punishment and reward, it will be continued in spite of the aversion associated with it until it becomes apparent that it no longer pays. However, the study tells us nothing about the effect of punishment as a corrective for transgressions. Hitting the Bobo doll was the central part of what was explicitly presented to the subject as a new game that would be fun. The subject thus cannot possibly have perceived it a transgression to punch the doll in the stomach, as instructed, and cannot have considered the contingent aversive stimulation as punishment for a misdeed. Actually, the study is largely compromised by the fact that the boys were told that receiving a marble would indicate that they were playing the game well and that the buzzer would show that they were playing it poorly. Assuming that the children were motivated to play well rather than poorly, it is conceivable that, for example, the flashing of green and red light signals—red for good and green for poor play or vice versa—would have produced similar results. Giving credence to the effect of the punisher, however, the findings are more relevant to the case in which a child avoids a hot stove after having been burned than to the case of his or her having committed a transgression.

There are numerous investigations that show that adults readily hold back aggressive reactions when this restraint holds promise of preventing, reducing, or eliminating aversive stimulation. Shortell, Epstein, and Taylor (1970) have shown that in aggression between males, merely knowing that an opponent is capable of massive retaliation reduces the aggressive behavior directed against him. Baron (1971c) found, again in intermale aggression, that aggressiveness was significantly lower when the victim's retaliation was considered possible and likely than when it was ruled out with certainty. Baron (1973) also observed that the apparent high likelihood of retaliation rather effectively curtails aggressive responses in males who are not angry but not in males experiencing acute anger toward the potential retaliator. Furthermore, Baron (1974c) demonstrated that a high likelihood of retaliation effectively curbs intermale aggressiveness when the attack yields only a small payoff but that it makes little difference when the incentives attached to aggression are high. Gaebelein and Hay (1974) presented data that suggest that regarding the tendency to minimize aversive stimulation, interfemale aggression parallels intermale aggression: Females vulnerable to counterattack displayed less aggressiveness than nonvulnerable females, the difference being minute in angry subjects and substantial in nonangry ones.

The possibility of retaliation for inflicting aversive stimulation upon another person generally exists, of course, because the aggressor is usually identified. If the aggressor is assured anonymity, retaliation is ruled out, and one would expect less inhibition of aggressive inclinations. In other words, establishing a potential attacker's identity in and of itself should reduce aggressive behavior. The consequences of the aggressor's identification vs. anonymity have in fact been ascertained. In studies conducted by Zimbardo (1969), females either wore hoods that prevented their being recognized or did not. It was found that the hooded, "deindividuated" females behaved far more punitively toward a victim than did their nonhooded counterparts. Similarly, Donnerstein, Donnerstein, Simon, and Ditrichs (1972) observed that when males were identified to the victim, they behaved less aggressively than when they were assured anonymity, particularly when the victim appeared to be dangerous.

Although there are some data that fail to confirm the aggression-suppressing effect of potential reprisals (Knott & Drost, 1972), the available evidence generally supports the view that likely retaliation prevents or reduces aggressiveness as long as the aggression is not connected with incentives or is associated with trivial incentives only. This effect diminishes as retaliation becomes more instrumental either in the termination of an annoyance (i.e., in rectifying mistreatment) or in the attainment of valued commodities or circumstances. The available evidence can also be seen as consistent with a *cost–benefit interpretation* of aggression: Conceiving of the victim's potential punitive reactions as a cost, the benefits produced by aggression must outweigh the cost to warrant aggressive action. It must be stressed, however, that the evidence again does not pertain to the effects of punishment for aggressive transgressions that the individual recognizes as such. In the research discussed, aggression was operationalized in the delivery of electric shock to another person, but this action was clearly legitimized in the context of the experiment.

The aversive control of aggression has been further examined in a revealing experiment conducted by Pisano and Taylor (1971). These investigators determined the effectiveness of different strategies of counteraggression in the curtailment of intermale aggression: Aggressive responses were: (a) matched in strength by the aggressive counterresponse, (b) countered with more intense aggressive responses, or (c) countered with less intense aggressive responses. The aggressor thus faced an opponent who was apparently determined to meet force with force, who behaved in a highly punitive manner, or who readily yielded. If it is assumed that the aggressor's primary concern is to minimize the aversion inflicted on him, he should reduce his own aggressiveness in proportion to the severity of the likely reprisal. Interestingly, this expectation was not confirmed. Highly punitive counteraggression proved to escalate rather than reduce aggressiveness. The opponent's apparent reluctance to pay back the aggressor, that is, the pacifistic type of reaction, only initially tended to reduce aggression but failed, overall, to control aggressiveness. Retaliation in line with the "an eye for an eye" formula, by contrast, suppressed aggression significantly. These effects, once established, held up throughout the interaction between the adversaries.

Apparently, in dealing with an aggressor, yielding does not pay. It removes the risk of aversive consequences from aggression. Aggression becomes safe, and inhibitions need not be applied. The finding that matching force with force (rather than yielding) lowered aggressiveness accords with the maxim of aversion minimization and is thus not surprising. The finding that does not accord with this maxim is that severe counteraggression escalates aggression. To understand this finding, we briefly analyze the procedural conditions of the experiment.

Pisano and Taylor employed a procedure in which two subjects compete in a reaction-time task (cf. Taylor, 1967). This procedure was detailed earlier in connection with Borden's (1975) experiment (see Section IIIA3 of this chapter). In this procedure, the subject and his opponent, an experimental accomplice, select shock intensities to deliver to each other, and the subject is informed of his opponent's selection. The opponent's degree of aggressiveness is thus very clear to the subject. Given this awareness of the intensity of countermeasures, the subject cannot perceive as a transgression the opponent's choice of shock intensities below or equal to those he himself has employed. This situation changes, however, for the punitive opponent. Here, the subject may readily perceive the opponent's choice of extreme countermeasures as uncalled for, unjustified, and objectionable—in short, as a transgression. As a consequence, the transgressor should be perceived as some "obnoxious guy" who deserves to be punished for his misbehavior. Conceivably, then, the observed escalation of aggression by severe counteraggression was mediated by moral considerations. However, since there are no data that could confirm that the highly punitive behavior was perceived as a transgression, this account is highly tentative. The observed escalation is also adequately explained with the assumption that the subject, forced to continue fighting as it were, felt that his best chance to reduce severe counteraggression was to increase his assaults in turn.

Whatever the ultimate explanation may be, the findings reported by Pisano and Taylor demonstrate quite convincingly that in intermale aggression, severe counteraggression further instigates aggression rather than diminishing it. In light of the sex differences in aggression we have already encountered, the findings may prove not to be generalizable to interfemale and male–female aggression. Females may be far less inclined to display toughness in punishing a punitive opponent, and their behavior may conform more closely to the aversion-minimization model. Unfortunately, conclusive data on this point do not exist.

There are many findings on aversive control that could be accounted for by the proposal that the effect of punitive actions is mediated by moral considerations. It has been observed, for example, that when punitive measures are applied by a friendly, liked person, they are more effective in reducing prohibited behaviors than when they are applied by a nonsupportive, potentially disliked person (e.g., Parke, 1969; Parke & Walters, 1967). The effect may be readily explained with the assumption that the punitive measures are perceived differently: as well intended and relatively justified when performed by the nurturant person and as relatively arbitrary when performed by the nonnurturant one. The treatment that appears more arbitrary should foster less compliance and possibly provoke hostile and aggressive reactions. Similarly, the finding that aggressive assaults are more effectively suppressed by brief periods of seclusion following the assaults than by repeated, longer seclusion periods (Pendergrass, 1971) should not be surprising. To the punished individual, the latter treatment must appear far more arbitrary and unwarranted than the former, and therefore it should promote aggression rather than nonaggressive compliance.

The proposed mediating function of moral judgment thus can provide an alternative explanation for earlier findings, but since it is used in a post facto fashion, the proposal cannot be considered implicated in any decisive way. It seems moot to seek further illustrations of probable confoundings of aversive control with moral considerations. Instead, one should involve findings that more directly relate to moral judgment in the effect of punishment. Such findings, however, are conspicuously absent. Reliable experimental data on the effectiveness of punishment for transgressions that the respondent recognizes as such and on the degree of acceptance of punitive treatments as a function of the respondent's awareness of having done wrong are not available. The reason for this lack of pertinent evidence is obvious: The investigation of transgressions and their punishment is severely restricted by concerns for the welfare of the human subjects involved. It would be highly unethical to manipulate well-adjusted children and adults to commit antisocial acts, to make them feel moral censure for so doing, and then to subject them to aversive stimulation in order to test the eventual decline in the frequency of their misdeeds. As a consequence, the available data tend to be restricted to hyperaggressive, deviant individuals and to have been obtained under insufficiently controlled conditions. Alternatively, they involve only mild forms of punishment and are confounded with the selective reinforcement of behavioral alternatives.

The study of physical punishment of more than trivial intensity is clearly confined to extreme cases such as one reported by Ludwig, Marx, Hill, and Browning (1969). After other measures to curb the unprovoked, potentially homicidal assaults of a schizophrenic female patient had failed, these investigators decided to administer aversive faradic shock upon the occurrence of the intolerable behavior. According to their report, the treatment eliminated the aggressive outbursts, and its side effects were entirely positive (i.e., the paranoid irritability and aggressiveness subsided, and the patient became generally friendly toward others). Physical punishment thus was effective in controlling violent behavior that the respondent recognized as transgressive. It is important to note that she *fully accepted* the punishment, recognizing the good intentions behind it. Conceivably, the absence of this recognition that the doctors were trying to make her "a human being" (her own words) would have produced very different results.

The generalizability of this and similar findings, which have been discussed in some detail by Bandura (1973a), is obviously quite limited. The findings are suggestive, at best, of the effect of accepted punishment in normally adjusted persons, but they tell us nothing about the consequences of physical punishment that is deemed unjustified, uncalled for, or overly harsh by the recipient. In Western cultures, it seems to be the rule that physical punishment prompts vehement objections and disapproval on the part of the punished person. Physical punishment is generally prohibited and denounced. When administered to adults, it amounts to an offense that, it seems, can only aggravate conflict and aggressiveness. When administered to children, its impact appears to depend on the extent to which the child has absorbed the prevalent social evaluation of physical punishment. In all likelihood, the child rather early comes to realize the general disapproval of such punishment and then applies the acquired evaluation to this type of punishment where it commonly occurs: in the family context (cf. Gil, 1973). As the child objects more and more to the application of physical punishment by parents and guardians, such punishment should come to be highly ineffective and should provoke hostile and aggressive reactions. All this is theoretical speculation, however. The available experimental evidence on the effects of accepted or rejected punishment for transgressions is simply inconclusive.

Since, generally speaking, society denies itself the use of physical punishment, the lack of data on its effect might be considered of little consequence. It is clearly more important to understand the effect of the forms of punishment that are consensually permissible, if not sanctioned: (a) punishment by hostile rather than aggressive action, and (b) negative punishment—that is, punishment through the removal of rewards. Both forms worsen the individual's experiential state, and they both can thus be treated as hostile measures. Here, as indicated earlier, the pertinent data tend to confound the effects of punishment and reinforcement. It has been shown with considerable consistency, for example, that hyperaggressive behavior, mainly in children, can be effectively curbed by the punishment of aggressive transgressions combined with the rewarding of constructive responses (e.g., Allison & Allison, 1971, Bostow & Bailey, 1969; Sloane, Johnston, & Bijou, 1967; Zeilberger, Sampen, & Sloane, 1968). Depriving persons of the privilege of interacting freely with others, characteristically their peers, proved to be a particularly effective punitive treatment. Prompt social exclusion was found to reduce aggressive behavior in delinquent boys greatly (Burchard & Tyler, 1965; Tyler & Brown, 1967). "Time out from reinforcement" even proved to break the aggressiveness of the leader of a gang of delinquents (Brown & Tyler, 1968). These effects were observed mostly under conditions in which the punishment, whether the recipients felt they deserved it or not, was backed up by considerable punitive power (e.g., in schools and correctional institutions). This is to say that resistance to the punishment or the display of hostile or aggressive reactions to it would, at least in the respondent's mind, have resulted in increasingly severe punitive measures. Under conditions in which the respondent cannot so readily be coerced into obedience—as, for example, in peer interactions—such punitive measures may prove less effective.

In this context, it is of interest to note that the rehabilitation of convicted criminal offenders largely relies on strategies that combine punishment with the selective reinforcement of constructive behaviors. These strategies are employed, for the most part, because they "appear reasonable" and not necessarily because they have been shown to be effective. Zimring (1971) has stressed the need to determine, through systematic research, the likelihood of success of the punitive measures that are intended to be corrective before they are widely applied.

The study of corrective strategies that involve both punishment and reinforcement appears to have great pragmatic value. The immobilizing, stifling effect of a no! can be prevented, it seems, through the simultaneous use of yes's. This relates back to the work with animals in which punishment without apparent avoidance routes proved maladaptive. Procedures involving both reward and punishment minimize the risk of maladaptive reactions by providing avenues for constructive behavior. They thus seem superior, in principle, to purely punitive techniques. Taking a pragmatic perspective, then, the lack of compelling evidence on the effect of pure punishment does not seem to be a problem. Educational and corrective strategies that combine the mild positive punishment and/or negative punishment of undesirable behaviors with the reinforcement of desirable activities have proven effective under a variety of conditions (cf. Bandura, 1973a). Much applied work is called for, however. What will have to be determined by future research are the specific combinations of punishment and reinforcement that are the most effective for particular purposes of behavior control.

Notwithstanding the scarcity of data on the effects of pure punishment for transgressions that the recipient, at least to some degree, recognizes as such, the evidence that punitive treatments that are perceived as arbitrary and unjustified instigate hostility and aggression is overwhelming. Unless the concept of punishment is reserved for the aversive control of transgressions (and usually it is not), unprovoked attack, whether by physical assault or personal insult, is considered a punitive treatment. In the framework of learning theory, such assaults and insults can of course be looked upon as punishers that should *suppress the responses that precede them.* This potential effect of unprovoked aggression or hostility, however, is characteristically of little interest to the aggression researcher. The aggression researcher is instead interested in the effect of unprovoked punitive treatments on the *hostile and aggressive reaction of the victim.* Here, as pointed out earlier, a large body of data shows with consistency that hostile or aggressive punitive behavior, when perceived as arbitrary or unjustified, provokes hostile and aggressive reactions (e.g., Burnstein & Worchel, 1962; Cohen, 1955; Kregarman & Worchel, 1961; Mallick & McCandless, 1966; Pastore, 1952; Zillmann, Bryant, Cantor, & Day, 1975; Zillmann & Cantor, 1976b). Unprovoked punitive treatments amount to attacks. They amount to the infliction of pain, torment, or annoyance. In short, they are hostility- and aggression-promoting actions, and they are accordingly used in the investigation of hostility and aggression. When it is necessary to provoke the experimental subject, it is usually done via the administration of unprovoked and hence unjustified punitive actions. All the investigations in which such a provocation treatment was effective in increasing hostility and aggressiveness (studies that are far too numerous even to attempt to list here) can be taken to support the proposal that unjustified punishment provokes hostility and aggression. This, however, is just another way of saying that hostility and aggression tend to produce counterhostility and counteraggression or that attack usually prompts retaliation.

Little is known, in terms of unequivocal data, about the effect of the threat of punishment on hostility and aggression. The explicit threat of physical punishment, that is, the communication that the performance of a particular behavior will result in the infliction of bodily harm, has not been studied—for apparent ethical reasons. The explicit threat of nonphysical positive and (mainly) negative punishment has been explored but rather unsystematically. Keirsey (1969; see also Blackham & Silberman, 1971), for example, has reported the successful reduction of transgressions by the following procedure: After the explanation of privileges and personal responsibilities, the respondent was carefully informed about the specific punitive consequences (mainly social exclusion) that specific transgressions would entail; this *contractual arrangement* was then strictly enforced without further justifications. Such findings are suggestive but unfortunately cannot be considered conclusive.

Explicit threats of adverse measures, which could be construed as hostile maneuvers or punishment, have been explored in systematic laboratory investigations (e.g., Deutsch & Krauss, 1960; Kelley, 1965; Shomer, Davis, & Kelley, 1966). However, it was the effect of such threats on bargaining that was being studied, and there are no compelling implications of these and similar studies for the effect of the threat of hostility and aggression on hostility and aggression. Some investigations, nonetheless, seem suggestive. Horai and Tedeschi (1969), for example, employed a modified Prisoner's Dilemma game in which the subject's opponent threatened the removal of valued points if the subject failed to execute an indicated choice. They observed that compliance with the directive increased as a linear function of the degree of credibility of the threat, that is, with the degree to which the subject believed the threatener would enforce the contingency expressed in the threat. There also was a tendency for compliance to increase with the severity of the disadvantageous measures threatened. The threat of punishment for transgressions, specifically those of a hostile or aggressive nature, may prove to be similarly affected by the threat's credibility and potential severity. But this remains to be demonstrated, especially in view of the fact that the available information derives from game situations in which the threats employed appeared legitimate. As is the case for punishment, the threat of punishment may be perceived as differentially legitimate or illegitimate, and this perceived legitimacy of the threat should potentially affect its impact on hostile and aggressive behavior.

This section on the deterrent value of punishment shows that there is considerable conceptual confusion in the use of the punishment concept. The use of *punishment* to denote a process equivalent, yet opposite in direction, to reinforcement seems to be an unfortunate choice of terms. So is the use of *punitive* as synonym for *aversive*. In fact, the inconsistent usage of the various terms can be held partly responsible for the at-times heated controversy about punishment. In summarizing the main points of this section now, we try to avoid "semantic problems" by using the concept of aversive control whenever possible and by indicating the various interpretations of *punishment* through appropriate qualifications.

1. Aversive stimulation that cannot be perceived as manipulated by persons or institutions to control the respondent's behavior suppresses the behavior that precedes and that apparently precipitates such stimulation. Aversive control in humans functions analogously to aversive control in subhuman species. Its effects on behavior can be strong and persistent, similar to the effects of reinforcement. The research evidence does not support the view that the aversive control of human behavior is ineffective and necessarily maladaptive.

2. Hostile and aggressive behavior are under aversive control. As long as the aversive control cannot be perceived as manipulative or does not involve stimuli sufficiently intense to prompt defensive aggressive reactions, aversive contingencies tend to suppress hostility and aggression.

3. Aversive control becomes ineffective as contingent aversions are matched or dominated by simultaneously operating reinforcement contingencies. Conceiving of aversion as a cost and reinforcement as a benefit, effective aversive control requires a cost dominance in a cost–benefits analogue.

4. Aversive stimulation perceived as manipulated by persons or institutions to control the respondent's behavior does not necessarily produce effects similar to those resulting from aversive stimulation not perceived in this way. The perceived legitimacy of the application of aversive stimulation appears to be a crucial variable in the effect of aversive treatments.

5. If aversive stimulation is perceived as legitimate or is recognized as ultimately beneficial by the respondent, manipulative aversive control may function analogously to nonmanipulative aversive control.

6. If aversive stimulation is perceived as unjustified and arbitrary by the respondent, it is likely to promote rather than suppress hostility and aggression.

7. Little is known about the effect of the punishment of transgressions. The perceived legitimacy of such punishment again seems to be of great importance. Physical punishment, because its legitimacy is generally questioned, is not likely to be an effective punitive measure; if such punishment is regarded as a violation of legitimacy, it should prompt hostile and aggressive reactions. Strategies employing mild positive punishment and negative punishment of transgressions together with the the reinforcement of constructive responses appear to be the most effective in the curtailment of hostility and aggression.

8. Threat of punishment may suppress hostile and aggressive behavior if the respondent perceives it as likely that the threatened contingency can and will be enforced by the threatener.

B. Stimulus Control of Aggression

In terms of instrumental learning, behavior is viewed as being controlled primarily by the consequences for the organism that are contingent upon the behavior. However, as an integral part of instrumental learning, it is recognized that environmental stimuli that precede reinforced (or punished) behavior can assume control over the behavior in question. As Skinner (1969) put it: "Prior stimuli are not irrelevant. Any stimulus present when an operant is reinforced acquires control in the sense that the rate will be higher when it is present [p. 7]." Skinner hastens, however, to point out that "such a stimulus does not act as a goad; it does not elicit the response in the sense of forcing it to occur. It is simply an essential aspect of the occasion upon which a response is made and reinforced [p. 7]." Environmental cues are thus conceived of as *discriminative* stimuli that mainly help the organism to respond as indicated by the prevailing contingencies of reinforcement (or punishment). Although these stimuli are seen to exert some degree of control, they are clearly assigned a secondary role. In classical conditioning, by contrast, contingent behavior is not an issue. An initially neutral stimulus assumes the power to elicit a reaction unique to an unconditioned stimulus solely through its repeated presentation with the unconditioned stimulus. The conditioned stimulus does not just serve as a discriminant cue, but exerts direct control over behavior. It functions as an *eliciting* stimulus.

It should be clear from this introduction that the classical-conditioning paradigm ascribes a more significant role to the stimulus control of behavior and applies more directly to this issue than does the theory of operant learning. It is thus not surprising to find that in considering the stimulus control of hostility and aggression, this paradigm is generally preferred.

Since there is no apparent reason to treat hostile and aggressive behavior as unique with regard to stimulus control, it must be expected that hostility and aggression, just like all other behaviors, *are* under stimulus control. Animal studies leave no doubt that this is indeed the case. Demonstrations of the classical conditioning of aggression were discussed earlier (Chapter 3). Very briefly, in most of the research (e.g., Creer, Hitzing, & Schaeffer, 1966; Farris, Gideon, & Ulrich, 1970; Lyon & Ozolins, 1970; Vernon & Ulrich, 1966), pairs of animals received electric shock that induced fighting. Shock was preceded by a stimulus that initially had no effect on fighting (e.g., a tone, a light, or both). The neutral stimulus acquired the power to induce fighting. The unconditioned aggressive response to shock had thus become conditioned to the initially neutral stimulus. It has also been shown, however, that this conditioned power of stimuli to elicit aggressive behavior vanishes rapidly under extinction (e.g., Farris, Fullmer, & Ulrich, 1970). Most of the research of this type has been conducted on lower vertebrates. An exception is Delgado's (1963) report of the classical conditioning of aggressive behavior in primates, with brain stimulation as the unconditioned stimulus.

The demonstration of the stimulus control of aggression in animals, together with anecdotal evidence in human behavior (such as Toch's [1969] report of a chronic aggressor who, having received a traumatic beating by a huge opponent as a youngster, was prone to attack large-sized people at minimal provocation), has been taken to suggest that hostility and aggression in humans are probably similarly controlled (Bandura, 1973a). Additionally, it has been suggested that the stimulus control of human aggression may largely operate through semiotic mediation: The individual is conditioned to display negative reactions to words and possibly to nonverbal cues, and as these words or cues are applied to a human target, the target assumes negative valence and ultimately draws hostile and aggressive reactions. This view, which has been expressed by Bandura (1973a) and Berkowitz (1973b), is based on research in semantic conditioning. This research has shown that the connotative meaning of entities can be altered through pairings with words of either positive or negative hedonic valence (e.g., Das & Nanda, 1963; Lang, Geer, & Hnatiow, 1963; Staats & Staats, 1958, 1957). It leads to the expectation that the mere negative characterization of persons makes them more suitable targets for aggression. Recently, this prediction has been experimentally supported (Bandura, Underwood, & Fromson, 1975). The findings are open to numerous alternative explanations, however, and it remains to be shown whether the aggression-facilitating effect of derogation is in fact due to semantic conditioning.

In Bandura's approach to aggression, stimulus control, especially through classical conditioning, is assigned a relatively minor role, however. In contrast, Berkowitz, who has always entertained what could be considered a stimulus-control theory of aggression (e.g., 1962, 1965a), has recently committed himself more explicitly than earlier to the paradigm of classical conditioning of aggressive responses and to stimulus control generally (e.g., 1970, 1973b, 1974). In Berkowitz's recent thinking, the conditioning of the power to elicit hostile and aggressive reactions to potentially any initially neutral stimulus is the nucleus of the theory; secondary, modifying factors, such as the degree of aggressive instigation or anger arousal, are organized around it. Particularly in connection with the discussion of "impulsive aggression" (i.e., unpremeditated annoyance-motivated aggression), Berkowitz (1970, 1973a) has suggested that operant learning has been greatly overemphasized and that a classical-conditioning model would be the superior explanatory mechanism. In his view (1970), the aggressor "reacts impulsively to particular stimuli in his environment, not because his inhibitions have been weakened or because he anticipates the pleasures arising from his actions, but because situational stimuli have evoked the response he is predisposed or set to make in that setting [p. 104]." The automaticity of such aggression is emphasized: The individual is said (1967) to react "to these stimuli without considering what he wants or does not want to do, and with no regard for the possible adaptive significance of his behavior [p. 243]." In this view, then, through the manipulated or incidental pairing of initially neutral environmental stimuli with aggression-evoking cues, the stimuli assume the power to trigger aggressive reactions in a highly automatic fashion. The stimuli act as a goad. They force aggression out of the organism. The organism cannot help itself, so to speak. In this view, cognitive processes that could intervene and guide behavior are clearly denied a critical function. Although their existence is occasionally acknowledged, they apparently are viewed as lacking the capacity to inhibit an aggressive course of action. Man's aggressive behavior is seen as being controlled primarily by environmental stimuli just as it is in subhuman species. There is a difference with regard to the use of sign systems, however. Unlike other species, man apparently can readily manipulate the "aggressive meaning" of events. Through linguistic operations and the arbitrary use of symbols, he can link events to aggression, and this capability, so it seems, makes him all the more vulnerable to being seduced into violent actions.

Berkowitz (1970, 1973a, 1974) has drawn mainly upon findings that were obtained in connection with the study of cue-mediation (e.g., Berkowitz & Geen, 1967; Geen & Berkowitz, 1966) and the so-called weapons effect (e.g., Berkowitz & LePage, 1967) to support his proposal of the classical conditioning of impulsive aggression. These studies have been discussed earlier (Section IIA3 of Chapter 4). An inspection of the procedures employed in these studies reveals no direct parallels with classical conditioning. There is no systematic pairing of an unconditioned and a conditioned stimulus and hence no conditioning of aggression. As a consequence, these studies cannot be considered supportive of a conditioning explanation in any decisive way. Instead, they can be viewed as having produced findings that are consistent with a conditioning interpretation in the weak sense that if it is assumed that the aggressive words and aggressive cues (e.g., guns and the like) functioned as conditioned stimuli, their presence contributed to the intensity of aggressive reactions. Such an assumption seems quite arbitrary, however. This is especially apparent when the case of aggression facilitation through the mediation of labels and names is considered. As will be recalled, such mediation was observed, for example, when the subject was told, after seeing a film of a prizefight, that his opponent's name was "Kirk" or "Kelley"—the same as that of the losing protagonist. At best, this is one-trial, backward conditioning of a possible vicarious aggressive response. The correspondence of this procedure with the basic paradigm of classical conditioning is obviously quite loose.

We now briefly review the investigations that have been interpreted as more direct tests of the proposed automatic stimulus control of aggression (e.g., Berkowitz, 1970).

Loew (1967) conducted an investigation in which male subjects first were "reinforced" for selecting from a set of words either an aggressive or a nonaggressive word. Reinforcement consisted of the experimenter's comment "Correct." Under the guise of a teaching task, subjects then administered electric shock to another person without having been provoked by this person. It was found that whether or not the teaching task involved a frustration, subjects who had been reinforced for selecting the aggressive words administered shocks of greater intensity than those who had been reinforced for nonaggressive choices.

Geen and Pigg (1970) reversed the order of the events in Loew's study. They either verbally reinforced or did not reinforce male subjects for administering intense shock to another person, and thereafter they assessed the use of aggressive words in an association task. It was found that subjects who had been reinforced for behaving aggressively exhibited a higher frequency of aggressive associates than subjects who had not been reinforced.

Although the frequent occurrence of words with aggressive connotations in free association in the latter study cannot readily be considered a measure of hostile behavior, the two studies are taken to "show that the reinforcement of one kind of aggressive response increases the likelihood of other types of aggressive reactions as well" (Berkowitz, 1973b, p. 120). This extension of "automatic reactions" to cues is somehow viewed as due to conditioning, but it is left unclear which behavior is considered conditioned to which cues. Even if uttering an aggressive word in a learning or association task is taken as a manifestation of aggression comparable to the administration of electric shock to another person, and even if both manifestations, words and shock, are considered interchangeable as unconditioned and conditioned responses, it is unclear which external stimulus should have acquired the power to elicit aggressive reactions and thus extend the initially reinforced behavior. Taking Loew's findings at face value, should approving reactions to utterances that somehow relate to violence promote aggressive responses to *any* stimulus situation? Similarly, do the findings reported by Geen and Pigg suggest that the reinforcement of aggression will enhance aggression-related verbalizations regardless of the specific stimuli present at that time? The extension of "aggressiveness," automatic as it may seem, appears to be "pushed" more than "pulled" in these particular research situations.

Geen and Stonner (1971) conducted an experiment that avoids the ambiguities regarding the aggressive response. Male subjects were either verbally reinforced ("That's good" and "You're doing fine") or not reinforced for delivering intense electric shock to another person whenever a light went on. Thereafter, subjects delivered shock in response to either aggressive words (*choke, massacre, murder, stab,* and *torture*) or nonaggressive words (*wash, travel, walk, relax, sleep,* and *listen*), which were projected on a screen. It was found that reinforced subjects gave more intense shocks in response to aggressive words than in response to neutral words. If it is reasonable to assume that respondents are generally conditioned to respond aggressively to such words as *massacre,* this effect is indeed consistent with a conditioning explanation. Geen and Stonner also observed, however, that subjects who had not been reinforced for behaving aggressively administered less intense shocks in response to aggressive words than in response to neutral ones. This finding is at variance with the assumption that aggressive words are conditioned triggers of aggression. Following Geen and Stonner, the findings on reinforced subjects can be explained as the result of the extension of an aggressive habit formed during the reinforcement period. The findings obtained from nonreinforced subjects, however, do not accord with this suggestion. Considering all the information, the findings seem to be best explained as the result of transparency and evaluation apprehension: As suggested earlier, verbal reinforcement amounts to the approval and encouragement of aggression; once aggression is thus legitimized in one phase of the experiment, the legitimization apparently extends into later phases. Subjects who are not verbally encouraged to behave aggressively, on the other hand, should experience apprehension about their aggressive behavior, and this apprehension should become particularly salient when the subjects are exposed to words such as *massacre*. Thus, although the findings show that the encouragement of aggression in one encounter may promote aggressiveness in subsequent interactions, the interpretation of the findings as evidence for the response-mediated stimulus generalization of aggression (Berkowitz, 1970) appears premature and unwarranted.

A recent investigation by Swart and Berkowitz (1976) may seem to relate more directly to the classical conditioning of aggression than the earlier studies discussed. In this investigation, male subjects were either provoked or not provoked by receiving either 8 shocks or 1 shock, respectively, from a confederate who was evaluating their performance on a task. Sitting alone in a soundproof booth, they were then made to record the frequency of flashes of a white light (8 flashes). The meaning of this light signal was systematically varied by instructions:

1. The subject was told that the experimenter had to deliver shock to the other subject—that is, the confederate—and that the white light signaled the reception of painful electric shock.
2. The subject was also told that the confederate was receiving shock from the experimenter but that the record of the white-light flashes was needed for the calibration of a timer.
3. The subject was told that the confederate, being in a control condition, would not receive shock and that the white-light observation served the calibration of a timer.

Thereafter, subjects were required to deliver shock to a person who had not been involved up to this point in the described interactions. Shock was to be delivered in response to the familiar white light and to a novel blue light. Forty signals (20 flashes of each light) were presented in random order. Intensity and duration of the shocks delivered in response to these lights served as the measure of aggression.

Swart and Berkowitz assumed that information about the confederate's suffering was rewarding to the provoked subject, and they proposed that the stimuli associated with this gratification would come to control future aggression. Accordingly, the provoked subject was expected to behave more aggressively (i.e., deliver more intense and longer shocks) in response to the white light than in response to the blue light. The white signal was viewed as the conditioned stimulus that would trigger the aggressive reaction, and classical conditioning was said to be the mechanism through which such stimulus control was to come about.

We have seen earlier (Section IIIA2 of Chapter 4) that the assumption that the victim's expression of pain is reinforcing has not been supported experimentally. Notwithstanding the weakness of this assumption, it is difficult to see how the described procedure can be regarded as classical conditioning. How can the white light, the presumed reinforcer in provoked subjects, become a conditioned stimulus for *aggression?* If the light is considered a reinforcer, sitting and waiting for someone else to attack an annoyer (i.e., the actual behavior that preceded the reinforcer) should be reinforced. Regardless of specifics, it is the subject's *nonaggressive* behavior that should be strengthened. If the light is treated as a stimulus, one would expect the reaction it might prompt under the circumstances—namely enjoyment (of the fact that an obnoxious person is getting his due)—to become conditioned to it. The white light should come to trigger euphoric reactions, not aggressive ones.

To support a classical-conditioning model of aggression, the white light should have been connected with the triggering of *aggressive responses* by another stimulus, and it should have been shown that after repeated linkages, the presentation of the light alone came to trigger aggressive reactions. Clearly, the procedure employed in the discussed investigation did not do this, and thus the data simply cannot be interpreted in terms of classical conditioning. The references to this mechanism, in fact, must be considered careless and misleading.

Although the findings presented by Swart and Berkowitz have no bearing on the classical conditioning of aggression, the study can be viewed as a test of the mediation model discussed earlier (Section IIA3 of Chapter 4). The findings do not give unequivocal support to this model, however. It could be argued that for the annoyed subject, the white light came to be associated with justified and even enjoyable aggression when it signaled the punishment of the tormentor. This association in the later aggressive encounter may have promoted aggression because it made the aggression appear more justified and enjoyable. Consequently, one might expect that subjects would behave more aggressively in the presence of the white light than in the presence of the blue light. This difference would not be expected for unprovoked subjects who learned to associate the white light with the pain of an undeserving target or for provoked or unprovoked subjects for whom the white light never signaled pain. The findings were not in accord with this reasoning. The experimental manipulations had no effect on the duration of shocks. On the intensity measure, there was a significant interaction between the provocation treatments, the meanings of the white light in the initial period, and the colors of the light signal in the final period. The analysis of this interaction reveals that there were no reliable differences in the intensity of shocks delivered in response to the white and blue lights. In provoked subjects, the pain-associated white light failed to produce more intense shocks than the blue light. Also, in the conditions in which the tormentor ostensibly received shock, the intensity of shock delivered in response to the white light when it was associated with the tormentor's pain did not reliably differ from its intensity when the light was not associated with his pain, although the difference was in the predicted direction. Considering all the data, the critical comparisons do not support the mediation model. If there were associations between pain and aggression, they failed to exert automatic stimulus control.

Swart and Berkowitz arrived at a somewhat different assessment, which is largely based on the analysis of the shock intensity data in 4 blocks of 10 responses. Although there were no significant effects in blocks 1 through 3, the 4th block yielded the significant interaction that we have discussed. In this 4th block, provoked subjects who associated the white light with their tormentor's pain administered significantly more intense shock in response to the white light than in response to the blue light. This supportive finding is compromised, however, by directly related findings that were left unexplained. In the pain-association condition, unprovoked subjects administered significantly more intense shocks in response to the blue light than provoked subjects. The margin of difference was the same as that in the comparison of the effect of the two lights in provoked subjects. The aggression-triggering power of the white light in provoked subjects was thus virtually identical to that of the blue light in unprovoked subjects—a finding that can hardly be considered to show the proposed aggression-eliciting power of associative linkages.

But whatever the findings reported by Swart and Berkowitz show, they cannot be considered to establish the classical conditioning of human aggression. The white signal was not, as claimed, a conditioned stimulus for aggression. Since it was not, it is incongruous to suggest that the white light's elicitation power may have temporarily generalized to the blue light, thus "explaining" the lack of a difference between the aggression elicited by the "conditioned stimulus" and that elicited by the neutral one throughout the initial three-quarters of the response sequence. Such a suggestion shows to what extent investigators put faith in the classical conditioning of aggression and treat it as a truism: Negative evidence is not accepted as nonsupportive; rather, null effects are viewed as supporting a particular aspect of the theory and ultimately the theory as a whole. Since the classical conditioning of human aggression has not yet been rigorously demonstrated, it can only be an act of faith in the theory that has led Berkowitz (e.g., 1970, 1973b, 1974) to project a world in which people are helplessly drawn into violence by all the stimuli that in the past preceded or were otherwise linked to aggressive outbursts. Conditioning and stimulus control are so liberally interpreted that the mere mention of a word with aggressive connotations is viewed as having the power to trigger violent reactions, especially in those who have suffered frustrations. The individual is apparently at the mercy of an environment laden with cues that may liberate aggressive associations and ultimately violence. Berkowitz's reasoning on aggressive cues is preoccupied with showing that stimulus control is established and strengthened. The deterioration of such control is entirely ignored. As a consequence, all roads, in his projections, lead to violence. If, for example, a youngster has fought others in front of red brick walls, red brick walls should come to trigger attacks on anyone he encounters. The sight of weapons should instigate aggression. So should the sight of a black eye or a band-aid. A word such as *rape* and exposure to aggressive sports events (e.g., a football game) and fictional violence (e.g., a detective story) should also elicit aggression. As long as a stimulus can somehow be related to aggression, the individual who encounters it, especially the annoyed one, is apparently viewed as on his or her way to commit an aggressive act.

Such a projection of stimulus control appears grossly distorted. If aggression is viewed as controlled by conditioned and discriminative stimuli, nonaggressive reactions must be considered to be similarly controlled. Specifically, if attack can be conditioned, so can avoidance, withdrawal, and escape. If, for example, fighting in front of red brick walls proved painful and induced flight in the past, red brick walls should trigger flight. Furthermore, if we follow the suggestion of findings on animal behavior, stimulus control is of course subject to extinction. If red brick walls indeed assume the power to induce fight or flight, this power will not prevail forever; it should diminish steadily, especially when novel experiences with red brick walls (i.e., activities without potential opponents and aggression-provoking threats) intervene. Thus, in entertaining a stimulus-control theory of aggression, there are at least two qualifying factors that have to be acknowledged: (a) Stimulus control applies to nonaggressive behavior as well as to aggressive behavior; and (b) stimulus control is subject to extinction. The application of these obvious considerations alone should prevent much overgeneralization.

In entertaining a stimulus-control theory of aggression, it is also necessary to give some attention to naturally prevailing conditions. If it is reasonable to assume that children and adults, mainly under the influence of punishment contingencies, resist far more often than not the temptation to aggress against an annoyer, preceding stimuli should assume the power to elicit nonaggressive reactions to annoyance. This idea relates to Scott's (1958) notion of the *passive inhibition* of aggression: A habit of nonfighting is formed simply by not fighting; if no aggressive response is displayed, it cannot become subject to stimulus control (nor can it be reinforced). Only the behavior of individuals who respond aggressively to provocation with some consistency can come, for some time at least, under stimulus control. Similarly, the use of signs with aggressive referents or connotations, words in particular, cannot be viewed as consistently linked with fighting. When aggression-laden words are used in direct encounters, they may be associated as much with fear and escape as with anger and aggression. The same applies when the covert use of such words is considered. When aggression-laden signs are viewed as conditioned stimuli for aggression, the occurrence of every sign that is not followed by aggressive activities furthers extinction. In this connection, a stimulus-control model of aggression apparently leads to a view of the effect of exposure to "symbolic" aggression that is virtually opposite to the one that has been attributed to such a model. Media violence, for example, should be seen as "extinction training." The viewer, whether taking the fare he or she is exposed to calmly or being aroused about it, de facto practices nonaggressive responses to threats, assaults, and other aggression-related events. If these stimuli ever "pulled" aggression, their power to do so should have rapidly deteriorated. This, of course, is counter to Berkowitz's (e.g., 1965a, 1970, 1973b, 1974) proposal of the aggression-enhancing effect of exposure to aggressive events.

The strict application of the stimulus-control paradigm to aggression thus does not produce the bleak consequences projected by Berkowitz. Stimulus control is not partial to aggression. *If* it plays a significant role in human affairs, it seems to further the nonaggressive resolution of conflict more than the aggressive one. The degree to which it exerts its automatic influence on overt behavior is, however, precisely what is in dispute. When it comes to behavior that is apparently under volitional control, aggression being a case in point, is it reasonable to assume that human beings, like fish and birds, react mechanically to cues that happened to be present when aggressive behavior was performed previously? Is man unable to employ his cognitive skills to correct a behavioral inclination? If, for example, behavior is recognized as being nonrewarding and as involving a high risk of aversive consequences, must it still be executed in response to conditioned stimuli? Does the boy who was successfully aggressive against lesser peers in front of red brick walls take on a far superior opponent just because of the locale?

Presumably, there is some degree of stimulus control of aggression in humans. There is no reason to treat aggression as behavior that differs basically from other behaviors, and since many other behaviors have been shown to be under stimulus control, one should expect aggression to be similarly controlled. Although at this time decisive evidence of the stimulus control of aggression is lacking, it would seem possible to demonstrate it experimentally under conditions in which other factors are made nonsalient. It is the relative contribution that stimulus control can make in the evocation of human aggression that constitutes the critical domain of uncertainty. The evidence amassed to show the influence of nonimpulsive, cognitive mediation in the facilitation and curtailment of aggression (i.e., information about intent or mitigating circumstances) challenges the automaticity of stimulus control proposed by Berkowitz. It suggests very strongly that in general, cognitive processes readily override impulses that may arise due to stimulus control. The individual can and does apply considerations that make aggressive behavior far less irrational and maladaptive than the one-sided interpretation of automatic stimulus control projects. We discuss the various elements of cognitive guidance in aggressive behavior in the forthcoming chapters.

Our discussion of the stimulus control of aggression may be summarized as follows:

1. Conspecific fighting in animals has been shown to be under the control of discriminative and conditioned stimuli.
2. There is no evidence as yet that shows with decisiveness that human aggressive behavior is under stimulus control.
3. Proposals in which aggression is viewed as primarily under the control of discriminative and conditioned stimuli are not substantiated by research findings.
4. The degree to which stimulus control may exert an influence on human aggression remains to be determined.

C. Social Learning of Aggression

The most comprehensive theory of human aggression to date (although considered more a systematic position or even "a way of thinking about aggression" than a theory by some [e.g., Pepitone, 1974]) has been proposed by Bandura (1973a, 1973b). In his "social-learning theory of aggression," Bandura first endorsed the learning of aggression through direct experiences, in accord with the basic paradigms of learning. Aggression is viewed as largely controlled by reinforcement and punishment contingencies. It is also seen to be under stimulus control. However, as a point of departure from other approaches, Bandura added further mechanisms to account for aspects of aggressive behavior that seem uniquely human and that are not adequately explained by the basic learning paradigms. Apparently, much behavior, including aggression, is learned through observation alone—that is, *without direct experience*. Bandura (1965, 1969, 1971a, 1971c) has proposed various theoretical rationales to account for such "no-trial learning." Also, more than any other investigator outside the Freudian tradition, Bandura has acknowledged the unique human capacity for information processing, and he has elaborated its implications for the instigation, maintenance, modification, and control of aggression. We now briefly discuss Bandura's proposals concerning *observational learning* and *cognitive control* in aggression.

The premise in observational learning is that "observed outcomes influence behavior in much the same way as do directly experienced consequences"

(Bandura, 1973b, p. 235). The individual is seen not to be entirely dependent on making his or her own mistakes in a trial-and-error fashion. After observing others fail, the individual can correct his or her behavior so as to avoid failure. Similarly, after merely witnessing the success of others, he or she should be inclined to achieve similar success through the observed, apparently effective behavioral means. Observing a model perform a particular activity and then receive a reward should thus, as with direct reinforcement, increase the observer's response rate for that behavior; observing a model perform this activity and then be subjected to an aversive treatment should, as with direct punishment, decrease the response rate for that behavior. Talking about the effects of "vicarious reinforcement" and "vicarious punishment" on the *rate* of a response is somewhat misleading, however. If the response in question is already established in the observer's repertoire, the rate of its emission is indeed what should be affected. If, however, the response in question is not yet established, it is the likelihood of the occurrence of the response that should increase with witnessed contingent reinforcement and decrease with witnessed contingent punishment. In general terms, then, and with regard to aggressive behavior, "seeing aggression rewarded in others increases, and seeing it punished decreases, the tendency to behave in similar aggressive ways [Bandura, 1973b, pp. 235-236]."

Bandura (1971a, 1971c, 1971d) has developed various rationales to explain the proposed effects of vicarious reinforcement and vicarious punishment.

The first major rationale concerns the *informative function* of observed outcomes. By witnessing response consequences in others, the observer becomes aware of the prevailing contingencies of reinforcement and punishment and can arrange his or her own behavior so as to maximize rewards and minimize aversions in the observed environment without having directly experienced these contingencies. Knowledge about likely response consequences, obtained through observation, can thus serve to facilitate or inhibit responses similar to those witnessed. According to this view, it is the *anticipation of consequences* based on the observation of the behavior of others, not immediate past experience, that guides the individual's action. As Bandura (1971a) put it: "Unlike the operant conditioning interpretation, the social learning formulation assumes that imitative behavior is regulated by observers' judgments of probable consequences for prospective actions rather than being directly controlled by stimuli that were correlated with reinforcement [p. 49]."

In support of this view, it has been shown (e.g., Bandura & Barab, 1971; Kaufman, Baron, & Kopp, 1966) that contingencies of reinforcement and punishment that are *believed* to prevail do indeed control behavior; they can, in fact, override and dominate the controlling influence of the actually prevailing contingencies.

The second major rationale posits *motivational effects of the vicarious conditioning and extinction of emotional arousal.* Bandura (e.g., 1971c) acknowledged that much emotional behavior is learned on the basis of direct experiences but nonetheless suggested that *empathetic reactions* that effect the *vicarious conditioning of affective responses* are equally, if not more, important. It is assumed that witnessing others express emotions generally induces affective reactions in the observer. It is further assumed that these affective reactions in the observer are *concordant* (cf. Berger, 1962) with those displayed by the person whose behavior has been witnessed. (In this context, concordance of affect reduces to concordance of the hedonic valence of affect. Bandura [personal communication, 1977] assumes a high degree of affinity between witnessed affect and empathetic reaction but does not expect these behaviors to be necessarily identical in terms of a typology of affect. However, the proposed affinity assures hedonic compatibility.) Thus, the observer's empathetic reaction is taken to be hedonically congruent with the affective behavior that has been witnessed. Bandura based this crucial assumption on the speculation that in social situations, people tend to express the same kind of emotional behavior as those around them, and therefore another's expression of affect becomes a discriminative cue for concordant affect in the observer. In other words, in social situations, concordant affect is conditioned to witnessing the expression of affect in others. Bandura (1971c) stated:

> Affective social cues most likely acquire arousal value as a result of correlated experiences between people. That is, individuals who are in high spirits tend to treat others in amiable ways, which arouse in them similar pleasurable affects; conversely, when individuals are dejected, ailing, distressed, or angry, others are also likely to suffer in one way or another [pp. 13–14].

Under the assumption of conditioned concordant affective reactions, it is then proposed (Bandura, 1971a) that because "models generally exhibit emotional reactions while undergoing rewarding or punishing experiences [p. 50]": (a) witnessing a model being rewarded will evoke positive feelings, such as gratification, that promote the imitation of the model's behavior; and (b) witnessing a model being punished will evoke negative feelings, such as fear, that effect response suppression. Roughly speaking, then, a model who is rewarded for aggressive actions is expected to promote aggression, because aggression becomes associated with pleasant feelings; conversely, a model who is punished for aggressive actions is expected to reduce aggression, because aggression has become associated with feelings of discomfort and uneasiness. It is recognized, however, that conditioned vicarious affect, when not occasionally reinstated, is subject to rapid extinction. In fact, Bandura (1969, 1971b) has successfully built procedures for the modification of maladaptive affective behavior (e.g., for the reduction and elimination of unfounded fears and phobias) on the basis of the systematic extinction of conditioned affect.

Although there is evidence that shows that vicarious affective reactions can readily be conditioned (e.g., Bandura & Rosenthal, 1966; Barnett & Benedetti, 1960; Berger, 1962; Craig & Weinstein, 1965), the assumption that people generally react concordantly with the emotions displayed by others seems questionable in the light of recent findings. As indicated earlier, it has been observed (Zillmann & Cantor, 1977) that a negative disposition toward a potential model occasions discordant rather than concordant affective reactions. The apparent dispositional control of affective reactions (cf. Zillmann & Cantor, 1976a) suggests that the projections put forth in the vicarious-conditioning rationale apply only to positively, or at least nonnegatively, perceived models. In fact, the rationale's predictions should be reversed in the case of a rejected model who induces discordant affect: Response-suppressing negative feelings should become associated with aggression when aggression is consistently seen as rewarding for a resented model. Conversely, response-enhancing positive feelings should come to be associated with aggression when it is witnessed as punishing for such a model.

The remaining rationales proposed by Bandura (1971a, 1971c, 1971d) to explain modeling are secondary to these two primary rationales. They address the consequences, mainly in terms of person perception, of the fact that a model has been witnessed to receive rewards or punishments from some agent for his or her actions. The entire episode is viewed as altering the observer's perception of both the model and the reinforcing or punishing agent, and this altered perception is seen to influence modeling. The *model's status*, for example, is seen to increase as rewards are received for apparently well performed behaviors. The gain in social status should then make the model more appealing and influential. Conversely, punishment is seen to devalue the model, making him or her less worthy of emulation. Similarly, the *valuation of the reinforcing or punishing agent* can be enhanced through his or her apparent fairness in administering rewards and punishments. When these agents "misuse their power to reward and punish they undermine the legitimacy of their authority and generate strong resentment" (Bandura, 1971a, p. 51). Inequitable reward or punishment, then, is seen to be irritating and disturbing and hence to interfere with the modeling process. Inappropriate reward and punishment, in itself, is viewed as potentially promoting hostility and aggression. "Seeing inequitable punishment may free incensed observers from self-censure of their own actions, rather than prompting compliance, and thus increase transgressive behavior [1971a, p. 51]." Clearly, Bandura involves considerations of justice in projecting the effect of vicarious reinforcement and punishment. Equity in reward and in punishment must be perceived as such by the respondent. In case of perceived inequities, the predictions derived from the primary rationales can be modified and possibly overruled. The respondent's moral judgment is thus implicated with an important mediating function in modeling.

Bandura's (e.g., 1971a, 1971c, 1971d) analysis of motivational processes in social learning extends the proposal of behavior control by external and vicarious reinforcement and punishment to *self-reinforcement* and *self-punishment*. (1973a):

> At the highest level of psychological functioning, individuals regulate their own behavior by self-evaluative and other self-produced consequences ... In this process people set themselves certain standards of conduct and respond to their own behavior in self-satisfied or self-critical ways in accordance with their self-imposed demands [p. 48].

The individual is thus seen to internalize prevalent norms or possibly to construct his or her own system of reinforcement and punishment. Then, since the individual functions as the self-rewarding or -punishing agent, he or she behaves so as to maximize the pleasures of self-approval and to minimize the aversions of self-contempt. "Having adopted a self-monitoring system, they [people] do things that give them self-satisfaction and a feeling of self-worth; conversely, they refrain from behaving in ways that result in self-criticism and other self-devaluative consequences [Bandura, 1973b, p. 237]."

Bandura feels that self-reinforcement and self-punishment can readily dominate the influence of external reinforcement and punishment. "There is no more devastating punishment than self-contempt [1973a, p. 48]." External reinforcement and punishment are seen to exert their greatest influence on behavior when they are consonant with self-generated approval or contempt. Should external inducements, whether rewarding or punishing, prevail over dissonant self-regulatory influences, individuals may show "cheerless compliance"; and if they fail to "justify" it adequately to themselves, such compliance, in Bandura's view, may have maladaptive consequences.

In aggression, *self-reinforcement* is viewed as the primary motivating force whenever it is connected with personal pride. *Self-punishment* for aggression is in evidence when the individual suffers dysphoric feelings of regret and self-accusation upon recognizing his or her actions as a violation of his or her own stand against aggressive actions per se. Since in general, negative sanctions against aggression must be assumed to have been adopted through precept, reinforcement, and modeling, Bandura (1973a, 1973b) proposed various mechanisms to account for the apparent fact that in hostile and aggressive outbursts, self-imposed restrictions are often disregarded. "By engaging in a variety of self-deceptive cognitive maneuvers, humane, moral people can behave cruelly without self-condemnation [1973b, p. 238]." The self-absolving practices implicated with the *neutralization of self-condemnation for aggression* are as follows:

1. *Slighting aggression by advantageous comparison* is said to occur when aggressive actions are compared with more hideous deeds. The comparison is seen to minimize the transgression (in terms of internalized standards) that is being contemplated or that has been committed.

2. The *justification of aggression in terms of higher principles* is said to make violence morally palatable to the aggressor by declaring its objectives noble and righteous. Aggression, as a means, is thus justified through the ends it accomplishes.

3. The neutralization of self-condemnation for aggression, it is posited, can also be achieved through the *displacement of responsibility* to an authority who is seen as assuming full responsibility for the hostile or aggressive action contemplated or taken.

4. Similarly, *diffusion of responsibility* to others who take part in hostile and aggressive activities, or who are known to promote and support such activities, is viewed as diminishing self-criticisms.

5. Another way in which the aggressor is seen to prevent self-devaluation is in the *dehumanization of victims*. As victims are dispossessed of distinguishing, human characteristics—that is, as they are presented as degenerate, subhuman beings—self-reproach for aggression becomes inappropriate and inapplicable.

6. The *attribution of blame to victims* is said to neutralize self-condemnation when aggressors, who think of themselves as well-meaning, manage to perceive themselves to be "forced into punitive actions by villainous adversaries [1973b, p. 240]." The attribution of culpability is seen to spur feelings of indignation, which provide moral support for the aggressor's actions.

7. *Misrepresentation of consequences* has also been implicated. The injurious consequences of aggression may be played down to avoid self-reproach. In actions that have brought benefits and harm, the former may be exaggerated and the latter minimized.

8. Finally, Bandura proposed (1973b) a process of *graduated desensitization* through which initially nonaggressive persons may become increasingly aggressive. It is suggested that the marked behavioral changes thus brought about may go largely unnoticed by the individuals concerned.

Initially, individuals are prompted to perform aggressive acts they can tolerate without excessive self-censure. After their discomfort and self-reproof are extinguished through repeated performance, the level of aggression is progressively increased in this manner until eventually gruesome deeds, originally regarded as abhorrent, can be performed without much distress [p. 241].

With the exception of the final rationale (8), all these proposed mechanisms apparently can serve a dual function. First, the considerations involved can be applied to contemplated hostile and aggressive behaviors, in which case—because anticipations of self-reproach are minimized—aggressive behavior is freed from inhibition. In short, aggression is encouraged—or more literally, de-discouraged. Second, the considerations may be applied after hostile and aggressive acts have been performed. In this case, the proposed mechanisms can be seen to function analogously to Freudian defense mechanisms. The perceived magnitude of transgressions is generally reduced, making it easier, so to speak, for the individual to live with the fact of having committed malicious and violent transgressions. This effect, of course, feeds directly into the proposed process of iterative desensitization.

In advancing the mechanisms of vicarious reinforcement and punishment and self-reinforcement and self-punishment, Bandura (e.g., 1971a, 1971c) has stipulated the involvement of specific *cognitive processes*. For vicarious contingencies of reinforcement and punishment to take effect, the individual obviously must *attend* to the model whose behavior manifests the contingency in question. The individual must also have the capability to *retain* the information obtained through observation. Bandura suggests that in humans, this required retention is greatly facilitated by symbolic coding and the associated cognitive organization, and by symbolic rehearsal. However, he feels that motor rehearsal may be important as well. Finally, in order for modeling effects to be possible, the individual must be equipped for *motor reproduction*. Clearly, a modeling effect cannot materialize when the individual is physically unable to execute a response similar to the one observed and to employ feedback from his or her performance to match the model's response more closely.

More importantly here, Bandura (e.g., 1973a, 1973b) has stressed the involvement of cognitive processes in the mediation of the behavior-controlling power of the contingencies of reinforcement and punishment. These cognitive processes have been subsumed under the label "cognitive control." They are detailed as follows:

1. Probably the most significant factor of cognitive control entails the *cognitive representation of contingencies of reinforcement and punishment.* It is assumed that human beings are generally capable of recognizing prevailing contingencies and that as these contingencies are comprehended and an awareness of them is achieved, this *awareness of the identified contingencies will guide the individual's action.* Human behavior is thus seen, not as depending on lengthy, piecemeal learning, but as efficiently cut short

by insightful functioning. The awareness of contingencies of reinforcement and punishment is viewed as overriding the influence of the actually prevailing contingencies. Should the perception of these contingencies be erroneous, inappropriate behavior should result. However, as discrepancies between the individual's initial perception of contingencies and those found actually to prevail become apparent, the individual eventually should correct his or her perception. In Bandura's words (1973a):

"When actions are guided by anticipated consequences derived from predictors that do not accurately reflect existing contingencies of reinforcement, behavior is weakly controlled by its actual consequences until cumulative experiences produce more realistic expectations [p. 51]."

The thrust of the argument is that human behavior—hostility and aggression being cases in point—"is regulated to a large extent by *anticipated consequences of prospective actions* [Bandura, 1973a, p. 50; italics added]" rather than by the incidental history of contingent reinforcing and punishing external events. The anticipations are seen, of course, to be subject to distortion by acute desires and subject to judgmental error.

2. Another aspect of cognitive control, according to Bandura (e.g., 1973a), is the *cognitive guidance* of behavior. The superior human capacity to process information is said to produce a selective valuation of particular reinforcing or punishing experiences. Whereas in subhuman species, the impact of a reinforcing or punishing event seems to deteriorate mechanically with the passage of time, certain short-lived effects apparently can be arbitrarily extended in humans. Bandura suggests (1973a) that this is so because "transitory external events are coded and stored in symbolic form for memory representation [p. 52]." This type of representation is seen to facilitate the rehearsal and the reinstatement of particular events. As a result, single incidents that should have only a brief impact on behavior can exert a lasting influence. Some critical experiences, then, can guide behavior to a degree grossly disproportional to their immediate value in terms of reinforcement and punishment.

3. Bandura (e.g., 1973a) finally stresses the function of *mental problem solving* in the cognitive control of behavior. This function is analogous to Freudian *Probe-handeln*. The consequences of prospective actions are contemplated and anticipated in thought rather than determined through preliminary overt behavior. This human capability to probe various actions covertly rather than overtly enables the individual to form optimal hostile and aggressive strategies in accord with self-set criteria. Such strategies may be quite independent of the individual's direct experience with contingencies of reinforcement and punishment relating to the behaviors contemplated. "Alternative courses of action," Bandura wrote (1973a), "are generally tested in symbolic exploration and either discarded or retained on the basis of

III. AGGRESSION AS LEARNED BEHAVIOR 239

calculated consequences. The best symbolic solution is then executed in action [p. 52]."

In summary, Bandura's social-learning theory of aggression comprises the following elements:

1. Hostility and aggression are seen to be under the control of contingencies of *external* reinforcement and punishment. They are also seen to be under the control of external discriminative cues and conditioned stimuli.

2. Hostility and aggression are said to be similarly controlled by contingencies of *vicarious* reinforcement and punishment. Vicarious discriminative cues and conditioned stimuli are said to function analogously to external stimulus control.

3. Hostility and aggression may be under the control of *self*-reinforcement and *self*-punishment.

4. Hostility and aggression are under *cognitive* control. Cognitive control potentially dominates stimulus and reinforcement or punishment control. It results in rational, behavior-guiding strategies that are relatively independent of direct (or vicarious) experiences with contingencies of reinforcement and punishment.

Bandura (1973a, 1973b) has built a strong case for the social-learning theory of aggression. He has interpreted the evidence concerning the control of aggression through external events (i.e., through contingencies of direct reinforcement and punishment and through discriminative and conditioned stimuli) as consistent with and supportive of the social-learning approach. In what should be considered the most significant contribution of the social-learning theory of aggression to the elucidation of the phenomenon of aggression, he has aggregated an impressive body of findings that support the proposals concerning the effect of *vicarious* reinforcement, *vicarious* punishment, and *vicarious* discriminative and conditioned stimuli. The evidence that establishes the predicted consequences of *modeling* is highly consistent and quite convincing. The pertinent research has been presented and discussed in great detail by Bandura (1973a) and others (e.g., Baron, 1977). In view of the availability of such excellent, extensive reviews, which the interested reader is urged to consult, we avoid unnecessary redundancy and do not elaborate on the crucial findings here. Suffice it to say that there is compelling evidence that shows that *hostile and aggressive behaviors can be acquired, maintained, strengthened, weakened, and eliminated through modeling*. Hostility and aggression are thus, without a doubt, greatly influenced by exposure to models. The important determining factors of this exposure (i.e., what type of model achieves what effect under what circumstances?) have been delineated. With regard to the various mechanisms posited to explain the demonstrated modeling effects, there is still considerable ambiguity, however. In particular, it has remained quite unclear which of the proposed mechanisms is mainly responsible for the modeling effect. The informative function, vicarious conditioning, and changes in the perception of salient features of the agents involved in the paradigm are characteristically confounded. The various proposed mechanisms, it seems, operate in concert, and it may prove difficult if not impossible to separate them in order to test their involvement or their respective contributions. The status of the various proposed cognitive processes implicated with control functions is even more uncertain. Suggestive as some of the findings may be, the covert nature of these processes has caused them to elude compelling implications. Nonetheless, when these processes are treated as hypothetical constructs, their involvement may help to elucidate phenomena that otherwise would be left unexplained. Assumptions about specific cognitive processes appear warranted when they are made in order to predict outcomes. However, these posited processes often come to be employed in post hoc explanations, and when used in this fashion, they tend to provide "plausible" accounts that obscure rather than clarify matters.

5

Incentive- and Annoyance-Motivated Hostility and Aggression

In this chapter we delineate the various factors that seem to influence hostile and aggressive behavior in humans. We draw upon the distinction between incentive- and annoyance-motivated hostility and aggression developed earlier, and we detail the similarities and differences between these two types of behavior. We specify the elements that are common to both incentive- and annoyance-motivated actions and those that are uniquely related to one or the other activity.

I. ELEMENTS OF HUMAN HOSTILITY AND AGGRESSION

In agreement with Bandura's (1973a, 1973b) views on aggression, it is proposed that human hostility and aggression are immensely influenced by the uniquely advanced human capacity to process information representing events that are not immediately present. As Bandura pointed out, ignoring this capacity to employ sign aggregates in extremely deliberate ways can only result in an inadequate conception of human aggression. The general proposal expressed, then, implies that human hostility and aggression cannot be fully understood on the basis of learning mechanisms alone and that some form of *cognitive guidance* must be invoked to explain the human characteristics of the behavior in question. However, regarding the "cognitive control" of hostility and aggression, we present a view that differs considerably from the one espoused by Bandura.

Human hostility and aggression undoubtedly are greatly influenced by prevailing contingencies of reinforcement and punishment. Evidence to this effect has already been discussed. The degree to which hostility and aggression can be evoked through discriminative and conditioned stimuli alone has not been sufficiently ascertained, however. It may be assumed, nonetheless, that such processes come into play under conditions in which the interference from other potentially stronger determining factors is minimal. These other factors are subsumed under the label of "cognitive guidance." Cognitive-guidance processes are assumed to compete with purely learned reactions. Dependent on the circumstances, specified below, these guidance processes will be dominated by or they will dominate the learned behavioral tendencies. As we see later, the organism's state of physiological excitation is to be considered a crucial factor in the determination of the degree to which cognitive guidance will be ineffective or will dominate behavior control.

A. Cognitive Guidance and Attributional Process

In discussing cognitive guidance, it is assumed, in accord with attribution theory (cf. Heider, 1958; Jones & Davis, 1965; Kelley, 1967, 1971a, 1971b; Weiner, 1972, 1974b), that events that are consistently contiguous in time and space tend to be perceived as *causally related*. Specifically, a condition that follows a particular antecedent state with some regularity, and that occurs notably less likely in the absence of this antecedent state, tends to be interpreted as having been caused by that state. Applied to the perception of prevailing contingencies of reinforcement and punishment, this means that the individual will *recognize that a consistently reinforced or punished condition leads to rewards or aversions*. Once *aware* of a prevailing contingency, he or she is able to *anticipate the consequences* of this condition; and to the extent that the individual can control the condition in question, he or she can bring about its consequences or prevent them. *The anticipation of rewards through aggressive action should thus promote such behavior, and the anticipation of aversions should reduce or eliminate it.*

If the causal attribution of consequences to antecedents were entirely mechanical and functioned analogously to a learning trial, the expectations based on attribution-theoretical considerations would be identical to those derived from learning theory. The two systems would more or less accurately reflect the prevailing contingencies and would thus be totally redundant. However, as we have indicated earlier, the human capacity for making causal attributions does not simply replicate the mechanistic trial-by-trial emergence of a relationship. It short-cuts such a process. This short-cutting of learning efforts seems to increase immensely the efficiency of adaptation to a complex, changing physical and social environment. It is not, however, a procedure devoid of error and bias. Since erroneous attributions (i.e., erroneous to the outside observer who is considered unbiased) are as "valid" to the acting individual as appropriate attributions, they have the same effect on behavior. In the study of cognitive guidance, *causal misattributions* are thus as important as causal attributions. In fact, misattributions may be considered to be of particular significance, because it is mainly their unique impact that separates predictions derived from attribution theory from those based on more mechanistic systems.

It may be assumed that in early childhood, the individual's assessment of contingencies of reinforcement and punishment is rather mechanical, with prevailing schedules reflected in any "expectancies" of outcomes. As soon as the individual learns to make causal attributions, however, his or her assessment of relationships comes to be based more and more on the perception of stable traits in the environment and in his or her own behavior. Although such proceeding may constitute great economy of mental effort, it entails a relatively high risk of misassessment. Any misassessment, in fact, tends to promote further misassessments, thereby creating an artificially stable system that may at times prove maladaptive.

In terms of theory, the problem reduces to the fact that the causal attribution of observed contingencies is a function of earlier causal attributions (cf. Kelley, 1971a). This process is particularly clear in the attribution of success and failure to the individual's own action (cf. Weiner, 1974a; Weiner, Nierenberg, & Goldstein, 1976). Apparently, individuals first develop (through attributions of their own and/or through attributions suggested by others) relatively stable beliefs concerning their own power to effect changes in the environment and concerning the power of external factors that are not under their control. The consequences of success or failure then very much depend on the assessment of such matters as their ability, mood, fatigue, illness, and luck. After succeeding, for example, individuals should anticipate future success to a greater extent when the experienced success is ascribed to their skill or the easiness of the task than when their success is attributed to luck. Conversely, after a failure, individuals should anticipate future failure to a greater extent when the failure is ascribed to personal inabilities than when it is attributed to transitory states such as moods or fatigue or to bad luck. The behavior-modifying impact of the anticipation of outcomes, then, is dependent on the individual's perception. Furthermore, persons who attributed their successes to their own doing in the past will tend to overattribute their recent successes to their own efforts and become overly confident of their skills. Conversely, persons who blame themselves for their failures will tend to be overcritical of themselves and will come to underestimate their own skills. The perception of success and failure thus appears to be a function of earlier attributions of success and failure. Most importantly here, the behavior-guiding anticipations of success and failure are based, at least in part, on the assessment of particular causal circumstances, and they do not simply reflect manifest schedules of success and failure or, for that matter, prevailing contingencies of reinforcement and punishment.

The consideration of causal circumstances extends, of course, into the realm of social interaction. If consequences of relevance are not simply the result of incidental changes in the individual's physical environment but are produced by another person, the question arises whether these consequences came about accidentally or were intentionally created for the individual. As Jones and Davis (1965) have pointed out, the central assumption underlying the attribution of intent is that the person is viewed as confronted with multiple response alternatives, of which he or she deliberately chooses a particular one. If another person's apparently deliberate choice of a response benefits or harms the individual, one should expect a reaction to this response that is very different from that which would occur had the action been perceived as controlled by other forces. The difference in reaction is indeed quite dramatic. Whereas receiving benefits from a person who is perceived as acting freely may prompt the inclination to reciprocate the benefaction, being benefited by a person who is apparently pressured into such action is likely to be unpleasing or even annoying (cf. Jones, 1964; Jones & Davis, 1965). Similarly, *whereas being deliberately harmed by another person constitutes an assault that demands retaliatory measures, being harmed without apparent malice or by accident may be tolerated without punitive compensations* (cf. Jones & Davis, 1965; Kelley, 1971a). The evidence concerning the behavioral implications of the attribution of intent is consistent and compelling. It marks a further point of departure from mechanistic learning interpretations: In social interaction, rewards and aversions cannot be taken at face value (i.e., in terms of their absolute stimulus potential), and their amplification or attenuation through mediating cognitive processes must be recognized.

B. Cognitive Guidance and Moral Judgment

The attribution of specific intentions is closely related to, and in fact intertwined with, moral considerations. If a person is held accountable for actions that benefit or harm others, the moral acceptability (i.e., the judged "goodness" or "badness") of the ends served by these actions crucially affects the evaluation of the acts themselves (cf. Rule & Nesdale, 1976b). Benefaction deriving from "ulterior motives" may be condemned as bad, whereas the same action may be hailed as good when ascribed to the pure desire to help another person (e.g., Jones, 1964). *Hostility or aggression is likely to be condemned when it is ascribed to malice or negligence, but it may meet with approval when it is viewed as committed in pursuit of ultimately beneficial ends* (e.g., Pepitone & Sherberg, 1957; Rule & Duker, 1973). The *moral sanction of hostile and aggressive behavior,* which seems to have little to do with attributional processes as such and rather appears to follow from the comparison of a particular event with an established social norm or precept, has only recently been stressed as an important factor in the control of hostility and aggression (cf. Rule & Nesdale, 1976b).

The influence of moral sanctions on hostility and aggression is apparently twofold. First, the perceived goodness of some hostile or aggressive measures removes the need for the inhibition of these characteristically disapproved actions, setting the individual free to attack and punish others. The weakening of inhibitions then is seen to generalize to other hostile and aggressive actions that have not been specifically sanctioned. Hostility and aggression, in general, are thus promoted through disinhibition. Second, the declaration of the goodness of hostile or aggressive actions can follow their performance. As the individual succeeds in considering his or her hostile or aggressive activities as not only called for but "the right thing to do" (possibly in an effort to reduce postbehavioral conflict or "guilt"), the individual post facto legitimizes his or her own coercive and punitive actions. Any suspicion of the objectionable, transgressive nature of the behavior is removed. The practice of sanctioning hostility and aggression should again further disinhibition generally and thereby promote future hostile and aggressive behavior.

Recent findings concerning the moral evaluation of hostility and aggression are suggestive of such a mechanism (cf. Rule & Nesdale, 1976b). It has been observed, for example, that merely witnessing legitimate or justified aggression, as compared to seeing the same action presented as somewhat objectionable, can enhance unrelated retaliatory activities (e.g., Berkowitz, Corwin, & Heironimus, 1963; Hoyt, 1970; Meyer, 1972b). Presumably, the subjects' own inhibitions were temporarily relaxed when they saw the violent actions of others depicted as legitimate. It has also been shown that the infliction of an aversive treatment, when morally approved of by the person witnessing it, is not merely accepted as right but tends to generate mirthful reactions in the witness (cf. Zillmann & Bryant, 1975; Zillmann & Cantor, 1976a, 1977). The available research evidence, then, suggests that moral considerations are an important, integral part of hostility and aggression—a part that can no longer be ignored.

C. Essential Discriminations and Judgmental Processes

We now systematize and further elaborate the various elements of cognitive guidance discussed thus far. We begin with the analysis of the *discriminations* essential to the understanding of hostility and aggression and then turn to the analysis of *motivational* and *dispositional elements.*

Discrimination at the most basic level concerns the *identification of the target* for hostile or aggressive acts. As the individual is annoyed or attacked by a person, he or she obviously must perceive and commit to memory the distinguishing features of the annoyer or attacker in order to recognize him or her at a later time under different environmental circumstances. This recognition may serve the avoidance of that person, but more importantly here, it can guide any retaliatory or punitive actions against the *appropriate* target. It may seem unnecessary even to mention this basic human skill for individual recognition. It should be recognized, however, that the fact of such recognition is given little attention in models of displaced and impulsive aggression (see Chapter 4). In these models, aggression is viewed as readily evoked by a person who resembles the appropriate target. The emphasis on the *identification* of the appropriate target denies such stimulus generalization. Based on the identification of the appropriate target (i.e., an individual or a particular group), cognitive guidance is seen to *prevent* hostile or aggressive activities from being directed against inappropriate targets—no matter how strong the physical resemblance may be.

It is acknowledged, however, that an individual's identity may be incidental to his or her target properties. For example, a person may resent *all* members of the Ku Klux Klan and potentially treat them in a hostile or aggressive manner. In the confrontation with one particular member, this person may well behave aggressively without having been directly provoked. Such behavior could be viewed as resulting from stimulus generalization (i.e., as mediated by attire and similar cues). It could also be attributed to semantic generalization (i.e., as mediated by the labels and symbols involved). In terms of the identification of target characteristics, such behavior is readily explained as the result of attributions. For example: Regardless of the particular member's present behavior, his identification as a KKK member— mediated by salient cues or linguistically—leads to the attribution of specific beliefs and behavioral dispositions to that member. This attribution is based on the *identification of target properties,* and to the extent that a person is motivated to treat *all* people associated with such properites in a punitive fashion, hostile or aggressive behavior may be expected. It is thus not necessary to assume that this behavior is mechanically elicited by some form of generalization.

Further discriminations concern the *identification of transgressions,* the *extent to which norms or precepts are violated,* and the *extent to which violating the norms or precepts in question is socially disapproved.* The necessary assumptions are: (a) that the individual recognizes prevailing norms of socially sanctioned behavior and comprehends precepts (i.e., an endorsed "ought" system); (b) that he or she matches specific activities against a relevant norm or precept and perceives the magnitude of any discrepancies; and (c) that he or she recognizes the social consequences for the failure to adhere to norms or precepts and assesses the significance of particular violations in these terms.

The attribution of intent is crucial in the perception of transgressions, since the very concept of transgression is based on the assumption of free will. Obviously, a person who does not deliberately choose a certain socially condemned course of action, but who is coerced into such behavior, should not be accused—at least not fully—of having committed a transgression. This is to say that with the exception of children at the level of expiatory retribution and below (cf. Piaget, 1932), the inference or attribution of intent is a necessary condition in the perception of hostile and aggressive transgressions.

The judgment of transgressions and their magnitude is certainly subject to distortion. It has been found that aggression committed by a physically attractive person, for example, is considered less wrong and deserving of less punishment than that committed by an unattractive person (e.g., Dion, 1972; Nesdale, Rule, & McAra, 1975). Similarly, transgressions committed by personally appealing persons were judged as less objectionable and as less demanding of punitive measures than those committed by unappealing persons (e.g., Landy & Aronson, 1969; Nesdale & Rule, 1974; Zillmann, 1972a). Such distortions do not affect the *subjective validity* of the perception of transgressions, however, and it is of course this subjective validity that is crucial in the cognitive mediation of hostile and aggressive behavior.

The recognition of hostile or aggressive transgressions has apparent *motivational* consequences. When such transgressions are directed against the individual—that is, when the individual perceives the self being subjected to an unwarranted, deliberately inflicted aversive treatment—he or she not only seeks to terminate the aversive stimulation but is likely to engage in efforts to *reciprocate* by inflicting an aversive treatment of similar intensity upon his or her annoyer (see Chapter 3). It is generally considered a truism that the perceived magnitude of a transgression determines the magnitude of compensatory punitive measures (cf. Gouldner, 1960). This relationship has become an integral part of the theory of distributive justice (Homans, 1961) and equity theory (cf. Adams, 1965; Leventhal, 1976; Leventhal & Anderson, 1970; Walster, Berscheid, & Walster, 1976). Generally consistent with such approaches to justice, it is tentatively proposed: (a) that *the transgressive infliction of aversion upon an individual motivates him or her to apply compensatory aversive treatment to the transgressor;* and (b) that *the magnitude of the compensatory treatment the individual seeks to inflict is, in general, proportional to that of the transgressive treatment suffered.*

In this proposal, the *motivation to retaliate* against persons who commit hostile or aggressive transgressions is expressed in moral terms. Apparently, if the issue were merely to ward off an annoyer or to terminate annoyance, there would be no need to stipulate any particular quantitative relationship between provocation and retaliation (or more generally speaking, between transgression and punishment). The individual in a state of acute annoyance would simply continue to engage in counterresponses, hostile and aggressive measures included, until the annoying stimulation was terminated. Whether the aversion inflicted upon the annoyer was below, equal to, or above the level of aversion suffered would be of little moment. A person who managed to ward off a severe annoyance without doing much harm to the annoyer would be satisfied. The common observation that people are not content with such a situation but are willing to subject themselves to considerable torment to "get even with" their annoyer marks a characteristic feature of hostility and aggression that, for better or worse, distinguishes man from other species.

Retaliation and punishment are essentially *moral concepts*. The motivation to retaliate and to punish consequently appears to be primarily "cognitive" (cf. Weiner, 1972, 1974b). However, as we will see, the moral system of retaliation and punishment tends to be strictly enforced in societies (cf. LeVine & Campbell, 1972), and it thus comes under reinforcement and aversive control. Also, it should be recognized that independent of moral considerations, retaliation can often be accounted for as a preventive measure: A person may feel that through prompt retaliation, he or she can reduce the likelihood of future transgressions being directed against him or her. At the level of international conflict, this kind of thinking seems to determine much military policy and strategy. Nonetheless, the fact remains that retaliation is frequently employed to punish a transgressor regardless of future threats this transgressor could pose. In the standard paradigm of aggression research, for example, subjects are provoked and then retaliate against their tormentor even though they know that they will not interact with this tormentor again (cf. Geen & O'Neal, 1976).

The fact that recompense, retribution, retaliation, revenge, vengeance, and so on are moral concepts is further documented by recent findings concerning affective reactions to the observation of transgressions and punishment. It has been shown that the enjoyment occasioned by seeing a transgressor punished is a function of the moral sanction of the punishment (Zillmann & Bryant, 1975). Children at the developmental level of equitable retribution (7- and 8-year olds) enjoyed dramatic events only when the transgression involved was "fairly"—that is, equitably—punished. The enjoyment vanished when the events entailed either under- or overretaliation. It has also been observed that the punishment of transgressive behavior is enjoyed even when it does not come through the retaliatory action of the tormented person but occurs by accident (Zillmann & Cantor, 1977). It apparently does not matter how the punishing action comes about. What matters is that it does come about and in the appropriate magnitude. Witnessing a transgression go unpunished or inadequately punished or overpunished, then, seems to leave one's sense of justice disturbed—as Heider (1958) suggested.

The moral disturbance appears also to apply to the individual's own transgressions. Feelings of guilt can be viewed as the result of the individual's recognition that he or she has violated norms or precepts and has avoided the punishment deserved. Conceivably, feelings of guilt occasionally may become aversive enough to motivate the individual to seek out and accept punishment or even to administer it to him- or herself (cf. Bandura, 1973a). The individual can avoid such self-punishment, however, as Bandura has suggested, by distorting the perception of his or her own acts so as to make them appear legitimate.

It has been assumed or proposed that man's eagerness to see transgressions adequately punished derives mainly from the need to create stable, predictable environmental conditions in order to assure that every member of a particular social aggregate in which specific punitive contingencies are enforced can operate effectively (e.g., Blau, 1964; Merton, 1957; Piaget, 1932). A "just world" means reliable contingencies of reinforcement and punishment or of rewards and aversions. Only such reliability enables the members of a social aggregate to form workable strategies to maximize rewards and minimize aversions. This stability has been viewed as central to the social-contract concept. Some of the undesirable consequences of deteriorating beliefs in stable punitive contingencies (which are considered "just" mainly because they are applied to many individuals) have been detailed by Erikson (1950) and by Jessor, Graves, Hanson, and Jessor (1968), for example.

It would of course be an oversimplification to assume that in any complex social aggregate, especially at the societal level, the sanctioned contingencies of reinforcement and punishment apply *equally* to all people. Regulatory systems, especially in modern societies, characteristically stipulate *equal* rights (and thus equal punishment) for all. In practice, however, much preferential and discriminatory treatment is tolerated and even promoted. For example, as recent American history teaches us, a president's or vice-president's criminal transgressions can go entirely unpunished. Apparently, even under the law, there are differences among people. The institutional rank or the history of a person's "contributions to society" may well affect the interpretation of legal stipulations and ultimately affect the type and magnitude of punishment for committed transgressions. Equality of punitive treatments under the law is usually further compromised, at least in Western cultures, by the liberal use of the discretionary power of judges to sentence persons convicted of crimes (cf. Davis, 1959). With such discretion, personal idiosyncrasies can readily enter into the sentencing, and the punishment can be made to fit the criminal rather than the crime. Distortions toward that end, due to bias in perceiving the transgressor and to behavior unrelated to the transgression, have been amply documented (cf. Austin, Walster, & Utne, 1976).

These ambiguities concerning the application of penal law, which could be largely eliminated by the formulation of more precise, binding, sentencing principles that take into account only the crime and its immediate circumstances (cf. Austin et al., 1976; Wasserstrom, 1961) appear to be minor, however, when compared to the ambiguities in the *assessment of entitlements and dues at the personal level*. Formal prescriptions of such personal entitlements and dues are obviously nonexistent. The individual is largely alone in determining the magnitude of rewards to which people are entitled for the performance of socially valued activities. And similarly, the individual him- or herself judges the size of a penalty people should suffer for transgressions that have been committed. If it is assumed, as we have done earlier, that the individual judges the deservedness of rewards or punishments by relating the magnitude of a prosocial act or of a transgression to that of the associated compensation, it must be acknowledged that this judgmental process not only is highly complex but also involves extremely ambiguous elements. Who can, in concrete terms, specify the deserved reward for a person who, for example, has served in the Peace Corps or in the armed forces or for someone who has helped an old lady cross the street? Who can say exactly how much of which kind of aversion adequately compensates for inflicting a flesh wound upon one's adversary, for slapping him in the face, for stealing a car, for shoplifting a particular item, for beating one's spouse, for temporarily depriving one's child of her favorite toy, for belittling one's neighbor, or for ridiculing one's friend?

We could conceive of "units of suffering" and then try to determine the number of aversive units inflicted by a particular transgression. This number would then determine the severity of an equitable punitive treatment. In these terms, it would appear that to deter transgressors from further transgressions, the punitive aversion should at least equal the transgressive aversion. Although such a conceptual model may be considered meaningful for transgressions that do not involve incentives (i.e., the purely malicious infliction of harm or injury would be equitably avenged), it does not meaningfully relate to incentive-motivated transgressions. The apprehension of an incentive-motivated transgressor usually means that the transgressor is deprived of any tangible incentives he or she may have obtained. At this point, the transgression is without payoff—the "crime" did not pay. The generally practiced application of additional punishment as a deterrent for future incentive-motivated transgressions clearly violates equitable retribution in terms of aversions: Punitive aversions tend to exceed any aversions inflicted in the commission of an incentive-motivated transgression.

These *conceptual difficulties with equity considerations* seem to call into question the assumption that the individual engages in a quasi-objective assessment of the magnitude of a transgression and then uses this assessment to set an equitable punishment for the transgressor. The model of equitable retribution may, in fact, constitute a poor analogue for the cognitive processes executed by the individual who develops a notion of just, fair, and *deserved* punishment—a notion that ultimately motivates him or her to sanction the application of "equitable" punishment or to apply that punishment personally. In discussing the concept of deservingness and its involvement in forms of justice, Lerner, Miller, and Holmes (1976) acknowledged the discussed ambiguities in subjective assessments and have suggested that the individual who is faced with such ambiguities resorts to social comparisons (cf. Festinger, 1954; Pettigrew, 1967). If, because of ambiguities, a clear decision on a person's deserved punishment cannot be reached, the individual readily finds a stable referent in other people's behavior: He or she will consider a fair and deserved punishment that which, under similar circumstances, others have considered fair and deserved. Following social-comparison theory and its application by Lerner et al., it is proposed that individuals develop a *sense of deserving* on the basis of comparisons with others who are similar to them. They consider themselves entitled to the rewards that others like themselves obtain under the same circumstances. To receive more but particularly to receive less is perceived as unjust and unfair. Analogously, *individuals consider themselves to be deserving of the punishment that others like themselves suffer under the same circumstances*. To receive more than similar others would receive under the same circumstances is considered particularly unfair. This reasoning is readily extended to the sanctioning of rewards and punishments for others. In considering the punishment of witnessed transgressions, an aversive treatment is considered just if it approximates what is known to be considered fair by others when applied to persons like the transgressor and for similar transgressions. Such a model can account for moral judgments that appear incomprehensible in terms of more formal systems of ethics. It can explain, for example, why the pardon of a president who committed transgressions can be sanctioned by many people. Presidents are sufficiently dissimilar from other people, and any precedent of immunity from prosecution fosters the expectation that criminal presidents are entitled to pardons. Similarly, the social-comparison reasoning can explain why in some cultures, a wife's sexual infidelity will cause her husband to retaliate against the presumed real transgressor, her lover, possibly by killing him; whereas in other cultures the husband may merely display his anger about his wife's behavior. In both cases, the husband's view of just, "equitable" punishment reflects what others (his cultural peers, in this case) probably would have done in the same situation. In juvenile gangs, a disparaging comment—which might be considered a harmless, funny put-down in student circles—can start warfare that may result in the deaths of the offenders—all in the name of "just" retaliation. In more common social situations, comparison-based differences in the perception of fair and equitable punishment are less eye-catching, but they undoubtedly also exist. Parents who learn that their teenage children are "on drugs," for example, may be quite uncertain as to whether or not such behavior constitutes a transgression and the degree of punishment it warrants. They are thus highly susceptible to social influence, and they should take their orientation concerning fair and just retribution from their social environment. If this immediate environment fails to provide cues, they may well take their orientation from fiction, as presented on television, which is likely to depict people like themselves in a similar dilemma. As a consequence, in one social grouping a child's use of drugs may result in severe punishment; in another it may prompt mild reproach; and in yet another, it may induce guilt-ridden parents to blame themselves and to try to express greater love toward their children. In terms of the individual's subjective assessment of deservingness, there seems to be equity in all of these punitive outcomes. It would appear, however, that considerations of equity that neglect social-comparison processes cannot adequately account for the vast differences in moral judgments of punishment and retaliatory action.

The psychological mechanics involved in moral judgments based on social-comparison processes may appear simplistic compared to those involved in judgments based on equity considerations and quasi-rational, individual decision making. In fact, the proposal that people essentially emulate their peers in making moral decisions might be considered rather primitive. Such "aesthetic" evaluations notwithstanding, the moral judgment of punitive and retaliatory actions that is mediated through social-comparison processes seems to constitute a highly adaptive system. On a grand social scale, this system may well prove superior to individualistic ethical decision making, because it entails the *consensual endorsement of what ought to be done in terms of punishment and retaliation.* Social comparison confines the individual to punitive or retaliatory actions that others apparently approve of or condone, and whatever others approve of or condone has presumably emerged as socially workable and hence adaptive. This is to say that in the final analysis, the individual is compelled to judge as right and just a course of action that in the past has proved to produce a minimum of social reproach within a particular social system. And it produced the minimum of opposition because the contingencies of reinforcement and punishment endorsed in this system were the least violated. This also means that actions that follow "moral decisions" will maximize social approval and minimize social reproach. Moral judgments based on social comparison are thus ultimately under reinforcement and aversive control.

Although such a view may be troublesome for theoreticians of ethics who have based their rationales on the assumption of a "free will" in man (cf. Skinner, 1971), it should be recognized that the projected process of the construction of precepts, although it ultimately promotes the maximization of gratification and the minimization of aversion, potentially involves every member of a social system. At the very least, *many* individuals participate in the construction, maintenance, and modification of precepts to accommodate changing needs within the social system. Such a procedure amounts to consensual "validation." A *group*, regardless of its size, is de facto entrusted with setting its moral standards. As a consequence, the individual is socially restrained in legitimizing his or her own hostile or aggressive action. The individual cannot step out of line and apply excessive punishment or retaliation with a sanctimonious attitude. On the other hand, he or she may be forced to punish and retaliate simply in order to avoid the feeling of having failed to do what is expected.

The discussed restraint in viewing punitive and retaliatory action as legitimate apparently does not necessarily prevail when the individual's capacity for ethical reasoning is entrusted with the moral judgment of hostility and aggression. Potentially, extreme measures that are unlikely ever to find general moral approval can be legitimized by some individuals who either act alone or with small groups of disciples. Atrocities and heinous crimes are known to have been justified on the basis of obscure and bizarre individualistic moral convictions (e.g., the well-known Tate–LaBianca murders by the Manson group). Such deviant hostile and aggressive acts (i.e., deviant in the purely descriptive sense of being different from more customary behavior), which are of course incompatible with a social-comparison model of the legitimization of hostility and aggression, attest to the existence of personal ethical rationales and to their possible consequences for behavior. These personal ethical systems no doubt generate "deviant" beneficial behavior as well as generally condemned behavior. Instances of extreme altruism and self-sacrifice for the public good, or even for the benefit of wrongdoers, are unlikely to result from social comparison but tend to follow from personal precepts that may be self-constructed or adopted from others (e.g., the promoters of moralities connected with religious belief systems). With regard to hostility and aggression, extreme pacifism and self-castigation may also find little social precedent. Admirable as such self-guided actions may be, when it comes to punishment and retaliation, it appears that personal ethical convictions are associated with a high risk of distortion in the legitimization of hostile and aggressive measures and that the reliance on social comparison constitutes a superior adaptive mechanism that curtails the sanctioned infliction of aversion.

The implications for hostility and aggression of moral judgments based on individualistic decision making and those based on social comparison may seem totally unrelated. The two systems are not necessarily independent, however. They may be rather closely related at times; on other occasions, they may indeed prove to be independent. It is suggested here that society provides for a "free market place of moral ideas" (i.e., of decision-making systems that permit the generation of moral judgments) but that all conceivable rationales that declare a punitive action to be right or wrong, good or bad, appropriate or inappropriate, worthy of praise or rebuke, etc., are subject to consensual validation. Such validation, which is not unique to social-comparison processes, may occur at the societal level, in large organized groups, or in small informal aggregates. With the exception of very small groups of potentially deviant individuals, sanctions that would jeopardize the functioning and well-being of society at large, or at least large portions of it, are likely to be corrected quickly so as to assure the most advantageous conditions for all concerned. Proposals that give privileges to adherents at the expense of nonfollowers generally meet with the prompt social reproach of these nonfollowers, and only proposals that assign equal entitlements and dues to all will fare well in the long run.

Regulations designed to prevent the attainment of undeserved rewards, especially through deception or force, characteristically involve hostile and aggressive measures against the transgressor. In such regulations, the magnitude of a transgression is generally considered in setting the retribution. Since more or less formal ethical proposals, as suggested, are subject to de facto ratification by consensual validation, it might appear that such concepts as punitive and retaliatory equity are propagated equally by moral systems based on decisional procedures and those based on social comparison. In fact, there need be no discrepancy. Both systems can be concordant and prescribe, for example, "an eye for an eye" retaliation; that is, equity between the aversion inflicted and that to be suffered in return. Under the assumption that the decisions derived from the two systems largely coincide, our initial proposal concerning the motivational consequences of subjective moral judgment may hold up. It states that the individual seeks to inflict, in general, a compensatory treatment proportional to the transgressive aversive treatment suffered. Consensual validation may virtually force such equity upon the individual. This is to say that equity may not be a goal in itself, but it may be *dictated by the prevention of punitive and retaliatory inequity*. This prevention, in turn, is operating not simply as the consequence of consensual validation but as the result of its by-product: the potential social reproach of violations of consensually endorsed precepts.

However, although reciprocity of aversion in punishment and retaliation may be dominant and constitute "the rule," the moral judgment of hostility and aggression based both on decision-making and on social-comparison processes can sanction behaviors that are difficult to reconcile with even the most liberal interpretations of equity in aversion. The juvenile delinquent, for example, who has been denied access to desired commodities, may well perceive the hostile and aggressive transgressions that give him access to these commodities as justified. Having been exposed to societally endorsed precepts, he may appraise his actions, not as "good," but as "right"—the latter judgment being based on social comparison with his close affiliates. The obvious discrepancy between two value systems may then, of course, be clouded by rationalizations such as the charge that society at large, in depriving the wrongdoer of gratifications, had inflicted upon him undeserved suffering, which was reciprocated in the transgressive action. Given the vagueness of the judgmental entities involved (e.g., the degree of personal suffering), it would appear that such rationalizations are easy to justify and maintain. The grief caused by a snappy remark, for example, can be arbitrarily viewed as severe enough to "justify" beatings and ultimately murder. Not only can the transgressor justify his or her actions to the self, but in displaying grievances, he or she may well convince others of the rightness of these actions. The obviously suffering individual is usually granted some transgressive privileges and some punitive immunity (cf. Austin et al., 1976). Thus, in spite of the enormous vagueness in the subjective assessment of suffering, this assessment, together with its moral implications, seems to play a crucial role in the cognitive guidance of punitive and retaliatory behavior.

The discussed discrepancy between the two systems of moral judgment under consideration can also occur in reverse form: Instead of submitting to social-comparison guidance, the individual may truly "follow his or her conscience" and act in accord with endorsed precepts that typically are not followed. Like, for example, the wealthy man who gives all his belongings to the poor, the "noble" avenger of a transgression that has gone unpunished may place himself at considerable risk and self-castigation in order to achieve his valued objective. In reality, this type of behavior is probably very rare. It is more an element of fiction, which projects the maintenance of a just world by "ethical" others (cf. Zillmann & Bryant, 1975). The fact that the precept-enforcing actions of our "heroes" are generally applauded may indicate that people prefer to entrust others with moral mandates rather than to expose themselves to risks or aversions. Precepts may often stipulate that a witnessed transgression be punished, but the witness may be content to hope that justice will be achieved somehow—that is, without his or her own involvement and efforts. This is not to say, however, that there are not occasions on which, in the face of severe risk of aversion, a person will follow his or her moral precept rather than social comparison in bringing "justice" to a situation. Some violent political radicals seem to attest to this possibility.

In view of these eventualities concerning moral assessments, we rephrase our earlier proposal on the motivational implications of moral considerations for hostility and aggression. We also extend this proposal from the active application of punitive and retaliatory actions to motivational aspects of merely witnessing the application of such actions.

1. The transgressive infliction of aversion upon an individual motivates this individual to inflict compensatory aversive treatments upon the transgressor.
2. The magnitude of the compensatory aversive treatment the individual seeks to inflict is determined by personal or social precept and/or by social comparison.
3. The magnitude of the compensatory aversive treatment tends to be proportional to that of the transgressive aversive treatment. Disproportional compensation is possible, however. It will occur when prescribed by binding precepts, when dictated by social comparison, or when demanded by both systems of moral judgment.
4. The transgressive infliction of aversion upon an individual motivates this individual to sanction the infliction of compensatory aversive treatments upon the transgressor by others.
5. The magnitude of the compensatory aversive treatment the individual is motivated to sanction is determined by personal or social precept and/or by social comparison as specified under item 3.
6. The witnessed transgressive infliction of aversion upon others motivates the individual to sanction the infliction of compensatory aversive treatments upon the transgressor by others.
7. The magnitude of the sanctioned compensatory treatment is as specified under item 5.

In advancing these propositions, we have not stipulated that witnessing the transgressive infliction of aversion upon others motivates the individual to apply compensatory aversive treatments through his or her own action. Thus, although he or she generally sanctions a transgressor's punishment, the individual is said to seek to avenge only the mistreatments personally suffered. If he or she retaliates, this is done only on the individual's own behalf; and he or she merely hopes, so to speak, that someone else will bring justice to transgressive situations that do not concern him or her directly. This view is based on the fact that the infliction of compensatory aversion is potentially aversive itself. As we turn to the discussion of cognitive processes that are relatively independent of moral considerations, we now elaborate the specific consequences of this circumstance.

D. Anticipations and Their Behavioral Implications

The implications of moral judgment for hostility and aggression are largely restricted to occasions in which precepts and norms are perceived as having been violated. The primary situation is the one in which harm or injury is inflicted upon another person without apparent justification. Moral considerations are then involved in setting the appropriate recompense for such a transgression, and the resulting judgment is considered to have motivational consequences. In a secondary application, moral considerations are viewed as motivating the setting of compensations for earlier retributions that have proved transgressive (e.g., excessive punishment). Both conditions make it clear that the moral judgment of hostility and aggression presupposes the occurrence of some transgressive event or circumstance.

Obviously, this type of judgment does not apply to the initial commission of a transgression, and consequently, it cannot promote hostile and aggressive actions committed purely in pursuit of tangible or intangible rewards or, more generally, in pursuit of the maximization of gratification and the minimization of aversion. It is posited that in the pursuit of these ends, the *anticipation of outcomes*, based on causal attributions rather than on mechanics of learning, plays a crucial role in the cognitive guidance of hostility and aggression. The principal anticipations and their motivational implications, as we propose them, are summarized in Table 1. We now briefly discuss them as listed. In doing so, we emphasize the differences in incentive- and annoyance-motivated hostility and aggression. We further attempt to show that moral assessments can be conceived of in terms of anticipations of outcomes.

As discussed earlier, it is assumed that the cognitively competent individual who is exposed to certain circumstances spontaneously forms *anticipations* of consequences. It is further assumed that these anticipations are based on the prior perception of similar circumstances and their consequences or, more specifically, on the causal *attribution* of the consequences to the circumstances. Finally, it is assumed that these anticipations guide the individual's behavior selection and that this *guidance* serves the hedonic principle of the maximization of gratification and the minimization of aversion. All these

TABLE 1
Principal Elements of Cognitive Guidance in Hostility and Aggression

	Recognition Through Attribution	Dispositional Implication of Recognition
(a)	Contingencies of reinforcement and punishment	Anticipation of gratification or aversion
(b)	Coercive contingencies	Anticipation of success[a] or failure[b]
(c)	Stable abilities and inabilities of self	Anticipation of success or failure
(d)	Transitory abilities and inabilities of self	Anticipation of success or failure
(e)	Opposing situational forces	Anticipation of cost[c]
(f)	Punitive and retaliatory potentialities of others	Anticipation of cost
(g)	Contingencies of social approval and reproach	Anticipation of gratification or aversion

[a]Success ultimately translates into attainment of gratification or removal of aversion.
[b]Failure ultimately translates into removal of gratification or attainment of aversion.
[c]Cost ultimately translates into aversion.

assumptions concerning the attribution–anticipation–disposition chain of cognitive guidance relate to the following propositions:

A. It is proposed: (1) that the individual recognizes the contingencies of reinforcement and punishment that potentially apply to his or her own behavior; (2) that he or she consequently anticipates gratification or aversion to result from particular conditions; and (3) that he or she acts so as to increase gratification and/or decrease aversion.

Processes of cognitive guidance are thus viewed as *motivating the individual to commit coercive acts, if necessary, in order to obtain incentives or prevent annoyances*. The former case constitutes the basis for *incentive-motivated* hostility and aggression. It provides the initial impulse to force the compliance of others who are perceived as thwarting the attainment of circumstances expected to generate gratification. The latter case constitutes a special condition for *annoyance-motivated* hostility and aggression. Annoyance motivation, strictly speaking, presupposes a state of acute annoyance. Such a state seems absent when annoyance is only anticipated. However, the anticipation of annoyance might be conceived of as a state of annoyance itself. But even if the individual who anticipates aversion is assumed not to be annoyed, guidance processes are expected to motivate the individual to engage in efforts to prevent the anticipated aversive experience. Annoyance-motivated hostility and aggression may thus be seen to serve a dual function: First, they aim at the diminution and ultimately the *termination* of acute annoyances; and second, they aim at the reduction and ultimately the *prevention* of anticipated annoyances. The second function, since it involves the projection of future states, appears to be particularly dependent on cognitive-guidance processes.

B. It is proposed: (1) that the individual recognizes the contingencies between hostile or aggressive behaviors and the compliance and submission of others; (2) that he or she correspondingly anticipates his or her own hostile or aggressive actions to affect the behavior of others similarly; and (3) that he or she is motivated to perform such actions only if they hold promise of coercive success.

Whereas proposition A projects anticipation-based behavior under the hedonic principle generally, proposition B specifically addresses the motivating aspects of anticipations concerning hostile and aggressive actions. If specific hostile or aggressive maneuvers performed by others are consistently perceived as producing compliance with behavioral directives serving the attainment of gratification or the prevention of aversion, the individual should be inclined to perform similar coercive acts serving his or her interest. Stated this way, proposition B projects the no-trial social learning of hostile and aggressive behavior (cf. Bandura, 1965). Neither in proposition B nor in proposition A has it been stipulated, however, that recognition of the prevailing contingencies derives solely or even primarily from the observation of the behavior of others. This recognition surely entails all firsthand experiences concerning the contingency in question. In the cognitive guidance of hostility and aggression, the recognition of relevant contingencies characteristically confounds elements of observation and experience. For the purpose of general predictions, a conceptual separation between these elements is thus not necessary. It should be noticed, however, that propositions A and B could readily be modified to accommodate the conceptual distinction between *anticipations based on observation* and *anticipations based on primary experience*. This distinction must be made, of course, in proposals that separate the effect of observation from that of primary experience and that address the respective contributions of the two sources of information. In this connection, it should be recognized that the reduction of propositions A and B to observation-based anticipations amounts to expressing Bandura's (e.g., 1971a) model of the informative function of social learning in terms of cognitive guidance through anticipations. Returning now to recognition deriving from primary experiences, the involvement of this recognition of contingencies in hostility and aggression is further detailed in the following two propositions:

C. It is proposed: (1) that the individual perceives him- or herself as generally possessing a particular degree of ability or inability to perform hostile and aggressive actions to affect the behavior of others; (2) that he or she correspondingly anticipates his or her hostile and aggressive actions to be effective or ineffective; and (3) that he or she is motivated to perform such actions only if they hold promise of coercive success.

D. It is also proposed: (1) that the individual perceives his or her hostile and aggressive capabilities and deficiencies to vary as a function of temporary bodily states (e.g., alertness vs. fatigue or health vs. illness); and (2) that this perception has the consequences stipulated in proposition C under (2) and (3).

Propositions C and D are clearly secondary to proposition B. Essentially, they restrict B in stipulating that the individual's experience of the success or failure of his or her own hostile and aggressive actions tends to overrule any hostile or aggressive inclinations that may result from observed contingencies. In concrete terms, the individual who has observed that certain aggressive activities consistently produce coercive success for others, but who also has found that these very activities have produced failure when employed by him or her, should follow the anticipations based on his or her primary experience rather than those based on observation.

The following two propositions further restrict proposition B. In contrast to the preceding propositions, which focus on potentialities defined with the individual him- or herself, the following propositions address the potentialities of the external conditions (i.e., the physical and social environment that confronts the individual).

E. It is proposed: (1) that the individual, based on his or her observation of and experience with the circumstances in question, appraises the strength of the forces that would oppose his or her hostile or aggressive actions; and (2) that he or she will perform such actions only if the anticipated effort to overcome these opposing forces constitutes an aversion whose magnitude is perceived to be below that of the gratifications to be potentially gained or the aversions to be potentially removed by the actions.

F. It is further proposed: (1) that the individual appraises the likelihood and severity of punitive or retaliatory measures for his or her hostile or aggressive actions; and (2) that he or she will perform such actions only if the anticipated effort to avert or undergo the punitive or retaliatory measures constitutes an aversion whose magnitude is perceived to be below that of the gratifications to be potentially gained or the aversions to be potentially removed by the actions.

According to both propositions, the individual, prior to performing hostile or aggressive actions, considers the cost (i.e., effort and strain; ultimately, aversion) of his or her contemplated action and elects to pursue a course of action only if it is, in the long run, hedonically to his or her advantage. The difference between the propositions, it should be noted, concerns not only the kind of difficulty associated with hostility or aggression (resistance vs. retribution) but also the time at which aversive consequences are expected (immediate vs. delayed). We address the significance of the time distinction in a later section.

G. Finally, it is proposed: (1) that the individual recognizes the contingencies between his or her hostile or aggressive actions and their social approval or condemnation; (2) that he or she correspondingly anticipates such actions to produce gratification or aversion; and (3) that he or she acts so as to increase future gratification and/or decrease future aversion.

This last proposition relates back to the moral judgment of hostility and aggression. It can, in fact, be viewed as providing the motivational basis for social-comparison processes concerning such judgments. Consistent with this proposal, it may be argued that it is the anticipation of social approval or social reproach, and ultimately the anticipation of reward or punishment, respectively, that "forces" the individual to make social comparisons: Because *in doing what others would do under the circumstances, the individual can maximize the approval and minimize the reproach of his or her potential judges.* Moral assessments are thus placed under reinforcement and aversive control. Hostile and aggressive actions are considered morally justified (i.e., the right thing to do) when they are expected to produce social praise; conversely, they are considered morally unjustified (i.e., the wrong thing to do) when they are expected to prompt social condemnation.

In this view, "inner guidance" reduces to primarily attribution-based anticipations that enable the individual to pursue the maximization of gratification and the minimization of aversion. In other words, these anticipations ensure optimal pursuit of the hedonic principle. It should be recognized, however, that this pursuit concerns future events. It is only *in the long run*, so to speak, that the hedonic principle is served. In fact, behavior guided by the anticipation of future gratifications or aversions may well appear to violate the hedonic principle in the short run.

Considering implications for behavior, two aspects of anticipated outcomes seem to be of particular importance: first, the perceived likelihood of positive or negative consequences, and second, the perceived delay in their realization. Regarding the former, it appears that if persons consider it certain or very likely that they will be held accountable for contemplated hostile or aggressive actions, they should anticipate social repercussions and act accordingly. On the other hand, persons who are certain that they will not be identified as perpetrators of harm or injury should not anticipate social repercussions. As a consequence, they should be "morally free" to commit any hostile or aggressive act they have in mind. It should, of course, be nearly impossible for potential transgressors to be absolutely certain that their transgression will go undetected and remain undetected *forever*. There should always be some basis for fear of detection, and this apprehension should prompt concern about social reproach. As suggested earlier, this apprehension and concern should foster the motivation to do the "right" thing, that is, to behave in a morally proper way. Given that there is almost always cause for apprehension, the transgressor who is entirely free of moral constraints appears, for the most part, to be a theoretical construction of little pragmatic consequence.

Regarding the perceived delay of consequences, recent research, especially on the delay of gratification (cf. Mischel, 1974a, 1974b), shows that the anticipation of consequences can span considerable periods of time. Generally speaking, children are already capable of behaving toward delayed rewards as if they were immediately available. It has also been shown, however, that the consequences of the delay of gratification are mediated by processes of ideation: When arousing, consummatory aspects of the outcomes are stressed, delay impedes their effect; in contrast, when the emphasis is placed on nonarousing, nonconsummatory aspects, delay enhances the effect (Mischel, 1974a). These observations concerning ideational mediation suggest that whenever there exists a behavioral urgency (i.e., a state of arousal associated with arousal-reducing goal reactions), immediate outcomes will dominate delayed ones but that whenever such urgency is absent, the immediacy of outcomes will be relatively unimportant. It would appear, then, that the individual can indeed take his or her orientation from nonimmediate, considerably delayed gratifications and aversions and behave so as to obtain or avoid them except when a state of behavioral urgency exists. The exception seems to become the rule, however, when annoyance-motivated hostility or aggression is being considered. It is conceivable that a person who has been intensely annoyed in the past, but who now experiences no annoyance to speak of, can plan reprisals, rejoice in the anticipation of their impact, and delay the execution of the contemplated euphoric event for indefinite periods of time. But it would seem more reasonable to expect the recall of the intense annoyance suffered in the past to reinstate the affective elements of this annoyance, thereby producing a state of annoyance, albeit probably of lesser intensity than the original one. This reinstated annoyance should then create some behavioral urgency, favoring "immediate solutions." We return to this condition of interest as we discuss annoyance-motivated behavior in terms of a theory of emotion.

Taken together, our analysis of cognitive guidance in hostility and aggression (up to this point, at least) has been largely consistent with the general proposal of "rational man." In other words, man has been viewed, at least implicitly, as an intelligent decision maker who scrutinizes potential outcomes and then optimizes his outcomes by choosing the appropriate courses of action. Such a view, however, overstates the rationality that has been assumed to operate. It should be recalled that with the exception of the generation of judgments of equity in punishment and retaliation, explicit decision-making processes have not been assumed. Also, it has not been stipulated that there need be any awareness of decisional processes, particularly as they serve the hedonic principle. And finally, decisional fallacies and distorting factors in the perception of behavioral contingencies have been pointed out. The rationality that seems to emerge in cognitive guidance is thus more a theoretical construction designed to predict observed outcomes than it is the result of assumed deliberate decisional action of which the individual has awareness. It exists de facto in its consequences, but it is not necessarily manifest and empirically demonstrable in specific decision-making processes.

What is being proposed is very simply that *in the cognitive guidance of hostility and aggression, man's superior cognitive faculties de facto serve the hedonic principle* and that they do so primarily *through the anticipation of immediate and future consequences.* The anticipation of future consequences seems of particular significance in that it assures optimal *long-range* accomplishments.

E. Cognitive Guidance and Level of Excitation

We now turn to a rather radical qualification of the foregoing generalization. It is proposed that *the cognitive faculties involved in the cognitive guidance of hostility and aggression are critically affected by the organism's state of physiological excitation.* More specifically, it is posited that higher-order cognitive processes, such as anticipatory projections, presuppose favorable excitatory conditions. At very low levels of excitation (e.g, drowsiness), the execution of such processes is impaired. At very high levels of excitation (e.g., extreme fear, rage), it is likewise impeded. The performance of higher-order cognitive processes is thus restricted to a relatively narrow range of variation in physiological excitation. As a consequence, *the cognitive control of hostile and aggressive behavior is restricted to optimal levels of excitation.*

This proposal of course does not imply that lower-order cognitive processes are independent of level of excitation. Such processes are similarly restricted but to a lesser extent. The range at which they are functional is wider. Conceptually, the order of processes is inversely proportional to the range: that is, *the more complex the cognitive processes (high order), the narrower the range of physiological excitation at which they are functional.*

Consistent with this proposition, lower-order cognitive processes (e.g., the discrimination and identification of specific entities through the use of codes) may well span a good portion of the excitation continuum, but they should nonetheless be limited to a particular range, below and above which they are no longer operative. If it is assumed, for example, that generating equity-based moral judgments is more complex cognitively than anticipating the consequences of contemplated actions, and that such anticipations in turn are more complex than identifying appropriate targets, one would expect that as one moves from an optimal level of excitation to either very low or very high levels, moral considerations become inoperative first; anticipatory projections next; and finally, the identification processes cease to function. The cognitive control of hostility and aggression is expected to deteriorate accordingly. At very low and very high levels of excitation, moral considerations, the anticipation of consequences, and specific identifications should, in this order, drop out of the guidance process. As a consequence, at these extreme levels of excitation, one should expect hostile and aggressive reactions that appear "irrational" in that they violate established moral standards and disregard seemingly obvious repercussions. At especially extreme levels of excitation, one should also expect a person to "lash out" rather indiscriminately. In other words, the displacement of hostility and aggression should be expected under extreme excitatory conditions. Later, we discuss the evidence pertinent to the proposed dependency of cognitive guidance on level of excitation.

The proposal that the cognitive guidance of hostile and aggressive behavior is restricted to a range of suitable excitatory conditions should not be taken to mean that outside this range, such behavior is necessarily disorganized—that is, without guidance. It simply means that cognitive guidance is diminished and behavior is guided by forces that do not depend on cognitive mediation. It is suggested now that for the most part, these forces manifest themselves through the various learning mechanisms discussed earlier. To a lesser extent, unlearned reactions (e.g., warding off, through vigorous movement, immediately present persons or objects in response to physical pain) may also be involved. More specifically, it is proposed that *behavior control through learning extends further into very low and very high levels of physiological excitation than does behavior control through cognitive guidance.* Assuming that in general, the cognitive processes involved in mechanistic learning are comparatively noncomplex, this proposal is entirely consistent with the earlier one concerning the relationship between the complexity of cognitive processes and the narrowness of the range of excitation levels at which they can be executed. It should be noticed that one could draw distinctions regarding the degree of complexity of cognitive processes presumably involved in various learned behaviors and accordingly specify different ranges of excitation for these learned behaviors. Such distinctions are unnecessary for our purposes here, however.

The foregoing propositions relate to two widely accepted generalizations of empirical data: (a) the inverted-U relationship between arousal and behavioral efficiency (e.g., Freeman, 1940; Hebb, 1955, 1966; Malmo, 1959); and (b) Easterbrook's (1959) cue-utilization model.

In the framework of activation theory, it was suggested that *the organism's capacity to react adaptively to specific stimulus conditions successively increases with increments in arousal until arousal reaches an optimal point, but that after this point is reached, further increments in arousal cause the successive deterioration of adaptive reactions* (cf. Hebb, 1966). The relationship between arousal and behavioral efficiency thus was seen to be curvilinear, assuming the form of an inverted U when efficiency is expressed as a function of level of arousal. The end points of this relationship may seem trivial and uninteresting. In a state of acute drowsiness, the organism is obviously not an efficient "problem solver." Similarly, the organism is obviously incapacitated in a state of utmost excitation just short of physical collapse (e.g., in a state of panic). The relationship is highly instructive, however, for all less extreme conditions of excitation.

The inverted-U relationship between arousal and behavioral efficiency has been supported in work with both animals and human subjects. In the work with animals, physiological arousal was characteristically manipulated through external conditions (e.g., food or water deprivation or shock) and was assessed in such indices of excitation as heart rate. Behavioral efficiency was measured in instrumental bar pressing. The frequency of instrumental responses was found to increase up to an intermediate level of arousal and then to drop off as predicted (e.g., Bélanger & Feldman, 1962; Ducharme & Bélanger, 1961; Dufresne, 1961). In the work with human subjects, arousal was similarly manipulated and measured. For example, Freeman (1940) employed skin conductance to assess arousal and observed superior performance on a reaction-time task at intermediate as compared to more extreme levels of arousal. Stennett (1957) produced different levels of arousal as measured by skin conductance and muscle potentials and reported superior performance on a tracking task at intermediate levels. Burgess and

Hokanson (1964) reported similar findings on a digit–symbol task with heart rate as a measure of arousal. Wood and Hokanson (1965) manipulated arousal through muscle tension, which they induced by having the subjects pull weights. They observed that whereas heart rate increased linearly with muscle tension, performance on a simple symbol-matching task was curvilinearly related to muscle tension. Again, behavioral efficiency was highest at intermediate levels of arousal. Not all findings are entirely supportive, however (e.g., White, 1965; Wood, 1964). It is unclear, at times, what level of arousal might be optimal for the performance of specific complex tasks. As a consequence, the range of arousal selected for experimentation may fall entirely below or above this point, and in such cases, the experiment cannot possibly produce support for the curvilinear relationship between arousal and behavioral efficiency. Other problems with the model derive from the fact that the various indices of arousal employed do not perfectly agree with one another (cf. Lacey, 1967; Malmo & Bélanger, 1967). In spite of these difficulties, the inverted-U relationship between excitation and behavioral efficiency—or at the human level, between excitation and the performance of comparatively simple motor reactions in cognitively mediated behavior—is quite well substantiated.

Easterbrook's (1959) model of cue utilization addresses only one side of the inverted-U relationship: cognitive performance under conditions of elevated excitation. For such excitatory conditions, the model stipulates that the number of cues that are being processed is reduced as arousal increases. Applied to the cognitive guidance of behavior, the model projects that if guidance depends on the processing of only a small number of cues of limited variability, behavior control will be efficient; however, if guidance depends on the processing of a wide variety of cues, behavior control will be inefficient. Easterbrook suggested that for each specific task there exists an optimal range of cue utilization. If this range is narrow, as in a nondemanding task, increases in arousal may actually further performance by blocking out the potentially interfering, task-irrelevant cues. Elevated excitation may thus have an "organizing" effect on behavior. On the other hand, if this range is wide, as in complex cognitive tasks, increases in arousal are decisively detrimental to performance, because the organism fails to respond to all the cues involved. Under such conditions, behavior becomes "disorganized" in the sense that the response to the cue aggregate will be inappropriate since it is based on only a portion of the cues involved. According to Easterbrook (1959), "the range of cue utilization can be regarded as an index of cerebral competence [p. 198]," and the cue model can be rephrased to state that *cerebral competence is reduced at high levels of physiological excitation.*

Easterbrook has advanced his model as a generalization of empirical findings. The model was thus "preconfirmed." It also withstood later testing, however. For example, Agnew and Agnew (1963) observed that whereas there was a tendency for the performance of a nondemanding task to improve with increases in excitation, such increases greatly impaired the performance of a cognitively complex task.

We now combine the earlier proposal that the cognitive guidance of behavior, specifically, of hostility and aggression, is restricted to a comparatively narrow range of excitation with both the inverted-U and the cue-utilization models. The following propositions are made:

1. *The curvilinear relationship between level of excitation and cognitive competence determines a corresponding curvilinear relationship between level of excitation and behavior control through cognitive mediation.*
2. *There is an analogous correspondence between the curvilinearity of perceptual and motor competence (as a function of level of excitation) and that of behavior control through learning.*
3. *The range of excitation in which behavior control through cognitive mediation operates is narrower than that for behavior control through learning.*
4. *There is an intermediate, optimal range of excitation in which behavior control through cognitive mediation dominates behavior control through learning.*

The foregoing propositions may be summarized in model form. The resulting model of behavior guidance is presented in Fig. 1. As can be seen, the

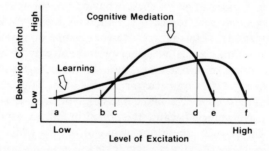

FIG. 1.   A dual-system model of behavior guidance. Curve a–f shows the presumed efficiency of response guidance acquired through learning (reinforcement, aversive, and stimulus control). Curve b–e shows the presumed efficiency of response guidance through cognitive mediation. Cognitive guidance of hostile and aggressive behavior is dominant in zone c–d. Zone d–f constitutes the primary domain of impulsive hostility and aggression. Zone a–c constitutes a secondary domain of such impulsive behavior.

hypothetical gradients associated with the proposed behavior control by cognitive mediation and by learning intersect in such a way that cognitive mediation dominates learned reactions only in a comparatively narrow middle range of excitation (points c–d). At more extreme levels of excitation, cognitive guidance yields to guidance established through the various mechanisms of learning. In this model, then, *learning is projected as a back-up system of behavior guidance that is drawn upon whenever cognitive guidance fails*. This relationship can also be expressed in very different terms. Behavior guidance through learning may be viewed to be the most fundamental system available to the organism for effective adaptation to environmental events. To a large extent, man shares this system with other species. In contrast to other species, however, man's cognitive faculties enable him to deal with these environmental events more effectively than mechanical learning would permit. But the superior adaptive skills require favorable excitatory conditions. They are lost when these conditions do not prevail. Rationality in hostility and aggression should consequently not be expected at extreme levels of excitation. According to the model presented, behavior-mediating cognitions drop out at high levels of excitation. Learned reactions to stimuli become dominant (points d–e), and with cognitive guidance becoming totally defunct (points e–f), the organism relies entirely on learned reactions. Since "irrational," impulsive aggression is characteristically associated with high levels of excitation, the zone in which cognitive mediation fails (points d–f) may be considered the *primary zone of impulsive aggression*. Impulsive aggression should also be expected at very low levels of excitation. The cognitively incapacitated individual (points a–c) again relies on learned reactions. In considering hostility and aggression, this lower end of the excitation continuum is not nearly as important as the upper end, however. This is so for two principal reasons: (a) The very performance of hostile and especially of aggressive actions requires energy that is only provided at somewhat higher levels of excitation; and (b) annoying treatments, which would evoke hostile or aggressive reactions, tend to elevate excitation (potentially to levels above point c), so that the behavior would come under cognitive guidance. We thus consider the lower end of the excitation continuum (points a–c) a *secondary zone of impulsive aggression*.

In principle, the model of behavior guidance just outlined *integrates* cognitive guidance and guidance through learning (i.e., reinforcement control, aversive control, and stimulus control), and it projects the dominance of one or the other controlling system as a function of level of excitation. We now apply this dual-system model of behavior guidance specifically to incentive-motivated and annoyance-motivated hostility and aggression.

II. A THEORY OF INCENTIVE-MOTIVATED
HOSTILITY AND AGGRESSION

It is proposed that incentive-motivated hostility and aggression generally fall into the intermediate range of excitation associated with cognitive behavior guidance. At very low levels of excitation, the organism characteristically does not pursue such objectives as the attainment of external rewards through elaborate maneuvers or through force. At very high levels of excitation, the organism is preoccupied with the experiential concomitants of this state of excitation. It thus appears likely that most incentive-motivated hostile and aggressive behavior is subject to mediating cognitive influences.

This is not to say, however, that all instances of incentive-motivated hostility and aggression are necessarily cognitively controlled. First, as has been stressed earlier, purely incentive-motivated hostile and aggressive behavior is a theoretical abstraction. Such behavior usually contains some elements of annoyance motivation. Even when hostile or aggressive actions are entirely based on the motivation merely to take control of incentives, complications in the execution of the transgression can readily create annoyances, and the associated elevation of excitation may foster impulsive actions that elude cognitive control. A calmly planned and carefully rehearsed bank robbery, for example, may result in a massacre if a robber is frightened by the movement of a customer, panics, and starts shooting. Or at a more common level, a child may grab a playmate's toy and then be provoked into violent actions when the playmate objects to the takeover. Second, incentive-motivated hostility and aggression may, of course, be under the control of learning mechanisms. Two developmental possibilities are apparent:

1. The individual, presumably as a child, may have been very successful in obtaining rewards through hostile and aggressive actions. Initially these actions may have been accidental rather than contemplated. Hostility and aggression thus came to be established through operant learning. Later, when the behavior came under cognitive control, cognitive mediation may have assumed the entirely secondary role of providing a rationalization or justification for the behavior. Since it appears, however, that cognitive control cannot sanction every learned transgressive reaction, it should function as a corrective for learned hostile and aggressive actions. Specifically, the anticipation of social reproach should come to discourage and inhibit transgressive activities.

2. The individual may initially contemplate the attainment of incentives and may, in doing so, apply most or all of the considerations comprising cognitive guidance. The gratifications obtained through the successful

execution of such plans for hostile or aggressive actions may then reinforce the behavior. Habits may thus become established, causing hostile and aggressive actions to be performed without much interference from cognitive considerations. The behavior may become "mechanical." The individual may cease to anticipate social reproach until such time as social reproach actually occurs. Then, in order to avoid further reproach, the individual is forced again to entertain the respective anticipations.

The foregoing rationales make it clear that the *potentiality* for cognitive control, which is associated with the intermediate range of excitation (*c–d* in Fig. 1), does not guarantee that every hostile or aggressive action is subject to cognitive guidance. Occasionally, learned responses may be dominant. As soon as the individual recognizes that these learned responses are in conflict with behavioral directives deriving from cognitive mediation, however, cognitive guidance should exert its controlling force and rule out discrepant courses of action. In the long run, then, hostile and aggressive behavior should be cognitively controlled under intermediate excitatory conditions. With this qualification in mind, we now turn to the propositions concerning cognitive guidance in incentive-motivated hostility and aggression.

A. *Incentive motivated hostility and aggression are motivated primarily by the anticipation of gratification.*

If such behavior should become "mechanical"—that is, if it is seemingly triggered without cognitive mediation, for example, by the sheer presence of incentives—it can still be interpreted as guided by the *expectation* of gratification (cf. Tolman, 1932, 1938). If the behavior in question were learned entirely through the contingent application of rewards, the organism would of course behave *as if it expected reward* for performing the behavior. The possible proposal that expectations are somehow involved in strictly re-inforcement-controlled hostile or aggressive actions adds nothing, however, to the account of the behavior in strict stimulus–response terms. Specifically, it fails to improve the predictive accuracy of a straightforward learning explanation, and it thus only detracts from the parsimony of explanation.

It should be recognized here that the anticipation of outcomes in the cognitive guidance of behavior has been proposed mainly to account for phenomena that elude explanation by learning theory. The anticipations in question may manifest themselves in overt or, more likely, in covert linguistic processes, and the individual may be fully aware of his or her anticipations. Thus conceived-of anticipation-guided behavior may differ substantially from responses mediated by learned connections, and the proposal of guidance through specific anticipations can further explanation. The domain of behavior in which this nonredundancy is particularly apparent is that of premeditated, novel activities directed at gaining incentives. This point is illustrated shortly.

B. *The individual who is motivated to obtain incentives and who recognizes that these incentives are accessible only through coercion will engage in hostile or aggressive actions directed at the usurpation or attainment of the incentives only if he or she is confident of being successful in his or her actions.*

The individual's subjective confidence may, of course, be conceived of in terms of subjective probabilities. In this context, confidence amounts to considering success to be very likely, if not certain. It is conceivable, however, that the degree of confidence required for committing an act of incentive-motivated hostility or aggression inversely varies, to some extent, with the magnitude of the incentive whose usurpation is attempted. A person might have to be quite sure of success before engaging in efforts to attain a minor reward through hostile or aggressive means but may be willing "to take a bit of a gamble" with such efforts when great rewards are involved.

C. *In assessing the likelihood of success in the usurpation or attainment of incentives, the individual takes into account his or her stable and transitory hostile and aggressive abilities.*

D. *Likewise, he or she takes into consideration the forces likely to obstruct his or her efforts and the possible measures of retribution.*

E. *Finally, the individual considers the likelihood of social approval and social reproach.* The anticipation of social approval furthers the motivation to usurp incentives. On occasion, it may function as the main motivating force. The anticipation of social reproach reduces the motivation to usurp incentives. Hostile and aggressive actions are inhibited when the anticipated social reproach constitutes an aversion whose intensity equals or exceeds that of the net gratification that is expected to be gained through the contemplated action.

Propositions A through E, expressed strictly in terms of gratifications and aversions, may be summarized as follows:

Incentive-motivated hostility and aggression will be enacted: (1) if gratifications are apparent; (2) if their successful attainment through coercive action is considered highly likely; and (3) if it seems likely that the coercive actions will be performed at a comparatively low cost in aversion.

The model, thus reduced, can of course be expressed in mathematical form. If it is assumed that gratifications and aversions constitute opposing forces, that these forces could be quantified, and that subjective probabilities could be determined, the magnitude of anticipated gratifications and anticipated costs in aversion (deriving from all the sources detailed earlier) could be weighted by their associated subjective probabilities. Aversions could be given negative value, and the various contributing factors could then simply be added up. For hostile or aggressive behavior to occur, the result would have to be positive; the higher its value, the more likely it would be for hostility or aggression to occur. However, in view of the difficulties—discussed earlier—in conceptualizing and measuring the magnitude of gratifications and aversions, and in view of the difficulties in assessing the subjective probabilities involved, such a formalization would give the impression of a degree of precision that, at this point, is simply not attainable. The formalization would have no practical value, and it thus seems uncalled for.

A. Experience and Observational Learning

In a model of cognitive guidance, the *factors that control the anticipation* of gratification or aversion, of success or failure, and of costs are of particular importance. It has been proposed earlier that the respective anticipations derive from the recognition of pertinent relationships (e.g., contingencies of gratification or aversion) that are largely based on causal attributions in the perception of related events. With regard to the informational basis of attributions, it has been suggested that the individual employs both primary experience and observational data. This dual information base seems to carry through all stages of the foregoing model. Concerning proposition A, for example, a youngster may see in a television drama that a juvenile gang member delights himself and the rest of the gang and enhances his own social status by stealing a car. The young viewer may well anticipate similar euphoric feelings to result from driving a stolen car and may thus be motivated to steal one. Concerning propositions B through D, he may, as the result of viewing the program, come to grossly overestimate the likelihood of success. He may be unaware of the difficulty of starting a car without the key and may severely misjudge the risk of getting caught. Concerning proposition E, he also may be misled into underestimating the severity of the social repercussions. It appears that the less direct experience the youngster has with the transgressive behavior in question, the more vulnerable he is to being misled in his anticipations. The juvenile delinquent who has been caught and has spent time in reformatory institutions would seem to be in a position to recognize the drama as misrepresenting the facts and should not be inclined to change his own anticipation of likely failure, which is based on primary experience. This illustration points up an important relationship that we assume to exist between immediate and mediated experience. Anticipations seem to be based primarily on immediate experience. *Only when these immediate experiences are lacking or are highly ambiguous is the individual susceptible to the suggestion of observed gratification and aversion or success and failure by the observation of others.* This critical relationship has generally eluded empirical testing, however. In fact, the distinction has been neglected in theory. Prominent views of hostility and aggression (e.g., Bandura, 1973a; Berkowitz, 1970) tend to project the influence of hostile and aggressive actions in fiction, especially those that are shown to be effective and approved of, as so pervasive that other potentially influential experiential factors appear secondary and powerless in preventing hostile or aggressive action.

The following propositions are advanced to fill the indicated theoretical void. They derive from the assumption: (1) that the individual distinguishes between immediate and mediated experiences relating to hostility and aggression; and (2) that immediate experiences, presumably because of their intuitive validity, exert a stronger influence on dependent anticipations than less direct, mediated experiences.

A. In the recognition of contingencies of reinforcement and punishment related to hostility and aggression—namely coercive contingencies, stable and transitory abilities and inabilities of the self, opposing situational forces, punitive and retaliatory potentialities of others, and contingencies of social approval and reproach—the individual distinguishes between at least four levels of apparent experiential validity: (1) his or her own primary experience, (2) the immediately witnessed experiences of others, (3) experiences of others stated by others to have actually occurred, and (4) experiences of others presented by others with the understanding that these experiences have been exaggerated, simplified, distorted, or entirely invented.

B. Experiences at level (1) exert the strongest influence on anticipations; the strength of the influence becomes successively less at the succeeding levels with experiences at level (4) exerting the weakest influence on anticipations.

C. Following proposition B, anticipations are primarily formed on the basis of the highest-order experience available.

D. Following further from proposition B, if there is inconsistent information at various levels of experience, the individual forms an anticipation on the basis of the available experience of the highest order.

In these propositions, then, more immediate experiences are posited to serve as correctives for less immediate experiences. As a consequence, information about hostility and aggression conveyed through fiction and hearsay should be of little consequence for the formation of behavior-guiding anticipations when it is contradicted by more direct experiences. On the other hand, the individual who has not directly experienced the contingencies in question, or who considers his or her experience atypical, should be receptive to the information provided through fiction and hearsay. For example, a boy who sees a movie in which someone gleefully tortures an animal without being criticized or punished for doing so may get the idea that torturing an animal is enjoyable and has no adverse consequences for some people. Concerning his own behavior, however, he should be inclined to imitate the witnessed action only if he has not directly experienced noxious reactions while witnessing an animal in pain and if his immediate experience with his social environment gives him reason to believe that imitation would not likely prompt reproach. The available evidence on this point (Cantor, 1974) shows that boys who witness a filmed model inflict pain upon an animal and apparently derive pleasure therefrom fail to display a greater degree of imitation than boys who see the same action produce sadness in the model. The anticipation of euphoria that the aggression-enjoyment film may have created was presumably overridden by more immediate experience with the behavioral contingency at hand.

The ease with which well-adjusted individuals manage to disregard the behavioral contingencies presented in fiction as atypical and unrepresentative is attested to by the fact that although so much entertainment fare in Western cultures depicts the attainment, at least temporarily, of almost every imaginable incentive by hostile or aggressive means, the depicted transgressions are not imitated on a massive scale. Most people apparently can dismiss the depicted contingencies as "fictional" (i.e., as having little or no validity) and can thus reduce or eliminate any consequences such presentations may have for the formation of anticipations.

All this is not to say that fiction or hearsay cannot decisively affect the motivation to obtain incentives through hostile or aggressive action. Nor is it to say that cognitive guidance can never be dominated by anticipations that derive mainly from nonimmediate experiences. As has been pointed out earlier, many immediate experiences may be ambiguous. At times, critical experiences may be lacking altogether, and the individual may be forced to generalize from potentially remote experiences. Most people, for example, have no immediate experience with extreme wealth, but they presumably entertain the notion that great wealth brings great happiness. This notion, together with the anticipations linked to it, may come predominantly out of fiction and from hearsay. The anticipation of happiness through the attainment of wealth, in turn, should motivate the individual to attain wealth—if necessary, through coercive means. Such a belief, erroneous though it may be, may produce potential liars, thieves, and killers. motivation is countered, however, by the anticipation of repercussions. Fear of detection, and ultimately, fear of punitive measures, is likely to inhibit coercive actions in those who risk worsening their condition by unsuccessful actions. But it might not deter those who have little or nothing to lose.

The relationship between incentive-motivated hostility and aggression and the risk of punitive compensation is nicely illustrated by the frequency of hijackings of airplanes in the late sixties and early seventies (cf. Bandura, 1973a). Detailed news reports of successful hijackings not only outlined an innovative course of coercive action for less inventive potential transgressors but also conveyed information that must have created the following anticipations in those who contemplated criminal coercion in order to get rich quickly: (1) The incentive is of enormous magnitude; (2) aversive cost, that is, the effort involved in the execution of the transgression, is minimal; (3) the action is quite safe; and (4) punitive repercussions can be readily avoided. This, of course, is the "golden formula" for incentive-motivated hostility and aggression: extremely high incentive at extremely low cost. Moreover, this recipe for a crime was apparently trustworthy; that is, it came out of the news, not out of fiction. It should not be surprising, then, to find that these newscasts triggered "an epidemic" of hijackings. It also is not surprising that the rate of hijackings dropped to near-zero levels after the introduction of changes in airport security that caused the failure of hijacking attempts. The news reports of these failures must be assumed to have changed the anticipations: Although the potential incentive was still there, the subjective probability of a successful hijacking had become low, and punitive repercussions were likely.

In this connection, it can readily be acknowledged that the fictional depiction of ingenious new ways to obtain incentives through transgressive means may also spark imitative hostile or aggressive actions. It would appear, however, that such imitation is likely only when the contingencies depicted in fiction do not clash with those deriving from more immediate experiences. This is to say that the individual may form anticipations pertaining to incentive-motivated hostility and aggression on the basis of fiction only if his or her primary experience *fails to falsify* these anticipations.

B. The Status of the Evidence

In concluding our discussion of incentive-motivated hostility and aggression, it should be pointed out that although the theoretical approach via cognitive guidance is entirely consistent with the empirical evidence available on this type of behavior, the approach is certainly not necessitated by decisive data. In fact, the data on hand seem adequately accounted for by more parsimonious approaches based on learning theory (e.g., Buss, 1961, 1971). We have discussed the pertinent evidence under "Incentive Theory" (Chapter 4, Section IIIA3). It may appear, then, that more complex proposals are unnecessary—indeed, undesirable. Such a verdict is considered premature, however, for at least two reasons. First, whereas the straightforward application of the operant-learning paradigm to incentive-motivated hostility and aggression may very parsimoniously explain the formation of specific hostile or aggressive habits, the initial occurrence of the reinforced actions is left to chance. In view of the fact that hostile and aggressive efforts toward the attainment of incentives tend to be complex and potentially entail *novel* activities varying considerably across situations, the reinforcement of past responses appears to be too narrow an explanation. Specifically, intelligent probing for superior plans of coercive action directed at gaining control of incentives, and the disciplined execution of the strategies arrived at, elude the reinforcement formula. References to shaping and generalization processes simply cannot bridge the gap to behaviors that apparently come about as the result of complex considerations. To deal effectively with the complexity of hostile and aggressive behavior, the invocation of some form of cognitive guidance seems unavoidable (cf. Bandura, 1973a), and the problems created by the involvement of concepts that are difficult to operationalize and to measure (e.g., anticipations) have to be accepted. This brings us directly to the second reason for the tentative adherence to a cognitive model. The available evidence does not directly support models of cognitive guidance in hostility and aggression, because the research was set up to test other notions. At this time, tests of aspects of cognitive mediation are rare but suggestive (e.g., Bandura, Underwood, & Fromson, 1975; Rule & Nesdale, 1976b; Zimbardo, 1969). It is hoped that specific proposals of cognitive guidance, such as the one presented, will promote further research into the cognitive mediation of hostility and aggression.

III. A THEORY OF ANNOYANCE-MOTIVATED HOSTILITY AND AGGRESSION

In accordance with our earlier discussion of response guidance in annoyance-motivated hostile and aggressive behavior (Chapter 5, Section IE), it is posited that such annoyance-motivated behavior is primarily under cognitive control when excitation is at intermediate levels but that when excitation is extremely low or, more importantly, extremely high, the behavior follows learned patterns and becomes impulsive. In addition to these differences in the control of behavior, the behavior seems to serve different purposes at the various levels of excitation. At intermediate levels of excitation, the individual appears to entertain anticipations, as in the case of incentive-motivated hostility and aggression. Once an annoyance is anticipated, the individual seems to be able to devise and follow a course of action through which the anticipated aversion can be avoided or at least minimized. If the individual has already suffered an aversion, he or she seems to be able to construct and carry out a course of action through which retribution is inflicted, this retribution being such that negative consequences to the self are kept to a minimum. At low and high levels of excitation, in contrast, the individual is apparently unable to entertain complex considerations. The organism seems preoccupied either with warding off a potential disturbance (at low levels) or with terminating an acute annoyance (at high levels). Responses that serve these ends *immediately,* regardless of their more remote implications, are likely to be performed (cf. Zillmann, 1972b). It is this difference in function at the three excitation levels that we now detail, along with the proposed differentiations in behavioral control.

A. Intermediate Levels of Excitation

1. *At intermediate levels of excitation, annoyance-motivated hostility and aggression are motivated primarily by the anticipation of the infliction of an annoyance or by the infliction of a moderate annoyance.*
2. *The individual who is motivated to avoid or terminate an aversion and who recognizes that this objective is attainable only through coercion will engage in hostile or aggressive actions directed at the avoidance or termination of the aversion only if he or she is confident of being successful in that action.*
3. *In assessing the likelihood of success in avoiding or terminating an aversion, the individual takes into account his or her stable and transitory hostile and aggressive abilities.*
4. *Likewise, the individual takes into consideration the forces likely to obstruct his or her efforts and the possible measures of retribution.*
5. *The individual furthermore considers the likelihood of social approval and social reproach.*

At intermediate levels of excitation, then, the control of hostile and aggressive behavior appears to be essentially the same for incentive-motivated and annoyance-motivated behaviors. Some characteristic differences do exist, however. These differences mainly concern moral considerations or, in more behavioral terms, the anticipation of approval or reproach.

In general, incentive-motivated hostile and aggressive behavior is transgressive, and perpetrators who are aware of the transgressive nature of their actions, should they be troubled by this awareness, can only try to "justify" the transgression by forcing it into line with some morally sanctioned objectives. The attainment of incentives is the primary motivating force, and such moral considerations as may be entertained appear to play the secondary role of freeing the individual from inhibitions to pursue his or her coercive efforts.

The situation is quite different in annoyance-motivated hostility and aggression. Characteristically, the individual resorts to the contemplation of hostile and aggressive actions to prevent an annoyance or to terminate a moderate annoyance only when the annoyance inflicted or anticipated to be inflicted upon him or her constitutes a transgression. Although the perception of what is and what is not transgressive is certainly subject to considerable distortion, the individual must keep general norms in mind. If he or she is annoyed by events caused by others whose actions are socially approved or at least not in violation of prevailing codes of conduct, he or she cannot readily resort to hostile or aggressive retaliatory actions. Under these circumstances, the actions would meet with strong social reproach. If, however, the annoyance is clearly identifiable as transgressive, the individual is freed from moral restraint: He or she can apply punitive measures, although not excessively, without the risk of reproach. The individual may, in fact, have cause to expect social approval for taking punitive actions. Moreover, the individual may rightfully expect social reproach if he or she fails to apply punitive measures or if he or she fails to apply them to a degree considered equitable (cf. this chapter, Sections IB through D). In simple words, the individual is under considerable social pressure to fight back when someone annoys him or her without apparent justification, and similarly, he or she is expected to do something about the threat of such annoyance. The anticipation of social approval and reproach, then, whether or not it is associated with explicit moral considerations, must be considered a motivating as well as a disinhibiting force.

The motivational properties of annoyance-motivated hostile and aggressive behavior are frequently presented as serving the maintenance of the self-concept. Feshbach (1970), for example, assumed that unwarranted mistreatment that annoys a person also inflicts a loss of self-esteem. He proposed that the individual is motivated to retaliate mainly to restore his or her self-esteem. Similarly, Bandura (1973a, 1973b) assumed that a person judges the merits of his or her own actions and correspondingly "rewards" or "punishes" the self. He suggested that when a situation mandates retaliation, aggression may be motivated by a desire to avoid punishing self-contempt. Both views depict the individual as internally driven to hostile or aggressive action, seemingly independent of social concerns. It appears, however, that such an impression is somewhat misleading. The individual may be predominantly concerned with gaining the esteem of others and with avoiding their contempt. In fact, this social concern may be held responsible for the development of stable retaliatory response tendencies. Once these tendencies are established, the individual may well believe them to be entirely self-determined. Regardless of such beliefs, however, the maintenance of a favorable self-concept must be viewed as socially motivated, in principle. Through hostile and aggressive action that seems to serve a favorable "self-concept," the individual ultimately furthers his or her social appeal. Potentially, the individual attains *social* approval and avoids *social* reproach as long as the behavior performed, which he or she may well believe to follow personal standards, does not violate the prevailing norms of *social* conduct. Personal standards tend to reflect the social norms of the groups the individual is a member of or, more importantly, aspires to be a member of; and to the extent that personal and social standards are redundant, hostile and aggressive behavior can be predicted on the basis of the anticipation of *social* approval and reproach. Concepts of self-esteem, self-reward, and self-punishment can thus be expressed in social terms.

Anticipations of social approval or reproach that effect the inhibition or disinhibition of annoyance-motivated hostile and aggressive behavior are operative mainly in the selection of an appropriate, effective course of action.

Whether the objective is to prevent or terminate an annoyance, the individual usually has many avenues of action open to him or her. Some possible actions would meet with social reproach for being too severe; others may be regarded as too weak. Some actions may be sanctioned; others may even be applauded. Courses of action that the individual considers likely to prompt reproach will be inhibited, and those that seem to hold promise of approval will more likely be carried out. In selecting a course of action, the individual should also respond to his or her anticipations regarding sucess and failure and cost.

At intermediate levels of excitation, annoyance-motivated behavior seems generally to be biased toward hostility. In other words, it appears unlikely that the individual who seeks to avoid discomfort or who wants to put an end to a moderate annoyance is inclined to fight physically. This is because: (a) the individual is unprepared excitationally to exert a large amount of energy quickly; and (b) maybe more importantly, he or she must expect social reproach for excessive punitive actions. With the exception of atypical codes of conduct in special groups (such as in the juvenile gangs discussed earlier, where a demeaning word or gesture calls for the death of the offender), the somewhat annoyed individual has to employ hostile rather than aggressive means as a deterrent or punishment. A person cannot simply lash out as he or she pleases. A young man, for example, who has been put down by an acquaintance in the presence of close friends cannot punch his annoyer in the nose. He may have to inhibit any physical form of retaliation because it would meet with the vehement disapproval of his friends. A quick comeback, in contrast, would not only be approved of but likely applauded by them. If the annoyer is a superior wit, the retaliator may have to resort to a blunt insult or to the less risky course of spreading malicious gossip at a later time. But unless the exchange of hostility escalates and the annoyance becomes severe (at which point, the individual should become highly aroused), retaliation cannot take the form of aggression without becoming transgressive and, potentially, a source of further annoyance. Generally speaking, the unwritten "laws" of conduct in human society favor nonviolent means of conflict resolution: They favor hostility over aggression. Only aggressive misconduct seems to justify the use of aggression as a deterrent or punishment. But since aggressive misconduct is expected to induce high levels of excitation in the victim, it should be mainly hostile transgressive behavior that produces annoyances associated with moderate levels of excitation, and consequently, hostile action should be the preferred mode of deterrent or punishment in this realm.

B. High Levels of Excitation

1. *At high levels of excitation, annoyance-motivated hostility and aggression are directed primarily at the immediate reduction and termination of the acute, motivating annoyance.*

2. *The individual's capacity to anticipate gratification and aversion, success and failure, and cost is diminished. As a consequence, response guidance through the anticipation of the consequences of a course of hostile or aggressive action is impaired. At extremely high levels of excitation, the individual disregards the nonimmediate consequences of his or her actions altogether.*

3. *The individual displays mainly learned reactions associated with great habit strength. At extremely high levels of excitation, cognitive mediation is minimal, and hostile and aggressive responses are impulsive.*

4. *Motor responses are vigorous. Their vigor is roughly proportional to the level of excitation prevailing at the time.*

Regarding response guidance, the hostile and aggressive behavior of the severely annoyed and highly aroused person is viewed as drastically different from that motivated by incentives or moderate annoyances. The individual behaves as if the high level of excitation being experienced—a level that, to be sure, he or she perceives as noxious—were "unbearable." Apparently, the individual behaves so as to rid him- or herself of this noxious arousal with little regard for the consequences of that behavior. In this disregard for the prevailing contingencies of gratification and aversion, for the likelihood of success and failure, and for the cost in effort, the extremely aroused individual readily violates the concept of "rational man." In "following his or her impulses," the person "gets carried away" and may inflict harm or injury to a degree that goes far beyond what equity considerations would prescribe. His or her behavior is likely to prompt social disapproval and even reprisal from the victim or the victim's associates. The highly aroused individual seems oblivious to the odds of being effective with hostile and aggressive actions. He or she fights, regardless of what the cost of that action may be, and he or she may make an all-out effort even in the face of certain defeat. It seems that extremely annoyed and angry persons "don't give a damn" about what happens to them after their attack. They behave as if they "couldn't care less" about the mess they might get themselves into. Outside intervention is usually refused, especially when it entails appeals to reason. As these highly aroused persons are being "unreasonable," they claim to know exactly what they are doing and consider their course of action reasonable. Characteristically, however, those who have "blown their top" come to regret their behavior ("I must have been out of my mind!") as soon as they calm down to intermediate levels of excitation and again adopt more normative standards of reasonableness. In terms of our model of response guidance, the individual regains anticipatory faculties as his or her excitation drops from very high to intermediate levels and recognizes the violation of "rational" objectives by his or her impulsive hostile and aggressive actions. The objectives that were violated are, of course, the long-range (i.e., nonimmediate) maximization of gratification and minimization of aversion.

The apparent *transitory cognitive incapacitation* seems invariably to accompany emotional outbursts. Characteristically, it causes the loss of otherwise effective inhibitions and thereby produces reckless behavior. This incapacitation can be viewed as a *lack of concern* that is brought about at high levels of excitation. It could be argued that the individual may well comprehend the consequences of his or her actions but *evaluates* them differently. Common observation seems to support this view. The highly aroused person often rejects appeals to consider the consequences of the hostile and aggressive acts he or she is about to commit. In such appeals, the specific consequences are often articulated, and the individual's inability to anticipate them thus seems to be overcome through the provision of this information by the person who attempts to intervene. Furthermore, the highly aroused person often appears to understand, yet nonetheless refuses to consider the implications. A youngster, for example, who has been deceived and insulted by a stronger peer may seethe with anger, ready to assault his annoyer. His friends' warnings that an attack would be foolish and that he would only be beaten up may prompt a response like "I don't care." Such a response would seem to show that the youngster comprehends the risk he is taking. But does he?

The observation that the articulation of consequences by others has prompted a verbal reaction does not prove that these consequences have been fully comprehended. Responses such as "I don't care!" merely show that the individual is determined to pursue a certain course of action and that he or she does not want to be interfered with. In fact, such responses can be viewed as attempts by the highly aroused individual to protect the self from "irrelevant" cues, to make possible a better response to the cues relevant to the acts he or she is set to perform. This view would be consistent with Easterbrook's (1959) model of cue utilization.

The earlier discussed research findings concerning the relationship between level of excitation and performance, especially cognitive performance, certainly suggest that the extremely excited person is unlikely to engage in the complex cognitive processes required to "evaluate" the implications of his or her actions—should he or she be able to understand them as they are presented. But in spite of this suggestion by the findings, it could be argued that the *evaluation* of the consequences of hostile and aggressive behavior varies as a function of level of excitation. Specifically, it could be argued that as excitation reaches high levels, the individual assesses the outcomes of his or her actions more favorably. It is at least conceivable that at high levels of excitation, the individual perceives the likelihood of success as higher and the cost attached as lower, if not as trivial. The aroused person would thus suffer from an "illusion of power," which would account for his or her recklessness. It should be noted here, however, that this very conception of an illusion of power in the excited individual also follows from the assumption that the individual in this state is unable to fully comprehend the implications of his or her action; or if a somewhat more conservative assumption is preferred, that he or she is so preoccupied with the pursuit of an immediate objective as simply to fail to attend to the nonimmediate aspects of his or her objective. These assumptions not only project the absence of anticipation-based inhibitions and recklessness; they also explain why these phenomena occur. What may appear to be a change in the evaluation of consequences and a move toward the acceptance of greater risks and greater cost is accounted for as the result of inability or inattentiveness. The extremely excited individual's illusion of power, then, is parsimoniously explained as the product of a temporary cognitive incapacitation.

Hostile and aggressive outbursts have occasionally been viewed as manifestations of mental illness. The temporarily incapacitated individual seems to display the behavior of persons whose incapacitation is more permanent. Cameron (1947), for example, compared emotional outbursts to hysterical seizures. He noted that the shared behavioral features of the two phenomena were the irresistible striving toward the completion of an immediate objective, the absence of inhibitions, the failure to respond to attempts by others to intervene, and recklessness. If the loss of anticipatory skills is critically involved in such "seizures," one should expect persons who have temporarily or permanently lost these skills, through intoxication or physical impairment, to exhibit frequent hostile and aggressive outbursts on minimal provocation. In general, evidence from correlational studies supports this interpretation. Whereas mental illness in general has not been found to be related to violent behavior, illnesses in which the loss of anticipatory skills is combined with unimpaired physical capabilities have been associated with violence (cf. Gulevich & Bourne, 1970). Similarly, although no relationship has been found between drugs in general and hostile and aggressive behavior, toxicants that cloud the anticipation of the consequences of the individual's actions without unduly hampering the motor skills have been linked to increased impulsive violence (cf. Tinklenberg & Stillman, 1970). In this connection, alcoholic intoxication has been noted for its "inhibition-releasing and judgment-altering effects" (Gulevich & Bourne, 1970, p. 319). Its facilitating effect on violent behavior is not in doubt (e.g., Guze, Tuason, Gatfield, Stewart, & Picken, 1962; Wolfgang & Strohm, 1956). Much violence, criminal homicide in particular, is committed in a state of alcoholic intoxication. But although this fact can be considered suggestive of the assailant's disregard for the nonimmediate implications of his or her actions, it certainly does not decisively implicate the impairment of the individual's cognitive faculties as the critical aggression-promoting force. It could be argued that the assailant was criminally inclined in the first place and that such criminally inclined people tend to drink. Following this argument, the consumption of alcohol would only be incidentally (not causally) related to violence. Controlled experimental investigations, which we discuss later, tend to rule out such an explanation, however.

But granted that violent reactions may greatly resemble certain manifestations of mental illness, the characterization of hostile and aggressive outbursts as a form of mental illness is a value judgment that adds nothing to our understanding of these outbursts. Normal or abnormal, emotional outbursts seem to occur to some extent in everyone's life. A statistical definition of normalcy would thus make them "normal." If a clinical definition that uses rationality as a criterion for normalcy is preferred, impulsive violent outbursts would indeed appear to be "abnormal." Such a classification is pragmatically inadvisable because it declares most people mentally ill. It is also inadvisable because it employs an arbitrary conception of rationality that can readily be challenged. Since we have used this conception of rationality implicitly, a clarifying comment seems in order.

The term *rational behavior* is commonly used to refer to behavior that serves the individual's self-interest. More precisely, as we indicated earlier, it serves the maximization of gratification and the minimization of aversion. The concept "rational" is characteristically applied to behavior that spans a considerable period of time (cf. Lewin, 1948). The verdict "rational" is rendered by an observer when a particular act appears to be in a person's best interest in the long run, potentially for the entire time course of an expected interaction. "Short-sighted" action—that is, action that produces immediate benefits at excessively high later cost—appears nonrational. The perception of rationality thus depends on the period of time scrutinized. In these terms, if the nonimmediate consequences of hostile and aggressive outbursts are being considered (and they usually are), such outbursts will be thought to violate rationality grossly. If, on the other hand, one were to look only at immediate results, most of the violent outbursts that occur could be classified as rational.

It seems that the individual who experiences an extremely high level of noxious arousal can in most instances improve his or her situation through violent action. In fact, such violent action may often be the only kind of action capable of accomplishing the immediate behavioral objective of stopping an *emergency* condition: the acute annoyance. If violent action fails to accomplish this goal, the individual's efforts should soon produce a state of exhaustion. Odd as it may seem, this state of exhaustion can be viewed as another resolution of the emergency situation. For physiological reasons (cf. Cannon, 1929; Freeman, 1948; Grossman, 1967), the individual is unable to maintain an extremely high level of sympathetic excitation for long periods of time. Arousal must return to more moderate levels, and the vigorous, energy-consuming action of violent outbursts can be expected to accelerate the normalization. Consequently, whereas the self-controlled person would continue to suffer from an acute annoyance for a considerable period of time, the individual who erupts in violent action will much sooner reach a point at which noxious arousal has diminished and has become "bearable." In addition, there is reason to believe (cf. Gellhorn, 1970) that the strenuous action associated with outbursts occasions muscular fatigue, which the individual experiences as relaxation. In brief, then, even if violent outbursts fail to terminate an annoyance by stopping the annoyer's actions, they can improve the individual's immediate condition. Violent outbursts can thus be viewed as serving a rational objective, because they alleviate an emergency condition of the organism.

The discussed reduction of annoyance through violent outbursts is expected primarily as the result of vigorous motor discharge. This discharge is commonly used as the defining characteristic of emotional outbursts, and it is thus by definition associated with violent reactions. More specifically, however, the discussed reduction of annoyance is viewed as resulting from motor discharge that is continued to the point of fatigue and exhaustion. Clearly, motor discharge is initially invigorating and arousing, and as long as this condition prevails, a reduction of annoyance should not be expected. On the contrary, invigorating motor activities must be expected to facilitate annoyance and, along with it, hostile and aggressive behavior. This expectation is amply supported by research evidence (e.g., Hornberger, 1959; Zillmann & Bryant, 1974; Zillmann, Katcher, & Milavsky, 1972). Counter to the widespread belief that all vigorous motor activities, and especially those that accompany the expression of annoyance and displaced hostile acts, have "cathartic value," such activities intensify feelings of annoyance, anger, and outrage. Only if they are performed to the point of exhaustion should one expect them to dissipate intense annoyances. Strictly speaking, it is the state of exhaustion that is considered to resolve the behavioral emergency created by the extreme annoyance. The instrumental value of a violent outburst that fails to stop the annoyer's action or otherwise terminate the annoyance is to be seen, then, in the fact that it quickly and effectively creates a state of exhaustion.

The characterization of violent outbursts as "nonrational behavior" should thus be treated with caution. Such outbursts do serve the individual's self-interest, and in the sense that they help resolve behavioral emergencies, they enable him or her to cope with intense annoyances even when they seem ineffective or "counterproductive."

Regarding our use of the term *incapacitation,* a further clarifying comment is indicated. Clearly, the concept of incapacitation has been applied in a specific manner. Higher-order cognitive processes, especially those mediating the anticipation of future events, were said to suffer impairment at high levels of excitation. Lower-order cognitive processes, such as those manifest in discrimination skills, were not viewed as being critically altered. The organism's ability to display coordinated actions was not seen to be impaired. This is in sharp contrast to the possible conception of intense emotional reactions as disruptive, disorganized behavior. Incapacitation, then, is specific to anticipation skills. It is not general. In fact, as has been implied all along, cognitive processes that serve vigorous motor behavior must be considered to be unimpaired at high levels of excitation, and the capacity for vigorous action must be viewed as enormously potentiated. In emergency situations, skills that are essential in coping with such situations seem sharpened, whereas nonessential skills seem temporarily retarded. Similarly, the emergency skills seem to be retarded and the more teleological skills reactivated as the organism's condition normalizes.

The view that the arousing properties of severe annoyances constitute a behavioral emergency that can be resolved through vigorous hostile or aggressive action derives, of course, from Cannon's (1929) well-known proposal regarding the emergency nature of emotional behavior generally. In accordance with Cannon's proposal, the excitatory reaction occasioned by a severe annoyance is conceived of primarily as heightened activity of the sympathetic nervous system that *prepares the organism for the temporary engagement in vigorous motor activities, such as those needed for fight or flight.* Both fight and flight are *adaptive* reactions to annoyance. Potentially, either reaction can resolve a behavioral emergency. In the evolution of man, the short-term potentiation of fight and flight reactions had obvious survival value. Only in complex, modern society has this potentiation become largely maladaptive—and hence branded as "nonrational." In most interactive situations, the severely annoyed individual can neither throw punches nor run away. Yet he or she is excitationally prepared for such action.

We analyze this condition and its implications for emotional behavior in detail in the next chapter. Suffice it here to say that at high levels of excitation, the annoyed individual is disposed to engage in vigorous action. To the extent that aggressive activities involve vigorous motor action more than do hostile activities, this preparedness for vigorous action would seem to favor aggressive responses over hostile ones. It might be misleading, however, to assume that aggressive activities are generally more vigorous than hostile ones. Permanent injury or death, for example, can be inflicted with the gentle pulling of an index finger that triggers a shotgun blast; and the destruction of an annoyer's property, a hostile act, may require considerable motor involvement. The preparedness for vigorous action that a high level of excitation provides, then, does not seem so much to favor aggression over hostility as it seems to favor vigorous aggressive and hostile behaviors over aggressive and hostile reactions associated with little action. Equally important, this preparedness seems to favor responses that produce immediate results over those with delayed consequences, and to the extent that immediately effective reactions involve greater vigor than those whose effect is delayed, it seems to favor vigorous hostile and aggressive behavior over the pursuit of a comparatively nonexerting course of hostile or aggressive action.

C. Low Levels of Excitation

1. *At low levels of excitation, annoyance-motivated hostility and aggression serve primarily the maintenance of a resting state.*
2. *As at high levels of excitation, anticipation skills are diminished, and cognitive response guidance is impaired.*
3. *The individual displays mainly learned reactions.*
4. *Motor responses are nonvigorous.*

Hostility and aggression at low levels of excitation are considered here for reasons of theoretical completeness rather than for their social significance. Obviously, at low levels of arousal, the organism is utterly unprepared for vigorous action. Additionally, any annoyance that would motivate hostile or aggressive reactions is comparatively mild. Under these conditions, one should expect habitual defensive reactions only, reactions that are unlikely to inflict severe harm or injury upon an annoyer. The individual simply wards off any disturbance of his or her tranquil state. The behavioral objective of such hostile or aggressive responses is well described by the verbal reaction typical under the described circumstances: "Leave me alone!"

If the individual is unable to ward off a disturbance through verbal responses or haphazard motor reactions, his or her annoyance, and along with it, the level of excitation, is expected to increase. Motor reactions especially should quickly elevate excitation to intermediate levels. As intermediate levels are reached, the earlier specified elements of cognitive control come into play. The initially nonaroused individual's *continued* annoyance is thus likely to produce hostile and aggressive reactions that are under cognitive control.

D. The Status of the Evidence

As was found to be the case with the theory of incentive-motivated hostility and aggression, research evidence consistent with the projections of the theory of annoyance-motivated hostility and aggression is abundant but fails to implicate decisively the cognitive mechanics proposed. The changing function of cognitive processes at different levels of excitation is strongly suggested by several investigations, however.

Research pertaining to the individual's anticipatory skills has been discussed earlier in some detail. As will be recalled (cf. Chapter 4, Section IIIA4), the investigation of the effects of the perceived likelihood and magnitude of reprisals revealed with great consistency that the individual readily controls his or her hostile and aggressive inclinations at intermediate levels of excitation, so as to minimize the aversive consequences of his or her actions. At intermediate levels of excitation, then, the individual is known to be highly sensitive to future aversions and cost. Studies discussed earlier demonstrate that a high likelihood of retaliation (e.g., Baron, 1973) or the possibility of a massive reprisal (e.g., Shortell, Epstein, & Taylor, 1970), both involving perceptions of the opponent and situational conditions, can curb an attack. There is also evidence that suggests that at intermediate levels of excitation, the individual takes his or her own hostile and aggressive capabilities into consideration. In a recent investigation, Dengerink, O'Leary, and Kasner (1975) separated subjects according to whether they perceived their behavior to be controlled mainly by themselves (internal locus of control) or by environmental factors (external locus of control). This distinction, it seems, can be translated into a contrast between individuals who are confident that they can affect their environment through their action and individuals who are less confident of being able to do so. In other words, persons who generally believe that they can, through their own action, control matters according to their wishes should also be confident of success in their hostile and aggressive actions. In contrast, persons who feel that their behavior is very much the result of external circumstances should be far less confident in this regard. Persons who are generally confident of success should thus be expected to behave more aggressively in situations of conflict than less confident individuals. This expectation received strong support in the investigation by Dengerink et al. Action-confident subjects displayed the same concerns for the consequences of their actions as nonconfident subjects but were generally more aggressive.

There is also some indication that a person's estimate of likely aggressive success is *temporarily* affected by preceding nonaggressive success and failure. In an investigation by Dengerink and Myers (Dengerink, 1976), subjects repeatedly succeeded or failed on an initial assignment and then competed on an aggression-measuring reaction-time task (cf. Taylor, 1967). Contrary to what the consideration of frustration would lead one to expect, subjects with a prior experience of success behaved more aggressively. This finding, which is otherwise difficult to account for, is readily explained when it is assumed that the experience of success temporarily boosts the individual's confidence in the efficacy of his or her actions, hostile and aggressive actions included.

Further findings that can be viewed as suggestive of the individual's consideration of the likely cost of an assault come from research on interracial aggression. It has been observed that the retaliatory behavior of a white person tends to be more severe against a black person than against a white person when the retaliator remains anonymous, but that when he is well identified, the white person's punitive actions are drastically lower against the black person than against the white person (Donnerstein & Donnerstein, 1976; Donnerstein, Donnerstein, Simon, & Ditrichs, 1972). Being known to the black person, "marked" as the potential target for reprisals, thus proved to have a strong inhibitory effect on the white person's aggressive actions. At intermediate levels of excitation, the white person appears to be quite apprehensive about the future interaction with his black opponent. Donnerstein et al. feel that their findings "support the conclusion that white persons have learned to fear black retaliation [p. 236]." Although "fear" may somewhat overstate the magnitude of the apprehension, the fact of apprehension seems not to be in doubt. It remains unclear, however, whether this anticipation of severe reprisals and/or of high cost derives from the white person's perception of the impulsiveness and the motor skills of his opponent or from the acknowledgment of his own hostile and aggressive limitations in a potential confrontation.

The implications of the proposed anticipation of social approval and reproach for hostility and aggression have been convincingly demonstrated in the investigation by Borden (1975) discussed earlier (cf. Chapter 4, Section IIIA3). As will be remembered, aggressive behavior was far more pronounced in the presence of an aggression-endorsing onlooker than in the presence of an aggression-rejecting witness. The aggression-facilitating effect of anticipated approval was further evidenced by the fact that the removal of the proaggressive onlooker prompted a significant decline in aggressiveness.

Data that suggest that the anticipation of social approval and reproach may affect hostile and aggressive behavior at the personality level have been presented by Fishman (1965). Female subjects were classified, according to their score on a social-desirability scale, as exhibiting either a low or a high need for approval. It was found that subjects high in need for approval were less hostile toward their annoyer than those less concerned with approval. Additionally, the excitatory reaction to the annoying treatment dissipated more rapidly after retaliation for the low-need-for-approval subjects. The latter observation seems to indicate that approval-oriented persons are more apprehensive about reproach for the hostile actions they have committed and hence maintain a state of elevated arousal for a longer period of time.

The study of attributional processes, especially of attributions regarding intent, directly addresses the cognitive mediation of hostile and aggressive behavior at intermediate levels of excitation. The punishment of aversion-producing actions meets with approval only if those actions are perceived as having been committed for the purpose of inflicting harm or injury. If the actions are not transgressive, that is, if no malicious intent is apparent, the punishment of aversion-producing acts can be expected to prompt social reproach. Under these contingencies of approval and reproach, the individual is obviously not free to burst out in hostile or aggressive reactions in response to any and every annoyance inflicted upon him or her. The individual is compelled to analyze the circumstances of the annoyance. He or she must determine whether the annoyer meant to annoy him or her or whether the annoyance suffered is the unintended by-product of actions directed at other, unrelated goals. More specifically, not only must the individual determine whether or not the annoyance was deliberately created, but if the annoyance-inflicting act cannot be perceived as outright malicious, he or she also must assess the degree to which mitigating circumstances might exist. The accidental infliction of an annoyance apparently does not inculpate the person who brought it about. Punitive measures accordingly are not indicated, and the individual who may be inclined to react in a hostile or aggressive manner must hold back his or her reaction to avoid social censure. Similarly, if an annoyance is inflicted by a person who is permanently handicapped or temporarily incapacitated, the inflicting act tends to be attributed to the annoyer's state of incapacitation rather than to be perceived as malice. Again, the annoyed individual has to refrain from punitive action to avoid reproach.

In this context, it is of great interest to note that in human society generally, the severely annoyed and hence highly aroused person, when tormenting others and conducting him- or herself in ways that are usually disapproved and censured, enjoys considerable "immunity from prosecution." Such tolerance seems to be based on the common recognition that cognitive functioning is impaired at high levels of excitation. Regarding the infliction of an annoyance by someone who is acutely annoyed or severely disturbed, the discussed tolerance would seem to make punitive actions against him or her inappropriate. Prompt punishment would meet with reproach, a circumstance that again forces the individual to inhibit retaliatory actions. The validity of these suggestions has been demonstrated in a recent investigation by Savitsky, Czyzewski, Dubord, and Kaminsky (1976). The punishment assigned for a particular offense was found to be far less severe when the offense in question was committed in a state of distress than when it was carried out in the absence of a mitigating condition. It is possible, however, that such a differentiation in punishment results not so much from a punishment-reducing effect of mitigating distress as from a punishment-enhancing effect of disturbing offenses committed "in cold blood" or with apparent enjoyment.

The implications of the presumed consideration of mitigating circumstances for annoyance-motivated hostility and aggression were first explored by Pastore (1952). In his investigation, subjects were furnished with descriptions of annoying situations. The infliction of each annoyance was depicted either as intentional and deliberate ("arbitrary") or as occurring under mitigating conditions ("nonarbitrary," nondeliberate). For example, an intimate friend was said to have spread demeaning rumors either while apparently sober (arbitrary annoyance) or while drunk (nonarbitrary annoyance). Subjects were instructed to try to imagine what their response would be. The results showed that those subjects who envisioned themselves as having been deliberately annoyed reported a readiness to behave more aggressively than those who envisioned themselves as having been annoyed by a person "with a good excuse." To the extent that such projections by nonannoyed persons reflect the response readiness of annoyed people, knowledge of mitigating circumstances seems to have had an inhibiting effect on aggression.

In a subsequent, very similar study by Cohen (1955), female subjects read descriptions of annoyances inflicted arbitrarily or nonarbitrarily and were instructed to report: (a) how another person, ideally, should respond; and (b) how other people actually would respond. Prescribed retaliatory hostile and aggressive behavior was found, overall, to be lower than that thought to actually occur under the circumstances. But within prescribed and predicted retaliation, the hostility- and aggression-reducing effect of mitigating information was again strongly evident.

Rothaus and Worchel (1960) combined the role-playing and projective techniques used in the earlier studies. Male and female subjects were instructed to tell how they themselves and how another person would feel and what they themselves and what another person would do in a given situation. Consistent with earlier findings, the responses of both male and female subjects revealed that an annoying treatment produces less anger and aggressiveness when mitigating circumstances are known than when the treatment is inflicted in an arbitrary fashion.

An investigation by Kregarman and Worchel (1961) introduced a critical improvement of the research procedure: Subjects were no longer asked to suppose that an annoyance occurred; they actually underwent an annoying treatment. While taking an intelligence test, male subjects were frequently interrupted by a pushy examiner who made several disparaging and derogatory comments. Subjects were led either to expect or not to expect the examiner's harassment. Additionally, the examiner's behavior was initially presented either as reasonable and nonarbitrary or as unreasonable and arbitrary. When the behavior was to be expected and to appear reasonable, it was said to be part of a study on the effect of distraction; when it was to be expected and to appear unreasonable, its function was said to be to prevent mind wandering. When the examiner's behavior was supposed to be unexpected and reasonable, it was hinted that the administration of the test "may seem strange [p. 184]" but that it would be standard; when it was supposed to be unexpected and unreasonable, no comment was made about the examiner's forthcoming conduct. The intended factorial variation of the expectedness and the arbitrariness of the annoying treatment was thus only approximate.

After the administration of the intelligence test, subjects completed a further test. The test included an evaluation of the examiner, and this evaluation served as a measure of the subjects' hostile inclinations. On this measure, it was found that hostility was lower when the annoying treatment was expected than when it was not expected. But although hostility tended to be lower when the annoying treatment was presented as reasonable than when it was presented as unreasonable, this difference failed to be reliable.

The failure to obtain the predicted main effect for the reasonableness variation, which could be interpreted as a failure to corroborate earlier findings, proves inconclusive, however. As has been pointed out, the variation was not really factorial. For example, whereas the appearance of reasonableness in one conditon was accomplished by furnishing a very convincing justification for the examiner's rude behavior (i.e., it serves the purpose of research), the examiner's behavior was not similarly justified in the corresponding condition (i.e., it is declared peculiar but standard). The success of the latter manipulation in making an annoying treatment appear reasonable seems questionable. If it is assumed that this manipulation attempt failed and that subjects considered the examiner's "strange" behavior to be unreasonable, the finding of comparatively high hostility in this condition—and along with it, the dependent failure to observe a reduction in hostility as the consequence of the nonarbitrariness of an annoying treatment—would be accounted for.

These problems with manipulation do not exist in an innovative investigation by Burnstein and Worchel (1962). Male subjects were: (a) arbitrarily annoyed, (b) nonarbitrarily annoyed, or (c) not annoyed. They then were provided with an opportunity to behave in a hostile manner. The annoyance treatment was applied in group discussions in which a unanimous decision had to be reached in a limited period of time. During this discussion, an experimental confederate, ostensibly another subject, behaved in one of three ways. (a) In the arbitrary-annoyance condition, he thwarted the decision through frequent requests for clarification that were apparently necessary because he was not paying attention. (b) In the nonarbitrary-annoyance condition, it was obvious that he suffered from a hearing impediment; he thwarted the decision through frequent requests for clarification necessitated by a defective hearing aid. (c) In the no-annoyance condition, he participated unobtrusively as an average group member and did not interfere with the deliberations. After the discussion, subjects were told that they were to participate in another similar test session at a later date and that they could determine who of the present group should or should not be a member of the future group. Subjects could thus reject members of the group. The frequency of rejection of the confederate, which was assessed both under public (i.e., expressed openly in the group) and private conditions, served as the measure of hostility.

The findings support the view that essentially the same annoying treatment can produce very different hostile and aggressive reactions. In particular, when the treatment is perceived as nondeliberate or nonarbitrary, it is likely to prompt only minimally intense hostile or aggressive responses. Annoyance, when occasioned by the annoyer's handicap, went virtually unpunished. In contrast to the person who had arbitrarily annoyed the group and who suffered some public rejection for it, the handicapped person was not publicly rejected at all. This outcome could be regarded as somewhat misleading, however, since it is possible that subjects publicly complied with the social precept to be kind to disadvantaged people. This potential bias should be less involved in the anonymous, private responses. Private rejection, as should be expected, overall was higher than public rejection. But these responses showed again that whereas the arbitrary annoyer was completely rejected, the handicapped person was hardly ever rejected. Public hostility directed against the handicapped annoyer was thus entirely absent, and private hostility against him was nearly as low as that against the person who had not inflicted an annoyance.

The foregoing findings were fully corroborated by the results of a recent investigation by Rule, Dyck, and Nesdale (1978). In this study, male subjects were deliberately or nondeliberately annoyed by a confederate and then were given an opportunity to treat him, publicly or privately, in a hostile manner. The confederate was to teach a concept to the subject, and a monetary incentive was set for successful completion of the task. The deliberate infliction of annoyance was accomplished by the confederate's apparent lack of concern and unwillingness to cooperate. The nondeliberate annoyance was created by his uncertainty about the instructions he was to follow. The subject later evaluated the confederate in the context of recommending him for a research-related job. The recommendation was either anonymous or not. In the nonanonymous condition, the subject had to give his name and identification number and provide reasons for his recommendation to a professor.

Using rejection (that is, the subject's recommendation that the confederate not be employed) as the measure of hostility, the findings again show that hostility is lower under public conditions than under private conditions. More importantly, they show that a deliberately inflicted annoyance produces far stronger hostile reactions than one inflicted unintentionally. Rule et al. (1978) further observed that the deliberate annoyer was perceived far less favorably than the nondeliberate annoyer, a difference in appeal that had not been found by Burnstein and Worchel. Specifically, the person who annoyed "on purpose" was judged to be less pleasant, less likable, less motivated, and less competent than the person who annoyed without apparent malice.

The hostility- and aggression-reducing effect of the knowledge that an aversion has not been inflicted deliberately has also been demonstrated in children. In an investigation by Mallick and McCandless (1966), male and female third graders were annoyed or not annoyed by a same-sex sixth grader, an experimental confederate. Through clumsiness, the confederate prevented the subjects from completing simple block-construction tasks. The failure to complete the tasks caused them to lose money. Additionally, the confederate made some sarcastic remarks in which the subjects were made to appear greedy. Following this treatment, subjects were placed in one of three conditions: (a) The experimenter chatted with the subjects and told them that the confederate was sleepy and upset; (b) the experimenter chatted with the subjects about matters not related to the confederate's behavior; (c) the subjects shot with guns at a target depicting a same-sex peer. Finally, the subjects were provided with an opportunity to hinder the confederate, who was now working on the block-construction tasks. Subjects could press buttons to thwart the confederate's efforts, and these attempts to foil his or her progress served as the measure of hostility.

The results show a strong mitigating effect of information about the annoyer's physical and emotional state, presumably because it brought about a reinterpretation of his or her motives. Hostility in the condition of mitigating information was comparable to that in the no-annoyance conditions. In contrast, substantially higher levels of hostility were observed in the conditions in which the annoyed subjects were engaged in conversation or in "aggressive" play. The latter condition was associated with particularly intense hostility, a finding that constitutes further evidence against catharsis theory. Regarding the strong effect of the mitigating information, it should be noted that the high level of hostility that was observed in the condition in which the annoyed subjects were engaged in mere conversation rules out the possibility that the reduction of hostility was due to the distracting (cf. Bryant & Zillmann, 1977) effects of the mitigating information. Mallick and McCandless also observed a pronounced negative relationship between hostile behavior and liking, a finding that is consistent with the person-perception data reported by Rule, Dyck, and Nesdale (1978).

These investigations, taken together, provide strong evidence in support of the proposal that at least at intermediate levels of excitation, the individual is quite sensitive to the particular circumstances under which an annoyance is inflicted and that his or her consideration of the circumstances can greatly modify hostile and aggressive reactions. More specifically, the discussed evidence is consistent with the view that the annoyed individual's retaliatory action is guided by his or her assessment of coercive contingencies and by anticipation of approval or reproach for possible courses of action. If the individual perceives an annoying treatment as deliberate, intended, or arbitrary, it apparently *constitutes a threat* that, through punitive action, is to be averted, stopped, or prevented in the future. If, however, the individual perceives it as nondeliberate, unintended, nonarbitrary, or accidental, it cannot be construed as a threat posed by the annoyer, and punitive actions are thus not called for. The perception of threat in an annoying treatment, then, should effect a corresponding degree of *instigation* to retaliate. Regarding the anticipation of approval and reproach, the annoyed individual who perceives the annoyance as deliberate has reason to consider his or her retaliatory action as socially approved as long as it does not become excessive. If, on the other hand, the annoyance is perceived as nondeliberate or accidental, he or she can only expect reproach for any punitive action against the annoyer. In anticipation of such reproach, the individual should *inhibit* the retaliatory actions he or she may be motivated to carry out.

It is apparent from this reasoning that the documented reduction of hostility and aggression brought about by knowledge of mitigating circumstances can be the result either of *reduced instigation* or of *inhibition*, or of both these factors to some degree. Notwithstanding claims to the contrary (e.g., Burnstein & Worchel, 1962), the research we have discussed does not decisively implicate either factor as the mechanism underlying the observed effect. In Chapter 6 we return to this controversial issue and present recent research findings that seem to resolve the controversy. Suffice it here to say that there is ample evidence suggesting that at intermediate levels of excitation, annoyance-motivated hostility and aggression are under cognitive control as we have specified it.

In our assessment of the evidence discussed thus far, we have *assumed* that excitation was at intermediate levels. As will be recalled, in the early investigations of the hostility- and aggression-reducing effect of mitigating circumstances (Cohen, 1955; Pastore, 1952; Rothaus & Worchel, 1960), the subjects who projected hostile and aggressive reactions did so in an unprovoked state. In the later studies, subjects were annoyed mainly as members of a group, and the annoyance did not pose a severe personal threat (Burnstein & Worchel, 1962; Kregarman & Worchel, 1961). Even in the study by Mallick and McCandless (1966), in which the annoyance was direct and personal, the annoyance appears to have been quite moderate. In all, it is very unlikely that the subjects in these investigations were severely annoyed and experienced extremely high levels of excitation. The findings thus cannot readily be generalized to intense annoyances capable of producing impulsive hostile and aggressive reactions.

To investigate the predicted deterioration of cognitive response guidance at extremely high levels of excitation, Zillmann, Bryant, Cantor, and Day (1975) conducted an experiment in which male subjects were severely provoked, placed in either an intermediate or extremely high state of excitation, either provided with mitigating information or not, and then given an opportunity to retaliate. The subjects were annoyed by an extremely rude experimenter who was apparently irritated with his job. He administered an auditory acuity test in which the subject was to perform a motor response to cues that were supposed to be easily detectable. Specifically, the subject listened via headphones to music in which extraneous noises were interspersed. Some of these cues were rather obtrusive, others were faint. There were 12 cues, and on the average, about half of them were detected by the subject. After a look at the event recorder that displayed the subject's responses, the experimenter stated with contempt that there were 29 cues on the tape. His comment was usually followed by embarrassed laughter on the part of the subject, a reaction that prompted a harsh remark by the experimenter to the effect that there was nothing funny about the subject's performance and that the research laboratory was no place to "goof off." Any protest from the subject was ignored. The experimenter accused the subject of a total lack of cooperation and said that they might as well forget about the acuity test and go on to the next part of the experiment. This next part consisted of either a rather dull disc-threading task, known to have no appreciable arousing properties, or a strenuous physical-exercise task (i.e., riding a bicycle ergometer), known to produce a substantial elevation of sympathetic activity (cf. Zillmann & Bryant, 1974). The subject then witnessed the experimenter lose his temper in an interaction with another person who had come to administer a questionnaire. This outburst provided the opportunity to unobtrusively inform the subject of mitigating circumstances. In the appropriate conditions, the person administering the questionnaire said, as if to explain the experimenter's rude behavior toward her, "He's really uptight about his prelims." In the no-mitigation conditions, she made no remark about the rude experimenter's behavior. She then asked the subject to fill in a form purportedly from the university's Human-Subjects Committee. The administration of the questionnaire was said to serve the protection of subjects and to be standard procedure on campus. With the anonymity of his reactions assured, the subject evaluated the experimenter's performance, filed any complaints against him, and recommended in favor of or against his reappointment as a research assistant. The latter response, through which the subject was led to believe he could adversely affect his annoyer's future, was considered the most direct measure of retaliation.

The findings, which are displayed in Fig. 2, fully support the proposal that the reduction of annoyance-motivated hostility through knowledge of mitigating circumstances applies to intermediate levels of excitation only. At

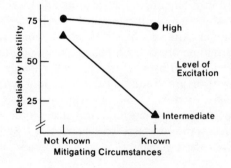

FIG. 2. Impairment of cognitive response guidance in hostile behavior at high levels of excitation. Retaliatory hostility was measured in the subject's recommendation against his annoyer's reappointment as a research assistant. (Adapted from Zillmann, Bryant, Cantor, & Day, 1975.)

high levels of excitation, presumably because the necessary cognitive mediation is greatly impaired, the reduction does not occur. As can be seen from the figure, the mitigating information caused subjects who had been strongly provoked but not further aroused to retaliate substantially less than those who had been similarly treated but who had not learned about the mitigating circumstances. In these moderately aroused subjects, the hostility-reducing effect of mitigating information removed nearly all the hostility in the subjects' response. Up to this point, the findings give further evidence of the power of cognitive operations in the mediation of hostile (and aggressive) reactions to annoyance treatments. It is, of course, this cognitive mediation that is expected to be greatly impaired or entirely lost at high levels of excitation. The findings certainly support this expectation. To the severely annoyed and highly aroused subjects, it was apparently of little moment whether their acute annoyance was deliberate or inflicted by someone with an excuse. The annoyer had made them suffer intensely, and they punished him for this, regardless of his specific intentions.

This apparent lack of sensitivity to the motivational underpinnings of the infliction of the annoyance was manifest not only in the findings on retaliation but also surfaced in ways that had not been anticipated. With considerable regularity, the severely annoyed and highly aroused subject "rejected" the mitigating information with a reaction such as "That's too bad!" and he took the first opportunity provided (i.e., the absence of the experimenter and the presence of the person soliciting the evaluations) to express his annoyance verbally. In the presence of the interviewer (a woman in her late twenties), subjects erupted with some of the most "colorful" and vulgar expressions the English language has to offer. These outbursts seem to attest to the fact that the subjects in the high-excitation conditions were more intensely annoyed than in earlier investigations and that in this state of extreme annoyance, they no longer cared about etiquette and propriety. Apparently, they had reached a point at which they "couldn't have cared less" and "didn't give a damn" about the possibility that their retaliatory actions against the "poor, somewhat agitated" annoyer might be considered as overly severe—or, for that matter, about the likelihood that their profanities would make a bad impression on an attractive member of the opposite sex.

The discussed experiment seems to be the only one available at this time that investigates retaliatory behavior at very high levels of excitation. The reason for this scarcity of evidence resides not only in the fact that the consistently observed hostility- and aggression-reducing effect of mitigating information was not expected to deteriorate at high levels of excitation but, more likely, in the difficulties associated with provoking experimental subjects so severely that they display emotional reactions that they cannot control very well. Obviously, ethical considerations impose restrictions upon the investigator. But there are practical limitations, too. Experimental subjects, who seem to be growing more and more sophisticated regarding deceptions, may readily recognize the purpose of a necessarily obtrusive, severe provocation, or they may know that such a treatment must be fake, since such things do not happen by accident in the laboratory. Indeed, ethical and practical considerations may combine to make an investigation unfeasible. Such a situation developed when we attempted to conduct the investigation just described with female subjects. The severe annoyance produced by a same-sex experimenter prompted most female subjects to burst into tears, and the experiment was halted as soon as this became clear. But had the experiment not been halted for ethical reasons, it might have had to be discontinued for practical ones: Midway through the experiment, the intensely annoyed female subjects tended to rush out of the laboratory, making it impossible to assess the extent to which they would retaliate if provided with the opportunity. Given such experiences with female subjects, in retrospect it appears that the males who had been subjected to the same annoying treatment must also have suffered intensely—for some time at least. But since they had not expressed their suffering by crying or escaping as the females had done, there was no cue to suggest discontinuation of the experiment. Our experience supports the view that females are less inhibited than males in expressing intense annoyances, and it would seem to be wise to use their greater expressiveness to counsel against the future use of excessively severe annoying treatments for both females and males. The experience also would seem to suggest that the investigator who studies hostile and aggressive behavior at very high levels of excitation not use laboratory techniques that force him or her to induce these extreme states. Instead, he or she should employ techniques based on the observation of naturally occurring hostile and aggressive outbursts.

If experimental evidence regarding annoyance-motivated hostile and aggressive behavior at extremely high levels of excitation is scarce, it is virtually nonexistent for such behavior at extremely low levels of excitation. States of acute fatigue and exhaustion are difficult to create in the laboratory, and presumably for this reason, their implications for hostility and aggression have not been explored. There is an approach to hostility and aggression, however, that seems to bear on low-excitation behavior. The investigation of the effects of certain intoxicants can be considered to produce conditions that create, to a high degree, the impairment or inefficiency of cognitive processes that is characteristically associated with extremely low levels of excitation. Behavior under conditions of alcoholic intoxication, in particular, may be viewed as an approximation of behavior at low levels of excitation. But this approximation is to be treated with considerable caution. Although the ingestion of alcohol indeed reduces sympathetic activity, it would seem unreasonable to assume that small or moderate doses reduce it to extremely low levels. Alcoholic intoxication appears to effect an impairment of cognitive processes more directly, possibly more rapidly, and certainly to a greater degree than it causes an incapacitating decline of sympathetic excitation. Such intoxication might thus be construed as a special case in which arousal declines to rather low levels and cognitive capabilities drop to a point generally associated with even lower levels of excitation. Qualified in this manner, the effect of alcoholic intoxication on the response to annoyance may be treated as a potentially informative analogue to hostility and aggression at low levels of excitation.

Although alcoholic intoxication has not always been found to affect hostile and aggressive behavior (e.g., Bennett, Buss, & Carpenter, 1969), a series of experiments conducted by Taylor and his associates leaves little doubt that moderate to high degrees of intoxication can substantially promote aggressive behavior. In a first study (Shuntich & Taylor, 1972), male subjects ingested either bourbon or a placebo. In an additional control condition, they ingested nothing and simply waited. The subjects then performed the competitive reaction-time task. In response to a stepped-up attack by the opponent, the intoxicated subjects exhibited far more aggressiveness than those in the placebo or waiting conditions. This finding was corroborated and extended in a follow-up experiment that involved vodka in addition to bourbon and also varied the degree of intoxication (Taylor & Gammon, 1975). The effects of the latter variation suggest that the enhancement of aggression brought about by alcoholic intoxication may be restricted to moderate and high doses and that the ingestion of smaller doses may actually produce a reduction of aggressiveness. Further data in support of the effect of dosage (i.e., aggression reduction for small doses vs. aggression enhancement for greater amounts) have recently been reported (Taylor, Vardaris, Rawtich, Gammon, Cranston, & Lubetkin, 1976).

An experiment that convincingly demonstrates that the facilitation of aggression by alcoholic intoxication is not indiscriminate but specific to annoyance has been reported by Taylor, Gammon, and Capasso (1976). Male subjects ingested either a substantial dosage of vodka or a placebo. They then performed the competitive reaction-time task, either under standard conditions or under conditions free from threat of assault by the opponent. This latter condition was accomplished through an inquiry the confederate addressed to the experimenter in the subject's presence. Specifically, the confederate said he had "strong convictions about hurting people [p. 940]" and that he would feel better about the whole matter if he could keep the intensity of the electric shock that his opponent, the subject, was to receive at the lowest possible level. In response to the question of whether this would bother the experiment, the experimenter answered that it would not. The subject was thus assured that his opponent would not suddenly launch a vicious attack on him. Under these circumstances, the opponent did not pose a threat and did not create an annoyance. The results reveal that alcoholic intoxication has no effect at all on the aggressive behavior of persons who are not threatened or annoyed. Undisturbed intoxicated subjects were as peaceful as their unintoxicated counterparts. Under conditions of threat and annoyance, in contrast, the same degree of alcoholic intoxication proved to have a strong aggression-facilitating effect.

In these investigations on the effects of alcoholic intoxication, subjects were first intoxicated and then subjected to an annoying treatment whose impact they could minimize through aggressive actions. Given that the annoyance was not overly severe (mild electric shock was received if the opponent responded faster to a signal) and that the ingestion of alcohol reduced sympathetic activity, the level of excitation that prevailed while aggressive responses were performed indeed seems to have been rather low. Although it is undoubtedly of import to understand the mechanics of aggressive behavior under these circumstances, it appears that the sequence of events that is mostly responsible for violent outbursts under the influence of alcohol has not yet been explored. Characteristically, severe annoyances occasion the ingestion of larger doses of alcohol, and the substantially intoxicated individual becomes violent when he or she reconfronts the annoyer. It appears that whereas persons are inhibited from acting aggressively against their annoyers when sober, after intoxication their inhibitions fail, presumably because they have become poor judges of the consequences of their actions, and they erupt in violence. Alcoholic intoxication is viewed here as an inhibition remover, not as a motivator. This view seems to be generally held now (cf. Tucker, 1970), especially by those who studied high-intensity annoyance-motivated aggression in the family context (e.g., Gelles, 1974; Straus, 1974). The consideration of excitation is entirely consistent with this interpretation. The ingestion of alcohol does not excite and incite action but can only lower arousal and dampen the emergency nature of the annoyance.

This analysis suggests that persons who are first substantially annoyed and then intoxicated, even though they do not experience an extremely high level of arousal, will display the impulsive hostile and aggressive reactions characteristic of extremely high levels of excitation. Initially annoyed, intoxicated persons, then, may well experience intermediate levels of excitation but nonetheless be prone to react violently. Drinking "to drown" one's acute annoyances may thus constitute a dangerous precondition for hostile and aggressive behavior—unless, of course, it is pursued to a point of total motor incapacitation or done under conditions where the likelihood of encountering the annoyer is nil.

To sum up, it can be said that evidence that demonstrates the cognitive mediation of hostile and aggressive behavior at intermediate levels of excitation is abundant. The evidence further shows that this mediation fails at extremely high levels of excitation, and it suggests that hostile and aggressive reactions at these levels become impulsive. The mechanics of hostility and aggression at very low levels of excitation remain to be explored empirically.

Alcohol appears to be an intoxicant that selectively impairs cognitive skills: Anticipatory skills that mediate the inhibition of hostile and aggressive actions seem impaired to a greater extent than the more basic "cognitive" operations required for coordinated motor activity. As a result, hostile and aggressive actions are disinhibited by alcoholic intoxication at all levels of excitation. It would appear that generally speaking, all toxic substances that impair anticipatory and judgmental skills to a greater extent than motor skills, and that do not induce euphoric states that potentially neutralize the experience of annoyance (cf. Taylor, Vardaris, Rawtich, Gammon, Cranston, & Lubetkin, 1976), will increase the likelihood and extent of hostile and aggressive behavior because of their detrimental effect on cognitive response guidance.

As has been said earlier in connection with incentive-motivated hostility and aggression, decisive evidence that would directly demonstrate the operation or dysfunction of the proposed cognitive mediation in hostile and aggressive behavior at different levels of excitation is unavailable. The operation of mediating processes is indirectly demonstrated through the observable effects that these presumed processes produce. Such processes, then, should be treated as hypothetical constructs and not as empirical facts.

E. Observational Learning

In Section IIA of this chapter, we discussed the likely involvement of observational learning in the anticipation of gratification and aversion, success and failure, and cost. Our assessment of this involvement in incentive-motivated hostility and aggression fully applies to hostile and aggressive behavior that is motivated by annoyance. In particular, the dominance of anticipations regarding contingencies that have been experienced over those that have been only witnessed applies equally to both domains of hostile and aggressive behavior.

Generally speaking, it appears that unless observational learning mediated the acquisition of hostile and aggressive habits at intermediate levels of excitation, it is unlikely to exert a strong influence on impulsive reactions at extreme levels of excitation. In the following chapter, we analyze more closely the acquisition of impulsive hostile and aggressive response tendencies.

6

Hostility and Aggression as Emotions

Contrary to the impression created by violence-ridden fiction (cf. Donner, 1976) and television drama in particular (cf. Gerbner & Gross, 1976), aggressive behavior is not primarily motivated by the pursuit of incentives. Although a look at the *Uniform Crime Reports for the United States* (e.g., 1975) of any recent year leaves no doubt about the abundance of incentive-motivated transgressions in society, it also reveals clearly that these incentive-motivated criminal actions are largely nonviolent. Crimes against property (i.e., larceny, theft, burglary, robbery), which are incentive motivated by definition, can be seen as hostile activities that only in the exception entail aggressive behavior. The analysis of violent crimes, especially criminal homicide, makes it abundantly clear that aggressive actions that inflict severe consequences upon the victim are primarily motivated by annoyance (cf. Mulvihill, Tumin, & Curtis, 1969).

The U.S. Uniform Crime Reports, along with the statistics on violent crime in other nations (e.g., *Criminal Statistics: England and Wales,* 1976; *European Committee on Crime Problems,* 1974; *Statistics Canada,* 1973), show murder to be predominantly an annoyance-motivated crime. Roughly speaking, only one-fifth of all murders are linked to incentive-motivated crimes. If those murders suspected to be at least in part motivated by incentives are included, the ratio rises only to one-fourth. This means that at least three-fourths of all murders committed are primarily motivated by annoyance. With great consistency across time (i.e., years) and regions (i.e., sections of the United States), these annoyance-motivated homicides are the result of acute conflict, especially between persons who know each other well (cf. Goode, 1969). Arguments within the family (mainly between spouses but also between parents and children) and lovers' quarrels make up an impressive portion of murders: roughly one-third. Additionally, murder deriving from conflict between people who had been acquainted with each other for some time is more characteristic than murder resulting from conflict between strangers. The figures that show that intense arguing can readily escalate into murder are staggering: More than one-third of criminal homicide is apparently thus motivated by sheer annoyance.

Wolfgang's (1958) well-known, meticulous analysis of motives in criminal homicide corroborates the pattern projected by the official crime statistics. The killing of close friends was found to be most frequent. Similarly frequent were killings within the family. The killing of an acquaintance is markedly less characteristic and even less so, that of a stranger. The killing of a personal enemy is obtrusively atypical. In this context, Wolfgang's data regarding the circumstances that apparently led to homicide are particularly revealing. By far the most frequent antecedent of a killing (more than one-third of all instances) was the annoying "altercation of relatively trivial origin; insult, curse, jostling, etc. [p. 376]." Domestic quarrels, jealousy, and bickering over money were rather characteristic. Interestingly, revenge proved to be a relatively infrequent antecedent condition of homicide (about 5% of all instances). Homicide connected with incentive-motivated hostile activities was again found to amount to less than one-fourth of all killings. The analysis of the locations in which killings occur makes it further clear that the place of criminal homicide is not the proverbial dark alley but the home and its modern extension, the car. Killings were reported to occur most frequently in and around cars, in the bedroom, in the living room, and in the kitchen.

The fact that homicide is predominantly annoyance motivated is also attested to by Wolfgang's analysis of sentencing. The greatest number of homicides (more than one-third of all instances) were ruled to constitute voluntary manslaughter, a crime defined as "the unlawful killing of another *in a sudden heat of anger,* without premeditation, malice or depravity of heart [Wolfgang, 1958, pp. 23–24; italics added]." Similarly frequent (nearly one-third of all instances) was the ruling of murder in the second degree, which entails the felonious and malicious killing of a human being without the specific intent to take life. The willful, deliberate, and premeditated killing of a human being, murder in the first degree, is far less characteristic than usually presumed. Only about one-fifth of all homicides were ruled first-degree murder. Annoyance- and incentive-motivated murders are confounded in this figure, and it can only be speculated that a good portion of the total constitutes behavior motivated by annoyance.

The dominance of annoyance-motivated aggression is apparent not only in the data on homicide. Analyses of the criminal infliction of bodily injury show the same pattern. If anything, they show an even greater dominance of annoyance motivation. To illustrate: Detailed recent data from Austria (cf.

European Committee on Crime Problems, 1974) document that as was the case for killing, willful wounding occurs mostly in the course of a quarrel. For example, quarrel-precipitated injury proved to be about 150 times as frequent as injury inflicted in the course of armed robbery and about 200 times that associated with rape.

The phenomenon of so-called normal violence (cf. Sarles, 1976), that is, injury-inflicting action that occurs within the family or between "intimates" and that is not reported or recognized as criminal behavior, gives further evidence to the pronounced dominance of annoyance motivation in aggression. Child abuse and wife beating, two domains of aggressive behavior of great public concern, are quite widespread. Although there are characteristic differences in the frequency of occurrence, both child abuse and wife beating permeate all conceivable social strata (e.g., Fontana, 1971; Gelles, 1974; Gil, 1973; Steinmetz & Straus, 1974; Straus, 1974; Zalba, 1966). The classification of the antecedent conditions of such "normal" aggressive behavior makes it very clear that nearly all the battering that occurs is precipitated by acute annoyance. Gil (1973) lists, as the major type of abusive behavior, assaults that grow out of disciplinary action by caretakers who *"respond in uncontrolled anger* [p. 126; italics added]" to the presumably annoying misconduct of a child. About three-fourths of all incidents of child abuse were attributed to the "inadequately controlled anger" of the abusive person. The second type of abuse is also related to anger: It is the assault upon a child because of a negative affective disposition toward him or her, that is, because of general resentment and rejection (cf. Miller & Swanson, 1960). Given such a negative general disposition, abusive behavior appears to be triggered by rather trivial forms of annoying conduct that are readily interpreted as *mis*conduct. The same circumstances, generally speaking, prevail in wife beating (cf. Gelles, 1974).

An inspection of the data regarding the criminal and quasi-criminal infliction of pain and injury, then, leaves no doubt about the fact that aggressive and violent behaviors are performed primarily to terminate annoyances and not to attain incentives. This generalization is of import, because at least within psychology, it has occasionally been suggested that aggressive behavior is almost entirely governed by incentive attainment. In particular, Buss (1971) has proposed that aggression is controlled by three principal reinforcers: money, prestige, and status. He has further suggested that through the deliberate management of these reinforcers, aggression can readily be curtailed. Moreover, Buss (1961) has argued that the concept of anger is not particularly useful in the analysis of aggression. Such a view, no matter how liberally the concept "incentive" is interpreted, seems to misconstrue greatly the phenomena of aggression and violence in society. The descriptive analysis of the circumstances under which acts of aggression and violence occur urges a very different assessment: Unquestionably, injurious behavior is motivated mainly by acute annoyance and performed in order to discontinue this experience. It is usually not planned or premeditated, and presumably, it occurs most often when the individual experiences rather high levels of activity in the sympathetic nervous system. Under these circumstances, the individual rarely pursues incentives. Whether the offense is manslaughter, child abuse, or wife beating, the aggressor hardly ever gains money, prestige, or status. On the contrary, an uncontrolled aggressive outburst in the family or between close friends usually inflicts a loss of prestige and status on the aggressor, and it leaves relationships in disarray and affiliations in jeopardy (cf. Scratton, 1976). Even in the extreme case of violent juvenile gangs, aggressive action appears to be prestigious and status enhancing only if it is displayed in response to adequate provocation, that is, when it is precipitated by annoyance (cf. Klein, 1969). In short, it appears that generally speaking, aggression does not pay. Granted that killing and wounding can greatly facilitate the criminal attainment of incentives, the far more common annoyance-motivated infliction of injury has no apparent payoff—other than the likelihood of terminating a particular acute annoyance. Assaultive behavior performed on the spur of an excited moment not only strains and disrupts personal bonds but is likely to incite retaliation and punishment at some later time. The fact that in spite of all these negative consequences, destructive outbursts are as ubiquitous as they are would seem to suggest that the concepts of anger and emotional disturbance, or the concept of emotion generally, must be involved in efforts to provide an adequate explanation of such behavior. The vast majority of incidents in which an individual inflicts injury or death upon another human being simply cannot be construed as actions instrumental in the attainment of incentives. These incidents, it appears, can be more readily comprehended and explained when they are treated as "normal" defensive, affective reactions of considerable intensity, and as emotional outbursts in the extreme. In fact, these incidents seem to *demand* an analysis in emotional terms.

We now turn to an analysis of annoyance-motivated hostile and aggressive reactions as emotional behavior. A three-factor theory of hostility and aggression is presented and discussed in terms of pertinent evidence. We then investigate the specific involvement of sympathetic excitation in hostile and aggressive behavior. Hostile and aggressive "overreactions" are of particular interest. Finally, we explore the formation and maintenance of hostile and aggressive habits.

I. THREE-FACTOR THEORY OF HOSTILITY AND AGGRESSION

The theory presented below is an application of the more inclusive three-factor theory of emotion (Zillmann, 1978) to hostility and aggression. Essentially, the three-factor approach integrates the two-factor theory of emotion (Schachter, 1964) with behavior theory (e.g., Brown, 1961; Hull,

1943, 1952; Spence, 1956). In this integration, the strengths of both approaches are combined, and their inadequacies are avoided. For a full discussion of the advantages of the three-factor approach over the earlier models on which it is based, the reader should consult the original presentation of the theory. Here, after applying the theory as indicated, we develop the specific advantages of this approach in the discussion of the research evidence regarding hostile and aggressive behavior.

The three-factor theory of emotion, and hence of hostility and aggression when viewed as emotions, projects emotional experience and emotional behavior as the result of the interaction of three principal components of emotional state: the *dispositional,* the *excitatory,* and the *experiential* components.

1. The dispositional component is conceived of as a response-guiding mechanism. It is assumed that the motor aspects of behavior are unconditional or acquired through learning. Connections between the emotion-inducing stimulus and the overt emotional response are thus viewed as preexisting (as, for example, in the case of defensive and attack motions in response to peripheral pain; cf. Hutchinson, 1972) or—much more likely in human behavior—as established but without the involvement of "cognitive operations at higher levels" (i.e., inferential or attributional processes). As a consequence, the organism is seen to be capable of displaying emotional motor reactions directly and without appreciable latency upon the presentation of the emotion-inducing stimulus.

2. The excitatory component is conceived of as the response-energizing mechanism. It is assumed that excitatory reactions, like motor reactions, are either unconditional or acquired through learning. If the connection between the emotion-inducing stimulus and the covert emotional response is established through learning, it is again assumed that higher-level cognitive processes are not involved (cf. Kimmel, 1974; Miller, 1969a). In accordance with Cannon's (1929) proposal of the "emergency" nature of emotional behavior, the excitatory reaction associated with emotional states is conceived of as heightened activity, primarily of the sympathetic nervous system, that prepares the organism for the temporary engagement in vigorous motor activities, such as those needed for "fight or flight."

3. The experiential component of emotional behavior is conceptualized as the conscious experience of either the motor or the excitatory reaction, or of both these aspects of the response to a stimulus condition (cf. Ádám, 1967). Both exteroceptive and interoceptive stimuli are thus assumed to reach the awareness level. The individual's awareness of his or her emotional response (i.e., of its motor and/or excitatory manifestations), the so-called feeling state, is viewed as potentially initiating further cognitive operations at the awareness level. Under conditions that we specify shortly, these operations

may serve the appraisal of the emotional reaction, and this appraisal in turn may effect changes in the motor and/or excitatory manifestations of the initial emotional reaction. In principle, then, the experiential component of emotions is viewed as a modifier or as a corrective that, within limits, controls the more archaic, basic emotional responsiveness governed by unlearned and learned S-R connections.

The essential interations and interdependencies of these three components of emotional behavior are described in the following propositions:

1. A stimulus condition that evokes a specific motor response without evoking an excitatory reaction will produce nonvigorous behavior that the individual is unlikely to experience as emotional.

2. A stimulus condition that evokes a specific motor response and an excitatory reaction will produce vigorous, "emotional" behavior. As the individual becomes aware of the state of elevated excitation, that individual will appraise his or her reaction. If he or she deems the behavior appropriate, he or she will continue to respond emotionally. If the behavior is deemed inappropriate, the individual will change his or her mode of reacting both motorically and excitationally.

3. A stimulus condition that evokes an excitatory reaction without evoking a specific motor response will produce a state of acute response ambiguity marked by motor restlessness. As the individual becomes aware of his or her aimless, excited behavior, he or she is likely to perform an epistemic search directed at the comprehension of the induction of this state of elevated excitation. The adopted explanation will guide further activities both at the motor and the excitatory levels.

In these propositions, it is generally assumed: (a) that most complex motor reactions are under voluntary control; (b) that excitatory reactions are usually not thus controlled by the individual; (c) that the linguistically mature individual habitually appraises the appropriateness of his or her behavior; and (d) that unless motor reactions are voluntarily controlled as the result of an appraisal process, their vigor is a simple function of the level of sympathetic excitation prevailing at that time. It is further assumed that the intensity of feelings, that is, the intensity of the subjective experience of emotional actions and reactions, is approximately proportional to the perceived magnitude of increases in excitation.

The interaction between the dispositional and the excitatory components may be regarded as a "primitive heritage of man." The basic response tendencies that are delineated by this interaction, as Cannon (1929) so persuasively argued, must have had great survival value. In the evolution of species, man included, it was obviously essential to respond to endangering circumstances with a sudden burst of energy that made effective escape or attack possible. Only in recent history, under the conditions of life in modern society, have these reactions largely lost their adaptive value. However, along with the evolution of rational capabilities in man, the capacity to modify emotional behavior through the appraisal of its effectiveness and appropriateness has evolved. The experiential component, then, is viewed as more than the mere awareness of a behavioral state associated with elevated excitation. It is considered to serve as a *corrective* of emotional reactions that are appraised as inappropriate. It is further seen to *provide guidance* in situations in which a specific response disposition does not exist. These two functions of appraisal can be viewed as an evolutionary adjustment that assures that in man, the more archaic response mechanisms (i.e., the dispositional and the excitatory components, in interaction) do not become overly maladaptive.

In considering annoyance-motivated hostile and aggressive behavior specifically, we conceptually separate the motivating emotional experience of annoyance and the motivated emotional behavior, and we trace both elements of the emotional reaction independently. Additionally, since the intensity of the reaction is of particular importance, we involve the assumptions regarding response intensity in the propositions themselves. Before we come to the formulation of propositions, however, we have to make a principal assumption regarding the evocation of excitatory reactions generally associated with annoyance.

A. The Induction of Annoyance

There is little doubt that heightened sympathetic activity has "survival value" or, more modestly expressed, that it can greatly aid the individual's well-being when he or she is confronted with life-endangering or potentially injurious conditions. Excitatory reactions in response to the mere anticipation of such conditions would seem to be similarly meaningful. These reactions, since they potentially facilitate the individual's ability to terminate or avoid harmful stimulation, may be viewed as having instrumental value even in the case of actual or anticipated moderate physical pain or minor bodily discomforts. There are, however, innumerable instances of annoyance-linked excitatory reactions that appear to be utterly devoid of instrumental value. The student, for example, who receives a grade that is far worse than expected may become intensely aroused when she receives the news. But how can this "burst of energy" help her to cope with the situation? Or, what is the instrumental value of the arousal of a husband who learns twenty years after the fact that his wife had a love affair with someone who has since died? Finally, what good is there in the excitatory reaction of a professor who is told that a colleague at another institution makes twice as much money as he does?

Such excitatory reactions not only lack utility, but in many cases they may be counterproductive: They seem to aggravate a situation that cannot be changed with a burst of high-intensity action. Why, then, do people respond in an excited fashion to circumstances under which such a reaction is noninstrumental or maladaptive? Why has man not evolved to adapt to the circumstances in question? Why are excitatory reactions not reserved for situations in which elevated sympathetic activity is required to ward off danger, pain, and discomfort effectively?

It is suggested that the mechanics of comparatively short-lived elevations in the level of sympathetic excitation indeed reach back to the fight-or-flight response as originally conceived by Cannon (1929). If such an energizing reaction had survival value, it did so because it aided the organism in attaining and retaining food, mate, and shelter (through fight) and in eluding discomfort and harm (through flight). Vigorous motor behavior had adaptive value, and to the extent that an arousal reaction increased the capacity for such behavior, the arousal reaction furthered the adaptive value of the motor behavior. Ideally, such an energizing mechanism should have been activated whenever the organism's well-being was threatened or the successful attainment and control of food, mate, and shelter was placed in jeopardy. Presumably, this is the way it once worked and still works. The basis for the excitatory reaction associated with annoyance is thus seen in the threat posed by members of the same or another species, or by environmental events, to the well-being of the individual or to the commodities and conditions vital to his or her well-being. Regarding threat, life in contemporary societies may have become an extremely complex affair, but the principal conditions for annoyance have not changed. The individual is still frequently exposed to risks to personal well-being and the well-being of those entities essential to his or her welfare. He or she daily confronts a multitude of incommodious and disadvantageous social conditions and is subjected to uncounted inconveniences and discomforts. But the adaptive value of punching, shoving, kicking, and lunging and, for that matter, of running away has vanished for the most part. Such archaic coping reactions may be frequent and even effective in peer interactions during childhood and adolescence. To the adult in modern society, however, they are largely barred and thus have no instrumental value. Unless the individual is willing to employ socially disapproved or criminal actions, he or she simply cannot avoid all annoyances through physical assaults upon his or her annoyers—or by running away.

This situation creates a dilemma. The individual (in any society in which punitive contingencies for violent actions have been constructed and are being enforced) reacts to the unavoidably numerous threats to his or her comfort and well-being with temporary increases in sympathetic activity. But, thus prepared for vigorous motor action, the individual generally cannot engage in the "fight-or-flight" behavior for which he or she is prepared—mainly because of the societal censure of such actions. The "primitive heritage of man" alluded to earlier is apparent in the fact that "people get excited" about countless matters that somehow seem to pose a threat to their well-being and that they get excited *whether or not physical actions constitute a useful means of coping with the threat.* In this context, a threat to the individual's well-being is conceived of in very general terms. Treatments that are likely to produce inconvenience and discomfort, for example, and events that place accomplishments and the success of goal-directed efforts in jeopardy are viewed as constituting such a threat as well as the direct endangerment of the individual's bodily welfare. The archaic nature of the excitatory reaction is particularly apparent in cases where physical actions are not only devoid of instrumental value but increase the likelihood of unfavorable outcomes in the individual's confrontation with threat.

Generally speaking, the archaic excitatory reaction to the endangerment of the individual's well-being constitutes the basis for much emotional behavior. It certainly constitutes the basis for the emotional experience of annoyance and, indirectly, for the motivational consequences thereof. We discuss the mechanism of this experience shortly. First, we summarize the discussion regarding the excitatory component of annoyance in more formal assumptions.

A. It is assumed that *the endangerment of the individual's well-being produces a temporary increase in sympathetic excitation.* Endangerment entails: (1) the immediate experience of pain, discomfort, or debasement; (2) the experience of impending distress of these kinds; (3) the vivid anticipation of such distress; (4) the immediate experience of the removal or the impediment of a gratifier; (5) the experience of the impending removal or impediment of a gratifier; and/or (6) the vivid anticipation of the removal or the impediment of a gratifier. To the extent that witnessing or anticipating a distressing treatment applied to another living being impedes the gratification that this being provides or is expected to provide, it may also be considered an endangerment of the individual's well-being. Similarly, to the extent that witnessing or anticipating a destructive treatment applied to an inanimate entity impedes the gratification that this entity provides or is expected to provide, it may be considered an endangerment. The individual, furthermore, may perceive his or her well-being endangered when, in comparing the gratifications enjoyed personally with those enjoyed by others, he or she judges the witnessed gratifications of others to be excessive and/or his or her own gratifications insufficient.

B. It is assumed that the magnitude of the excitatory reaction induced by the individual's endangerment is roughly proportional to the intensity of the aversion entailed or the amount of gratification jeopardized. The direct experience of an endangerment is expected to induce more intense excitatory reactions than probable or possible endangerment of the same kind. Other things being equal, the greater the perceived likelihood of an endangerment, the more intense should be the excitatory reaction it produces. The immediacy of an endangerment is likely to modify further the excitatory reaction. Immediately impending endangerments are expected to produce more intense reactions than the same endangerments anticipated to occur at a later time.

These assumptions are inclusive enough to encompass such diverse arousing conditions as being assaulted in the street, being exposed to the noisy play of the neighbors' children, being insulted by a stranger, recognizing that there's not enough gas to get to the next filling station, anticipating the bizarre reactions of an adversary at a forthcoming encounter, being deserted by a lover, fearing deceit by a friend, learning that one's daughter has been molested, fearing that the neighbor's cat might raid the robin's nest at the window, being robbed of money, worrying that one's teenage son might wreck the new car, and finding out that the boat one has just bought is being sold for a substantially lower price by another dealer. The assumptions regarding the magnitude of the excitatory reaction enable us to expect, for example, that the threat of a physical assault is more arousing than the threat of an insult or that, no matter who is responsible, wrecking the big new car is more arousing than wrecking the little old car. They further enable us to expect, for example, that apprehension-linked arousal will increase to a greater degree if the neighbor's cat frequently sneaks around the robin's nest than if it rarely does so and that arousal will increase more when abandonment by a lover is anticipated to happen at any moment than when it is expected to occur sometime next year.

In this section we have concentrated on the evocation of the excitatory reaction to the actual or anticipated endangerment of the individual. This reaction in itself, however, does not constitute annoyance, anger, or fear. We can treat the excitatory reaction to endangerment as a necessary but not sufficient condition for annoyance. Annoyance, as an affective or emotional experience, involves cognitive manifestations as well. We now incorporate these manifestations into our analysis.

B. The Experience of Annoyance

1. A condition of endangerment that fails to produce a discernible excitatory reaction, regardless of any motor reaction evoked, is unlikely to be experienced as an acute annoyance by the individual.

This first proposition simply expresses the dependence of annoyance as an emotional experience on an appreciable excitatory reaction: Such a reaction is *necessary*.

2. A condition of endangerment that evokes a specific motor response and a discernible excitatory reaction, and that is recognized as a threat, will produce the experience of annoyance. The intensity of this experience is determined by the magnitude of the excitatory reaction. If the motor reaction reflects the tendency to act on the condition apparently creating the annoyance so as to reduce or terminate this experiential state, the individual will appraise his or her feelings as anger. If the motor reaction reflects the tendency to avoid or withdraw from the condition apparently creating the annoyance, the individual will appraise his or her feelings as fear. If the individual deems his or her feelings and course of action appropriate, he or she will continue to respond angrily or fearfully. If they are deemed inappropriate, the individual will inhibit the motor reactions in question and experience a reduction of excitedness.

In this proposal it is assumed that the stimuli that constitute a condition of endangerment are *unambiguous* and evoke mainly learned motor responses. The motor response may be expressive only (e.g., reactions in the facial musculature) or may involve target-specific actions (e.g., warding-off motions with the arms and hands). The acquired response may also be one of alert motor readiness, however. Unlearned and learned motor reactions should occur without appreciable latency. Once they have occurred, they are subject to appraisal. The individual who recognizes—from the assessment of the threat to his or her well-being and from the initial reaction to that threat— that he or she is angry, and who deems his or her reaction appropriate or at least not inappropriate, should continue to be angry and be inclined to further act on the condition of endangerment so as to minimize or abolish the threat it poses. Analogously, the individual who recognizes from this assessment that he or she is afraid, and who deems his or her reaction appropriate, should continue to be afraid and to seek to elude the threat posed by the condition of endangerment. If the individual assesses his or her initial reaction as inappropriate, response corrections are likely to occur. It should be recalled here, however, that the appraisal function may be impaired at very high levels of excitation. Under extreme excitatory conditions, then, response correc- tions might not occur. When they occur at more moderate levels of excitation, they may derive from the assessment that either an apparent threat is not severe enough to warrant the course of action taken or that it is more severe and demands greater coping efforts. In the first case, behavioral reactions should be inhibited, and arousal should dissipate; in the latter case, behavioral reactions should be stepped up, and arousal should increase. These corrections are expected to occur whether the experience of annoyance is converted into anger or into fear.

3. A stimulus condition that evokes a marked excitatory reaction without eliciting specific motor reactions will produce a state of acute response ambiguity that, in turn, will motivate the individual to appraise his or her

experiential state. Specifically, it will motivate him or her to determine a cause for the excitatory reaction, and this process of determination is likely to result in the attribution of this reaction to a particular inducing stimulus condition. If the stimulus condition is construed as an endangerment, the individual will experience annoyance. The intensity of this experience of annoyance is again determined by the magnitude of the excitatory reaction.

Clearly, in the latter propositions, it is assumed that the individual is confronted with a highly *ambiguous* situation. Whereas in many domains of emotional behavior such circumstances may have great significance, it would appear that in the realm of hostile and aggressive behavior, the annoyance-inducing condition is generally obtrusive and immediately apparent to the respondent. Characteristically, an endangerment that induces arousal, even if it fails to evoke expressive or protective reactions, imposes itself on the individual. It cannot easily be overlooked. Stimulus conditions that produce acute annoyance, then, appear to be almost always unambiguous. There is the possibility, however, that the circumstances of an endangerment are complex and subtle to a point where the individual is forced to employ attributional and inferential techniques to determine whether the situation he or she deals with amounts to a threat or not. In fact, the ambiguity of a situation can considerably contribute to the respondent's state of excitation (cf. Leventhal, 1974). If, under such conditions of uncertainty, the individual resolves the ambiguity through the attribution of the excitatory reaction to an endangerment, he or she will experience annoyance. Mere arousal thus is viewed as an *insufficient* condition for the experience of annoyance.

The proposal that in ambiguous response situations, the threat status of a stimulus condition is arrived at through inferential processes implies that prior to the threat attribution, the stimuli were too ambiguous to permit the individual to display habitual modes of responding in annoyance. Once the attribution is made, the individual may resort to learned coping responses. It would appear, however, that after having conducted an appraisal of the circumstances of his or her annoyance, the individual is well prepared to choose an appropriate course of action to cope with the situation. The individual cannot be surprised by quasi-spontaneous, unlearned or learned hostile or aggressive reactions, and consequently, there is no need for the correction of his or her feelings or actions. This is not to say that in cases of initial ambiguity in the reaction to an endangerment there is no need for reappraisals, especially when the circumstances of an annoyance undergo change. It is, instead, to point out the principal difference in the chain of events between the confrontation with an unambiguous vs. an ambiguous induction of an arousal reaction. In the former case, the individual is likely to display learned reactions to an endangerment and then apply an appraisal as a potential corrective of the experience of annoyance and the behavior it motivates. In the latter case, the individual is forced to apply an appraisal initially, and this appraisal then determines his or her experience of annoyance and guides the behavior it motivates. One should expect, then, that endangerments that unambiguously produce acute annoyance are likely to result, at least initially, in hostile and aggressive reactions (or in fear and escape) that are mainly controlled by learning. Ambiguous conditions, in contrast, might be expected to produce reactions that are predominantly under cognitive control. The danger of uncontrolled, impulsive hostile or aggressive outbursts seems to reside mainly in the individual's sudden endangerment under entirely unambiguous circumstances.

Regarding the ambiguous induction of excitatory reactions, it is conceivable of course that the individual will erroneously attribute a particular reaction to an endangerment. In such a case, the individual might experience annoyance when he or she should not. Or if there is a basis for annoyance, the individual may attribute his or her reaction to the actions of the wrong person and then retaliate against this presumed annoyer. In short, the individual may not be a reliable judge of the causes of his or her excitatory reaction and may often *misattribute* excitation and *misrespond* emotionally as a consequence. We analyze this potential dilemma and its implications for hostility and aggression in our discussion of excitation-transfer phenomena (Section II of this chapter).

C. Behavioral Implications of Annoyance

It should be clear from the preceding discussion that adaptive reactions to the experience of annoyance (i.e., reactions that diminish or terminate this aversive experience) can take two principal forms: Either the annoying stimulus condition can be acted on so as to minimize or eliminate its aversive impact, or the individual can withdraw from stimulus exposure without altering the properties of the stimulus condition as such. The experience–behavior sequence of fear and avoidance thus parallels that of anger and attack. Although this parallelism should prove instructive in the analysis of coping reactions, we do not pursue it here but rather concentrate on the experience of anger and its implications for hostile and aggressive behavior.

Following our earlier discussion of the motivational properties of aversive states, it is posited that as the experience of annoyance converts to anger, the individual becomes motivated to minimize or terminate the aversive state he or she suffers by acting upon the agents and events that create the annoyance. Under conditions where low-cost, noncoercive maneuvers (e.g., appeals to the annoyer) hold little or no promise of success, the individual is likely to resort to hostile and aggressive actions to achieve his or her goal. The intensity of actions and the harm inflicted through them appear to depend on at least two principal factors: *impulsiveness* and *immediacy*. The way in which impulsive vs. appraisal-guided and immediate vs. delayed hostile and aggressive actions are likely to differ is expressed in the following propositions.

1. The vigor of an annoyance-motivated hostile or aggressive reaction that is evoked by an unconditional or conditioned stimulus condition is a simple function of level of excitation. To the extent that vigor furthers the individual's capacity to inflict harm and injury, the amount of harm and injury inflicted is approximately proportional to the magnitude of the excitatory reaction associated with the annoyance suffered.

This first proposition covers impulsive hostility and aggression. Such behavior, by definition, is not cognitively mediated. As a consequence, it can be "blindly" vigorous, or it can be instrumental but cause devastation far beyond that required for its instrumentality. A severely annoyed and angry person may, for example, "pound the walls" in rage and thus express his anger without affecting the conditions responsible for his experiential state. On the other hand, a guardian may be so enraged about a mishap caused by a child that he brutally beats and injures the child—a reaction that is certainly not justifiable as an act to terminate an acute annoyance. Or in a similar vein, a student who has been provoked by her roommate may display a bout of temper in which she destroys much of her annoyer's property. In such an outburst, a proportionality between the intensity of an annoyance and the amount of harm and injury inflicted depends largely on the involvement of tools and weapons. Obviously, the use of mechanical aids in hostile and aggressive behavior removes any correspondence between level of excitation and amount of harm inflicted. A capacity for vigorous action, for example, is essential for punching and kicking, even for clubbing and stabbing, but not for pulling the trigger of a gun. As tools and weapons become involved in impulsive hostile and aggressive actions, the suffering inflicted upon an annoyer (and possibly on bystanders as well) is likely to get out of hand and regarding the behavioral objective of diminishing or abolishing an acute annoyance, to be very much in excess of the amount necessary to terminate the annoyer's action.

2. The intensity of an annoyance-motivated hostile or aggressive reaction that is mediated by an appraisal is proportional to the magnitude of the excitatory reaction associated with the annoyance suffered only if the defensive or punitive action in question accords with moral considerations. If the individual anticipates social reproach for such action, the intensity of hostile and aggressive behavior will be below the level to be expected on the basis of proportionality with his or her excitatory reaction; if he or she anticipates social approval, the intensity of hostile and aggressive behavior may be above that level. This anticipation-mediated correction diminishes as excitation increases to extreme levels.

3. If defensive or punitive actions cannot be carried out at the time of acute annoyance and anger, an appraisal—especially the moral considerations that

it entails—may urge punitive action at a later time. The deferred punitive actions may then be applied when opportunities arise. The intensity of hostile and aggressive measures in deferred punitive actions tends to be proportional to the magnitude of the excitatory reaction associated with the annoyance suffered. However, because the deferred punitive action is characteristically taken when excitation is not at very high levels, the hostility- and aggression-reducing correction based on the anticipation of social reproach and approval should generally be applied.

In these latter propositions, appraisal-mediated hostile and aggressive actions are characterized as punitive when they are not instrumental in the alleviation of an acute annoyance. Deferred actions are usually devoid of such instrumental value. At best, they can be regarded as instrumental in functioning as a deterrent in future encounters with the annoyer. It appears likely, however, that hostile and aggressive actions that do not directly serve the individual's well-being (i.e., alleviation of aversion) are motivated by moral considerations. Punishment seems to be applied not so much as a defensive measure as "to get even" with an annoyer (cf. Chapter 5, Sections IB and ID).

The comparison between impulsive and appraisal-mediated hostility and aggression shows that the danger of "uncontrolled" destructive emotional reactions lies in the *sudden* endangerment of the individual's well-being. If impulsive destructive reactions can be avoided at this time of intense annoyance (e.g., by the absence of the annoyer or the unavailability of weapons), the appraisal of the circumstances that follows would seem to remove the possibility of impulsive reactions and thereby moderate the infliction of harm and injury. Paradoxically, however, as the potential for violent reactions is diffused by an appraisal process, this process may further the infliction of harm and injury in prescribing immediate or delayed punitive actions that are alien to the defensive nature of impulsive hostile and aggressive reactions.

D. Supportive Evidence

The proposed excitatory properties of the endangerment of the individual's well-being have been abundantly documented. In numerous investigations (e.g., Hokanson & Burgess, 1962a; Hokanson & Shetler, 1961; Vantress & Williams, 1972; Zillmann & Johnson, 1973; Zillmann & Sapolsky, 1977) in which the excitatory reaction to threatening conditions was operationalized in various indices of autonomic activity (mainly systolic blood pressure but also diastolic blood pressure, heart rate, and vasoconstriction), attacks, frustrations, and insults were found to produce strong effects on arousal. Counterevidence showing a decline in autonomic activity brought about by such situations is conspicuously absent. There is no reason, then, to doubt that annoying treatments generally elevate the level of sympathetic excitation.

It is further clear from the investigation of autonomic reactions to threatening conditions that the excitatory reaction is not maintained indefinitely but is in fact comparatively short-lived (e.g., Hokanson & Edelman, 1966; Kahn, 1966). The dissipation of annoyance-related arousal is by no means mechanical, however, and the factors that accelerate and impede the decay of excitation have been the subject of considerable exploratory efforts. Hokanson and his associates (cf. Hokanson, 1970) have pioneered the work on the decay of excitation after the commission of hostile or hostility-related activities. In their work, they have treated autonomic activity connected with annoyance as hostility-motivating "tension," and they have equated the dissipation of such activity as a (drive) reduction in the instigation to aggression. Together with the research efforts of others (cf. Quanty, 1976), their findings show that hostile and aggressive actions effect a prompt reduction in annoyance-associated sympathetic excitation only under specific circumstances. After an extensive review of pertinent research, Geen and Quanty (1977) enumerated the following conditions under which a speedy excitatory recovery from annoyance does *not* occur after retaliation: (a) when the annoyer is of higher social status than the annoyed person; (b) when hostile or aggressive reactions are manifestly inappropriate under the prevailing circumstances; and (c) when the annoyed person is predisposed to feel guilty about acting in a hostile manner. These investigators then concluded that the common element in these recovery-hampering conditions is the annoyed person's experience of *anxiety*. Although this generalization of the findings appears to be largely valid, the universal involvement of anxiety as the arousal-maintaining force may be called into question. We briefly analyze some of the crucial findings and explain them in terms of three-factor theory.

The social status of the annoyer emerged as a relevant variable in an investigation by Hokanson and Shetler (1961). Male and female subjects were annoyed or not annoyed by an experimenter, and they then aggressed or did not aggress against him through the administration of electric shock. The experimenter was either "a distinguished appearing male of 48 years [p. 446]" who posed as a visiting professor (high status) or an undergraduate psychology major (low status). It was found that the performance of retaliatory aggressive responses led to a prompt and speedy recovery from excitation only when the annoyer was of low status. Specifically, it was observed that after the delivery of shock, systolic blood pressure quickly dropped to a level comparable to that in the no-annoyance conditions. Subjects who had been annoyed by the low-status experimenter, and who had no opportunity to retaliate for the mistreatment they had suffered, failed to exhibit any appreciable recovery. In contrast, subjects who had been annoyed by the high-status experimenter recovered whether or not they retaliated against him. There was, in fact, a slight tendency for recovery to be more complete when the annoyer was not attacked.

These initial findings are actually at variance with the generalization that aggression against annoyers of superior rank is not followed by a prompt diminution of arousal. But more importantly, anxiety apparently cannot account for the unexpected prompt excitatory recovery of the annoyed subjects who could not retaliate against the high-status annoyer. One explanation of this observation is offered by Hokanson and Shetler themselves: Students may have learned that there is usually little occasion to retaliate against persons of very high status. They do not expect "to get a chance to get even," and they thus give up on the idea and display a "withdrawal response [p. 448]." According to this line of reasoning, recovery can be prompted by a learned *nonaggressive* reaction—a proposal that we explore in greater detail in Section III of this chapter. The observation in question can also be explained as the result of a reappraisal, however. When the undergraduate assistant harassed the subjects about their performance on a task, they may have perceived him as a bully who took advantage of the situation. When the dignified professor treated them in the same manner, they may have viewed the treatment as an effort on his part to make them work more efficiently. In short, they may have regarded the annoying treatment as more malicious when it was administered by the peer than when it came from a superior preoccupied with a research objective. The appraisal or reappraisal of the high-status annoyer's action as a nonthreat, comparatively speaking, should have prompted the observed recovery from the initial arousal reaction.

A follow-up study by Hokanson and Burgess (1962a) clarifies the situation greatly. Male and female subjects were: (a) annoyed by a personal attack, (b) annoyed by the blocking of a goal, or (c) not annoyed. They then were given or not given an opportunity to behave in a hostile manner toward their annoyer. The annoyer's social status was again varied but to a less extreme degree: The experimenter was either a new, young faculty member (high) or a psychology student (low). As in the earlier investigation, the annoying treatment was administered in the experimenter–student interaction. But in contrast to the procedure employed in the earlier study, the opportunity to retaliate came in the form of a questionnaire in which subjects could file complaints about the experimenter. Subjects who did not receive such an opportunity filled out a questionnaire on an unrelated, innocuous topic. Systolic blood pressure and heart rate served as measures of changes in sympathetic excitation.

Contrary to the generalization offered by Geen and Quanty (1977), the findings show that those subjects who did not have an opportunity to retaliate against the annoyer who had harassed them with apparent malice, whether he was of low or high status, maintained their level of excitation. Those subjects who retaliated against this annoyer, again whether he was of low or high status, exhibited pronounced recovery from annoyance-produced excitation. There is evidence, then, that if an annoyance is attributable to malice, retaliation prompts a reduction in arousal regardless of the social status of the annoyer. Interestingly, this pattern of effects does not apply to annoyances devoid of malice. Mere goal blocking by the low-status annoyer proved to be as arousing as the explicitly malicious treatment, presumably because it was attributed to malice anyway. Moreover, arousal was maintained when subjects could not retaliate, and it diminished when they retaliated. In contrast, those subjects who were frustrated by the high-status experimenter and who had no opportunity to retaliate showed pronounced recovery. In those who were frustrated by this experimenter and who retaliated, arousal remained at comparatively high levels. This finding regarding hostility after frustration accords with Geen and Quanty's generalization. But since the findings regarding hostility after malicious annoyance deviate from it, a modification of the generalization seems in order: It appears that in the excitatory reaction to annoyance and the recovery from excitation following retaliation, the social status of the annoyer is of little moment when the annoyance is unambiguously attributed to malice. However, if the circumstances of the annoyance are somewhat ambiguous, malice may be more readily attributed to a low-status than to a high-status annoyer. As a result, only if the annoyer is of relatively low status will annoyance-produced arousal be maintained in the absence of an opportunity to retaliate and will arousal promptly drop after retaliation.

It is likely that this modified generalization will require further modification. According to the interpretation of the findings in terms of three-factor theory, recovery from annoyance-produced excitation depends on an appraisal of the circumstances: If the annoying treatment is perceived as a personal threat, excitation tends to be maintained as long as this threat is acute, and it will dissipate when this threat is averted or the annoyer is duly punished. If, on the other hand, an annoying treatment is not regarded as a personal threat, any initial arousal reaction should rapidly dissipate regardless of retaliatory opportunities. The critical variation in the perception of threat may have been coincidental with the variation of social status. But it would appear that the status level of an annoyer is generally not negatively related to the perception of threat. One might expect the reverse to be more characteristic: Persons of high status tend to be persons in authority (in many everyday social situations), and the infliction of annoyance by "a person in authority" should be highly threatening. Statements about the implications of an annoyer's status for emotional reactions must thus be treated as very tentative.

Since the findings presented by Hokanson and Burgess (1962a) show a prompt reduction in the level of excitation following retaliation against both the high- and low-status annoyer, the data are not adequately accounted for either by the proposal that the subjects dealing with the professor as an "authority figure" displayed a withdrawal reaction or by the suggestion that these subjects experienced anxiety. However, the argument of Geen and Quanty (1977) that anxiety may prevent the decay of excitation seems to be supported by the observation that arousal was at a comparatively high level in those subjects who retaliated against the high-status annoyer who had merely frustrated them on a task. Especially as measured by heart rate, arousal was at a substantially lower level in those subjects who were treated in the same manner but had no opportunity to retaliate. If arousal were solely retaliation motivating, it should have dissipated after retaliation. The fact that it did not, whereas it did when retaliatory actions were not taken, suggests that the retaliating subjects may have been apprehensive about the appropriateness of their behavior and that this state of apprehension maintained or produced arousal.

This assessment points to a problem that greatly compromises the interpretation of arousal as an aggression-*motivating* force: In the measured autonomic activities, various potential sources of excitation are confounded. What might be regarded as a maintenance of annoyance-produced arousal may in fact be anxiety-generated arousal that compensates for the quickly dissipating arousal deriving from annoyance. In the discussed research, this problem is accentuated by the observation that the mere interaction with a high-status person (in the no-annoyance conditions) proved to be highly arousing.

Geen and Quanty's (1977) generalization that recovery from annoyance-produced excitation does not occur when a hostile or aggressive response is inappropriate or when it induces feelings of guilt derives mainly from the observation that prompt recovery is most characteristic when the annoyed person retaliates for an obviously transgressive act against him or her. The annoyed person's hostile or aggressive reactions, when not so justified, fail to induce recovery.

The fact that aggressive behavior per se is not arousal reducing has been demonstrated by Hokanson, Burgess, and Cohen (1963). Male and female subjects were annoyed by an experimenter and then aggressed either against their annoyer, his assistant, a psychology major, or a nonpsychology undergraduate. In another condition, they did not aggress at all. Only direct retaliation (i.e., aggression directed at the annoyer) was found to reduce arousal significantly. Regardless of the degree of relatedness between the annoyer and the substitute target, the same aggressive responses directed at these substitute targets (i.e., identical amounts of electric shock were delivered) failed to lower arousal appreciably below the level associated with no aggression.

It is possible that those subjects who aggressed against a person who had done them no harm, as required by the experimental procedure, felt guilty of some wrongdoing. This is not likely, however, since in additional experimental conditions in which subjects were not annoyed, equally uncalled-for attacks upon the various target persons failed to elevate arousal notably. These subjects were apparently not disturbed. Presumably because their aggressive behavior was socially sanctioned in the experimental situation, they could perceive their responses as appropriate.

The findings are readily explained by three-factor theory: The individual's endangerment mobilizes behavior-energizing arousal, and only the repulsion or the punishment of this endangerment should prompt fast recovery. An assault upon another person or upon any inanimate object that brings no harm to the annoyer neither discourages nor punishes the annoyer. It simply does not constitute retaliation. Only a retaliatory attack upon the annoyer himself has the required instrumental value. "Displaced aggression" lacks this utility, and therefore arousal should be maintained at comparatively high levels as long as the acute threat prevails.

In direct support of this utility account of retaliation, Baker and Schaie (1969) observed that males promptly recovered from an annoyance-induced state of heightened excitation after punitive actions against the annoyer were taken, and they recovered equally whether they themselves or an accomplice of theirs administered the punishment. Geen, Stonner, and Shope (1975), however, failed to confirm these findings. In their investigation, annoyed and aroused males recovered considerably after witnessing another person aggress against their annoyer but showed far greater recovery (in fact, they displayed a relaxation-type reaction) after they personally retaliated. These observations were made only on changes in diastolic blood pressure as the measure of autonomic activity. This measure has proved troublesome in the investigation of annoyance-produced arousal, however (e.g., Hokanson & Edelman, 1966; Zillmann & Cantor, 1976b; Zillmann & Johnson, 1973), a circumstance that dictates caution. But regardless of potential problems with the reliance on diastolic blood pressure as the sole measure of arousal, a recent investigation by Worchel, Arnold, and Harrison (1978) makes it appear likely that punitive actions administered by the annoyed person him- or herself cause a speedier recovery from annoyance-produced arousal than the same punishment administered by another person.

In the study by Worchel et al., male subjects were provoked and then provided with an opportunity to retaliate. One condition of retaliation was straightforward: The subjects aggressed against their annoyer via the administration of electric shock, believing that the annoyer knew their identity. In the other condition, the subjects had the same opportunity to retaliate but were led to believe that the annoyer thought that the shocks were being delivered by another person. The subjects in the latter condition were thus anonymous and not accountable for the punishment they administered. In the former condition, they were identified and accountable.

Worchel et al. proposed that the attacked and debased individual should seek to reassert the self and reestablish his or her lost power. One way of doing this is through retaliation but only if the annoyer knows the retaliator's identity. Thus, although the anonymous avenger need not fear the annoyer's reprisal for the punitive action, this "safe" attack has less utility than one for which he or she takes full responsibility. Because the individual's open retaliation has greater utility than an anonymous assault, aggression should be more intense in the former condition. The findings reported by Worchel et al. confirm this expectation for males. Clearly, this outcome is contrary to what is to be expected on the basis of anxiety considerations.

One of the differences between the experiment by Baker and Schaie (1969) and the one by Geen, Stonner, and Shope (1975) is that in the former study, the annoyer was an experimenter, and in the latter he was a peer. If subjects regarded the experimenter as a superior, they may have felt that assertive efforts were pointless under the circumstances. As a result, they may have been content to see him get his just deserts, no matter how or by whose hands. This contentedness is less likely in the interaction between peers. In the study by Geen et al., annoyer and subject met face to face, and to the extent that the annoyer's assault motivated the debased subject to restore his status, the subject could terminate his annoyance, and with it his state of heightened excitation, only through his own punitive action. The findings reported by Geen et al., then, accord with a three-factor analysis and need not be viewed as challenging earlier observations.

In summary, it appears that in coping with intense annoyances through hostile and aggressive actions, the individual will experience a prompt reduction of arousal and relief from acute feelings of anger: (a) if his or her actions effectively turn back a threat or adequately punish the annoyer; and (b) if his or her actions do not produce the apprehension of further endangerment by the annoyer or the expectation of social reproach. But as we have indicated earlier, even if retaliation neither has utility nor is free from the expectation of further annoyance, the maintenance of arousal cannot last for extended periods of time. Excitation will eventually return to basal levels because of fatigue alone. Characteristically, however, arousal deriving from an unresolved annoyance is not left to "decay by fatigue" but is modified by continued appraisals of the prevailing endangerment. In a state of acute annoyance, the individual presumably rehearses his or her grievance and thereby perpetuates both the state of elevated excitation and the dependent, intense feelings of anger. One would expect that any stimulation that promotes this assumed rehearsal process would prevent recovery. Any disruption of the rehearsal of grievances, on the other hand, should accelerate the decay of excitation.

These expectations have been confirmed in numerous investigations. Studies exploring the effects of aggressive fantasies on recovery from annoyance-produced excitation have shown that the induction of such fantasies maintains arousal at high levels (e.g., Baker & Schaie, 1969; Hokanson & Burgess, 1962b). Apparently, the rehearsal of grievances is not only furthered by explicitly induced or invited aggression-related cognitions; it is readily maintained by salient stimuli. Vantress and Williams (1972) observed that the mere presence of the annoyer prevented excitatory recovery. Even waiting under minimally distracting circumstances has been shown to be a condition in which excitation associated with annoyance can be perpetuated, presumably because rehearsal remains undisturbed. In an investigation by Sapolsky, Stocking, and Zillmann (1977), males and females were provoked and given a chance to retaliate either immediately following provocation or after 6 minutes of waiting in solitude. Waiting failed to reduce excitation in males. In females, however, it did reduce excitation. This difference in the effect of waiting on recovery suggests that males may be more prone than females to ruminate about mistreatments they have suffered and/or about their inability to retaliate against their annoyer.

Research on the hostility- and aggression-modifying effect of the annoyed individual's exposure to communication provides further evidence in support of the notion that brooding, or the rehearsal of grievances, impedes recovery from annoyance-produced excitation. Complex stimuli such as documentaries or fictional films differ considerably in the degree to which they involve and absorb the viewer, and to the extent that they do, they potentially intervene in and disrupt the rehearsal of grievances in a state of acute annoyance to different degrees. In general, the more involving a communication, the more it is expected to disrupt the rehearsal of grievances and the more it should facilitate recovery from annoyance-produced excitation and thus lower feelings of annoyance and aggressiveness. There is, however, a notable exception to this rule: Communications involving *contents that relate to the individual's acute emotional state potentially reiterate arousal-maintaining cognitions* (cf. Zillmann & Johnson, 1973). In the case of annoyance, this means that films that feature provocation and retaliation, annoyance and anger, mistreatment, hostility, aggression, and violence are unlikely to disrupt the maintenance of annoyance and anger even if they are otherwise involving, because they tend to remind the viewer of his or her own feelings. In other words, they simply do not let the viewer forget about the mistreatment he or she has suffered and/or about any reprisals he or she may have contemplated, but was unable to carry out. This reasoning leads to the following expectations:

1. Exposure of the annoyed individual to materials featuring hostile and aggressive behavior perpetuates his or her state of elevated excitation. Exposure to nonhostile and nonaggressive fare, in contrast, induces excitatory recovery. If annoyance and anger are cognitively reinstated after

exposure, as by the individual's reconfrontration with his or her annoyer, the intensity of these feelings will be determined by the arousal prevailing at that time. The hostile and aggressive actions mediated by these emotional states are thus more intense and severe after exposure to hostile than to nonhostile fare.

2. By the same mechanics, exposure of the annoyed individual to a nonhostile communication induces excitatory recovery in proportion to the communication's capacity to involve and absorb the individual, and it lowers feelings of annoyance and anger together with the severity of hostile and aggressive actions accordingly. Of any two nonhostile communications, then, the more involving one will produce the more complete recovery from annoyance-produced excitation and thus result in less subsequent anger and aggressiveness.

The expectations regarding the effects of exposure to films with hostile vs. nonhostile contents have received support in an investigation by Zillmann and Johnson (1973). Male subjects were either minimally or severely provoked; exposed to (a) fictional violence, (b) a travelogue, or (c) no film at all; and then reconfronted by their annoyer and provided with an opportunity to aggress against him. Minimal provocation had a trivial effect on excitation, and although there was some indication that the violent film produced some arousal, exposure to the films did not appreciably alter level of excitation. Subsequent aggressive reactions were predictably low in all communication conditions. In contrast, the severely provoked subjects exhibited a sharp increase in excitation. This state of elevated excitation, as measured by systolic blood pressure and vasoconstriction, was largely maintained during exposure to the violent action, whereas exposure to the nonhostile film produced full recovery. The intensity of aggressive responses, measured in the delivery of electric shock to the annoyer, was a simple function of this difference in level of excitation after exposure. Annoyed subjects who had seen the fictional violence were as aggressive as (but not more aggressive than) those who had not seen a film. Those who had been exposed to the nonhostile travelogue, in contrast, behaved significantly less aggressively than the annoyed subjects in both other conditions. These findings regarding aggressive behavior have been fully replicated in a more recent study by Donnerstein, Donnerstein, and Barrett (1976).

The expectations regarding the consequences of exposure to differentially absorbing nonhostile communication contents have been confirmed in an investigation by Bryant and Zillmann (1977). Male subjects were annoyed, exposed to one of six 10-minute film segments, and then given an opportunity to retaliate against their annoyer. The following films were employed: (a) a monotonous stimulus consisting of soundless, slowly moving, wave patterns on a blue screen; (b) a nature film depicting fish, with a narrative in Korean;

(c) a comedy show featuring nonhostile routines by various comedians; (d) a nonaggressive sport show featuring figure skating; (e) a daytime quiz show; and (f) a rough-and-tumble ice-hockey game that included some fistfights. As determined through pretesting, communications (a) and (b) proved to be minimally absorbing, whereas communications (e) and (f) exhibited a high capacity to intervene in and disrupt cognitive preoccupation with events prior to and during exposure. The intervention potential of communications (c) and (d) was found to be at intermediate levels. Entirely as predicted, exposure of provoked subjects to communications with nonhostile contents resulted in greater reduction of annoyance-produced excitation, the greater the communication's intervention potential. Also as predicted, exposure to the aggressive communication, although it was highly involving to the unprovoked person, maintained the level of excitation. Recovery in this condition was comparable to that in the conditions in which the subjects were exposed to the minimally involving communications, which presumably did little to stop the rehearsal of grievances. Finally, as is evident from Fig. 3, retaliation again proved to be a simple function of the prevailing level of excitation. In terms of three-factor theory, when the annoyed subject was

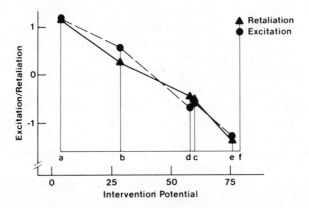

FIG. 3. Level of excitation and retaliatory behavior as a function of the intervention potential of communications. The greater the capacity of nonhostile contents to absorb the respondent (points connected by gradients), the greater the recovery from annoyance-produced excitation (circles) and the less severe the postexposure retaliation against the annoyer (triangles). Contents featuring hostilities were absorbing to the nonannoyed subjects but failed to induce efficient recovery from excitation and failed to lower the level of retaliatory behavior in annoyed subjects (isolated points on coordinate f). The communications were: (a) a monotonous stimulus, (b) a nature film, (c) a comedy show, (d) a program featuring nonaggressive sport, (e) a quiz show, and (f) a program featuring contact sport entailing aggressive actions beyond the legitimate sports activity. Excitation and retaliation are expressed in z scores for ease of comparison. (Adapted from Bryant & Zillmann, 1977.)

reconfronted by his annoyer, feelings of annoyance and anger were cognitively reinstated; the intensity of these feelings, which mediates the severity of retaliatory measures, was then determined by the excitation manifest at that time.

These findings accord well with the proposal that exposure of the annoyed person to communications whose content does not relate to his or her experiential state tends to lower the level of excitation, diminish feelings of annoyance and anger, and ultimately reduce retaliatory inclinations, because it disrupts the rehearsal of grievances and the construction of retaliatory plans. However, they challenge the view that exposure to aggressive fare generally *facilitates* aggressive behavior (e.g., Berkowitz, 1965a, 1973b). Apparently, exposure of the angry person to communications featuring hostile, aggressive, and violent actions does not make the person angrier or more prone to attack his or her annoyer, the annoyer's affiliates or belongings, or any other convenient target (cf. Bryant & Zillmann, 1977). The exposure does not trigger violent reactions but instead *perpetuates* a negative emotional experience and with it a readiness to retaliate against the annoyer. The annoyed person who wants to "get his or her mind off" the disturbing experience is thus ill advised to try to calm down by watching highly aggressive materials. But because arousal in a state of acute annoyance is generally at a higher level than after exposure to "exciting" films (cf. Bryant & Zillmann, 1977; Zillmann, Hoyt, & Day, 1974), it is unlikely that this, comparatively speaking, excitement-reducing exposure will increase the individual's eagerness to engage in retaliatory efforts.

The notion that the so-called aggressive cues contained in communications featuring hostilities, violence, and destruction *increase* subsequent aggressiveness is believed to be supported (e.g., Berkowitz, 1965a, 1973b; Geen, 1976; Goranson, 1970) because the impact of these cues has been assessed relative to the wrong controls. In the standard research paradigm, the annoyed subjects' aggressiveness after exposure to aggressive materials is compared with their aggressiveness after exposure to neutral—that is, nonaggressive—materials. Notwithstanding rare exceptions (e.g., Feshbach, 1961), the evidence consistently shows aggressiveness to be higher after exposure to aggressive than after exposure to nonaggressive fare (cf. Tannenbaum & Zillmann, 1975). It has apparently been assumed that exposure to nonaggressive stimuli has a negligible effect on aggressiveness. Only such an assumption warrants the conclusion that the relatively higher level of aggressiveness after exposure to aggressive stimuli represents an increase in aggression. This crucial assumption is faulty, however, as the studies by Zillmann and Johnson (1973) and Donnerstein, Donnerstein, and Barrett (1976) have shown. Compared to no exposure to communication, it is the aggressive material that has a negligible effect on the annoyed person's aggressiveness and the nonaggressive material that alters aggressiveness.

What appeared to be an increase in aggression after exposure to aggressive cues proved to be a reduction of aggression after exposure to nonaggressive stimuli.

Exposure to communications with nonhostile contents, then, presumably because it is distracting, appears to have a beneficial effect on the acutely annoyed individual: It dissipates feelings of anger and diminishes the urgency of retaliation. Nature films appear to be extremely calming (e.g., Levi, 1965). Game shows and aesthetic rather than combatlike sports displays effectively lower annoyance-produced arousal (e.g., Bryant & Zillmann, 1977). Humor and comedy have been found to pacify the irritated person (e.g., Baron, 1978; Baron & Ball, 1974; Bryant & Zillmann, 1977; Mueller & Donnerstein, 1977a). Reduced aggressiveness has also been observed after exposure to mild erotica (e.g., Baron, 1974b; Baron & Bell, 1973, 1977; Donnerstein, Donnerstein, & Evans, 1975). These aggression-reducing effects of the consumption of primarily entertaining fare are limited, however. Aggressive and arousing sports events appear to lack the power to reduce annoyance and aggressiveness (cf. Zillmann, Bryant, & Sapolsky, 1978). So do arousing humor (e.g., Levi, 1965; Mueller & Donnerstein, 1977b; Tannenbaum & Zillmann, 1975) and arousing erotica (e.g., Donnerstein, Donnerstein, & Evans, 1975; Meyer, 1972a; Zillmann, 1971). It also must be acknowledged that the annoyance- and aggressiveness-reducing effect of exposure to comparatively nonarousing materials is probably not totally due to the disruption of the rehearsal of grievances. It is conceivable that a relaxation type of reaction (in physiological terms) is conditioned to tranquil nature scenes and generalizes to communication stimuli such as nature films. Furthermore, recent research findings suggest that the aggression-dissipating effect of mild erotica is mediated by their positive hedonic valence rather than by their capacity to absorb the respondent cognitively (cf. Zillmann & Sapolsky, 1977). On the other hand, it should be noted that the beneficial effect of distracting stimulation is by no means restricted to exposure to communication. The discussed mechanics lead to the expectation that the reduction of annoyance and aggressiveness is proportional to the capacity of *any* nonaggressive activity to absorb the initially annoyed individual without producing sizable increases in arousal. In accord with this proposal, Konečni (1975a) observed that annoyed subjects behaved less aggressively after having been kept busy with a mathematical task than after waiting for the same period of time. Waiting appears to invite arousal-maintaining brooding over a mistreatment (cf. Holmes, 1966; Sapolsky, Stocking, & Zillmann, 1977).

Leaving acutely annoyed persons to themselves seems to be a rather ineffective method of controlling emotional outbursts. (Only the continued confrontation with annoyers or annoyance-linked conditions must be expected to be less effective.) Any nonarousing distraction, in contrast, appears to be of value in the control of outbursts. But although it is clear that the disruption of the annoyance-perpetuating rehearsal of grievances *can* help to curtail hostile and aggressive reactions, it is not necessarily of great importance in the curtailment of violence. Unlike in the laboratory where the annoyed subject is coerced into exposure to stimuli or compelled to perform certain activities, under natural conditions persons are free to do what they want. They may or may not be inclined to perform activities that would effectively reduce their excitation and feelings of annoyance and hostility. It is conceivable that acutely annoyed persons avoid distraction in order to cope more effectively with their situation. If the rehearsal of grievances is not particularly adaptive, the preparation of responses that resolve the individual's predicament, hostile and aggressive or not, certainly has instrumental value. Acutely annoyed persons, then, may well shield themselves against stimuli that could intervene in their consideration of the response alternatives open to them. As a consequence, in this state they might avoid exposing themselves to communications depicting relaxing wildlife, comedy, game shows, ballet, and mild erotica; and they might avoid solving riddles and math problems, playing chess, or doing needlepoint. In short, it seems likely that the acutely annoyed and angry individual might persevere in the preoccupation with his or her emotional state, thinking about terminating it and/or punishing the annoyer, until he or she has come up with a solution or until a distracting treatment forces itself upon that individual. Unless it can be shown that annoyed persons readily accept or even seek out distractions from their "state of mind," the demonstration of the hostility- and aggression-reducing capacity of the various stimulus conditions outlined seems of little moment in the control of harm-inflicting behavior in society.

Clearly, this assessment does not apply to situations in which the individual's environment can be *managed,* to some degree at least, by intervening parties. For example, a nursery-school teacher can send an annoyed and angry child to another room "to cool off" *or* involve her in absorbing play. Similarly, a raging teenager at home could be left to himself *or* engaged in a game of badminton or poker by the members of his family or by friends. Whenever such intervention choices exist, the selection of the most absorbing, least provocation-related activity may be expected to produce the strongest anger-dissipating effect. The selection of effective annoyance-diminishing activities is thus guided by the intervention rationale. The application of this rationale, then, mainly by persons who interact with an acutely irritated and upset individual and attempt to improve his or her condition, can aid in the control of hostile and aggressive outbursts.

Earlier it was proposed that the magnitude of the excitatory reaction to the individual's endangerment tends to be proportional to the intensity of an aversion or the amount of gratification lost or placed in jeopardy. Compelling evidence on this point is lacking, mainly because experimentation is restricted to a comparatively narrow range of excitatory reactions of moderate intensity. The level of autonomic activity associated with the extreme annoyances that characteristically precipitate impulsive beatings, woundings, and killings is obviously not subject to manipulation and detailed inspection. There are observational data, however, that have some bearing on the proposed relationship. In his pioneering investigation of homicide, Wolfgang (1958) noted that the slaying of spouses and lovers was significantly more violent and cruel than other killings. Victims who had been intimately linked with their assailants tended to be shot and stabbed more often or otherwise mutilated to a greater degree than other victims. Although it can only be speculated that the more violent and cruel murders occurred when the assailant was experiencing exceedingly high levels of excitation, this observation is entirely consistent with the contention that the greater the endangerment, the greater the resulting annoyance and ultimately, the more intense the hostile or aggressive behavior. The closer a person is (or was) to his or her spouse or lover, the greater the gratification he or she presumably provided; and as this greater gratifier is lost or seen to be threatened, annoyance of higher intensity should develop and motivate more violent assaults. Greater love, because it produces greater satisfaction, is thus, in a conflict situation, converted to greater hate and greater violence. A person who has little to lose, in contrast, should be able to contain his or her destructive inclinations more easily.

The evidence presented thus far has demonstrated or assumed a direct correspondence between excitatory state and the intensity of annoyance, anger, or aggressiveness. Such a correspondence cannot generally be expected, however.

First, it is clear that prevailing excitation can affect the intensity of annoyance, anger, and aggressiveness only if these reactions are displayed in direct response to environmental cues or are arrived at through an appraisal of the behavioral situation. Put simply, arousal can intensify the experience of annoyance only if the aroused person experiences annoyance. The same applies to anger and aggressiveness or to any other emotional experience or emotional behavior. This seems a moot point, but on occasion, arousal has been expected to intensify responses that the individual was not predisposed to perform (e.g., Mueller, Nelson, & Donnerstein, 1977).

The dependence of the facilitation of aggression through arousal upon a *disposition* to aggress is evident in an investigation by Zillmann, Katcher, and Milavsky (1972). Male subjects were either provoked or treated in a neutral manner. They then either engaged in strenuous physical exercise or not. After a brief delay, they were provided with an opportunity to aggress against the person they had interacted with earlier. Obviously, the elevated sympathetic activity from exercise could intensify feelings of hostility only in the subjects who had been provoked. Only the provoked subjects were predisposed to retaliate. The elevation of excitation could thus "energize" aggression only in these subjects. In the unprovoked subjects, the elevation of excitation should have been of no consequence, simply because it could not intensify feelings of annoyance and anger. The findings fully confirmed these expectations. Many other investigations give further evidence to the dispositional dependence of behavior intensification through excitation (cf. Tannenbaum & Zillmann, 1975).

Second, a close correspondence between level of excitation and intensity of annoyance and, in turn, annoyance-motivated hostile and aggressive reactions should not be expected when the individual perceives his or her state of excitation to be induced by events that are not related to the annoyance. Suppose, for example, that an annoyed male is exposed to erotic stimuli and becomes aware of his reaction of sexual excitement through obtrusive intero- and exteroceptive cues. It is unlikely, under these conditions, that he will experience intense feelings of annoyance when reconfronted by his annoyer as long as he believes himself to be sexually aroused. Similarly, the person who experiences a high level of excitation because of fever might not attribute all his arousal to his annoyance, and hence he should behave less aggressively than would be predicted from his level of excitation.

The fact that high levels of excitation do not necessarily intensify feelings of anger and aggressiveness even in the provoked person is evident from an investigation by Zillmann, Johnson, and Day (1974a). Severely provoked male subjects were made to perform strenuous physical exercise and were provided with an opportunity to aggress against their annoyer either im- mediately after exercise or after a delay of 6 minutes. The time between provocation and retaliation was kept constant, however. Sympathetic excitation was at an extremely high level immediately after exercise. After the delay period, only the subjects in superior physical condition had fully recovered. In the less fit subjects, arousal was still elevated but far less pronounced than immediately after exercise. If, as the drive models discussed earlier suggest, arousal by necessity were to energize any and every behavior the individual performs, it would be expected that retaliatory aggression immediately after exercise would be much more intense than after a delay. The opposite was observed to be the case, however. Aggressive behavior, measured by the administration of electric shock to the annoyer, was found to be at a very low level when engaged in *immediately* after exercise. It was comparable to that exhibited by subjects of superior physical fitness after they had fully recovered. In sharp contrast, the aggressive behavior of those subjects who had waited but had not fully recovered was of significantly higher intensity.

These findings are readily explained by the assumption that the highly aroused subjects, being short of breath and feeling their hearts pound vigorously, could not help but attribute their arousal state to the exercise. Since they were not provided with such obtrusive and unmistakable manifestations of the portion of their arousal that stemmed from their annoyance, they could not parcel out the arousal that would have appropriately intensified feelings of anger and aggressiveness. In the reconfrontation with their annoyer, these feelings of anger and aggressiveness were cognitively reinstated; but devoid of their excitatory component, they lacked intensity. Those subjects who waited, and whose excitation had partially decayed, were caught in a different attributional dilemma: They no longer were provided with obtrusive intero- and exteroceptive cues of their excitatory reaction to the exercise, cues that would have compelled them to attribute this reaction to exertion. Instead, when they were reconfronted by their annoyer, nothing prevented them from behaving as though all the arousal prevailing at that time were caused by the annoyance. The validity of this explanation has been demonstrated outside the domain of hostility and aggression (cf. Cantor, Zillmann, & Bryant, 1975; Zillmann, 1978).

The effects of cognitive mediation, as specified in three-factor theory, on the individual's excitatory reaction to endangerment, on the experience of annoyance, on feelings of anger, and ultimately on his or her retaliatory behavior have been demonstrated most directly in an investigation by Zillmann and Cantor (1976b). It will be remembered from our earlier discussion (Chapter 5, Section IIID) that it is well established that an annoyance produces less retaliatory behavior, at least at intermediate levels of excitation, when it is inflicted under mitigating circumstances than when it is produced with apparent malice (e.g., Kregarman & Worchel, 1961; Pastore, 1952; Zillmann, Bryant, Cantor, & Day, 1975). The mechanism for this documented effect was less certain, however. Specifically, it was unclear whether the effect is due to a reduction in the instigation to aggression or derives from the inhibition of instigated aggression. Cohen (1955) favored the view that knowledge of mitigating circumstances diminishes the strength of aggressive impulses, whereas Burnstein and Worchel (1962) espoused the position that knowledge of mitigating circumstances fails to reduce annoyance and aggressive impulses but forces the individual to inhibit the behavior he or she is motivated to perform.

Burnstein and Worchel believed they had supported their view by showing that when retaliation was socially disapproved, subjects tended to displace their hostility upon alternative, "innocent" targets. Clearly, they assumed: (a) that the annoyed person who is aware of mitigating circumstances is just as aggressively instigated as one who regards the annoyance as maliciously inflicted; (b) that the likelihood of social reproach forces him or her to hold back reprisals against the nonarbitrary annoyer; and (c) that the activated aggressive forces compel him or her to act out inhibited impulses elsewhere by attacking a substitute target. It remains unclear in this line of reasoning why the annoyed individual is viewed to be forced to inhibit punitive actions against his or her annoyer by considerations of social reproach but is seemingly unrestrained by such considerations in assaults upon "innocent" targets. But more importantly, the entire argument hinges upon the supposition that any inhibition of "aggressive drive" is futile and by necessity produces displacements against alternative targets. As we have seen earlier (Chapter 4), such a supposition is totally unfounded, a circumstance that renders the measurement of inhibition through displacement spurious and the inhibition argument by Burnstein and Worchel unacceptable.

The investigation by Zillmann and Cantor sought to resolve the lowered instigation vs. inhibition controversy regarding the aggression-reducing effect of mitigating circumstances: (a) by tracing the individual's excitatory reactions, and (b) by assessing the retaliatory behavior assumed to be mediated by them. In a procedure similar to the one employed in the study by Zillmann, Bryant, Cantor, and Day (1975), described in Section ID of this chapter, male subjects were severely annoyed by an obnoxious experimenter. They were later provided with an opportunity to retaliate against him by filing complaints that ostensibly affected his financial and academic future adversely. In one experimental condition, subjects were not informed of mitigating circumstances underlying their annoyer's demeaning behavior. In a second condition, subjects were "incidentally" informed about mitigating circumstances for the behavior of their annoyer (he was said to be disturbed about forthcoming exams) *before* they interacted with him and were treated in a demeaning manner. In a third condition, subjects were "incidentally" informed about the same mitigating circumstances *after* they had been mistreated. The time between provocation and retaliation was kept constant across conditions, however. Measures of excitation (blood pressure and heart rate) were taken at various critical times throughout the experiment.

Under these experimental conditions, the inhibition rationale leads to the expectation that the provision of information about mitigating circumstances prior to provocation will not prevent intense feelings of annoyance from developing. The excitatory reaction to provocation in this condition should thus be similar to that in the other two conditions. Furthermore, whether mitigating information is provided before or after provocation should make no appreciable difference in retaliatory behavior: In both conditions, knowledge of mitigating circumstances should simply force the inhibition of hostile actions against the annoyer. Consequently, whereas annoyance-intensifying and hostility-motivating excitation is expected to be similarly elevated in all experimental conditions, retaliation in the two mitigation conditions should be significantly lower than in the condition in which mitigating circumstances are not known. In sharp contrast, the rationale that knowledge of mitigating circumstances keeps aggressive instigation at a low level leads to the expectation that primarily in the condition in which knowledge of mitigating circumstances is provided prior to provocation, and to a lesser degree in the condition in which it is provided after provocation, annoyance and retaliation will be of comparatively low intensity.

The mechanics of this expectation of reduced aggression instigation are explicit in three-factor theory. Prior mitigation *prepares* the individual for an attack, a condition that is associated with low emotional responsiveness (cf. Leventhal, 1974). But more importantly, through prior mitigation the attack is *preattributed to causes other than the victim's behavior.* The attacked person can thus perceive the attack as a *minimal endangerment. Excitatory reactions* are consequently *not intense.* In turn, *feelings of annoyance are of low intensity,* and since these feelings are considered to mediate the motivation to retaliate, *minimal retaliatory efforts* are expected. In contrast, the individual who is attacked without knowing of mitigating circumstances at the time is likely to suffer the full impact of being surprised and of perceiving him- or herself as being personally assaulted. This person should display an intense excitatory reaction and thus experience intense feelings of annoyance and anger. Furthermore, he or she should be motivated to behave in a highly hostile manner and given an opportunity, should take strong punitive actions against the annoyer. When the acutely annoyed individual learns of mitigation, he or she is likely to reappraise his or her endangerment. If this reappraisal diminishes or removes the threat status of the annoying treatment, the individual should experience excitatory recovery. The intensity of feelings of annoyance and of hostile inclinations should likewise decline. However, two exceptions are conceivable in the specified effect of the provision of mitigating information *after* annoyance: (1) The individual may be so intensely annoyed that the ability to conduct a reappraisal is impaired, and he or she thus fails to perceive a reduction of endangerment (cf. Chapter 5, Section IIIB and Section IIID). (2) The individual may have contemplated punitive actions while in a state of acute annoyance and committed him- or herself to retaliation (cf. Section IB and Section IC of this chapter). Both lines of reasoning lead to the same conclusion: The individual who has been intensely annoyed and learns of mitigating circumstances only after the fact may, when he or she learns of mitigation, efficiently recover from excitation but nonetheless react highly punitively. According to this reasoning, then, the provision of mitigating information after provocation should have a comparatively poor retaliation-restraining effect.

The findings are summarized in Fig. 4. As can be seen, they fully support the expectations derived from the three-factor theory of hostility and aggression. In addition, they provide compelling evidence against the inhibition rationale. Prior mitigation was found to prevent intense excitatory reactions. As is evident from the *absence of retaliation* (the obnoxious experimenter was favorably evaluated, and *no complaints* were filed about his conduct), prior knowledge of mitigating information held feelings of

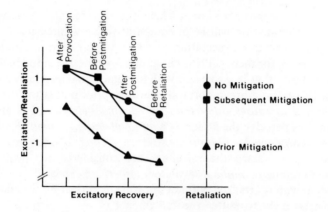

FIG. 4.   The effect of mitigating information on excitatory reactions to annoyance and on retaliatory hostility. The provision of mitigating information prior to provocation prevented intense annoyance and kept retaliation to a minimum. The subsequent provision of mitigating information accelerated the decay of excitation but failed to reduce retaliation effectively. Excitation and retaliation are expressed in z scores for ease of comparison. (Adapted from Zillmann & Cantor, 1976b.)

annoyance to extremely low and tolerable levels. Postannoyance mitigation proved to initiate speedy recovery from excitation but failed to bring retaliation down to a low level. Compared to the condition in which subjects never learned of mitigation, the provision of mitigating information after provocation did have a tendency to reduce retaliation but actually failed to do so reliably. This finding supports the view that the individual who has suffered through intense annoyance is unable or unwilling to curtail the infliction of annoyance upon his or her annoyer in return. It should be recalled that there is evidence that shows that a reappraisal of annoyance "after the fact" can curb hostile behavior (e.g., Mallick & McCandless, 1966). The present findings strongly suggest, however, that the annoyance- and hostility-reducing effect of the provision of mitigating information prior to annoyance is far more powerful than that of the subsequent provision of such information.

An investigation by Zillmann and Bryant (1974) gives further evidence to the postponement of retaliatory activities as predicted by three-factor theory. Male subjects either were placed in a state of elevated excitation or were not aroused, and they were then either attacked by a peer or treated by him in a neutral manner. The time of provocation was arranged so as to assure the (mis)attribution of excitation from prior activity to the annoyance (cf. Cantor, Zillmann, & Bryant, 1975). The opportunity to aggress against the peer was delayed to a point at which subjects had fully recovered from the elevation of excitation induced earlier. Emotionally neutral physical exercise was employed to elevate excitation. The specific times for the provocation and retaliation were determined in a pretest. In summary, subjects were either provoked or not at a time when excitation was either at a high or low level, and they retaliated at a later time when the initial arousal differentiation had disappeared.

The findings are presented in Fig. 5. As can be seen, delayed retaliatory aggression was substantially more intense when provocation (but not necessarily retaliation) was associated with a higher level of excitation. Consistent with three-factor theory, the higher level of excitation prevailing at the time of provocation (created by means unrelated to annoyance) must have intensified feelings of annoyance. These feelings must have been intense enough to activate the definite intention to get back at the annoyer. When the opportunity for retaliation arose later, this retaliatory inclination prompted pronounced aggression in spite of the fact that the intensity of accompanying feelings of annoyance was presumably relatively low because the added-in excitation had subsided. Although it remains unclear whether intense feelings of annoyance are merely recalled and then urge retaliation, whether the reconfrontation with a past annoyer reinstates excitatory elements of the annoyance as well as its cognitive aspects, whether annoyance experienced at high levels results in enduring endocrine arousal reactions that are not readily detected in peripheral manifestations, or whether annoyance experienced at very high levels of excitation interacts with elements of excitation that do not derive from annoyance in such a way that their decay is held up, it is apparent that individuals who have been severely provoked delay highly punitive actions. These individuals appear to be able to hold back on actions contemplated or planned "in the heat of anger" and perform these actions later "in cold blood."

The delay of retaliation has been further explored in a recent investigation (Bryant & Zillmann, 1978) involving both male and female subjects. By means of exposure to nonarousing, somewhat arousing, and substantially

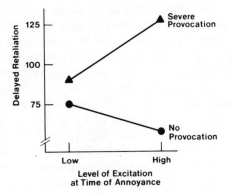

FIG. 5. Delayed retaliatory aggression as a function of the level of excitation at the time of provocation. Excitation was measured in peripheral manifestations. Retaliatory aggression was assessed by the administration of electric shock. (Adapted from Zillmann & Bryant, 1974.)

arousing films, students were placed at different levels of excitation. They were then provoked or not provoked by a guest lecturer. The opportunity to retaliate against the visitor was delayed for an entire week. This was done mainly to rule out the possibility that through whatever mediating process, the excitatory differentiation prevailing at the time of provocation could be maintained to the time of retaliation and thereby influence the intensity of hostile reactions.

As expected, the level of excitation experienced during provocation critically affected delayed hostile behavior. Subjects were provided with the opportunity to prevent the guest lecturer's appointment to a superior position. It was found that those subjects who were provoked while still aroused from prior stimulation opposed his appointment more strongly than subjects who were equally provoked but who experienced less arousal at the time this treatment was applied. The effect was observed for both males and females. Regardless of the respondent's sex, the higher the level of excitation prevailing at provocation, the more intense the delayed hostile reaction tended to be—presumably because the arousal intensified feelings of annoyance and anger. In unprovoked subjects, level of excitation was of no consequence, as should be expected. These findings on substantially delayed retaliatory behavior fully corroborate those of the earlier reported investigation in which retaliation was held up for a comparatively short period of time.

It is clear from these studies on delayed retaliation that *the likelihood of retaliatory actions and the severity of these actions does not simply diminish in close correspondence with the dissipation of annoyance-linked sympathetic excitation.* But whereas annoyance-motivated hostile or aggressive actions can and occasionally do go beyond the emotional "emergency period," it would appear that "uncontrolled" and overly severe retaliatory hostile and aggressive actions become less likely as time goes by. There are two reasons for this expectation: (1) The likelihood and frequency of reappraisals increases with time after an acute annoyance; these reappraisals, which are conducted at intermediate levels of excitation and thus entail the various facets of cognitive guidance, should effect a moderation of retaliatory intentions. (2) The memory of an annoyance is likely to become less vivid with the passage of time, and habituation to the recall of the specific arousing events should successfully reduce the excitatory component of recalling the annoying experience. In short, as the individual has time to think about an intensely disturbing incident and the memory of it becomes less and less disturbing, he or she is likely to correct any "unreasonable" plans of vengeance that may have been entertained when the individual was acutely annoyed. It appears that plans of vengeance conceived of in the heat of anger will be adhered to and executed in cold blood at a later time only when the annoyance suffered was very severe and inflicted with unquestionable malice, or when these plans have been conveyed to others who have manifested reproach-and-approval pressures upon the avenger to carry out his or her intentions. Only under such conditions should extreme retaliatory plans survive the hostility- and aggression-moderating effect of the repeated reappraisal of annoyance.

The relationship between excitation and hostility or aggression is further explored in the next section. A theory that addresses the confounding of potentially many sources of excitation in the excitatory activity that intensifies a particular emotional experience or emotional behavior, especially in sequences of emotional reactions, is detailed. Research findings that support this theory, and that also support three-factor theory in general, are then presented.

II. EXCITATION TRANSFER IN HOSTILITY AND AGGRESSION

In the discussion of research findings in the preceding section, it was suggested that the excitatory reaction to stimuli that are unrelated to a particular annoying treatment *can, but need not, combine* with the excitatory reaction to that treatment. Excitatory reactions unrelated to annoyance as such thus *may* intensify feelings of anger and, ultimately, hostile and aggressive behavior. We now specify more precisely the conditions under which such an aggression-enhancing integration of arousal from different sources occurs or does not occur. We briefly outline a theoretical model of excitation transfer (cf. Zillmann, 1971, 1972b, 1978) and then apply it to hostility and aggression specifically.

A. Excitation-Transfer Theory of Hostility and Aggression

Essentially, excitation-transfer theory is the application of the three-factor theory of emotion to the experience of all conceivable emotional states *in sequence.* The theory predicts under what conditions residues of sympathetic excitation from a preceding emotional state, whatever that state may be, will intensify a subsequent emotional state, whatever that state may be. The paradigm has been explored and has been supported under a great variety of circumstances. It has been shown, for example, that residues of excitation from physical exertion can intensify feelings of anger and aggressive behavior (Zillmann & Bryant, 1974; Zillmann, Johnson, & Day, 1974a; Zillmann, Katcher, & Milavsky, 1972), can enhance the experience of sexual excitement (Cantor, Zillmann, & Bryant, 1975), and can increase altruistic inclinations (Borden & Sloan, 1977). Residues from arousing comedy have been found to intensify aggressiveness (Mueller & Donnerstein, 1977b; Tannenbaum & Zillmann, 1975). It has also been demonstrated that residues of fear-associated arousal can enhance sexual behavior (Barfield & Sachs, 1968; Crowley, Popolow, & Ward, 1973). Furthermore, it has been shown that residues of sexual arousal can potentiate aggression (Meyer, 1972a; Zillmann, 1971; Zillmann, Hoyt, & Day, 1974) and prosocial behavior (Mueller & Donnerstein, 1978); and that residues from either sexual arousal or disgust reactions can facilitate such diverse experiences as the enjoyment of music (Cantor & Zillmann, 1973), the appreciation of humor (Cantor, Bryant, & Zillmann, 1974), and dysphoric empathy (Zillmann, Mody, & Cantor, 1974). We do not concern ourselves here with the variety of emotional reactions that can be facilitated by prior emotional states, however, but instead concentrate on the potentiation of annoyance and annoyance-related reactions. Accordingly, we rephrase the transfer paradigm to accommodate all conceivable emotions as antecedent conditions to the experience of annoyance and anger, and to hostile and aggressive behavior.

The transfer paradigm is based on the following assumptions:

1. Regarding emotions, the interoception of excitatory reactions is generally nonspecific. This interoceptive nonspecificity is largely due to a high degree of nonspecificity of the excitatory reactions themselves.

2. The individual can determine the intensity of his or her excitatory reaction through interoception. However, only comparatively gross changes in the level of excitation will draw the individual's attention and produce an awareness of his or her state of excitation.

3. The individual relates an excitatory reaction of which he or she becomes aware to the apparent inducing condition and recalls this connection at later times.

4. The individual generally does not partition excitation compounded from reactions to different inducing conditions. More specifically, the individual does not identify all factors that contribute to an experienced state of excitation; nor does he or she apportion that excitation to the various contributing factors. Instead, the individual tends to ascribe his or her entire excitatory reaction to one particular inducing condition.

5. Intense excitatory reactions do not terminate abruptly. Because of slow humoral processes involved in the control of sympathetic excitation, excitation decays comparatively slowly. Residues of this slowly decaying excitation, then, may enter into subsequent, potentially independent experiential states.

Whereas these assumptions apply to transfer to and from any emotional state, the following propositions are specific to annoyance, anger, and aggressiveness. The more general transfer propositions can be found elsewhere (Zillmann, 1978).

1. Given a situation in which: (a) an individual responds to an endangerment and appraises his or her reactions as annoyance; (b) he or she experiences a level of sympathetic arousal that is still elevated from prior stimulation; and (c) he or she is not provided with apparent extero- and/or interoceptive cues that would indicate that this arousal results from prior stimulation, excitatory residues from prior arousal will combine inseparably with the excitatory response to the endangerment. As a consequence, these residues will intensify the experience of annoyance, and to the extent that the individual seeks to resolve his or her annoyance through hostile and aggressive behavior, these residues will intensify such behavior.

2. The experience of anger and hostile or aggressive behavior will be enhanced in proportion to the magnitude of the prevailing residual excitation.

3. Both the period of time in which transfer can manifest itself and the magnitude of transferable residues are a function of: (a) the magnitude of the preceding excitatory response, and/or (b) the rate of recovery from the excitatory state.

4. The individual's potential for transfer is: (a) proportional to his or her excitatory responsiveness, and (b) inversely proportional to his or her proficiency to recover from excitatory states.

A model of the additive integration of residual excitation and excitation specific to the current state is presented in Fig. 6. Additive integration can be viewed as a parsimonious projection of arousal integration. There may be a

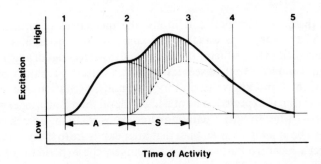

FIG. 6. A model of excitation transfer in which residual excitation from a preceding excitatory reaction combines additively with the excitatory reaction to current stimulation. An antecedent stimulus condition (A), persisting from time 1 to time 2, is assumed to produce excitatory activity that has entirely decayed only at time 4. Similarly, a subsequent stimulus condition (S), persisting from time 2 to time 3, is assumed to produce excitatory activity that has entirely decayed only at time 5. Residual excitation from condition A and excitation specific to condition S combine from time 2 to time 4. The extent to which the transfer of residues from condition A increases the excitatory activity associated with condition S is shown in the shaded area.

considerable deviation from additivity, however. Nonadditivity is suggested, for example, whenever the sum of residual and annoyance-specific excitation exceeds the upper threshold of excitability. Models in which the annoyance-specific excitatory reaction is considered a function of prevailing levels of excitation can readily accommodate range restrictions of excitability, and they may thus be called for under certain circumstances. Probably because of considerable imprecision in the assessment of sympathetic excitation at this time, the additive model is quite sufficient in the explanation of pertinent findings, and we employ it as a practical working hypothesis.

B. Supportive Evidence

In the initial experimental test of the excitation-transfer paradigm (Zillmann, 1971), residues of sexual arousal were transferred into aggressive behavior. Male subjects were provoked by a same-sex peer; exposed to a neutral, aggressive, or erotic communication; and then provided with an opportunity to aggress against their annoyer. The neutral communication was an innocuous travelogue, the aggressive communication featured a prizefight, and the erotic communication depicted a young couple engaged in gentle precoital behavior. It was determined in a pretest that the excitatory potential of the erotic film exceeded that of the aggressive film and that, in turn, the excitatory potential of the aggressive film was above that of the neutral film. The excitatory reaction to the films was measured in peripheral manifestations of arousal. Measures of blood pressure and measures combining blood pressure and heart rate were significantly differentiated for the films, as described.

Under these experimental conditions, the mechanics of transfer are as follows: As the subject is attacked, he appraises his reaction, and by the process specified in three-factor theory, he arrives at feelings of anger directed against his annoyer. He then sees a film with a certain excitatory potential. Because of the films' known excitatory potentials, excitation after exposure to the erotic film is expected to be at a higher level than that after exposure to the aggressive film. In turn, excitation after exposure to the aggressive film is expected to be at a higher level than that after exposure to the neutral film. In the subject's reconfrontation with his annoyer, the experience of anger is cognitively reinstated. The intensity of feelings of anger is now determined by any excitatory reaction that accompanies the reinstatement of anger *and by residual excitation from exposure to communication.* Higher residues will produce more intense feelings of anger, and more intense feelings of anger will motivate more intense retaliatory aggression. It is to be expected, then, that equally provoked subjects will behave more aggressively after exposure to the erotic film than after exposure to the aggressive film. In turn, they should behave more aggressively after exposure to the aggressive film than after exposure to the neutral film.

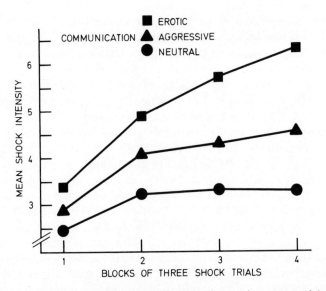

FIG. 7. Retaliatory aggression as a function of the excitatory potential of communications. Exposure to communication was interpolated between provocation and retaliation. Excitation, measured in peripheral manifestations, was at a higher level after exposure to the erotic communication than after exposure to the aggressive communication, and in turn, at a higher level after exposure to the aggressive communication than after exposure to the neutral communication. (Reprinted from Zillmann, 1971, with permission.)

The findings, shown in Fig. 7, are entirely as predicted from the excitation-transfer paradigm. In contrast, they are highly nonsupportive of both the notion of symbolic catharsis (cf. Feshbach, 1955, 1956) and that of cue elicitation (cf. Berkowitz, 1965a, 1973b). According to the former model, aggressiveness after exposure to the aggressive film should have been lower than aggressiveness after exposure to either of the other films, because only the aggressive film provided action for the supposedly cathartic "vicarious participation." According to the latter model, the aggressive film should have increased aggressiveness to a level above that after either of the other films, because only this film contained supposedly aggression-enhancing aggressive cues.

The finding that motivated aggression can be intensified by residues of excitation from exposure to highly arousing erotica has been corroborated in further similar investigations (Meyer, 1972a; Rosene, 1971; Zillmann, Hoyt, & Day, 1974). It should be recognized, however, that this intensification is rather short-lived. The potentiality for the intensification of emotional experiences and emotional behaviors by residual excitation dissipates, of course, with the decay of these residues. Aggression-enhancing residual excitation from exposure to aggressive and violent fare dissipates in a few minutes (Day, 1976; Zillmann, Hoyt, & Day, 1974). As mentioned earlier, residues of humor-induced excitation have also been shown to enhance motivated aggression (Mueller & Donnerstein, 1977b; Tannenbaum & Zillmann, 1975). The potentiality for such effects should be similarly short-lived.

In the investigation of the effects of communications on hostile and aggressive behavior, the described experimental paradigm has been employed almost exclusively. Subjects are first either provoked or not, then exposed to communication, and finally provided with an opportunity to aggress. Generally speaking, it has been found that whereas unprovoked subjects are not appreciably affected by exposure to communication, provoked subjects display temporarily intensified hostile and aggressive reactions when arousing stimuli are interpolated between provocation and retaliation (cf. Tannenbaum & Zillmann, 1975). Another sequence of events in which exposure to communication may influence hostile and aggressive behavior has received little attention. The individual may first be exposed to communication and then be provoked and receive an opportunity to retaliate. The transfer paradigm applies to this sequence more directly. Exposure brings about a certain level of excitation, and as the individual is provoked, residues transfer into anger and aggressiveness. The reinstatement of anger is not an issue in this sequence.

One of the rare studies in which the communication/provocation/retaliation sequence has been employed was conducted by Donnerstein, Donnerstein, and Barrett (1976). Male subjects were exposed to either an aggressive or a neutral communication, or were not exposed to communication. They were then provoked and permitted to retaliate. Prior exposure to the aggressive film resulted in pronouncedly more intense retaliatory aggression than prior exposure to the neutral film or no exposure. Aggressiveness after the neutral film was particularly low. If it is assumed that the aggressive film elevated excitation and the neutral film reduced it, the transfer paradigm accounts for the findings. But since excitation was not measured, there is no direct evidence that communication-induced arousal corresponded with the observed level of aggressiveness. The assumed differentiation of arousal is suggested, however, by the assessment of the excitatory potential of the aggressive film and of similar neutral films in other investigations (e.g., Zillmann, Hoyt, & Day, 1974).

An investigation by Cantor, Zillmann, and Einsiedel (1978) avoided these interpretative ambiguities by directly assessing peripheral manifestations of sympathetic excitation after exposure to communication. Female subjects were exposed to a neutral, aggressive, or erotic film; were provoked or not provoked by a same-sex peer; and were immediately provided with an opportunity to aggress against this peer. The erotic film proved to be substantially more arousing than the aggressive film. Level of excitation following exposure to the aggressive film was especially low. In fact, this level fell slightly, but not reliably, below that associated with the neutral film. This failure on the part of the females to respond excitationally to violent fare is in sharp contrast to the characteristic reaction of males. It seems that unlike males, females are not emotionally moved by the display of aggressive behaviors such as fistfighting, behaviors that have been a male preoccupation. In terms of aggressive behavior, the excitatory reaction to the various films was of no consequence for unprovoked females. As with males, if an aggressive disposition is not established through an endangerment of some sort, feelings of anger do not develop, and hence they cannot be intensified. For the provoked females, in contrast, retaliatory aggression was modified in accord with the magnitude of residual excitation from exposure to communication. Arousing erotica greatly facilitated motivated aggressiveness. Aggression was at significantly lower levels in both other conditions. In line with the arousal differentiation, it was slightly, but not reliably, lower after exposure to the aggressive film than after exposure to the neutral film. The findings, then, are fully in accord with excitation-transfer expectations. But beyond theoretical considerations, the findings also urge a reassessment of some of the generalizations regarding the impact of media violence on "normal" adults, since these generalizations are almost entirely based on the investigation of the behavior of males (cf. Goranson, 1970). In such a reassessment, it must be recognized, however, that the aggressive and violent transgressions that are of great public concern are mostly committed by males.

In the investigation of excitation transfer in hostility and aggression outside the realm of communication effects, emotionally neutral physical exercise has been the most commonly used source of sympathetic excitation for transfer into subsequent emotional states. The earlier discussed studies by Zillmann, Katcher, and Milavsky (1972) and Zillmann, Johnson, and Day (1974a) give strong support to the transfer model (cf. Section ID of this chapter). The findings of the former study are summarized in Fig. 8. As can be seen, residues of exertion-induced sympathetic excitation did not indiscriminately "energize" aggressive responses, but intensified these responses only when they were motivated through the mediation of intensified feelings of anger.

The fact that arousal does not "automatically" lead to increased hostility and aggression is further attested to in an investigation by Konečni (1975b). Male and female subjects were annoyed and were exposed to noises known to have arousing properties while they were making retaliatory choices. In a control condition, the subjects were not exposed to noise. These stimulus conditions were also applied to nonannoyed subjects. The presence of arousing noise was found to have no appreciable effect on the aggressive behavior of these nonannoyed subjects. In contrast, arousing noise was observed to increase retaliatory aggression, relative to the no-noise controls, in those subjects who had been annoyed.

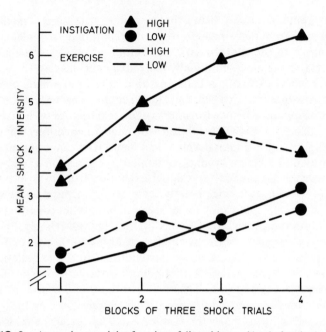

FIG. 8.   Aggression as a joint function of disposition and level of excitation. Excitatory residues from strenuous physical exercise were present during the period of time in which aggressive responses were performed. Residual excitation intensified aggressive behavior when it was motivated through provocation. When aggression was not thus motivated, residual excitation had no appreciable effect on aggression. (Reprinted from Zillmann, Katcher, & Milavsky, 1972, with permission.)

Although the findings of this study demonstrate that arousal—even when it derives from exposure to noxious stimuli—does not further hostile behavior when such behavior is not motivated, they do not necessarily implicate arousal as the intensifier of motivated aggression. In fact, the findings are open to several equally plausible explanations. First, it could be argued that arousal was indeed the mediator of intensified aggression. The angry subject, when exposed to arousing noise, displayed an excitatory reaction that was not recognized as due to the noise but instead was de facto misattributed to anger, thereby intensifying this experience. Arousal was thus quasi-instantaneously transferred into anger and aggressiveness. Second, it is conceivable that arousal was not critically involved but that instead the exposure to complex and/or loud noise simply distracted the subject from an appraisal of the circumstances, which might have moderated aggressiveness (cf. Zillmann, 1972b). Angry subjects not thus distracted may have been advantaged in applying inhibitions to their aggressive behavior and consequently displayed less aggressiveness. Third, it is possible and even likely that the hedonic properties of the stimuli were chiefly responsible for the effects obtained. Exposure to complex loud noise was undoubtedly annoying to the subjects. If they were not provoked, this noise-induced annoyance could not possibly be blamed on the person they had to treat punitively. It thus could not readily intensify aggressiveness. If they were provoked, however, the additional annoyance could more readily be construed as a part of the acute annoyance suffered. To the extent that an unrelated annoyance (and not necessarily any associated arousal) was misattributed to the main source of anger, that is, to the annoyer, aggressiveness should indeed have increased as observed. The findings, then, suggest that aversive and potentially arousing stimulation that is received at the time motivated hostile or aggressive responses are being performed tends to enhance these responses. But although various possible mechanisms, all deriving from three-factor theoretical considerations, can be implicated to some degree, it remains unclear exactly which of these mechanisms, or which combination thereof, mediates this effect.

The dispositional dependency of the intensification of hostile and aggressive behavior through excitation transfer from unrelated experiences, apparent in the investigations that have been discussed, may be considered evidence against the behavior-theoretical view (cf. Zillmann, 1978) that arousal facilitates any and every behavior the individual is led to perform. In the experiments already reported, aggressiveness was forced into a prime location in the response hierarchy even when subjects were not provoked. Subjects, after all, *had to* perform punitive acts. They had to deliver electric shock, and they were only free to vary the frequency and/or the intensity and/or the duration of shock. According to the behavior-theoretical formulation, aggression, since it was performed, should have been energized by arousal in nonannoyed subjects also. This reasoning may appear forced, however. It could be argued that in the unprovoked subjects, the aggressive responses performed were not occasioned by aggression-eliciting stimuli and that a response energization should only be expected if aggression is triggered by salient cues. Phrased in this manner, the behavior-theoretical formulation can explain, for example, the findings reported by Zillmann, Katcher, and Milavsky (1972) and Konečni (1975b). As long as arousal is increased immediately prior to or during the individual's performance of hostile or aggressive activities, the behavior-theoretical view appears to provide a parsimonious alternative explanation.

This alternative explanation is ruled out, however, in the investigations by Zillmann and Bryant (1975) and Bryant and Zillmann (1978) discussed earlier (Section ID of this chapter). As will be recalled, residual excitation was transferred into annoyance, and retaliatory aggression was delayed until the transferred residues had decayed. Arousal was thus employed to intensify the experience of annoyance and anger. It did not energize retaliation. But retaliation was nonetheless intensified through the mediation of intensified prior anger (cf. Fig. 5).

The implications of the propositions of transfer theory regarding individual differences have been explored in an investigation by Zillmann, Johnson, and Day (1974a). According to the theory, individuals who readily experience increased sympathetic activity and who recover from that state of elevated excitation slowly are especially vulnerable to displaying excitation transfer into anger and aggressiveness. The person who becomes more aroused and whose arousal lasts longer is prone to display more intense transfer reactions for a longer period of time than the comparatively unexcitable person. To the extent that sympathetic excitability is adequately operationalized in the responsiveness of the cardiovascular system, these expectations regarding individual differences may be expressed in terms of cardiovascular responsiveness, or inversely in terms of *cardiovascular fitness*. The person of good cardiovascular fitness should display autonomic reactions of low intensity not only to exertion but also to emotion-inducing stimuli. Similarly, he or she should exhibit speedy autonomic recovery after exertion and after emotion-inducing stimuli. It has been shown that cardiovascular fitness indeed generalizes to emotional reactions that are independent of motoric exertion (Cantor, Zillmann, & Day, 1978).

Regardless of the nature of the prior induction of autonomic arousal, then, the residues for transfer into subsequent reactions should be more pronounced and prevail longer, the greater the respondent's cardiovascular responsiveness. The intensification of hostility and aggression through transferred excitation is thus viewed as inversely proportional to cardiovascular fitness. The proposed relationship is further explicated in Fig. 9.

In testing this relationship, male subjects were provoked by a same-sex peer, engaged in strenuous physical exercise, and were given the opportunity to aggress against their annoyer either immediately following exertion or after a delay of 6 minutes, with the time between provocation and retaliation kept constant. In a pretest, the subjects' cardiovascular reactions to and recovery from the strenuous task were monitored (i.e., in blood pressure and heart rate); and on the basis of the subjects' measured proficiency to recover, three levels of cardiovascular fitness were distinguished. Six minutes after completion of the strenuous task, cardiovascular activity was found to be maximally differentiated between the three recovery-proficiency groups: In the high-proficiency condition, subjects had fully recovered (in fact, some subjects were below basal levels on systolic blood pressure). In the intermediate-recovery condition, subjects were still aroused from exercise: Excitation was above the level in the high-proficiency group. In the low-proficiency condition, subjects were still highly aroused, with excitation being above that in both the high- and the intermediate-proficiency groups. These

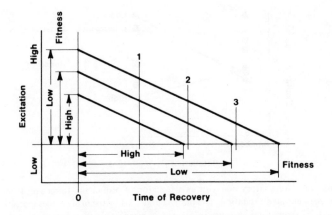

FIG. 9. Illustration of the hypothesized inverse relationship between cardiovascular fitness and the propensity for transfer. As shown in the simplified decay gradients, the excitatory reaction to a particular stimulus (time 0) and the time of recovery from that reaction decrease as cardiovascular fitness increases. At time 1, residual excitation for transfer exists in all fitness conditions in differing amounts. At time 2, recovery to basal levels of excitation is complete for high fitness, but the propensity for transfer is maintained, to different degrees, for intermediate and low fitness. At time 3, the propensity for transfer is maintained only for low fitness.

arousal conditions were recreated in the main experiment, which was conducted on the same subjects 1 week after the pretest.

The findings are presented in Fig. 10. As reported earlier in connection with attributional considerations (Section ID of this chapter), immediately after exertion, residual excitation failed to intensify aggressive reactions, because arousal could not be misattributed. This expected lack of transfer was observed in all conditions of recovery proficiency. It evidently applies regardless of the magnitude of prevailing residues. In contrast, the respondent's cardiovascular fitness did affect aggressive behavior when retaliation was delayed to a point where awareness of the major source of residual arousal no longer prevailed and prevented transfer. Subjects of superior cardiovascular fitness, who had fully recovered, behaved significantly less aggressively than the less fit subjects, in whom transferable residues persisted. This finding supports the main theoretical expectation. The secondary expectation that in the low-fitness condition, aggression should be intensified to a higher degree than in the intermediate-fitness condition was not confirmed, however. In spite of greater residual excitation, retaliatory aggression in the low-fitness condition, although slightly higher, did not reliably exceed that in the intermediate-fitness condition.

The findings, taken together, are fully consistent with the proposed negative relationship between cardiovascular fitness and aggressiveness. In

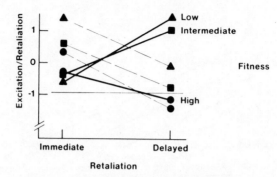

FIG. 10.   Retaliatory behavior as a function of proficiency to recover from states of elevated excitation. The points connected by the broken lines indicate levels of sympathetic activity (measured in systolic blood pressure) immediately following strenuous physical exercise and after a recovery period. The points connected by the solid lines indicate levels of retaliatory behavior (measured in the intensity of electric shock ostensibly administered to the annoyer) at the corresponding times. Excitation and retaliation are expressed in z scores for ease of comparison. Immediately after exertion, when residual excitation could only be attributed to its actual source, retaliatory behavior was minimal in spite of very high levels of excitation. After partial recovery, retaliatory behavior was intensified by residual excitation that could not readily be connected with exertion. In the condition of high cardiovascular fitness (circles), recovery from exertion-produced excitation was complete (the horizontal line indicates the basal level of excitation), and in the absence of transferable residues, retaliatory behavior was negligible. (Adapted from Zillmann, Johnson, & Day, 1974a.)

more general terms, they support the view that the person of good cardiovascular (or excitational) fitness is less prone to experience high levels of excitation during and after the induction of emotional responses, and he or she is thus protected against overly intense and "irrational" reactions. To the extent that such excitational fitness is correlated with physical fitness, the rationale projects physical fitness as a causal, contributory condition to emotional stability—stability being construed as the absence of frequent uncontrolled outbursts. But although the proposed mechanism may be viewed as elucidating the link between physical fitness and mental health, a linkage assumed to exist by countless educators since the ancient Greeks (cf. Layman, 1972), it should be clear that physical fitness is no assurance of emotional stability. Excitational fitness must be viewed as a contributing factor that operates in conjunction with potentially many other factors.

In considering other contributing factors, one that can readily dominate any aggression-curtailing effect of physical fitness is the development of aggressive habits. This has been shown in an investigation by Zillmann, Johnson, and Day (1974b). The behavior of male athletes was compared to that of equally intelligent male nonathletes. Athletes were subdivided into those involved in so-called contact sports (members of varsity football and wrestling teams) and those engaged in non-contact sports (from varsity teams in swimming, tennis, track, gymnastics, baseball, and basketball). On a measure of cardiovascular fitness, the contact-sport athletes proved to be the most fit; with non-contact-sport athletes following; and nonathletes, as one would expect, being the least fit. Subjects were provoked or not provoked by a same-sex peer and then provided with an opportunity to aggress against him. When subjects were not provoked, there was no appreciable difference in aggressiveness among the three groups. When provoked, nonathletes displayed the highest level of retaliatory aggression. They behaved more punitively than the combined groups of athletes. Provoked non-contact-sport athletes exhibited the least aggressiveness. Their behavior was far less punitive than that of the provoked nonathletes. Provoked contact-sport athletes, however, though they were somewhat less punitive than the provoked nonathletes, failed to be reliably less aggressive than this latter group.

Clearly, cardiovascular fitness alone cannot explain such findings. Although the lower level of retaliatory aggression in the combined groups of athletes is in line with their superior fitness, the most fit athletes, those involved in football and wrestling, failed to behave in accord with their superlative fitness. It appears that any emotion-curtailing influence their fitness may have exerted was counteracted by strong aggressive habits (and skills) formed in the pursuit of their athletic objectives (cf. Zillmann, Bryant, & Sapolsky, 1978).

In the following section, we analyze the formation and maintenance of such aggressive habits. We first present a theory of habit formation that explains the development of aggressive *and nonaggressive* habits on the basis of reactions to annoyance, and we then discuss the pertinent research evidence.

III. THE FORMATION OF HOSTILE AND AGGRESSIVE HABITS

There should be little doubt that in man, almost all hostile and aggressive behavior patterns are ontogenetically determined. The individual acquires characteristic ways of reacting to annoyance, and this acquisition is governed by the learning mechanisms discussed earlier (mainly in Chapters 4 and 5). *Incentive-motivated hostile and aggressive behavior patterns emerge and are strengthened as they prove successful in the attainment of rewards, and they are weakened as they fail to accomplish this objective or as they prompt punishment. Analogously, annoyance-motivated hostile and aggressive behavior patterns emerge and are strengthened as they effectively terminate annoyances, and they are weakened as they fail in this regard or produce further annoyance.* The formation and maintenance of hostile and aggressive habits, then, may be viewed as a continuous process in which every incidence of hostile or aggressive action or reaction modifies habit strength. Regarding the strength of hostile and aggressive habits thus controlled by reward and punishment, the habit-controlling events are, in principle, *favorable environmental changes* that are brought about by habit-associated actions. Both the attainment of incentives and the avoidance or termination of an aversive treatment are events that amount to an adaptive rearrangement of the external world. But although this operant control of hostile and aggressive habits through external stimulus changes is undoubtedly of immense importance, in annoyance-motivated behavior, *internal changes* also appear to play a significant role. To the extent that high levels of sympathetic excitation constitute an aversion, the alleviation of this internal aversive state should exert a strong effect on the formation and maintenance of associated habits.

In the study of human hostility and aggression, it was Hokanson (1970) who promoted the concept of a dual control of habit in annoyance-motivated behavior. He proposed that:

> when a person carries out a behavior that successfully "turns off" another's aggression, two types of learning hypothetically take place: (1) the successful removal of noxious stimulation reinforces the instrumental response; and (2) the pairing of the instrumental response with the physical arousal reduction that normally takes place when noxious stimulation is removed defines a Pavlovian conditioning paradigm [p. 81].

In addition to operant control, then, Hokanson invoked classical conditioning. Specifically, the dissipation of arousal is viewed as becoming classically conditioned to the performance of acts that are followed with some regularity by a dissipation of arousal. Such acts may be hostile or aggressive, but as Hokanson has stressed (1970), they may also be nonhostile and nonaggressive: "Depending on the idiosyncratic learning history of the person, *any social response* to others' aggression is potentially capable of acquiring tension-reducing concomitants [p. 81; italics added]."

Actually, the response need not be social (i.e., it need not be displayed in a social context with consequences for others), and it need not be precipitated by the aggressive behavior of others. The proposed mechanism is general enough to encompass all conceivable annoyances. Any response displayed in a state of acute annoyance that, for whatever reason, is followed with some consistency by a reduction in arousal should eventually come to induce an arousal reduction. If, for example, an acutely annoyed person were to sit down and twiddle his thumbs until arousal returned to basal levels, and if he were to do so repeatedly, the combination of sitting and thumb twiddling would soon assume some power to initiate and speed up the decay of excitation; and this quickened decay should come about whether the excitation derived from a physical assault, from a verbal insult, from some very bad news, or from apprehensions regarding future events. It should be clear, however, that not all activities lend themselves equally to this conditioning of relief. Thumb twiddling, in fact, may be a very poor choice of activity, because it has a very low capacity to intervene in the rehearsal of grievances or to disrupt the anticipatory involvement with endangerments. A prompt reduction of annoyance-induced arousal should be more readily achieved with such activities as solving puzzles or watching television.

Hokanson's proposal has some very interesting implicatons. It projects nonhostile and nonaggressive reactions to endangerment as being basically equivalent to hostile and aggressive reactions in the control of annoyance and annoyance-motivated behavior. This is in sharp contrast to the view that annoyance motivates specific hostile and aggressive behaviors (e.g., Dollard, Doob, Miller, Mowrer, & Sears, 1939), an impetus that is satisfied only when the annoyer is hurt (e.g., Berkowitz, 1965a). The social significance of the proposal should be apparent. If annoyances can indeed be reduced or terminated by nonhostile and even by so-called prosocial acts as well as by hostile actions, important guidelines for the treatment and control of annoyance and its behavioral implications may be devised. It would seem to be an oversimplification, however, to regard the arousal reduction that may be conditioned to stimuli associated with instrumental responses as a primary hostility- and aggression-controlling mechanism. We discuss the likely restrictions of the power of this mechanism when we conceive of it within the framework of three-factor theory.

A. Habit Formation Through the Alleviation of Annoyance

According to three-factor theory, the intensity of an unambiguous emotional experience is a simple function of prevailing sympathetic excitation. The intensity of the experience of annoyance is thus seen to vary with changes in sympathetic activity. Any decline of sympathetic activity is expected to effect a reduction in the intensity of experienced annoyance. This excitation-mediated reduction of the intensity of annoyance, then, constitutes *relief*. It is assumed that any appreciable reduction of the intensity of an acute annoyance is experienced as relief.

The following propositions employ this conception of relief:

1. Any response that is performed in a state of acute annoyance and that is followed by relief is reinforced.
2. Relief is conditioned to the proprioceptive stimuli of any response that is performed in a state of acute annoyance and that is followed by relief.

It should be clear that in these propositions, it is *not* stipulated that the response in question be causally involved in the evocation of relief. A causal connection between response and relief may, but need not, exist. The response, then, need not be instrumental in the sense of contributing to the cessation of the annoying stimulation. The formation of coping habits is expected on the basis of the response–relief contiguity alone.

But though response instrumentality is not a necessary condition for habit formation through the classical conditioning of relief, it appears that instrumental responses are generally favored in the paradigm. Responses that cause the reduction or termination of annoying treatments are more likely to be consistently linked with the experience of prompt relief than responses that relate to relief only by coincidence. Additionally, instrumental reactions tend to be closely associated with the circumstances in which they are instrumental. Noninstrumental reactions, in contrast, often occur in different behavioral contexts; and every occurrence in these other contexts, because it is not associated with relief, is to be regarded as an extinction trial. This fact should greatly detract from their use as coping reactions. But regardless of the instrumental value of a response, reactions that are more or less specific to annoyance should suffer less extinction interference than behaviors performed in more general contexts.

As long as only elementary instrumental or noninstrumental reactions (e.g., pushing, shoving, punching, kicking, or turning away) are being considered, it seems that the paradigm can be rather unambiguously applied. If, for example, hitting one's annoyer always leads to the termination of an acute annoyance, hitting responses to annoyance should not only be reinforced and develop into strong habits; they should also acquire the power to induce arousal reductions when performed in similar or different behavioral contexts. The expressive hitting of substitute targets should thus reduce the level of arousal and, ultimately, the intensity of annoyance, anger, and hostile behavior. On the other hand, such expressive behavior should tend to weaken the conditioned connection between hitting and arousal reduction. Unless this connection is occasionally reinstated, the effectiveness of the expressive use of a reaction whose proprioceptive cues trigger a dissipation of arousal should rapidly deteriorate. In practice, however, hitting one's annoyer is unlikely to initiate prompt relief with any regularity. It is conceivable that for people who are well developed physically, reactions such as hitting are dominantly instrumental in the reduction of annoyance. For most people, however, hitting is more likely to produce further annoyance, be it fear of retaliation, fear of social reproach, or simply an escalation of the annoyer's activity. Be this as it may, even if hitting should have great instrumental value, it is unlikely that such a basic response form is uniquely linked to annoyance. Hitting is also likely to occur in leisure activities and during participation in sports. Pitching a tent and playing tennis entail motor operations that are proprioceptively very similar, if not identical, to those of hitting in a violent confrontation. If proprioceptive cues are considered the stimuli to which the reduction of arousal is conditioned, any conditioned connection must be expected to suffer immensely from the extinction imposed by the frequent occurrence of these stimuli in situations devoid of annoyance and unrelated to elevated excitation.

The direct application of a conditioning paradigm to the experience of relief is further compromised by the nature of the conditioned response. The dissipation of excitation is a comparatively slow, time-consuming process. The point at which an arousal reduction is to be regarded as having been achieved is conceptually ambiguous. There are potentially many points in time at which excitation could be experienced as having subsided, and accordingly, there are many stimuli that could be implicated with the elicitation of the dissipation. In short, the conditioned capacity to induce relief can be projected onto a great variety of stimuli that precede or accompany the decay of excitation. In the face of such ambiguity, the choice of a "conditioned stimulus" appears to be very arbitrary.

The purpose of the foregoing discussion is, not to challenge the validity of the conditioning approach to relief, but to call its practicality into question. As suggested earlier, there is no reason to doubt the usefulness of the application of the paradigm of operant conditioning to the formation and maintenance of hostile and aggressive habits. With regard to the classical conditioning of relief, the situation is different, however. Although such conditioning may be presumed to be operative, the circumstances under which it occurs are so complex and ambiguous as to render attempts at the prediction of specific outcomes nearly impossible. This assessment applies also to the classical conditioning of relief to cues that are other than proprioceptive. If the dissipation of arousal is assumed to be conditioned to external stimuli that precede or accompany relief as well as to proprioceptive cues, the same ambiguity exists regarding the time at which the conditioned response supposedly occurs. Additionally, it is unlikely that specific external stimuli are uniquely linked with relief. The circumstances under which conditioning presumably manifests itself are thus even more complex and ambiguous than when only proprioceptive stimuli are considered.

In the application of learning paradigms to the phenomenon of relief, it is of course assumed that certain responses are strengthened and that certain stimuli develop the capacity to induce relief without any awareness on the part of the individual about these processes that control his or her behavior. If some awareness exists, it is generally assumed not to have an appreciable effect. This is where an emotion-theoretical analysis departs from learning theory. If relief is conceived of as an emotional *experience,* it is generally assumed that the individual *is aware* of his or her experiential state. In such an analysis, it is further assumed that the awareness of relief may lead to its conscious attribution to an inducing stimulus. If a conscious connection between stimulus and response is made, the consequences of an association through learning may be altered or overpowered. We now present an emotion-theoretical model of the function of relief in the formation and maintenance of annoyance-motivated habits. This model parallels the learning-theoretical approach, but as we will see, it avoids the ambiguities that the application of the paradigm of classical conditioning creates.

It is assumed that barring obtrusive annoyance-resolving outside intervention, the acutely annoyed individual who experiences relief *attributes this experience of relief to the course of action he or she has taken.*

The following propositions are based on this assumption:

3. Any course of action that is taken in a state of acute annoyance and that is followed by the experience of relief is strengthened, and the likelihood of its occurrence increases.
4. Any course of action that in the past has been followed with some regularity by the experience of relief evokes the anticipation of relief and initiates relief.

It would appear that the units of analysis in these propositions are immediately meaningful and are more useful for the purpose of prediction than the vaguely described units associated with the application of learning paradigms. The concept of "course of action" accommodates goal-directed activities from a snide remark or a slap in the face to elaborate strategies of hostile or aggressive action. It also accommodates "doing nothing" or responses such as praying and "turning the other cheek." In the application of learning paradigms, these more elaborate schemes of behavior are meaningless entities. Strictly speaking, if relief is classically conditioned, it is conditioned to stimuli that are more or less immediately antecedent. Similarly, reinforcement favors immediately preceding actions. The fact that in the application of these paradigms, much more is typically implied attests to their rather careless usage.

The stipulation that relief be experienced in order to be of consequence is the other change in the unit of analysis from learning to emotional theory. Relief is viewed as being experienced or not, and if it is experienced, it is viewed as being experienced at a particular point in time. This conceptualization avoids the earlier discussed ambiguities regarding the timing of the manifestation of relief.

In summing up, it is suggested that relief probably controls responses and is controlled by stimuli as specified in the discussed learning mechanisms but that the application of learning paradigms is of little predictive value, especially when complex patterns of hostility or aggression are being considered. Consistent with this view, the initial propositions (1 and 2) should be regarded as impractical rather than faulty. The latter two propositions (3 and 4) do not render the initial ones superfluous, however. Instead, they should be recognized as adding attributional processes to those involved in learning. As suggested earlier, attributional processes are assumed to override the mechanics of learning. If, for whatever reason, the experience of relief is not attributed to an inducing condition, the linkage between stimulus and response is governed by the more basic mechanisms of learning. Analogously to the relationship between behavior control through cognitive mediation and through learning (cf. Chapter 5, Section I), the mechanisms of learning are viewed as a back-up system to which the individual resorts by default when the superior cognitive apparatus fails or is not employed.

The discussed complementarity of learning and attributional systems is expressed in the following proposition:

5. The attribution or misattribution of the experience of relief to a particular course of action establishes a causal or pseudocausal connection that, in the control of behavior, dominates the effect of any competing learned associations. In the absence of the conscious experience of relief and the attributional considerations it is expected to prompt, relief and its implications are governed by learning mechanisms.

The ontogenetic implications of this model of habit formation are straightforward: Those responses to annoyance into which the individual, especially the child, is frequently coerced or that he or she frequently performs for whatever reason are most likely to develop into coping habits. This is because arousal eventually *has to dissipate*—if for no other reason, to achieve homeostasis. A reinforcing "drive reduction" or the experience of relief thus must follow, in principle, any activity performed by the individual. Notwithstanding the fact that activities may differ greatly in their capacity to accelerate or delay the annoyance-draining decay of excitation (cf. Section ID of this chapter), relief will follow annoyance and strengthen the behavior performed during annoyance regardless of its character. If fighting is repeatedly followed by relief, habits of fighting will be formed, and they will be maintained if fighting continues to lead to relief. If withdrawal and submission are repeatedly followed by relief, submissive habits will be formed, and if they continue to provide relief, they will be maintained. Even doing nothing about an annoyance, that is, letting it pass or hoping for a resolution through the intervention of a third party, should develop into a habitually practiced coping reaction. The latter conditions manifest Scott's (1958) principle of the passive inhibition of aggression: If hostile and aggressive modes of reaction are not practiced, they are not reinforced, and hence they cannot grow into strong habits.

The intriguing aspect of this reasoning is that *in coping with annoyance, hostile and aggressive reactions are not necessarily superior to nonhostile or nonaggressive reactions.* In fact, *because in contemporary society, hostile and aggressive reactions usually entail a greater risk of endangerment through direct reprisal or social reproach, and because they also tend to be higher in cost than nonhostile and nonaggressive reactions, the former type of response may be viewed as less intelligent and less adaptive than the latter type.*

We now turn to the discussion of the evidence on this point. Can nonaggressive reactions to annoyance, or even prosocial reactions, indeed form coping habits that alleviate annoyance as effectively as aggressive reactions?

B. Supportive Evidence

Evidence in support of the model of habit formation just presented comes chiefly from a series of experiments conducted by Hokanson and his associates (cf. Hokanson, 1970). Initially, the use of a new research procedure that was employed in the investigation of recovery from annoyance-induced excitation (cf. Section ID of this chapter) produced some unexpected results that prompted speculations regarding habit formation. Later studies were then specifically designed to test the learning interpretation of habit formation as proposed by Hokanson (propositions 1 and 2 of the foregoing model).

The critical change of research procedure was made in an investigation by Hokanson and Edelman (1966). Whereas in earlier research the annoyed subjects were *required* to perform a certain activity (e.g., administer electric shock or not), they were now *offered a choice* between an aggressive response, a quasi-beneficial response, and no response. In the context of an interaction simulation with a peer, subjects could respond—whenever they were attacked with electric shock by their interactant—by pushing buttons labeled "shock," "reward," or "no response." It was explained that pushing the "reward" button would signal an effort "to do something nice," in short, friendliness, to the interactant. In a control group, the annoyed subjects had no opportunity to take action of any kind toward their annoyer. Excitatory reactions, mainly assessed through systolic blood pressure, were recorded and traced for the particular responses the subjects elected to perform.

The consistently punitive behavior of the subject's opponent prompted marked elevations of arousal in both male and female subjects. Consistent with earlier findings (e.g., Hokanson & Burgess, 1962a), excitatory recovery in male subjects was the most pronounced after aggressive counterresponses. Nonaggressive reactions (i.e., signaling friendliness or electing to do nothing) failed to accelerate the decay of excitation. Recovery after nonaggressive reactions did not appreciably differ from that in the control condition, in which subjects could do nothing about being attacked. In sharp contrast and unexpectedly, female subjects exhibited efficient recovery no matter what counterresponse they chose. Without appreciable differences in the decay of excitation after particular chosen reactions, recovery was substantially faster after all these choices than in the control condition.

In an effort to explain the unexpected sex difference in the recovery from annoyance-induced arousal, and especially the surprising finding that annoyed females apparently recovered very efficiently after answering an attack with a friendly response, Hokanson implicated the differential, sex-specific upbringing in Western societies (Hokanson, Willers, & Koropsak, 1968):

> Females undergo a set of learning experiences in which making nonaggressive responses to someone else's aggression is rewarded: in the specific sense of thereby effectively reducing the other person's aversive behavior, and in the general sense that this behavior conforms to cultural norms and expectations. Males, on the other hand, evidently have learned that meeting another's aggression with counter-aggression is both an effective and a socially sanctioned means of controlling a peer's aversive behavior [p. 388].

Clearly, the observed sex difference in the recovery from annoyance is not projected as the result of different genetic endowments. It is instead explained as the consequence of conditioning histories with different sets of reinforcement (and punishment) contingencies. Since the prevailing cultural norms of social conduct—which undoubtedly are arbitrarily instituted and subject to change—favor males to be aggressive and females to be friendly toward an annoyer, sex differences in coping with annoyance must be expected. If males are socially rewarded for aggression (esteemed for being tough) and socially punished for failing to fight (devalued for being "sissies"), males should readily develop aggressive habits and, when provoked, should experience relief only after retaliation. Analogously, if females are punished for aggression (devalued as "bitchy") and rewarded for failing to fight (admired for behaving in a subdued manner), females should indeed become nonaggressive. They should, when provoked, take a submissive route out of annoyance and experience relief (cf. Maccoby & Jacklin, 1974).

If acculturation can thus be held responsible for the females' efficient excitatory recovery after countering an attack with a friendly reaction, the creation of different contingencies of reinforcement and punishment should alter the behavior in question. If females suddenly find themselves in a social environment where submissiveness fails to reduce annoyance whereas aggression proves effective, they should readily adapt to the new contingencies and become aggressive. Analogously, if males are placed in a social situation where being friendly reduces annoyance whereas being aggressive does not, they should quickly desert aggression and become more friendly. Hokanson, Willers, and Koropsak (1968) designed and conducted an experiment that provides a direct test of these expectations.

Male and female subjects underwent the interaction-simulating procedure. In a first phase of the experiment, a same-sex peer, actually a confederate who followed a prepared "random" schedule of "responses," attacked the subjects through the administration of electric shock. Subjects could choose either an aggressive (pushing a button labeled "shock") or a friendly (pushing a button labeled "reward") counterresponse. In a second phase, the so-called conditioning phase, the confederate punished the females whenever they displayed a friendly counterresponse to annoyance (in 90% of all such instances) and rewarded them whenever they responded aggressively (also in 90% of such instances). The male subjects received the opposite treatment. Whenever they reacted aggressively the confederate punished them, and whenever they exhibited a friendly reaction he rewarded them. In the third and final phase, the confederate returned to a random schedule of reward and punishment. The excitatory reaction to annoyance and recovery after counterresponding, measured in plethysmographically recorded vasoconstriction, was traced throughout all phases.

The findings fully corroborated the theoretical expectations. Consistent with earlier findings, females in the first phase exhibited superior recovery after friendly counterresponses, whereas recovery in males was superior after aggressive reactions in this phase. In the course of the second phase, this pattern was reversed: Females recovered more efficiently after aggressive than after friendly responses, and males recovered more efficiently after friendly than after aggressive responses. In the third phase, both female and male subjects quickly returned to their preconditioning behavior patterns.

In a very similar investigation, Stone and Hokanson (1969) provided annoyed subjects with a choice between an aggressive and a self-punitive counterresponse (i.e., the subjects administered electric shock either to their annoyer or to themselves). During the second phase of the experiment, when the subjects could avoid receiving more severe shock from their annoyer through the self-administration of shock, both female and male subjects resorted to the initially disturbing infliction of pain upon themselves. This self-infliction of pain came to induce more efficient recovery from excitation than the aggressive counterresponse upon the annoyer. This pattern of effects quickly vanished in the third phase of the experiment when the self-infliction of pain had lost the instrumental value of preventing attack.

An investigation by Sosa (1968) lends further support to the view that the recovery from annoyance-induced arousal after particular counterresponses is determined by ontogenetically established behavior patterns. Male prison inmates served as subjects. They were selected on the basis of their case histories and divided into two groups according to their characteristic past reactions to threats posed by others—those who had a history of violent reactions to endangerment and those who had a record of passive responses. It was found that recovery from annoyance-induced arousal after aggressive or nonaggressive counterresponses was consistent with the subject's past behavior in the sense that the characteristically practiced behavior proved arousal reducing. The finding that in passive, nonviolent subjects, a nonaggressive counterresponse induced efficient recovery is most revealing and again shows that the punitive treatment of an annoyer is not necessarily an efficient way to terminate or reduce an acute annoyance.

All these findings are very suggestive of the influence of prevailing contingencies of reinforcement and punishment in the formation of aggressive and nonaggressive habits, and in this sense, they support the proposed model of habit formation. It is not clear, however, exactly which of the propositions have been supported. Specifically, it is unclear whether the research evidence supports propositions 1 and 2 or propositions 3 and 4. Hokanson (e.g., 1970) apparently regarded the conditioning model to be supported (propositions 1 and 2), but this interpretation faces at least two counterarguments. First, it would appear that the contingencies of reinforcement and punishment created in the laboratory were quite obtrusive (e.g., Hokanson et al., 1968) and that the subjects could readily *recognize* the prevailing conditions. It is likely that the subjects were aware of the contingencies and acted in accord with their *appraisal* of the circumstances. Second, it seems unlikely that habits assumed to be based on a "lifetime conditioning history" can readily be reversed by just a few learning trials under the opposite contingencies of reinforcement and punishment. It seems more reasonable, then, to assume that subjects recognized the prevailing contingencies and thus could select an annoyance-minimizing response. Regardless of the nature of this response (aggressive or friendly), it should prompt recovery from excitation, because it lessens the threat of being attacked further. In this reasoning, *it is the knowledge of having reduced an endangerment and/or the anticipation of relief from annoyance that prompts the decay of excitation.* The evidence may thus be regarded as more likely to support propositions 3 and 4 than 1 and 2. But be this as it may, the evidence is certainly supportive of the overall model of habit formation.

We pointed out earlier that the intensity of hostile or aggressive behavior is not necessarily a simple function of prevailing arousal, and we have specified conditions under which such a correspondence should not be expected (cf. Section IIA of this chapter). Efficient recovery from annoyance-induced excitation thus does *not necessarily* bring with it a reduction of hostile or aggressive inclinations (cf. Bryant & Zillmann, 1978; Zillmann & Bryant, 1974; Zillmann & Cantor, 1976b). In line with this statement of caution, recent findings (Sapolsky, Stocking, & Zillmann, 1977) suggest that the documented superior nonaggressive coping skills of females do not necessarily reduce later retaliation when the retaliatory activities are entirely legitimate and without repercussions. Female and male subjects were provoked and either waited or did not wait before they could retaliate.

Females recovered more efficiently from annoyance-induced excitation during the waiting period than did males. However, when the opportunity arose to punish the annoyer, the females employed as much hostility as the males.

The cliché of the submissive female who "takes the beating" and readily "turns the other cheek" appears to be a gross oversimplification and certainly does not follow from the research data. Instead, the data show the female to be an effective minimizer of annoyance. If conditions require it, she behaves nonaggressively and even self-punitively. But as the findings reported by Stone and Hokanson (1969) show, she does so no more than the male. In fact the occurrence of self-punitive behavior was found to be lower in females than in males. It is the male, then, rather than the female who often behaves in what may be considered *nonintelligent* ways. It appears that culture, through the enforcement of the prevailing contingencies of reinforcement and punishment already discussed, forces upon the male hostile and aggressive habits that clearly run counter to the minimization of annoyance. The annoyed male is forced into efforts "to get even" regardless of whether retaliatory action constitutes intelligent behavior. He often counters an attack even when it appears that he can only become further aggravated and suffer more intensely, and he does so for such intangible manifestations of social approval and reproach as "pride" and "honor." If the minimization of aversion is employed as a yardstick of adaptive intelligence, it is not the behavior of the female but the hostile and aggressive modes of reaction of the male that are questionable and that call for correction.

7

A Comment on the Control of Hostility and Aggression

As we have seen, many writers (e.g., Dollard, Doob, Miller, Mowrer, & Sears, 1939; Freud, 1915a/1946, 1915b/1946, 1933/1950; Lorenz, 1963) have viewed hostile and aggressive behavior as manifestations of aggression instincts or aggressive drives. The individual, in these views, is presented as a creature inclined or compelled to injure anyone or to destroy anything that obstructs the attainment of his or her desires or goals. The prevalence of destructive behavior in society is seen, by and large, to be the direct result of inborn mechanisms. Such views may acknowledge that learning can modify the individual's hostile and aggressive inclinations; but clearly, the modification of these inclinations through learning is ascribed an entirely secondary role. Essentially, the individual is seen to be forced into hostile and aggressive actions by his or her very nature. The message ultimately reads that we are destructive "because of the way we are *built.*" According to such views, then, we *must* aggress, and our only hope is to *rechannel* our destructive urges so as to render them harmless.

The writers who have committed themselves to the notion of aggression instincts or specific aggressive drives thus find themselves compelled to present the related mechanisms of *displacement* and *catharsis* as the grand solutions for the curtailment of hostility and aggression in man. As we have seen, the available research evidence on the efficacy of these presumed mechanisms is decidedly negative and challenges the validity of the proposals that are derived from them. But despite this, displacement and catharsis tend to be treated as unquestionable psychological dynamics, and the projection of their beneficial effects is widely accepted.

In psychotherapy, treatments based on displacement and catharsis are more popular than ever—or so it seems. It is mainly the noninjurious expression of violence, from ripping dolls to shreds to shouting obscenities in the face of an adversary, that is believed to have great aggression-purging properties. A look at the pertinent evidence regarding the effect of hostile expressions on hostile and aggressive behavior (cf. Ebbesen, Duncan, & Konečni, 1975; Geen & Quanty, 1977) suggests that such therapy furthers rather than controls aggressiveness. But since the "aggression therapies" in question entail the vivid display of human conflict, a kind of display that has the essential characteristics of great drama, they have received much attention. The entertainment media, television in particular, have popularized the view that aggressiveness can be discharged through intense expressive actions; and to the extent that cathartic modes of conflict resolution have been adopted (through processes such as those specified in social-learning theory; cf. Bandura, 1969, 1971a), unfounded views regarding the nature of human aggression may do far more damage than good. The issue is complicated by the fact that the aggression therapies under consideration may well produce feelings of relief and subjective assessments of dissipated anger. Apparently, many patients have come to believe that the technique works for them, and their reports of the benefits of the therapeutic treatment seem to be more convincing to the lay-person than the usually poorly popularized research evidence. But although *beliefs*—such as that beating an annoyer or some substitute target with a styrofoam bat lowers the desire to harm him or her—may occasionally produce a "placebo effect" by convincing patients that they have "let it out" and that further hostile behavior is unnecessary for their well-being, the research evidence taken as a whole simply does not support the view that pseudoattacks on appropriate targets or real attacks on substitute targets lower the likelihood of further annoyance-motivated hostile or aggressive behavior.

According to Lorenz (1963) and Storr (1968), one of the greatest achievements of civilization lies in the invention of sports and sportslike competition. Such competition is viewed as "ritualized combat" in which the combatants are confined by arbitrarily set rules. These rules prevent the actual infliction of harm and injury, while the action, even when experienced only vicariously, is said to vent pent-up hostile and aggressive urges. Again, when tested empirically, these ideas have proved to be unfounded (cf. Zillmann, Bryant, & Sapolsky, 1978). The available evidence suggests that intense competition, especially when it involves elements of aggression, is likely to enhance rather than curtail hostility and aggression. Competition produces losers and with it, annoyance, debasement, humiliation, and the motivation to retaliate and avenge. The proposal that international competition, whether through sports (Lorenz) or through such matters of national pride as space exploration (Storr), can only promote international understanding reveals great faith in theoretical convictions, but it amounts to a risky proposition indeed.

The advocates of the catharsis doctrine have placed their trust in a number of further remedies, the foremost of which is humor. Lorenz (1963) presented humor as a blessing to mankind, and he suggested that we had better take it more seriously. Laughing is seen as a ritualized threat gesture, and it is said to produce sudden relief. Other researchers (e.g., Fry, 1977) have suggested that laughter is an appeasement gesture and that it can pacify the annoyed. But it appears that humor can as readily, if not more readily, be employed as a demeaning, punishing, and hence aggression-instigating treatment (Bergson, 1908; Zillmann, 1977; Zillmann & Cantor, 1976a). Regardless of such objections, however, it is unclear how the use of humor, even if it should have a beneficial effect under specific social circumstances, could be instituted so as to help curb violence in society. The same applies to other projected cathartic remedies such as involvement in fine arts or the sciences (Lorenz, 1963). How could an interest in art or educational involvement be instilled in the annoyed or angry person? And how could laughter be forced upon those ready to strike? The suggestion that hostility and aggression in society can be curtailed through laughter, art, and epistemic curiosity, idealistic as it may be, not only rests on shaky theoretical grounds; it also would be difficult if not impossible to implement.

It has been our position that aggressive instincts or specific aggressive drives do not exist in man. Remedial solutions to such presumed, inherent destructive forces thus are pointless and unnecessary. Needless to say, any attempt to obtain aggression catharsis through ritualized or displaced activity per se is futile in our view. Hostility and aggression in society are likely to be unaltered—or may possibly increase—after all the dolls have been ripped apart, all the china smashed, and all the obscenities shouted. But the lack of a grand design for remedies does not mean that effective solutions to the problem of hostility and aggression cannot be projected. We now outline some measures that, if taken, should help to curtail harm- and injury-inflicting behaviors.

First of all, it should be clear from our analysis of hostility and aggression that these behaviors will be with us as long as the essential functions they serve prevail. Thus, although we deny that man must aggress because of his nature, he *will*, in all probability, aggress and behave in hostile ways because these behaviors will continue to be instrumental: (a) in helping him gain incentives at low cost, and (b) in providing a comparatively efficient means of ridding himself of annoyance. Man is hostile and aggressive, then, not because he follows inborn impulses, but because these behaviors have *utility*. It may be conjectured that if they had no utility, they would long ago have vanished in the evolution of man. But as we have argued earlier, it is unlikely that these behaviors will ever lose their utility. Hostility and aggression, then, are not viewed as residues of man's "dark" past, residues that are dwindling as we advance to presumably higher levels of civilization. On the contrary, hostility and aggression are here to stay, and we must devise strategies for the effective control of these behaviors. In the event that we succeed in curtailing harm- and injury-inflicting behaviors, we are well advised to remember that we have not erased their motivational bases and that potentially, any re-creation of the conditions that give them utility will lead to new eruptions of violence and destruction.

The solution to the problems of hostility and aggression is simple in principle: These behaviors have to be deprived of their utility. In practice, however, the implementation of this objective is enormously complex. From the outset, we have to separate the two basic forms of utility we have discussed: the attainment of incentives and the alleviation of annoyance. These two forms of utility have usually been confounded in recommendations for hostility- and aggression-controlling strategies, and the issue has consequently been blurred.

The *reduction of incentive-motivated hostility and aggression* has two principal solutions: (a) Valued commodities and services must be distributed equitably; and (b) any gain through the coercive actions in question must be nullified and/or the actions must be equitably and consistently punished.

With regard to the first part of this solution, it appears that incentive-motivated transgressions will be the most frequent when commodities and services are inequitably distributed and those who are deprived perceive themselves to be entitled to the commodities and services controlled by the privileged. Any appreciable change toward a more equitable distribution, then, may be expected to produce a notable reduction of the frequency of incentive-motivated transgressions within a social system.

It would seem naive, however, to assume that even if an entirely equitable distribution of valued commodities and services could be reached, incentive-motivated transgressions would cease to occur. Theoretically speaking, as long as a social system includes some convenience-minded individuals who feel that they need to contribute less and/or are entitled to more (and surely there will be some), hostile and aggressive transgressions will occur. The valued commodities and services can, of course, be protected so as to make their attainment more effortful. Characteristically, however, any protection is economically limited to a portion of the cash value of the protected entity, and this leaves room for a "profit" (gain minus effort) of transgressive actions. Thus, no matter how ideal the distribution of valued commodities and services may be, the temptation to gain further incentives through coercive action, especially when it entails minimal effort, will not be eliminated.

But notwithstanding the foregoing consideration of a hypothetical situation, there should be little doubt that any progress toward a more equitable distribution of obligations and benefits in society will help curb incentive-motivated violent transgressions (and along with it, a good deal of related annoyance-motivated hostility and aggression). A look at recent history, especially at the many social reforms that have taken place (often in the aftermath of considerable violence), shows that great strides have been made in narrowing the gap between the great wealth of a few and the extreme poverty of so many. It appears that such progress has been made regardless of the particular political doctrines that have prevailed in the various "progressive" nations around the world. However, a look at contemporary societies leaves no doubt about the fact that gross inequities in the distribution of obligations and benefits, in services rendered and in privileges attained, still exist. Although the magnitude of the problem may differ from nation to nation, it seems that modern society is still faced with the acute problem of controlling incentive-motivated crime and political violence by reducing the discrepancy between the extreme wealth of some (i.e., wealth far beyond that needed to achieve "a high standard of living") and the extreme poverty of others (i.e., a lack of means to maintain good health).

A reduction in the existing vast variation of personal "buying power" (i.e., the individual's capacity to attain sought commodities and services through noncoercive means) appears to be necessary if high levels of interpersonal (and possibly international) violence are to be curbed over extended periods of time. Clearly, there can be no return to the antiquated acceptance of birthrights and similar institutions that grant "unearned" privileges to some. The informed citizen of modern society, unlike the subjects of kings and other noblemen of earlier times, cannot tolerate what he or she recognizes as arbitrarily granted privileges. And although some remnants of ancient birthrights, manifest in inheritance laws, have survived and are generally not recognized as such, the citizen of modern society possesses a keener sense of fairness regarding the relationship between services rendered and compensations granted. Apparently, this citizen can accept *earned* wealth, that is, wealth attained by someone for providing valued services. But it seems that this citizen grows increasingly intolerant of benefits granted to people who cannot be considered deserving of them. Seeing those who were "born rich," who "make money on money," and who "get richer" without ever doing anything constructive seems to fuel much incentive-motivated violence in society. It also gives the perpetrators of this violence cause to perceive their actions as rectifying a grave injustice: their being disprivileged by birth.

Given the uncensored use of the media of communication, it is inconceivable that the public could be kept ignorant of gross economic disparities that exist. (If anything, the media may exaggerate existing disparities, especially in the context of dramatic fare.) Public awareness is likely to breed social and political unrest that ultimately leads to hostilities and to violence. But though minor eruptions of such violence may be "economically tolerable" (i.e., the destruction they cause can be readily absorbed by the prevailing economic system without requiring changes), in considering the welfare of all the people in the long run, it seems that there is no alternative to the greatest possible equity in obligations and benefits.

Regarding the second part of the proposed solution, it appears that punishment of some form is essential to increase the cost of incentive-motivated transgressions and thereby deter such action. If the transgression has been committed, any gain, particularly when the incentives usurped have already been consumed, must be compensated for through punishment. The latter is necessary if only to assure the deterrent value of punishment.

We have seen that likely aversive consequences are an effective deterrent to hostile and aggressive behavior. Punishment works; and projections to the contrary (e.g., Skinner, 1953)—which in any event derive mainly from the consideration of annoyance-motivated actions—are simply misleading. Skinner's proposal of alternatives to punishment, for example, is entirely unworkable for incentive-motivated transgressions. Neither forgetting, nor extinction, nor the conditioning of incompatible behavior will help solve the problem of incentive-motivated noncriminal or criminal transgressions. The lure of great incentives attainable without the risk of punishment is unlikely to deteriorate mechanically as time passes; extinction is not to be expected if the coercive attainment of incentives succeeds at minimal cost; and the conditioning of innumerable, potentially less reinforced alternative reactions must be regarded as a totally hopeless undertaking. It appears that a society that deprives itself, for whatever ethical reasons, of the use of punishment to curtail incentive-motivated hostile and aggressive transgressions will have to accept a high incidence of such transgressions. On the other hand, there is little doubt that incentive-motivated coercive behavior can be effectively reduced through punishment. If the use of punishment is accepted in principle, the moral issue becomes one of making it humane and equitable and of applying it consistently. The problems with inequitable and inconsistently applied punishment have long been recognized (e.g., Bentham, 1789/1948) but certainly have not been resolved.

In the controversy over punishment, two distinct functions of punishment have not been separated as they should have been, and this has led to considerable confusion. Punishment can be treated as a *corrective* or as a *deterrent*, and its efficacy can be measured in the degree to which it serves one or the other function. It should be measured in the degree to which it serves *both* functions. In practice, however, presumably because data on the corrective function abound and data on the deterrent function are scarce, the overall effectiveness of punishment has been judged mainly by its corrective value (or, to be more accurate, by the apparent lack thereof).

We have indicated the plight of reformatory institutions earlier. Apparently, punishment is *not* an effective means of converting a hardened criminal into a law-abiding citizen. And it may well be that the punitive measures of parents, educators, and supervisors fail to lower the future incidence of transgressive actions that their perpetrators consider likely to go undetected. But even if punishment has little or no corrective value (in the sense of reducing the likelihood of future transgressions by the punished transgressor), it does not follow in any compelling way that its deterrent value is also negligible. In fact, even if it were true, as some have suggested, that punitive treatments further rather than diminish the transgressive inclinations in question, the demonstrated anticipation-based power of punishment as a deterrent remains unaltered. The two functions of punishment, then, are largely independent, and the hasty dismissal of its deterrent value on the basis of its questionable corrective value is unwarranted.

In light of the doubtful corrective value of punishment, it may indeed smack of "retaliation" and appear inhumane to punish severely those who have committed transgressions in which others were harmed. As a convicted killer who shot the proprietor of a liquor store in cold blood recently put it in a televised interview: "Putting me in jail don't bring him back to life!" Since it would presumably also fail to prevent the killer's future engagement in similar criminal transgressions, punishment seems to have only the practical value of "keeping him off the streets" for some time.

Such an assessment is faulty, however. First, reformatory efforts may not be as ineffective and futile as some have alleged, and it would seem possible to improve on the effectiveness of existing programs. But some basic considerations are more important. Although leniency and forgivingness toward convicted criminals, and for that matter, toward those who have transgressed in the family context or in educational settings, may be regarded as a humanitarian gesture (in the case of criminal transgressions, it may be economically advantageous, too), it clearly *undermines the deterrent value of punishment*. The failure to punish or the failure to apply the full amount of a designated punishment to some transgressors signals to all other potential transgressors the absence of punitive consequences or at least the absence of severe punitive consequences (cf. Bandura, 1973a). The failure to punish a few, then, encourages transgressive actions by many others.

Leniency and forgivingness in the application of the punishment that is prescribed for particular transgressions by formal or informal stipulations (i.e., by legal specifications or by prevailing rules of social conduct) are usually presented as acts of great virtue. But although such acts accord with some moral systems and consequently bring recognition and esteem to those who advocate and practice them (not to mention that it also tends to be convenient not to have to go through the potentially distressing actions of punishing those who need to be punished), they may also be construed as immoral. Clearly, if within a social system it is attempted to prevent certain harm-inflicting and destructive actions by placing them under specified penalties, and if those who elect to violate the punitive arrangements in pursuit of personal gain are not punished (or not punished in full), an injustice is inflicted upon all those who resisted the temptation of furthering their self-interest through similar violations. The conception of a so-called just world, in which punitive contingencies are created to eliminate socially undesirable behaviors, requires that these contingencies *be applied* under the appropriate circumstances—or that they be changed or removed for *all* individuals, so that *all* can act in accord with the altered contingencies.

As we have pointed out earlier, a punitive contingency amounts to a contractual arrangement between two parties: the one to whom the contingency applies and the other who enforces it. In a just world, all individuals *must* enjoy the same rights. One of these rights is the right to protection from harm and injury by others. To assure that this protection is extended to all individuals, it is each individual's obligation to accept and act in accordance with the punitive contingencies set up to apply equally to all. Obviously, a just world cannot be built when transgressors are sometimes punished in full, sometimes in part, and sometimes not at all. A system of contractual arrangements that is inconsistently used fails to serve justice, and it is likely to breed discontent, annoyance, and overt hostilities.

Since—in order to control excessive hostility, aggression, and violence in human society—the use of some form of punishment seems inevitable, and since the "ethics of punishment" manifest in the controversy over punishment appear to be in disarray, the punishment issue is in dire need of reassessment. In such a reassessment, the analysis of the following three aspects of punishment should prove particularly informative: (1) What are *humane* forms of punishment? (2) What are the implications of *equity* in punishment? And (3), what are the consequences of the *consistent use* of punishment?

Punishment, by definition, entails the infliction of aversion. Forms of hostility (mainly the withholding or removing of gratifying entities or conditions that does not involve the infliction of physical pain or injury), although their use may be judged as inappropriate by some, may be considered effective punishers. Some forms of aggression may be equally effective, but their use may more readily be branded as inhumane. Regardless of ethical considerations, however, the infliction of pain and injury, as we have seen earlier, is likely to serve as an instigation to further hostility and aggression. Punitive aggression must be expected to produce intense aversions that are associated with high levels of excitation. Such aversions tend to prompt counteraggression. Under the circumstances, counteraggression amounts to further transgression, which in turn calls for increased punitive aggression. But punitive aggression is not only likely to escalate aggression; it is also likely to be perceived as inappropriate and unjust by the punished party. This should further the experience of annoyance and suggest retaliatory action. Perhaps most importantly, punitive aggression may readily get out of hand, mainly because of the punishing agent's excitatory experience, and become excessive (as has been so often observed in the abusive punitive treatment of children). Taken together, the effectiveness of punishment through aggression is doubtful. If the risk of injury is added, the cost of human suffering inflicted by punitive aggression appears to outweigh by far the benefits that can possibly be attained through it. If one further considers the nondestructive, noninjurious punitive alternatives available, the use of pain- and injury-inflicting punishment must be regarded as impractical and unnecessary, if not as intolerable and inhumane. In the family context, in educational settings, and especially in the control of criminal transgressions, the use of physical force may well be required and justified in preventing or in terminating destructive behaviors and in subduing the perpetrators; but it seems that society is well advised to avoid altogether the use of any pain- or injury-inflicting punishment as a corrective or as a deterrent.

As has been noted earlier, the concept of equity in punishment is difficult to operationalize. It is easy to say that the punishment should fit the crime, but any "fit," it seems, can be viewed in different ways and meet with the approval of some and the contempt of others. These difficulties notwithstanding, there may exist a considerable degree of consensus as to what constitutes equitable punishment for which transgression.

In order to be effective as a corrective, punishment must accord with such a consensus on equity. Only if the transgressor regards him- or herself as deserving of punishment and perceives the punishment itself as equitable (the latter being most likely when a high degree of consensus exists) will the punishment be accepted as a retributive measure. If it is considered too severe, it is likely to instigate hostility and aggression rather than help control these behaviors. As Bentham (e.g., 1789/1948) has insisted, "unreasonable" penalties, which tend not to be applied because they cannot be considered equitable punishment, foil the entire punitive system.

Bentham's argument applies to the use of punishment as a deterrent as well. If penalties are so severe that judges, educators, and supervisors fail to apply them, the punishment cannot be an effective deterrent. But unlike in the analysis of punishment as a corrective, the equity of punishment is of little moment in its deterrent function. In fact, if designated punishments were consistently applied, the deterrent value of punishment would increase with its severity. If, for example, a year in prison were considered an equitable punishment for bank robbery, a ten-year term would obviously be a greater deterrent; and a twenty-year term that might be considered grossly inequitable by most would serve as an even greater deterrent in spite of its possible moral inappropriateness.

This brings us back to consistency in the use of punishment. Only if punishment is *consistently employed* on all occasions and across all members of a social system can it be hoped that it will function as an effective deterrent.

Only if it is employed consistently can one expect that it will be widely perceived as just, and only if it is perceived as just can it be hoped to serve a corrective function. Great variability in sentencing criminal transgressors, whatever the cause of such variability may be, can only have detrimental effects. Likewise, the educator and supervisor who punishes only some transgressions creates an unjust punitive system of low efficacy, and the parents who threaten their children with stiff penalties that they will not carry out destroy the very conditions under which punishment as a deterrent can be effective.

In summary, it appears that incentive-motivated hostility and aggression in society can be curbed: (a) through a reduction of existing disparities in nontransgressive access to valued commodities and services, and (b) through punishment. Punishment as a deterrent is likely to be effective: (a) when it is consistently applied; (b) when it is severe; and (c) when it does not entail the infliction of physical pain or injury. Punishment appears to be a rather ineffective corrective. It should be the least ineffective: (a) when consistently applied, (b) when perceived as equitable, and (c) when not entailing forms of aggression. In combining the deterrent and corrective functions of punishment, the main stipulations for effective punishment are: (a) that it be consistently used; (b) that its magnitude be within reason; and (c) that it be devoid of elements of aggression. The consistent use of punishment appears to be the most critical factor in establishing an effective deterrent system. It should be recognized that an effective deterrent system, by reducing the incidence of punishable transgressions, minimizes the actual use of punishment. Also, as fewer transgressors need be punished, the doubtful corrective function of punishment is less drawn upon.

The *reduction of annoyance-motivated hostility and aggression* appears to be even more complex an issue than that of incentive-motivated transgressions. In considering the transgressive behaviors that are precipitated by annoyance, it is instructive to distinguish between hostile and aggressive behavior that seeks to *terminate an acute annoyance* and that which is performed to *punish an annoyer* for the purpose of retribution. The former type of behavior is characteristically associated with high levels of excitation. Since anticipatory skills are impaired in such a state, punitive consequences are not fully recognized. Under these circumstances, punishment should be a poor deterrent indeed. In contrast, retaliatory behavior that serves the punishment of an annoyer is mostly performed after the annoyed individual has partially or fully recovered from the excitatory reaction associated with the annoyance. The individual should have regained his or her anticipatory skills and should be sensitive and responsive to punitive contingencies.

As we have pointed out, the motivation to punish an annoyer for having inflicted an aversive experience is mainly mediated by moral considerations.

In a sense, the individual who entertains intuitive or more formal notions of justice is a vigilante. He or she is intolerant of annoyers and unforgiving, punishing according to his or her moral convictions. As long as the individual's convictions correspond with societal rules of social conduct, the punitive actions obviously meet with social approval. If such a correspondence does not exist, however, and punitive actions against annoyers are excessive in terms of the prevailing rules of conduct, the problem of curtailment arises. Since retaliatory, punitive actions are characteristically taken when the individual is experiencing intermediate levels of excitation, and his or her anticipatory skills are intact, there is no reason to doubt that punishment would function effectively as a deterrent to excessive punitive actions. It appears, then, that the use of excessive punishment can be controlled by threatening the punisher with punishment.

Our analysis of the effectiveness of punishment both as a deterrent and as a corrective in the curtailment of incentive-motivated hostility and aggression fully applies to the control of annoyance-motivated hostility and aggression as long as such behavior is associated with intermediate levels of excitation. These excitatory conditions, which are of course those that favor cognitive response guidance through the anticipation of aversive consequences, should be more likely *after* an acute annoyance than *during* such an experience. As a consequence, the anticipation-based deterrent value of punishment is likely to be more critically involved in the curtailment of retaliatory actions than in that of hostility and aggression aimed at terminating acute annoyances.

As we have stressed earlier, annoyance-motivated hostile and aggressive behavior is the most destructive and uncontrolled when the associated excitatory reactions are extremely intense. The severely annoyed, enraged individual resorts to learned coping reactions and punitive habits that may inflict considerable harm, injury, or devastation. In short, hostility and aggression are the most dangerous when they become highly emotional affairs. Because of the impairment of anticipatory skills, the deterrent value of punishment is minimal and may become entirely negligible. The key factor in the control of this type of hostility and aggression thus becomes to *prevent* the annoyed individual from becoming highly excited or if this cannot be accomplished, to *prevent* him or her from acting destructively as long as the state of extreme excitation prevails.

There have been some radical proposals with regard to the de-emotionalization of hostility and aggression. Pharmaceutical and surgical procedures have been suggested (e.g., Moyer, 1971) to keep excitatory reactions under control. In pathological cases, drug treatments and surgical intervention have in some cases produced favorable results. An analogous treatment of the population at large, with the consent of the people involved, remains the pharmacologist's and brain surgeon's utopia, however. It is, politically speaking, unrealistic and naive. It also is misleading in that it projects a nonviolent *and* happy society. Apparently, it is assumed that the pharmaceutical and surgical intervention in hostility and aggression would be highly specific (in the sense of de-emotionalizing hostile and aggressive behavior only). This, in all probability, is overly optimistic. It is far more likely that the chemical and surgical neutralization of the affective component of hostility and aggression would affect other emotions as well. As experiences of annoyance and anger are deprived of their excitatory concomitants, experiences of joy and happiness are likely to be similarly deprived of their excitatory basis. In other words, the pharmaceutical and surgical prevention of intensely felt annoyances will make other feelings "flat". and "empty," including those that are deemed highly desirable.

Barring the use of drugs and surgical intervention, the research evidence suggests a powerful means of preventing impulsive destructive behavior in the early provision of information that diminishes the threat that can be perceived in an annoyance. If, as will be recalled, information about any existing mitigating circumstances is supplied *prior to* a person's annoying conduct (e.g., that the conduct is due to some handicap or to a disturbance the annoyer is suffering—but not to malice), excitatory reactions will be quite moderate. Feelings of anger, in turn, will lack intensity, and the hostile and aggressive reactions they mediate will be comparatively weak. The extreme arousal reactions that are accompanied by the temporary impairment of cognitive faculties are thus averted because: (a) the individual is *prepared* for what might happen (a condition known to prevent strong arousal reactions; cf. Leventhal, 1974); and (b) he or she has preappraised the happenings as *nonthreatening*. The person who has recognized the annoyer's dilemma, and who is prepared for a nonmalicious annoyance, is likely to be quite tolerant and possibly even compassionate. If an annoying treatment can only be attributed to malice, however, an emotional reaction can probably not be avoided. Under these circumstances, the annoyance constitutes an endangerment, and a nonemotional reaction of tolerance and compassion might be maladaptive.

The suggestion that impulsive hostile and aggressive behavior be controlled through the early provision of mitigating information may appear to be a very modest proposal. It should be recalled, however, that annoyance-motivated violence in society is primarily an emotional affair between intimates and that it often occurs when the parties in conflict are aroused to a point where they perceive more malice than actually exists. It should also be recalled that such violence (homicide and assault resulting in severe injury, in particular) is frequently precipitated by an initially trivial conflict. It would appear, then, that much extreme anger, and ultimately much tragedy, can be avoided by alerting those who suffer annoyances to their annoyers' predicaments and shortcomings. In this context, it would seem that the expression of personal grievances and acute irritations is beneficial and should be encouraged. Disturbed persons who annoy others without letting them know about their own problems are likely to be perceived as behaving maliciously and to become targets for apparently justified retaliatory assaults.

If extreme excitatory reactions to threatening, annoying treatments and consequently intensely experienced annoyances cannot be prevented, two principal objectives in the control of impulsive hostile and aggressive behavior are immediately apparent: First, efforts must be made to *minimize the opportunity for destructive action*; and second, efforts must be made to *initiate and facilitate the dissipation of the extreme excitatory activity*. The latter objective serves to *restore* the individual's cognitive faculties. More specifically, it serves to restore anticipatory skills and thus to *reestablish cognitive response guidance*.

The wisdom expressed in this proposal is very old indeed. The impulsiveness of the reactions of extremely aroused persons has long been understood on an intuitive basis. This is apparent in such typical advice of a third party as to "simmer down" or to "sleep on it" before actions are taken. Surely, as we have said earlier, such advice is generally not appreciated, and it tends to be rejected by acutely annoyed persons. Acutely annoyed individuals are motivated to act so as to terminate their experiential state, and they are acutely ready to act. They are unlikely to seek conditions that deter them from acting out their response dispositions. Deterrence is often imposed upon them by their immediate environment, however. It is manifest in third-party intervention and in distracting stimulation generally.

Effective third-party intervention can be achieved either by temporarily separating the antagonistic parties or by depriving the annoyed person of means of inflicting severe harm or injury upon the annoyer.

Regarding the separation of the potential assailant and available targets, the removal of these targets is certainly preferable to attempts to physically restrain the aroused, annoyed individual. An effort to constrain an enraged person is likely to be treated as an annoyance itself, and it tends to prompt the impulsive person to lash out at those who are attempting to thwart the initial hostile or aggressive goal reactions.

The removal of weapons is obviously a measure to be taken. The destructive potential of an unarmed raging individual may be considerable, but it is minor when compared to that of such a person equipped with a dagger, a pitchfork, or a gun. The devastating consequences of the ready availability of all kinds of firearms are beyond doubt. In the United States and in many other countries, the number of heated arguments that are settled with the blast of a handgun is staggering. Such conflicts might terminate with black eyes and bloody noses if the weapons were a bit harder to come by.

Instead, these weapons are waiting in the pockets of so many people who easily become upset and are ready to use them to resolve their immediate problems with little regard for what happens thereafter.

Beyond rearranging the annoyed and aroused person's physical environment so as to make impulsive destructive reactions unlikely or impossible, third-party intervention can be effective through the provision of information. Reports of mitigating circumstances that may exist (which could also be supplied by the annoyer him- or herself) should initiate the decay of noxious arousal and thus provide relief. Although the hostility- and aggression-reducing effect of such information presented during or after annoyance is less pronounced than when the information is known beforehand, there is little doubt that it has a strong pacifying, calming effect. Furthermore, mere distraction may have highly beneficial consequences. It will be recalled that brooding over a mistreatment can maintain excitation at elevated levels. The suggestion that acutely annoyed persons be left to themselves appears to be poor advice, because being alone fosters ideal conditions for the arousal-perpetuating rehearsal of threats and grievances. As we have seen earlier, any distracting stimulation that does not relate to the individual's experiential state tends to have a calming effect, and the more absorbing it is, the more pacifying it is. The hedonic properties of the intervening stimulation seem important, too. The calming effect is likely to be stronger, the more pleasant the affective responses evoked by the distracting stimuli. Needless to say, noncommunicative absorbing activities should produce similar consequences.

The fact that in the discussion of the control of impulsive hostility and aggression, we have focused on third-party intervention does not mean that the potential victim of an assault or the annoyed person him- or herself cannot act so as to lower the likelihood of outbursts or prevent them altogether. We have pointed out already that the potential victim may be the party who presents information about mitigating conditions. The most effective maneuver on the potential victim's part is, no doubt, to avoid any further instigating actions. In fact, he or she should avoid any further confrontation and withdraw, if possible, until the acute annoyance has dissipated. But whereas withdrawal is an obviously effective means of preventing violent action, the potential victim's efforts to calm down an acutely annoyed person through distraction seem bound to fail, because the target's reminding presence is likely to nullify any beneficial effect the distracting stimulation may have.

Conceivably, impulsive destructive behavior can also be curtailed by the annoyed person's own precautionary actions. If highly disturbing interactions can be anticipated, the person who expects to suffer unavoidable annoyances could manage his or her own environment, so to speak. He or she could remove weapons and arrange for absorbing distractions. The individual could also develop interoceptive sensitivity (informally by paying close attention to cues that precede emotional outbursts, or more formally through programs such as biofeedback training) and then escape from a confrontation that seems to be leading to violent reactions. But these possible precautionary measures are unlikely to be critically involved in the curtailment of violence because: (a) they can be taken only if extreme annoyances can be anticipated (and characteristically, they cannot); and (b) they require an extraordinary degree of self-discipline on the part of the potential assailant. Such extreme self-discipline is certainly the exception rather than the rule, and even in those who can master it, it can only serve in the described precautionary function. Additionally, even those persons distinguished by the utmost of foresight and discipline should behave impulsively once their excitatory activity reaches extremely high levels. It is possible, however, that particularly "impulsive" individuals (i.e., persons who experience outbursts frequently and at seemingly minor provocation) can greatly benefit from acquiring a higher degree of interoceptive sensitivity, so that they can be alerted to their propensity for violent action and can take any preventive actions they may be motivated to take.

In summary, it appears that annoyance-motivated hostility and aggression in society can be curtailed mainly: (a) through punishment, and (b) through maneuvers that deprive potentially impulsive reactions of their excitatory component. Our specification of the deterrent and corrective value of punishment for incentive-motivated transgressions fully applies to annoyance-motivated hostile and aggressive behaviors that are associated with intermediate levels of excitation. In brief, primarily because anticipatory skills are intact, the stipulations for effective punishment are: (a) that it be consistently used; (b) that its magnitude be within reason; and (c) that it be devoid of aggression. In sharp contrast, the deterrent value of punishment is considered negligible for actions taken under extreme excitatory conditions. However, punishment may have a corrective effect under these circumstances: As an aversive contingency, it should be expected to reduce the strength of hostile and aggressive habits. Impulsive destructive actions can be prevented, in principle: (a) by holding excitation to moderate levels, thereby keeping cognitive response guidance intact; (b) by promoting the dissipation of noxious arrousal, thereby restoring cognitive response guidance; and (c) by minimizing the opportunity for destructive assaults during extreme annoyance.

In the foregoing discussion of the curtailment of *impulsive* destructive behavior, we have treated this behavior as a widespread phenomenon in society. As the records on impulsive homicide and impulsive beatings in various social contexts show, the magnitude of the phenomenon together with its societal significance cannot be denied. But the fact that impulsive destructive behavior is widespread and penetrates all social strata and all facets of life should not be taken to mean that we have to accept impulsive reactions as a "natural occurrence." If, as we have argued, cognitive response guidance diminishes and fails under conditions of extreme excitation and behavior comes to be controlled mainly by acquired habits, impulsive destructive behavior can be prevented by *preventing hostile and aggressive habits from developing.*

The prevention of the formation of impulsive destructive response tendencies may well constitute the most effective societal means of curtailing violence. Plainly, if impulsive destructive habits are not acquired, they cannot come into play as the cognitive guidance of behavior is impaired. As we have pointed out, the transitory cognitive incapacitation is not only a typical accompaniment of extreme arousal states, but relatively independent of prevailing excitatory conditions, it also is the result of many forms of intoxication. Again, when cognitive faculties are impaired through intoxication, impulsive destructive reactions cannot be performed if they have not been acquired beforehand. In fact, it appears that the only effective way of curbing the societal violence connected with various forms of intoxication (especially with alcoholic intoxication) is to prevent the formation of destructive habits (if the intoxication itself cannot be prevented).

In theory, as we have seen earlier, the conditions under which hostile and aggressive habits can*not* be formed are very clear. They are well expressed in Scott's (1958) passive-inhibition principle. Obviously, if the performance of hostile and aggressive reactions can be prevented through social disapproval and, if necessary, the threat of more severe contingent punishment, such reactions cannot be reinforced and come under stimulus control. In practice, however, the required conditions are difficult to institute. It is mainly in the family and in school contexts that hostile and aggressive habits are likely to be formed; and in spite of the parents' and educators' efforts to discourage and prevent destructive behavior, such behavior may be greatly reinforced in peer interactions—at least in some children. In particular, it is difficult to see how in countless interactions that are not supervised by parents or teachers, the physically superior child, who can readily get things his or her way through force and the threat of force, could be prevented from developing coercive and potentially destructive aggressive habits. It seems that the peer-interaction conditions that must be assumed to exist in many families and in schools generally favor the development of impulsive aggressive habits in firstborn children, especially when the next born is substantially younger, and in children whose physical development is ahead of that of their peers. But such difficulties in the implementation of Scott's proposal should not detract from the fact that it presents a basic solution to the problem of violence in society. Every step we can take toward eliminating the formation of impulsive hostile and aggressive habits should bring progress in the curtailment of impulsive destructive violence.

The work of Hokanson (1970), whose implications for the curtailment of violence appear to have been largely neglected, complements and extends Scott's proposal in that it shows the relief-inducing capacity of nonhostile and nonaggressive reactions to annoyance to be potentially equivalent to that of destructive reactions. But nonhostile and nonaggressive reactions will provide relief only if they have been practiced under conditions of acute annoyance. In other words, they will be effective only if habits of nonviolent reactions to provocation have been formed. The acquisition of such habits, then, must be the objective of efforts to curtail violence in society. Not only must we discourage and prevent destructive reactions altogether; we also must encourage and support all nondestructive actions taken in response to provocation and under conditions of acute annoyance.

In summary, it appears that impulsive destructive behavior can be effectively curtailed: (a) by preventing violent habits from developing, and (b) by assuring the development of alternative nonviolent habits. It should be recognized that this proposal is diametrically opposed to that of the curtailment of aggression through the uninhibited display of hostile and aggressive substitute actions. And it should further be recognized that in contrast to the "aggression therapies" discussed earlier, which stand on shaky theoretical and empirical grounds, the foregoing proposal is founded on research findings and accords well with the evidence at hand.

In our discussion of the various proposals for controlling hostility and aggression in society, we have pointed out the difficulties associated with their implementation. Violence-curtailing measures cannot be instituted simply by informing the public about them and their beneficial effects. They cannot be instituted by appeals alone. People cannot simply be told to be more sensitive to the problems others may cope with. They cannot be instructed to be more tolerant and compassionate. When annoyed, they cannot readily be talked into postponing the violent actions they may be prepared to perform. They also cannot simply be told to play the part of a benevolent intermediary in the potentially hostile and aggressive conflicts of others. It seems that social sensitivity and responsibility cannot be created through education and persuasion only. They can conceivably be created, however, by setting up contingencies of approval and reproach that, in contrast to the status quo, condemn rather than glorify machismo and that support rather than punish the resolution of conflict through tolerance and compassion. These contingencies, in order to be effective, must penetrate all domains of human life, all facets of human affairs. They must be continually present in the home, in the school, on the job, and in public places.

This amounts to suggesting that in order to curtail hostile and aggressive behaviors, we ought to change our societal and cultural values regarding them. Such a suggestion is easily made, but change in the indicated direction is unlikely to occur. First, it is highly improbable that the entertainment arts, which may be regarded as the primary displayers of prevailing values in society, will advocate change. The commercial nature of the entertainment media assures their adherence to hostility and aggression in the context of established values, as elements of a best-selling formula (cf. Zillmann, Bryant, & Sapolsky, 1978). Attempts to censure violence are bound to fail under these circumstances. Moreover, it remains questionable whether the entertainment media could be effective in instituting (rather than reflecting) social change. Second, it is unlikely that formal and informal education can do much more than it has done all along, namely pay lip service to the peaceful resolution of conflict. Educational efforts are hampered by the fact that hostility and aggression have utility, and any misrepresentation of this fact would violate the principal value of education: truthfulness. Hostile and aggressive behavior, as we have seen, cannot always be denied on rational grounds.

Education can do much more, however, than advocate a canon of "oughts" and "ought nots" regarding hostility and aggression. It can correct distorted views of hostility, aggression, violence, and emotion. It can call into question the popular convictions concerning catharsis. It can challenge the currently fashionable reverence for "deep" gut reactions and feelings as substitutes for reason. And it can make a case for impulse control by projecting the devastation invited by popular maxims such as "Let it all hang out!"

In the realm of hostility and aggression, we cannot permit total freedom. The laissez faire philosophy that has proved to be very convenient for the educator is unworkable in this domain. A person's right to punch obviously must end where another person's nose starts. No one can be permitted to inflict harm and injury on impulse. No one has a right to coerce others into actions in conflict with the others' interests. Unless we are willing to return to the rule of the fist, we must condemn destructive emotional outbursts and calculated coercive efforts. Although we should meet the acutely annoyed person's behavior with compassion, we must show contempt for those who coerce, punish, harm, or injure without adequate provocation. We must learn to let the perpetrator of hostile and aggressive actions feel the sting of social disapproval rather than continuing to idolize those who "make it to the top" at everyone else's expense.

But regardless of value changes that eventually might make hostile and aggressive behavior appear more obtrusively transgressive, it seems that an enormous educational accomplishment would already be achieved if hostility and aggression were no longer construed as an undeniable part of human nature. Great strides would be made if it were not believed that the inhibition of supposedly built-in or reactive destructive urges is ultimately pathogenic and if it were recognized that the destructive treatment of adversaries, suitable substitutes, or the self is not necessarily a "healthy" means of coping. In short, we have a great deal to gain if a view of human hostility and aggressiveness more closely in line with the evidence at hand is adopted by the public at large.

References

Ádám, G. *Interoception and behavior: An experimental study.* Budapest: Publishing House of the Hungarian Academy of Sciences, 1967.

Adams, D. B. Cells related to fighting behavior recorded from midbrain central gray neuropil of cat. *Science,* 1968, *159,* 894–896.

Adams, J. S. Inequity in social exchange. In L. Berkowitz (Ed.), *Advances in experimental social psychology* (Vol. 2). New York: Academic Press, 1965.

Adler, A. *The practice and theory of individual psychology.* New York: Harcourt, Brace, 1927. (a)

Adler, A. *Understanding human nature.* Garden City, N. Y.: Garden City Publishing, 1927. (b)

Agnew, N., & Agnew, M. Drive level effects on tasks of narrow and broad attention. *Quarterly Journal of Experimental Psychology,* 1963, *15,* 58–62.

Alexander, R. D. The search for an evolutionary philosophy of man. *Proceedings of the Royal Society of Victoria,* 1971, *84*(1), 99–120.

Allee, W. C. *Co-operation among animals.* New York: Schuman, 1951.

Allison, T. S., & Allison, S. L. Time-out from reinforcement: Effect on sibling aggression. *Psychological Record,* 1971, *21,* 81–86.

Altmann, S. A field study of the sociobiology of rhesus monkeys, *Macaca mulatta. Annals of the New York Academy of Sciences,* 1962, *102,* 338–435.

Amsel, A., & Work, M. S. The role of learned factors in "spontaneous" activity. *Journal of Comparative and Physiological Psychology,* 1961, *54,* 527–532.

Andrew, R. J. Influence of hunger on aggressive behavior in certain buntings of the genus *Emberiza. Physiological Zoology,* 1957, *30,* 177–185.

Anger, D. The role of temporal discriminations in the reinforcement of Sidman avoidance behavior. *Journal of the Experimental Analysis of Behavior,* 1963, *6,* 477–505.

Appel, J. B. Punishment in the squirrel monkey *Saimiri sciurea. Science,* 1961, *133,* 36–37.

Appel, J. B., & Peterson, N. J. Punishment: Effects of shock intensity on response suppression. *Psychological Reports,* 1965, *16,* 721–730.

Ardrey, R. *The territorial imperative.* New York: Atheneum, 1966.

Atz, J. W. The application of the idea of homology to behavior. In L. R. Aronson, E. Tobach, D. S. Lehrman, & J. S. Rosenblatt (Eds.), *Development and evolution of behavior: Essays in memory of T. C. Schneirla.* San Francisco: Freeman, 1970.

377

Austin, W., Walster, E., & Utne, M. K. Equity and the law: The effect of a harmdoer's "suffering in the act" on liking and assigned punishment. In L. Berkowitz & E. Walster (Eds.), *Advances in experimental social psychology* (Vol. 9). *Equity theory: Toward a general theory of social interaction.* New York: Academic Press, 1976.

Ayllon, T., & Azrin, N. *The token economy: A motivational system for therapy and rehabilitation.* New York: Appleton-Century-Crofts, 1968.

Azrin, N. H. Some effects of two intermittent schedules of immediate and non-immediate punishment. *Journal of Psychology*, 1956, *42*, 3–21.

Azrin, N. H. Effects of punishment intensity during variable-interval reinforcement. *Journal of the Experimental Analysis of Behavior*, 1960, *3*, 123–142.

Azrin, N. H. Aggressive responses of paired animals. In *Symposium on medical aspects of stress in the military climate.* Washington, D.C.: Walter Reed Army Institute of Research, 1964.

Azrin, N. H., Hake, D. F., & Hutchinson, R. R. Elicitation of aggression by a physical blow. *Journal of the Experimental Analysis of Behavior*, 1965, *8*, 55–57.

Azrin, N. H., & Holz, W. C. Punishment. In W. K. Honig (Ed.), *Operant behavior: Areas of research and application.* New York: Appleton-Century-Crofts, 1966.

Azrin, N. H., Holz, W. C., & Hake, D. F. Fixed-ratio punishment. *Journal of the Experimental Analysis of Behavior*, 1963, *6*, 141–148.

Azrin, N. H., & Hutchinson, R. R. Conditioning of the aggressive behavior of pigeons by a fixed-interval schedule of reinforcement. *Journal of the Experimental Analysis of Behavior*, 1967, *10*, 395–402.

Azrin, N. H., Hutchinson, R. R., & Hake, D. F. Extinction-induced aggression. *Journal of the Experimental Analysis of Behavior*, 1966, *9*, 191–204.

Azrin, N. H., Hutchinson, R. R., & Hake, D. F. Attack avoidance and escape reactions to aversive shock. *Journal of the Experimental Analysis of Behavior*, 1967, *10*, 131–148.

Azrin, N. H., Hutchinson, R. R., & McLaughlin, R. The opportunity for aggression as an operant reinforcer during aversive stimulation. *Journal of the Experimental Analysis of Behavior*, 1965, *8*, 171–180.

Azrin, N. H., Hutchinson, R. R., & Sallery, R. D. Pain-aggression toward inanimate objects. *Journal of the Experimental Analysis of Behavior*, 1964, *7*, 223–228.

Bach, G. R., & Goldberg, H. *Creative aggression.* New York: Avon Books, 1974.

Baenninger, L. P. The reliability of dominance orders in rats. *Animal Behavior*, 1966, *14*, 367–371.

Baker, J. W., & Schaie, K. W. Effects of aggressing "alone" or "with another" on physiological and psychological arousal. *Journal of Personality and Social Psychology*, 1969, *12*, 80–86.

Bandura, A. Vicarious processes: A case of no-trial learning. In L. Berkowitz (Ed.), *Advances in experimental social psychology* (Vol. 2). New York: Academic Press, 1965.

Bandura, A. *Principles of behavior modification.* New York: Holt, Rinehart & Winston, 1969.

Bandura, A. Analysis of modeling processes. In A. Bandura (Ed.), *Psychological modeling: Conflicting theories.* Chicago: Aldine, 1971. (a)

Bandura, A. Psychotherapy based upon modeling principles. In A. E. Bergin & S. L. Garfield (Eds.), *Handbook of psychotherapy and behavior change.* New York: Wiley, 1971. (b)

Bandura, A. *Social learning theory.* Morristown, N.J.: General Learning Press, 1971. (c)

Bandura, A. Vicarious and self-reinforcement processes. In R. Glaser (Ed.), *The nature of reinforcement.* New York: Academic Press, 1971. (d)

Bandura, A. *Aggression: A social learning analysis.* Englewood Cliffs, N.J.: Prentice-Hall, 1973. (a)

Bandura, A. Social learning theory of aggression. In J. F. Knutson (Ed.), *The control of aggression: Implications from basic research.* Chicago: Aldine, 1973. (b)

Bandura, A. Personal communication, 1977.

Bandura, A., & Barab, P. G. Conditions governing nonreinforced imitation. *Developmental Psychology*, 1971, *5*, 244–255.

Bandura, A., & Rosenthal, T. L. Vicarious classical conditioning as a function of arousal level. *Journal of Personality and Social Psychology*, 1966, *3*, 54–62.

Bandura, A., Underwood, B., & Fromson, M. E. Disinhibition of aggression through diffusion of responsibility and dehumanization of victims. *Journal of Research in Personality*, 1975, *9*, 253–269.

Bandura, A., & Walters, R. H. *Adolescent aggression*. New York: Ronald Press, 1959.

Bandura, A., & Walters, R. H. Aggression. In H. W. Stevenson (Ed.), *Child psychology* (Vol. 62). *Yearbook of the National Society for the Study of Education*. Chicago: University of Chicago Press, 1963. (a)

Bandura, A., & Walters, R. H. *Social learning and personality development*. New York: Holt, Rinehart & Winston, 1963. (b)

Barfield, R. J., & Sachs, B. D. Sexual behavior: Stimulation by painful electrical shock to skin in male rats. *Science*, 1968, *161*, 392–393.

Barker, R., Dembo, T., & Lewin, K. Frustration and regression: An experiment with young children. *University of Iowa Studies in Child Welfare*, 1941, *18*(1, Whole No. 386).

Barnett, P., & Benedetti, D. T. *Vicarious conditioning of the GSR to a sound*. Paper presented to the Rocky Mountain Psychological Association, Glenwood Springs, Colorado, May 1960.

Barnett, S. A. Attack and defense in animal societies. In C. D. Clemente & D. B. Lindsley (Eds.), *Aggression and defense: Neural mechanisms and social patterns* (Vol. 5). *Brain function*. Berkeley: University of California Press, 1967.

Baron, R. A. Aggression as a function of audience presence and prior anger arousal. *Journal of Experimental Social Psychology*, 1971, *7*, 515–523. (a)

Baron, R. A. Aggression as a function of magnitude of victim's pain cues, level of prior anger arousal, and aggressor–victim similarity. *Journal of Personality and Social Psychology*, 1971, *18*, 48–54. (b)

Baron, R. A. Exposure to an aggressive model and apparent probability of retaliation from the victim as determinants of adult aggressive behavior. *Journal of Experimental Social Psychology*, 1971, *7*, 343–355. (c)

Baron, R. A. Magnitude of victim's pain cues and level of prior anger arousal as determinants of adult aggressive behavior. *Journal of Personality and Social Psychology*, 1971, *17*, 236–243. (d)

Baron, R. A. Threatened retaliation from the victim as an inhibitor of physical aggression. *Journal of Research in Personality*, 1973, *7*, 103–115.

Baron, R. A. Aggression as a function of victim's pain cues, level of prior anger arousal, and exposure to an aggressive model. *Journal of Personality and Social Psychology*, 1974, *29*, 117–124. (a)

Baron, R. A. The aggression-inhibiting influence of heightened sexual arousal. *Journal of Personality and Social Psychology*, 1974, *30*, 318–322. (b)

Baron, R. A. Threatened retaliation as an inhibitor of human aggression: Mediating effects of the instrumental value of aggression. *Bulletin of the Psychonomic Society*, 1974, *3*, 217–219. (c)

Baron, R. A. *Human aggression*. New York: Plenum, 1977.

Baron, R. A. The aggression-inhibiting influence of sexual humor. *Journal of Personality and Social Psychology*, 1978, *36*, 189–197.

Baron, R. A., & Ball, R. L. The aggression-inhibiting influence of nonhostile humor. *Journal of Experimental Social Psychology*, 1974, *10*, 23–33.

Baron, R. A., & Bell, P. A. Effects of heightened sexual arousal on physical aggression. *Proceedings of the 81st Annual Convention of the American Psychological Association*, 1973, *8*, 171–172.

Baron, R. A., & Bell, P. A. Sexual arousal and aggression by males: Effects of type of erotic stimuli and prior provocation. *Journal of Personality and Social Psychology*, 1977, *35*, 79–87.

Becker, W. C., Peterson, D. R., Luria, Z., Shoemaker, D. J., & Hellmer, L. A. Relations of factors derived from parent-interview ratings to behavior problems of five-year-olds. *Child Development*, 1962, *33*, 509–535.

Beeman, E. A. The effect of male hormone on aggressive behavior in mice. *Physiological Zoology*, 1947, *20*, 373–405.

Bélanger, D., & Feldman, S. M. Effects of water deprivation upon heart rate and instrumental activity in the rat. *Journal of Comparative and Physiological Psychology*, 1962, *55*, 220–225.

Bennett, R. M., Buss, A. H., & Carpenter, J. A. Alcohol and human physical aggression. *Quarterly Journal of Studies on Alcohol*, 1969, *30*(4), 870–877.

Bentham, J. *An introduction to the principles of morals and legislation.* New York: Hafner, 1948. (Originally published, 1789.)

Beres, D. Clinical notes on aggression in children. *Psychoanalytic Study of the Child*, 1952, *7*, 241–263.

Berger, S. M. Conditioning through vicarious instigation. *Psychological Review*, 1962, *69*, 450–466.

Bergson, H. *Le rire, essai sur la signification du comique.* Paris: Alcan, 1908.

Berkowitz, L. The expression and reduction of hostility. *Psychological Bulletin*, 1958, *55*, 257–283.

Berkowitz, L. *Aggression: A social psychological analysis.* New York: McGraw-Hill, 1962.

Berkowitz, L. The concept of aggressive drive: Some additional considerations. In L. Berkowitz (Ed.), *Advances in experimental social psychology* (Vol. 2). New York: Academic Press, 1965. (a)

Berkowitz, L. Some aspects of observed agression. *Journal of Personality and Social Psychology*, 1965, *2*, 359–369. (b)

Berkowitz, L. Experiments on automatism and intent in human aggression. In C. D. Clemente & D. B. Lindsley (Eds.), *Aggression and defense: Neural mechanisms and social patterns* (Vol. 5). *Brain function.* Berkeley: University of California Press, 1967.

Berkowitz, L. Impulse, aggression and the gun. *Psychology Today*, 1968, *2*(4), 18–22.

Berkowitz, L. The frustration–aggression hypothesis revisited. In L. Berkowitz (Ed.), *Roots of aggression: A re-examination of the frustration–aggression hypothesis.* New York: Atherton, 1969. (a)

Berkowitz, L. Simple views of aggression. *American Scientist*, 1969, *57*, 372–383. (b)

Berkowitz, L. The contagion of violence: An S–R mediational analysis of some effects of observed aggression. In W. J. Arnold & M. M. Page (Eds.), *Nebraska Symposium on Motivation, 1970.* Lincoln: University of Nebraska Press, 1970.

Berkowitz, L. The "weapons effect," demand characteristics, and the myth of the compliant subject. *Journal of Personality and Social Psychology*, 1971, *20*, 332–338.

Berkowitz, L. The case for bottling up rage. *Psychology Today*, 1973, *7*(2), 24–31. (a)

Berkowitz, L. Words and symbols as stimuli to aggressive responses. In J. F. Knutson (Ed.), *The control of aggression: Implications from basic research.* Chicago: Aldine, 1973. (b)

Berkowitz, L. Some determinants of impulsive aggression: Role of mediated associations with reinforcement for aggression. *Psychological Review*, 1974, *81*, 165–176.

Berkowitz, L., & Alioto, J. T. The meaning of an observed event as a determinant of its aggressive consequences. *Journal of Personality and Social Psychology*, 1973, *28*, 206–217.

Berkowitz, L., Corwin, R., & Heironimus, M. Film violence and subsequent aggressive tendencies. *Public Opinion Quarterly*, 1963, *27*, 217–229.

Berkowitz, L, & Geen, R. G. Film violence and the cue properties of available targets. *Journal of Personality and Social Psychology*, 1966, *3*, 525–530.

Berkowitz, L., & Geen, R. G. Stimulus qualities of the target of aggression: A further study. *Journal of Personality and Social Psychology*, 1967, *5*, 364–368.

Berkowitz, L., & Knurek, D. A. Label-mediated hostility generalization. *Journal of Personality and Social Psychology*, 1969, *13*, 200–206.

Berkowitz, L., & LePage, A. Weapons as aggression-eliciting stimuli. *Journal of Personality and Social Psychology*, 1967, *7*, 202–207.

Berlyne, D. E. *Conflict, arousal, and curiosity*. New York: McGraw-Hill, 1960.

Bernard, L. L. *Instinct: A study in social psychology*. New York: Holt, 1924.

Bernard, L. L. *An introduction to social psychology*. New York: Holt, 1926.

Bevan, J. M., Bevan, W., & Williams, B. F. Spontaneous aggressiveness in young castrate C_3H male mice treated with three dose levels of testosterone. *Physiological Zoology*, 1958, *31*, 284–288.

Bigelow, R. *The dawn warriors: Man's evolution toward peace*. Boston: Little, Brown, 1969.

Bigelow, R. The evolution of cooperation, aggression, and self-control. In J. K. Cole & D. D. Jensen (Eds.), *Nebraska Symposium on Motivation, 1972*. Lincoln: University of Nebraska Press, 1972.

Bindra, D. *Motivation: A systematic reinterpretation*. New York: Ronald Press, 1959.

Birch, H. G., & Clark, G. Hormonal modifications of social behavior. II. The effects of sex-hormone administration on the social dominance status of the female-castrate chimpanzee. *Psychosomatic Medicine*, 1946, *8*, 320–331.

Blackham, G. J., & Silberman, A. *Modification of child behavior*. Belmont, Calif.: Wadsworth, 1971.

Blau, P. M. *Exchange and power in social life*. New York: Wiley, 1964.

Boelkins, R. C., & Heiser, J. F. Biological bases of aggression. In D. N. Daniels, M. F. Gilula, & F. M. Ochberg (Eds.), *Violence and the struggle for existence*. Boston: Little, Brown, 1970.

Bolles, R. C. Effect of food deprivation upon the rat's behavior in its home cage. *Journal of Comparative and Physiological Psychology*, 1963, *56*, 456–460.

Bolles, R. C. Effects of deprivation conditions upon the rat's home cage behavior. *Journal of Comparative and Physiological Psychology*, 1965, *60*, 244–248.

Bolles, R. C. *Theory of motivation*. New York: Harper & Row, 1967.

Bolles, R. C., & Grossen, N. E. Effects of an informational stimulus on the acquisition of avoidance behavior in rats. *Journal of Comparative and Physiological Psychology*, 1969, *68*, 90–99.

Bolles, R. C., Stokes, L. W., & Younger, M. S. Does CS-termination reinforce avoidance behavior? *Journal of Comparative and Physiological Psychology*, 1966, *62*, 201–207.

Borden, M. A., & Sloan, L. R. *Unjustified violence and physiological arousal increase the impact of altruistic appeals: Perhaps some televised sensationalism is good*. Paper presented at the meeting of the Midwestern Psychological Association, Chicago, May 1977.

Borden, R. J. Witnessed aggression: Influence of an observer's sex and values on aggressive responding. *Journal of Personality and Social Psychology*, 1975, *31*, 567–573.

Borden, R. J., & Taylor, S. P. The social instigation and control of physical aggression. *Journal of Applied Social Psychology*, 1973, *3*, 354–361.

Boshka, S. C., Weisman, M. H., & Thor, D. H. A technique for inducing aggression in rats utilizing morphine withdrawal. *Psychological Record*, 1966, *16*, 541–543.

Bostow, D. E., & Bailey, J. S. Modification of severe disruptive and aggressive behavior using brief timeout and reinforcement procedures. *Journal of Applied Behavior Analysis*, 1969, *2*, 31–37.

Boulenger, E. G. *Apes and monkeys*. New York: McBride, 1937.

Brady, J. V. Endocrine and autonomic correlates of emotional behavior. In P. Black (Ed.), *Physiological correlates of emotion*. New York: Academic Press, 1970.

Bramel, D., Taub, B., & Blum, B. An observer's reaction to the suffering of his enemy. *Journal of Personality and Social Psychology*, 1968, *8*, 384–392.

Brehm, A. E. *Tierleben* (Band 4). *Säugetiere*. Leipzig: Bibliographisches Institut, 1916.

Bronowski, J. *The ascent of man*. Boston: Little, Brown, 1973.

Bronson, F. H., & Desjardins, C. Aggression in adult mice: Modification by neonatal injections of gonadal hormones. *Science*, 1968, *161*, 705–706.

Bronson, F. H., & Desjardins, C. Steroid hormones and aggressive behavior in mammals. In B. E. Eleftheriou & J. P. Scott (Eds.), *The physiology of aggression and defeat.* New York: Plenum, 1971.

Bronson, F. H., & Eleftheriou, B. E. Adrenal response to fighting in mice: Separation of physical and psychological causes. *Science,* 1965, *147,* 627–628. (a)

Bronson, F. H., & Eleftheriou, B. E. Relative effects of fighting on bound and unbound corticosterone in mice. *Proceedings of the Society for Experimental Biology and Medicine,* 1965, *118,* 146–149. (b)

Brown, G. D., & Tyler, V. O., Jr. Time out from reinforcement: A technique for dethroning the "duke" of an institutionalized delinquent group. *Journal of Child Psychology and Psychiatry and Allied Disciplines,* 1968, *9,* 203–211.

Brown, J. L., & Hunsperger, R. W. Neuroethology and the motivation of agnostic behaviour. *Animal Behaviour,* 1963, *11,* 439–448.

Brown, J. S. *The motivation of behavior.* New York: McGraw-Hill, 1961.

Brown, J. S., & Farber, I. E. Emotions conceptualized as intervening variables—with suggestions toward a theory of frustration. *Psychological Bulletin,* 1951, *48,* 465–495.

Bryant, J., & Zillmann, D. The mediating effect of the intervention potential of communications on displaced aggressiveness and retaliatory behavior. In B. D. Ruben (Ed.), *Communication Yearbook 1.* New Brunswick, N.J.: ICA-Transaction Press, 1977.

Bryant, J., & Zillmann, D. *The effect of the intensification of annoyance through residual excitation from unrelated prior stimulation on substantially delayed hostile behavior.* Unpublished manuscript, Indiana University, 1978.

Burchard, J., & Tyler, V. O., Jr. The modification of delinquent behavior through operant conditioning. *Behavior Research and Therapy,* 1965, *2,* 245–250.

Burgess, M., & Hokanson, J. E. Effects of increased heart rate on intellectual performance. *Journal of Abnormal and Social Psychology,* 1964, *68,* 85–91.

Burnstein, E., & Worchel, P. Arbitrariness of frustration and its consequences for aggression in a social situation. *Journal of Personality,* 1962, *30,* 528–540.

Buss, A. H. *The psychology of aggression.* New York: Wiley, 1961.

Buss, A. H. Physical aggression in relation to different frustrations. *Journal of Abnormal and Social Psychology,* 1963, *67,* 1–7.

Buss, A. H. The effect of harm on subsequent aggression. *Journal of Experimental Research in Personality,* 1966, *1,* 249–255. (a)

Buss, A. H. Instrumentality of aggression, feedback, and frustration as determinants of physical aggression. *Journal of Personality and Social Psychology,* 1966, *3,* 153–162. (b)

Buss, A. H. Aggression pays. In J. L. Singer (Ed.), *The control of aggression and violence: Cognitive and physiological factors.* New York: Academic Press, 1971.

Buss, A., Booker, A., & Buss, E. Firing a weapon and aggression. *Journal of Personality and Social Psychology,* 1972, *22,* 296–302.

Cairns, R. B. Development, maintenance and extinction of social attachment behavior in sheep. *Journal of Comparative and Physiological Psychology,* 1966, *62,* 298–306.

Cairns, R. B. Fighting and punishment from a developmental perspective. In J. K. Cole & D. D. Jensen (Eds.), *Nebraska Symposium on Motivation, 1972.* Lincoln: University of Nebraska Press, 1972.

Cameron, N. *The psychology of behavior disorders.* Boston: Houghton Mifflin, 1947.

Candland, D. K., & Bloomquist, D. W. Interspecies comparisons of the reliability of dominance orders. *Journal of Comparative and Physiological Psychology,* 1965, *59,* 135–137.

Cannon, W. B. *Bodily changes in pain, hunger, fear and rage: An account of researches into the function of emotional excitement* (2nd ed.). New York: Appleton-Century, 1929.

Cannon, W. B. *The wisdom of the body.* New York: Norton, 1932.

Cantor, J. R. *Imitation of aggression as a function of exposure to a model's emotional expressions contingent upon his performance of aggressive acts.* Unpublished doctoral dissertation, Indiana University, 1974.

Cantor, J. R., Bryant, J., & Zillmann, D. Enhancement of humor appreciation by transferred excitation. *Journal of Personality and Social Psychology*, 1974, *30*, 812–821.

Cantor, J. R., & Zillmann, D. The effect of affective state and emotional arousal on music appreciation. *Journal of General Psychology*, 1973, *89*, 97–108.

Cantor, J. R., Zillmann, D., & Bryant, J. Enhancement of experienced sexual arousal in response to erotic stimuli through misattribution of unrelated residual excitation. *Journal of Personality and Social Psychology*, 1975, *32*, 69–75.

Cantor, J. R., Zillmann, D., & Day, K. D. Relationship between cardiorespiratory fitness and physiological responses to films. *Perceptual and Motor Skills*, 1978, *46*, 1123–1130.

Cantor, J. R., Zillmann, D., & Einsiedel, E. Female responses to provocation after exposure to aggressive and erotic films. *Communication Research*, 1978, *5*, 395–412.

Carpenter, C. R. A field study of the behavior and social relations of howling monkeys (*Alouatta palliata*). *Comparative Psychology Monographs*, 1934, *10*(2), 1–168.

Carpenter, C. R. Behavior of the red spider monkey (*Ateles geoffroyi*) in Panama. *Journal of Mammalogy*, 1935, *16*, 171–180.

Carpenter, C. R. A field study in Siam of the behavior and social relations of the gibbon (*Hylobates lar*). *Comparative Psychology Monographs*, 1940, *16*(5), 1–212.

Carthy, J. D., & Ebling, F. J. (Eds.). *The natural history of aggression*. London: Academic Press, 1964.

Caspari, E. W. Behavioral consequences of genetic differences in man: A summary. In J. N. Spuhler (Ed.), *Genetic diversity and human behavior*. Chicago: Aldine, 1967.

Christian, J. J. The adreno-pituitary system and population cycles in mammals. *Journal of Mammalogy*, 1950, *31*, 247–259.

Christian, J. J. Endocrine adaptive mechanisms and the physiologic regulation of population growth. In W. V. Mayer & R. G. Van Gelder (Eds.), *Physiological Mammalogy* (Vol. 1). *Mammalian populations*. New York: Academic Press, 1963.

Christian, J. J., Lloyd, J. A., & Davis, D. E. The role of endocrines in the self-regulation of mammalian populations. *Recent Progress in Hormone Research*, 1965, *21*, 501–578.

Christy, P. R., Gelfand, D. M., & Hartmann, D. P. Effects of competition-induced frustration on two classes of modeled behavior. *Developmental Psychology*, 1971, *5*, 104–111.

Clark, L. D. Experimental studies of the behavior of an aggressive predatory mouse, *onychomys leucogaster*. In E. L. Bliss (Ed.), *Roots of behavior*. New York: Hoeber, 1962.

Clark, W. E. L. *The fossil evidence of human evolution: An introduction to the study of palaeoanthropology*. Chicago: University of Chicago Press, 1955.

Cloudsley-Thompson, J. L. *Animal conflict and adaptation*. Chester Springs, Pa.: Dufour, 1965.

Cofer, C. N., & Appley, M. H. *Motivation: Theory and research*. New York: Wiley, 1964.

Cohen, A. R. Social norms, arbitrariness of frustration, and status of the agent of frustration in the frustration–aggression hypothesis. *Journal of Abnormal and Social Psychology*, 1955, *51*, 222–226.

Cohen, P. S. Punishment: The interactive effects of delay and intensity of shock. *Journal of the Experimental Analysis of Behavior*, 1968, *11*, 789–799.

Cole, J. M., & Parker, B. K. Schedule-induced aggression: Access to an attackable target bird as a positive reinforcer. *Psychonomic Science*, 1971, *22*, 33–35.

Collias, N. E. Aggressive behavior among vertebrate animals. *Physiological Zoology*, 1944, *17*, 83–123.

Conner, R. L. Hormones, biogenic amines, and aggression. In S. Levine (Ed.), *Hormones and behavior*. New York: Academic Press, 1972.

Conner, R. L., & Levine, S. Hormonal influences on aggressive behaviour. In S. Garattini & E. B. Sigg (Eds.), *Aggressive behaviour*. New York: Wiley, 1969.

Conner, R. L., Vernikos-Danellis, J., & Levine, S. Stress, fighting and neuroendocrine function. *Nature*, 1971, *234*, 564–566.

Cowan, P. A., & Walters, R. H. Studies of reinforcement of aggression: I. Effects of scheduling. *Child Development,* 1963, *34,* 543–551.

Craig, K. D., & Weinstein, M. S. Conditioning vicarious affective arousal. *Psychological Reports,* 1965, *17,* 955–963.

Craig,W. Appetites and aversions as constituents of instincts. *Biological Bulletin,* 1918, *34,* 91–107.

Craig. W. Why do animals fight? *International Journal of Ethics,* 1921, *31,* 264–278.

Creer, T. L., Hitzing, E. W., & Schaeffer, R. W. Classical conditioning of reflexive fighting. *Psychonomic Science,* 1966, *4,* 89–90.

Criminal statistics: England and Wales, 1975. London: Her Majesty's Stationery Office, 1976.

Crowley, W. R., Popolow, H. B., & Ward, O. B., Jr. From dud to stud: Copulatory behavior elicited through conditioned arousal in sexually inactive male rats. *Physiology and Behavior,* 1973, *10,* 391–394.

Cullen, E. Final Report, Contract AF 61 (052)-29, USAFRDC, 1-23 (1961).

D'Amato, M. R., Fazzaro, J., & Etkin, M. Discriminated bar-press avoidance maintenance and extinction in rats as a function of shock intensity. *Journal of Comparative and Physiological Psychology,* 1967, *63,* 351–354.

Darling, F. F. *A herd of red deer.* London: Oxford University Press, 1937.

Dart, R. A. Australopithecus africanus: The man-ape of South Africa. *Nature,* 1925, *115,* 195–199. (a)

Dart, R. A. A note on Makapansgat: A site of early human occupation. *South African Journal of Science,* 1925, *22,* 454. (b)

Dart. R. A. Taungs and its significance. *Natural History,* 1926,*26,* 315–327.

Dart, R. A. An Australopithecus from the Central Transvaal. *South African Science,* 1948, *1,* 200–201.

Dart, R. A. Innominate fragments of *Australopithecus prometheus. American Journal of Physical Anthropology,* 1949, *7,* 301–334. (a)

Dart, R. A. The predatory implemental technique of *Australopithecus. American Journal of Physical Anthropology,* 1949, *7,* 1–38. (b)

Dart, R. A. The predatory transition from ape to man. *International Anthropological and Linguistic Review,* 1953, *1,* 201–219.

Dart, R. A. The Kisoro pattern of mountain gorilla preservation. *Current Anthropology,* 1961, *2,* 510–511.

Darwin, C. *On the origin of species by means of natural selection.* New York: Appleton, 1887. (Originally published, 1859.)

Das, J. P., & Nanda, P. C. Mediated transfer of attitudes. *Journal of Abnormal and Social Psychology,* 1963, *66,* 12–16.

Davis, D. E. The role of density in aggressive behaviour of house mice. *Animal Behavior,* 1958, *6,* 207–210.

Davis, D. E. The physiological analysis of aggressive behavior. In W. Etkin (Ed.), *Social behavior and organization among vertebrates.* Chicago: University of Chicago Press, 1964.

Davis, D. E., & Christian, J. J. Relation of adrenal weight to social rank of mice. *Proceedings of the Society of Experimental Biology and Medicine,* 1957, *94,* 728–731.

Davis, D. E., & Domm, L. V. The influence of hormones on the sexual behavior of domestic fowl. In *Essays in biology: In honor of Herbert M. Evans.* Berkeley: University of California Press, 1943.

Davis, K. C. *Discretionary justice: A preliminary inquiry.* Baton Rouge: Louisiana State University Press, 1959.

Davitz, J. R. The effects of previous training on postfrustration behavior. *Journal of Abnormal and Social Psychology,* 1952, *47,* 309–315.

Day, K. D. Short-lived facilitation of aggressive behavior by violent communications. *Psychological Reports,* 1976, *38,* 1068–1070.

Delgado, J. M. R. Cerebral heterostimulation in a monkey colony, *Science*, 1963, *141*, 161–163.

Delgado, J. M. R. Aggression and defense under cerebral radio control. In C. D. Clemente & D. B. Lindsley (Eds.), *Aggression and defense: Neural mechanisms and social patterns* (Vol. 5). *Brain function*. Berkeley: University of California Press, 1967. (a)

Delgado, J. M. R. Social rank and radio-stimulated aggressiveness in monkeys. *Journal of Nervous and Mental Disease,*1967, *144*, 383–390. (b)

Delgado, J. M. R. Electrical stimulation of the limbic system. *Proceedings of the XXIV International Congress of Physiological Sciences*, 1968, *6*, 222–223.

Delgado, J. M. R. Offensive–defensive behaviour in free monkeys and chimpanzees induced by radio stimulation of the brain. In S. Garattini & E. B. Sigg (Eds.), *Aggressive behaviour*. New York: Wiley, 1969.

Denenberg, V. H. Animal studies on developmental determinants of behavioral adaptability. In O. J. Harvey (Ed.), *Experience, structure, and adaptability*. New York: Springer, 1966.

Denenberg, V. H., Hudgens, G. A., & Zarrow, M. X. Mice reared with rats: Modification of behavior by early experience with another species. *Science*, 1964, *143*, 380–381.

Denenberg, V. H., Paschke, R. E., & Zarrow, M. X. Killing of mice by rats prevented by early interaction between the two species. *Psychonomic Science*, 1968, *11*, 39.

Dengerink, H. A. Personality variables as mediators of attack-instigated aggression. In R. G. Geen & E. C. O'Neal (Eds.), *Perspectives on aggression*. New York: Academic Press, 1976.

Dengerink, H. A., O'Leary, M. R., & Kasner, K. H. Individual differences in aggressive responses to attack: Internal–external locus of control and field dependence–independence. *Journal of Research in Personality*, 1975, *9*, 191–199.

Deur, J. L., & Parke, R. D. Effects of inconsistent punishment on aggression in children. *Developmental Psychology*, 1970, *2*, 403–411.

Deutsch, M., & Krauss, R. M. The effect of threat upon interpersonal bargaining. *Journal of Abnormal and Social Psychology*, 1960, *61*, 181–189.

DeVore, I. (Ed.). *Primate behavior: Field studies of monkeys and apes*. New York: Holt, Rinehart & Winston, 1965.

DeVore, I. Quest for the roots of society. In *The marvels of animal behavior*. Washington, D. C.: National Geographic Society, 1972.

DeVore, I., & Hall, K. R. L. Baboon ecology. In I. DeVore (Ed.), *Primate behavior: Field studies in monkeys and apes*. New York: Holt, Rinehart & Winston, 1965.

Dinsmoor, J. A. Punishment: I. The avoidance hypothesis. *Psychological Review*, 1954, *61*, 34–46.

Dinsmoor, J. A. Punishment: II. An interpretation of empirical findings. *Psychological Review*, 1955, *62*, 96–105.

Dion, K. K. Physical attractiveness and evaluation of children's transgressions. *Journal of Personality and Social Psychology*, 1972, *24*, 207–213.

Dollard, J., Doob, L. W., Miller, N. E., Mowrer, O. H., & Sears, R. R. *Frustration and aggression*. New Haven, Conn.: Yale University Press, 1939.

Donner, L. Violence in the media. In D. J. Madden & J. R. Lion (Eds.), *Rage, hate, assault and other forms of violence*. New York: Spectrum Publications, 1976.

Donnerstein, E., & Donnerstein, M. Research in the control of interracial aggression. In R. G. Geen & E. C. O'Neal (Eds.), *Perspectives on aggression*. New York: Academic Press, 1976.

Donnerstein, E., Donnerstein, M., & Barrett, G. Where is the facilitation of media violence: The effects of nonexposure and placement of anger arousal. *Journal of Research in Personality*, 1976, *10*, 386–398.

Donnerstein, E., Donnerstein, M., & Evans, R. Erotic stimuli and aggression: Facilitation or inhibition. *Journal of Personality and Social Psychology*, 1975, *32*, 237–244.

Donnerstein, E., Donnerstein, M., Simon, S., & Ditrichs, R. Variables in interracial aggression: Anonymity, expected retaliation, and a riot. *Journal of Personality and Social Psychology*, 1972, *22*, 236–245.

Doob, A. N., & Kirshenbaum, H. M. The effects on arousal of frustration and aggressive films. *Journal of Experimental Social Psychology*, 1973, *9*, 57–64.

Dreyer, P. I., & Church, R. W. Reinforcement of shock-induced fighting. *Psychonomic Science*, 1970, *18*, 147–148.

Ducharme, R., & Bélanger, D. Influence d'une stimulation électrique sur le niveau d'activation et la performance. *Canadian Journal of Psychology*, 1961, *15*, 61–68.

Duffy, E. Emotion: An example of the need for reorientation in psychology. *Psychological Review*, 1934, *41*, 184–198.

Duffy, E. The psychological significance of the concept of "arousal" or "activation." *Psychological Review*, 1957, *64*, 265–275.

Duffy, E. *Activation and behavior.* New York: Wiley, 1962.

Dufresne, C. *Influence de la privation de nourriture sur le rythme cardiaque et l'activité instrumentale.* Unpublished master's thesis, Université de Montreal, 1961.

Dulany, D. E., Jr. Hypotheses and habits in verbal "operant conditioning." *Journal of Abnormal and Social Psychology*, 1961, *63*, 251–263.

Dunham, P. J. Punishment: Method and theory. *Psychological Review*, 1971, *78*, 58–70.

Easterbrook, J. A. The effect of emotion on cue utilization and the organization of behavior. *Psychological Review*, 1959, *66*, 183–201.

Ebbesen, E. G., Duncan, B., & Konečni, V. J. Effects of content of verbal aggression on future verbal aggression: A field experiment. *Journal of Experimental Social Psychology*, 1975, *11*, 192–204.

Egger, M. D., & Flynn, J. P. Effect of electrical stimulation of the amygdala on hypothalamically elicited attack behavior in cats. *Journal of Neurophysiology*, 1963, *26*, 705–720.

Eibl-Eibesfeldt, I. Aggressive behavior and ritualized fighting in animals. In J. H. Masserman (Ed.), *Science and psychoanalysis* (Vol. 6). *Violence and war.* New York: Grune & Stratton, 1963. (a)

Eibl-Eibesfeldt, I. Angeborenes und Erworbenes im Verhalten einiger Säuger. *Zeitschrift für Tierpsychologie*, 1963, *20*, 705–754. (b)

Eibl-Eibesfeldt, I. *Ethology: The biology of behavior.* New York: Holt, Rinehart & Winston, 1970.

Eibl-Eibesfeldt, I. *Love and hate: The natural history of behavior patterns.* New York: Holt, Rinehart & Winston, 1971.

Ellis, D. P., Weinir, P., & Miller, L. Does the trigger pull the finger? An experimental test of weapons as aggression-eliciting stimuli. *Sociometry*, 1971, *34*, 453–465.

Emley, G. S., Hutchinson, R. R., & Brannan, I. B. Aggression: Effects of acute and chronic morphine. *Michigan Mental Health Research Bulletin*, 1970, *4*, 23–26.

Erikson, E. H. *Childhood and society.* New York: Norton, 1950.

Eron, L. D., Banta, T. J., Walder, L. O., & Laulicht, J. H. Comparison of data obtained from mothers and fathers on childrearing practices and their relation to child aggression. *Child Development*, 1961, *32*, 457–472.

Estes, R. D. Territorial behavior of the wildebeest (*Connochaetes taurinus Burchell*) 1923. *Zeitschrift für Tierpsychologie*, 1969, *26*, 284–370.

Estes, W. K. An experimental study of punishment. *Psychological Monographs*, 1944, *57*(3).

Estes, W. K., & Skinner, B. F. Some quantitative properties of anxiety. *Journal of Experimental Psychology*, 1941, *29*, 390–400.

Etkin, W. Co-operation and competition in social behavior. In W. Etkin (Ed.), *Social behavior and organization among vertebrates.* Chicago: University of Chicago Press, 1964.

European Committee on Crime Problems. *Collected studies in criminological research* (Vol. 11). *Violence in society.* Strasbourg: Council of Europe, 1974.

Evans, L. T. Social behavior of the normal and castrated lizard, *Anolis carolinensis. Science*, 1936, *83*, 104.

Fantino, E. Aversive control. In J. A. Nevin (Ed.), *The study of behavior: Learning, motivation, emotion, and instinct.* Glenview, Ill.: Scott, Foresman, 1973.

Farris, H. E., Fullmer, W. H., & Ulrich, R. E. Extinction of classically conditioned aggression: Results from two procedures. *Proceedings of the 78th Annual Convention of the American Psychological Association.* Washington, D. C.: American Psychological Association, 1970.

Farris, H. E., Gideon, B. E., & Ulrich, R. E. Classical conditioning of aggression: A developmental study. *Psychological Record,* 1970, *20,* 63–67.

Fenichel, O. *The psychoanalytic theory of neurosis.* New York: Norton, 1945.

Fenigstein, A., & Buss, A. H. Association and affect as determinants of displaced aggression. *Journal of Research in Personality,* 1974, *7,* 306–313.

Ferson, J. E. *The displacement of hostility.* Unpublished doctoral dissertation, University of Texas, 1958.

Ferster, C. B. Withdrawal of positive reinforcement as punishment. *Science,* 1957, *126,* 509.

Ferster, C. B., & Skinner, B. F. *Schedules of reinforcement.* New York: Appleton-Century-Crofts, 1957.

Feshbach, S. The drive-reducing function of fantasy behavior. *Journal of Abnormal and Social Psychology,* 1955, *50,* 3–12.

Feshbach, S. The catharsis hypothesis and some consequences of interaction with aggressive and neutral play objects. *Journal of Personality,* 1956, *24,* 449–462.

Feshbach, S. The stimulating versus cathartic effects of a vicarious aggressive activity. *Journal of Abnormal and Social Psychology,* 1961, *63,* 381–385.

Feshbach, S. The function of aggression and the regulation of aggressive drive. *Psychological Review,* 1964, *71,* 257–272.

Feshbach, S. Aggression. In P. H. Mussen (Ed.), *Carmichael's manual of child psychology* (Vol. 2). New York: Wiley, 1970.

Feshbach, S. Dynamics and morality of violence and aggression: Some psychological considerations. *American Psychologist,* 1971, *26,* 281–292.

Feshbach, S., Stiles, W. B., & Bitter, E. The reinforcing effect of witnessing aggression. *Journal of Experimental Research in Personality,* 1967, *2,* 133–139.

Festinger, L. A theory of social comparison processes. *Human Relations,* 1954, *7,* 117–140.

Filby, Y., & Appel, J. B. Variable-interval punishment during variable-interval reinforcement. *Journal of the Experimental Analysis of Behavior,* 1966, *9,* 521–527.

Fishman, C. G. Need for approval and the expression of aggression under varying conditions of frustration. *Journal of Personality and Social Psychology,* 1965, *2,* 809–816.

Flickinger, G. L. Effect of grouping on adrenals and gonads of chickens. *General and Comparative Endocrinology,* 1961, *1,* 332–340.

Fontana, V. J. *The maltreated child.* Springfield, Ill.: Charles C. Thomas, 1971.

Fredericson, E. The effects of food deprivation upon competitive and spontaneous combat in C57 black mice. *Journal of Psychology,* 1950, *29,* 89–100.

Freeman, D. Human aggression in anthropological perspective. In J. D. Carthy & F. J. Ebling (Eds.), *The natural history of aggression.* New York: Academic Press, 1964.

Freeman, G. L. The relationship between performance level and bodily activity level. *Journal of Experimental Psychology,* 1940, *26,* 602–608.

Freeman, G. L. *The energetics of human behavior.* Ithaca, N.Y.: Cornell University Press, 1948.

Freud, S. Drei Abhandlungen zur Sexualtheorie. In *Gesammelte Werke* (Vol. 5). London: Imago, 1942. (Originally published, 1905.)

Freud, S. Triebe und Triebschicksale. In *Gesammelte Werke* (Vol. 10). London: Imago, 1946. (Originally published, 1915.) (a)

Freud, S. Zeitgemässes über Krieg und Tod. In *Gesammelte Werke* (Vol. 10). London: Imago, 1946. (Originally published, 1915.) (b)

Freud, S. Vorlesungen zur Einführung in die Psychoanalyse. In *Gesammelte Werke* (Vol. 11). London: Imago, 1940. (Originally published, 1917.)

Freud, S. Jenseits des Lustprinzips. In *Gesammelte Werke* (Vol. 13). London: Imago, 1940. (Originally published, 1920.)

Freud, S. Das Unbehagen in der Kultur. In *Gesammelte Werke* (Vol. 14). London: Imago, 1948. (Originally published, 1930.)

Freud, S. Warum Krieg? In *Gesammelte Werke* (Vol. 16). London: Imago, 1950. (Originally published, 1933.)

Fry, W. F., Jr. The appeasement function of mirthful laughter. In A. J. Chapman & H. C. Foot (Eds.), *It's a funny thing, humor.* Oxford: Pergamon Press, 1977.

Gaebelein, J. W. Instigative aggression in females. *Psychological Reports,* 1973, *33,* 619-622. (a)

Gaebelein, J. W. Third-party instigation of aggression: An experimental approach. *Journal of Personality and Social Psychology,* 1973, *27,* 389-395. (b)

Gaebelein, J. W., & Hay, W. M. Third-party instigation of aggression as a function of attack and vulnerability. *Journal of Research in Personality,* 1974, *7,* 324-333.

Gallup. G., & Altomari, T. Activity as a post-situation measure of frustrative nonreward. *Journal of Comparative and Physiological Psychology,* 1969, *68,* 382-384.

Garattini, S., & Sigg, E. B. (Eds.). *Aggressive behaviour.* New York: Wiley, 1969.

Garland, H., & Brown, B. R. Face-saving as affected by subjects' sex, audiences' sex, and audience expertise. *Sociometry,* 1972, *35,* 280-289.

Geen, R. G. Effects of frustration, attack, and prior training in aggressiveness upon aggressive behavior. *Journal of Personality and Social Psychology,* 1968, *9,* 316-321.

Geen, R. G. Perceived suffering of the victim as an inhibitor of attack-induced aggression. *Journal of Social Psychology,* 1970, *81,* 209-215.

Geen, R. G. *Aggression.* Morristown, N.J.: General Learning Press, 1972.

Geen, R. G. Observing violence in the mass media: Implications of basic research. In R. G. Geen & E. C. O'Neal (Eds.), *Perspectives on aggression.* New York: Academic Press, 1976.

Geen, R., & Berkowitz, L. Name-mediated aggressive cue properties. *Journal of Personality,* 1966, *34,* 456-465.

Geen, R., & Berkowitz, L. Some conditions facilitating the occurrence of aggression after the observation of violence. *Journal of Personality,* 1967, *35,* 666-676.

Geen, R. G., & O'Neal, E. C. Activation of cue-elicited aggression by general arousal. *Journal of Personality and Social Psychology,* 1969, *11,* 289-292.

Geen, R. G., & O'Neal, E. C. (Eds.). *Perspectives on aggression.* New York: Academic Press, 1976.

Geen, R. G., & Pigg, R. Acquisition of an aggressive response and its generalization to verbal behavior. *Journal of Personality and Social Psychology,* 1970, *15,* 165-170.

Geen, R. G., & Quanty, M. B. The catharsis of aggression: An evaluation of a hypothesis. In L. Berkowitz (Ed.), *Advances in experimental social psychology* (Vol. 10). New York: Academic Press, 1977.

Geen, R. G., & Stonner, D. Effects of aggressiveness habit strength on behavior in the presence of aggression-related stimuli. *Journal of Personality and Social Psychology,* 1971, *17,* 149-153.

Geen, R. G., & Stonner, D. Reactions to aggression-related stimuli following reinforcement of aggression. *Journal of Psychology,* 1973, *83,* 95-102.

Geen, R. G., Stonner, D., & Shope, G. L. The facilitation of aggression by aggression: Evidence against the catharsis hypothesis. *Journal of Personality and Social Psychology,* 1975, *31,* 721-726.

Gelles, R. J. *The violent home: A study of physical aggression between husbands and wives.* Beverly Hills, Calif.: Sage Publications, 1974.

Gellhorn, E. The emotions and the ergotropic and trophotropic systems. *Psychologische Forschung,* 1970, *34,* 48-94.

Gerbner, G., & Gross, L. Living with television: The violence profile. *Journal of Communication,* 1976, *26*(2), 173-199.

Gil, D. G. *Violence against children: Physical child abuse in the United States.* Cambridge, Mass.: Harvard University Press, 1973.

Ginsburg, B., & Allee, W. C. Some effects of conditioning on social dominance and subordination in inbred strains of mice. *Physiological Zoology,* 1942, *15,* 485–506.

Glickman, S. E., & Schiff, B. A biological theory of reinforcement. *Psychological Review,* 1967, *74,* 81–109.

Goldberg, M. E., & Salama, A. I. Norepinephrine turnover and brain monoamine levels in aggressive mouse-killing rats. *Biochemical Pharmacology,* 1969, *18,* 532–534.

Goode, W. Violence among intimates. In D. J. Mulvihill, M. M. Tumin, & L. A. Curtis (Eds.), *Crimes of violence* (Vol. 13). Washington, D. C.: U.S. Government Printing Office, 1969.

Goranson, R. E. Media violence and aggressive behavior: A review of experimental research. In L. Berkowitz (Ed.), *Advances in experimental social psychology* (Vol. 5). New York: Academic Press, 1970.

Gouldner, A. W. The norm of reciprocity: a preliminary statement. *American Sociological Review,* 1960, *25,* 161–178.

Greenspoon, J. The reinforcing effect of two spoken sounds on the frequency of two responses. *American Journal of Psychology,* 1955, *68,* 409–416.

Greenspoon, J. Verbal conditioning and clinical psychology. In A. J. Bachrach (Ed.), *Experimental foundations of clinical psychology.* New York: Basic Books, 1962.

Grossman, S. P. *A textbook of physiological psychology.* New York: Wiley, 1967.

Guhl, A. M. The social order of chickens. *Scientific American,* 1956, *194,* 42–46.

Guhl, A. M. The behaviour of chickens. In E. S. E. Hafez (Ed.), *The behaviour of domestic animals.* London: Baillière, Tindall, & Cox, 1962.

Gulevich, G. D., & Bourne, P. G. Mental illness and violence. In D. N. Daniels, M. F. Gilula, & F. M. Ochberg (Eds.), *Violence and the struggle for existence.* Boston: Little, Brown, 1970.

Guze, S. B., Tuason, V. B., Gatfield, P. D., Stewart, M. A., & Picken, B. Psychiatric illness and crime with particular reference to alcoholism: A study of 223 criminals. *Journal of Nervous and Mental Disease,* 1962, *134,* 512–521.

Hafez, E. S. E., & Scott, J. P. The behaviour of sheep and goats. In E. S. E. Hafez (Ed.), *The behaviour of domestic animals.* London: Baillière, Tindall, & Cox, 1962.

Hailman, J. P. Comments on the coding of releasing stimuli. In L. R. Aronson, E. Tobach, D. S. Lehrman, & J. S. Rosenblatt (Eds.), *Development and evolution of behavior: Essays in memory of T. C. Schneirla.* San Francisco: Freeman, 1970.

Hake, D. F., & Azrin, N. H. Conditioned punishment. *Journal of the Experimental Analysis of Behavior,* 1965, *8,* 279–293.

Hall, K. R. L. Aggression in monkey and ape societies. In J. D. Carthy & F. J. Ebling (Eds.), *The natural history of aggression.* New York: Academic Press, 1964.

Hall, K. R. L. Social organization of the old-world monkeys and apes. In P. C. Jay (Ed.), *Primates: Studies in adaptation and variability.* New York: Holt, Rinehart & Winston, 1968. (a)

Hall, K. R. L. Tool-using performances as indicators of behavioral adaptability. In P. C. Jay (Ed.), *Primates: Studies in adaptation and variability.* New York: Holt, Rinehart & Winston, 1968. (b)

Hall, K. R. L., & DeVore, I. Baboon social behavior. In I. DeVore (Ed.), *Primate behavior: Field studies of monkeys and apes.* New York: Holt, Rinehart & Winston, 1965.

Haner, C. F., & Brown, P. A. Clarification of the instigation to action concept in the frustration–aggression hypothesis. *Journal of Abnormal and Social Psychology,* 1955, *51,* 204–206.

Harlow, H. F., & Harlow, M. K. The affectional systems. In A. M. Schrier, H. F. Harlow, & F. Stollnitz (Eds.), *Behavior of nonhuman primates: Modern research trends* (Vol. 2). New York: Academic Press, 1965.

Hartman, H., Kris, E., & Loewenstein, R. Notes on the theory of aggression. *Psychoanalytic Study of the Child,* 1949, *3,* 9–36.

Hebb, D. O. Drives and the C. N. S. (conceptual nervous system). *Psychological Review,* 1955, *62,* 243–254.

Hebb, D. O. *A textbook of psychology* (2nd ed.). Philadelphia, Pa.: Saunders, 1966.

Heider, F. *The psychology of interpersonal relations.* New York: Wiley, 1958.

Heimstra, N. A further investigation of the development of mouse killing in rats. *Psychonomic Science,* 1965, *2,* 179–180.

Heimstra, N. W., & Newton, G. Effects of prior food competition on the rat's killing response to the white mouse. *Behaviour,* 1961, *17,* 95–102.

Hendry, D. P., & Hendry, L. S. Partial negative reinforcement: Fixed-ratio escape. *Journal of the Experimental Analysis of Behavior,* 1963, *6,* 519–523.

Herrnstein, R. J. Secondary reinforcement and rate of primary reinforcement. *Journal of the Expermental Analysis of Behavior,* 1964, *7,* 27–36.

Herrnstein, R. J. Method and theory in the study of avoidance. *Psychological Review,* 1969, *76,* 49–60.

Herrnstein, R. J., & Hineline, P. N. Negative reinforcement as shock-frequency reduction. *Journal of the Experimental Analysis of Behavior,* 1966, *9,* 421–430.

Hinde, R. A. Energy models of motivation. *Symposia of the Society for Experimental Biology,* 1960, *14,* 199–213.

Hinde, R. A. The nature of aggression. *New Society,* 1967, *9,* 302–304.

Hinde, R. A. *Animal behaviour: A synthesis of ethology and comparative psychology* (2nd ed.). New York: McGraw-Hill, 1970.

Hingston, R. E. G. *A naturalist in Himalaya.* Boston: Small, 1920.

Hokanson, J. E. *The physiological bases of motivation.* New York: Wiley, 1969.

Hokanson, J. E. Psychophysiological evaluation of the catharsis hypothesis. In E. I. Megargee & J. E. Hokanson (Eds.), *The dynamics of aggression: Individual, group, and international analyses.* New York: Harper & Row, 1970.

Hokanson, J. E., & Burgess, M. The effects of status, type of frustration, and aggression on vascular processes. *Journal of Abnormal and Social Psychology,* 1962, *65,* 232–237. (a)

Hokanson, J. E., & Burgess, M. The effects of three types of aggression on vascular processes. *Journal of Abnormal and Social Psychology,* 1962, *64,* 446–449. (b)

Hokanson, J. E., Burgess, M., & Cohen, M. F. Effects of displaced aggression on systolic blood pressure. *Journal of Abnormal and Social Psychology,* 1963, *67,* 214–218.

Hokanson, J. E., & Edelman, R. Effects of three social responses on vascular processes. *Journal of Personality and Social Psychology,* 1966, *3,* 442–447.

Hokanson, J. E., & Shetler, S. The effect of overt aggression on physiological arousal level. *Journal of Abnormal and Social Psychology,* 1961, *63,* 446–448.

Hokanson, J. E., Willers, K. R., & Koropsak, E. The modification of autonomic responses during aggressive interchange. *Journal of Personality,* 1968, *36,* 386–404.

Holmes, D. S. Effects of overt aggression on level of physiological arousal. *Journal of Personality and Social Psychology,* 1966, *4,* 189–194.

Holst, E. v., & Saint Paul, U. v. Vom Wirkungsgefüge der Triebe. *Naturwissenschaften,* 1960, *47*(18), 409–422.

Holz, W. C., & Azrin, N. H. Discriminative properties of punishment. *Journal of the Experimental Analysis of Behavior,* 1961, *4,* 225–232.

Holz, W. C., Azrin, N. H., & Ulrich, R. E. Punishment of temporally spaced responding. *Journal of the Experimental Analysis of Behavior,* 1963, *6,* 115–122.

Homans, G. C. *Social behavior: Its elementary forms.* New York: Harcourt, Brace & World, 1961.

Honig, W. K. (Ed.). *Operant behavior: Areas of research and application.* New York: Appleton-Century-Crofts, 1966.

Honig, W. K., & Slivka, R. M. Stimulus generalization of the effects of punishment. *Journal of the Experimental Analysis of Behavior,* 1964, *7,* 21–25.

Horai, J., & Tedeschi, J. T. Effects of credibility and magnitude of punishment on compliance to threats. *Journal of Personality and Social Psychology,* 1969, *12,* 164–169.

Hornaday, W. T. *The minds and manners of wild animals.* New York: Scribner's, 1922.

Hornberger, R. H. The differential reduction of aggressive responses as a function of interpolated activities. *American Psychologist,* 1959, *14,* 354.

Horney, K. *New ways in psychoanalysis.* New York: Norton, 1939.

Howard, D. *Territory in bird life.* London: Murray, 1920.

Hoyt, J. L. Effect of media "justification" on aggression. *Journal of Broadcasting,* 1970, *6,* 455–464.

Hull, C. L. *Principles of behavior: An introduction to behavior theory.* New York: Appleton-Century-Crofts, 1943.

Hull, C. L. *A behavior system: An introduction to behavior theory concerning the individual organism.* New York: Wiley, 1952.

Huston, J. P., DeSisto, M. J., & Meyer, E. *Frog-killing by rats as influenced by territorial variables.* Paper presented to the Eastern Psychological Association, Philadelphia, April 1965.

Hutchinson, R. R. The environmental causes of aggression. In J. K. Cole & D. D. Jensen (Eds.), *Nebraska Symposium on Motivation, 1972.* Lincoln: University of Nebraska Press, 1972.

Hutchinson, R. R., Azrin, N. H., & Hake, D. F. An automatic method for the study of aggression in squirrel monkeys. *Journal of the Experimental Analysis of Behavior,* 1966, *9,* 233–237.

Hutchinson, R. R., Azrin, N. H., & Hunt, G. M. Attack produced by intermittent reinforcement of a concurrent operant response. *Journal of the Experimental Analysis of Behavior,* 1968, *11,* 489–495.

Hutchinson, R. R., & Emley, G. Effects of nicotine on avoidance, conditioned suppression, and aggression response measures in animals and man. In Council for Tobacco Research, *Conference on motivation in cigarette smoking.* New York: Academic Press, 1972.

Hutchinson, R. R., & Pierce, G. E. *Jaw clenching in humans: Its measurement, and effects produced by conditions of reinforcement and extinction.* Paper presented at the meeting of the American Psychological Association, Washington, D.C., August 1971.

Hutchinson, R. R., & Renfrew, J. W. Stalking attack and eating behavior elicited from the same sites in the hypothalamus. *Journal of Comparative and Physiological Psychology,* 1966, *61,* 300–367.

Hutchinson, R. R., Renfrew, J. W., & Young, G. A. Effects of long-term shock and associated stimuli on aggressive and manual responses. *Journal of the Experimental Analysis of Behavior,* 1971, *15,* 141–166.

Hutchinson, R. R., Ulrich, R., & Azrin, N. H. Effects of age and related factors on the pain–aggression reaction. *Journal of Comparative and Physiological Psychology,* 1965, *59,* 365–369.

Imanishi, K. Social organization of subhuman primates in their natural habitat. *Current Anthropology,* 1960, *1,* 393–407.

Jacobs, B. L., & Farel, P. B. Motivated behaviors produced by increased arousal in the presence of goal objects. *Physiology and Behavior,* 1971, *6,* 473–476.

Jakobi, U., Selg, H., & Belschner, W. Triebmodelle der Aggression. In H. Selg (Ed.), *Zur Aggression verdammt?: Psychologische Ansätze einer Friedensforschung.* Stuttgart: Kohlhammer, 1971.

James, W. *The principles of psychology.* New York: Holt, 1890. (Originally published, 1844.)

Jay, P. Field studies. In A. M. Schrier, H. F. Harlow, & F. Stollnitz (Eds.), *Behavior of nonhuman primates: Modern research trends* (Vol. 2). New York: Academic Press, 1965.

Jessor, R., Graves, T. D., Hanson, R. C., & Jessor, S. L. *Society, personality and deviant behavior: A study of a tri-ethnic community.* New York: Holt, Rinehart & Winston, 1968.

Johnson, R. N. *Aggression in man and animals.* Philadelphia, Pa.: Saunders, 1972.

Joléaud, L. Etudes de Géographie Zoologique sur la Berbérie. Les Primates: Le Magot. *Proceedings of the International Congress of Geography, Paris,* 1931, *2*(2), 851–663.

Jones, E. *Sigmund Freud.* London: Hogarth Press, 1955.

Jones, E. E. *Ingratiation: A social psychological analysis.* New York: Appleton-Century-Crofts, 1964.

Jones, E. E., & Davis, K. E. From acts to dispositions: The attribution process in person perception. In L. Berkowitz (Ed.), *Advances in experimental social psychology* (Vol. 2). New York: Academic Press, 1965.

Kaada, B. Brain mechanisms related to aggressive behavior. In C. D. Clemente & D. B. Lindsley (Eds.), *Aggression and defense: Neural mechanisms and social patterns.* Berkeley: University of California Press, 1967.

Kahn, M. W. The effect of severe defeat at various age levels on the aggressive behavior of mice. *Journal of Genetic Psychology,* 1951, *79,* 117–130.

Kahn, M. The physiology of catharsis. *Journal of Personality and Social Psychology,* 1966, *3,* 278–286.

Kamin, L. J. The effects of termination of the CS and avoidance of the US on avoidance learning. *Journal of Comparative and Physiological Psychology,* 1956, *49,* 420–424.

Kamin, L. J. The effects of termination of the CS and avoidance of the US on avoidance learning: An extension. *Canadian Journal of Psychology,* 1957, *11,* 48–56.

Kanfer, F. H. Verbal conditioning: A review of its current status. In T. R. Dixon & D. L. Horton (Eds.), *Verbal behavior and general behavior theory.* Englewood Cliffs, N.J.: Prentice-Hall, 1968.

Kant, I. Grundlegung zur Metaphysik der Sitten. In *Immanuel Kant's sämtliche Werke* (Vol. 5). Leipzig: Inselverlag, 1922. (Originally published, 1785.)

Karli, P. The Norway rat's killing response to the white mouse. *Behaviour,* 1956, *10,* 81–103.

Karli, P. Hormones stéroides et comportement d'aggression interspecifique rat-souris. *Journal de Physiologie et de Pathologie Generale,* 1958, *50,* 346–357.

Karli, P., & Vergnes, M. Nouvelles données sur les bases neurophysiologiques du comportement d'aggression interspécifique rat-souris. *Journal de Physiologie,* 1964, *56,* 384.

Kaufman, A., Baron, A., & Kopp, R. E. Some effects of instructions on human operant behavior. *Psychonomic Monograph Supplements,* 1966,*1,* 243–250.

Kaufmann, H. *Aggression and altruism: A psychological analysis.* New York: Holt, Rinehart & Winston, 1970.

Kaufmann, J. H. Ecology and social behavior of the coati, *Nasua narica,* on Barro Colorado Island, Panama. *University of California Publications in Zoology,* 1962, *60,* 95–222.

Keirsey, D. W. Systematic exclusion: Eliminating chronic classroom disruptions. In J. D. Krumboltz & C. E. Thoresen (Eds.), *Behavioral counseling: Cases and techniques.* New York: Holt, Rinehart & Winston, 1969.

Kelley, H. H. Experimental studies of threats in interpersonal negotiations. *Journal of Conflict Resolution,* 1965, *9,* 79–105.

Kelley, H. H. Attribution theory in social psychology. In D. Levine (Ed.), *Nebraska Symposium on Motivation, 1967.* Lincoln: University of Nebraska Press, 1967.

Kelley, H. H. Attribution in social interaction. In E. E. Jones, D. E. Kanouse, H. H. Kelley, R. E. Nisbett, S. Valins, & B. Weiner, *Attribution: Perceiving the causes of behavior.* Morristown, N.J.: General Learning Press, 1971. (a)

Kelley, H. H. Causal schemata and the attribution process. In E. E. Jones, D. E. Kanouse, H. H. Kelley, R. E. Nisbett, S. Valins, & B. Weiner, *Attribution: Perceiving the causes of behavior.* Morristown, N.J.: General Learning Press, 1971. (b)

Kelly, J. F., & Hake, D. F. An extinction-induced increase in an aggressive response with humans. *Journal of the Experimental Analysis of Behavior,* 1970, *14,* 153–164.

Kimmel, H. D. Instrumental conditioning of autonomically mediated responses in human beings. *American Psychologist,* 1974, *29,* 325–335.

Kislak, J. W., & Beach, F. A. Inhibition of aggressiveness by ovarian hormones. *Endocrinology,* 1955, *56,* 684–692.

Kitzler, G. Die Paarungsbiologie einiger Eidechsen. *Zeitschrift für Tierpsychologie,* 1942, *4,* 353–402.

Klein, M. *Contributions to psycho-analysis.* London: Hogarth Press, 1950.

Klein, M. *Envy and gratitude.* London: Tavistock, 1957.

Klein, M. W. Violence in American juvenile gangs. In D. J. Mulvihill, M. M. Tumin, & L. A. Curtis (Eds.), *Crimes of violence* (Vol. 13). Washington, D. C.: U.S. Government Printing Office, 1969.

Knott, P. D., & Drost, B. A. Effects of varying intensity of attack and fear arousal on the intensity of counter aggression. *Journal of Personality,* 1972, *40,* 27–37.

Koehler, O. Prototypes of human communication systems in animals. In H. Friedrich (Ed.), *Man and animal: Studies in behaviour.* New York: St. Martin's, 1968.

Kohlberg, L. Development of moral character and moral ideology. In M. L. Hoffman & L. W. Hoffman (Eds.), *Review of child development research* (Vol. 1). New York: Russell Sage Foundation, 1964.

Konečni, V. J. Annoyance, type and duration of postannoyance activity, and aggression: The "cathartic effect." *Journal of Experimental Psychology: General,* 1975, *104,* 76–102. (a)

Konečni, V. J. The mediation of aggressive behavior: Arousal level versus anger and cognitive labeling. *Journal of Personality and Social Psychology,* 1975, *32,* 706–712. (b)

Kortlandt, A., & Kooij, M. Protohominid behaviour in primates. *Symposia of the Zoological Society of London,* 1963, *10,* 61–88.

Kostowski, W. Myotropic and neurotropic action of certain steroids. *Dissertationes Pharmaceuticae et Pharmacologicae,* 1967, *19,* 619–623.

Krasner, L. A technique for investigating the relationship between the behavior cues of the examiner and the verbal behavior of the patient. *Journal of Consulting Psychology,* 1958, *22,* 364–366.

Krebs, D. L. Altrusim: An examination of the concept and a review of the literature. *Psychological Bulletin,* 1970, *73,* 258–302.

Kregarman, J. J., & Worchel, P. Arbitrariness of frustration and aggression. *Journal of Abnormal and Social Psychology,* 1961, *63,* 183–187.

Kruijt, J. P. Ontogeny of social behavior in Burmese Red Jungle Fowl (*Gallus gallus spadiceus*). *Behaviour,* 1964, Suppl. No. 12.

Kulkarni, A. S. Satiation of instinctive mouse killing in rats. *Psychological Revue,* 1968, *18,* 385–388.

Kuo, Z. Y. The genesis of the cat's response toward the rat. *Journal of Comparative Psychology,* 1930, *15,* 1–35.

Kuo, Z. Y. Further study on the behavior of the cat towards the rat. *Journal of Comparative Psychology,* 1938, *25,* 1–8.

Kuo, Z. Y. Studies on the basic factors in animal fighting: Parts I–IV. *Journal of Genetic Psychology,* 1960, *96,* 210–239.

Kuo, Z. Y. *The dynamics of behavior development.* New York: Random House, 1967.

Lacey, J. I. Somatic response patterning and stress: Some revisions of activation theory. In M. H. Appley & R. Trumbull (Eds.), *Psychological stress: Issues in research.* New York: Appleton-Century-Crofts, 1967.

Lagerspetz, K. M. J. Aggression and aggressiveness in laboratory mice. In S. Garattini & E. B. Sigg (Eds.), *Aggressive behaviour.* New York: Wiley, 1969.

Lancaster, J. B. Primate communication systems and the emergence of human language. In P. C. Jay (Ed.), *Primates: Studies in adaptation and variability.* New York: Holt, Rinehart & Winston, 1968.

Landy, D. & Aronson, E. The influence of the character of the criminal and his victim on the decisions of simulated jurors. *Journal of Experimental Social Psychology*, 1969, *5*, 141-152.

Lang, P. J., Geer, J., & Hnatiow, M. Semantic generalization of conditioned autonomic responses. *Journal of Experimental Psychology*, 1963, *65*, 552-558.

Lashley, K. S. Experimental analysis of instinctive behavior. *Psychological Review*, 1938, *45*, 445-471.

Lawick-Goodall, J. van. The behavior of free-living chimpanzees in the Gombe Stream Reserve. *Animal Behaviour Monographs*, 1968, *1*(3), 161-311.

Layman, E. M. The contribution of play and sports to emotional health. In J. E. Kane (Ed.), *Psychological aspects of physical education and sport*. London: Routledge & Kegan Paul, 1972.

Leaf, R. C., Lerner, L., & Horovitz, Z. P. The role of the amygdala in the pharmacological and endocrinological manipulation of aggression. In S. Garattini & E. B. Sigg (Eds.), *Aggressive behaviour*. New York: Wiley, 1969.

Leakey, L. S. B. *Olduvai Gorge*. Cambridge: Cambridge University Press, 1951.

Leakey, L. S. B. A new fossil skull from Olduvai. *Nature*, 1959, *183*, 491-493.

Leakey, L. S. B. Develpment of aggression as a factor in early human and pre-human evolution. In C. D. Clemente & D. B. Lindsley (Eds.), *Aggression and defense: Neural mechanisms and social patterns* (Vol. 5). *Brain function*. Berkeley: University of California Press, 1967.

Legrand, R. Successful aggression as the reinforcer for runway behavior of mice. *Psychonomic Science*, 1970, *20*, 303-305.

Lehrman, D. S. A critique of Konrad Lorenz's theory of instinctive behavior, *Quarterly Review of Biology*, 1953, *28*, 337-363.

Lehrman, D. S. Semantic and conceptual issues in the nature-nurture problem. In L. R. Aronson, E. Tobach, D. S. Lehrman, & J. S. Rosenblatt (Eds.), *Development and evolution of behavior: Essays in memory of T. C. Schneirla*. San Francisco: Freeman, 1970.

Lerner, M. J., Miller, D. T., & Holmes, J. G. Deserving and the emergence of justice. In L. Berkowitz & E. Walster (Eds.), *Advances in experimental social psychology* (Vol. 9). *Equity theory: Toward a general theory of social interaction*. New York: Academic Press, 1976.

Leventhal, G. S. The distribution of rewards and resources in groups and organizations. In L. Berkowitz & E. Walster (Eds.), *Advances in experimental social psychology* (Vol. 9). *Equity theory: Toward a general theory of social interaction*. New York: Academic Press, 1976.

Leventhal, G. S., & Anderson, D. Self-interest and the maintenance of equity. *Journal of Personality and Social Psychology*, 1970, *15*, 57-62.

Leventhal, H. Emotions: A basic problem for social psychology. In C. Nemeth (Ed.), *Social psychology: Classic and contemporary integrations*. Skokie, Ill.: Rand McNally, 1974.

Levi, L. The urinary output of adrenalin and noradrenalin during pleasant and unpleasant emotional states. *Psychosomatic Medicine*, 1965, *27*, 80-85.

LeVine, R. A., & Campbell, D. T. *Ethnocentrism: Theories of conflict, ethnic attitudes, and group behavior*. New York: Wiley, 1972.

Levison, P. K., & Flynn, J. P. The objects attacked by cats during stimulation of the hypothalamus. *Animal Behavior*, 1965, *13*, 217-220.

Levy, J., & King, J. A. The effects of testosterone propionate on fighting behaviour in young male C57BL/10 mice. *Anatomical Record*, 1953, *117*, 562-563. (Abstract)

Lewin, K. *Resolving social conflicts*. New York: Harper, 1948.

Lewin, K. *Field theory in social science*. New York: Harper & Row, 1951.

Lindsley, D. B. Emotion. In S. S. Stevens (Ed.), *Handbook of experimental psychology*. New York: Wiley, 1951.

Lindsley, D. B. Psychophysiology and motivation. In M. R. Jones (Ed.), *Nebraska Symposium on Motivation, 1957*. Lincoln: University of Nebraska Press, 1957.

Loew, C. A. Acquisition of a hostile attitude and its relationship to aggressive behavior. *Journal of Personality and Social Psychology*, 1967, *5*, 335-341.

Loewenstein, R. The vital or somatic instincts. *International Journal of Psycho-Analysis*, 1940, *21*, 377–400.

Lorenz, K. Der Kumpan in der Umwelt des Vogels: Der Artgenosse als auslösendes Moment sozialer Verhaltensweisen. In K. Lorenz, *Über tierisches und menschliches Verhalten: Aus dem Werdegang der Verhaltenslehre* (Vol. 1). München: Piper, 1965. (Originally published, 1935.)

Lorenz, K. Die angeborenen Formen möglicher Erfahrung. *Zeitschrift für Tierpsychologie*, 1942, *5*, 260–409.

Lorenz, K. Z. The comparative method in studying innate behavior patterns. *Symposia of the Society for Experimental Biology*, 1950, *4*, 221–268.

Lorenz, K. Psychologie und Stammesgeschichte. In K. Lorenz, *Über tierisches und menschliches Verhalten: Aus dem Werdegang der Verhaltenslehre* (Vol. 2). München: Piper, 1965. (Originally published, 1954.)

Lorenz, K. Z. Phylogenetische Anpassung und adaptive Modifikation des Verhaltens. *Zeitschrift für Tierpsychologie*, 1961, *18*, 139–187.

Lorenz, K. *Das sogenannte Böse: Zur Naturgeschichte der Aggression*. Wien: Borotha-Schoeler, 1963.

Lorenz, K. Ritualized fighting. In J. D. Carthy & F. J. Ebling (Eds.), *The natural history of aggression*. New York: Academic Press, 1964.

Lorenz, K. Z. *Evolution and modification of behavior*. Chicago: University of Chicago Press, 1965. (a)

Lorenz, K. *Über tierisches und menschliches Verhalten: Aus dem Werdegang der Verhaltenslehre* (Vols. 1 & 2). München: Piper, 1965. (b)

Lorenz, K. Zur Naturgeschichte der Aggression. *Neue Sammlung*, 1965, *5*, 296–308. (c)

Louch, C. D., & Higginbotham, M. The relation between social rank and plasma corticosterone levels in mice. *General and Comparative Endocrinology*, 1967, *8*, 441–444.

Lowen, A. *Betrayal of the body*. New York: Macmillan, 1967.

Lowen, A. *Pleasure*. New York: Coward-McCann, 1970.

Lowen, A. Bio-energetic group therapy. In H. M. Ruitenback (Ed.), *Group therapy today*. New York: Atherton, 1971.

Ludwig, A. M., Marx, A. J., Hill, P. A., & Browning, R. M. The control of violent behavior through faradic shock. *Journal of Nervous and Mental Disease*, 1969, *148*, 624–637.

Lunde, D. T. Our murder boom. *Psychology Today*, 1975, *9*(2), 35–42.

Lyon, D. O., & Ozolins, D. Pavlovian conditioning of shock-elicited aggression: A discrimination procedure. *Journal of the Experimental Analysis of Behavior*, 1970, *13*, 325–331.

Maccoby, E. E., & Jacklin, C. N. *The psychology of sex differences*. Stanford, Calif.: Stanford University Press, 1974.

Magoun, H. W. The ascending reticular system and wakefulness. In J. F. Delafresnaye (Ed.), *Brain mechanisms and consciousness*. Springfield, Ill.: Charles C. Thomas, 1954.

Maier, N. R. F. *Frustration: The study of behavior without a goal*. New York: McGraw-Hill, 1949.

Mallick, S. K., & McCandless, B. R. A study of catharsis of aggression. *Journal of Personality and Social Psychology*, 1966, *4*, 591–596.

Malmo, R. B. Activation: A neuropsychological dimension. *Psychological Review*, 1959, *66*, 367–386.

Malmo, R. B. Physiological gradients and behavior. *Psychological Bulletin*, 1965, *64*, 225–234.

Malmo, R. B., & Bélanger, D. Related physiological and behavioral changes: What are their determinants? In S. S. Kety, E. V. Evarts, & H. L. William (Eds.), *Sleep and altered states of consciousness*. Baltimore, Md.: Williams & Wilkins, 1967.

Maltzman, I. Theoretical conceptions of semantic conditioning and generalization. In T. R. Dixon & D. L. Horton (Eds.), *Verbal behavior and general behavior theory*. Englewood Cliffs, N.J.: Prentice-Hall, 1968.

Marler, P. Studies of fighting in chaffinches. (1) Behaviour in relation to the social hierarchy. *British Journal of Animal Behaviour*, 1955, *3*, 111, 117.

Marler, P. Studies of fighting in chaffinches. (3) Proximity as a cause of aggression. *British Journal of Animal Behaviour*, 1956, *4*, 23–30.

Marler, P. Studies of fighting in chaffinches. (4) Appetitive and consummatory behaviour. *British Journal of Animal Behaviour*, 1957, *5*, 29–37.

Marler, P. On aggression in birds. In V. G. Dethier (Ed.), *Topics in animal behavior*. New York: Harper & Row, 1971.

Marler, P., & Hamilton, W. J. *Mechanisms of animal behavior*. New York: Wiley, 1968.

Marx, M. H., & Hillix, W. A. *Systems and theories in psychology*. New York: McGraw-Hill, 1963.

Masling, J. Role-related behavior of the subject and psychologist and its effect upon psychological data. In D. Levine (Ed.), *Nebraska Symposium on Motivation, 1966*. Lincoln: University of Nebraska Press, 1966.

Maslow, A. H. Deprivation, threat and frustration. *Psychological Review*, 1941, *48*, 364–366.

Mason, W. A., & Green, P. C. The effects of social restriction on the behavior of rhesus monkeys. IV. Responses to a novel environment and to an alien species. *Journal of Comparative and Physiological Psychology*, 1962, *55*, 363–368.

McBride, G. A general theory of social organization and behaviour. *University of Queensland Papers: Faculty of Veterinary Science*, 1964, *1*(2), 75–110.

McDougall, W. *An introduction to social psychology*. London: Methuen, 1908.

McKearney, J. W. Fixed-interval schedules of electric shock presentation: Extinction and recovery of performance under different shock intensities and fixed interval durations. *Journal of the Experimental Analysis of Behavior*, 1969, *12*, 301–313.

McNeil, E. B. Psychology and aggression. *Journal of Conflict Resolution*, 1959, *3*, 195–293.

Megargee, E. I. Undercontrolled and overcontrolled personality types in extreme antisocial aggression. *Psychological Monographs*, 1966, *80*(3, Whole No. 611).

Megargee, E. I. The role of inhibition in the assessment and understanding of violence. In J. L. Singer (Ed.), *The control of aggression and violence: Cognitive and physiological factors*. New York: Academic Press, 1971.

Mendelson, J. Role of hunger in T-maze learning for food by rats. *Journal of Comparative and Physiological Psychology*, 1966, *62*, 341–349.

Merfield, F. G., & Miller, H. *Gorilla hunter*. London: Arnold, 1956.

Merton, R. K. *Social theory and social structure*. Glencoe, Ill.: Free Press, 1957.

Meyer, T. P. The effects of sexually arousing and violent films on aggressive behavior. *Journal of Sex Research*, 1972, *8*, 324–331. (a)

Meyer, T. P. Effects of viewing justified and unjustified real film violence on aggressive behavior. *Journal of Personality and Social Psychology*, 1972, *23*, 21–29. (b)

Michael, R. P. Effects of gonadal hormones on displaced and direct aggression in pairs of rhesus monkeys of opposite sex. In S. Garattini & E. B. Sigg (Eds.), *Aggressive behaviour*. New York: Wiley, 1969.

Miller, D., & Swanson, G. *Inner conflict and defense*. New York: Holt, Rinehart & Winston, 1960.

Miller, G. A., Galanter, E., & Pribram, K. H. *Plans and the structure of behavior*. New York: Holt, 1960.

Miller, N. E. The frustration–aggression hypothesis. *Psychological Review*, 1941, *48*, 337–342.

Miller, N. E. Experimental studies of conflict. In J. McV. Hunt (Ed.), *Personality and the behavior disorders*. New York: Ronald Press, 1944.

Miller, N. E. Theory and experiment relating psychoanalytic displacement to stimulus–response generalization. *Journal of Abnormal and Social Psychology*, 1948, *43*, 155–178.

Miller, N. E. Liberalization of basic S–R concepts: Extensions to conflict behavior, motivation, and social learning. In S. Koch (Ed.), *Psychology: A study of a science* (Vol. 2). *General systematic formulations, learning, and special processes*. New York: McGraw-Hill, 1959.

Miller, N. E. Learning of visceral and glandular responses. *Science,* 1969, *163,* 434–445 (a)

Miller, N. E. Psychosomatic effects of specific types of training. *Annals of the New York Academy of Sciences,* 1969, *159,* 1025–1040. (b)

Miller, N. E., & Dollard, J. *Social learning and imitation.* New Haven, Conn.: Yale University Press, 1941.

Miller, W. B. Lower class culture as a generating milieu of gang delinquency. *Journal of Social Issues,* 1958, *14,* 5–19.

Miller, W. B., Geertz, H., & Cutter, H. S. G. Aggression in a boys' streetcorner group. *Psychiatry,* 1961, *24,* 282–298.

Mirsky, A. F. The influence of sex hormones on social behavior in monkeys. *Journal of Comparative and Physiological Psychology,* 1955, *48,* 327–335.

Mischel, W. Cognitive appraisals and transformations in self-control. In B. Weiner (Ed.), *Cognitive views of human motivation.* New York: Academic Press, 1974. (a)

Mischel, W. Processes in delay of gratification. In L. Berkowitz (Ed.), *Advances in experimental social psychology* (Vol. 7). New York: Academic Press, 1974. (b)

Mitscherlich, A. *Auf dem Weg zur vaterlosen Gesellschaft: Ideen zur Sozialpsychologie.* München: Piper, 1963.

Morgan, C. T. Physiological theory of drive. In S. Koch (Ed.), *Psychology: A study of a science* (Vol. 1). *Sensory, perceptual, and physiological formulations.* New York: McGraw-Hill, 1959.

Morris, D. *The naked ape.* New York: McGraw-Hill, 1968.

Moruzzi, G. Reticular influences on the EEG. *Electroencephalography and Clinical Neurophysiology,* 1964, *16,* 2–17.

Moruzzi, G., & Magoun, H. W. Brain stem reticular formation and activation of the EEG. *Electroencephalography and Clinical Neurophysiology,* 1949, *1,* 455–473.

Mowrer, O. H. On the dual nature of learning a reinterpretation of "conditioning" and "problem-solving." *Harvard Educational Review,* 1947, *17,* 102–148.

Mowrer, O. H., & Lamoreaux, R. R. Fear as an intervening variable in avoidance conditioning. *Journal of Comparative and Physiological Psychology,* 1946, *39,* 29–50.

Moyer, K. E. *The physiology of hostility.* Chicago: Markham, 1971.

Mueller, C., & Donnerstein, E. The effects of humor-induced arousal upon aggressive behavior. *Journal of Research in Personality,* 1977, *11,* 73–82. (a)

Mueller, C., & Donnerstein, E. *Media violence and subsequent behavior: A test of competing theories.* Paper presented at the meeting of the Midwestern Psychological Assocation, Chicago, May 1977. (b)

Mueller, C., & Donnerstein, E. *Film-facilitated arousal and prosocial behavior.* Paper presented at the meeting of the Midwestern Psychological Association, Chicago, May 1978.

Mueller, C., Nelson, R., & Donnerstein, E. Facilitative effects of media violence on helping. *Psychological Reports,* 1977, *40,* 775–778.

Mugford, R. A., & Nowell, N. W. The aggression of male mice against androgenized females. *Psychonomic Science,* 1970, *20,* 191–192. (a)

Mugford, R. A., & Nowell, N. W. Pheromones and their effect on aggression in mice. *Nature,* 1970, *226,* 967–968. (b)

Mulvihill, D. J., Tumin, M. M., & Curtis, L. A. (Eds.). *Crimes of violence* (Vol. 13). Washington, D. C.: U.S. Government Printing Office, 1969.

Murie, A. *The wolves of Mt. McKinley* (U.S.D.I. Fauna Series No. 4). Washington, D.C.: U.S. Government Printing Office, 1944.

Murray, E. J. A case study in the behavioral analysis of psychotherapy. *Journal of Abnormal and Social Psychology,* 1954, *49,* 305–310.

Murray, E. J., & Berkun, M. M. Displacement as a function of conflict. *Journal of Abnormal and Social Psychology,* 1955, *51,* 47–56.

Myer, J. S. Early experience and the development of mouse killing by rats. *Journal of Comparative and Physiological Psychology,* 1969, *67,* 46–49.

Myer, J. S., & White, R. T. Aggressive motivation in the rat. *Animal Behaviour*, 1965, *13*, 430–433.

Nagel, E. *The structure of science: Problems in the logic of scientific explanation*. London: Routledge & Kegan Paul, 1961.

Nagra, C. L., Baum, G. T., & Meyer, R. K. Corticosterone levels in adrenal effluent blood of some gallinaceous birds. *Proceedings of the Society for Experimental Biology and Medicine*, 1960, *105*, 68–70.

Nesdale, A. R., & Rule, B. G. The effects of an aggressor's characteristics and an observer's accountability on judgments of aggression. *Canadian Journal of Behavioral Science*, 1974, *6*, 342–351.

Nesdale, A. R., Rule, B. G., & McAra, M. Moral judgments of aggression: Personal and situational determinants. *European Journal of Social Psychology*, 1975, *5*, 339–349.

Neuringer, A. J. Delayed reinforcement versus reinforcement after a fixed interval. *Journal of the Experimental Analysis of Behavior*, 1969, *12*, 375–383.

Nevin, J. A. Stimulus control. In J. A. Nevin (Ed.), *The study of behavior: Learning, motivation, emotion, and instinct*. Glenview, Ill.: Scott, Foresman, 1973.

Noble, G. K. Courtship and sexual selection of the flicker (*Colaptes auratus luteus*). *Auk*, 1936, *53*, 269–282.

Noble, G. K., & Bradley, H. T. The mating behavior of lizards: Its bearing on the theory of sexual selection. *Annals of the New York Academy of Sciences*, 1933, *35*, 25–100.

Nunberg, H. *Principles of psychoanalysis*. New York: International Unversity Press, 1955.

O'Kelly, L. W., & Steckle, L. C. A note on long-enduring emotional responses in the rat. *Journal of Psychology*, 1939, *8*, 125–131.

Oken, D. The psychophysiology and psychoendocrinology of stress and emotion. In M. H. Appley & R. Trumbull (Eds.), *Psychological stress: Issues in research*. New York: Appleton-Century-Crofts, 1967.

O'Neal, E., McDonald, P., Hori, R., & McClinton, B. *Arousal and imitation of aggression*. Unpublished manuscript, Tulane University, 1978.

Orne, M. T. On the social psychology of the psychological experiment: With particular reference to demand characteristics and their implications. *American Psychologist*, 1962, *17*, 776–783.

Page, M. M., & Scheidt, R. J. The elusive weapons effect: Demand awareness, evaluation apprehension, and slightly sophisticated subjects. *Journal of Personality and Social Psychology*, 1971, *20*, 304–318.

Palmer, S. Frustration, aggression, and murder. *Journal of Abnormal and Social Psychology*, 1960, *60*, 430–432.

Parke, R. D. Effectiveness of punishment as an interaction of intensity, timing, agent nurturance, and cognitive structuring. *Child Development*, 1969, *40*, 213–235.

Parke, R. D., & Walters, R. H. Some factors influencing the efficacy of punishment training for inducing response inhibition. *Monographs of the Society for Research in Child Development*, 1967, *32* (1, Serial No. 109).

Pastore, N. The role of arbitrariness in the frustration–aggression hypothesis. *Journal of Abnormal and Social Psychology*, 1952, *47*, 728–731.

Patterson, G. R., & Cobb, J. A. A dyadic analysis of "aggressive" behaviors: An additional step toward a theory of aggression. In J. P. Hill (Ed.), *Minnesota Symposia on Child Psychology* (Vol. 5). Minneapolis: University of Minnesota Press, 1971.

Patterson, G. R., & Cobb, J. A. Stimulus control for classes of noxious behaviors. In J. F. Knutson (Ed.), *The control of aggression: Implications from basic research*. Chicago: Aldine, 1973.

Patterson, G. R., Littman, R. A., & Bricker, W. Assertive behavior in children: A step toward a theory of aggression. *Monographs of the Society for Research in Child Devlopment*, 1967, *32*(Whole No. 113).

Patterson, G. R., Ludwig, M., & Sonoda, B. *Reinforcement of aggression in children*. Unpublished manuscript, University of Oregon, 1961.

Patterson, G. R., & Reid, J. B. Reciprocity and coercion: Two facets of social systems. In C. Neuringer & J. Michael (Eds.), *Behavior modification in clinical psychology.* New York: Appleton-Century-Crofts, 1970.

Paul, L. Predatory attack by rats: Its relationship to feeding and type of prey. *Journal of Comparative and Physiological Psychology,* 1972, *78,* 69–76.

Paul, L., Miley, W., & Baenninger, R. Mouse-killing by rats: Roles of hunger and thirst in its initiation and maintenance. *Journal of Comparative and Physiological Psychology,* 1971,*76,* 242–249.

Pelkwijk, J. J. ter, & Tinbergen, N. Eine reizbiologische Analyse einiger Verhaltensweisen von *Gasterosteus aculeatus L. Zeitschrift für Tierpsychologie,* 1937, *1,* 193–200.

Pendergrass, V. E. Effect of length of time-out from positive reinforcement and schedule of application in suppression of aggressive behavior. *Psychological Record,* 1971, *21,* 75–80.

Pepitone, A. *Attraction and hostility.* New York: Atherton, 1964.

Pepitone, A. Aggression—a matter of stimulus and reinforcement control. (Review of *Aggression: A social learning analysis* by A. Bandura). *Contemporary Psychology,* 1974,*19,* 769–771.

Pepitone, A., & Sherberg, J. Intentionality, responsibility, and interpersonal attraction. *Journal of Personality,* 1957, *25,* 757–766.

Perls, F. *Gestalt therapy verbatim.* Lafayette, Calif.: Real People Press, 1969. (a)

Perls, F. *In and out of the garbage pail.* Lafayette, Calif.: Real People Press, 1969. (b)

Pettigrew, T. Social evaluation theory: Convergences and applications. In D. Levine (Ed.), *Nebraska Symposium on Motivation, 1967.* Lincoln: University of Nebraska Press, 1967.

Phillips, R. E. "Wildness" in the mallard duck: Effects of brain lesions and stimulation on "escape behavior" and reproduction. *Journal of Comparative Neurology,* 1964, *122,* 139–155.

Piaget, J. *The moral judgment of the child.* London: Routledge & Kegan Paul, 1932.

Pisano, R., & Taylor, S. P. Reduction of physical aggression: The effects of four strategies. *Journal of Personality and Social Psychology,* 1971, *19,* 237–242.

Plack, A. *Die Gesellschaft und das Böse: Eine Kritik der herrschenden Moral* (4th ed.). München: List, 1969.

Plotnik, R. Changes in social behavior of squirrel monkeys after anterior temporal lobectomy. *Journal of Comparative and Physiological Psychology,* 1968, *66,* 369–377.

Plotnik, R., Mir, D., & Delgado, J. M. R. Aggression, noxiousness, and brain stimulation in unrestrained rhesus monkeys. In B. E. Eleftheriou & J. P. Scott (Eds.), *The physiology of aggression and defeat.* New York: Plenum, 1971.

Powell, D. A., Francis, J., & Schneiderman, N. The effects of castration, neonatal injections of testosterone, and previous experience with fighting on shock-elicted aggression. *Communications in Behavioral Biology,* 1971, *5,* 311–377.

Premack, D. Reversibility of the reinforcement relation. *Science,* 1962, *136,* 255–257.

Quanty, M. B. Aggression catharsis: Experimental investigatons and implications. In R. G. Geen & E. C. O'Neal (Eds.), *Perspectives on aggression.* New York: Academic Press, 1976.

Rapoport, A. Models of conflict: Cataclysmic and strategic. In A. de Reuck & J. Knight (Eds.), *Conflict in society.* Boston: Little, Brown, 1966.

Rasa, O. A. E. The effect of pair isolation on reproductive success in *Etroplus maculatus (Cichlidae). Zeitschrift für Tierpsychologie,* 1969, *26,* 846–852.

Reichenbach, H. *Elements of symbolic logic.* New York: Macmillan, 1947.

Renfrew, J. W. The intensity function and reinforcing properties of brain stimulation that elicits attack. *Physiology and Behavior,* 1969, *4,* 509–515.

Rescorla, R. A., & Solomon, R. L. Two process learning theory: Relationships between Pavlovian conditioning and instrumental learning. *Psychological Review,* 1967,*74,* 151–182.

Reynolds, G. S., Catania, A. C., & Skinner, B. F. Conditioned and unconditioned aggression in pigeons. *Journal of the Experimental Analysis of Behavior,* 1963, *1,* 73–75.

Richter, C. P. Total self-regulatory functions in animals and human beings. *The Harvey Lectures Series,* 1942, *38,* 63–103.

Roberts, W. W., & Kiess, H. O. Motivational properties of hypothalamic aggression in cats. *Journal of Comparative and Physiological Psychology,* 1964, *58,* 187–193.

Robinson, B. W. *The physiology of fighting and defeat: Summary and overview.* Paper presented at the AAAS Symposium on the Physiology of Fighting and Defeat, Dallas, December 1968.

Roper, M. K. A survey of the evidence for intrahuman killing in the Pleistocene. *Current Anthropology,* 1969, *10,* 427–459.

Rosenberg, M. J. When dissonance fails: On eliminating evaluation apprehension from attitude measurement. *Journal of Personality and Social Psychology,* 1965, *1,* 28–42.

Rosenberg, M. J. The conditions and consequences of evaluation apprehension. In R. Rosenthal & R. L. Rosnow (Eds.), *Artifact in behavioral research.* New York: Academic Press, 1969.

Rosene, J. M. *The effects of violent and sexually arousing film content: An experimental study.* Unpublished doctoral dissertation, Ohio University, 1971.

Rosenthal, R. *Experimenter effects in behavioral research.* New York: Appleton, 1966.

Rosenzweig, S. An outline of frustration theory. In J. McV. Hunt (Ed.), *Personality and the behavior disorders.* New York: Ronald Press, 1944.

Rosvold, H. E., Mirsky, A. F., & Pribram, K. H. Influences of amygdalectomy on social interaction in a monkey group. *Journal of Comparative and Physiological Psychology,* 1954, *47,* 173–178.

Rothaus, P., & Worchel, P. The inhibition of aggression under nonarbitrary frustration. *Journal of Personality,* 1960, *28,* 108–117.

Rothballer, A. B. Aggression, defense and neurohumors. In C. D. Clemente & D. B. Lindsley (Eds.), *Aggression and defense: Neural mechanisms and social patterns* (Vol. 5). *Brain function.* Berkeley: University of California Press, 1967.

Rowland, G. L. *The effects of total social isolation upon learning and social behavior of rhesus monkeys.* Unpublished doctoral dissertation, University of Wisconsin, 1964.

Rule, B. G. The hostile and instrumental functions of human aggression. In J. De Wit & W. W. Hartup (Eds.), *Determinants and origins of aggressive behavior.* The Hague: Mouton, 1974.

Rule, B. G., & Duker, P. Effects of intentions and consequences on children's evaluations of aggressors. *Journal of Personality and Social Psychology,* 1973, *27,* 184–189.

Rule, B. G., & Leger, G. J. Pain cues and differing functions of aggression. *Canadian Journal of Behavioral Science,* 1976, *8,* 213–223.

Rule, B. G., & Nesdale, A. R. Differing functions of aggression. *Journal of Personality,* 1974, *42,* 467–481.

Rule, B. G., & Nesdale, A. R. Emotional arousal and aggressive behavior. *Psychological Bulletin,* 1976, *83,* 851–863. (a)

Rule, B. G., & Nesdale, A. R. Moral judgment of aggressive behavior. In R. G. Geen & E. C. O'Neal (Eds.), *Perspectives on aggression.* New York: Academic Press, 1976. (b)

Rule, B. G., Dyck, R., & Nesdale, A. R. Arbitrariness of frustration: Inhibition or instigation effects on aggression. *European Journal of Social Psychology,* 1978, *8,* 237–244.

Rule, B. G., & Percival, E. The effects of frustration and attack on physical aggression. *Journal of Experimental Research in Personality,* 1971, *5,* 111–118.

Sabine, W. S. The winter society of the Oregon junco: Intolerance, dominance, and the pecking order. *Condor,* 1959, *61,* 110–135.

Sade, D. S. Determinants of dominance in a group of free-ranging rhesus monkeys. In S. A. Altmann (Ed.), *Social communication among primates.* Chicago: University of Chicago Press, 1967.

Sapolsky, B. S., Stocking, S. H., & Zillmann, D. Immediate vs delayed retaliation in male and female adults. *Psychological Reports,* 1977, *40,* 197–198.

Sarles, R. M.   Child abuse. In D. J. Madden & J. R. Lion (Eds.), *Rage, hate, assault and other forms of violence*. New York: Spectrum Publications, 1976.

Sassenrath, E. N.   Increased adrenal responsiveness related to social stress in rhesus monkeys. *Hormones and Behavior*, 1970, *1*, 283–298.

Savitsky, J. C., Czyzewski, D., Dubord, D., & Kaminsky, S.   Age and emotion of an offender as determinants of adult punitive reactions. *Journal of Personality*, 1976, *44*, 311–320.

Schaar, J. H.   *Escape from authority: The perspectives of Erich Fromm*. New York: Basic Books, 1961.

Schachter, S.   The interaction of cognitive and physiological determinants of emotional state. In L. Berkowitz (Ed.), *Advances in experimental social psychology* (Vol. 1). New York: Academic Press, 1964.

Schaller, G. B.   The orangutan in Sarawak. *Zoologica*, 1961, *46*, 73–82.

Schaller, G. B.   *The mountain gorilla*. Chicago: University of Chicago Press, 1963.

Schaller, G. B.   The behavior of the mountain gorilla. In I. DeVore (Ed.), *Primate behavior: Field studies of monkeys and apes*. New York: Holt, Rinehart & Winston, 1965.

Schaller, G. B.   Life with the king of beasts. *National Geographic*, 1969, *135*, 494–519.

Schein, M. W., & Fohrman, M. H.   Social dominance relationships in a herd of dairy cattle. *British Journal of Animal Behaviour*, 1956, *3*, 45–55.

Schenkel, R.   Zum Problem der Territorialität und des Markierens bei Säugern—am Beispiel des Schwarzen Nashorns und des Löwen. *Zeitschrift für Tierpsychologie*, 1966, *23*, 593–626.

Schenkel, R.   Submission: Its features and functions in the wolf and dog. *American Zoologist*, 1967, *7*, 319–329.

Schneirla, T. C.   An evolutionary and developmental theory of biphasic processes underlying approach and withdrawal. In M. R. Jones (Ed.), *Nebraska Symposium on Motivation, 1959*. Lincoln: University of Nebraska Press, 1959.

Schneirla, T. C.   Instinct and aggression. In A. Montagu (Ed.), *Man and aggression* (2nd ed.). New York: Oxford University Press, 1973.

Schoenfeld, W. N.   Some old work for modern conditioning theory. *Conditional Reflex*, 1966, *1*(4), 219–223.

Schreiner, L., & Kling, A.   Behavioral changes following rhinencephalic injury in cat. *Journal of Neurophysiology*, 1953, *16*, 643–658.

Schultz-Hencke, H.   *Der gehemmte Mensch: Grundlagen einer Desmologie als Beitrag zur Tiefenpsychologie*. Leipzig: Thieme, 1940.

Schultz-Hencke, H.   *Lehrbuch der analytischen Psychotherapie*. Stuttgart. Thieme, 1951.

Schuster, R., & Rachlin, H.   Indifference between punishment and free shock: Evidence for the negative law of effect. *Journal of the Experimental Analysis of Behavior*, 1968, *11*, 777–786.

Scott, J. P.   Social behavior, organization, and leadership in a small flock of domestic sheep. *Comparative Psychology Monographs*, 1945, *18*(4), 1–29.

Scott, J. P.   The social behavior of dogs and wolves: An illustration of sociobiological systematics. *Annals of the New York Academy of Sciences*, 1950, *51*, 1009–1021.

Scott, J. P.   *Aggression*. Chicago: University of Chicago Press, 1958.

Scott, J. P.   Agonistic behavior of mice and rats: A review. *American Zoologist*, 1966, *6*, 683.

Scott, J. P.   That old-time aggression. *Nation*, January 9, 1967, pp. 53–54.

Scott, J. P.   Biological basis of human warfare: An interdisciplinary problem. In M. Sherif & C. W. Sherif (Eds.), *Interdisciplinary relationships in the social sciences*. Chicago: Aldine, 1969. (a)

Scott, J. P.   The social psychology of infrahuman animals. In G. Lindzey & E. Aronson (Eds.), *The handbook of social psychology* (2nd ed., Vol. 4). Reading, Mass.: Addison-Wesley, 1969. (b)

Scott, J. P.   Theoretical issues concerning the origin and causes of fighting. In B. E. Eleftheriou & J. P. Scott (Eds.), *The physiology of aggression and defeat*. New York: Plenum, 1971.

Scott, J. P.   Hostility and aggression. In B. Wolman (Ed.), *Handbook of general psychology*. Englewood Cliffs, N.J.: Prentice-Hall, 1973.

Scott, J. P. Personal communication, February 26, 1976.

Scott, J. P., & Fredericson, E. The causes of fighting in mice and rats. *Physiological Zoology*, 1951, *24*, 273–309.

Scott, J. P., & Fuller, J. L. *Genetics and the social behavior of the dog*. Chicago: University of Chicago Press, 1965.

Scott, J. P., & Marston, M. V. Nonadaptive behavior resulting from a series of defeats in fighting mice. *Journal of Abnormal and Social Psychology*, 1953, *48*, 417–428.

Scratton, J. Violence in the family. In D. J. Madden & J. R. Lion (Eds.), *Rage, hate, assault and other forms of violence*. New York: Spectrum Publications, 1976.

Sears, R. R. Personality development in the family. In J. M. Seidman (Ed.), *The child*. New York: Rinehart, 1958.

Sears, R. R., Maccoby, E. E., & Levin, H. *Patterns of child rearing*. Evanston, Ill.: Row, Peterson, 1957.

Sears, R. R., Rau, L., & Alpert, R. *Identification and child rearing*. Stanford, Ca.: Stanford University Press, 1965.

Selg, H. Die Frustrations–Aggressions Theorie. In H. Selg (Ed.), *Zur Aggression verdammt?: Psychologische Ansätze einer Friedensforschung*. Stuttgart: Kohlhammer, 1971.

Selye, H. *The physiology and pathology of exposure to stress*. Montreal: Acta, 1950.

Selye, H. *The stress of life*. New York: McGraw-Hill, 1956.

Shaw, C. E. The male combat "dance" of some crotalid snakes. *Herpetologica*, 1948, *4*, 137–145.

Sheffield, F. D., & Campbell, B. A. The role of experience in the "spontaneous" activity of hungry rats. *Journal of Comparative and Physiological Psychology*, 1954, *47*, 97–100.

Sherrington, C. *The integrative action of the nervous system*. London: Scribner's, 1906.

Shomer, R. W., Davis, A. H., & Kelley, H. H. Threats and the development of coordination: Further studies of the Deutsch and Krauss trucking game. *Journal of Personality and Social Psychology*, 1966, *4*, 119–126.

Short, J. F., Jr., & Strodtbeck, F. L. Why gangs fight. *Transaction*, 1964, *1*(6), 25–29.

Shortell, J., Epstein, S., & Taylor, S. P. Instigation to aggression as a function of degree of defeat and the capacity for massive retaliation. *Journal of Personality*, 1970, *38*, 313–328.

Shuntich, R. J., & Taylor, S. P. The effects of alcohol on human physical aggression. *Journal of Experimental Research in Personality*, 1972, *6*, 34–38.

Sigall, H., Aronson, E., & VanHoose, T. The cooperative subject: Myth or reality? *Journal of Experimental Social Psychology*, 1970, *6*, 1–10.

Sigg, E. B. Relationship of aggressive behaviour to adrenal and gonadal function in male mice. In S. Garattini & E. B. Sigg (Eds.), *Aggressive behaviour*. New York: Wiley, 1969.

Simonds, P. E. The bonnet macaque in South India. In I. DeVore (Ed.), *Primate behavior: Field studies of monkeys and apes*. New York: Holt, Rinehart & Winston, 1965.

Skinner, B. F. *The behavior of organisms*. New York: Appleton-Century-Crofts, 1938.

Skinner, B. F. *Science and human behavior*. New York: Macmillan, 1953.

Skinner, B. F. *Contingencies of reinforcement: A theoretical analysis*. New York: Appleton-Century-Crofts, 1969.

Skinner, B. F. *Beyond freedom and dignity*. New York: Knopf, 1971.

Sloane, H. N., Johnston, M. K., & Bijou, S. W. Successive modification of aggressive behavior and aggressive fantasy play by management of contingencies. *Journal of Child Psychology and Psychiatry and Allied Disciplines*, 1967, *8*, 217–226.

Sofia, R. D. Structural relationship and potency of agents which selectively block mouse killing (muricide) behavior in rats. *Life Sciences*, 1969, *8*, 1201–1210.

Solomon, R. L. Punishment. *American Psychologist*, 1964, *19*, 239–253.

Sosa, J. N. *Vascular effects of aggression and passivity in a prison population*. Unpublished master's thesis, Florida State University, 1968.

Southwick, C. H. Experimental studies of intragroup aggression in rhesus monkeys. *American Zoologist*, 1966, *6*, 301.

Southwick, C. H. Aggressive behaviour of rhesus monkeys in natural and captive groups. In S. Garattini & E. B. Sigg (Eds.), *Aggressive behaviour.* New York: Wiley, 1969.

Southwick, C. H., Beg, M. A., & Siddiqi, M. R. Rhesus monkeys in North India. In I. DeVore (Ed.), *Primate behavior: Field studies of monkeys and apes.* New York: Holt, Rinehart & Winston, 1965.

Spence, K. W. *Behavior theory and conditioning.* New Haven, Conn.: Yale University Press, 1956.

Spence, K. W. *Behavior theory and learning.* Englewood Cliffs, N.J.: Prentice-Hall, 1960.

Spielberger, C. D. Theoretical and epistemological issues in verbal conditioning. In S. Rosenberg (Ed.), *Directions in psycholinguistics.* New York: Macmillan, 1965.

Squires, N., & Fantino, E. A model for choice in simple concurrent and concurrent-chains schedules. *Journal of the Experimental Analysis of Behavior,* 1971, *15,* 27–38.

Staats, A. W., & Staats, C. K. Attitudes established by classical conditioning. *Journal of Abnormal and Social Psychology,* 1958, *57,* 37–40.

Staats, C. K., & Staats, A. W. Meaning established by classical conditioning. *Journal of Experimental Psychology,* 1957, *54,* 74–80.

Stachnik, T. J., Ulrich, R. E., & Mabry, J. H. Reinforcement of aggression through intracranial stimulation. *Psychonomic Science,* 1966, *5,* 101–102. (a)

Stachnik, T. J., Ulrich, R., & Mabry, J. H. Reinforcement of intra- and inter-species aggression with intracranial stimulation. *American Zoologist,* 1966, *6,* 663–668. (b)

Staples, F. R., & Walters, R. H. Influence of positive reinforcement of aggression on subjects differing in initial aggression level. *Journal of Consulting Psychology,* 1964, *28,* 547–552.

Statistics Canada. *Murder statistics: 1961–1970.* Ottawa: Author, 1973.

Steinmetz, S. K., & Straus, M. A. *Violence in the family.* New York: Dodd, Mead, 1974.

Stennett, R. G. The relationship of performance level to level of arousal. *Journal of Experimental Psychology,* 1957, *54,* 54–61.

Sternbach, R. A. *Pain: A psychophysiological analysis.* New York: Academic Press, 1968.

Stone, G. R. The effect of negative incentives in serial learning: VII. Theory of punishment. *Journal of General Psychology,* 1953, *48,* 133–161.

Stone, G. R., & Walters, N. J. The effect of negative incentives in serial learning: VI. Response repetition as a function of an isolated electric shock punishment. *Journal of Experimental Psychology,* 1951, *41,* 411–418.

Stone, L. Reflections on the psychoanalytic concept of aggression. *Psychoanalytic Quarterly,* 1971, *40,* 195–244.

Stone, L. J., & Hokanson, J. E. Arousal reduction via self-punitive behavior. *Journal of Personality and Social Psychology,* 1969, *12,* 72–79.

Storms, L. H., Boroczi, G., & Broen, W. E., Jr. Punishment inhibits an instrumental response in hooded rats. *Science,* 1962, *135,* 1133–1134.

Storr, A. *Human aggression.* New York: Atheneum, 1968.

Stotland, E. Exploratory investigations of empathy. In L. Berkowitz (Ed.), *Advances in experimental social psychology* (Vol. 4). New York: Academic Press, 1969.

Straus, M. A. Cultural and social organizational influences on violence between family members. In R. Prince & D. Barrier (Eds.), *Configurations: Biological and cultural factors in sexuality and family life.* Lexington, Mass.: Lexington Books, 1974.

Suchowsky, G. K., Pegrassi, L., & Bonsignori, A. The effect of steroids on aggressive behaviour in isolated male mice. In S. Garattini & E. B. Sigg (Eds.), *Aggressive behaviour.* New York: Wiley, 1969.

Sugiyama, Y. Social organization of Hanuman langurs. In S. A. Altmann (Ed.), *Social communication among primates.* Chicago: University of Chicago Press, 1967.

Swart, C., & Berkowitz, L. The effects of a stimulus associated with a victim's pain on later aggression. *Journal of Personality and Social Psychology,* 1976, *33,* 623–631.

Tannenbaum, P. H. Studies in film- and television-mediated arousal and aggression: A progress report. In G. A. Comstock, E. A. Rubinstein, & J. P. Murray (Eds.), *Television and social behavior* (Vol. 5). *Television's effects: Further explorations.* Washington, D.C.: U.S. Government Printing Office, 1972.

Tannenbaum, P. H., & Zillmann, D. Emotional arousal in the facilitation of aggression through communication. In L. Berkowitz (Ed.), *Advances in experimental social psychology* (Vol. 8). New York: Academic Press, 1975.

Taylor, S. P. Aggressive behavior and physiological arousal as a function of provocation and the tendency to inhibit aggression. *Journal of Personality,* 1967, *35,* 474–486.

Taylor, S. P., & Gammon, C. B. Effects of type and dose of alcohol on human physical aggression. *Journal of Personality and Social Psychology,* 1975, *32,* 169–175.

Taylor, S. P., Gammon, C. B., & Capasso, D. R. Aggression as a function of the interaction of alcohol and threat. *Journal of Personality and Social Psychology,* 1976, *34,* 938–941.

Taylor, S. P., Vardaris, R. M., Rawtich, A. B., Gammon, C. B., Cranston, J. W., & Lubetkin, A. I. The effects of alcohol and delta-9-tetrahydrocannabinol on human physical aggression. *Aggressive Behavior,* 1976, *2,* 153–161.

Tedeschi, J. T. Threats and promises. In P. Swingle (Ed.), *The structure of conflict.* New York: Academic Press, 1970.

Tedeschi, J. T., Smith, R. B., III, & Brown, R. C., Jr. A reinterpretation of research on aggression. *Psychological Bulletin,* 1974, *81,* 540–562.

Teghtsoonian, R., & Campbell, B. A. Random activity of the rat during food deprivation as a function of environmental conditions. *Journal of Comparative and Physiological Psychology,* 1960, *53,* 242–244.

Teleki, G. *The predatory behavior of wild chimpanzees.* Lewisburg, Pa.: Bucknell University Press, 1973.

Tellegen, A., Horn, J. M., & Legrand, R. G. Opportunity for aggression as a reinforcer in mice. *Psychonomic Science,* 1969, *14,* 104–105.

Terdiman, A. M., & Levy, J. V. The effects of estrogen on fighting behavior in young male C57F1-10 mice. *Proceedings of the West Virginia Academy of Science,* 1954, *26,* 15. (Abstract)

Thompson, R. F. *Foundations of physiological psychology.* New York: Harper & Row, 1967.

Thompson, T. Visual reinforcement in Siamese fighting fish. *Science,* 1963, *141,* 55–57.

Thompson, T. Visual reinforcement in fighting cocks. *Journal of the Experimental Analysis of Behavior,* 1964, *7,* 45–49.

Thorndike, E. L. *Animal intelligence.* New York: Macmillan, 1911.

Thorndike, E. L. *Educational psychology* (Vol. 2). *The psychology of learning.* New York: Columbia University, Teacher's College, Bureau of Publications, 1913.

Thorndike, E. L. *The fundamentals of learning.* New York: Columbia University, Teacher's College, Bureau of Publications, 1932.

Tinbergen, N. *The study of instinct.* Oxford: Clarendon Press, 1951.

Tinbergen, N. Fighting and threat in animals. *New Biology,* 1953, *14,* 9–24. (a)

Tinbergen, N. *Social behavior in animals.* London: Methuen, 1953. (b)

Tinbergen, N. On war and peace in animals and man: An ethologist's approach to the biology of aggression. *Science,* 1968, *160,* 1411–1418.

Tinklenberg, J. R., & Stillman, R. C. Drug use and violence. In D. N. Daniels, M. F. Gilula, & F. M. Ochberg (Eds.), *Violence and the struggle for existence.* Boston: Little, Brown, 1970.

Toch, H. *Violent men.* Chicago: Aldine, 1969.

Tolman, E. C. *Purposive behavior in animals and men.* New York: Appleton-Century-Crofts, 1932.

Tolman, E. C. The determiners of behavior at a choice point. *Psychological Review,* 1938, *45,* 1–41.

Toman, W. *Dynamik der Motive: Eine Einführung in die klinische Psychologie.* Frankfurt: Humboldt, 1954.

Tucker, I. F. *Adjustment, models and mechanisms.* New York: Academic Press, 1970.

Turner, C. W., Layton, J. F., & Simons, L. S. Naturalistic studies of aggressive behavior: Aggressive stimuli, victim visibility, and horn honking. *Journal of Personality and Social Psychology,* 1975, *31,* 1098–1107.

Turner, C. W., & Simons, L. S. Effects of subject sophistication and evaluation apprehension on aggressive responses to weapons. *Journal of Personality and Social Psychology,* 1974, *30,* 341–348.

Tyler, V. O., Jr., & Brown, G. D. The use of swift, brief isolation as a group control device for institutionalized delinquents. *Behavior Research and Therapy,* 1967, *5,* 1–9.

Uexküll, J. von. *Streifzüge durch die Umwelten von Tieren und Menschen.* Hamburg: Rowohlt, 1956.

Uhrich, J. The social hierarchy in albino mice. *Journal of Comparative Psychology,* 1938, *25,* 373–413.

Ulrich, R. Reflexive fighting in response to aversive stimulation. *Dissertation Abstracts,* 1961, *22,* 4421.

Ulrich, R. Pain as a cause of aggression. *American Zoologist,* 1966, *6,* 643–662.

Ulrich, R., & Azrin, N. H. Reflexive fighting in response to aversive stimulation. *Journal of the Experimental Analysis of Behavior,* 1962, *5,* 511–520.

Ulrich, R., Dulaney, S., Arnett, M., & Mueller, K. An experimental analysis of nonhuman and human aggression. In J. F. Knutson (Ed.), *The control of aggression: Implications from basic research.* Chicago: Aldine, 1973.

Ulrich, R., Hutchinson, R. R., & Azrin, N. H. Pain-elicited aggression. *Psychological Record,* 1965, *15,* 111–126.

Ulrich, R., Johnston, M., Richardson, J., & Wolff, P. C. The operant conditioning of fighting behavior in rats. *Psychological Record,* 1963, *13,* 465–470.

Ulrich, R., & Symannek, B. Pain as a stimulus for aggression. In S. Garattini & E. B. Sigg (Eds.), *Aggressive behaviour.* New York: Wiley, 1969.

Uniform Crime Reports for the United States. Washington, D.C.: U.S. Government Printing Office, 1975.

Ursin, H. The effect of amygdaloid lesions on flight and defense behavior in cats. *Experimental Neurology,* 1965, *11,* 61–79.

Ursin, H., & Kaada, B. R. Functional localization within the amygdaloid complex in the cat. *Electroencephalography and Clinical Neurophysiology,* 1960, *12,* 1–20.

Van Hemel, P. E. Aggression as a reinforcer: Operant behavior in the mouse-killing rat. *Journal of the Experimental Analysis of Behavior,* 1972, *17,* 237–245.

Van Hemel, P. E., & Myer, J. S. Satiation of mouse killing by rats in an operant situation. *Psychonomic Science,* 1970, *21,* 129–130.

Vantress, F. E., & Williams, C. B. The effect of the presence of the provocator and the opportunity to counteraggress on systolic blood pressure. *Journal of General Psychology,* 1972, *86,* 63–68.

Varley, M., & Symmes, D. The hierarchy of dominance in a group of macaques. *Behaviour,* 1966, *27,* 54–75.

Vernon, W., & Ulrich, R. Classical conditioning of pain-elicited aggression. *Science,* 1966, *152,* 668–669.

Waelder, R. Critical discussion of the concept of an instinct of destruction. *Bulletin of the Philadelphia Association for Psychoanalysis,* 1956, *6,* 97–109.

Wahlsten, D., Cole, M., Sharp, D., & Fantino, E. J. Facilitation of bar-press avoidance by handling during the intertrial interval. *Journal of Comparative and Physiological Psychology,* 1968, *65,* 170–175.

Wallace, A. R. *The Malay Archipelago.* New York: Macmillan, 1902.

Walster, E., Berscheid, E., & Walster, G. W. New directions in equity research. In L. Berkowitz & E. Walster (Eds.), *Advances in experimental social psychology* (Vol. 9). *Equity theory: Toward a general theory of social interaction.* New York: Academic Press, 1976.

Walters, R. H., & Brown, M. Studies of reinforcement of aggression: III. Transfer of responses to an interpersonal situation. *Child Development,* 1963, *34,* 563-571.

Walther, F. Zum Kampf- und Paarungsverhalten einiger Antilopen. *Zeitschrift für Tierpsychologie,* 1958, *15,* 340-380.

Washburn, S. L., & DeVore, I. The social life of baboons. *Scientific American,* 1961, *204,* 62-71.

Washburn, S. L., & Hamburg, D. A. Aggressive behavior in old world monkeys and apes. In P. C. Jay (Ed.), *Primates: Studies in adaptation and variability.* New York: Holt, Rinehart & Winston, 1968.

Wasman, M., & Flynn, J. P. Directed attack elicited from hypothalamus. *Archives of Neurology,* 1962, *6,* 220-227.

Wasserstrom, R. A. *The judicial decision: Toward a theory of legal justification.* Stanford, Ca.: Stanford University Press, 1961.

Weiner, B. *Theories of motivation: From mechanism to cognition.* Skokie, Ill.: Rand McNally, 1972.

Weiner, B. An attributional interpretation of expectancy-value theory. In B. Weiner (Ed.), *Cognitive views of human motivation.* New York: Academic Press, 1974. (a)

Weiner, B. (Ed.). *Cognitive views of human motivation.* New York: Academic Press, 1974. (b)

Weiner, B., Nierenberg, R., & Goldstein, M. Social learning (locus of control) versus attributional (causal stability) interpretations of expectancy of success. *Journal of Personality,* 1976, *44,* 52-68.

Welch, A. S., & Welch, B. L. Effect of stress and parachlorophenyl-alanine upon brain serotonin, 5-hydroxyindoleacetic acid and catecholamines in grouped and isolated mice. *Biochemical Pharmacology,* 1968, *17,* 699-708. (a)

Welch, A. S., & Welch, B. L. Isolation, reactivity and aggression: Evidence for an involvement of brain catecholamines and serotonin. In B. E. Eleftheriou & J. P. Scott (Eds.), *The physiology of aggression and defeat.* New York: Plenum, 1971.

Welch, B. L. Psychophysiological response to the mean level of environmental stimulation: A theory of environmental integration. In *Symposium on medical aspects of stress in the military climate.* Washington, D.C.: Walter Reed Army Institute of Research, 1964.

Welch, B. L., & Welch, A. S. Differential activation by restraint stress of a mechanism to conserve brain catecholamines and serotonin in mice differing in excitability. *Nature,* 1968, *218,* 575-577. (b)

Welch, B. L., & Welch, A. S. Aggression and the biogenic amines. In S. Garattini & E. B. Sigg (Eds.), *Aggressive behaviour.* New York: Wiley, 1969. (a)

Welch, B. L., & Welch, A. S. Fighting: Preferential lowering of norepinephrine and dopamine in the brain stem, concomitant with a depletion of epinephrine from the adrenal medulla. *Communications in Behavioral Biology,* 1969, *3,* 125-130. (b)

Weltman, A. S., Sackler, A. M., Schwartz, R., & Owens, H. Effects of isolation stress on female albino mice. *Laboratory Animal Care,* 1968, *18,* 426-435.

Wernimont, P. F., & Fitzpatrick, S. The meaning of money. *Journal of Applied Psychology,* 1972, *56,* 218-226.

Westby, B. W. M., & Box, H. O. Prediction of dominance in social groups of the electric fish. *Psychonomic Science,* 1970, *21,* 181-183.

Whalen, R. E., & Fehr, H. The development of the mouse killing response in rats. *Psychonomic Science,* 1964, *1,* 77-78.

Wheatley, M. D. The hypothalamus and affective behavior in cats. *Archives of Neurology and Psychiatry,* 1944, *52,* 296-316.

White, J. F. *The effects of induced muscular tension on heart rate and concept formation.* Unpublished doctoral dissertation, Florida State University, 1965.

Wolfgang, M. E. *Patterns in criminal homicide.* Philadelphia, Pa.: University of Pennsylvania, 1958.

Wolfgang, M. E., & Ferracuti, F. *The subculture of violence: Towards an integrated theory in criminology.* London: Tavistock, 1967.

Wolfgang, M. E., & Strohm, R. B. The relationship between alcohol and criminal homicide. *Quarterly Journal of Studies on Alcohol,* 1956, *17,* 411–425.

Wood, C. G. *The effects of induced muscular tension on learning and recall.* Unpublished doctoral dissertation, Florida State University, 1964.

Wood, C. G., & Hokanson, J. E. Effects of induced muscular tension on performance and the inverted U function. *Journal of Personality and Social Psychology,* 1965, *1,* 506–510.

Worchel, S., Arnold, S. E., & Harrison, W. Aggression and power restoration: The effects of identifiability and timing on aggressive behavior. *Journal of Experimental Social Psychology,* 1978, *14,* 43–52.

Wurtman, R. J. Brain monoamines and endocrine function: Neuro-endocrine transduction: An essay. *Neurosciences Research Bulletin,* 1971, *9,* 182–187.

Wynne-Edwards, V. C. *Animal dispersion in relation to social behavior.* New York: Hafner, 1962.

Yablonsky, L. *The violent gang.* New York: Macmillan, 1962.

Yasukochi, G. Emotional responses elicited by electrical stimulation of the hypothalamus of cat. *Folia Psychiatrica et Neurologica Japonica,* 1960, *14,* 260–267.

Yen, H. C. Y., Day, C. A., & Sigg, E. B. Influence of endocrine factors on development of fighting behavior in rodents. *Pharmacologist,* 1962, *4,* 173.

Yoshiba, K. Local and intertroop variability in ecology and social behavior of common Indian langurs. In P. C. Jay (Ed.), *Primates: Studies in adaptation and variability.* New York: Holt, Rinehart & Winston, 1968.

Zalba, S. R. The abused child: A survey of the problem. *Social Work,* 1966, *11,* 3–16.

Zeilberger, J., Sampen, S. E., & Sloane, H. N., Jr. Modification of a child's problem behaviors in the home with the mother as therapist. *Journal of Applied Behavior Analysis,* 1968, *1,* 47–53.

Zillmann, D. Excitation transfer in communication-mediated aggressive behavior. *Journal of Experimental Social Psychology,* 1971, *7,* 419–434.

Zillmann, D. Rhetorical elicitation of agreement in persuasion. *Journal of Personality and Social Psychology,* 1972, *21,* 159–165. (a)

Zillmann, D. The role of excitation in aggressive behavior. In *Proceedings of the Seventeenth International Congress of Applied Psychology, 1971.* Brussels: Editest, 1972. (b)

Zillmann, D. Humor and communication. In T. Chapman & H. Foot (Eds.), *It's a funny thing, humor.* Oxford: Pergamon Press, 1977.

Zillmann, D. Attribution and misattribution of excitatory reactions. In J. H. Harvey, W. J. Ickes, & R. F. Kidd (Eds.), *New directions in attribution research* (Vol. 2). Hillsdale, N.J.: Lawrence Erlbaum Associates, 1978.

Zillmann, D., & Bryant, J. Effect of residual excitation on the emotional response to provocation and delayed aggressive behavior. *Journal of Personality and Social Psychology,* 1974, *30,* 782–791.

Zillmann, D., & Bryant, J. Viewer's moral sanction of retribution in the appreciation of dramatic presentations. *Journal of Experimental Social Psychology,* 1975, *11,* 572–582.

Zillmann, D., Bryant, J., Cantor, J. R., & Day, K. D. Irrelevance of mitigating circumstances in retaliatory behavior at high levels of excitation. *Journal of Research in Personality,* 1975, *9,* 282–293.

Zillmann, D., Bryant J., & Sapolsky, B. S. The enjoyment of watching sport contests. In J. Goldstein (Ed.), *Sports, games and play.* Hillsdale, N.J.: Lawrence Erlbaum Associates, 1978.

Zillmann, D., & Cantor, J. R. A disposition theory of humor and mirth. In A. J. Chapman & H. C. Foot (Eds.), *Humor and laughter: Theory, research and applications.* London: Wiley, 1976. (a)

Zillmann, D., & Cantor, J. R. Effect of timing of information about mitigating circumstances on emotional responses to provocation and retaliatory behavior. *Journal of Experimental Social Psychology,* 1976, *12,* 38–55. (b)

Zillmann, D., & Cantor, J. R. Affective responses to the emotions of a protagonist. *Journal of Experimental Social Psychology,* 1977, *13,* 155–165.

Zillmann, D., Hoyt, J. L., & Day, K. D. Strength and duration of the effect of aggressive, violent, and erotic communications on subsequent aggressive behavior. *Communication Research,* 1974, *1,* 286–306.

Zillmann, D., & Johnson, R. C. Motivated aggressiveness perpetuated by exposure to aggressive films and reduced by exposure to nonaggressive films. *Journal of Research in Personality,* 1973, *7,* 261–276.

Zillmann, D., Johnson, R. C., & Day, K. D. Attribution of apparent arousal and proficiency of recovery from sympathetic activation affecting excitation transfer to aggressive behavior. *Journal of Experimental Social Psychology,* 1974, *10,* 503–515. (a)

Zillmann, D., Johnson, R. C., & Day, K. D. Provoked and unprovoked aggressiveness in athletes. *Journal of Research in Personality,* 1974, *8,* 139–152. (b)

Zillmann, D., Katcher, A. H., & Milavsky, B. Excitation transfer from physical exercise to subsequent aggressive behavior. *Journal of Experimental Social Psychology,* 1972, *8,* 247–259.

Zillmann, D., Mody, B., & Cantor, J. R. Empathetic perception of emotional displays in films as a function of hedonic and excitatory state prior to exposure. *Journal of Research in Personality,* 1974, *8,* 335–349.

Zillmann, D., & Sapolsky, B. S. What mediates the effect of mild erotica on annoyance and hostile behavior in males? *Journal of Personality and Social Psychology,* 1977, *35,* 587–596.

Zimbardo, P. G. The human choice: Individuation, reason, and order versus deindividuation, impulse, and chaos. In W. J. Arnold & D. Levine (Eds.), *Nebraska Symposium on Motivation, 1969.* Lincoln: University of Nebraska Press, 1969.

Zimring, F. E. *Perspectives on deterrence.* Washington, D.C.: U.S. Government Printing Office, 1971.

Author Index

409

Subject Index